'A kaleidoscopic biography, studded with vivid portraits and entertaining footnotes. The writing is as elegant and as attentive to cadence as Runciman's ... Minoo Dinshaw has triumphed. He conjures up the worlds, works and harlequin career of Runciman with a magical touch of his own' James Howard-Johnston, *Literary Review*

'Minoo Dinshaw's biography is itself a splendid mosaic, a careful and well-written account ... a splendid book, to be put at once onto the Wolfson Prize shortlist' Norman Stone, *Oldie*

'An astonishing feat of empathy as well as research ... What keeps the reader's interest on every page is, precisely, this biographer's sensitivity to atmosphere and his humorous awareness ... Near-omniscient thoroughness, gentle humour and psychological precision' Noel Malcolm, *New Statesman*

'This biography is both funny and erudite and empathetic but critical as it chronicles a fascinating caste of dangerously charming spies, poet-scholars, scheming Oxbridge academics, dashing majors and clever queens ... delves beneath the gossip to shed new light on a fascinating and complex personality' Barnaby Rogerson, *Country Life*

'A lively life of a colourful British historian who was best known for his work on the Crusades, by a promising young author. A debut to be proud of' *Economist* Books of the Year

'Dinshaw does a superb job ... The account of Runciman's old age (he died, aged 97, in 2000), playing the laird and host at his Borders tower Elshieshields, couldn't be bettered ... vividly brings alive this secretive, ludic man, making good his case that Runciman, like all the best historians, should be considered, first and foremost, as a writer' Jane Ridley, *Spectator*

'There are times, reading this assured biography of Sir Steven Runciman, when one's attention swerves from the life and times of the great Byzantinist to focus on his biographer. Who is the young Proteus of research, in the name of the ... line wit? Runciman was famous ... Dinshaw himself writes with ... We are dealing with a h ... is more rare, with ... vin, *Cornucopia*

D1421567

'A superb study does justice to Steven Runciman – historian, laird and dabbler in the dark arts ... More than a biography: it is also a substantial work of literary criticism ... I have been riveted by this book from start to finish, and leave the reader with one word of advice. Watch Minoo Dinshaw. He will go far' John Julius Norwich, *Sunday Telegraph*

'Seventeen years after his death, Runciman has found a suitably inquisitive and industrious biographer. Minoo Dinshaw's immense book leaves no source untapped, no incident unexplored, no book undefended, and no character, however fleeting the appearance or walk-on part, unidentified ... He captures both Runciman's kaleidoscopic social world and his elusive nature – ludic but paradoxically serious – with acuteness ... for those interested in elite British life in the twentieth century, there is much to instruct, intrigue, and entertain' Christopher Tyerman, *First Things*

'Mr Dinshaw's choice of subject for his first book is an inspired one. He interweaves the strands of a long and variegated life with sympathy, elegance and awareness of the wider picture ... Mr Dinshaw has done Runciman proud. To whom will he turn his attention next?' *Economist*

'Dinshaw reveals his fibs and foibles with a robust honesty and engaging sense of humour ... shows unwavering and infectious enthusiasm for Runciman the historian' Noonie Minogue, *The Tablet*

ABOUT THE AUTHOR

Minoo Dinshaw lives in London and *Outlandish Knight* is his first book.

# MINOO DINSHAW

# Outlandish Knight
## *The Byzantine Life of Steven Runciman*

PENGUIN BOOKS

## PENGUIN BOOKS

UK | USA | Canada | Ireland | Australia
India | New Zealand | South Africa

Penguin Books is part of the Penguin Random House group of companies
whose addresses can be found at global.penguinrandomhouse.com.

First published by Allen Lane 2016
Published in Penguin Books 2017
001

Set in 9.35/12.47 pt Sabon LT Std
Typeset by Jouve (UK), Milton Keynes
Printed in Great Britain by Clays Ltd, St Ives plc

A CIP catalogue record for this book is available from the British Library

ISBN: 978-0-141-97947-2

*For Ann Shukman*

*An outlandish knight came from the north lands . . .*

Traditional folk song

# Contents

# CONTENTS

# List of Illustrations

# STEVEN RUNCIMAN'S BOOKS

# Author's Note

Steven Runciman was born just south of the Border but brought up highly conscious of his family's origin to its north. Later on he enjoyed a forty-year relationship with Eigg, one of the Small Isles of the Hebrides, and passed his last three and a half decades in a tower-house on the Scottish West March, complete with a beacon platform to warn of English incursions. Dying in Warwickshire, he was buried in Lochmaben, according to the Scots Presbyterian rite. In the pursuit of his life I came increasingly to locate this playfully elusive figure amongst his Border extraction and allegiances. Lecturing in the still wilder frontier country of Peshawar, Runciman gave it as his opinion that:

> Life in a frontier-land, wherever it may be, and whether it is divided by a political boundary or boundaries or none at all, has always some of the same characteristics. Frontier-folk usually show the same tendencies. Their love of freedom is greater than their respect for authority; they admire personal gallantry more than civic virtue; romance and poetry mean more to them than tomes of philosophy and law. (I speak as a frontiersman myself. I was born and brought up on the historic border between England and Scotland – on the wrong side of it ... I grew up among all the legends and traditions that survive there from the good old lawless days.)

As I considered a childhood passed and a retirement spent in the 'Debatable Land', a title associated with one of the oldest and oddest of the Border ballads collected by Child, *The Outlandish Knight*, came to mind. It seemed to me to capture Runciman's contradictions, characteristics and enthusiasms with remarkable felicity: his uneasily sceptical attraction to chivalric romance; his preference for the exotic over the parochial; for the multivalent over the monolithic; for the poetic truth over the literal fact, and the organic tradition over the codified doctrine. It was a phrase quite as hauntingly peculiar as the man who had come to preoccupy me. As I reacquainted myself with the ancient ballad's actual incidents, the congruence seemed less happy. It tells of a typically grim Border affair, and Steven was no false knight upon the road. But my choice of title seeks after an air, not an analogy; and I feel that the presence in this old song of a parrot in a gilt cage given to tittle-tattle would have appealed to my subject's uncanny sense of humour.

# I

# The High Priestess

*Northumberland, Scotswood 1903–9,*
*Doxford 1909–23*

> She is the Secret Tradition and the higher sense of the
> instituted Mysteries.
>     The scroll in her hands . . . is partly covered by her mantle,
> to show that some things are implied and some spoken.
>
> Arthur Waite, *The Key to the Tarot*, 1920

Long ago in Northumberland a forest was cleared and a village settled, built out of the most easterly fragments of the Roman Wall, and
named for the people Hadrian had debarred. The nineteenth century
brought Scotswood prosperity, effective absorption by Newcastle-
upon-Tyne, and a large new manor house, West Denton Hall. In 1901
the lease on the house was taken by an ambitious, serious-minded,
comfortably circumstanced couple in their early thirties. The wife
was a year the elder, the stronger character and more brilliant mind,
winner of a first-class degree from Cambridge, though owing to her
sex she could not graduate. She had met her husband on one of the
newly created Educational Boards, then the only public bodies to
which women could be voted by an exclusively male electorate. They
had married not long afterwards, and by now had a son; they intended
to acquire more children and at least one Parliamentary constituency.
Eight years later Hilda Runciman had borne four children and her
husband, Walter, had become President of the Board of Education in
Asquith's first Cabinet. The family now moved north and into the
country, to Doxford Hall. The big house at Scotswood was first
turned into an enclosed convent, and then, in 2007, entered its most
recent incarnation as the Alan Shearer Centre, a specialist facility for

the care of the disabled. Steven Runciman, who was born there in the summer of 1903, did not quite live to hear of this last development, but he would surely have appreciated another transformation so in keeping with the spirit of the age.

For Steven the 1909 move from West Denton and from the loom of the Emperor Hadrian was to prove, however, doubly welcome. He had never warmed to the place as a small child; he remembered it in old age as 'a vast edifice with huge rooms and a formidable stair-case, while the slope outside, at the bottom of which there was a rose-garden, looked like a mountain-side'. Though his father showed some perceptiveness in trying to interest his younger son in their house from the historical point of view, Steven found Walter's well-meaning stories of Roman carvings hidden in the cellar rather sinister. Doxford, an early product of the distinguished Newcastle neo-classical architect John Dobson, lay further both from the city and from the ghosts of the Wall. The new house carried a reasonable price but a rocky recent history. Its last owner, Henry Percy Warren, had been committed to an asylum after displaying an indecent degree of interest in females of various ages and species. His predecessors, the Browns, had retreated from Doxford amid stories of murdered horses and poisoned wells. No such melodrama was in prospect under the new regime; the Runciman family had become justly proud of cultivating order from unpromising beginnings.

The move was welcome to Steven and his siblings less because of the change of scene than of governess. As at West Denton they were still in the care of their beloved Nannie Laight, whom Steven recalled as 'the most important person in our early lives'.* Their father was in perpetual demand from the Liberal Cabinet or the electors of Dews-bury.† Their mother never hesitated to aver that 'her first duty was to her husband' – and nor was she uninterested in politics, twice contest-ing and once securing a seat of her own. Nannie Laight filled the

*In Steven's case this was almost an understatement; he had been born weeks early, and only Nannie Laight had been on hand to deliver him.

† Newly appointed or promoted Ministers were obliged to stand for confirmation of their seats at by-elections in some or all cases until 1926. Walter Runciman was promoted five times, and so elected for Dewsbury six, before the First World War.

breach; but the children were approaching an age that required education as well as solicitude. Steven disapproved of their first governess, Miss Neligan at West Denton, 'a lady with red hair who liked to wear green and who took us for Nature Walks', on both aesthetic and intellectual grounds; she pointed out birds that the children could recognize for themselves, and wildflowers that were without interest for them. This flame-headed botanist was soon poached by the wife of one of Walter's Cabinet colleagues, Lord Beauchamp.* Steven would never lose his annoyance with those who tried to teach him what he felt sure he knew in greater detail already. The next governess at the new house never committed this error.

She was named Miss Rebecca (shortened among intimates to 'Reay' or 'Ray') Fraser Forbes. Her lisping pupils immediately rechristened her Torby. She was quite different from the insubstantial Miss Neligan, being, apart from anything else, a generation older.† Far from dragging Steven over stale ground, she represented not just new fields of knowledge, but a whole new cultural strain in the household. Walter Runciman, like his father, a formidable shipping magnate of the same name, was a teetotal Methodist. Hilda's family, the Stevensons, had for centuries been canny, hard-working, sober Presbyterians. Nannie Laight, who had simple Broad Church sympathies, was divided from her charges by class and, as an Englishwoman, by heritage and, they thought, by character. In his eighties Steven was quite firm in asserting that his whole family had regarded themselves as entirely Scottish (though both Walters Runciman were, by birthplace, Geordies). 'I've lived a great deal of my life in England, but I'm not English. The English are immensely illogical.'

* Miss Neligan's new charges, the Lygon children, were to share the accolade of inspiring the Flytes of Brideshead. It is unlikely she had an easier time of it at Madresfield, where the turnover of governesses was rapid and the replacements chosen by the Countess purely on the basis of appearance (much as her husband selected the footmen). Lady Beauchamp, who liked her children's governesses to 'look like the Madonna', must have differed from Steven as to the attractiveness of Miss Neligan's hair.
† Born in 1862, Miss Forbes was almost a decade older than her employers Walter and Hilda Runciman, although she had clipped five years off her real age for their benefit.

An illogical Englishwoman Nannie Laight may have been, but Miss Forbes was a wilder specimen. As far as Steven remembered in his unpublished memoirs, Torby had been born and brought up near the Highland village of Bonar Bridge in Sutherland, the daughter of an Episcopalian clergyman who had graduated from Edinburgh University. She could not follow her father to that institution, because, despite the efforts of such campaigners as the 'Edinburgh Seven' and Louisa Stevenson (Hilda Runciman's aunt), the University did not award degrees to women until the last years of the nineteenth century. But Mr Forbes, who took a more enlightened view, taught her himself, and in consequence Rebecca Forbes became one of the very few women in 1900s Scotland to be both fluent in Gaelic, her mother-tongue, and accomplished in Greek, her father's discipline. Steven believed that her father had remained attached to the University after graduation, which explained Torby's wide and enduring acquaintance there. Among her Edinburgh friends was the botanist David Prain, later to be knighted and appointed to the directorship of Kew Gardens. Torby had lived and studied abroad, was 'more or less bi-lingual' in French and German, and was au fait with contemporary painting and sculpture.

Steven's memories make for an instructive contrast with the surviving documents. He does not seem to have known that Torby's real Christian name was Rebecca. He was not far wrong about her birthplace, at Rosehall, a few miles inland from Bonar Bridge and rather less cosmopolitan. But although a fierce High Churchwoman by the time she entered the Runciman household, Rebecca Forbes had, in fact, been born into the ascetic ranks of the Free Church of Scotland (or Wee Frees). Her father, John Forbes, was not a learned university clergyman, but the Rosehall village schoolteacher. Rebecca got her classical education not from him, but through the sponsorship of her maternal uncle, a surgeon in Wark. It was through this uncle, a member of the Edinburgh Royal College of Physicians, that she must have met David Prain. She went to school in Aberdeen, and after a stint as a governess there had saved enough for her brief French and German tour. After her return she had tried her luck in the south, teaching English and classics for some years at a preparatory school in Aldeburgh, where her pupils included the future novelist Theodore Powys.

Torby's interests were academic though not dry, her instincts artistic but not fanciful. She treated her adopted Episcopalian religion in a spirit of hereditary romance; her politics, accordingly, were entirely traditional. The firmly Liberal Runcimans had entrusted the education of their children to one of the last seventeenth-century Tories in Britain. Torby maintained an unservile frankness, and, despite the fondness she was to develop for her employers over twelve years, 'she could not bring herself to approve of the Liberal government of which my father was a member.' This arrangement was not entirely paradoxical. Inherent in Walter and Hilda's large-L Liberal principles was a benign, interested ecumenism that encouraged them to balance the English Nannie with the Highland governess, the Anglican rite of both against their own dissenting preferences, and to retain a High Tory at the hearth for education's sake. The Runcimans were stern and sure of their own views, but no bigots, unless it were, in the inchoate way shared by so many of their countrymen and their class, against the Jews.* Irritated by the 'narrow-mindedness' of the nearest Presbyterian minister, Hilda soon allowed, even encouraged, both Nannie and Torby to take the children to the Church of England services near by at Ellingham. Later on, during the Runciman proprietorship of Eigg, Walter and Hilda were on consistently excellent terms with the island's Catholic priest. Most importantly, the Runciman parents urged not just tolerance towards, but engagement with, the heterodox and unaccustomed when it came to foreign travel, to which they and all their children were devoted.

Conscious of their own relative lack of continental polish, Walter and Hilda were determined that their children should be better equipped. Neither husband nor wife – for all the foreign remit of Walter's later ministerial responsibilities – was fluent in French; the eccentricities of any governess were worth enduring to undo such a handicap in the next generation, and Steven in his nineties could not remember ever 'not knowing some French' as a result. Throughout

---

* The Runciman parents' correspondence is prone to unthinking anti-Semitism, a casual prejudice they transmitted to their children. This did not prevent Walter and Hilda enjoying cordial relations with Jewish Liberal grandees, including Edwin Montagu and Herbert Samuel.

their lives, whenever they travelled without their children, both parents (but especially Hilda) made sure to send detailed, somewhat didactic descriptions back in their barrages of letters; and, when writing to each other, they often comment on the progress shown by their offspring. Thus Hilda to her husband, from an excursion into France in 1913:

> Leslie is an observant creature, he greatly enjoyed the French men of war at Toulon. Steven is more keen on the architecture and notices the church more for instance, but Leslie is very keen on the fortifications. Margaret *shows* the least interest, but I am sure she enjoys it very much.

There is an element of selective vision in this comparison. Twelve-year-old Leslie, the elder son, physically more robust and (Steven thought) already much better looking, is a model of the English schoolboy (he had just started boarding at Summer Fields), interested above all in ships, castles and, by implication, war, public service and patriotism. Steven, younger, ganglier, odder, is being encouraged in a more bookish, even clerical, direction. The second child and eldest daughter is a hard case in a hard place. Leslie is his father's pride, Steven his mother's joy, but Margie (whom Hilda usually calls, alone of her children, by her formal name, Margaret) remains a puzzle to her parents – although, unbeknown to them, she is the favourite sibling of both her brothers.

The advent of Torby was, to Steven, a life-changing delight. Of the rest of the family, Kitty, the daughter born at Doxford, responded well to her lessons, and Hilda respected Miss Forbes's learning and rigour. But Ruth ('Ruie'), the short-sighted middle daughter, struggled with Torby's stern attentions; less enamoured, too, were Margie and Nannie Laight. Both felt their positions in Steven's favours to be threatened by the new governess, Nannie as a primary parental figure and ethical guide, Margie as co-conspirator. Nannie, 'essentially English', was frosty towards the Celtic interloper. Margie, who had more in common with Torby than she knew, resented the alterations that an intellectually ambitious governess imposed both on the pattern of her own days and on her alliance with Steven. Her younger brother was already, as proved by the letters Hilda demanded as soon as he could write, an unusually fully formed personality for his age. He was now cast into a definite intellectual shape. Torby was a woman of strong passions, perhaps especially (roughly in order) for language, antiquity, drama, tradition and aesthetics. Close attention to her tutelage left Steven not so much expert in Latin and Greek as fluent in the way that a linguist with both brilliance and diligence becomes in a living language. Torby's method in bringing Steven so far was as much narrative as grammatical. 'She would talk to us about the Romans and the ancient Greeks almost as though they were people living in our own time,' Steven recalls, exactly describing his own idiom as a narrator of medieval history.

Torby brought an opposite, and equally useful, perspective to bear on modern English. As it was her second language after Gaelic, she was inclined to treat it with a scholarly, anatomical exactitude that was rare even at the dawn of the twentieth century. Steven seems to have regarded her as his master in the discipline of prose until her death, and even until his own. He submitted the proofs of his first three books to her for corrections. In 1958, he admonished an old friend, Stewart Perowne: 'Don't ever write "of course". My governess, a Highland lady of great wisdom, told me when I was very young that a statement which included "of course" was a statement which *ipso facto* was not worth making, and ever since then I've had a wild prejudice against the phrase.' Asked about the chief influence on his prose style, Runciman told David Plante that it was Daniel Defoe, and Anthony Bryer that it was Beatrix Potter. It is a safe bet that both these answers were in some measure code for Torby, who combined Defoe's Scottishness and zeal (if not his political persuasion) with Potter's rural, unpretentious verbal chastity.

Torby's taste, and flair for the theatrical in idea and gesture, was one of her most compelling qualities, if also, at times, her greatest limitation. She taught Latin and French with the help of short plays, taken from primers such as Mary Letitia Newman's *Easy Latin Plays* or Josette Eugénie Spink's *French Plays for Children*, salted with her own multilingual touches. Even Margie was charmed by these productions. Torby had the capacity to turn objects of her disapproval to good pedagogical use. She considered the children's relationship to the animal kingdom excessive and sentimental, but when one of their kittens died she put the ensuing grief to work, insisting that proper rites be respected and helping Steven and Margie to compose a Latin epitaph. For all her verbal precision, Torby was unable to extend her gift of inspiration to mathematics lessons, which were merely 'perfunctory'. History, in her old-fashioned way, she left Steven to infer from classical exemplars and his own reading; the past was to her a vital battleground of sharp dichotomies and romantic partisanship.

Torby's stagey disposition, which Steven associated with her Highland birth and upbringing, also came with a 'temper that could be terrifying when roused'. This was a new and alarming factor in the lives of the Runciman children, who were a little frightened of their paternal grandfather but much less so of their parents, and had rarely, before Torby, encountered shouting or physical chastisement. The children found her spells of fury unpredictable, though in retrospect, Steven came to think, 'not unjustified'. She was as entertained by some of their crimes as annoyed by others, and this was an amusement Steven became adept at exploiting. Even though Torby was now responsible for their church attendance – and gave Steven a Greek New Testament for his tenth birthday – she viewed with approbation Steven and Margie's invention of a neo-pagan religion based around poultry. But when she caught them muddying themselves in an attempt at pig-racing, Torby was so wrathful that the children's new term for her rages became 'having a sow'. A sow she certainly had, when brother and sister contrived to feed whisky to a turkey-cock (a not very contrite Steven admits in his unpublished memoirs that 'I still remember with delight the behaviour of the inebriated bird'). Torby may have felt this episode particularly risked impugning her reputation in the eyes of the Runciman parents; unlike them, she was not teetotal.

Steven's memories of his governess are not merely grateful, but wistful, almost regretful. As a boy he enjoyed her style, her teaching and the diversion she provided, but six and a half decades allowed him to approach understanding and even, perhaps, identification. Interspersed with his happiest Torby vignettes there is a consciousness – coming from a man who, though enlightened for his own time and imaginative for any, could hardly have been described as a feminist – that this remarkable woman may have been wasted in the life of a governess, and felt less satisfied with her pupils than they were with her. 'I think – I certainly hope – that she was happy with us,' he writes with eloquent uncertainty. He noticed even as a boy that she seemed more contented when the family – increasingly often – removed to London than when they were in Northumberland. In the capital she could whisk the children off to the National Gallery and the Wallace Collection, dilating to them on her favourite paintings (though museums seemed to bore her). She introduced them to Sir David Prain at Kew Gardens, where they were subsequently let in by the Director's gate; she brought them for tea to a certain lady-artist, 'large . . . dressed in scarves and bangles . . . who liked to be called Amaryllis. She had a house full of fascinating bric-a-brac; and it was there that we first tasted olives.' At Doxford Torby was more solitary and irritable, shutting herself up to read as often as she could, away from the children and their animals.

Torby changed over her thirteen years with the Runcimans as surely as her pupils. At the outbreak of the First World War this thwarted bohemian, well travelled in Germany, fluent in its language and a devotee of Goethe and Heine, transformed into a rabid jingoist, and accused Hilda's sympathetic, novel-reading Polish lady's maid, Paula, of spying for Germany. Torby left the Runcimans in 1923, when Kitty, the youngest daughter and, like Steven, a favoured pupil, was sent to boarding-school; she retired at first among the delights of London, but they seemed no longer to exercise the same charm for her. She settled finally near distant relations in the Lake District, and for the last two decades of her life would not, it seems, seek more intellectual or artistic novelty than was contained in Steven's occasional parcels of proofs from Cambridge. When Kitty became engaged in 1930, Torby wrote with fond urgency advising her to confide in Steven above anyone else. She died aged eighty during the war, at Newcastle, in the summer of 1942; Steven guessed in his unpublished memoirs that it had been about ten years earlier. The Professor of Byzantine Studies at Istanbul had evidently by then lost touch with his first mentor, but he never forgot her precepts, or ceased to acknowledge his debt.

# 2

# The Empress

*Northumberland; France, spring 1913; Oxfordshire,*
*Summer Fields and Sutton Courtenay, 1913–16*

> The Empress, who is sometimes represented with full face,
> while her correspondence, the Emperor, is in profile.
> . . . There is no direct message which has been given to
> man like that which is borne by woman . . .
>
> Arthur Waite, *The Key to the Tarot*, 1920

> Their religion, for all its severity, suited the people of Langue-
> doc, just as they were later to welcome the stern doctrine of
> Calvin, and fitted in well with the melancholy gaiety of the
> troubadours.
>
> Steven Runciman, *The Medieval Manichee*, 1947

Neither of Hilda and Walter's sons went by their formal first names.
Leslie, always called by his middle name, was, like his father, his
grandfather and his great-grandfather, a Walter. Steven was in fact
James Cochran Stevenson, after his mother's father. That James had
shown superb ability as a chemist at Glasgow University, but *his*
father, another James and a successful mill owner, had obliged him to
help transform the family concern into a chemical works, rather than
bury himself in a laboratory. Steven did not know his maternal grandfather and namesake, but over both him and Leslie there loomed a
precedent of obedience to family before academe. 'We all have ancestors,' Steven reflects in his unpublished memoirs, and neither Leslie
nor he was likely to forget it.

Named for his mother's father, Steven was most evidently his
mother's son. His earliest letter to her is grandly dated '11 November

1911 AD'. It must then have seemed a splendid day, its significance purely, delightfully numerological. Hilda is in London with her husband; Steven is enduring the routine of Doxford with feigned petulance and actual high spirits. The letter postdates Hilda's breach with the too-austere Presbyterian minister, for Steven takes up, as an already traditional theme, the boredom induced by the Anglican vicar – 'We have been to church, all of us have been. Mr Magonigle said 4 ums in the sermon.' Here Steven supported the rebellion of Margie over the reign of Torby; both children were unimpressed by the vicar of their governess's rite, 'a charmless bearded Ulsterman': 'Margie and I used to listen attentively, one of us counting the "ums" and the other the "ers" in competition to see which prevailed.' Steven unhesitatingly describes this mutiny to his mother, whose decision the church attendance had been, and who had small tolerance for her eldest daughter's truculence. He was already using his affinity for the ludicrous to entertain his parents while gently subverting their rules.

This letter from an eight-year-old as secure in his mother's affection as in his own wit has all the hallmarks that continue to characterize Steven's correspondence with Hilda (a woman everybody else, from her daughters to Lloyd George, tended to approach with caution). It is outwardly frivolous but revealing. Hilda could be furious, needy and, to her husband, emasculating. She rebuked Walter for his 'carelessness' in not writing to her in Carcassonne in April 1913, telling him it was 'humiliating to be missed so little'. But in the '1911 AD' letter, Steven turns the tables on her – 'Why have you not wrote to me?' The bad grammar is not a genuine error by this already alarmingly literate child, but a pose, a music-hall Cockney guying; Steven deliberately excludes conventional manners and inhibitions from the inner world he shares with his mother. 'H'aint I wrote this letter well c'os its private. Love from your goodest wisest beautifullest nicest he who wishes to be a "η".'*

* The ambisexual implications of the Greek feminine pronoun bring to mind a record Pamela Glenconner made of a conversation between her son, Stephen Tennant, and his childhood friend Malcolm Murray. 'Stephen and Malcolm, talking together, Glen 1913. Malcolm: "Don't tell Nannie or anyone, but you know I'm a little girl, really, all the time!" Stephen: "How do you know?" Malcolm: "Don't you know I wear a ribbing in my hair at night?"' (Pamela Glenconner, personal writings,

If Steven's bond with his mother was one of singular intimacy, then to the world his usual companion and accomplice was his elder sister. Though both loved and admired their elder brother, Steven's unpublished memoirs give an impression of mischievous collaboration from which the better-behaved, more responsible Leslie was excluded. 'Leslie was a beautiful, rather serious and very virtuous little boy. Margie and I lacked these qualities.' They shared instead a love of stories, animals and escapades, and a worldly sense of humour. When Margie was eight and Steven six, they declared that their toy monkeys, which had been married, were divorcing, 'because divorce sounded glamorous and slightly improper. Neither Nannie nor mother was willing to tell us much about divorce, so we invented our own grounds.' Margie and even the virtuous Leslie were destined to discover the full truth of this mystery one day, while their brother was to lead a still more glamorous and improper life. In the meantime Steven's monkey was naturally the aggrieved and neglected divorcee, Margie's the errant husband. 'Soon afterwards both of them disintegrated and had to be given funerals.'

Funerals were just one facet of Steven and Margie's next grand conceit. They invented an independent realm called the Kokish World, or Kokland, 'owing to our liking for poultry'. Such realms sometimes emerge as the preoccupation of a solitary and precocious child, hungry for company, stimulated by imagination and used to absolute power and order. Steven and Margie, however, were not of this type at all. Their Kokland was a collaborative endeavour, organic and chaotic, a patchwork of affection, idiosyncrasy and compromise, given essential shape by the differing fantasies of its two sibling creators. Steven and Margie awarded each other distinct but adjoining islands. Margie's island was Bulkoks, Steven's Lilu, but he, rather like the Crusading barons whose careers he would later popularize, had larger territorial ambitions. He announced that the Queen of Lilu,

---

quoted in Philip Hoare, *Serious Pleasures* (Hamish Hamilton, 1990), p. 11.) Stephen and Malcolm were seven years old at the time of this dialogue. Malcolm followed his father, a distinguished general, into the army, and married first Lady Grizel Boyle, then Zofia, one of the several Countesses Tarnowska. Stephen's quite different and, in the event, more beribboned path would overlap with Steven's.

Seleryr (celery was his favourite vegetable), had inherited from her mother a supplementary kingdom, Abaerba, on the transoceanic continent of Firkoks.

Margie and Steven were too busy inventing drastic deaths and unexpected lines of descent for their monarchs to waste time *being* them, and so, logically enough, they decided that the Kokish World worshipped a sibling god and goddess, Guronos and Gurene. Steven thought these names 'beautifully Greek' (at seven, he had just begun to learn the language from Torby). The Kokish, or Guronaic, religion employed much ritualistic ceremony, owing more to the Church of England than to the Runciman parents' non-conformism. Margie and Steven wrote and composed hymns and built a wicker chapel in the woods outside Doxford; Steven was the keeper of the 'ritual books'. Margie's latest pet, a billy-goat, was allowed full rights of worship (the exclusion of animals from prayers and communion in any Christian denomination had for some time been a sore point with both siblings). Nannie Laight regarded these goings-on as flagrant blasphemy, but she was overruled by the Runciman parents and Torby, who all found the Kokish Rite quietly amusing.

In the spring of 1913 Hilda took her three eldest children on a cruise from Rouen to Carcassonne, by way of southern Spain, reuniting the younger two with Leslie, who had finished his second year at boarding school, and consoling them for their own imminent departures from home. Steven was to follow his brother to the relatively civilized precincts of Summer Fields, a preparatory school on the fringes of Oxford, while Margie was to be schooled in a manner more pleasing to the eldest generation of Runcimans, at the Mount, a Quaker school in Yorkshire. Hilda had already taken the trouble to ensure as smooth a reception as possible for Steven. She had worked out a scheme with the Prime Minister's wife, Margot Asquith, whereby Leslie would look after Margot's son Anthony – always called 'Puffin' – and Puffin was in turn instructed to show Steven every kindness.

The main target of Margie and Steven's mockery on this cruise was yet another denominationally varied new domestic, Susie, a Plymouth Brother ('they do not seem to have Sisters,' Steven observed). Steven, at least, enjoyed the paradox of Susie's pleasant nature and the horrifying visions of Hell he teased out of her. Hilda overlooked this theological controversy-mongering, and her letters home to Walter struggle fair-mindedly but unavailingly with her evident favouritism of her second son:

> Steven is full of interest, perhaps not more than the others, but he is so eager to get all the information he can about what he sees. He constantly studies the chart stuck up at the smoke room door and carefully informs us of the height of each mountain we see ... The children enjoyed the drive greatly, they liked (especially the 2 younger) to see oranges growing in the open, cactus and palm trees and all the rest ... we got some tangerines in the market, Steven was charmed with the attraction which their being picked with leaves attached gives to them ... Steven is in great form, he laughs and jokes all day long ...

Oddly enough, Hilda's preference did not provoke the irritation of his elder siblings, who both seem, on the whole, to have been on better terms with Steven than with each other. By his siblings as well as by his mother, he was accepted as a wag rather than a bore, even if it is a pity that the testimony of Susie the Plymouth Brother is lost to posterity.

History and French were the twin staples of the holiday's curriculum. Hilda describes Steven and Margie entertaining themselves in a strikingly post-modern manner by *pretending* to be English tourists abroad, 'seeking pleasant tours in France which they choose after long consultations with Baedeker (in French) & then they write to Leslie or me for tours in French. They will learn a lot of French that way & it keeps them very happy!' But this sounds suspiciously convenient, and it is tempting to wonder whether this was either an official 'game' pressed on the children by their mother and adopted with less relish than she claims to her husband, or another example of the anarchic younger pair slyly mocking their mother and staid elder brother. As for history, Hilda was both interested in and surprisingly well informed about the medieval and ancient associations of the ports of the Midi:

> We saw dungeons and the actual chains which bound the Inquisition victims to the stone pillar. This is the country of Albigensian heresy &

Troubadours & Courts of Love & is full of romance . . . At Arles we go back to Greek civilisation. The theatre I believe is Greek & then there is a Roman amphitheatre & the whole district is alive with legends of saints & knights & of Popes & gay ladies of all descriptions! Petrarch loved his Laura near here & Dante got some of his ideas from an ancient cemetery at Arles.

. . . Arles has its fascination – and the children are thoroughly interested – they carefully scan the Arlisienne girls who are said to inherit Grecian beauty & indeed there are a number of really pretty people here.

This thoroughly romantic appreciation may not exactly approach the nuance, sophistication and originality of her son's portraits of the same region in *The Medieval Manichee* and *The Sicilian Vespers*, but a family resemblance may be discerned.

The Hilda whose imagination is so easily stimulated by 'Courts of Love', 'Popes & gay ladies of all descriptions!', Petrarch and 'his Laura', Dante and 'his ideas' and 'Grecian beauty' is at first glance hard to reconcile with the forbidding figure she presents elsewhere: of a ferociously loyal Liberal spouse, the first to sit alongside her husband in the Commons, a short-tempered wife, mother and grandmother, and a, if not *the*, Lady Macbeth, of the old Liberal Party's final tragedy. But Hilda's florid yet genuine historical consciousness was entirely of a piece with her public incarnation as a warrior, political fixer and matriarch. Already in these letters she is urging her husband (then President of the Board of Agriculture and Fisheries) against their party's most outstanding talent, who would be forced, partly by her hostility, into the role of Walter Runciman's implacable enemy; and there is something unpleasantly *de haut en bas* in Hilda's visceral distaste for David Lloyd George. 'How sadly undignified the little creature is,' she hisses from Provence, with all the pride of a woman who, though not so very much grander by caste than the Welsh Wizard, has always been a good deal richer; whose husband is the country neighbour of Sir Edward Grey, the Foreign Secretary, and who may rely in easing her favourite son's schooldays on an alliance with Margot Asquith. Mrs Asquith, née Tennant, was sprung, in fact, from a family not entirely dissimilar to the Stevensons and Runcimans, though even more successful; and the Prime Minister's father was a Congregationalist woollen-mill owner. These Liberal grandees had developed into high political dynasties at a more sedate pace than Lloyd George's vertigo-inducing ascent, and distrusted him with the zeal of fairly recent converts to an old order.

Whatever might be said to Hilda Runciman's disadvantage, she offered her second son unstinting love and encouragement. She knew when to retreat as well as when to grasp tight; when Steven, manifesting his first signs of schoolboy conformism, asked her to stop writing so many and such long letters, she readily wrote to Leslie instead, including messages to be passed on to her younger son (Leslie's absolute, rather than qualified, loathing for his prep school made him more relaxed about receiving frequent letters from home). One such message, in a letter of April 1914, written off Ithaca from Walter's yacht, contains a piece of advice which endears Hilda to any biographer: 'Keep my letters as they will be the only record I shall have of our life.'

Hilda goes on to show a combination of political naivety and offhand prophecy about world affairs, a reminder that the wives of Cabinet Ministers have neither much more nor much less awareness of the future than anyone else:

> At Corfu we went to a café where there were lots of Germans, I suppose the Kaiser has made it fashionable ... Tell Steven that the husband of the 'heaviest royal Lady in Europe' doesn't seem to be making a good start in Albania, everyone seems to think he is very stupid. I wonder how long he will have his country, or if they will not all begin to fight again very soon.*

Steven's first reaction to Summer Fields had been one of boredom, discomfort and the particular boys' school malaise of loneliness

---

* Prince Wilhelm of Wied had become Vidi I, Prince of Albania, that March. He was the Albanians' second choice after the adventurer and Conservative MP Aubrey Herbert, who, although interested, declined the throne after representations both from his party's whips and from Asquith, the father of his best friend, Raymond. Prince Wilhelm's wife was Princess Sophie of Schönberg-Waldenburg. She had distant Albanian ancestry and was slender, elegant and relatively popular; Hilda may have mixed her up with the Queen of Greece. This letter is the earliest sign of Steven's unceasing interest in European royalty.

combined with the sudden deprivation of privacy. He was an individualist by nature, who had so far lived mainly in the care and company of women – his mother, his sister, Nannie and Torby – and who had been educated, to an exceptional standard, through unconventional methods. Now that education was itself taken, at least in part, to be suspect. Steven was mocked by the other boys, as Leslie had been before him, for his too-accurate French accent, 'pretentious and a bit too fluent'. He found the classics teaching, after Torby's regime, unchallenging and dispiriting – 'stern and orderly' rather than humane. In his unpublished memoirs, Steven describes his attitude to Summer Fields as that of a voluntary outcast – 'I was not a satisfactory school-boy. I loathed organized games. I was unwilling to conform with my fellows. I was shy of the masters and was rather pert in my lessons.' While the last claim rings true, being entirely consistent with every other glimpse we get of Steven as a student and, indeed, of Runciman as a mature scholar, Steven, like George Orwell in *Such, Such Were the Joys*, exaggerates the awfulness and isolation of his prep school experience. He writes jokily to his father near the end of his first term, describing a catalogue of academic successes before adding, 'Besides this I have written a poem whose first line is "Oh! Woe is me, that I was born".' In truth he fitted in at Summer Fields with more success than Leslie. The reason for this was the spectacular success of his mother's intrigue. In Puffin Asquith, Hilda had arranged a friend for Steven who could palliate all the disadvantages of boarding school on his own.

Summer Fields was more comfortable than most preparatory schools of the period, and, as the pre-eminent 'feeder' for Eton, Winchester, Harrow, Radley and Sherborne, it had good intellectual credentials, too. But it was distinctly Tory, having been founded by a Scots fencing master to cater for the sons of the Oxfordshire squirearchy, unlike the neighbouring Dragon School which specialized in the children of dons. This meant it was not invariably congenial for a Liberal Cabinet minister's son. Leslie was persecuted on his arrival for stinking of cattle and old fish: the Summerfieldian wits' reaction to his father's portfolio, Agriculture and Fisheries. But even these wags, being also snobs, afforded the Prime Minister's son respect, though Puffin was hardly heroic in schoolboy terms. 'He had enormous natural charm and beautiful manners,' Steven remembered, but 'he was not good-looking and was no good at games; yet all the boys liked him.'

Puffin had other advantages. He must have been one of the few Summerfieldians that year with a mother more formidable than Steven's. Margot Asquith was one of the most famous, or notorious, women in the country. Late in life, Steven was asked by a new acquaintance what man and woman he would most like to dine with in all history; he was expected to choose some obscurely fascinating pair of Byzantine figures. Instead, he at once named Diaghilev and Margot Asquith, both of whom he had known quite well. It was Margot who had rechristened Anthony, her only surviving son, as Puffin, on account of his prominent hooked Tennant nose. Steven always maintained that she had muddled her ornithology and had really meant to dub her son Pipit; the pipit, a small, slender cousin of the wagtail, indeed has more of the Tennant look.

Though Steven and Puffin had not properly met before Summer Fields, few boys can have been so well placed to sympathize with each other's circumstances. Like Steven, Puffin had grown up among parents thoroughly distracted by the exertions and machinations of Liberal politics; had benefited from the teaching of an exceptional governess, Fräulein Anna Heinsius; and was the inseparable comrade of his elder sister, Elizabeth. The Asquith and Runciman children had overlapping, if divergent, memories concerning the campaigns of the suffragettes. Margot was so outspoken an anti-suffragist that Elizabeth and Puffin were threatened with kidnapping, whereas Margie and Steven showed such enthusiasm for the cause – displaying teddy-bears on their bedroom balconies draped in Mrs Pankhurst's green, white and purple tricolour – that Walter Runciman's house on Barton Street in Westminster was the only Cabinet Minister's residence to evade a window-smashing.

When Margot descended to take her son and his new friend out for a treat – which she tended to do practically every weekend, since the Asquiths had a convenient bolt-hole, the Wharf, close by at Sutton Courtenay – none could gainsay her, least of all the fawning head-master Dr Williams. One of the first women in Britain to smoke in public, she had rarely stopped since (she was later to precipitate a riot in 1920s Roumania by igniting a cigar at the theatre). Steven remembered the contrast of her strikingly innovative costumes with her uncompromising, beaky looks. One Sunday she appeared at the school dressed in a *jupe-sultane*, flowing harem pants which 'suited her thin boyish figure, but did not fit so well with her ageing aquiline face'.

In the summer terms, she removed the boys from Oxford altogether to spend their Sunday afternoons at the Wharf. This Thames-side house was pretty and comfortable rather than grand; Margot, whose wild expenditure plagued her husband, had acquired it in 1911 with money she did not possess, advanced by an old admirer, J. Pierpont Morgan, and had it redesigned by another, Walter Cave. It was to become the most consistent home of the large and complicated Asquith household, and the scene of many of Margot's most memorable parties.\* At such parties many worlds met. Steven recalled seeing the writer Maurice Baring's lean, ascetic figure alongside the spherical portentousness of Viscount Haldane, the Lord Chancellor, and feeling intimidated into silence by both of them. Baring had a few years earlier been the *Morning Post*'s correspondent at Constantinople, a city Steven had not yet seen, though he was already attracted to its history. Among the Asquiths, Baring's closest friend was not Margot but her eldest stepson, Raymond, a prodigy of talent and charm;† and another of Raymond's circle was Lady Diana Manners, generally thought to be the most beautiful woman in England. The last of the Souls, the presiding clique, in both intellectual and social terms, of Margot's youth, mingled here with the paragons of the next generation, sometimes called the Coterie.

Towards the end of that first summer term at Summer Fields, Steven and Puffin gravely noted the assassination of the Archduke Franz Ferdinand of Austria, Puffin because his father had warned

---

\* The Mill House – the main part of the Wharf, without the converted barn where Margot accommodated supernumerary guests – is now owned by Helena Bonham Carter, H. H. Asquith's great-granddaughter. The Asquiths are buried in the village churchyard at Sutton Courtenay, along with Eric Blair, who as a child enjoyed fishing there.

† Raymond and his wife Katharine inherited Nannie Laight from the Runcimans in early 1914.

him of 'terrible consequences', Steven because he was already addicted to the bible of European noble lineages, the *Almanach de Gotha*. Returning to Doxford for the holidays by way of the Runciman townhouse at Barton Street, Westminster, Steven and Leslie lunched with their father and their country neighbour Sir Edward Grey; and the Foreign Secretary confirmed what the more circumspect Prime Minister had only hinted. The prospect of war sent Steven reeling from the table, overcome with nausea; but its actuality did not greatly change the pattern of his life at Summer Fields. Leslie had now proceeded to Eton, but Puffin was still a gentle, amusing, enthusiastic presence. Both boys were reprimanded – though, owing to their fathers' positions, not very fiercely – for singing comic songs under the protective swell of the chapel organ. 'Puffin scored a Duck against the Dragons' went one zoological and regular refrain. The friends occasionally quarrelled about the arrangement of a small garden for which they shared responsibility; Puffin resented the fact that Steven always got his way. The increasingly elderly teachers now began preparing these two clever pupils to sit scholarships to the great schools: Steven was to follow Leslie to Eton; Puffin had the more distant examples of four Wykehamist half-brothers.

A letter from Steven to a temporarily absent Puffin, in March 1916, near the end of their penultimate term, gives an insight into their school lives:

> Dovey, sweety, lovebird . . .
>
> Doctor has just been jawing us because we, the whole Vth form room, were all bullying, in words chiefly, a little in deeds, Forrester. He found him blubbing at the vinery [Summerfieldian for lavatory], shirking the walk.
>
> . . . In the sham schols I beat you by 50 marks in IInd Maths, and in Verses by about 15.
>
> *Nihil est sayere; itaque vale; tuus almissimus pater salutem dicit plurimum.*

Few men of letters were quite as unhappy at school as they later claim, perhaps even fewer as innocent as they care to remember. This contemporary glimpse reveals Steven hunting with the pack, not immune to the effect of three years at an English boarding school. His pithy turn of phrase and independent character were already in place, intellectually confident, humorous, observant, with the capacity for both cruelty and kindness, and a marked taste for romance. He had inherited these qualities, in large part, from his mother.

# 3

# The Emperor

*Northumberland and the sea; Eton and
London, 1916*

> ... the cards are a medley of old and new emblems ... Hereof
> is the lordship of thought rather than of the animal world.
>
> Arthur Waite, *The Key to the Tarot*, 1920

When Steven Runciman was three years old, his father flogged him
with the end of a rope, as he relates in his unpublished memoirs but
claims not to recall: 'The experience did not produce any traumatic
result. Indeed I remember nothing about it myself.' The account is
deliberately blasé. They were on the Runciman yacht, *Sunbeam*,
where Steven apparently persisted in bawling, in defiance of his captain and father's orders. Steven would grow up without self-pity,
sceptical, rather than ignorant, of psychological dogmas; when Nikos
Stangos, a much younger friend and publisher, told him he was about
to start a course of Kleinian analysis, Steven recommended instead
the remedy he had himself undertaken as a young man: 'a long sea
voyage'. But, repressed or not, this first maritime and paternal experience stands in strong contrast to its successors, which Steven
remembered in, for him, unusually immoderate terms:

> What I really hated was when my father took me for day trips on a
> small sailing boat up and down the bleak Northumberland coast. My
> mother, when I complained, told me not to disappoint him. But I think
> that he must have found me a sullen companion; and it kept me from
> feeling any intimacy with him for years to come. It was sad, as my
> brother in spite of his sea-sickness loved being on the sea ... and
> would gladly have taken my place.

The Runciman parents were hardly unusual in allotting imagined talents and preferences to their children for simplicity's sake. It must have seemed fortunate to Walter Runciman that his unusual younger son, so obviously closer to his mother, was suited, and to all appearances willing, to join him in one of his dearest pleasures, sailing – especially as seafaring had such great importance, sentimental, historic and economic, for the whole family. Given Hilda's stubborn adherence to *omertà*, Walter could not know that Steven was flagging not from seasickness but from more complicated complaints, boredom and guilt.

It was probably Steven's lifelong difficulties with his father that helped him to understand the younger Walter's ambiguous relationship with the elder one, Steven's grandfather, founder of the family's success. In summing up the younger Walter's childhood, Steven all but describes his own feelings for his parents: 'My father's relations with his father were never very easy. He was devoted to his mother, but as a boy he had seen little of his father, who spent most of the time away at sea.' Walter Runciman, junior, as much a sailor as his father, spent his working life on the ship of state. Its vagaries kept him, in turn, away from his children. Steven did not shy away from charting the connection. 'On leaving Cambridge my father went into the family business. He was too loyal to admit it, but he seems to have found it difficult to work in harmony with his very autocratic father. Partly from a sense of public duty, but also as a means of escape, he began to interest himself in politics.' To that interest the Runciman children owed their existence; their father had met their mother in Liberal circles. Steven, in this sense the product of one paternal estrangement, could not help developing another.

Steven's theory makes sense of much about the younger Walter's character and the course of his life and career. It explains the motive which drove this cautious, introverted, earnest man to seek high office; and the inevitable scruples and animosities that led to his regular defeat at the hands of swashbuckling, roguish extroverts. Winston Churchill and Lloyd George, megalomaniacs of self-love and monsters of ability, were more like the elder Walter. While offering this neat, plausible, even somewhat Freudian analysis, Steven made certain that aspects of the younger Walter would remain unknowable, by destroying the letters his father wrote to him.

Their uneasy connection was a private matter, and he made sure it remained so.

Steven's grandfather, the elder Walter, was in his way a conscientious historian. He had many tales to tell, plenty of time to deliver them, and a captive audience in his wide and dependent family. 'He was a remarkable man,' his grandson remembered, 'energetic to the last, courageous, ready to take risks, strictly honest and very generous, but often ruthless and inconsiderate, and wholly egotistical.' When the elder Walter was made first a baronet and then a baron, his grandchildren were covertly amused and irreverent about 'the Old Gentleman' in a way they were not about their own father's preferments. But though they might find their grandfather comical for reasons that had much to do with class, the Runciman children never quite dropped their nervous respect, or their faint suspicion that he was right when he hinted to them that he possessed powers out of the ordinary. They enjoyed the story that a Norwegian sailor – some gnarled ocean-Viking wizard, like their mother's reputedly piratical forebear, Captain Andersen out of sixteenth-century Norroway – had taught him 'the curse that kills in a year and a day'; and they quietly speculated about which maritime and mercantile rivals their grandfather might have used it on.

For all the dissimilarity between this ludicrous, unavoidably impressive pantomime ogre and his hesitant, careful son, the children recognized something intangible and peculiar which their father and grandfather had in common – a faculty that they considered had been passed down, indeed, to them, bypassing mere Runcimans by marriage like Hilda. It touched a family legend of a kind of knack, even second sight, inherited perhaps from Walter the coastguard and Methodist preacher, perhaps from earlier still. Runcimans exacted obedience from animals. They knew the tricks of the land as well as the sea. They were hard to fool. They were not lightly denied when they had a certain look of command or reproach in their eye. This, in part, explains the leniency, relative to the time, with which Steven and Margie, mischievous children by disposition, were brought up. Generally one of these glances from Walter was enough to discourage a repeated offence, without any need for any less subtle punishment. The whole family took part in a proud self-consciousness, a tradition of toughness within their work and unexpectedness beyond it. Steven called the Runcimans in his unpublished memoirs 'a typical Scottish family of no pretensions, probably quite well educated, with a taste for music and the arts, but restless and with a liking for sea-faring'. The studied neutrality of this summary betrays the extent to which he shared the family identity, that collective pride which of course includes the boasted independence from 'pretensions'.*

Whatever Steven's difficulties in 'feeling any intimacy' with his father, his letters to him still show some; but their humour is of a more calculated, restrained kind than the display of gleaming inner life he habitually offered his mother. In one pert tease he doodles a portrait of his father and asks, 'Will you whack me for this?' Steven also appears from the first to be proud of, and intrigued by, his father's political calling, declaring in an early letter of November 1911, 'What fun the rows in the House of Commons must be!' With the outbreak of the First World War, Walter's experiences in the Commons were to become more rowdy even than his younger son imagined. His friend and Cabinet colleague the Liberal socialist John Burns, whom Steven remembered as 'charming and erudite', well versed in the works of Chaucer, resigned in protest at the declaration of war, and Walter was promoted into his place, the Presidency of the Board of Trade. In the October of 1914 Winston Churchill, then First Lord of the Admiralty, who privately considered Walter Runciman to be a 'little goose', attempted, in an access of contrition for causing the capture of a British garrison at Antwerp, to resign and take personal command of a continental army. He proposed that Runciman replace him, but Asquith hurriedly dismissed the whole idea.

Six months later, the Prime Minister was compelled, in the wake of Churchill's next brainchild, the Gallipoli campaign, to form a war-time coalition of all parties. Lloyd George schemed to have Walter shifted to the new Ministry of Munitions, but ended up having to accept this post himself. At the end of 1915, Walter and Lloyd George

---

* Steven's niece Ann Shukman has described this verdict as a defensive exercise in 'embourgeoisement', eliding the deep poverty and basic levels of self-education among the Runcimans prior to the success of Steven's grandfather, the 1st Baron Runciman. She also notes that this shipping magnate's various writings, for all their claims to bluff maritime honesty, skim over the desperate circumstances of a family background beset by deprivation, alcoholism and tuberculosis.

clashed again over the crucial question of conscription, which Walter, Reginald McKenna, the Chancellor of the Exchequer, and Sir John Simon, the Home Secretary, all opposed.* Lloyd George persuaded the Prime Minister that compulsory military service was essential if victory were to be achieved, and succeeded in framing his three adversaries – all hitherto distinguished by intense personal loyalty to Asquith – as uncooperative reactionaries. In truth, Lloyd George's contempt embraced his Prime Minister too. He wrote to his secretary and mistress Frances Stevenson that if Asquith 'were in the pay of the Germans he could not be of more complete use to them'.

At the same time, Margot Asquith, to whom clan allegiance was of immeasurably greater importance than personal dignity or scrupulosity, busied herself in trying to apply straightforward emotional blackmail to Walter Runciman. 'How can you find it in your heart to desert Henry', her stepdaughter Cynthia recalled her reproaching him, 'when Puffin has been such a friend of your little boy's!' After some face-saving concessions, few of which related to goings-on at Summer Fields, Walter and McKenna, though not Simon, remained in the Cabinet. It was a ministry, as it turned out, with just under a year left to run. Even within that period Walter had reason to doubt his Prime Minister's stability, and consequently that of his own tenure at the Board of Trade. After the Easter Rising in Dublin in 1916, and the honourable but despairing resignation of the Chief Secretary for Ireland, Augustine Birrell, Runciman was one of several Cabinet Ministers whom Asquith managed thoroughly to discompose by suggesting that he be sent out as Birrell's successor.

Scarcely less competitive than these War Cabinet manoeuvres were the scholarship examinations for which Summer Fields was now cramming Steven and Puffin. 'By this time,' Steven remarks with deceptive blitheness, 'I had been more or less adopted by the Asquiths,' but a geographical separation, at least, from Puffin was now inevitable. The results in July announced their double triumph – by a strange

---

* Simon was absolutely opposed to any conscription on moral and liberal principles; Walter Runciman and McKenna, economic rather than social liberals, argued that the malign effect of conscription upon the country's productivity would outweigh any military advantage.

coincidence, both boys had been elected as the third best scholar at their destinations, Eton and Winchester. Raymond Asquith wrote from the Western Front to congratulate his little brother and his not-very-beloved stepmother, assuring Margot that Puffin would be much happier at the public school he remembered with much affection than at Summer Fields. On the last day of that summer term, Steven was invited to accompany Puffin back to his family's metropolitan residence, 10 Downing Street. The Bright Young Things of *Vile Bodies* inadvertently drop in on the place in the mid-1920s; Steven had anticipated Evelyn Waugh's characters by a decade. Margot Asquith's salon was quite as disconcerting as Margot Metroland's, and Steven contrived to lose his way until a footman retrieved him an hour or so into lunch, and found him space next to the glacial beauty Lady Diana Manners.

The beginning of the long summer holidays of 1916 may have brought Steven perturbation, but their end would throw the Asquiths into mourning. On the last Sunday before he was to start Winchester, Puffin was with his parents and the usual assemblage of luminaries at the Wharf, about to begin a parlour-game, when Margot was summoned to the telephone. It was the sort of call that had become dully, achingly familiar all over Europe. Raymond Asquith had been shot dead, hit through the chest while leading a platoon of Grenadier Guards, on the first day of the Battle of Flers-Courcelette, the beginning of the 'third phase' of the Somme Offensive. He left his grieving widow, Katharine, three children and Nannie Laight, formerly of the Runciman household. Nannie Laight would be discomfited when Katharine converted to Catholicism, taking her children with her, at the urgent suggestion of her and Raymond's close friend Maurice Baring. But Nannie stayed on anyway, and would eventually be buried in the same churchyard as her last employer.

The dreadful news affected the Runciman family at the political, personal and domestic levels; it must have exacerbated the already overwhelming unpleasantness of Steven's first weeks at Eton. 'I may have disliked Summer Fields, but my first half [Etonian for term] at Eton was sheer misery.' Only now did he recognize that his 'adoption' by the Asquiths had greatly diluted the usual trials of boarding school – the specific humiliations of the fagging system, the preponderance of physical punishment, the inedible food, the pointless regulations and the impossible standard of collective honour. The bluff, handsome, rather vain Head Master, Dr Alington, was adored by the school's athletes but sneered at by its intellectuals; probably the greatest practical difference his reforming tenure had made to the boys was his decision to bring back birching. Leslie was a scholar in the election (College parlance for a year group) two years ahead of Steven, and was enjoying himself far more than he had at Summer Fields. He was by now a byword for schoolboy success, intelligent, physically capable, good-looking and famous for never provoking a beating. He paid his brother little attention; his only worry was that the war might end before he could distinguish himself in it. Steven, on the other hand, worried about everything, including, unsurprisingly given what had just befallen his best friend, the prospect of *his* elder brother's death in the event of the war being prolonged.

In mid-November 1916, towards the end of his first half, Steven wrote a stoical account to his father at Doxford:

> My games are much improved now. I actually got quite a good goal while playing in a disgustingly horrible snowstorm . . . I asked for early bed leave on Thursday evening, saying that I had a headache and a cold, nothing extraordinary. But Miss Oughteson, after taking my temperature, quite normal, said that I had better miss early school next morning, – presumably because I am (or look) so anemic [sic]. – Then afterwards, next morning, she said I had better miss all the schools . . . and so I got off all Friday schools for very little more than nothing.
>
> Please tell Mammy Love to send me 'Saints & Sinners of R. History' also could she send me some jams. I personally feel that I cannot spend money on such stuff as jam, when my father is making such statements about confectionery, but I trust that her conscience is not so delicate . . . Please forgive my writing in green ink, but as it is perfumed, I couldn't resist the temptation.

Miss Oughteson, the Matron-in-College, Steven was to describe in his unpublished memoirs as 'one of the few people I have known whom I thoroughly disliked'. In his quip about his father's responsibilities as President of the Board of Trade, in the colour and perfume of his ink and in every crevice of his syntax, Steven had already developed into an idiosyncratic personality, one his father would accept with hesitant, half-comprehending decency.

Physically, too, Steven developed with inconvenient speed. The Runcimans were of tall and bony stock, and Steven was inheriting the unruly physique of a Scots Borderer – he grew by 5 inches that first half – yoked to his own fastidious, even valetudinarian temperament. Well trained and naturally gifted, but lacking particular motivation, he found himself constitutionally unequal to throwing off headaches, exhaustion and the ordeal of the Eton diet. Steven was not used to being told what to do or what to eat. Any such indignities at Summer Fields had been moderated by the nearby shielding sway of the Asquiths. Subjection to authoritarian Sixth-Form fag-masters and survival on the sort of sustenance he had scarcely seen before – especially among the discipline and shortages of war – must have seemed all of a nauseating piece.

> I greatly resented fagging and thought it monstrous that older boys should be able to order me about, and, worse, that they were entitled to beat one if they decided that one had committed a misdemeanour. The food was awful . . . I became anorexic, refusing to eat the slabs of red meat, coming from heaven knows what animal, and a horribly greasy steam pudding, known as Wagstaff . . .

Steven's later eagerness to alight upon medical terminology in explaining his pickiness about food may invite scepticism, but there was something more than simple disgust to the oddities of his eating at this period. He had a lifelong distaste for dairy products, and cannot have reacted well to being made to drink milk daily.* His specific reaction to the declaration of war had been a desire to vomit. While Steven's dietary anxieties cannot precisely be linked, as anorexia is, to sensations of self-disgust, the school's process of hierarchical pupation, the transformation from despised fag, dressed in a short 'bumfreezer' jacket, to a waistcoated, wing-collared dragonfly among youths, was hardly calculated at the outset to bolster a young

---

* Steven's closest Eton friend, Eric Blair, quite differed from him in this respect, subsisting partly on the cheese that he secretly manufactured in his room.

adolescent's physical self-confidence.* Good, at least, almost immediately came out of ill; the doctor summoned to examine Steven
during his first holidays from Eton insisted there was no question of
his going back to school for the time being. When he eventually did
return, weeks into the next half, medical instructions protected him
from the twin torments of competitive games and fagging.

Even at their worst, Steven's sufferings were slighter than they
might have been. Eton tolerated a greater degree of heterodoxy than
most other public schools would have allowed, especially in a scholar;
and its College, King Henry VI's original foundation, the most academically and architecturally impressive part of the school, was much
the best place for Steven. King's Scholars not only lived apart from
the full-fee-paying Oppidans (or town-dwellers); they ate apart, often
learnt apart, and dressed apart, with flowing black scholars' gowns
over the tailcoats every boy wore in mourning for King George III.
By letting their boys become 'KSes', or 'tugs' (for their gowns or
*togae*), a more intellectual but theoretically less grand breed, the
Runcimans showed that, rich as they might be, they still had more
sense than money. Their decision placed Steven in one of the most
remarkable and, happily, best-documented elections the College at
Eton has ever seen.

At the top of the 1916 scholarship paper had come Denis Dannreuther, the son of Sir Sigmund, the Financial Secretary at Lloyd
George's Ministry, and the grandson of a German pianist from Strasbourg, the tutor of Hubert Parry.† Dannreuther had dark good looks,
was lithe and quick at games, and thoroughly liberal-minded. After
him was Athelstan Caroe, son of a Danish grain merchant resident in
Liverpool. He worked hard and played well, but was not widely liked,
and Steven thought him dull. After Runciman minor KS was Roger
Mynors, son of the Vicar of Bridstow in Herefordshire; Steven would
soon consider him 'the best scholar of the whole election'. George

---

* Anorexia nervosa had been known about for decades (the term was coined by Sir
William Gull, one of Queen Victoria's physicians, in 1873).
† Denis Dannreuther's grandmother, Chlariclea Ionides, might have been of greater
interest to Steven; she was a Phanariot Greek by blood, born into a family of refugees from Constantinople.

Wansbrough was another clergyman's son, a talkative all-rounder becoming interested in Marxist economics. Frederick Burgess was mainly notable for his acting. Bobbie Longden, an admiral's son, was another skilful classicist; Steven was to describe him as 'red-haired and freckled, attractive rather than good-looking, sweet, vague and charming'. Ralph Cazalet was praised and dismissed by Steven as 'a quiet unexciting boy whom it was impossible not to like'. Denys Nettleton had an elder brother in Leslie's year, but the younger brothers did not get on so well as the older ones; Steven found Denys 'a good comic artist, but without his brother's solid qualities . . . I was never entirely at ease with him.'* James Gibson was another of the heartier, sportier Collegers, a tubby boy despite his sporting abilities, who was teased in a pseudonymous article by another member of the election for being callous enough, hypothetically, to kick his new-born son in the head to stop it wailing. This satirist, who came from a more straitened background than any of the others, and did not hesitate to emphasize this, was Eric Blair.

After George Orwell had reached the height of his posthumous fame, Steven, by then a distinguished old man, quickly became impatient with the swarm of biographers eager for hagiographical fragments from this English worthy's boyhood. He often professed himself bored with the Orwell industry, and at the release of every new account he exchanged wry postcards with Anthony Powell – an Oppidan survivor from the same era at Eton – about what parts they were likely to be allotted in the latest 'Orwelliad'. Sometimes he would play down the extent of this early bond; sometimes he preferred to encourage extravagantly close interpretations. In 1997, he tartly reminded one Orwellologist that he had not met Eric Blair for seventy-seven years. At the time, like many schoolboy friendships, the accord between Runciman minor and Blair was a matter less of

---

* Denys Nettleton was so called at the time of his admission to Eton, but he was né King-Farlow, and soon would revert to that name. His father, Sir Sydney King-Farlow, the ex-Chief Justice of Gibraltar but not quite confident in his social position, had changed the whole family's name after his wife was left a small estate in Kent, traversed by a Nettleton Road. Eventually his wife and children prevailed upon him to change it back. King-Farlow or Nettleton, the family came to know the Runcimans more intimately, and Roddy, Denys's elder brother, married Margie in 1925.

common ground than of defensive pact, and perhaps all the more important for that.

Blair arrived only in the second, Lent half, having transferred from Wellington, to which more militaristic establishment he had first won a scholarship. He made his first impression on the rest of the election in a manner that belies the intellectual aloofness later attributed to him by Steven, among others. New 'tugs' underwent a mild initiation ceremony called 'Chamber Singing', in which they entertained their fellow scholars with a song and, if that proved unsatisfactory, were pelted with shoes, books and food. Steven left no record of his own performance, but for all his shyness he probably managed adequately – he had recently had plenty of practice in this sort of exploit with the Asquiths, to the accompaniment of Puffin's piano and Margot's 'Castilian' dances. When his turn came, Blair, for his part, much impressed the Chamber; a passionate follower of music-hall comedy, he had little difficulty in belting out 'Riding Home from Bangor', a nineteenth-century classic from Maine.

As a harbinger of acceptance and popularity, this first glimpse was misleading. The main unifying force between Steven and Blair was their deliberate preference for isolation from their peers. They were both markedly better read than the rest, which their masters noted – as often with annoyance as with appreciation. Blair was more advanced outside the curriculum; Steven remembers being guided by his new friend, a much dimmer academic talent, towards Samuel Butler's *The Way of All Flesh*. It was a recommendation he would come to see as typical of Blair's style: bracing, satirical, rational and a touch earnest. 'Blair, though he always had wit and irony, was lacking in lightness of humour, anything that smacked of frivolity.'

Soon after Blair's arrival, he and Steven were involved in a curious and macabre incident. Philip Yorke, an older Colleger, good-looking, sporting and intelligent but disliked even by his brothers Gerald and Henry as a verbal and physical bully, called Steven by 'a particularly unpleasant name'. Blair, already indefatigable in pursuit of justice, declared that Yorke must be punished. The plot of a ghost story in the *Ingoldsby Legends*, which Blair had lent to him, occurred to Steven, and he suggested that they employ a waxen voodoo doll. When Blair was about to pierce the resultant object, melted from a candle, with a steel pin through its heart, Steven deflected this extreme plan, and the boys contented themselves with snapping off its leg. Within days Yorke broke his leg playing the more tactile Eton variant of football, the Field Game; and not long afterwards he happened to die of leukaemia. His brothers, perhaps severally impressed, were to become a novelist and an occultist. Blair and Steven were regarded with a certain cautious respect from then on. Unchastened, they exchanged enthusiastic letters and scholarly recommendations about lycanthropy and vampirism.

Denys King-Farlow has recalled Blair as a put-upon, aggrieved figure, all too willing to bring up the subject of money, whose disappointing Eton career and rejection of a university education can be attributed to a mixture of financial and personal considerations. But the Blair Steven describes is a romancer of a more thorough kind. Steven neither believed his contemporary's relative poverty to be genuine nor regarded it, as King-Farlow and others did, as Blair's driving concern. He considered Blair, in the end, to be an impersonal character amid all his idealism, who felt more 'pity for the human condition than for the individual human', and whose actions were motivated mainly by a desire for escape, independence and travel, especially to the East. This was certainly a desire Steven felt himself, and he too would escape Eton early, though not, unlike Blair, in the first instance for the orient.

Meanwhile, Steven's home life at Doxford and Barton Street was subject to fluctuations of power at Westminster. His father had been a Liberal MP since 1899, with a short interval in 1900–1902 when he was defeated by his persistent opponent, the then-and-future-Tory Winston Churchill. Churchill, according to Steven, chivalrously told his conceding adversary that 'the world will be hearing from both of us again' (though other accounts make this compliment Walter's to Churchill). For eleven years from 1905, Walter enjoyed patronage and exercised power under Sir Henry Campbell-Bannerman and, especially, Asquith. He was a serious man of dedicated industry, proven experience and intellectual substance. With the unstinting aid of his similarly disposed, equally competent wife, he seemed to have escaped from the shadow of his comic-opera tycoon father.

Walter did not resemble his brilliant but rather unstraightforward leader, Asquith, in terms of character, abilities or even ideals. He was more isolated than he knew; his closest political ally was the

Chancellor, McKenna, and both represented a kind of old-fashioned, laissez-faire Victorian businessman's Liberalism that had, almost without knowing it, already succumbed to war and to history. The Tory Prime Minister and later Leader of the Opposition Arthur Balfour, who, with his grand background as Lord Salisbury's favourite nephew, was much more to Asquith's liking at the human level, dismissed McKenna as 'an able accountant'; and Asquith, confronted with the sort of business-minded motives that represented the anchor of McKenna's and Walter's public career, had once branded them 'not disgraceful, but disgusting'. In a note to his young inamorata Venetia Stanley, rating his Cabinet 'as if it were an examination ... like a Tripos at Cambridge', Asquith ranked Runciman a not especially complimentary ninth equal. Had it been only Asquiths and Balfours with whom Walter Runciman had to do, he might well have lasted the course, without necessarily reaching the distinguished heights he was coming to consider his due. But these too were yesterday's men, and, partly because of Hilda's indelible prejudice, Runciman had made an enemy of the rising sun, Lloyd George.

By the end of 1916, Lloyd George had added to his popularity and reputation for ruthless efficiency the support of the populist, right-wing Northcliffe press and of the Tories, under their obscure new Canadian-born leader, Andrew Bonar Law. Together they successfully forced the Prime Minister to accede to the appointment of an inner War Committee, of which the Minister of Munitions would be chairman. The question arose, and was fiercely fought, as to who would have ultimate control of the war's direction, the Committee Chairman or the Prime Minister. It was to be a struggle that cost Asquith his remaining authority. When Lloyd George, with seeming inevitability, replaced him as Prime Minister at the head of a new coalition with only a minority of Liberal support, Runciman was among those who urged Asquith to accept no subordinate post in the new government, and who themselves ostentatiously refused to serve. Judging by Lloyd George's letters to Miss Stevenson at the time, the new Prime Minister was little troubled by this self-denying ordinance. Walter Runciman was out of government and, in common with many fellow Asquithians, destined to be ejected from Parliament at the 1918 election. Steven would recuperate from his first uncomfortable half at Eton in a much sobered household.

# 4
# Temperance

*Eton, 1918–21; Cambridge, 1921*

Under that rule we know in our rational part something of
whence we came and whither we are going.

Arthur Waite, *The Key to the Tarot*, 1920

The Great War was over at last, but, even if the time was free, the
boys of the Eton College Officer Training Corps, as yet, were not. For
Steven's election of Collegers, the years after the war were a frustrating interlude of enforced subjection to structures they had disavowed.
Politics manifested itself more vehemently, and coherently, than
among previous generations of schoolboys. Christopher Hollis, a
member of Sixth Form in 1918, was one of the few 'liberals' in a
largely 'reactionary' election that included Leslie Runciman. He
recalls even the headmaster, Dr Alington, having some sympathy
with the new mood abroad, sensing the contradiction between a
world changed by war but a school culture, if anything, ossified by it:

Alington . . . had a capacity for amused and ironic observation. I remember him coming out of Chapel one day after the boys had all sung the
*Magnificat* and commenting on 'the curiosity of a thousand rich boys
daily thanking the Almighty for putting down the mighty from their seat,
when they all intended to devote the rest of their lives to seeing that nothing of the sort ever happened'. He thought it funny and we, who were
passing through our mood of parlour bolshevism, also thought it funny,
but it never occurred either to him or to us to do anything about it.

The Sixth Form of 1920 was made of other metal. They were not
content to 'pass through' their sense of the injustice and incompetence

that had precipitated the disaster of the war with no more active response than sophisticated laughter.

Their leader was not Eric Blair and certainly not Steven Runciman, but Denis Dannreuther, the prodigious scholar of Strasbourg German and Phanariot Greek descent who stood at the top of the election. One of Dannreuther's most ardent disciples came, twenty years later, to describe a version of the 'manifesto' advocated by the liberal 'Caucus' – that is, Dannreuther himself, Roger Mynors, Ralph Cazalet, Bobbie Longden and James Gibson. The manifesto's most immediate target was the College election system of vigilantly segregated year groups, which, the liberals maintained, 'created a sense of guilt in those who had innocent relationships outside ... though bullying, like immorality, was commonest among boys of the same age'.

The chronicler of Dannreuther's programme was a prep-school friend of Eric Blair's in the election below. He was idle, unathletic, sharp-tongued, an unsleeping intriguer and, Steven thought, 'quite the ugliest schoolboy I've ever seen'. Cyril Connolly knew how to make the best of his talents. Originally one of the 'reactionary' faction, he changed sides because he too chafed at the restrictions against Collegers making friends of disparate ages. In Connolly's case, 'immorality' – what he called 'the thrill, not untinged by apprehension, by which the romantic recognises reciprocated love' – was the driving motive. 'I could not give a picture of Eton', he declares, 'if I did not emphasise how much time was devoted to planning meetings with people of another year or in another house; the intrigues were worthy of Versailles or Yildiz.'*

Connolly was in pursuit of Noel Blakiston, a coy, godly cricketer in the year below; but he also admired the glamorous figures who adorned the election above. His hero-worship of the Caucus had survived undimmed for two decades when he wrote in *Enemies of Promise*:

---

* Yıldız, the Star Palace, was the favourite residence of the Ottoman Sultans in the late nineteenth century.

our own senior election, the year above us, whom as yet we hardly
knew, contained heroic fighters for liberty and justice. It bristled with
Pyms and Hampdens and the feudal system was powerless there.

... They were a remarkable set of boys ... animated, unlike the
rulers of college, by post-war opinions. They hated bullying, beating,
fagging, the election system, militarism, and infringements of liberty,
and believed in the ultimate victory of human reason.*

In the view of the Caucus, the bitterest outrage against human reason they had to endure was the perpetuation of the compulsory OTC
cadet force after the war. Blair aside, they were not necessarily 'parlour bolshevists' or even left-wingers, but they had developed an
enduring pacifism, further entrenched by the patriotic celebrations
the school laid on. Encouraged to sing 'Land of Hope and Glory' as
a cadet procession marched by in December 1918, Etonians broke
into a medley of subversive alternatives.

Steven's near-contemporary Lord Longford (Edward Pakenham,
elder brother of the more celebrated Frank) had succeeded to his earl-
dom in 1915 upon the death of his father at Gallipoli. The late Earl's
last words were said to have been 'Don't bother ducking, the men
don't like it and it doesn't do any good.' But his heir ducked on principle, becoming the first Etonian cadet to resign from the OTC and
achieving heroic stature among the school's liberals. Steven, thinking
back on that immediate post-war atmosphere in later interviews,
maintained his distance from all extremes. He considered young
Longford 'a silly boy'; but, though he had known Churchill in his
father's Liberal circles since early childhood, he always thought it
'difficult to forgive him over the Dardanelles'.

In the Lent term of 1918, when the Colleger cadets were sent for
training at Blackdown Camp in Surrey, Cyril Connolly seized his
chance for social preferment among the Caucus. His father Major
Matthew Connolly was a retired officer, chronic drinker and expert

---

* Christopher Hollis, the older, resigned pragmatist to Connolly's star-struck
younger acolyte, came to put matters in quite different terms. 'The reforms of which
we spoke were not something to be done. They were rather something to be advocated. Talking about projects was an end in itself' (Christopher Hollis, *A Study of
George Orwell* (Hollis & Carter, 1956), p. 16).

in the classification of snails. His chief faults, according to his son, included 'worldliness, insincerity, meanness ... vulgarity ... vanity, cowardice and greed'. But he had geography in his favour: he lived near the Camp. Hospitable in his bibulous way, the Major was delighted, at his son's suggestion, to receive Roger Mynors, George Wansbrough, Bobbie Longden, Steven Runciman and George Rylands for a dinner-party.

Young Connolly's most notable social conquest by way of this deft manoeuvre was not Runciman but Rylands. The most approachable, most distinguished and best-looking member of the 1915 election – between Leslie and Steven Runciman's years – Rylands, called 'Dadie' by his intimate friends, a lisped variant of 'Baby', stood wearily aloof from the great societal struggle in College, serving the higher cause of Art, and already offering to it many victorious garlands. He seemed to win both prizes and affection without trying. Academically and theatrically, he was Eton's leading Shakespearean. His golden-headed Viola had made a lasting impression upon Provost Sheppard of King's, Cambridge. Dadie's humane, vital influence was beginning to eclipse, in its appeal to Steven, the severe spirit of resistance incarnated in Eric Blair (whom Dadie, less than coincidentally, was to remember as 'aloof and unsympathetic').

At first, like Blair, Steven had allowed his disapproval of the school system to prevail over his desire and ability to flourish there. 'With a sad mixture of haughtiness and diffidence', he avoided competing for any prizes except, in an impish spirit, those for Harmony, Counterpoint and Composition – where he contended in a field of one. Perhaps a trace of nostalgia for his bouts of singing and piano-playing with Puffin and Margot Asquith may be discerned here; in any case his main achievements in the musical sphere were 'a very simple fugue, and some short, simple songs, settings of poems by Walter de la Mare'. Steven contributed much less than Mynors, Wansbrough, King-Farlow or even Blair to school magazines and 'ephemerals' (single-number productions that were more idiosyncratic than the official organs). Steering clear of any more controversial schoolboy journalism, he confined himself to a single short story, 'The She-Devil', under the puckish pseudonym 'Rita Galsworthy, authoress of *The Mountain of Tears*, *Divorce*, *The Sin of Laura Paton*, etc'.

This lightly swipes at Blair's enjoyment of *The Forsyte Saga*, while the story's content mocks Caroe and Dannreuther more directly. Steven borrows Caroe's Christian name Athelstan for the wronged husband, and appears to gender-bend Dannreuther into Denise, the treacherous wife and 'she-devil' of the title. Denise and her wicked lover Count Vilnovitch are presumed dead in a shipwreck, while Athelstan, a dullard lawyer, rapidly consoles himself with a rich second wife. Inevitably, though, Denise returns to complicate the situation. This production represented the height of Steven's social success at Eton, and he was volubly proud of it, sending Margie a detailed letter full of worldly-wise authorial tips:

> How is your story for the Babies [that is, Ruth and Kitty] getting on? Have you thought of an excellent plot? Have a few railway accidents and murders and the house catching fire every now and then; they all add to the interest of the story. A tragic end always makes one's belief in the writer far stronger too. Think what triumphant sensations you would have if Ruthie wept on reading the last chapter. You should have a promising title too: 'Too Late, a story of an Orphan' or 'The Under-petticoat, or An Unclaimed Baby'. Very few titles have anything to do with the actual plot.

While the war was still in progress, some of the 'eccentric temporary masters' provided entertainment if not education. Science and French, the two most disregarded subjects in the Eton curriculum ('French', according to Hollis, 'was so meanly thought of that the teaching of it was actually entrusted to Frenchmen'), attracted two of the oddest masters, or beaks. These were respectively John Christie, the future founder of Glyndebourne Opera, who, Steven thought, possessed more enthusiasm than aptitude for scientific experimentation, and Aldous Huxley, who was incapable of exercising classroom discipline but won Steven's covert admiration for 'the elegance of his English' – 'he taught us strange and rare words in a rather reflective way.' Christie had been lamed at the front, and Huxley was all but blind. Steven remembers Blair sticking up for this unusual, original young man with his huge, useless blue eyes against a throng of less scrupulous Etonian practical jokers, while he himself lacked the courage to intervene. It is a neat image: the prophet of

*Brave New World* shielded by the creator of *1984* – perhaps a little too neat.

Steven made most of his intellectual progress alone in the library during term ('learning far more from history books there than I ever did from history masters'), or else in the considerable holidays his frail health continued to parlay for him. He had in the summer of 1915 begun to learn Russian from a Madame Vera Donnet, née Polianov, a theatrical director and singer, who had been first exiled from Russia for subversive sympathies, and then divorced by her Swiss husband for her literary enthusiasms. Hilda Runciman, ever obedient to her younger son's desires, had located her. 'She was far from good looking,' Steven remembered, and he was equally dismissive of Vera's voice, but 'she had style ... We were all enchanted by her.'* She returned in the summer holidays of 1916 and 1917, after which Steven decided that his reading Russian, at least, was sufficient. She remained, though, a useful and intriguing friend whose invitations to tea could relieve the Runciman brothers' Etonian sufferings. Leslie found Vera a little alarming; when she materialized to rescue both brothers from the exertions of the OTC, Steven was amused by her effect: 'very interesting, very scented, and very inquisitive. I don't think she made a single remark to poor Lellie that wasn't a question.'

Connolly was perceptive enough to notice the disaffection and detachment from the school felt by Runciman and Blair, though he did not distinguish between their distinct characters. He contented himself with the observation that both lacked 'the ape-like virtues without which no one can enjoy a private school ... a mixture of enthusiasm with moral cowardice and social sense. The enthusiasm is

---

* When Vera Donnet married the orientalist scholar Harold Bowen, she became an object of curiosity to the whole Bloomsbury set, especially Maynard Keynes, who had a Russian wife of his own, the ballerina Lydia Lopokova. Steven told Keynes that he 'thought it an example of [Vera's] remarkable talent that although she had no voice at all and was not musical, she could keep up appearances with her singing' (Steven Runciman paraphrased in letter from John Maynard Keynes to Lydia Lopokova, 16 November 1924, in *Lydia and Maynard*, ed. Richard Keynes and Polly Hill (André Deutsch, 1989), p. 255). Steven also seems to have been convinced, without foundation, that Vera's father owned a vast expanse of Ukrainian mines. Vera Bowen and Lydia Keynes were to become close, if often fractious, friends.

for personalities, for a schoolboy is a novelist too busy to write.' In fact, Steven, who always regarded himself as interested in people and stories above all else, would have resented the implication that he was too aloof to appreciate the narrative eventfulness of school life; but he would probably have agreed that Connolly's verdict applied to Blair, who, as Steven was to tell the Orwell biographer Gordon Bowker, 'didn't really like people'. Of the three, it was the impersonal ideologue Blair who would make a novelist.

The Master-in-College, John Crace, was not regarded with affection by Blair, Connolly or Runciman. But Connolly's distaste for their housemaster had in it more than a little self-abasement:

> He was a Jesuitical, conscientious and deceitful man, not at peace with himself, and perpetually torn between an idealistic and a cynical attitude to boys. He was religious, unmarried, Celtic, a Browning addict and, like myself, obviously a virgin. He would come round, when I had been beaten, whistling in a quizzical way; it was unnerving to discover that he knew all about it, and perhaps had even suggested it. He loved tickling small boys, and the squeals of the tickled were agonising music for the bullied and the persecuted like myself. I was never really tickle-worthy.

Neither Blair nor the younger Runciman were tickle-worthy either. Crace's taste ran more predictably to the luscious Dadie, the fresh-faced Noel Blakiston or Bobbie Longden, the handsome redhead and object of Connolly's maturing attentions. In the Lent half of 1920 Blair and King-Farlow were to persecute Crace's known tendresse by placing a mock-advertisement in a college magazine, 'A. R.D. – After rooms – Janney', the initials of Crace's then favourite coupled with a derisive nickname for the Master. The implication was a forbidden tryst after lights out. As Orwell's biographer Bernard Crick observed, this was 'a baited hook – for to punish the slanderer would be to broadcast the accusation'.

Crace does not in fact come across as a particularly malevolent or predatory figure.* He was no match for active cynics like Blair,

---

* Even Crace had had his hour; in 1900 he had been wildly praised as the bewitchingly feminine Cassandra of a Cambridge *Agamemnon*. As for handsome Bobbie

King-Farlow or, in his subversive, double-sided way, Connolly. How-ever, for an essentially civilized, well-mannered, law-abiding original, like Steven, Crace's lack of imagination made existence a good deal more inconvenient than it had to be. Steven expressed a relatively mild series of revenge fantasies by beginning to keep a detailed dream diary, and absent-mindedly leaving it around in the sight of close friends at school and of his sisters at home; it contained unlikely entries such as 'a thrilling dream about Crace eloping with an unknown female'. Crace was suspicious of Steven's recurring ill-nesses, and Steven every now and again implored his parents to write to Crace in support of their genuineness. An altogether nastier type of master was the most learned and caustic of the classical tutors, A. S. F. 'Grannie' Gow. Steven thought Gow's shortcomings were opposite in nature to Crace's. Though Gow was 'a good but not a remarkable scholar, a competent but not stimulating teacher . . . [he] disliked little boys. He didn't understand them at all.' In particu-lar, 'Eric was everything Gow couldn't understand.'

As the Michaelmas half of September 1919 began, Steven's closest friend among the older boys was Dadie Rylands, and among the younger ones, Connolly. Steven credited Dadie with having 'taken the trouble to see to my literary education' around this time. Blair, who had also lent him books and helped to form his taste, was now dis-placed as mentor by the far more glamorous theatrical aesthete. As for Connolly, almost forty years later he remembered with gratitude both Steven's hospitality and his historical erudition. However reserved and untribal he found this older, quieter friend, the compen-sations of Steven's company more than outweighed, for him, their different dispositions. Always easily won over through his stomach, Connolly recalled Steven's generosity with bananas and cream, and added that 'some of my most enlightening moments were spent' in Steven's 'small, high rooms'. Both Rylands and Connolly now pos-sessed a degree of sexual experience with other Etonians. Steven seems to have been aware, but faintly censorious, of Connolly's affair

---

Longden, he would grow up to be a famously popular and flirtatious Master of Wellington; his notes to favourites were discovered in school library books there for years after his untimely death.

with Bobbie Longden, about which Anthony Powell phlegmatically remarked that 'a lot of manual labour went on'. Both Rylands and Steven found Connolly physically beyond the pale, so that the usually well-informed Connolly mistook Dadie for a prude, nicknaming him 'the Old Testament'.

By this year, Steven's third at Eton, his election were ready for academic specialization. Along with practically every other element of the school life, academic decisions had specific social ramifications. As Hollis recalled it,

> there was a strange snobbery about the classics at Eton ... Not only were the majority of the masters classical, but they made no bones about it that they thought of themselves as a superior sort of master to those who taught other subjects. The best boys were made, almost willy-nilly, to specialise in classics. Those who could not quite make the grade were allowed to become History Specialists without loss of social caste.

Steven, overtaken by Roger Mynors but still the fourth strongest scholar in his election and so by no means unable to make the grade, had never thoroughly enjoyed classics since Torby's narrative, dramatic and experimental techniques had given way at Summer Fields and Eton to the hard grind offered by the likes of Grannie Gow. 'I decided to quit the rat-race and to become a History specialist,' Steven explained in his unpublished memoirs, 'rightly seeing that thereby I need not work so hard.' He thus presented the beginning of his commitment to the discipline that shaped his life and career as a short-term tactical manoeuvre, no doubt hoping to annoy the younger, keener historians among his readers. But the sentiment still rings true, and shows that Steven's friendships with the more happily institutionalized Rylands and Connolly had not allayed the basic distaste for Eton and its regimentation that he still shared with Blair.

The most famous of the Eton history masters of this era was G. W. 'Tuppy' Headlam. Headlam had perfected a bonhomous mask and enjoyed wide popularity with the boys. His casual cynicism appeared to his admirers to render life as well as thought more comfortable. Asked what he thought of the afterlife, he once remarked, 'Doubtless I shall inherit eternal bliss, but I prefer not to meditate upon so wholly melancholy a prospect.' His success was sealed by the hard-drinking, unpredictable quality of his social life, whose leading adornment was the Chinese-American film star Anna May Wong. The young Steven's attitude to this 'character' was unforgiving: 'None of us took him very seriously.' For his part, Tuppy wrote of Steven to Walter Runciman in a 1919 school report that 'I wish this boy were kinder to me.' Headlam's favourite subject was the history of Renaissance Italy. Under his instruction both Connolly and Denys King-Farlow became absorbed in Machiavelli, whom Connolly studied with a view to getting into the school's elective elite, the Eton Society, better known as 'Pop'. Eight of the then twenty-five members of Pop had Headlam as their personal tutor, though this probably related only indirectly to their mastery of Machiavelli. Steven's engagement with the period was lighter-hearted but also more sophisticated. He wrote to his mother a couple of weeks into term to describe his latest work:

> This week, instead of writing an essay, which we usually have to do, we have to write a historical play, of the time of the Tudors, in England or abroad. I am writing rather a melodramatic affair about Milan in 1494, introducing Charles VIII of France, Beatrice D'Este and Leonardo da Vinci. There is only one murder (by poison); and the play differs from true melodrama by having a tragic ending. It has only one perversion of history, in making a married couple live at Milan, when they ought to be living at Pavia.

The letter reveals Steven kicking against the parochial quality of history at Eton ('of the time of the Tudors, in England or abroad'), a slant from which he would dissent even more emphatically while at Cambridge. With the natural desire of an advanced sixteen-year-old to display his command of form, Steven lays down the law on the genre of melodrama and the details of chronology, but does not seem to take either literary or historical concerns unduly seriously. At heart he is still guying the whole system.

As a history specialist, Steven was finally permitting himself to draw upon his competitive instincts. His attempt at the Rosebery Prize in the Lent half of 1920 reveals further interest in Italian history, though by now he had abandoned Renaissance 'melodrama' for the peninsula's scarcely less eventful later nineteenth century, concentrating on Count Cavour and Garibaldi. At his request Hilda sent him a recent work by G. M. Trevelyan on the subject; Steven had soon decided that Garibaldi 'would have been an intolerable man to have known: I much prefer Cavour.' Evidently, for all his disapproval of the jovial Tuppy, Steven no less than Headlam subscribed to 'the history of personalities', whose total dominance at Eton Connolly described in *Enemies of Promise*.

The next Michaelmas Steven scented an above-board chance at escape, and he took it. Dadie Rylands was going up to Cambridge for an interview to read classics at King's; he had every reason to be confident of success there. Eton had a traditional sibling relationship with Henry VI's Cambridge foundation, and many places there were reserved for its products. The college was also becoming fashionable in a new mode, exemplified by the theatre-loving Provost, John Sheppard (who had so admired Dadie's Viola), and the new Bursar, Maynard Keynes. Steven, although a year younger than Dadie, had determined to apply for a place at Trinity – his father's and now his brother's college, arguably even grander than King's – at the same time. Headlam, as his academic tutor, and Crace as his personal one, both told him he would do better to wait. But he appealed over their heads to Dr Alington. Though Alington was sneered at on intellectual grounds by some of the school's most exalted scholars, Steven rightly suspected that this jovial, charismatic Head Master harboured a liking for him.

Together with Roger Mynors and Bobbie Longden, Steven had earlier initiated the unusual step, in Eton's monastic society, of entering into friendly relations with Mrs Alington ('a large lady with a red face and flaming red hair, rather careless about her clothes, but full of good sense and kindliness') and, especially, her three daughters, Kathleen, Elizabeth and Lavinia. After the Alingtons had entertained the Collegers to tea, Steven, with Mynors and Longden, his two best friends among Connolly's Caucus, had simply issued a return invitation. It was a polite, harmless and amusing way of undermining the stultifying codes upheld in College by Crace and the reactionaries, and the little Alington girls (the eldest of whom was ten at the time of the first tea-party) took to it extremely well. Twenty-five years on, the youngest of the three, Lavinia, married Roger Mynors.* For the pres-

---

* Elizabeth, the middle daughter, married an Oppidan of the same generation, Lord Dunglass, later, as Sir Alec Douglas-Home, to become Prime Minister. Connolly

ent, Mrs Alington and her daughters provided a pleasant consolation for the feminine home life Steven missed, and to which he decamped whenever possible. They also constituted a useful channel of communication to the increasingly well-disposed Head Master.

Just as Steven had hoped, Alington supported him on the subject of Cambridge and informed Walter and Hilda Runciman that there could be no possible drawback to their able younger son trying for Trinity early. Steven travelled up to Cambridge with Dadie, who was then invited by Sheppard, more or less on the spot, to begin residence at King's the very next term, at the beginning of 1921. It seemed that the theatre-struck Provost needed an Electra in a hurry for an *Oresteia* he was about to put on, and no one but the golden Rylands would do. Younger, taller, lanky and shy, with the heavily boned Runciman face and his uncompromisingly Caledonian auburn mop, Steven – not favoured to Dadie's smoothly 'Athenian' extent at either Eton or Cambridge – had to fall back on merit.

Trinity might be a place of fabled majesty – its scornfully beautiful Great Court still bringing to mind its most glamorous son, Lord Byron, and his domestic bear – but its accommodation of applicants was rather more cheerless. A young émigré 'White' Russian, Vladimir Nabokov, who had come up the previous year, recalled the glumness of exchanging a Revolution for a small bed, an ashtray embossed with the college arms, a sea shell and a water-jug topped with a frangible wafer of ice. For running, as opposed to freezing, water, both on his first visit and during his undergraduate residence, Steven had to walk across a wide court; and, to reach his interview, he was bidden further off to some of the most gorgeous rooms in college, overlooking both the Great Court and the lush greenery of the Backs. This appointment was with Jim Butler, a thirty-year-old Prize Fellow, a decorated and demobilized hero of Gallipoli, Egypt and France, and

---

had, with an unwitting combination of prescience and error, observed of Dunglass that 'in the 18th century he would have become Prime Minister before he was 30. As it was, he appeared honourably ineligible for the struggle of life' (Cyril Connolly, *Enemies of Promise* (Routledge, 1938), p. 228). Steven's favourite among the Alington sisters was the eldest, Kathleen, 'bright and amusing . . . a first class pianist' (SR, 'Footnotes to a Long Life', Elshieshields Archive, Lochnaben, p. 42), who died at thirty of anorexia, possibly after a disappointment in love.

a son of Trinity less figuratively than Byron or any other graduate –
Butler had been born in the Master's Lodge. Butler's favourite area of
historical study, the Great Reform Act, was not attuned to Steven's
already more exotic interests. The other history interviewers, Denys
Winstanley and the supremely urbane East Coast American aristocrat Gaillard (pronounced Galyard) Lapsley, were also experts on the
constitutional details of English history, from which Steven shied.
Nonetheless, he impressed all three easily with his quality. 'We all
thought your son's work extraordinarily good, and indeed brilliant,
and (in confidence) put him easily first of all the historians,' Butler
wrote, without compromise or hesitation, to Walter.

All the same, Steven's stylish exit from Eton was handicapped both
by his tender age, seventeen, and by the continuing antipathy of the
Master-in-College. The day after the arrival of Butler's encomium,
the Runciman parents received a letter of reluctant congratulation
from Crace: 'Steven's very remarkable success at Trinity is in itself the
best comment upon the real merit of his work: and however much he
may puzzle us here – and he is a most puzzling person to understand –
he has made a sufficiently definite impression at Cambridge . . . ' But
now that evidence of Runciman minor's talents, puzzling though they
seemed to him, had been formally acknowledged by a higher authority, Crace was even less willing to set this enigmatic prodigy free.
Steven had not, like Dadie, been invited to take up residence immediately and would have to endure two more Eton halves; but Crace
wanted him to go through the orthodox glories of Sixth Form
until the summer of 1922, joining the struggle for school prizes that
must now have sounded, to the new Trinity scholar, achingly
parochial.

Unlike Connolly, whose liberal phase faded instantaneously with
his election to Pop, Steven still genuinely disapproved of the powers
he would be expected to exercise in Sixth Form. Even Blair stayed on
and reconciled himself to a year of seniority, before pursuing the
unknown romance of a career with the Imperial Police in Burma.
Steven – whose aggression was all intellectual – had visceral rather
than ideological objections to this stage among the gods, which most
Etonians regard as a long overdue reward.

But the question was not really about what he wanted. He was an obedient son, and his parents would fall in with the advice of his masters, even the stumbling conformities of a Crace; they agreed that he was still too young for university. So it was to his intense relief that he heard that Trinity refused to hold his place beyond 1921. Perhaps he had, during that eager display above the Great Court, conveyed a little of his dilemma to the genial Butler or the socially beady Lapsley; in any case, they declared that his time was now or never. Steven's gratitude brought on a delighted physical collapse. He was obliged to spend a good portion of his 'last year' at Eton recuperating at Château-d'Oex, in the Swiss canton of Vaud, accompanied by Margie who was perfecting her French there. 'I have always found that the delights of convalescence outweigh the tiresomeness of being ill.' But he returned in time to satisfy his curiosity about the Japanese Crown Prince, Hirohito, who visited Eton in late May, and to lay on a final courteous tease for Crace and the conformists, delivering to the Essay Society a paper of studied peculiarity on 'The Evil Eye'.

# 5

# The Lovers

*Cambridge, 1921–4*

The Cupid is of love beginning rather than of love in its
fulness, guarding the fruit thereof.

Arthur Waite, *The Key to the Tarot*, 1920

'I am really very fond of being at Cambridge,' Steven wrote to his
paternal grandmother, whose own education had been confined to
devotional exercises. 'I would prefer being at home of course, but
compared to school – which I didn't like very much – I think Cambridge really delightful . . . ' To Dadie Rylands Steven described his
home-life in a would-be-sophisticated strain of revulsion: 'It has
come as a horrid shock to me how ugly this house [Doxford] and its
very immediate neighbourhood is.' Neither sentiment was straightforwardly hypocritical. Steven's pattern of life had altered at an
accelerated pace; consistency of feeling was hard to come by, and
even harder to express.

One agreeable side-effect during the interval between leaving Eton
in the summer of 1921 and arriving at Trinity in October was Steven's first step towards relative financial emancipation. He and his
siblings now received the proceeds from a trust fund set up by their
grandfather. Administered by a seasoned Runciman employee named
Humble, it was rapidly dubbed the Humble Pie. Armed with an
income of £300 a year (about £12,000 today), Steven took to borrowing the family chauffeur to explore country-house sales, where he
acquired furniture, crockery and ornaments for his future life at
Cambridge. It was an excuse to escape from Doxford and to put his
Dadie-trained aestheticism into practice. His eye tended at this stage

to grandeur, and his husbandry of the Humble Pie to ambition rather than prudence. Steven retailed news of his best finds to Dadie with blasé prodigality ('I've found a tea set of Dresden-Watteau . . . magnificent but I think ugly'). His disingenuous deprecation of his home was really aimed at enticing Dadie to visit. The Birrells, father and son, were the best he could offer by way of diversion; the father, Augustine, a celebrated if superannuated elder statesman and a persistent man of letters;* the son, Frankie, one of the youngest of the Bloomsbury set, a dilettantish reviewer and bookseller, but a more glamorous lure as far as Steven and Dadie were concerned.

Dadie, for his part, was at this point probably too distracted to notice these carefully nuanced invitations. The *Oresteia* produced by the Provost of King's, John Sheppard, which had precipitated Dadie's translation to Cambridge as a typically gilded Electra, led also to a more serious love-affair than the 'manual labour' of schooldays – although not, whatever the Provost might have hoped, with Sheppard. Cambridge theatre, untouched by the tastes of Charles II, was still all male, but Dadie was considered to have more than made up for any dearth. In particular his Electra caught the notice of one of the non-speaking guards, Roland Penrose, himself included in the play largely as dogsbody to its costume designer, his elder brother Alec. The Penroses were strict Quakers, and Roland had briefly experienced the First World War as a non-combatant orderly serving under the command of G. M. Trevelyan. Of any other kind of experience, however, he was at this point entirely innocent. By contrast Dadie, as humanely as he was classically educated, initiated a physical relationship that lasted over the next year.

Penrose remembered an intoxicating blend of first love, sexual disinhibition and confidential friendship, perfected by Dadie's 'beautiful manners. He was modest, not at all egotistical – a completely sympathetic person.' This *preux chevalier* impression was not universally shared; several men and at least one woman would accuse the young

---

* Like Walter Runciman, Augustine Birrell had struggled in vain with the contentious Education brief; as Chief Secretary of Ireland he enjoyed much greater success, but took responsibility for the Easter Rising of 1916 and did not contest the 1918 election.

Dadie of narcissism and callousness. He was compared to both Lord Byron and Shakespeare's Fair Youth, while the less deluded Eddy Sackville-West would refer to any dumping of a lover as 'doing a Dadie'.* Virginia Woolf remarked in her diary that 'Dadie has an ingratiating manner of pawing ladies old enough to be his mother,' describing him as a splendid construction of his own vanity: 'Dadie in his silver grey suits, pink shirts, with his powdered pink and white face, his nerves, his manners, his love of praise'. Frances Marshall (later Partridge) was introduced to Dadie in the summer of 1921, and noted especially his 'condescension towards us ... girls' and the over-neat harmony of his attire, 'pink-shirted to match his complexion'.

It was Dr Sheppard's habit to alternate high-flown Greek or Jacobean tragedy with parodic, even more transvestite skits, and Steven visited Cambridge to watch one of these just after leaving Eton. He professed himself to Dadie 'quite fascinated' by what he had seen and heard:

> My one grief and sorrow was that being tired and a little ill as well as absurdly shy, I must have appeared unutterably stupid ... But (this with a pious air) no doubt a rebuff or two is good for one of my conceited self-consciousness. I loved seeing you act, you and your little friends, and I'll tactfully withhold my biting criticism which of course spares no one. You make a distressingly lifelike loose woman.

The arch, pre-emptive self-protection in this letter suggests that 'a rebuff or two' was just what Steven feared from his ever-popular friend and Dadie's glamorous new undergraduate associates. Though the balance of power was, for the moment, hopelessly unequal, Steven was confident enough to tease Dadie on paper. Dadie in turn poked fun at Steven's epistolary style with its dependence on 'epithets', a criticism that provoked Steven into fits of mock-hesitation in subsequent pen-sketches of Doxford life. Leslie's economics supervisor, Dennis Robertson, a friend and later opponent of Keynes, did

---

* In the 1922 Marlowe Society production of *Troilus and Cressida*, Dadie was given the apt role of the ruthless seducer Diomedes. Steven was more impressed by Joe Ackerley's Achilles, 'a heroic figure who glamorized all Cambridge' (Steven Runciman quoted in Peter Parker, *Ackerley* (Constable, 1989), p. 48).

come to visit. 'I haven't properly had time to catalogue him, though he awes me; I feel he might see through me . . . '

This apprehension may have contained a touch of youthful solipsism, as Robertson was probably concentrating too much upon Leslie, his handsome, good-natured, rather dogged pupil, to take much notice of the younger Runciman. Robertson was an admirable, alarming presence. Only a decade Steven's senior, he already seemed older owing to experience, achievement and complication. A relentless all-rounder at Eton, Robertson had at Cambridge mastered, besides his many academic distinctions, the closely allied skills of amateur dramatics and Liberal Party politics. In August 1914, two months after taking up his inevitable fellowship at Trinity, he had volunteered to serve in a war of which he entirely disapproved. He had commanded men in Egypt, Palestine and Constantinople and won the Military Cross at Gaza. He had a soldier's stern, Roman face; in his works of economics he stuck to a clean, unpretentious prose that displayed his lucid and wide-ranging thought, while arousing the suspicion of his colleagues.

Robertson, Steven soon realized, was 'married to the college'. He regarded his pupils as his family, remaining boyishly one of them as long as he could, while his feelings for several grew more and more entangled. He kept to a playful tradition, which more austere rival authorities regarded as arch nonsense, of illustrating economic models by recourse to *Alice in Wonderland* and *Through the Looking Glass*. The most faithful exegete of Robertson's legacy, Gordon Fletcher, observes of this motif:

> [The 'Alice' books] were a by-product of Dodgson's attempt to come to terms with his life's predicament. Robertson was able to enjoy the fruits of Dodgson's literary genius as a means of coming to terms with his own problems. In the 'Alice' books, Robertson found both a nostalgic refuge in the dreamy half-world of childhood but also a practical philosophy for coping with the harsh world of reality.

Steven only 'realised later that [Robertson's] was a lonely and unhappy life, much of it spent in trying to suppress unsuitable passions for certain undergraduates'. Robertson would come to succeed Penrose as yet another of Dadie's swains, a loyal if often unwanted admirer. In the meantime Robertson's nonchalant role as a 'literary economist' and his taste for the company of younger men made him the most approachable of superiors. After that first sticky weekend in Northumberland, he was the first don in front of whom Steven lowered his guard.

The Runciman brothers, so different in temperament and intellect, shared a preference for the conversation of savants like Robertson to the political side of life at Doxford and in Barton Street. Both were already determined to resist absorption into the creaking Liberal Party whose machinery and reversals continued to obsess their parents. Steven delivered to Dadie a haughtily glum account of a Doxford Liberal tea-party:

> We have been undergoing a terrible ordeal today – a political tea-party to about a hundred Liberals of this very respectable constituency, which my father is now taking on. A dreadful time – taking relays of dull women round the garden with the same cycle of remarks, and then a stodgy meal that lasts till you can bear the sight of munching no longer, and a blizzard of tea cups, to hand this way and that, and the grand climax of speeches. Avoid political doings.

It was all, in any case, for naught – for all the complacency of Steven's allusion to his father 'taking on' a constituency, Walter and Hilda had made too many enemies in the course of the increasingly vicious, petty and directionless affray into which the Liberal Party was collapsing. Walter was not even selected for the 1922 general election, and crept back into the House as the member, not for local and 'respectable' Sunderland but for far-off Swansea West, only in 1924.*

Steven looked forward to escaping from this parochial and futile

---

* A flavour of the bitterness of the struggle among the Liberals, and the abrasive behaviour of Hilda in particular, is captured by a note to her from Lord Beauchamp: 'I came to see you at your request. I was advised not to come by those who knew you. In your own home to which you had invited me, you entertained me to an hour and a half of studied insolence such as I have never experienced in a varied life. You took advantage of the fact that you were a lady to whom I must speak with respect in her own house. I hope I may never have such an experience again. I am afraid we must disagree as much on the principles of hospitality as we do on our ideas of what Liberalism means' (quoted in John Campbell, *Lloyd George* (Jonathan Cape, 1977), p. 215).

scrum into the unknown liberties of Cambridge – but this expectancy was not without qualification. He was caught between trepidation and unconventionality; his last days of holiday found him in a febrile temper. His slice of Humble Pie led him to consume some of the even humbler variety, as he overdrew his account, much to his father's annoyance, by buying an impractically huge Breton oak sideboard, a piano, a selection of silk dressing-gowns ('my only whim'), the various tea-sets he had rescued at north-country auctions, and shelves of books on 'Chinese porcelain and Japanese prints'. He wrote 'short-lived' music, and a short story called simply 'Red', which has not survived (although it piques the interest that Steven apologized to Dadie about it, worried that his friend would find the theme 'a little obvious'). The companion of his farmyard adventures as a child, Margie, was living in Paris, so Steven indulged his nostalgia for the past alone, spending hours out of doors feeding and petting the Doxford goats. He grew his hair in a fringe rather than a parting in a modest step towards open if merely dandiacal rebellion. He admitted to Dadie with what looks like abrupt sincerity that 'I dread the future.'

Steven's fearfulness vied with the impish side to his nature during his first weeks at Cambridge in October. He was well looked after; his brother was a popular member of Trinity, successful both on stage and on the river, prized particularly highly by the Trinity Senior Tutor Ernest Harrison (whom Nabokov, incidentally, had dubbed 'Spy Harrison', 'an extraordinarily stupid, vile man'). Although Leslie moved with a hearty rowing set, which he kept separate from Steven for the good of all concerned, he was now less bound by the unfraternal conventions of boarding school. His Runciman family spirit manifested itself in enthusiastic introductions of Steven to both undergraduates and dons. The most celebrated of these new acquaintances was a recently appointed college Bursar, who, though he found Walter Runciman heavy going, scrupulously acknowledged a favour owed from wartime politics at the Treasury, and was ready to be hospitable to his sons. Steven would come to remember John Maynard Keynes as the most brilliant talker he had ever encountered; but Keynes was at first only an intimidating, if exciting, occasional host. More important was a friendship brokered by Dadie during

Steven's second week at Cambridge. Dadie's looks, theatrical talent and (in respectable third place) learning had already interested Cambridge's most famous, and perhaps most misunderstood, secret society, the Apostles (also known, less self-importantly, as the Conversazione Society). One of the younger members was F. L. 'Peter' Lucas, whom Virginia Woolf called 'pure Cambridge: as clean and sharp as a breadknife'; Lucas had married a much less typically Cantabrigian figure.

Emily Beatrix Coursolles Lucas, née Jones, whom everyone called 'Topsy', was one of the six nieces of Robert Ross, Oscar Wilde's literary executor and *fidus Achates*. She had published poetry and, in 1920, a first novel, *Quiet Interior*, which, according to Rebecca West, perfectly described 'the tone of life as it is lived among pretty young people with enough money to give them power to amuse themselves, but not so much money that they need move out of Bayswater'. Topsy enjoyed the company, flirtation and homage of young men, and if they often turned out to prefer one another, she was lightly possessive, but not jealous and certainly not shocked. She was a self-appointed mother-substitute who never quite retracted the claw of her sexuality: dark-haired, deep-voiced, free with advice and hospitality, and growing bored with the unswervingly intellectual husband she publicly revered.

Steven does not seem to have cared much for the friendship of his contemporaries at Trinity, as opposed to the older undergraduates, dons and dons' wives he met through Leslie and Dadie. He was still virtually teetotal (unlike Roland Penrose, who was permanently marked by the stark transition from dry Quakerism to tremendous drinking bouts in Cambridge and abroad). A vestige of the aloofness he had maintained at Eton led him to avoid the Apostles and their hermetic rites, shunning their grand secrecy as silliness. Steven much preferred the Heretics, an intellectual avant-garde whose proceedings were carried out with breezy publicity; their speakers were to include Dr Marie Stopes and Virginia Woolf. With the patronage of both Dadie and Leslie (who had played Agamemnon to Dadie's Electra), he had a slight foothold in the University's theatrical world, and in the interconnected spheres of young academics like the Lucases, overlapping, though certainly not identical, with Bloomsbury.

In later decades, Steven often remarked that he had made his 'debut' among the Bloomsburies. In so doing, he was contributing to what was by then a long-established tradition. The game was played by insiders, outsiders, liminal onlookers, enemies, voyeurs, reviewers and gossip columnists, and its object was to codify the unclassifiable. This self-conscious pursuit ran on from the very inception of the group's self-proclaimed identity. In 1928 the Bloomsburyish critic Raymond Mortimer, writing for an American audience at the *Dial*, impersonated an anonymous scholar quoting him himself ('Sir Raymond Mortimer . . . trustworthy if academic') in 1960. In so doing Mortimer laid out, for almost the first time, the elusive nature of the Bloomsbury Rules: 'It is impossible to say where Bloomsbury begins, and where it ends. Are the painters and journalists of a younger generation to be included? Arthur Waley? Francis Birrell? George Rylands? Douglas Davidson? Are old and intimate friends who have never become imbued entirely with the Bloomsbury spirit? And what precisely is this spirit?' Waley, Birrell, Rylands, Davidson, those four names reeled off the top of Mortimer's head to prove a point about definition, shadowy though they may indeed sound to the modern ear, did not belong to mere youths on the fringes. The company often carelessly described as 'Second Generation Bloomsbury' in fact possessed internal coherence and external independence.

Arthur Waley, half a generation older than Dadie and Steven, was a poet and translator from Chinese and Japanese literature whose work was extolled by those wildly variant forces, the Sitwell siblings and Ezra Pound; he was also the bosom friend of Harold Bowen, who had married Vera Donnet, Steven's one-time Russian teacher. Frankie Birrell – like Steven – occupied intriguing common territory between the fading Liberal establishment and the intellectual avant-garde; at the end of the decade, he would be among the reviewers of Steven's first book. Dadie Rylands, despite or because of his youth, was becoming a social prize and an impresario in his own right. Douglas Davidson, shortly to become, alongside Dadie, Steven's closest friend in Cambridge, was a painter in the manner of Duncan Grant (briefly his lover); his brother Angus was a skilful translator from Italian who would take over from Dadie as assistant at the Hogarth Press in 1924. Like most young, ambitious, gregarious people, these 'Bloomsbury connections' saw themselves as fixed points in their own lives and dramas, not satellites in some stronger, overarching orbit.

It is not incidental that almost all these friends belonged to what Maurice Bowra was about to dub 'the Homintern', and that Arthur Waley, unusually heterosexual by contrast, encountered considerable resistance in his persistent attempts to incorporate his long-time mistress, Beryl de Zoete, into the fold (she was ten years his senior, which along with her South African heritage encouraged various ungallant jokes about her having come out before the Boer War). At the same time, it would be a gross over-simplification to assume that sexual attraction rather than general sympathy was the driving motive behind this younger group's formation. Dadie's success with various distinguished elders, of both sexes, in the 1920s left him relatively little time to dally with his own generation. Frankie Birrell had a consummated but unhappy love-affair with Keynes, and received a violent rebuff from D. H. Lawrence, but his importance in the younger set was primarily as a fixer, dabbler, belletrist and bookseller.

Douglas Davidson, a Magdalene undergraduate two years Steven's senior, was assumed by Topsy Lucas to have been his lover. After one party of Steven's attended by Davidson, Topsy complained of 'moments of loneliness, when S. et al all disappeared and I longed for someone to hold my hand'; she then stated in a rattling staccato, 'I love Steven. Douglas has been with him. Steven has been seedy.' In one of his few more or less frank comments on his own love life in his unpublished memoirs, Steven seems to deny this – 'It was a perfectly straightforward friendship, untrammelled by any emotional complication.' This is scarcely a perfectly straightforward sentence. Steven complained to his sisters of disagreeable obligations comforting Davidson through low spirits and poor health, suggesting that their bond could at times be as onerous as it was close. Topsy herself was hardly a disinterested party. She had already succumbed to the Zeitgeist by becoming attracted to Dadie, though she avoided declaring herself, for the time being, because she was 'unwilling to join the throng of Herberts & Herbertinas of all sexes and sizes'. Steven's friendship with Davidson was not, at least primarily, sexual. He was mercilessly condescending towards Davidson's painting (admired by Dadie and by Davidson's mentor, Duncan Grant), admitting only that 'Douglas had a charming talent for painting trays and boxes.' But he acknowledged that 'we had many of the same tastes and the same sense of humour. He was ready to reprove me when I was silly or tiresome, but in so kindly a way that I was grateful for his reproofs.' With these words Steven exhibited some of the highest praise he ever allowed, and some of the most genuine humility he ever showed about himself. It seems that Douglas Davidson functioned as a kind of moral preceptor, a better self and a force for restraint and charity.

For all his recollections of shyness, Steven allowed elements of a more extroverted and mischievous spirit to reveal themselves throughout his first year. His scholarship entitled him to rooms in the Great Court of Trinity, but, as he was not a musical scholar, the college authorities forbade him to keep his new piano there. He responded by consulting a Cambridge antique-dealer and swapping his instrument for a sort of proto-piano called a dulcitone, 'roughly speaking, a dulcimer on legs', which, passing unmentioned in the college regulations, could not be forbidden. More than a century before, Lord Byron had used a similar loophole to accommodate Bruin the Bear in the same Great Court turret (there were rules against dogs, but not bears); Steven, who nightly looked out for a sight or a sound of that bear's ghost, was contributing in an understated way to the same vein of gentlemanly absurdity.

Later in the Michaelmas term Steven was talent-spotted by two older Trinity undergraduates, Paul Paget and John Seely, and handed the small but, to the already Sinophile Steven, intensely satisfying role of the Emperor of China in a pantomime of Aladdin which the pair were superintending. Steven enjoyed himself immensely, but fell out with one of the elder performers, a Fellow of King's, the production's director and Widow Twankey, Frank Birch. Birch was to be described by Penelope Fitzgerald in *The Knox Brothers* as 'a rather dull historian, an acceptable drinking companion, a mysterious private personality, a brilliant talker and a born actor. In his impersonations, as in those of all great comedians, there was a frightening element.' Steven 'admired his talents though not his personality'.* It was Birch

---

* The dislike between Steven and Birch remained mutual, but Steven often visited the older man's wife Vera when her husband was out. Birch became an intelligence

who was to dub Steven and Dadie Rylands, with both malice and grudging admiration, the 'Tea Party Cats', named for their velvety urbanity.

Steven was not as yet in this year regarded by Trinity dons as a reliable academic talent, and indeed in some ways he would never become one. He found Part I of the History Tripos a sorry chore, admitting to his father in a June letter that 'I have been working slightly feverishly during the last week, in an endeavour to improve my knowledge of English constitutional history – much my worst subject – it is so hard really to be thrilled by the functions of the Privy Council under Charles II!'

Constitutional history took first place at Trinity under the instruction both of Denys Winstanley, 'a hospitable little man with a curious vocal impediment', who identified King's College with Babylon and violently disapproved of Steven's fraternizing there, and of Gaillard Lapsley, who treated the minutiae of the High Middle Ages as letters of marque to British society. Their scepticism about Steven was conveyed by Dr Harrison in his report to Walter Runciman. He preferred Leslie, 'a most valuable member of the college' owing to his proven abilities at the Amateur Dramatic Club, at the Union and on the river, in spite of the dampening assertion that 'for economics he has no great gift'. Leslie was particularly commended for taking a firm position against racial prejudice towards 'black' (mostly Indian) members of Trinity. Steven, by contrast, was accorded grudging academic praise undermined with a general implication of skittishness, rather as he had been at Eton: 'Steven is thought by those who see his work to have very great possibilities. He has certainly literary taste and gifts. Whether he has the taste for the *grind* that is wanted for a mastery of history, is not so clear . . . ' But if Harrison thought to pin down the fringe-wearing, dulcitone-tinkling young dandy and coerce

---

recruiter before the Second World War and a cryptographer at Bletchley during it. Steven thought Mrs Birch enjoyed his company largely in order to have someone to beat at chess. He was privately disloyal about both sides of the couple – 'Vera Birch, the niceish bright quite stupid wife of a clever nasty don at Kings' (SR to Ruth Runciman, 24 February 1924, Elshieshields) – but remained drawn to Vera's aristocratic cachet.

him into proper, applied '*grind*', he was, like many such Harrisons, to be disappointed.

At the beginning of his second year Steven inadvertently caught the attention of a spectacular new arrival at Cambridge, who spotted him during a history lecture. Steven, for his part, took in Cecil Beaton slightly later. Passing St John's College undergraduate accommodation on Bridge Street, he glimpsed a dissolute figure flinging a cigarette end out of a window; it set a passing lady's church straw hat on fire. Steven remembered Beaton as, from the first, 'shamelessly, almost stridently eccentric', 'wilfully eager to shock and rather embarrassing', but passed over much of this sense of alarm in his admiration for Beaton's artistic talent. Writing to his sister, he patronized his new acquaintance while acknowledging both his talent and the nascent connection between them: 'affected clever conceited Mr Cecil Beaton, who rather likes me'. There was a defensiveness about Beaton, who since Harrow had felt driven to transmute his middle-class background into a mysteriously sourced aura. A friend of Steven's at Corpus Christi, Stewart Perowne, obliquely remarked that 'Cecil had none of the advantages of his contemporaries.'* Beaton came from quite as much money as many of his friends – his father was a timber-merchant – but he deliberately projected, and indeed seems inwardly to have felt, the sense of insecure, extravagant, *novus homo* self-creation to which Perowne and Steven were alert. Scarcely a week after arriving at Cambridge Beaton had confided to his diary that 'I don't want people to know me as I really am but as I'm trying and pretending to be.'

Theirs was still a tentative and youthful world, where dismissive epigrams in public easily coincided with covert, actual interest. Under these circumstances the terms in which Beaton first considered Steven become particularly revealing. He thought the slightly older boy's fringe 'absurd-looking', but appeared to entertain an ironical but sincere appreciation for some *jolie laide* quality: 'He

---

* Steven described Stewart Perowne in 1925 as one of his bêtes noires, an expansive category for him at that time, but they were on regular social terms from 1922 and would be close and convenient friends during and after the Second World War.

really is rather marvellous. I should adore to model him. He's so huge and ugly and strong with the most fruity voice.' Steven was certainly tall – the tallest member of a tall family – but his bony frame was never supplemented by much musculature, and as for 'ugly', his photographs – many of them Beaton's – show a face surely easier to decry as 'pretty'. There is, it is true, a strange discordance between Steven's typically stern, guarded, sidelong expressions and the badges of the aesthetic tribe with which he identified. Eddie Bates, a love-object of Steven's and of Dadie's in the 1930s, invoked in relation to his own alcoholism the psychological use to which make-up was put among undergraduates: 'Nowadays I am as done without alcohol as I used to be without rouge at Cambridge lunch-parties.' Steven followed a more decorous pattern than Eddie Bates, Beaton or, beyond Cambridge, the outstandingly effeminate Stephen Tennant; he was also, unlike them, almost entirely teetotal as a young man. There is about his tribal markings, for all their elegance, something of determined duty, of compulsory enjoyment, of conscious, wilful inhibition, and perhaps it was in part this contradictory aspect that drew Beaton's notice.

Though Beaton's was the more spectacular social success at Cambridge, Steven's position was considerably more assured. Beaton seems to have looked up to Steven, at least to begin with, with some of the same hero worship, the same intellectual and aesthetic attraction, as that which Steven felt for Dadie. Beaton began, in a small way, to follow Steven's lead, adopting the Fair Isle woollen jerseys Steven liked to wear against the fenland chill, and listening to his new friend's advice on academic, artistic and professional matters. He paid attention when Steven warned him against a talented rival actor in Cambridge theatrical circles, Adrian Bishop; and it was apparently for fear of Steven's scorn that, when Beaton was commissioned to design a cover for the Cambridge-based literary magazine *Granta*, he suppressed his name in the publication. Less than coincidentally, Beaton nursed an intermittent but intense envy of Dadie's theatrical triumphs. If Steven repaid Beaton's feeling of mentorship and attraction, he hid it almost completely, and his teasing of Beaton ranges from the affectionate to the acidic. When an outwardly respectable rowing hearty admitted his attraction to Beaton, Steven laughingly dismissed such tendresse for Cecil as an 'exotic taste', rather like, he thought, acting itself. When he met in 1925 the young artist Edward 'Boy' Le Bas, who may have been Beaton's first lover at Harrow, Steven thought him 'a dear, ridiculous creature', 'exquisite' (which was not a compliment). This is the language not of rivalry but of patronage, banishing Beaton alongside Le Bas to a less absorbing and less adult sphere than Steven's own ideal of sophistication.

Steven and Beaton first came to know each other well during an enterprise of uncomplicated, Bacchanalian display. Dennis Robertson was directing a stage version of Thackeray's baroquely satirical romance *The Rose and the Ring*, a fairy farce of love, misadventure and monarchy set in the Kingdoms of Paflagonia and Crim Tartary – which in their actual incarnations of Paphlagonia and Crimea would both come to feature in Steven's books. Beaton, whose school reputation for theatricality had been only magnified during his first weeks at Cambridge, was handed one of the leading roles, the beautiful and heartless Paflagonian Princess Angelica. As for Steven, he was cast as Angelica's mother, and hence rejoiced in the title of the Queen of Paflagonia. This was a small but irresistible part, indicative less of any histrionic talent than of Steven's height and spareness, which was, of course, 'stuffed out with cushions into a splendid embonpoint'. He wore a long chinoiserie gown, fringed with satin, a harbinger of travels, costumes and purchases yet to come. It is telling that, while Beaton took a genuinely feminine lead, Steven preferred the sort of comically exaggerated transvestitism within the traditional purlieu of drag. With his usual detachment Steven remembered it as 'a hilarious production, much enjoyed by the actors and, I hope, by the audience'.

Not long after *The Rose and the Ring*, Beaton chose Steven as the subject of the first photographic portrait he had taken outside his family. This initial picture was an uncompromising profile, without extravagance of costume or maquillage; but as the year progressed Beaton took further pictures, and their viewer now gains the unsettling, Wildean sense of a subject playing to, changing in accordance with, the camera. Steven soon faces it head on; he becomes visibly rouged, for all the sobriety of photographic black-and-white, and then enrobed; his hands are revealed, heavy now with rings. The

Beaton pictures show to advantage the new incumbent of Steven's rooms, Benedict the parakeet, a feathered response to Byron's ghostly Bruin. Verdant and garrulous, Benedict exemplified (and enjoyed) the increasingly extravagant atmosphere of Steven's rooms – Russian cigarettes and roseleaf jam at teatime. During the parakeet's most trying moments Steven tended to rebuke him ('he would try to eat my fingers, and it got a little painful') by way of quick, precise spanks with the side of a pencil. A few weeks into Steven's second Michaelmas term the bird seemed 'very well. His green is much more glossy now and his tail has grown a little larger. He is very tame; and considering everything, "accidents" don't happen very often. He is devoted to apples and to Swiss Roll.' Such a familiar was well suited to Steven's own flourishing character. When Beaton, in another devoted mood, progressed from photography and tried to paint him, Steven disconcerted his occasional disciple and glancing admirer by 'pursing up his mouth and staring as though mad'.

Steven's Trinity supervisor was now Gaillard Lapsley, whose fantastical snobbery made him a figure of fun among the undergraduate body. They disseminated a story that he had been born too far west of Boston to be received in polite American society, and so had washed up in England as second best. A Harvard protégé of Henry James, Lapsley had maintained a reverent friendship with the Master. He was a discreet receptacle of confidences who exchanged frank opinions on romantic ideals and sexual morality with the chronically repressed don and writer A. C. Benson; Benson described him upon their first meeting as 'glittering like a diamond, polished, hard as nails'. His academic field, unlike his wide acquaintance, crucially including Edith Wharton, held little interest for Steven. Lapsley was an expert on the English constitution of the High Middle Ages. Domestic English history of the traditional Cambridge school wearied Steven, both as an undergraduate and later on, when he had to teach it. It might be thought that the reigns of Charles II and, especially, of Edward II under Lapsley encompassed personal high politics that would have appealed to Steven. In his memoirs Steven keeps to a modesty as disingenuous as it is disarming, making out that he preferred obscurer topics in order to avoid more challenging fields of competition. Boredom, not idleness or lack of ambition, was evidently his real obstacle, a restless desire for the untrodden and the foreign which the relative freedoms of Cambridge had piqued but could not now appease.*

This ennui came to a head in a quarrel with Lapsley, who handled the outwardly well-mannered, covertly subversive young scholar well with a 'withering lecture' accusing him of 'bad manners'. It was a perfectly judged reprimand to Steven, who improved his rate of industry in the interest of *bella figura* while ignoring the substance of his supervisor's complaint. 'I think that [Lapsley] rather liked a scholar who had a disdain for work that he thought dull,' he wrote unrepentantly seventy years later. At any rate, a prickly professional relationship settled into friendship; in Steven's letters home Lapsley is transformed from 'that terrific snob' to 'my great friend'. Steven was accepted as an habitué at Lapsley's stiff, candlelit evenings, where nobly born undergraduates were most appreciated and, Steven points out, appreciative – 'grammar-school boys regarded his parties as being old-fashioned, somewhat oppressive and rather absurd'.

At the undergraduate institution of high tea – at which beer, but not wine, might be consumed, Steven himself sticking to cider or lemonade – the company was a good deal more various. One favourite catch, in November 1923, was Fredegond Shove, 'the soulful poetess', as Steven described her to Ruth, who 'says that having tea in my rooms is like coming to Fairyland'. To the less impressionable Margie, Mrs Shove got a more caustic billing as 'a woman who writes very good poetry, creeps about and whispers, and "found religion" lately'. Fredegond was the younger daughter of the great medieval legal historian F. W. Maitland; her elder sister was baptized Ermengard. Their mother had on widowhood remarried, to a Darwin, placing the family squarely in the Edwardian Cambridge of Gwen Raverat's *Period Piece*. Through Fredegond, Steven would come to know other members of this wider clan, including the Raverats, the Jebbs and the Cornfords.† Fredegond married the economist Gerald

---

* By contrast, Steven was fascinated by his occasional conversations with the Professor of Arabic, Ashley Bevan, who imparted to him various revelations about the queens of Madagascar which Steven was delighted to recycle for the rest of the century.

† This powerful and high-minded extended family would take the place of honour in Noel Annan's essay, 'The Intellectual Aristocracy' (1955).

Shove (pronounced as in Hove, not love). During the First World War, Gerald, a conscientious objector, worked as Lady Ottoline Morrell's poultry-keeper, and they lived in pastoral retreat at Garsington, harmonizing with Fredegond's taste and even her appearance. She had a long, equine face and gloomy eyes, but possessed an ecstatic, Georgian talent; Ralph Vaughan Williams, an uncle by marriage, set four of her poems to music. Her sister Ermengard, who became a Quaker, described Fredegond's life rather pointedly as 'the putting off of Bloomsbury, the putting on of Catholicism', but to Steven her fanaticism took only benevolent, if sometimes exacting, forms. 'In particular she was horrified by capital punishment. When any hanging was to take place in Britain, which was not seldom, I would be summoned to spend the previous evening with her, to distract her so that she would go to bed not thinking of what was to happen at dawn.'

Just as he had entertained masters' wives and daughters at Eton, Steven felt interested and secure at the tables of dons' wives in Cambridge. Nor did he dismiss female undergraduates of his own age, attending evenings at Newnham with friends such as Sylvia and Pamela Paget. He was to claim credit as a go-between and confidant during Sylvia's successful courtship by a much patronized schoolboy acquaintance, Christopher Chancellor. His mother's triumphant Girton career, and perhaps even his favourite sister Margie's less happy attendance there, left him with a comparatively enlightened attitude towards the intellectual equality of the sexes, and female society was always to be a desirable ingredient in his life. Where a lady of title was concerned, Steven was especially vigilant and attentive; in his memoirs he describes with particular relish a Newnham party for Princess Ileana of Roumania. He maintains that the Princess was frightened by the grotesque personal appearance of Jim Butler, the kindly, Christian Scientist Trinity Fellow, who was suffering from a swollen, untreated poisoned lip. She had to be consoled by Steven's own, naturally assiduous reassurances.

At the same time, Steven could be defensive and unforgiving with just those undergraduates who might have been assumed to possess similar artistic, social, even amatory tastes to his own. Roger Hinks was a Trinity scholar, who shared Steven's enthusiasm for art, antiquity and amateur dramatics. Often a harsh critic of his contemporaries, Hinks seems to have treated Steven with friendly respect, but this was rarely reciprocated. To Steven he was regularly 'horrid Mr Hinks, the most tiresome bore in the world'. Hinks had an unfortunately heavy, drooping appearance and his family background, though respectable and erudite, was not independently intriguing. Steven tended to think of him, too, as an intellectual fraud, one whose territory inclined him to ill-informed ventures into Steven's own, already emergent Byzantine interests. Worst of all, he could be sentimental. 'I lunched with a horror of a young man called Roger Hinks – I was being good and nice to him, but he doesn't deserve it.' Though Steven dismissed Hinks with disdain as 'my little enemy, or rather little slum', their careers, to his private annoyance, would consistently overlap for decades. Another irritant was a younger Etonian, Alan Clutton-Brock, later to be Slade Professor of Fine Art, who was also to be found in the orbit of Beaton. Steven found Clutton-Brock's daylight tippling of brandy affected, and was also repelled, as in the case of Hinks, by his ingratiating manners. 'I don't like him very much; he tries to impress one, and is dirty in his person.' Cleanliness, whether of habit or disposition, was almost always a decisive criterion. Sometimes Steven's delicate standards of physical perfection could be unreasonable, callow and rather nasty. When he got to know John Hayward, a twenty-year-old undergraduate who had just produced an edition of the poetry of Lord Rochester, Steven dismissed him as 'apt to be boring', 'just fairly clever' and, fatally, 'a cripple'.

Steven's last supervisor as an undergraduate was the leading 'character' among the dons of Trinity, F. A. 'Snipper' Simpson (the sobriquet deriving from his obsessive adjustments to the Trinity topiary). He was a figure so peculiar that Steven's memories of him represent, if anything, a muted version of the truth:

> a fine historian who when quite young had published two excellent volumes on the life of Louis Napoleon, but when the second volume received one or two unfavourable reviews refused to publish the third or any other historical work. His lectures were interesting but not easy to follow. As a supervisor he was alarming. While you read your essay to him he would wander round his room, going off sometimes into his bedroom or, if the curtains were drawn across the windows, he would hide behind them then suddenly reappear. Other pupils told of him

sometimes crouching under his grand piano and then jumping to his feet . . . in spite of his antics, he listened carefully to every word that you had said and came out with apposite and severe comments. I learnt a lot from these sessions; but I did not find them enjoyable.

What Steven is barely troubling to conceal here is that Snipper Simpson was a sudden and inveterate pouncer. The undergraduates tended to be more amused than not by this behaviour – especially as it was balanced by bouts of generosity – but the college servants, who had less defence against it and more onerous duties in covering up for it, were widely known to loathe him. He had also alienated Bloomsbury by his criticisms of Lytton Strachey's methods of research in *Eminent Victorians*. In Steven, Simpson would have recognized an adherent of an inimical party, whom he might bully personally, but not intimidate intellectually.

Though Steven's third-year supervision was thus a ramshackle and alarming affair, it hardly mattered. He had in great measure escaped his initial inhibitions and settled to a happy and glamorous pattern of entertainment. He continued to dabble in amateur theatre, portraying a flirtatious Regan in a private evening performance of *King Lear* with Dadie and the Lucases, and finally finding favour with Sheppard at King's, who granted him 'the small but amusing part' of Prometheus in *The Birds* (a role which involved hiding from the fury of Zeus beneath a parasol, while wrapped in a kimono). He kept alight his reputation for left-of-field excellence by delivering a paper on papal nephews to his college's Historical Society. But he remembered with more genuine excitement being taken by Sebastian Sprott, a postgraduate student of psychology who had been well disposed to him since his arrival at Cambridge, to dine with Keynes, who though always courteous still frightened Steven into speechlessness, and Lytton Strachey. The latter he had often met before with Leslie, whose rowing physique and looks, he realized, made him a more genuine object of interest than a mere 'striving intellectual' like himself. But he had never before seen either Keynes or Strachey performing in full flight to each other.

I thought then, – rightly, – that I was unlikely ever again to listen to such brilliance of talk. But I have to admit that, brilliant as Lytton

was, Maynard was the more brilliant ... Lytton ... attacked Maynard on the subject of Higher Mathematics, which, he said, was an
artificial exercise in tautology. One invented symbols and one then
invented their reactions. It was very convincing; but Maynard demol-
ished his arguments and explained to us with great lucidity what was
the point and purpose of Higher Mathematics. I went back to my College that evening feeling wonderfully enlightened. But, alas, next
morning, the enlightenment vanished.

Steven's relationship with Keynes gained in fluency after the great
man married Lydia Lopokova. Though the ballerina was mocked by
many older pillars of Bloomsbury, Steven rated her grace and generosity highly.

Other encounters with celebrated figures in Steven's last months as an
undergraduate relate to his uncertainty about his future, and a search for
potential patrons. His parents, with their seriousness about public service and their conventional attitudes to its fulfilment, thought that Leslie
should, like his father and his grandfather, combine running the family
shipping line with a political career. Steven, the younger, more academically distinguished but less easily categorized son, was encouraged, with
his curiosity about foreign parts and knack for languages, to enter the
Foreign Service. The brothers were unenthusiastic about these plans. In
Steven's case the possible alternatives included the world of museums,
into which the dreaded Hinks had already progressed; a literary career
in writing or publishing; and further academic study. Only for the last
did he have any real vocation, but this would necessitate a First in his
final examinations, of which he was far from confident, and in any case
his parents were unconvinced about such a life's stability.

Accordingly, Steven arranged to meet Sydney Cockerell, the Director of the Fitzwilliam Museum in Cambridge, Raymond Mortimer,
the lead fiction reviewer at the *New Statesman*, and Professor J. B.
Bury, the only Byzantine expert in Cambridge. None of these meetings proved especially encouraging. Cockerell, Steven decided in
short order, was 'a ridiculous old man with *absolutely no* humour, &
a nice, much cleverer but downtrodden delicate wife' (the illuminator
Florence Kingsford, who was suffering from multiple sclerosis). Raymond Mortimer had been introduced by Frankie Birrell, which did

not necessarily recommend him. The interview with Bury was strange and demanding, but, as will be told later, decisive.

Steven's path towards academic life was smoothed by the games-manship with which he tackled his Part II exams:

> one or two of my examiners wanted not to give me a First on the grounds that I had obviously been rather idle. They were perhaps jus-tified; but I had rightly suspected that there is nothing more boring than having to deal with examination papers with almost all the can-didates answering the same obvious questions. So I made a point of choosing obscurer questions which few, if any, of the other candidates would attempt to answer. I suspect that I was saved by that tactic.

The agnosticism of the Runciman parents about Steven's further research was also offset by his acquisition of an unexpected ally, the often-mocked but still all-powerful elder Walter Runciman, 'from whom our material blessings flowed'. Himself the author of several 'somewhat amateurish historical works', as Steven ungratefully but accurately described them, old Sir Walter (he would be ennobled only in 1933) was much tickled by the idea of an historian proper as a grandson.

Steven's elder brother had lately asserted his own independence in a different direction. Early in 1923 Leslie had become friendly with one of Margie's Girton contemporaries, the elder sister of one of Ste-ven's least favourite Eton juniors, John Lehmann. Rosamond was one of the most renowned beauties in Cambridge. Steven readily called her 'the most glamorous of girl-undergraduates . . . tall and graceful, with a melodious speaking-voice, very intelligent, and with enormous personal charm'. Steven and Rosamond's first proper meeting went, as he told Margie, relatively well:

> Rosamond Lehmann has been up for the week, staying with a Mrs Gordon . . . who likes to know all the interesting people at Cambridge – I, I add conceitedly, count as one – and she's been trying to get at me for some time – so flattering – so Rosamond asked me to dine there last night . . . I like her on the whole; she is quite intelligent for her sex and sort; she asked lovingly after you.

These concessions to praise did not amount to an acceptance of Rosamond in the more important role of his brother's fiancée. When

Leslie first befriended Rosamond independently, she was recovering from an unhappy, semi-requited love-affair, and had now settled upon her friend's elder brother as an honourable, handsome, materially settled marital prospect. She was prepared, in theory, to love him. Leslie, though at this point uncertain if he believed in marriage and in particular determined not to father children, could not help falling more precipitately for her.

By April 1923 Leslie and Rosamond were secretly engaged. The Runciman parents were abroad, which may have bolstered their elder son's courage. But Leslie found his powers of discretion overtaxed, and his family annoyingly, characteristically alert. Kitty, the youngest of the siblings, and Torby, still employed as her governess, entangled him in a discussion about marriage. Was it a coincidence, or had they somehow intuited his situation? 'This continual effort to be my natural rather rude self about you as about other people is so hard,' Leslie complained to Rosamond. Worse was to come; Kitty and Torby proved delicate interrogators indeed compared to Leslie's mother, and his younger brother.

'Is Rosamond catching you? Mummie remarked in a letter to me that you were seeing a lot of her & what did I think? What shall I reply?' Steven teased his brother in late May, provoking no reply in turn. The tormented Leslie seems to have gone so far as to consider confiding in Torby, with whom, he admitted to Rosamond, he had embarked on an enigmatic and agonizing conversation about the nature of love. Steven was clearly the main gadfly now in his brother's view.* During the summer vacation Leslie took to slipping out, whenever Steven was at home, to telephone Rosamond from public boxes. Before long he bowed to the inevitable and told his parents; things went less disastrously than he expected, partly because his father quite obviously fancied his fiancée. His mother pretended, for the

---

* Leslie's frank warning to Rosamond that 'Steven is sure to be a monster' (LR to Rosamond Lehmann, undated, King's) stands in striking contrast to the more adoring and deferential view of Torby about her favourite charge. When Kitty got engaged, in 1930, to Oliver Farrer – a younger friend of Steven's whom he liked and supported – Torby unhesitatingly declared, 'I am very glad you have someone to talk to who will be all sympathy, I mean Steven.' (Rebecca Forbes to KR, 16 October 1930, Elshieshields)

moment, to display equal delight, though she was no actress. Leslie attempted to square her over a long, nocturnal talk, 'in the course of which I told her a good many things such as what I'd really like to do, and that I had no public spirit (which distressed her)'. Rosamond was thus instantly identified by her mother-in-law with Leslie's refusal to become a stalwart Liberal statesman.

After a wrangle between the rites of holy matrimony and Leslie's severely secular conscience – Steven brokered a compromise involving an unceremonious, crapulous family friend and Wesleyan divine, Dr Rattenbury – Leslie and Rosamond were married just before Christmas, 1923. Dr Rattenbury was heard to say that the match would be unlikely to last – or, at least, was heard to do so by Steven, who proceeded to tell everybody else. Steven later claimed that Rosamond had invited him to join them on their honeymoon, a suggestion he took as an early, inauspicious augury. Rosamond and Leslie had both already sensed that Steven disapproved of, mocked and meant to sabotage their marriage, so the idea coming from Rosamond does seem bizarre; but it makes about as much sense as the extreme defensive measure of an uncertain bride as it does as Steven's purely malicious invention. The young couple set up house in Liverpool, where Steven came to visit them after he came down from Cambridge. By this time they had been married six months. Steven reported his verdict to his younger sister Ruth:

> I've been out shopping with Rosamond, choosing curtain materials etc and seeing their bought furniture. I'm not at all sure of their taste, but I think it'll be all right. But when they've decided on things for themselves, it's terribly difficult to dissuade them. It amuses me here; but, to tell the truth, I'd be bored to death by Rosamond if I saw much of her; and I think they're terribly silly together.

It was a harbinger of his role in the brief, maimed marriage to come.

About this time Steven wrote, and, uncharacteristically, preserved, a regretful, oddly defiant lyric, 'The Loveless':

> The plains are very wide and stretch around us.
> O'er the wide plains in liberty we roam.

There is no fence or barrier to bound us;
There is no limit set upon our home.

They came to take us, but they never caught us.
They set us snares in which we never fell
The only lesson that the hunting taught us
Was how we could remain untameable.

Others were fresher when the hunters chased them.
The hunters captured them with scornful ease
In gilded cages round the walls they placed them
Surrounding them with pretty luxuries.

And so the captives live laden with treasures.
They never suffer loneliness again.
But they are slaves in spite of all their pleasures,
And we are left unconquered on the plain.

O you that love, wallowing in your prison,
How is it that you ever can forget
That feel of freedom when the sun had risen
Before you fell into the hunters' net?

The plains are bare indeed, but they are vaster
Than we can cross by travelling all the day.
In such a world how can you bear a master?
You love; and freedom is the price you pay.

The reddening sun swings down on the horizon.
There is a chilly strangeness in the light.
The hum of daytime hesitates and dies on
Into the silent bleakness of the night.

Would it not, now, be better to be dying
Warm in the cushioned comfort of the cage
With fond attendants comforting and sighing?
This freedom is a lonely heritage.

Cry out to me, cry that I have not wasted
This only little life that I have had,

Cry, it is better never to have tasted
Wine that is poisoned, pleasure that is sad.

Soon, very soon, the cruel night will numb me,
Let me be proud and cry triumphantly
That no one knew the way to overcome me.
Much I had missed, perhaps, but I am free.

If intended as a prophecy, this became self-fulfilling; if a credo, it was
kept with ascetic and absolute determination.

# 6

# The Hierophant

*Cambridge, 1924–9;* The Emperor Romanus
Lecapenus and his Reign *(written 1924–8,
published 1929)*

The proper meanings of this card have suffered woeful
admixture from nearly all hands . . . He is not, as it has been
thought, philosophy – except on the theological side; he is not
inspiration; and he is not religion, although he is a mode of its
expression.

Arthur Waite, *The Key to the Tarot*, 1920

In 1924, J. B. Bury, a Fellow of Trinity for almost forty years, and
Regius Professor of Greek and History for more than twenty, was
faced with a wearyingly persistent pupil. Having taken an outstanding First, young Runciman expressed his interest in further study
within Bury's own field, the Eastern Roman Empire. In *A Traveller's
Alphabet*, his 'partial memoirs' published in 1991, Steven claimed to
have been the only pupil Bury ever had in Cambridge: '[Bury] was a
frail shy man who many years ago when he had taught Classical history in Dublin may have had a few pupils; but after he had moved
into Byzantine studies he neither had nor wished to have any.* It was
an uneasy interview, as I too was shy.'

Steven was not in fact Bury's first pupil at Cambridge to study Eastern Rome (Bury utterly rejected the term 'Byzantine', arguing instead
for an unbroken descent from the Roman Empire). Bury's most gifted
earlier disciple, Norman Baynes, was, by the time Steven graduated,
already a reader in later Roman history at the University of London.

* At Dublin Bury had taught at least one pupil who would influence public awareness of Byzantium even more fundamentally than Steven: W. B. Yeats.

On first meeting the tall, handsome, fresh-faced Bury, Baynes took him for a dandiacal fellow undergraduate. As a young don at Cambridge, Steven would enjoy causing similar confusion. Their shyness once overcome, Bury and Runciman might have seemed well suited. Both were able classicists, omnivorous modern linguists, immaculate dressers and ceremoniously private beings, drawn to the same esoteric historical and geographical terrain. Friends of Bury remembered him strikingly akin to how Steven would come to be described; in character 'distinctive, but somewhat elusive', while in conversation 'a talk with Bury was almost like being present at the making of history.' Steven was no untried and frivolous undergraduate chancer, but already a star performer. But his brief pupillage under Bury was to be characterized by philosophical irreconcilability and farcical misadventure.

As an undergraduate, Bury had been a classicist of practically Housmanian perfectionism, grasp and dryness. At Trinity, Dublin he had provided much of the legwork for an edition of Euripides' *Hippolytus* by the great Professor Mahaffy (now mainly remembered, rather unfairly, as the tutor of Oscar Wilde). Bury won his Cambridge fellowship rummaging in the thorny texts of Pindar. His move to the history faculty at Cambridge signified no softening of discipline. Irritated by Whiggish liberal humanism, Bury advanced instead a rigorously philological Teutonic rival model, associated with Leopold von Ranke, which fiercely advocated 'the release of history from rhetoric'. 'History is not a branch of literature,' Bury had insisted in his 1902 inaugural lecture as Regius Professor, just before Steven was born. He maintained that 'so long as history was regarded as an art, the sanctions of truth and accuracy could not be severe.' Nearly eighty years later, Steven told a young novelist that 'History belongs in the English department, it belongs with literature.' The world might have changed out of measure in the interim, but Steven was still defying the long-dead Bury and his concept of historical science. In his introduction to the 1930 *Selected Essays* published in Bury's memory Harold Temperley wrote that Bury 'wished to put Clio [the Muse of History] in a laboratory, before allowing her to declaim in an Academy'. Steven would have found both sentiment and image as ungallant as they were unhelpful. He preferred to think of Clio as an intimate friend with pronounced personal idiosyncrasies, 'an awful snob'.

According to *A Traveller's Alphabet*, Bury conceded a grudging scintilla of admiration during their first, desperate-sounding meeting. 'He told me firmly that Byzantine studies were far too difficult for any innocent youth to try to undertake.' Perhaps it was understandable of Bury to bristle at the green young pretender intruding on his time and, worse, on his Eastern Roman ground. His next move was to declare that 'it was ridiculous for anyone to approach the subject unless he could read the Slavonic languages.' For the great majority of Steven's contemporaries, this warning would have settled the matter. Even the conscientious and talented Baynes had been cowed by a similar test: 'from that interview I retired somewhat dismayed by the prospect of the novitiate which a student of Byzantine history must serve.' Steven, on the other hand, had experienced a deeper training at the feet of Torby and the charming, *mondaine* Russian singer Vera Donnet. When Steven revealed that he read Russian, Bury sent him off to read a few articles in Bulgarian. From this successfully called bluff emerged the Bulgarian slant of Runciman's early research and writing. This was the first example of Runciman's habitual technique: identifying an exotic, unexpected perspective and sticking to it with flair and partiality.

In his later unpublished memoirs Steven admits that Bury did, from time to time, accept pupils, but explains that these unfortunates, Steven's less resourceful precursors, were never able to capture the savant's attention either in person or through written communication. Steven at last gathered that the problem lay with Mrs Bury, who kept her husband out of college, received no visitors and destroyed any letters from would-be disciples that reached her house. But Steven solved the riddle and located the sage by learning to ambush Bury during his favourite solitary walk, through the Cambridge Backs. These snatched perambulations, according to Steven, just about sufficed for occasional supervisions.

This fanciful vignette is typical of Steven; but there is certain plausibility to his recollections of these ambulatory occasions, which he came to prefer to more conventional supervisions indoors. He began to suspect that Bury 'enjoyed having company now and then'. The Professor would generally answer his questions fluently, only during occasional moments of weary impatience snatching pages from Steven's notebook, scribbling down his pupil's enquiry, and firing back an answer by postcard after an unpredictable interval. Steven recalls Bury lamenting his own patchy Arabic, impaired by failing eyesight, and his 'shock when I said that I was not prepared to take on Hungarian'. By the time he reluctantly took on Steven, Bury was mortally ill; he died less than a year into Steven's research, but those peculiar consultations on the Backs came to have a deep, verifiable effect on its direction.

The critical disagreement between supervisor and pupil lay in their attitudes to Gibbon. For Bury, Gibbon's *Decline and Fall of the Roman Empire* was the beginning of rational history, imperfect, certainly, but an important stride in the right direction. From 1896 until the end of his life Bury was Gibbon's most illustrious editor and reviser. He thought Gibbon's technique seriously impaired by the twin afflictions of rhetoric and didacticism: 'The idea of writing history for its own sake was strange to Gibbon.' But Gibbon, along with Voltaire, Montesquieu and Rousseau, was to Bury a forerunner of his *beau idéal*, what he called 'genetic history' – the idea that 'the present condition of the human race is simply and strictly the result of a causal series.' If Gibbon was a crucial link in the Rankean quest for 'what actually happened', Bury could still take him sternly enough to task for his cavalier preference for gossip over evidence: 'The principle of Gibbon was as follows: "Of these strange anecdotes a part may have been true because probable, and a part true because improbable . . . " This is plainly untenable . . . There is no direct reason why the author should not have invented; and deliberate invention on the part of *one* man is not the only alternative to the truth of the charges.' Where Gibbon made up in full for such failings was, for Bury, in his aversion to Christianity. Religion, Bury wrote, had been a shadow casting a wholly malign influence across the human intellect: 'Thought was rendered sterile and unproductive for centuries under the withering pressure of a monotonous and omnipresent idea.'

The first reviewers of *Romanus Lecapenus*, Runciman's fellowship thesis, published in 1929, tended to regard him as a faithful disciple of his late supervisor.* Even by 1933 Robert Byron would refer to him

---

* This book alludes to 'Steven' when discussing Steven Runciman as a biographical subject, partly to distinguish him from members of his family prominent in his story,

disobligingly as Bury's 'Elisha'. Like his supposed master, Runciman seemed to be sceptical in religion and Gibbonian in manner, as in this sally about the laws of the Khazars: 'Justice was administered by seven judges, two Jews who judged according to Hebrew law, two Christians who judged according to Gospel law, two Mahometans who judged according to Koran law, and one heathen who judged according to reason.' But to invoke Gibbon was in fact the least informed, as well as the most obvious, tactic. Steven's Bloomsbury acquaintance Francis Birrell, reviewing *Romanus Lecapenus* in the *Nation and Athenaeum*, was frank about his lack of expertise: 'I am quite unfit to review this book and only gratified my desire to do so on being informed that there were not more than half a dozen people in England really competent for the task, a statement I can well believe.' Birrell, naturally enough, resorted to Gibbon in his assessment of Steven: ' . . . Mr. Runciman has a feline, at times Gibbonian, wit, which prevents his enumeration of obscure events in remote and rebarbative provinces degenerating into a dreary and lifeless catalogue.' The *Times Literary Supplement* also invoked the resonant name of Gibbon: 'Mr. Runciman . . . is readable throughout, and many happy flashes, both of intuition and phrasing, show that he has studied his Gibbon to good effect without ever falling into the pit of slavish imitation.'

Steven had emerged into academic notice as a pupil of the supreme Gibbonian of his day. He could hardly have ignored *The Decline and Fall*. But his real attitude to the great historian was plainly stated on his first page: 'Gibbon's dark shadow has long weighed on posterity; his sweeping epigrams and entertaining sneers frightened even gentle nineteenth-century philhellenes into the adoption of an air of disapproval. All the historians in chorus treated of a thousand years of empire as a short sinister unbroken decline.' Part of Steven's motivation for pursuing Byzantine study was his almost instinctive dissent from Gibbon's position. When he first consulted Bury, he had not yet seen Istanbul – that pleasure was to come later that summer, cruising

---

partly to approach more nearly his mentality and that of his friends. By a similar principle, other personages are called by the names Steven would have used of them; and Steven himself becomes 'Runciman' when his writing and historiographical thought is under discussion.

aboard his grandfather's yacht, *Sunbeam*. Steven had always enjoyed Greek literature and been interested in the medieval era, so his claim that he early on sought to explore the natural combination, Greece in the Middle Ages, carries some credibility. But he admitted more often and more insistently to a negative propulsion – the maddening feeling that two famous writers before him had got Byzantium badly wrong. The first was Walter Scott, whose *Count Robert of Paris* he had considered 'a dreadful book' as a child; the second Gibbon, who he claimed had induced in him 'the same effect . . . a little later on'.

Part of Steven's reaction against Gibbon was undoubtedly provoked by the same anti-clericalism that so endeared the Enlightenment historian to Bury. In 1996, Steven described the lifelong ambiguity of his own religious allegiance with some nuance in an interview with Jonathan Riley-Smith: 'Neither Anglican nor Roman Catholic. I was brought up in the Church of Scotland, which is Calvinist, but my sympathies have been for many years with the Orthodox Church. I have always been greatly interested in religion, though not *pratiquant*.' The last point is more important than the wavering, if consistently anti-Catholic, trajectory implied before it: Steven felt keen *interest* in religion, and to his mind Gibbon's fulminations against Christianity of any kind would have seemed sadly philistine and a failure of the imagination. Ironically, by 2008 Riley-Smith would characterize Runciman over-simply as a Lowlands Calvinist bigot, who merely wrote 'what Walter Scott would have written, had he been more knowledgeable', nicely tying up the cycle of contempt.

Runciman does owe something of his lucid style and sardonic humour to Gibbon. He was however determined never to admit this, much preferring to proclaim his literary descent from Beatrix Potter. But Steven learnt more than he was willing to let on during those two dysfunctional terms with J. B. Bury, even if he was, in time, to discard the lessons just as surely as he retained the anecdotes.

In the summer of 1927 Bury died, and that autumn Steven was awarded a prize fellowship at Trinity. His only competitor in history had been an older Colleger at Eton – Gerald Yorke, whose eldest brother's untimely death was rumoured to have been connected with Steven and Eric Blair's passion for black magic. Yorke's study of the

Great Game was no match for one of the first fellowship theses Trinity dons had ever read that alluded to primary sources in Armenian and old Slavonic. For the next two years Steven, whose social life had become frenetic and who vanished abroad whenever he could arrange it, had two professional tasks: transforming the thesis into *Romanus*, and the education of undergraduates at Trinity. Not so very long had passed since he, by his own account an idle student, had irked Gaillard Lapsley by the discourtesy of his inattention. Now he had to endure the same frustrations.

As Steven wrote to a new London friend, Charlotte Bonham Carter: 'I interview and teach superior and frightening pupils all about European history . . . nine condescending and indolent young men at half an hour each. It has made me grow years older.' That counter-intuitive adjective, 'condescending', reveals Steven's sense of being ambushed in his new role, by a sudden reversal in matters of class. As an undergraduate, he had not been atypical in mocking the American Lapsley's social pretensions. Now he found that his own status as a leading Liberal politician's son counted for little with these pitiless, ignorant youths; he felt he might as well have been a village schoolmaster or upper servant. Of course there were compensations; a decent wage could be extracted by way of humorous observation: 'One of my bright young gentlemen – a quite bien né old Etonian with charming most polished manners asked me the other day: "What is Alsace? who does it belong to?"' In the context of the twentieth century, it was perhaps after all not so very bad a question; but it was not an enquiry of the sort Steven felt he had been placed on earth to answer. 'I fear I'm not a good teacher; I dislike some of them so much I can barely speak to them; and with the ones I do like I find myself always brightly digressing on to more amusing subjects than the Treaty of Westphalia or the diplomatic prelude to the 7 Years' War.' He claimed in his unpublished memoirs to have resorted to the old trick of supervising his ablest pupils early in the week, so as to plagiarize their labours when instructing the more backward ones.

Steven's letters to Lady Bonham Carter also indicate that he was, at this point, scarcely more confident in his writing than in his teaching. He did not rest content for long with the results of his *Romanus*.

He dismisses it as 'my dull Byz book', and a reader who made the mistake of taking Steven at his word might assume that *Romanus Lecapenus*, like so many theses-turned-first-monographs, is a dry production. There are good reasons why it has not been out of print in almost nine decades. These are not just the freshness and persuasiveness of its argument, or that the book filled a gap. Nor is it only as the first work of a famous pen that *Romanus* remains read by those interested in the political history of Byzantium.

Runciman's first book was a tautly experimental construct. Given the obscurity of its subject even to an academic audience, and the ambition of its geographic sweep, not yet known as a Runciman hallmark, it was startlingly readable. It drew the public admiration of Lytton Strachey, who had in 1918 revolutionized post-war popular history and biography with the stylistic concision, visual exactitude and psychological plausibility of his *Eminent Victorians*.* In its graceful form, compressed, compartmentalized and, as its young author put it, 'horizontal rather than vertical' (more thematic than chronological), *Romanus* was an independent advance from the monumental and monolithic works of Bury.

The young Byzantinist's fluency was recognized everywhere, but several authorities took it for flippancy. To the great and temperamental Belgian scholar Henri Grégoire, of whom Steven would come to know much more, Runciman displayed in *Romanus* 'une pétulance un peu juvénile'. The *Cambridge Review* warned that 'the pedant must overlook the queerest lapses into colloquialism'; but many pedants were afoot, and the *Journal of Hellenic Studies* could not restrain a curmudgeonly complaint against 'a certain modish frivolity of tone'. These doubters were the natural counterparts to the many reviewers who hailed Runciman, in a manner about which even Steven must have had misgivings, for rescuing Byzantium from a 'miasma of dullness'. Voices from the academy might object to the approachability of the idiom; but to Grub Street Runciman's Byzantium came as a revelation.

---

* Strachey was, however, as will be seen, a Janus-faced, disingenuous sort of champion to have. His praise for *Romanus*, while it gave great satisfaction to Steven, was in part a social performance.

If Strachey was the most prominent of the book's admirers, the academic objections to *Romanus* were incarnated in the forbidding figure of Norman Baynes, that earlier 'only pupil' of Bury. He had been appointed by Trinity to examine Runciman's fellowship thesis. Steven reported to Ruth that he found Baynes 'unattractive, conceited, but kindly'. To Kitty, Steven added that Baynes was 'to look at, quite unbelievably distasteful (a green complexion, fangs for teeth, and such dirty fingernails)'. Perhaps that 'kindly' represented a wishful bravado; Steven carefully acknowledged Baynes in his preface, and decades later he revealed why to a favourite protégé, Donald Nicol: 'it is not strict etiquette to review books in which one has been, however undeservedly, thanked – or so Norman Baynes used to say (one could always avoid one of his severe reviews by thanking him fulsomely in the preface).' In the coming decades Steven would not invariably succeed with this most tactical form of tact; Baynes had, in any case, a regiment of well-deployed pupils ready to damn at his pleasure.

The opening of *Romanus* establishes the practice of resonantly gnomic first lines in Runciman's work: clear in style, epic in resonance, cynical in import and without immediate application to the particulars of the subject. 'In the battles between truth and prejudice, waged on the field of history books, it must be confessed that the latter usually wins.' David Plante has observed with pardonable exaggeration that Runciman never employs metaphor. Runciman is a writer who tends to grasp his reader's interest with his plain and authoritative manner well before he lays out the practical details of his scene. He is unafraid to let his protagonist await the proper cue. The entrance of Romanus employs a favourite device, the dramatically binary comparison. Fifty pages in, all in good time, a Byzantine empress announces an expedition against the Bulgars. The two military leaders involved are described:

> The commander-in-chief of the army ... was Leo Phocas, son of the celebrated Nicephorus who had reconquered Italy. Though his many personal attractions included great bravery, his ability was generally doubted; but his high aristocratic connections ... kept him in his position, and lately he had commanded with some success in the east ...

> The navy was under a much less distinguished command; the Grand
> Admiral ... was an Armenian peasant's son, who by painstaking
> merit and a few scraps of imperial favour had worked his way up ...
> He was called Romanus Lecapenus, and everyone ignored him as
> being an excellent officer and no more.

Steven had decided upon the reign of Romanus I Lecapenus as the
subject for his fellowship thesis during that first, wary conversation
with Bury in the summer of 1924: Bury agreed with Steven that the
Emperor was 'interesting, and never has been properly done'. Steven
had begun the reading, but not writing, by the time of his sea-voyage
for China in the autumn of 1925; this was theoretically motivated by
his fragile health, but more importantly by Steven's own interest in
the Far East. It was an interest that had led him to experience a city
under siege, observe a civil war, befriend an Imperial tutor, loot the
Empress Dowager's wardrobe and, it seems fairly clear, greatly
enlarge the extent of his amatory experience. The young scholar who
returned to concentrate on Romanus in the spring of 1926 was a
rather different figure from the dainty and more easily intimidated
undergraduate.

Whether the subject of Romanus was Bury's suggestion or Steven's
own idea is uncertain. While the importance of Bulgaria to his reign
seems to be consistent with Bury's emphasis on the importance of
Slavonic sources, various aspects of Romanus' character, career and
reputation make it likely that he appealed especially to Steven.
Romanus had been vilified by Gibbon. His atypical origins, as an
Armenian of obscure lineage, played to Steven's consistent feel for
social ambiguity; and Romanus was the hero of an episode that came
to exemplify Steven's portrayal of Byzantine diplomacy, statecraft
and civilization. Faced with invasion by the Bulgarian Tsar Symeon,
who had defeated every Byzantine force sent against him and was
poised to attack Constantinople, Romanus drew on the authority of
history, and the moral power of Christianity, to abash the opponent
he could not defeat. As Runciman tells it,

> Romanus, instead of begging for peace, reproved [Tsar Symeon] as a
> schoolmaster might reprove a naughty pupil (though he skilfully
> inserted an offer to pay a larger tribute) ...

... Romanus's speech was not mere bravado. With a thousand years of imperial rule behind him, he genuinely thought it apposite to remind the monarch of the mushroom Bulgaria that 'tomorrow you are dust' ... to treat Symeon as a recalcitrant spiritual subordinate, and to talk to the old barbarian of death and of the Hell that awaits the wicked. It never occurred to the Byzantines that the Emperor was actually a beaten man begging for the best terms that he could secure ...

Throughout his decades of engagement with the Byzantine Empire, Steven was to see its rulers, at their best, as simultaneously sincere in their piety and realistic in their policy. The somewhat disdainful tone, with which in this first book he treats, among many others, the Bulgars, would soon be moderated by travel and time, but his attraction towards Byzantine religion, integrity and pragmatism would not waver.

Here, at his first emergence, Runciman, unlike more tentative academic beginners, is swift and crisp in judgement, as much so with historiographical predecessors as with the civilizations that rival his favoured Empire. F. H. Marshall complained with aggrieved dignity that 'some rather vehement criticism of other researchers might, perhaps, have been toned down with advantage.' In *Romanus Lecapenus* Runciman's French precursors receive the severest drubbing, in part because, more enterprising and linguistically proficient than their English contemporaries, they happen to be in possession of the relevant intellectual territory. Alfred Rambaud, the only scholar who might be said to have covered Romanus I's reign in critical depth before Runciman's advent, is at one point damned as 'garbled'; the scholar-priest Vitalien Laurent is described as writing 'fantastic nonsense'.

The study of the past is apt to stir up passions in the present, and these sallies are not unusual coming from a keen young historian ostentatiously breaking fresh ground neglected by his elders. But Runciman is already in this book idiosyncratically prone to similar lunges – somewhere between the professional and the personal – against primary sources and historical personages. Already he has mastered what would become his favourite device, one especially useful for a medieval narrative historian, of treating chroniclers as characters, characters as chroniclers, and both as intriguing but fallible acquaintances. The gamiest example of this technique in *Romanus* is Runciman's description of Liudprand, Bishop of Cremona:

> Liudprand ... twice visited Constantinople, and his father and step-father had been ambassadors there before him; he thus had admirable opportunities for collecting first-hand information. He was, however, credulous and gossipy and rather prejudiced, and saw love affairs wherever he looked; so though he is the most entertaining as well as one of the most vital of the sources, he must be treated with a little circumspection.

As a proactive diplomat, politician and author, Liudprand represents Runciman's ideal subject, and target, as a primary source – one who got engaged in, and compromised by, the action of his own story.

Still more deeply embedded within the political narrative Runciman traces were the Patriarch of Constantinople, Nicholas Mysticus, and John, the Catholicus, or chief bishop, of the separated Armenian Church. In his comparison of these rival hierophants' qualities, Runciman is sharply judgemental in his vision of competing civilizations at distinct stages of development (such contrasts are practically always made to Constantinople's advantage):

> [Armenia] was on a much lower level; the recitals of any of the historians show how childish and improvident the policies of Armenian statesmen were ... Nicholas's letter is terse and to the point, showing a wide comprehension of the problems of Armenia and reasonable schemes for their solution. John's ... is extremely long and diffuse, full of crude flattery and scriptural quotations that point rather to ignorance than to knowledge of the Bible. Even in his history he thus innocently shows up the backwardness of his country.

'Childish', 'improvident', 'backward' – these hard words would come to be more nuanced in Runciman's next book, *The First Bulgarian Empire*; eventually they would reappear in all their unforgiving condescension aimed not at Armenians or Bulgars, but at Western Crusaders. Runciman would later come to be admired by critics of Western triumphalism from Eric Hobsbawm to Edward Said as a friend to cultural diversity and equality and a stern sceptic of narratives of occidental progress. But had they read his first book, Hobsbawm and especially Said would have found much of which to disapprove. The young Runciman's stout Byzantine partisanship involves an aggressive revision of scholarship sympathetic to Islam and the tenth-century Arab world: 'Prejudice has descended; the conventional view in Western Europe, introduced by jealous Crusaders and firmly rooted in their descendants, is to regard every Arab as a hero and every Byzantine as a corrupt and incompetent coward, and to interpret their history accordingly.'

Occasionally Runciman replicates exactly the same kind of generalizing invective he so keenly resents when it is aimed at Byzantium. The results make exciting reading, but are scarcely dispassionate: 'to a nation [Black Bulgaria] so primitively oriental in its tastes, Islam with its bellicosity and polygamy was bound to be more seductive than Christianity.' But neither is Islam quite at the bottom of the array of religions that Runciman so often seems to characterize in terms of social hierarchy. One tribal monarch, we are told, became a Muslim on the grounds that 'a civilized potentate should have a higher class religion than Altaic naturalism.'

But if, viewed in retrospect, Runciman's opinions about relative 'levels of civilization' may have preserved in aspic both his relative inexperience and the assumptions of his time, *Romanus* also evinces a habit of coming to the defence of unexpected and thought-provoking causes. In the first chapter Runciman champions the efficacy and conscientiousness in government of eunuchs, defying a millennium of Western suspicion:

> Eunuchs were an ideal class in that they had no family life, left no descendants, and could never aspire to be Emperor.
>
> . . . The eunuchs were the weapon that kept feudalism at bay . . . It was only in the late eleventh century that the Empire had to taste the rule of feudal families – a taste that was poison. Eunuchs might intrigue for their brothers and nephews, but collaterals never have the same appeal to the instincts as descendants.
>
> . . . It is not the place here to discuss the psychological results of castration . . . It has long been the custom to talk of eunuchs as always having a demoralizing influence all round . . . Such generalizations are a disgrace to the historians that make them.

Runciman does not name the 'historians' he attacks here with such virulence; but he is toying with the long-established Gibbonian horror at the decadence of human castration – an attitude whose supposed compassion, he suggests, barely conceals narrow-minded disgust. By considering eunuchs in terms of their political expediency, he in fact restores to them a natural human dignity; castration, he indicates, is a professional step in the *cursus honorum*, rather than a demeaning surgical humiliation.

Romanus Lecapenus' youngest son Theophylact was castrated as a prelude to advancement in the Church. The boy's subsequent record as Patriarch of Constantinople was chequered, but Runciman is quick to empathize with his position: 'it seems unreasonable to expect a high-spirited, probably spoilt boy of fifteen to turn at once into a dignified and respectable ecclesiastic. And Theophylact had one good quality lacking in all his brothers – unbroken filial loyalty . . . ' The curious implication here is that Theophylact's castration had something to do with his dutifulness as a son, a psychological observation comparable in its compression to Runciman's previous remark that 'collaterals never have the same appeal to the instincts as descendants.' There is an undeniable force to this political argument, that eunuchs were a useful barrier against the chaos threatened by dynastic ambition. Steven's sly support for a sexually heterodox part of society is attractive, if scarcely surprising; and the whole operates as both an esoteric joke and an imaginative exercise, a successful insinuation into a thoroughly Byzantine point of view. Nor is it only with the Byzantines that Runciman can accomplish this form of intellectual ventriloquism; he is equally empathetic with the Armenian loathing of 'Greek heretics and Arab infidels'.

Steven's Liberal, cautiously suffragist, non-conformist parents might have been a little nonplussed by the disquisition on eunuchs, but would doubtless have recognized with approval his spirited picture of Byzantium as a beacon of female education and social opportunity:

> In the West, women were the frail sex set apart by chivalry and owing their privileges to their frailty; but in Byzantium women were men's intellectual equals. Girls usually received the same education as their

brothers; and Byzantine history can point to several authoresses of distinction.

> . . . A lack of snobbishness was characteristic of the whole of Byzantine society. It is true that later chroniclers, wishing to insult [the Empress] Theophano, called her an innkeeper's daughter; but society would have to be very democratic where such a past would not be considered a little undignified for an Empress . . . It was lack of education rather than lack of birth that was considered a subject for mockery . . .

This was another position which, once occupied, Runciman refused to evacuate; writing on the role of the Byzantine Empress in the mid-1970s, he compared the position of Byzantine women favourably to the lot of women in late Victorian Britain. One wonders what Hilda Runciman or Torby, children of the 1860s, might have thought of that comparison had they lived to read it.

For all its liveliness and daring, it must be admitted that *Romanus Lecapenus* is a difficult book, the product of a difficult early phase for its author: a cold Cantabrigian spell spent enduring the incompetence and indifference of haughty undergraduates, robed about in that *snobisme* from which Runciman, contrary to stereotype, dissociates Byzantium; or sitting through lonely High Table evenings at Trinity, where in the worst case one might find oneself stranded next to A. E. Housman, a sage unlikely to surrender a syllable of wisdom or even conversation. Bury's unappeasable spirit has discouraged Runciman from exploiting as yet his full narrative fluency, but left him determined to infiltrate indigestible and opaque linguistic and cultural matter. It is hard to disagree with the reviewer of the *Near East and India*, to whom it seemed that 'the task of making an interesting consecutive narrative out of the intricacies of the Armenian maze has proved too much even for [Runciman]' – both the criticism and the implied compliment are fair. Lytton Strachey's private verdict, written for the benefit of his lover Roger Senhouse, was more treacherous: 'I've just finished Steven Runciman's book on the Emperor Romanus Lecapenus or possibly Lackapenis – incredible learning and industry is displayed, but one doesn't really in the least gather what those odd beings were like. I've now relapsed into my beautiful old Gibbon to see how *he* treats the subject.' At least

Strachey had caught what Birrell missed, that Runciman aimed to be a corrective to Gibbon, not his follower. But if 'those odd beings' did, and do, for many readers of *Romanus* remain pretty odd, the book is still notable as the point of embarkation on a long and illuminating pilgrimage on behalf of the general reader.

# 7

# The Sun

*Wilsford, 1925–7; London, 1925–38;*
*France, 1925–33*

the great and holy light which goes before the endless procession of humanity, coming out from the walled garden of the
sensitive life and passing on the journey home.

Arthur Waite, *The Key to the Tarot*, 1920

Oh, life is a glorious cycle of song,
A medley of extemporanea,
And love is a thing that can never go wrong,
And I am Marie of Roumania.

Dorothy Parker, 'Comment', *c.* 1926

Cambridge is proverbially a dampening place, and Steven was a
believer in human photosynthesis. In part this motivated the far-off
settings and adventurous field-trips of his early research. 'I want to go
to Bulgaria in the height of summer,' he declared to Charlotte Bonham Carter. 'I love heat, but my family all shriek at the idea, saying
that I shall certainly die of dreadful diseases on the way.' But shrieks
and heat were also to be found closer to home; one noteworthy source
of both was Wilsford, the Wiltshire idyll of the Tennant family.

The Tennants, an industrial dynasty even more spectacularly hard
of nose than the Runciman family, were, like many of the Runcimans'
grander friends, Liberal Party connections. Margot Asquith had been
born a Tennant, and the clan included Pamela Lady Glenconner (née
Wyndham) and her clutch of variously remarkable children. The older
Runcimans reacted with dismay when Pamela married her long-time
*cavaliere servente*, Lord Grey, in 1922. Viscount Grey of Fallodon

was the Runcimans' north-country neighbour and Walter's unfailing political ally. Remembered by history as the most elegiac warmonger in Europe, Grey was unanimously regarded by his Cabinet colleague's family as a kind and honourable man. Steven enjoyed walking beside the ageing statesman's lake at Fallodon, admiring the sleek, kempt figures of his ducks and listening to his recitations of Wordsworth's *Prelude*, 'a work which I doubt if otherwise I would ever have read right through'. In due course Steven found himself in a position to repay this kindness; his host became almost completely blind, and welcomed his young friend's precise descriptions of his waterfowls' number, appearance and state of health.

Lord Grey was, among his other accomplishments, a writer about the country and, especially, its birds, and Lady Glenconner shared his avian interests. Steven perceived this common ground with sympathy and, being also an admirer of Pamela Glenconner's poetry, he was quicker than his parents to accept her roosting in their old friend's life. Bereft by war of her beloved eldest son Bim, Pamela had taken to spiritualism with an ardour that disturbed Walter and Hilda. Steven, by contrast, was receptive to her oddness, though he did find it eerie that Lady Glenconner appeared to have brought up her youngest child, his own near namesake, Stephen, to resemble and replace her eldest, Clare, a beauty long since married. Although Pamela Glenconner's 'philosophy . . . was never to notice anything that was unpleasant', she regarded this daughter with frank dislike: 'Clare has the face of an angel and the soul of a devil.' Her determination to instil unquestionably angelic qualities in her baby had, Steven thought, left her youngest child befuddled, 'giving the impression of not quite knowing to which sex he belonged'.

Though Stephen Tennant was only three years younger than Steven, and they shared many friends, relations on Steven's side were cautious. In some ways the younger man was a warning to him of the perils of getting one's way. Like Steven, Stephen had found public school uncivilized and authoritarian; like Steven, he knew the value of 'enjoying ill health'.* But while Steven had learnt to excel wherever

---

* The Stev/phens were similarly tall, though Stephen was the slighter; both grew up physically very fast in early adolescence, a development that was blamed for their delicate constitutions.

he could with the greatest pleasure and least effort, Stephen Tennant, encouraged by Pamela to evade anything he found distasteful, had assumed the role of *fainéant* enchanted prince, for whom action would break his all-important spell. Cyril Connolly remembered Steven's impatience at Eton with 'the stupids and the sillies'; the cosseted Stephen was translucently a silly.

At the end of his life, some of Steven's interviewers, knowing no better, treated him as the Last of Bloomsbury, the First Bright Young Thing and, as such, a variant on a Stephen Tennantesque theme; James Owen at the *Spectator* called him (alongside Cecil Beaton) 'another beautiful young man'. Steven found this embarrassing. His ambitions, unlike Stephen's, by far outreached the merely beautiful. Closer to his own mother than to anybody else, Steven still felt that the maternal influence upon Stephen was worrying in itself, and cause for alarm over 'what would happen to him if he ever got free of Pamela ... if the glass in the conservatory got broken'. He found himself in the paradoxical position of admiring the mother while deploring her effect on the son whom he liked less.

Steven's qualms about Stephen's fragility and self-indulgence were not shared by more overt and less scrupulous pleasure-seekers in their circle. Foremost among these was Cecil Beaton (Steven snidely reported to Ruth that 'dear Mr Beaton, as you know, has been taken up in those [that is, Tennant] circles'), who experienced Stephen's figure, garb, complexion, cosmetics, friends and house as love-objects destined for his lens. Rosamond Lehmann, Steven's increasingly unwelcome sister-in-law, was another courtier at Wilsford; indeed she was already a court favourite of its recumbent prince, who could not resist the attraction of so universally acknowledged a beauty. Worse still, the friendship between these beauties had been forged in their common dislike of Hilda Runciman.

Walter and Hilda Runciman, as non-conformist Liberals, had not at first been received into the most exalted society in Northumberland.* But, as Walter grew more eminent, good manners dictated a

---

* It is a curiosity worth noting that Hugh Trevor-Roper, Steven's academic ally and uneasy friend, spent his (miserable) childhood with an accepted if subordinate role in this society, as the son of the Duke of Northumberland's GP at Alnwick.

relaxation of etiquette. By the summer of 1925 Hilda was confident enough in her friendship with the Duke and Duchess of Northumberland to take over the superintendence of a historical pageant at Alnwick Castle. With a characteristic blend of historical romanticism and wifely feminism, Hilda decided to stage the forlorn defence of Bamburgh Castle against the wicked King William Rufus by the valiant Matilda, Countess of Northumberland. One northern stronghold, after all, was perfectly capable of standing in for another. With either determined naivety or a detached complaisance to equal her elder son Leslie's, Hilda cast her daughter-in-law's handsome and histrionic lover, Wogan Philipps, as the captive young Earl of Northumberland. Rosamond herself was allotted an almost speechless male Herald. 'The Hon. S. Tennant', just over from his stepfather's house, was, Steven recalled, 'a very fetching young soldier'.

The two beautiful mechanicals had not yet been formally introduced, but soon got into a protracted conversation, more hilarious than witty, about colour, inspired by the homespun tunics Hilda had provided. Their parts were tiny, and amid their giggles they both quite missed their cues, much to the displeasure of the (contemporary) Duke of Northumberland. 'I don't think we were forgiven,' Rosamond observed sixty years later. Whether she felt forgiveness had been withheld by her ducal host, her mother-in-law, her lover as leading man or her brother-in-law Steven with his refined historical sensibility, she did not specify.

After returning from the Far East in the spring of 1926, Steven settled down to his Trinity fellowship thesis. But rather than go back to the solitude of Cambridge before it was absolutely necessary, he chose for the time being to move into his parents' house at Barton Street. He spent his days working at the London Library, 'that most valuable institution', of which he had been a member since his twentieth birthday. Living with his parents among their earnest and Liberal friends might appear to have been a retrograde development after six months of independent travel. But Steven's range of acquaintances in London had expanded with his confidence at an exciting time to be young and metropolitan. 'In London a group of those who could afford it, and many who could not, came together to give parties and to enjoy themselves, earning the title, in the gossip columns, of Bright Young People.'

It is worth observing that, though Steven, like Evelyn Waugh in *Vile Bodies*, accepts the popular term – 'and on the whole they were very bright' – he has a distinct set in mind. 'It was the golden age for aestheticism in Oxford; in Cambridge we were slightly more restrained.' Steven shared Waugh's contempt for the pointless attitudinizing of the period; few among his new friends had not earned their place by some conspicuous, if not invariably substantial, accomplishment: 'writers such as the Sitwells, Peter Quennell and Harold Acton, musicians such as William Walton and Constant Lambert, painters as diverse as Mark Gertler and Rex Whistler, and dancers such as Freddie Ashton'.* Steven's evening companions had purposefulness foreign to Waugh's Adam, Nina and Agatha Runcible, in the exercise of their pleasures as well as their talents. Steven hints at a more sexually fulfilled scene than the brittle innocence of Waugh's creations ('All this fuss about sleeping together. For physical pleasure I'd sooner go to my dentist any day'):

> As an outcome of the recent war, young women had escaped from the former era of chaperonage. Many of them now had jobs and were free to go out with their boy-friends without the watchful eyes of their elders. They were joined by other young persons whose sexual tastes would not have been admitted in the past. In comparison with modern standards, their sexual activities, whatever they might be, were conducted on the whole with discretion. Their parties were lively and informal but seldom orgiastic.

Steven's detached tone does not entirely occlude the racy attractions of the London circles he was now discovering, though it

---

* Of these, Steven preferred the male Sitwells to Edith and Sacheverell to Osbert; regarded Acton as a rather dishonest friend (and was thought of similarly in turn); thought Quennell by and large 'tiresome'; liked Walton but took against Lambert (whose compositions he however preferred); found Gertler 'neurotic', one of Steven's most frequent and sternest terms of rebuke; was much taken with Whistler and maintained an enjoyable rivalry with Ashton. At Steven's eightieth birthday party the by then Sir Frederick Ashton observed to him that 'we are the only two of the Bright Young People to have made good' (SR, 'Footnotes', p. 68).

establishes his continuing sense of separation: seldom has a 'seldom' been more pointedly nuanced.

Stephen Tennant's was a separation of another sort. Although by common consent, Steven says, 'the youngest and the brightest of the Bright Young Things', Stephen reclined at a tangent to their air of modernity and action. Steven described his namesake's most endearing qualities as his 'love of fantasy, and infectious light-heartedness, all combined with very good manners'. But though he had an original mind, drew skilfully and had surprised everybody by attending a few of his lectures at the Slade School of Art, Stephen Tennant was quite deliberately neither for anything nor headed anywhere. With Wilsford at his command, he had small need to be.

Steven disapproved of those, like Cecil Beaton, Dadie Rylands, Rosamond and Wogan Philipps, who availed themselves of the earthly paradise at Wilsford without the long-established family knowledge he considered necessary for the negotiation of its serpents. Steven had known the younger Tennants from their births, and avoided intimacy with them. His Trinity contemporary David, elder brother of Stephen, the founder of the Gargoyle Club, a sophisticated metropolitan night-spot, was another kind of Tennant, more naturally along Leslie's sort of line; while Steven and Stephen, superficially similar by nature, increasingly different by choice, had never exactly been friends, for all their Liberal quasi-cousinage. Wilsford was a fatherless house, the domain of the Younger Set; Steven still preferred the company of his elders, or contemporaries with an eye for the past. His was an avant-garde already overtaken, Bloomsbury in aesthetics, Liberal in politics, Yeatsian in metaphysics. It was only in the sphere of international high culture, like Diaghilev's Russian Ballet, that Steven concerned himself with keeping up to date; and even this case of balletomania led back to older connections, like the Keyneses and the Bowens. It was an older friend, too, who would facilitate the relaxation of Steven's attitude towards Wilsford.

Eleanor 'Baba' Brougham was a middle-aged spinster with exalted connections and strong affections; she combined a traditional poetic sensibility, leaning to the sentimental, with a surprisingly advanced ear for prose. Baba had once been lady-in-waiting to Queen Ena of Spain, and had in her youth possessed the reputation in gossip columns on both sides of the Atlantic of being a 'conversationalist of talent'. Steven described her as 'looking like a large-boned, well-bred horse, with remarkably elegant legs'. In 1925 Stephen Tennant had less charitably observed, to his notional fiancée Elizabeth Lowndes, that '[Baba's] father thinks she's pretty & her mother thinks her clever and she's neither it's rather a joke! Isn't it? Not for her, of course, but for us!' Baba wrote aphorisms, anthologized ballads, introduced Vita Sackville-West to the essays of Walter Pater and insti-gated Steven's close friendship with the novelist Fred (E. F.) Benson; Stephen Tennant, according to Steven, owed to her his craze for Willa Cather. She was alternately an admirer of and at war with the Sitwell siblings. A dear friend of Lady Grey's, Baba was staying at Wilsford when Steven first visited the house in June 1925. A letter to Kitty reveals him at first frozen with diffidence, but rapidly thawed by astonishment:

> That afternoon we went to a garden party with Sir Oliver Lodge, the scientist spiritualist* In the evening three young females arrived – Cynthia Noble, Mrs Saxton Noble's daughter – she tries so hard to be cultured† – a female called Meraud Guinness, of the rich banking and brewing family, and her friend, an odious American . . . Stephen is still rather unwell and has to rest a great deal and drink milk . . . I walked with Stephen in the morning; and in the afternoon we all sight saw at old Sarum. Lord Grey arrived with a Lord Stanley – a 1st creation – with a horrid face but a kind heart. Today we are going to Stonehenge.
> . . . I was so frightened at first, but Lady Grey is very kind, and Stephen so charming, that my shyness has worn off and I quite enjoy it. I eat strawberries all day long. The house is only quite nice, but the garden really rather beautiful. One has to gush a great deal about birds, but I'm good at that. Stephen keeps pet alligators, but they are very small.

* A friend of Lady Grey's, Sir Oliver Lodge, one of the pioneers of radio, had like his hostess lost a beloved son in the First World War and had become convinced that he could establish contact with his spirit from the afterlife, a process described in his *Raymond, or Life and Death* (1916).
† Later Cynthia Gladwyn; her husband, Gladwyn Jebb, Baron Gladwyn, was nick-named 'Jebb the deb' owing to his reputation as the most etiolated diplomat in the Foreign Service. Both Gladwyns would be lifelong and demanding friends of Steven.

Though Steven does not mention Baba Brougham in this first impression, on subsequent visits he contrived to overlap with her. Her grandeur seemed passé to her young host, but Steven found her company a considerable relief.

On a chilly January weekend in 1927, Steven went up from Waterloo with Baba Brougham, Cecil Beaton and a new acquaintance, physically somewhat in Baba's mould, 'no chicken and not slender', but with a spectacular heredity. This was Dolly Wilde, niece of Oscar. She had achieved a precarious celebrity as a 1920s reincarnation of her uncle, exhibiting his looks, mannerisms and ripostes. Steven thought her physique more Wildean than her intellect, and was as sharp about Stephen Tennant's latest bohemian prize as Stephen was about Baba. Steven had been sceptical of the cult of Oscar since his schooldays. Dolly's exhibitionist lesbianism and heroin habit annoyed him further. Cecil Beaton, more extrovert than Steven, found Dolly's presence an indispensable part of the weekend's allure. To him Dolly's talk seemed to be of a quality as high as it was unaffected: 'never expecting that she might have inherited her uncle's wit, she continually managed to say clever, funny things as if by a fluke. Her eyes widened with astonishment at each bon mot, and she exploded as heartily as anyone in the ensuing laughter.'

Dolly Wilde's biographer reprimands Beaton, and, by association, 'all the young men around Stephen Tennant', for their hypocrisy in pillorying Dolly's appearance – as Beaton had it in his journal, 'raven hair shingled, oyster face plastered in powder, she wore vitriolic purple and reclined like a decadent Roman empress.' After all, these youths all 'painted and powdered and creamed their faces at night, then seriously discussed their complexions in the morning'. This is over-defensive; Beaton clearly intended his evocation of exaggerated colour as an unadulterated compliment. Steven was not so sure. Unlike Beaton, he had grown used to the Wilsford circus and by now found its unrelenting frolics increasingly hard work.

It was not that Steven was unskilled at the succession of games that kept the party going. Looking back on the weekend's talk, Beaton quoted only Steven's conversation, among that of the young guests, for its content rather than its manner. He rattled off 'historical anecdotes', with hints both of the regal and the macabre; Beaton records a story about the accidental ingestion of the heart of Louis XIV, when a myopic English parson mistook it for a scone. Steven was competing with Lady Grey, who 'regaled us with nonsense', such as 'the woman who wanted to have diamonds put in her teeth so that she could even say "Good morning" brilliantly'. This was conversation as the older generation practised it: the gentle passing and capping of anecdotes. The countervalent craze of the Younger Set was already for self-analysis. 'All the weekend we talked and talked and talked about ourselves and each other,' Steven related with exhaustion, 'or played the sort of games that one does play at Wilsford.' It was not coincidental that the Sun King had come into his mind. A connoisseur of courts past and present, Steven felt cramped by the protocol of Wilsford, broadcasting its outrageousness while enforcing its physical and intellectual limitations. The fairy prince's delicacy heightened, rather than mellowed, his tyranny: 'Baba was remarkably silent, being ill with a cold (which of course you have to pretend not to have at Wilsford, for fear Stephen gets it).'

Steven and Beaton at least satisfied their young host's aesthetic whims. Indeed Beaton secured his perpetual inclusion in Tennant parties with a horizontal, aquatic, frolicsome photograph of the Stev/phens, gambolling with the two most famous beauties present, the Jungman sisters. Of all the novelties Wilsford offered on this occasion, these two 'society young ladies' caught Steven's most lingering, if ambivalent, attention: ' . . . Miss Zita and Miss "Baby" (that's the only name I know) [she was baptised Teresa] Jungman, stepdaughters of one of the Guinness family. Zita is very beautiful and rather intelligent and altogether quite pleasant . . . Baby rather a little horror, of the fluffy calculating sort.' Three years later, Evelyn Waugh would find himself bewitched by Baby's fluffiness. Like Steven, Beaton seems to have been more impressed by Zita, 'with her page's cap of hair . . . a gentle quiet voice like honey, or milk that is slightly off'. Zita Jungman continued to mix with Stephen Tennant and the Sitwells in London; seven years later, she and Steven would share a godchild.

Two of the 'sort of games that one does play at Wilsford' were 'Analogies' and 'Interesting Questions'. The second's innuendo-tinged title was a tease: its difficulties were more lexical than psychological. The first complemented the Freudian self-absorption of the young people's conversation. The players were asked to describe each other with reference, or 'analogy', to certain categories. The categories Beaton mentions give an idea of the parameters of the Wilsford universe: 'My Mother; My Father; My Teacher; My Governess; My Skeleton in the Cupboard; What Would I Save from the Fire'. Beaton remembers that in Steven's observant fantasy he became the child of Sybil Colefax and Cardinal Mazarin; 'My Skeleton: a kind heart. What I Would Save from the Fire: Myself.'

The last attraction that Stephen had laid on arrived late. Borden Harriman, an obscure American actor, was, however, well behaved, good looking and impeccably connected. He made little impression on Beaton, but Steven took to him at once, thinking him 'soft-voiced and ingenuous . . . a little lost, but enjoying it and us all'. It must have come as a relief to the young American to find in Steven a serious young man, superficially resembling Stephen Tennant and Cecil Beaton, but blessedly willing to make polite rather than purely expressive conversation. 'Everyone was very happy and felt popular, and Cecil took photographs of us all,' Steven concluded his account of the weekend, not without a hint of claustrophobic distaste.

Still more distasteful, to Steven's mind, was his elder brother's marriage. At first Steven and Rosamond, although instinctively suspicious of each other, felt a wary mutual appreciation. They amused each other, enjoyed similar circles and shared many friends, most importantly Dadie Rylands. In early 1925 Leslie inflicted mortal damage on this delicate union, already a brave assertion of good will over misunderstanding, by insisting that his pregnant wife undergo an abortion, in order to assuage what he termed his 'paedophobia', a horror of propagating the human race in a world of wretchedness. Rosamond longed for a child, and Leslie attempted in later life to describe this termination as a natural miscarriage, but the surviving correspondence does not bear him out. When Rosamond had recovered (if only physically) from the operation, she left her husband in his Runciman headquarters at Newcastle, a city she had always loathed. Leslie hoped Rosamond might return in time, in the flesh and in spirit. Uncertain about his future, and craving sympathetic company, he was delighted by the appearance of a promising confrère – a young scapegrace who had been sent to him for training in commercial conscience.

Wogan Philipps, 'the inevitable Wogan', was the easy-going son and heir of a shipowner and insurance-broking mogul, Sir Laurence Philipps, a father much like the elder Walter Runciman in his ferocity and grip. Sir Laurence first extracted his son from the softening distractions of Oxford, then even more precipitately from the enticements of metropolitan life and the likelihood of an inopportune marriage. Wogan was sent out to South America, and subsequently to Newcastle to buckle down under Leslie, a fellow shipping heir reputed, even by his Cambridge supervisors, to be a steadying influence. It was to prove a decisive course, if not in the way Sir Laurence had anticipated. Less than two years later, Wogan would be living in a sort of *ménage à trois*; he had learnt relatively little about the shipping trade, but was the acknowledged paramour of the most beautiful female Cambridge graduate of her day, his great good looks fawned over by the dangerous bohemians whose influence upon his heir Sir Laurence had thought to have curtailed. As though in confirmation of Sir Laurence's worst fears, Wogan would end up as the British Communist Party's first, and to date only, spokesman in the House of Lords.

Wogan found neither difficulty nor contradiction in the various roles his new situation called upon him to fulfil. At first he was the agreeable, if less than competent, shipping apprentice, and the inseparable companion, of the lonely and self-contained Leslie – a younger brother substitute, without the inconveniencies of Steven's intellectual head-start and delight in subversive teasing. With Rosamond's reluctant return to Newcastle, he was perfectly situated to be the male lead to her ill-used romantic heroine. She felt he had barely noticed her at their first meeting. Few men ever failed to notice Rosamond, but Wogan was a practised flirt. He would later claim that about the time their affair began he provided his services as amanuensis for Rosamond's first novel, *Dusty Answer* – an imperfectly transfigured account of the unhappy Cambridge love-affair that had driven her to marry Leslie. Before Steven left for China in the autumn of 1925, he was aware of the state of his brother's marriage and 'irritated to find Leslie putting up with it. But in those days he was modest and without much self-confidence, and he was still in love with Rosamond and wanted her to be happy.'

Apprentice and friend, lover and secretary Wogan might already be, but by the summer of 1926 – which found all three holidaying in a cottage outside Hexham – he showed himself willing to adopt an additional guise. Stephen Tennant called on the young Runciman couple, still enchanted by Rosamond's style and spirit; not far behind came Steven, accompanied by Dadie Rylands. Although Steven had already groused to his friends, sisters and acquaintances about Wogan and Rosamond, he remained more intrigued than he admitted by his sister-in-law. His visit to the northern *locus amoenus* was motivated half by fraternal loyalty – unsolicited by Leslie – and half by social curiosity. This desire to accumulate stray gossip was punished in an exasperating manner when Dadie, himself accustomed to playing the fascinating and callous lover, fell headlong for Wogan, who, flexible as ever, did not altogether rebuff him. Whatever Steven had felt for Dadie as a schoolboy and an undergraduate, their friendship was now too mature to be physical, but this made it all the more galling that Dadie could so lightly transfer his sympathies to the enemy, admiring Rosamond and adoring Wogan. As for Leslie, he continued, it seemed, to enjoy Wogan's presence, and during the next year he embarked on some kind of flirtation with his rival's cousin, Honor Philipps. Steven was now isolated in his distaste for Wogan, and in his rejection of his elder brother's conciliatory position.

Dadie made things worse by bestowing the blessing of Bloomsbury on the lovers. Lytton Strachey called by the summer cottage, and embellished its rococo erotic architecture by deciding that the real beauty of the household was Leslie:

Mr and Mrs R. share the establishment with a young man called Wogan Philipps – quite nice . . . Leslie is to me extremely attractive – in character, even, as well as appearance. But I don't suppose many would agree with this. He is pompous, moody, flies into tempers, and is not mentally entertaining by any means. Perhaps you would be bored by the poor fellow. But oh! he's so strong, and his difficulties are so curious – and his eyelashes . . . there's a childishness about him that – I daresay all grown-up people are childish in some way or other – I find endearing. Rosamond is a much brighter character . . . though not as good-looking – gay, enthusiastic, and full of fun. She and Dadie get on like a house on fire. Wogan lies vaguely and sympathetically at their feet. And dear Leslie makes a pompous remark, to which no attention is paid, looks divine, scowls, until I long to fling my arms around his neck.

The cosiness of all this was worse than upsetting to Steven – it was maddening. His responsible elder brother, much beloved but something of a plodder, the reliable heir to the family business, was now outclassing him in indifference to convention. Or, rather, Leslie was against all expectation succeeding in being adopted into an alternative convention, one which Steven himself found attractive but could not regard without irony or follow without insecurity.

Strachey's account of this tableau, Wogan 'lying vaguely and sympathetically' at the feet of the two beauties in love with him, is in part an idealization of the Bloomsbury model – such a one as Strachey himself enjoyed with Dora Carrington and Ralph Partridge. Strachey himself is playful about the ambiguity, half suggesting that the arrangement was consensual to all parties – as, indeed, it half was – while recording every twinge of Leslie's painful, embarrassing exclusion with a peculiar admixture of sympathy and sadism. Strachey's correspondent, Carrington, did not much like Steven, regarding him with suspicion as a latter-day intruder, 'a mushroom growth'. Among the Keynes-led Bloomsbury–Cambridge set, whose kindness Steven acknowledged and whose standards of wit and civilization he accepted, he was privately damned with the unflattering nickname 'Robot Runciman'. It was, perhaps, a question of the 'childishness' Strachey found so lovable in Leslie. Steven lacked, and was aware of lacking, such childishness; and by Strachey's logic this meant he could not be perceived as fully grown up. It was this void that left Steven with a basic allergy to Stephen Tennant, and an immunity to Wogan's stripe of animal charm: he thought Wogan 'such a public schoolboy . . . cold and bloodless and moist'. Now, for all the misery and indignity of his position, Leslie was at least regarded by none other than Lytton Strachey as possessing the innocence requisite for entry to a funny sort of paradise. And all this was arranged by Dadie, Steven's oldest, closest friend, one of the youngest yet most integrated of Bloomsbury muses, while Steven himself would always emphasize that 'I was never one of them'. Feeling betrayed and bored by the squalor of it all, this unconventional younger brother began to resort to convention after all.

In April 1927, about the time that Leslie finally allowed himself to be persuaded that his marriage was irreparable, *Dusty Answer* was published under Rosamond's maiden name, with a dedication to Dadie Rylands. It became a best-seller in short order, partly through the good offices of Alfred Noyes, the popular poet, a friend of Rosamond's father, who produced an early and unstinting encomium in the *Sunday Times*, but mainly due to its flawed, but inarguable, sincerity and power. Steven, who at this point was still in the throes of contending for the Trinity fellowship, about which he did not feel confident, reacted to *Dusty Answer* with personal annoyance tinged with professional competition. He had thought Rosamond beautiful and accomplished, but never witty, let alone brilliant; now she appeared to be the coming young novelist, and his best friend was her dedicatee. Steven consoled himself with a burst of haughty patronage in a letter to Ruth:

Rosamond's novel is a *succès fou* – real best seller! Glowing reviews, though many older people are shocked, and all the characters depicted (you know everyone is somebody) are furious, I believe. You must tell people that R&L are separated, and say (as delicately as you can) that it's because she has another young man. She's telling her friends that she has left Lellie 'and it wouldn't be fair to Leslie to tell you the reason just yet'! So, though silly Lellie wants it to be called a mutual separation, I'm going to risk his displeasure and tell the truth.

The reviews were not all so very glowing; one of the nastiest came from Rose Macaulay, and though Rosamond's publisher tried to soothe his new star by assuring her that this reviewer was 'unco' spinsterish', Macaulay was also a devoted friend to Steven. Not all Steven's intimates had followed Dadie's lead. In the meantime, Steven showed no compunction in defying his brother and sister-in-law's wishes, speaking freely to family and friends about a subject that was assuredly more the separated couple's business than his.

At first they endeavoured to placate him; during one party at the Lehmann parents' house, Rosamond persisted in tête-à-tête with Steven 'for about twenty minutes . . . making herself very pleasant to me'. This proved of limited use, and now Steven's ill-natured garrulity seriously hindered Leslie and Rosamond's wishes. Left to himself, Leslie was perfectly willing to obey the gentlemanly convention of the day and provide grounds to be divorced by his wife, a device to which Wogan's pretty cousin, Honor Philipps, seemed willing to contribute. This would permit divorce proceedings to begin with Rosamond as the wronged party, which, in light of the secret and regretted abortion, she in at least one undeniable respect was. Steven's refusal to play along, in informing practically everyone he met of his construction of the facts, would either force the shabby pretence of the marriage to continue, or inflict the full disgrace on Rosamond herself, a disgrace in the late 1920s still far more disadvantageous to a woman than a man.

Desperate for her malicious young brother-in-law to show her mercy, Rosamond sought Steven out at a grander party in Belgravia. It was an eventful and raucous occasion; the light-jazz singer and pianist Leslie 'Hutch' Hutchinson had put himself up for auction, and was narrowly won by a notorious society heroin addict, Brenda Dean Paul. 'Rumour maintained', Steven recalled, 'that they rushed to an upper floor to consummate the auction and opened a door into a bedroom where our host's parents were vainly trying to sleep.' Rosamond fought her way to Steven and imparted a long and garbled version of the whole truth, but he was as offended by her indiscretion as determined to persist in his own:

> Our darling sister-in-law is telling all her friends that she has left Leslie, giving as the reason either . . . that he cared for some other woman, or he wouldn't let her have a baby. No mention of Wogan. So I have felt obliged to tell all my friends the facts (as far as one decently can) because her stories are being spread very thoroughly. It's very funny, isn't it, how she is proving herself really to be a far nastier creature than one ever imagined even when one supposed that one thought the worst of her! I'm afraid she may do poor Lellie a great deal of harm.

The 'other woman' to whom Rosamond alluded was presumably

Honor Philipps, and this was a weak line of complaint; Leslie's relations with Honor had been hesitant, inconclusive and painstakingly encouraged by Wogan and Rosamond herself. The whole story of the real grievance, the abortion, was almost impossible to confide to an ear as unsympathetic as Steven's. Partly because of her dramatic looks and her unexpected literary success, anything Rosamond could say would be treated by Steven as a lie, enjoining upon him a corresponding obligation to counter it with 'the facts'. As for 'poor Lellie', Steven more than 'risked his displeasure'. The morning after the Hutch auction party, he marched straight to Leslie's flat in Haymarket and repeated to his brother all that he could reconstruct of 'Rosamond's diatribe'. Leslie's loyalty still attached, vestigially, to his wife, and he vowed in his fury never to speak to his younger brother again. Though this threat was in the moment sincerely made, within the close matriarchy of the Runciman family it was never really practicable.

As Wogan's involvement emerged into public knowledge through a mixture of Steven's meddling and Rosamond's harassed naivety, Walter Runciman entirely refused to co-operate with Rosamond divorcing Leslie rather than vice versa. The victory of Steven and the elder Runcimans over Leslie and his unfortunate first wife was total; Leslie was obliged to begin divorce proceedings in late 1927, and, when attempting to do the honourable thing at least in terms of financial support, was freshly humiliated when Rosamond brushed him aside to live independently on her then-considerable literary earnings. Decades later, Steven and Rosamond would achieve a surprising degree of friendship. He would end up treating her with more imagination and kindness than the beloved but tricky Dadie. But Steven never expressed, nor indeed felt, contrition for his interfering behaviour in the 1920s, that series of long thin scratches that never quite stopped stinging his ex-sister-in-law. He considered till the end that he had helped to rescue his elder brother from a 'silly' and 'vicarious' form of romanticism. Contemplating her projected biography by Selina Hastings in 1987, Rosamond wrote to Steven that 'there was – is – so much misunderstanding and (for me) suffering that probably only you could throw light on.'

If Steven's conduct during the disintegration of his brother's marriage illustrated his least attractive personal qualities – envy, indiscretion and mischief-making – he cultivated the better side of his nature in his friendship with a novelist who made of such weaknesses some of his most celebrated material. This was E. F. Benson, Fred to his intimates, son of a famously odd family, and, as the creator of Mapp and Lucia, a cult success of a stylish and specific kind. Steven and he were introduced at a party of Baba Brougham's in late 1928, Baba being a neighbour of Benson's in Brompton Square, and over the next decade, whenever Steven escaped Cambridge for London, he was likely to find a place at Fred Benson's table. The novelist remained, to Steven, firmly Mr Benson, but Steven was rapidly beStevened.

Fred Benson was short and solid, and looked older than his fifty-odd years, his sage though humorous face adorned with clipped, respectable grey whiskers. Steven recalls that his parents were quietly frank in their disapproval of this new association; he attributed this antipathy to a form of class and political *omertà*, as in his novels *Dodo* and *Dodo the Second* Benson had appeared to satirize Margot Tennant, later Asquith, and the rest of the Souls.* But a more probable motive for the Runciman parents' reservations than the fading obscurities of Liberal feuding may be found in their trepidation about their talented, aesthetical younger son associating so much in private with an older male novelist, and a Benson at that.

Fred was, by now, the last of the Bensons; his elder brother A. C. Benson, the friend and confidant of Steven's old supervisor Gaillard Lapsley and one of the most distinguished among Dadie's legion of adorers, had died in 1925. The Benson children, progeny of an Archbishop of Canterbury and Mary Sidgwick, the woman Gladstone had accounted 'the cleverest in Europe', had earned a collective renown for restless intellect, prolific literary activity, religious complexity, sporadic madness and sexual non-conformity. Both the children's mother and the surviving Benson daughter, Margaret, were

---

* Certainly Steven accepted this identification of the character Dodo, 'though Mr. Benson always denied it' (SR to Tony Reavell, 6 February 1984, Elshieshields). Another guest Steven encountered at Fred Benson's occasions, the composer and suffragette Ethel Smyth, was quite clearly the model for Dodo's androgynous friend Edith Staines; she took this as a compliment.

able to live more or less openly with female companions. Robert Hugh Benson, the youngest of the children, after his ordination into the Catholic priesthood became, at the very least, emotionally entwined with the notorious Frederick Rolfe, Baron Corvo; A. C. and E. F. Benson, men of greater worldly comfort and romantic timidity, lived all but celibate existences punctuated by crushes, rationalization and guilt.

Steven was aware, at the time and later, that his relations with Mr Benson were readily open to misconstruction; but he always insisted on the entire propriety of their acquaintanceship, and, indeed, so far as he could tell, on Fred Benson's lack of sexual connection to anybody. He did feel that he was always the youngest guest present at these Brompton Square gatherings, and was much interested decades later to discover that he had been one of quite a number of youthful protégés whom Fred had carefully avoided introducing to one another. Steven felt Mr Benson to be almost morbidly chaste; he seemed averse even to touching or being touched:

> ... EFB always seemed to me to have a fastidious distaste for physical contacts. I think I was quite a personable youth whom a lecherous homosexual might have desired. But I don't recall that he ever touched me except when we shook hands ... I wonder, indeed, if he was ever deeply involved emotionally with anyone ... I don't think that passion, either physical or emotional, played a part in his life – and perhaps that shows in his books. I think that he probably was more attracted by young men than by young women; but it was a very innocent attraction. His brother Arthur did rather like to paw young men – a bit embarrassingly – but Mr. Benson ... quite clearly had no such desire.

Steven had good authority for A. C.'s pawing in the elder Benson brother's besotted and unhappy courtship of Dadie. A. C. had regarded Dadie as 'gracefully puritanical' yet 'eager ... a loveable creature altogether'; he had comforted himself with the (mistaken) supposition that Dadie was unpopular with his own contemporaries, 'thought haughty – he likes older people better,' and was agonized when he appeared at last to lose Dadie to the Bloomsbury set, with their 'bird-like morals'.

To an earlier favourite, Geoffrey Madan, A. C. had pronounced two unforgiving aphorisms about Fred:

> E. F. never lived his life at all; only stayed with it and dined with it.
>
> . . . [his] idea of a good conversation: when neither party remembers a word of what was said afterwards.

This fraternal view may be more than a little jaundiced, and pepped up for Madan's delectation; Steven certainly had no difficulty remembering the gossip he heard at E. F.'s table.

> [E. F.] was, I think, the best company of anyone whom I have known. He had himself known everyone of interest in his time . . . and had an immensely observant eye and . . . an unending store of anecdotes, all highly entertaining and some pretty libellous, though he was always discreet. 'Kindly' is not an adjective that leaps to the mind, though he was always kind to me. His humour was a bit too sharp for that. But there was no basic malice in him, only a delight in the ridiculous.

Steven claimed to have found various acquaintances throughout the century, some celebrated, some attractive, some both, 'the best company'; they included Margot Asquith, Diaghilev, Keynes and Peter Montgomery, a boyishly handsome Irish squire who conducted a long affair with Anthony Blunt. But some additional sincerity is conveyed here by the cohesion of this account of Fred Benson with the standards, of hospitality, conversation, morality and generosity, which Steven would attempt to uphold all through his long life. The withdrawn fastidiousness about love-affairs which, he half avouches, half speculates, was Benson's is part of the same picture – the beautifully mannered *beau idéal* Steven strove to exemplify. He often felt he had fallen short of it; he was to recall to a Benson biographer a swift reprimand from the genial Mr Benson, after Steven had delivered an ill-timed, unfavourable verdict on another guest. Steven's exterior self-deprecation thinly covered, as David Plante among others sensed, self-regard; but, below this in turn, Steven judged himself by iron-hard standards. Whatever he felt were his own lapses into unkindness or unworthiness, Steven identified with E. F. Benson's Edwardian manners and determined, as best he could, to perpetuate them.

Steven knew Fred Benson during the decade of 1928–38, his own twenty-fifth to thirty-fifth years: the difference between the last of youth and the cusp of middle age. His account of the friendship traces his own development from callow certainty towards sophisticated nuance. To begin with Steven had recoiled from the heartiness of the novelist's Brompton Square decor: 'I remember now that neo-Jacobean fireplace (and thinking it rather hideous) and the china on the shelves and the over-mantle [sic] ... As a highbrow purist youth I did not admire it; but there was something welcoming about it, largely because [Benson] was so welcoming.'

Steven was no longer the boy who had tried to amuse Dadie by mocking his parents' dowdy furniture. He was beginning to absorb that 'delight in the ridiculous' in which Benson was implicitly educating him. Benson had an especially subtle and maturing influence on one subject that always interested Steven – the supernatural:

> EFB certainly 'believed' in ghosts. He talked to me several times about the subject. He certainly was convinced that the chair in the garden room was haunted, and he told me of other experiences which he certainly had not invented – he could supply place and date. But he had no cut and dried *theory* about them. He took the line (very properly, in my opinion) that it would be arrogant and pointless to try to explain what they were, and he had no sympathy for spiritualistic séances, which he thought dangerous. I think that he liked the supernatural to remain a mystery. It is, I can confidently attest, nonsense to say that he only talked and wrote about it for dramatic effect.

Many of these Bensonian elements would become hallmarks of Steven's cast of thought, both as a writer and as a raconteur. There is that intriguing combination, less contradictory than at first sight, of a love of formal accuracy ('he could supply place and date') with faith in the essentially 'apophatic', the ineffable and unsayable ('he liked the supernatural to remain a mystery'). Steven adopted some of Benson's suspicion and distaste for spiritualism – which he had previously found rather an intriguing subject and a useful way of disconcerting his parents – and he would always retain that curiously theatrical, deadpan seriousness, which would make his listeners suspect that they were being bamboozled even as they experienced a twinge of genuine alarm.

Fred Benson might have been a last survivor and a period piece, but his friendship led Steven to many avant-garde introductions. E. F.'s female acquaintances, perhaps owing to the effect upon him of his deceased, beloved but overpowering mother and sister, were frequently lesbian or bisexual. This was in part a matter of coincidence; Radclyffe Hall and Una Troubridge lived not far from Fred's seaside bolthole at Rye, fit models at hand for 'Quaint Irene', the unkempt voice of candour in the Lucia novels. Musical expertise also played a part; Fred often entertained, in addition to Ethel Smyth, the harpsichordist Violet Gordon-Woodhouse and Lady Dean Paul. This last was a Belgian pianist born Régine Wieniawski but better known as Madame Poldowski, and the mother of the debauched Brenda, the beneficiary of the Hutch auction.

Benson's most lasting achievement has become the Mapp and Lucia series, still the subject of a cult, though the machinery of their humour, protagonists and plot is of an exquisitely period construction. Benson himself called these novels 'frivolous' and 'preposterous', adjectives he intended as high marks of artistic perfectionism adding that 'there was nothing faked or sentimental about them'. This is certainly fair – while the six Lucia novels are composed in a mood of extreme mannerism that is not suited to every palette, they cannot be accused of falsity or emotional incontinence. Steven felt that Mr Benson was aware of his talent's limits, and would have liked to surpass them; but the Lucia series met his own taste for contained hilarity. He particularly approved of a denouement when the eponymous protagonists are, all of a sudden, swept away by a flood, floating on an upturned kitchen table.

The flood of taste dispatched Benson himself into relative oblivion for a time, his reputation barely afloat, clinging to one of those heavy Victorian sideboards of which the young Steven had disapproved. But Steven himself did not forget Mr Benson, that timely source of moral and conversational reorientation, whose impact upon his character, if not his writing, was to prove far more enduring than that of any Cambridge don. His biographical recollections of the novelist were eventually, to his delight, to contribute to something of a revival, which found its apotheosis after his death in a 2014 BBC TV series starring Anna Chancellor, the daughter of Steven's godson John.

In August 1927 Steven had written to Dadie, with whom he was still on relatively equivocal terms over the Rosamond affair:

> after the silly fellowship exam . . . I'm going abroad, to be away when the result is out, – going with a young man who has a sumptuous car; but I shan't tell you who it is, because you'll be horrified.* I shall feel very cross and rather let down if, as I fear seems likely, I don't get my fellowship. But, apart from the slight humiliation, I shouldn't really be sorry . . . The idea of living in Cambridge is really rather horrible – I would only know you there, and you would be too busy to come and comfort me all day long . . . whereas in London one can always find consolation.

Indeed, Steven's London social life had developed from shy beginnings to acquire an ever-more discernible pattern. On the evening of his twenty-fourth birthday, he graced someone else's party at the Ivy. Other guests included Cecil Beaton, a whisky-soused Frankie Birrell, Rex Whistler, Osbert and Sacheverell Sitwell, Sacheverell's Canadian wife Georgia, and Zita Jungman. The occasion had been arranged for Edith Olivier, who was typical of Steven's preferred hostesses in the 1920s – an older, socially selective novelist, shy, dry and queenly – by another girl friend who was most atypical. This was the wispily englamoured American poetess and novelist, a confection as much of her atmosphere as of her oeuvre, Elinor Wylie. Of her, Olivier observed that 'one could not follow her on foot – wings were needed.'

It seems at first glance strange that Steven, who had shown so little patience for Rosamond, should not only have tolerated but have befriended Elinor Wylie, an infinitely more extravagant, capricious, egotistical and doom-laden figure. Doubtless fortunately, she was not married to his brother. One of her husbands had killed himself and the other two had become exhausted by the furtherance of her genuine but baroque talent. Her corporeal muse was now a colonel living in the country, Henry de Clifford Woodhouse, half American but thoroughly English, married elsewhere and too prudent to defect. Though in fact Steven knew several of Woodhouse's cousins, the Youngs of Formosa Place, and even met them in Elinor's company, 'I was not allowed to meet [Woodhouse], nor even to know his name.' Elinor Wylie's truest

---

* This was Sir Basil Bartlett, baronet and actor, of whom more below.

love, Percy Bysshe Shelley, the dedicatee of one of her novels and the subject of another, was more safely yet beyond her reach, though she claimed to have achieved sporadic trysts with his ghost. Steven believed that Elinor's interest in Stephen Tennant had its origins in her desire to use this latter-day angelic youth as a model for Shelley in the novel she wrote about her adored poetical predecessor, *The Orphan Angel*, published not long after her first appearance at Wilsford.

She was tall and of avian, fragile thinness, with luminous white skin, black hair waved and bobbed, stern, enormous, shaded eyes and, in her opinion, far more refined details of countenance, costume and conversation than anybody else's. Olivier remembered the wearying, paradoxically rewarding process of accompanying her over her toilette: 'She enjoyed nothing more than a serious discussion of her own personal appearance. We talked for hours about her each separate feature – her nose, eyes, mouth, cheekbones, wrists, or hair. Each part of her became like a separate person to be discussed or argued over . . . ' Fuelled as it was by insecurity that amounted almost to paranoia, this self-absorbed spell was very difficult to reverse. Many rebelled against Elinor's highly coloured charm. When she was introduced to Virginia Woolf, each was irritated by the other flaunting ignorance of her work. When Steven first met Elinor at Wilsford, Rosamond was also in attendance. Unused, perhaps, to so dramatic a rival for male attention, Rosamond took against Elinor and teased her by proposing that she ought to be worshipped as a fertility goddess at nearby Stonehenge. It was a vain challenge; Elinor accepted divine honours with equanimity and Steven amused himself with designing an elaborate ceremonial, perhaps bringing back fond memories of the poultry-derived paganism he had so enjoyed with Margie as a child. By overshadowing his irksome sister-in-law, Elinor can only have distinguished herself in Steven's playful classification of feminine fowl.* Steven and Elinor were soon well enough disposed to

---

* On this weekend Steven also encountered for the first time Sir Arthur and Lady Colefax ('he an amiable bore, she already determined to be acquainted with everyone of distinction. I cannot say that I liked her' (SR, 'Footnotes', p. 66)) and, most tantalizingly, Lord Berners, 'composer and grand eccentric, whom I found fascinating but frightening; I regret that I was too shy ever to get to know him well.'

each other to exchange confidences about the marital misfortunes of their siblings.

By the 1927 summer party at the Ivy, Elinor was established among carefully chosen friends; mistress of her own court rather than merely decorating Stephen Tennant's; but her confidence was enamelled, not adamant. Attired in characteristically chilly silver and eau-de-Nil chiffon, she performed several of her own poems, one of which reduced her to 'convulsive laughter'. When Cecil Beaton, with rather unkind vigilance, reprimanded her for nervously ripping her nails, she 'spoke of nothing else for hours'. Harold Acton put in an appearance, and unwisely remarked that Shelley had suffered from acne; he found himself facing a tirade from Elinor, who called him a Papist bigot incapable of comprehending holiness. Frankie Birrell she considered odiously alcoholic and 'untrue to her'. She identified the stylish Canadian Georgia Sitwell as a direct sartorial threat, and suspected the Sitwell brothers 'of jibing at her – as they do!' All in all she contrived to be at her most trying, and Steven in his report of the evening to Ruth despairingly wrote her off as 'completely mad'. But for all that, he would continue to see her regularly over the rest of her British sojourn, and to be counted, despite her many dictatorial alterations of whim, among her few trustworthy, affectionate and lasting friends in the country. After a quarrel with the long-suffering Edith Olivier, she ranked Steven and the fantasy writer Eleanor Chilton as 'my only friends, the only ones I really like'.

Late 1927 found Elinor downcast about the lack of advancement in her relations with Woodhouse – although she considered her sonnets to him 'the best poetry of my life' – while Steven was feeling solitary and discontented, after his fellowship had been achieved and he had embarked upon the lonely Cantabrigian period he had so gloomily prophesied to Dadie. He asked Elinor down to Trinity, and she was delighted with what she found there, quite as Fredegond Shove had been with Steven's 'Fairy Land' in his undergraduate days. Steven offered his guest a black Russian cigarette, Zakaznija No. 10, from a lacquered Chinese case, and Elinor was so impressed that she took up smoking on the spot. The weather was unrelentingly wet, but Elinor did not mind in the least: 'How I loved the rainy day and the fire and the peace and the poetry and the mysterious swaying Tree in the middle of Trinity – is it a plane-tree or a chest-nut? Never mind, it is all heavenly.' She professed to find Cambridge life infinitely preferable to the rhythm of the capital: 'who would leave such peace and spiritual plenty as yours at Cambridge for a horrid little dinner in Chelsea?' She promised to return when the weather was finer, 'and be good about Milton and Newton and everyone, but meanwhile our day remains quite perfect'. 'Of course,' she was to add in another meditation on her envy of the Trinity don's existence, 'one has to be a Man to attain such felicity . . . '

But Elinor Wylie's second, brighter trip to Cambridge would never come to pass. She had hoped and planned to make a visit the next March, but found herself too exhausted to travel. 'Personally I think such a day would be well worth dying for,' she declared, 'much less being wearied for, but I suppose that neither you nor Bill [her husband] agree with me.' In fact, it was much more a question of life and death than Elinor's dramatizing tone made it seem. When Steven and Elinor had shared each other's favourite complaints about health, Elinor proudly confided to Steven that she 'possessed the blood pressure of a parrot'. It seems that this time she did not exaggerate. Little more than a year later, midway through a party thrown at the apartment of her detached third husband, William Rose Benét, she collapsed to the floor. As Steven retold the moment in all its ghoulish comedy: 'A guest noticed and said, "Oh, Elinor's dead", and the party went on.'

Literary Ediths abounded between the wars. There was Edith Olivier, in whose dignified shade even Elinor Wylie could relax her performance; she was a modest, unifying presence, a cool observer, liberated late in life by the deaths of a martinet father and an invalid sister. Far more conspicuous was Edith Sitwell, her own performance coiled, constant and always bravely at the ready, in pursuit of something odder and more lasting than beauty or, despite the opinions of her many detractors, fame. Steven gamely partook of the atmosphere she and her brothers toiled to project and promote, while acknowledging its modish transience: 'In the evening I'm taking Rex Whistler to the Sitwells' play – just on for four nights, and every ticket sold. But bad, I expect . . . ' But Steven revered above all the others the Edith whose literary place in the sun had become embodied in a physical one, Gaillard Lapsley's friend of a quarter of a century's standing, Mrs Wharton.

Lapsley's enthusiasm for the company of this rich, transatlantic widowed novelist had seemed to his wary friend A. C. Benson to show a disappointing want of taste. But it was hardly surprising that Lapsley, that intimate of Henry James and exemplar of Jamesian conflict, an East Coast American embedded in Cambridge and devoted to medieval English history, should attend upon Edith Wharton with affectionate, if sometimes sardonic, interest. Like several other 'Jacobites', Lapsley regarded Wharton, partly on the grounds of her sex, as the Master's dogged and imperfect pupil. But there was also the sheer charm and comfort of her French and expatriate milieu to be considered, especially after her purchase, in 1927, of the villa of Sainte-Claire du Château at Hyères. Here the old jokes, rituals and ceremonial courtships of James's household and circle could, to a great extent, survive – flavoured by the addition of, on the one hand, the formal and discerning local *gratin* and, on the other, talented and good-looking young Englishmen.

In March 1925 Steven gained his opportunity to exploit Lapsley's social range when his mother happened to pick Hyères as a suitable spring refuge ('preferable to the smarter resorts further east') for her delicate son and débutante daughter Ruth. Hilda, as ever, was busying herself about the prospects of her husband and the Liberal Party, and soon returned to London, leaving her children to the supervision of another Liberal wife, Lady Emmott. This wardress being less exigent than their mother, Steven and his sister found themselves able to pass the next four 'restful and happy weeks' very much as they chose, and Steven soon put in an appearance, Lapsley's letter of introduction in his pocket, at the 'enchanting house on the castle rock'. Mrs Wharton, a regal figure in her early sixties, received him with pleasure, though his sartorial pride might have been injured had he seen the first impression of him she sent to his former supervisor, 'a nice looking youth with rumpled hair and dimpled socks'. But her praise for the 'brilliance and erudition' of his conversation was less faint, and he was often asked back from then on, both to Hyères and to the northern hunting box that complemented Mrs Wharton's villa, 'an exquisite *pavillon* in the forest of Montmorency'.

Edith Wharton played a benevolent part in her latest young acquaintance's career when, in the autumn of 1927, he was awaiting – and avoiding – the decision as to whether or not he had won a prize fellowship at Trinity. Immediately after the final exam, Steven abandoned Cambridge for a restorative French tour, by ship to Bordeaux and then back north by car. He had arranged to be driven by Basil Bartlett, an undergraduate loathed by Dadie, but whose appearance, baronetcy and automobile recommended him to Steven. Though Steven usually avoided dancing in nightclubs, he occasionally made an exception to dance with Sir Basil, of whom he admitted he was very fond, finding him foolish but 'extremely charming'. Bartlett had all Dadie's theatrical enthusiasm, and even more confidence, but, if at least one of his directors is to be believed, almost none of the ability necessary for a stage career: 'a wealthy stage-struck baronet who is the World's Worst Actor in any and every part which he has tried', having 'the flirtatious lightness of a hippopotamus with a headache. His actions on stage remind one of a dyspeptic stork stalking frogs in a marsh.'

Sir Basil was to prove an equally ill-starred chauffeur; his 'sumptuous car' broke down at Fontainebleau. Steven proceeded to Paris by train and alone. The delay all this occasioned left him with little time before he expected a telegram from the ever-serviceable economics don Dennis Robertson, announcing the decision of the Fellows of Trinity. Steven decided to spend the day of destiny with Mrs Wharton at her Pavillon Colombe, reasoning that 'the strain of living up to her standards could distract me from a time of frightening anxiety.' Sensing his nerves, she fed him with particular lavishness, then took him over her Chantilly gardens, carefully detailing their history and botany, and finally provided her car, less flashy and more resilient than the unfortunate baronet's, to return him to Paris. 'I feel eternal gratitude to her for her kindness to me that day,' Steven wrote in his unpublished memoirs. At Paris the news from Trinity was good.

Like Lytton Strachey, but with more sincerity, Edith Wharton kept abreast of and admired Runciman's early books, singling out *The First Bulgarian Empire* and (rather surprisingly) the more factually compendious *Byzantine Civilization* for particular praise. When he for his part praised her 1928 novel *The Children*, she was sufficiently flattered to expose to him a work in progress that she thought might be calculated to appeal to him, a historical romance set in Byzantine Cyprus, about the heady temptations of the Swedish mystic St Bridget. This was a story that perfectly suited Steven's own element of mystical whimsy; among his own experimental and abandoned fiction by this time was a fantasy novella called 'Victoria Robinson: Saint and Martyr', about a pious English spinster and werewolf-hunter. His consistent fondness for the capacious borderland between eroticism and religiosity is well exemplified – leaving his historical and theological writing for a moment aside – in an undergraduate poem, 'Repentance':

> To one who saw what I have seen
> What can my former pleasures mean?
> How can they sound to one who heard
> The very preaching of the Word?
> What is the old life now to me
> Who stood that night at Calvary?
>
> Yet even so, when all is said,
> Sometimes I shudder in my bed,
> Remembering with a stab of pain
> That I shall never see again
> The burning eyes of lustful men
> Nor hear them murmur 'Magdalen'.

Steven's praise for the story that would become the less than immortal 'Dieu d'Amour' was lavish, and extracted another confidence, even confession, from a much moved Mrs Wharton: 'I have a passion for romantic writing, & would give way to it continuously and without any encouragement.' She also passed on a shrewd piece of professional advice: 'novels are about development of character, short stories are about incident.' This last stage of her life, static but well constellated, had settled decidedly into novel form.

Steven passed the Christmas of 1933 at Sainte-Claire du Château among especially glamorous company, some of whom might well have made Hilda Runciman, had she known about them, regret her choice of a Hyères spring eight years previously. First there was Robert Norton, the diplomat and dilettante, and, by general consent, the best looking of the younger 'Jacobites' around Mrs Wharton. The ill-informed even hazarded some kind of physical relationship between the novelist and 'Beau Norts', whose dark-haired looks one Wharton biographer compared to those of Anthony Eden. Lapsley, who was also in attendance that Christmas, said of Norton that he had cultivated life as a fine art. He had also cultivated speculation as a fine trade, and could afford now to rest, turning his civilized languor to the benefit of his friends.

Much more spectacular was the presence over the New Year of Mrs Wharton's neighbours on the castle rock, the vicomte and vicomtesse de Noailles. There were many things about this couple that drew Steven's interest, but his immediate attention was caught by their dramatic genealogy: 'she descended from the Marquis de Sade, he related to Napoleon'. In the case of Marie-Laure de Noailles, this was scarcely a fraction of the story. She could claim not only Sade, but Petrarch's Laura as antecedents through her grandmother, accordingly named Laure de Sade, who was furthermore supposed to have been an original for Proust's duchesse de Guermantes. Steven already adored Proust, even as he enjoyed history itself as the greatest of all *romans fleuves*.

Marie-Laure de Noailles was not on the face of it naturally sympathetic to Edith Wharton, her friends or the passing age they still managed to inhabit. In their study of *La Côte d'Azur des écrivains*, Christian Arthaud and Eric Paul observed that the short walk from Sainte-Claire to the Noailles' 'Cubist château', Saint-Bernard, in fact spanned the gulf between the nineteenth and twentieth centuries. Madame de Noailles' biographer, Laurence Benaïm, notes an early mutual loathing between the two universally acknowledged 'great ladies', attributable again to a fundamental historical disharmony. The Noailles were never quite forgiven by Mrs Wharton for facilitating a practical joke in which Cocteau had lectured her and Bernard Berenson on the non-existent merits of a patently false 'Picasso collage' formed out of nailed-up newspapers.

By the time Steven encountered this most advanced confluence of the *gratin*, all had been settled on a more amiable footing, partly by means of Robert Norton's considerable diplomatic powers, and partly because whatever cultural, even epochal, disjunctions lay between Mrs Wharton and the Noailles were as nothing beside their shared enthusiasm for their gardens. The vicomte sought out Edith Wharton's advice with special regularity; the common Parisian witticism went that whenever Madame de Noailles was asked whether her husband liked men or women, she replied, 'Oh, il aime les fleurs' (though the wags rarely failed to add that this was the wrong answer, and that Marie-Laure, having caught her husband in bed with at least one domestic, was perfectly apprised of the fact).

Marie-Laure has been described with an evocative lack of gallantry by several of the sexually manoeuvrable younger adventurers who encountered her after the Second World War as a presiding queen of Parisian salons. James Lord depicts her as a warm but untrustworthy power, with something compromised about her, her taste and her milieu, 'the redoubtable viscountess', in her 'undistinguished Cubist extravaganza of reinforced concrete . . . within the ancient walls of a Saracen fortress'. He also testifies to her dizzying influence: 'I told her, certainly, far too much, and I regretted it almost immediately, because my interlocutor was too conspicuously pleased.' Alexis, baron de Rédé, who, like Lord, boasts of Marie-Laure's tendresse for him, provides physical, as well as psychological and social, detail:

> She was not good-looking, with a heavy-set face, jolie-laide . . . She had a poor figure due to a tumour in her stomach, which made her look permanently pregnant, yet she had a certain presence. Some said she looked like Louis XIV.
>
> . . . a fascinating and complicated creature, by degrees confident and controlling, yet equally nervous and insecure . . . unconventional, sometimes badly behaved, not always kind, and a great trial to her friends . . .
>
> . . . much of her group's time was spent indulging in whims and pleasure, a more than muddled love life, and speculating about the love lives of others.

When Steven met her at the end of 1933 she was thirty-one (a year his elder), a decade into her surprisingly satisfactory marriage, and delighted with her new villa, garden and friends, all (with the exception of the unlikely Whartonian alliance) in the best worst contemporary taste procurable. She announced to Steven that she was planning to produce a 'blasphemous film about Christ'. In the years to come he gamely awaited this avatar but it never appeared. Steven's later impression was that Mrs Wharton 'was devoted to Marie-Laure, deploring, if enjoying, her vagaries'; he recalled too that his hostess liked to remind him that the vicomtesse was descended not only from Sade and Laura, but from a renowned wife-murderer, the duc de Praslin, into the bargain.

By now Mrs Wharton expressed an interest in returning her young friend's visits, and calling upon him in Britain, to where she was atavistically as well as culturally drawn. Rumours, of which she was aware and which she did not altogether discourage, ascribed her paternity not to the official candidate, a complacent New York layabout, George Frederic Jones, but to one of two Britons. The wider-spread and more spectacular report was that a cultivated private tutor from England, possibly named James Blake, had impregnated Edith's haughty mother, Lucretia, sought refuge from the scandal in the ranks of General Custer's army and met his end at the Battle of Little Big Horn. The other version, staider but grander, was naturally preferred by Steven as it had a bearing upon his immediate circle – this made Edith's father the eighty-two-year-old Lord Brougham, wintering at Cannes, who was none other than the great-uncle of Steven's friend Baba.

In any case, Mrs Wharton's voyage to England, and indeed to Northumberland, in the autumn of 1934, proved ill timed from Steven's point of view, finding him at a conference in Roumania; all he could do was half-mischievously to recommend her to the society of his family. He had made her acquaintance on the rock at Hyères, and now she accompanied the Runciman family, Walter, Hilda and their unmarried younger daughters, on a trip to the promontory upon Lindisfarne. It was not a very successful occasion. Hilda's ferocious love for her younger son rarely by now restricted his independence, but nonetheless made it unlikely that she would welcome his friendship with an American lady novelist of her own age. Her gloomy expectations were, she felt, fully borne out by Mrs Wharton's high-handed behaviour. The novelist invited herself on an impromptu visit to the startled castellan of Holy Island, the banker Sir Edward de Stein. Hilda recognized in Mrs Wharton an imperiousness to match her own: ' . . . I fancy she is accustomed to taking charge. Do you love her dearly Steven? I found her rather the hard type of American, certainly interesting but we felt all her sympathy and humanity had gone into her novels and she had not much interest in real alive actual beings!' When pressed in old age, Steven would admit that his friendship with Mrs Wharton had foundered when he slighted her 'evil-tempered Pekinese dog'; it is hard not to wonder if a deeper fissure opened when Edith Wharton slighted Steven's evil-tempered mother.

At this exact point, though, it was all light comedy, and Steven was setting about adding an element of exalted farce. He wrote delighted letters, to his sister, his mother, his grandfather and Mrs Wharton alike, 'from the bedroom of a reigning queen', neither novelist nor vicomtesse, but a proper queen consort who had long ago secured his undying obeisance, Marie of Roumania.

# 8

# The Moon

*SS* **Patroclus**, *China, Japan, 1925–6*

> The card represents life of the imagination apart from life of
> the spirit.
>
> Arthur Waite, *The Key to the Tarot*, 1920

The summer of 1925 had, Steven thought, been 'one of the few
periods in my life when my enjoyment of things was clouded over'.
Still uncertain about his prospects, academic or otherwise, he was
subject to a deepening gloom with a visible effect on his health. His
parents still spoke of the Diplomatic Service, but their individualistic
younger son's response was discouraging: 'I had no wish to join the
ranks of a complacent bureaucracy with its own standards of correc-
titude.' Steven's pessimism seemed ominous; the older Runcimans
began to worry if he might not be, like his brother-in-law Roddy
King-Farlow, succumbing to tuberculosis. The remedy proposed by
the family physician, quickly approved by Walter and Hilda, was
extended maritime travel. The Runciman family motto, adopted at
the ennoblement of the elder Walter in 1933, was *By Sea*, and Steven's
parents retained 'faith in the sea's curative powers'. In addition it
seemed that their son, sharp but shy, regarded by his Cambridge
supervisors as brilliant but hardly steady, and in social terms hesitant
and young for his age, might benefit from a period of self-reliance.
Steven was not at all sure that he agreed with any of this, but he was
increasingly certain where he wanted to go, if go he must. 'I realised
it could give me an opportunity that might never recur. I agreed,
therefore, on condition that I might go to China.'

For a supposedly delicate twenty-two-year-old easily startled by strange company, a journey into 1920s China was a courageous choice of sanatorium. In retrospect, there are signs that Steven had harboured an interest in this direction. He would tell Orwell's biographers that his schoolfriend 'had no intention of going to the university . . . He wanted to go to the East'; this may have expressed a corresponding attitude of his own. Arthur Waley, one of Steven's most admired older friends, was the best-known translator from Chinese and Japanese poetry of his day. In several Beaton photographs, Steven is draped in silk against a world of undergraduate chinoiserie. In amateur theatricals he had impersonated, as well as the Queen of Paflagonia, the Emperor of China from *Aladdin*. But the difference between this aestheticized experiment in costume and attitude and the actual China of 1925 – an empire fallen past decadence into anarchy and war, a field that called for adventurers and journalists, not flâneurs – was a gulf almost as wide as the physical ocean Steven now prepared to cross.

For the next month Steven was confined to the less perilous or picturesque environs of the SS *Patroclus*, of the Blue Funnel Line. The vessel's proprietors, the Holt family, were long-time business associates of the Runcimans, and had given Leslie his apprenticeship in the business. Steven was, at least in theory, guaranteed a comfortable journey, but he was scarcely enthusiastic about his fellow passengers. On his first night aboard, 'lonely and apprehensive', he was soaked by a bursting hot-water bottle, 'and felt sure that the journey was doomed'. For all the week out to Gibraltar, the weather was vilely grey, and Steven sulked, 'reading unsociably in my cabin'. A foray to dine at the captain's table as they passed Finisterre provoked his first assessment of his shipmates:

> They are my little cross to bear. They fall into two classes, the vulgar and the dowdy. The men are mostly vulgar, drinking a lot and eternally playing bridge or being rather gallant . . . Of the women, one naturally notices the vulgar most – strident jolly women that nothing can tire; I don't even believe they'll wilt in the Red Sea . . .
>
> . . . my most intimate friend so far is a young bride (one of the vulgars) who loves poetry, and knew I must too from my face; her husband who is a *dear* doesn't really appreciate it, and it is so nice to find someone who does, especially as such *splendid* poetry is being written

nowadays; it sounds *so* silly, but she even writes some herself. And so we get on well together, while the husband (who, I think, has married beneath him) looks on amiably silent.

... My first night I was next a flamboyant lady who was unquench-able – 'I always think what a true saying it is that it's a long lane that has no turning. Don't you agree with me? don't you?' 'England's going to her ruin; we have no strong men; all these politicians, they're so weak. What we need is strong men' and so on, variations of no great variety ...

Steven was not at this point the most appealing or broad-minded of travellers, but he was chafing against his own family shipping back-ground, with its stuffy, unintentionally comic version of travel *en luxe*. He had not yet managed to achieve independence from this world, for though already hundreds of miles from home, he was jour-neying in Runciman fashion by Runciman decree.

Steven's morale rose with the sun as the ship passed into the Medi-terranean. He dodged various deck-games but began to enjoy observing their players. Some passengers, including Mr and Mrs Edwardes, the poetical bride and her 'amiably silent' husband, he now recognized as social equals. Arthur Edwardes was acting head of the Chinese Cus-toms, then a British preserve; his wife Sybil was his cousin, both of them, Steven gathered with delight, being grandchildren of the Mar-quess of Ormonde. This disproved Steven's earlier theory that the husband had 'married beneath him', and that the wife was 'slightly Levantine or Eurasian' – her 'curiously untraceable accent' being merely Anglo-Irish. Steven found Mr Edwardes to be 'a jolly manly man', as amateurishly eager about history as his wife was about art and poetry, and when the *Patroclus* reached Malta at dawn this future Chinese Customs Inspector General treated the historian-to-be of the Crusades to an enthusiastic lecture on the Knights of Malta, the Great Siege and the foundation of Valetta. More welcome was the offer the Edwardeses extended of eventual hospitality in Peking.

At Port Said Steven and the Edwardeses enjoyed another early-morning stroll, in 'the famous emporium of Simon Artz [*sic*], where one was sup-posed to be able to buy anything that one wanted cheaper than anywhere else in the world; but there was nothing I wanted to buy.' They encoun-tered, however, an Indian clairvoyant, his most persuasive and lucrative forecasts being traced out 'in patterns on the sand'. Steven reported most of the results to Hilda:

> I had my fortune told by an Indian said to be excellent. It gave no impressive details about the past, except to assign me 1 brother and 3 sisters, and vaguely to be correct. Next February I shall have a piece of delightful news, and something else extraordinarily nice will happen in 1926, due to a large extent to the ever-present help and inspiration given me by one of my parents (you and Father can fight that out.) I may marry when I'm 28, but not before and perhaps never. Soon I shall burst suddenly famous on a hitherto sceptical world. I shall never be a millionaire but never poor. And so on, good on the whole. He had an air about him.

Steven suppressed only the fact that he had also been warned by the sand-doodling magus against disreputable friends, a prediction he was in later life to associate with his close friendship with Guy Burgess and his slighter relations with the other Cambridge spies. Leaving the disappointing bazaar behind him to seek the generally promising future he had been promised, he was charmed by his first sight and touch of the Red Sea. 'I was always told that it was the same temperature as Hell, but if so I shall not trouble to be good.'

As the *Patroclus* crossed the Indian Ocean, Steven found himself bowing to the vessel's *esprit de corps*; he helped to rig up a Sports Day for the thirty-three children, 'which has improved my social position', painted a Union Jack on to a shield for a version of St George and the Dragon, and, no doubt inspired by his benign experience at the Port Said bazaar, consented during 'the inevitable fancy-dress ball' to tell fortunes, both by palmistry and by the tarot. The Captain was well pleased with the upshot of his hand, but Steven did not care to stick altogether to the reassuring treatment he had lately received himself:

> I was not in a very good fortune telling mood ... but was managing all right, as most of my victims gave themselves away by the sort of questions that they asked, and with one or two I established a sort of telepathic connection. Then a woman came who was one of the few who wanted cards as well. As I laid out her cards I felt suddenly inspired. Without stopping to think what I was saying I told her that she would be a widow soon. Her friends rightly rebuked me for giving

> her a fright . . . to my horror, when we reached Singapore she received
> a message to say that her husband was seriously ill. She left at once to
> go up-country to the station where he worked. Whether he survived or
> not I do not know. It was a salutary lesson for me. Thereafter I kept
> control over what I said.

This would be far from the only instance when Steven felt he had predicted a death. Even as he liked to say that his grandfather (whose death he was to claim he and all his siblings had also intuited) possessed knowledge of 'the curse that kills in a year and a day', there was some connection in his mind, thoroughly disturbing to himself, between the foreknowledge of death and its causation. The unfortunate wife he had warned, and possibly widowed, on this occasion was the 'unquenchable' and 'flamboyant lady' who had so irked him off the coast of Galicia with her demands for the salvation of England by strong men.

As the *Patroclus* passed through Penang, Singapore and Shanghai, the nervous atmosphere of the dying Chinese Empire, at chaotic and inconsistent war with itself, became impossible to ignore. The first allusions to the wider situation's volatility that Steven sent home are jocular, the detached commentary of a cool-headed observer, whose dominant impression of the country is one of incongruity, inefficiency and unreality. Steven's debonair scepticism brings to mind the sort of jittery gallows-humour that, fifteen years later, would greet the looming anti-climax of the Phoney War in Britain: 'It is a remarkable innovation to have a civil war in the depth of winter, and no-one thinks it can last . . . But we live in stirring times; it is even said that some people have been killed in the war lately – a quite unheard of event.' Steven's carefully affected sangfroid evidently masks some awareness about the true magnitude, complexity and danger of the Chinese Civil War, but how much is harder to divine. In speaking of his Chinese journey as 'an opportunity that might never recur', he may have indicated his desire to see an ancient culture and before it was annihilated. He seems rarely to have felt in any personal danger, secure in his position as an intrigued and impartial guest, doubly protected as a British citizen in general and a well-connected Runciman in particular.

Penang's main attraction proved to be its Snake Temple, where Steven much enjoyed the 'mass of brilliant snakes intertwining everywhere, doped with the incense'. He thought Sumatra's misty, wooded coast remarkably similar to Norway's, with which he was familiar by way of his father's yacht. At Singapore, he was entertained for lunch by the Blue Funnel Line agent, who introduced him to a disappointing bishop and 'the vastest and vastest-bearded Dutchman, Mr. Wuntzberg, who claims to smoke 3,600 cigarettes a month', 'a tall voracious man, like God'. Steven left a characteristic description of supper in the colonial tropics, with a hint of uncomfortable self-consciousness:

> the kind agent man took me out to tea and dinner at his house, where he and his wife were very charming to me (though I don't think he thought me quite manly enough).
>
> . . . The evening there was like living on a stage – huge open pillared rooms, across the back of which Chinese servants would pass noiselessly. Great bats flew in and out from the open walls, and on the ceiling strange lizards, the Checha lizard, clucked. The crickets chirped unceasingly, and far off a drum was rhythmically beating, in honour of a Malay wedding feast. Then suddenly a tropical thunderstorm burst overhead . . .

At about this point of the voyage a woman passenger revealed herself to be unexpectedly, even disconcertingly diverting:

> There was a glamorous Dutch lady, aged about forty, with the strange Christian name of Femme, going out to Shanghai to join her husband, for whom she did not seem to have much affection. I found her entertaining but rather fey. She wore a large, rather ugly ring with a cat's-eye stone set in it, which, she said, had been bequeathed to her by a friend who had lived in Java. She told me that ever since she had acquired it she had been suffering from nightmares and nervous crises, and that, shortly before she left Holland, a woman whom she had never seen before had come up to her in a restaurant and begged her to throw the ring away. It was cursed and evil, she said. I persuaded Femme to let me wear the ring for a night. I passed a very unpleasant night, waking at intervals with the sensation that someone was trying to throttle me.

The sensation may well have been self-induced as I believed the ring to be sinister. But when I returned it to her and told her about my experience she said that she had often had exactly the same feeling. Two nights later she was found by a sailor sleep-walking on deck and apparently about to throw herself overboard. Next morning she gave me the ring and I flung it into the sea.

It was not the last occult experience of Steven's voyage, nor the last magic ring of his life. As for fey Femme, after surviving her brush with fatality she would depart, as planned, at Shanghai, which was, Steven noted, 'a twin city to Liverpool – handsome in a commercial way, but devoid of charm'. From the Astor Hotel Steven wrote to comfort Kitty, who was having a miserable time at school in St Andrews but had not persuaded Hilda to remove her: ' . . . I heard that Mummie's visit to St Andrew's [sic] had been without good result on the main issue. I am dreadful sorry and sympathetic; you must be as unmiserable as possible. Be charming with your little friends so that they confide in you; that was how I used to divert myself at Eton when I was bored and depressed.'

At Shanghai Steven stayed for some days with a Mr Shaw, the local director of the mighty import-export firm Butterfield & Swire, who could advise him on the Chinese political outlook, and its implications for his itinerary, in greater detail. Steven had hoped to travel further up the Yangtze, a river he found to possess an unexpectedly nostalgic charm ('ornamented with tree-clumps reminiscent of the Thames at Eton'), with the aim of swiftly reaching the chief object of his travels, Peking, or, as he still considered it, the Xanadu of Marco Polo. But Shaw urged him instead to stick with the *Patroclus* as it entered the Yellow Sea, and to accept Tientsin, for the present, as a safe and practical stepping-stone on the way to the former Imperial capital. Tientsin itself had points both of convenience and interest for Steven – a first cousin of Hilda's, Bill Ker, was British Consul there, while in the Japanese concession the city still sheltered the melancholy figure of the boy-Emperor.

Steven accepted this plan, though it began with another disappointment: the Yellow Sea was 'no more Yellow than the Black Sea is Black'. Its waters were dark and shallow, rippled by a freezing wind and loured over by unremitting cloud. The *Patroclus* could not negotiate its bulk all the way up the ever less substantial River Pei-ho, and its passengers now proceeded in lighter, flat-bottomed launches. Northern China in winter was not the ideal setting for even the most enterprising of invalids, and Steven contracted a cold which became feverish, with a rocketing temperature. 'The journey that afternoon was an unreal experience for me . . . there was gunfire to be heard all around, and a few shots seemed to be directed against our launch.' But the reports quietened as the city neared.

Still scarcely coherent, immediately on landing Steven telephoned his kinsman at the Consulate. The Kers were experienced, kindly and no-nonsense; Bill had married a Canadian, Lucy Murray, who was to become a target of her young cousin-by-marriage's mild satire, but whose formidable exterior had been shaped by courage and suffering. When, in 1900, the foreign legations had been besieged during the Boxer Rebellion, the Kers' two-year-old son had died of scarlet fever. Despite this trial, the Kers had determinedly embedded themselves in their adopted country; according to Steven, 'they bore no resentment against the Chinese in general . . . and even kept a grudging admiration for the monstrous old Empress-Dowager, whom they had met on several occasions.' They were prepared to face any further disasters the Civil War might threaten. This was as well, because, while Steven was undergoing a relapse of the fever, the Christian warlord Feng Yü-hsiang determined that the moment had come to take Tientsin. As Feng's devout army closed about the city, Steven was, to his exasperation, advised to prepare for an indefinite stay.

Though it was frustrating to be held up only a short sea-voyage from his goal of Peking, Steven found many compensations and plenty of gossip in the now besieged Tientsin, which had many of the aspects of an impromptu capital – an air especially apparent at the British Consulate. 'One met most of the British residents in Tientsin at their house, and many Americans too, as the United States was too officially anti-imperialist to have a Quarter of its own.' Steven described the town and the British concession to Kitty:

> The monde of Tientsin, though not chic and gay like the world of Shanghai, is rather intellectual, and very respectable – I am sure that divorcées are not received in Tientsin society – certainly I have met none – whereas Shanghai – not fit for jeunes filles.

... We are the Royal Family here as regards the English Concession; as Consul-General Cousin Bill leads society. And so of course,
when there was a memorial service for our dear late Queen-Mother, I
had to attend looking my blackest (we are very loyal in these distant
parts; and even in Her honour put off the St Andrews Day (Scotch)
ball – though we all ate haggis (ugh!) all day.)

... Food (a subject on which I know you lay a certain stress) is plentiful and good – we ought to be having pheasant daily, but that nasty
civil war is interrupting the supply from Mongolia.

On his first night out of bed, Steven dined with the Kers and Major
Valentine Burkhart, the head of British intelligence in northern
China. Two nights later the Kers introduced him to a figure of lesser
executive power but, to Steven, far greater interest. Reginald John-
ston, a native of Edinburgh and graduate of its University, had, by
way of the Colonial Service, ended up as tutor to the young Emperor
Pu-Yi. Prior to Feng's capture of Peking the previous autumn, he and
Isabel Ingram, the American tutor to Pu-Yi's little-loved Empress
Wanrong, became the first Westerners to infiltrate the inner apart-
ments of the Forbidden City. Steven took to Johnston at once,
considering him 'a shy hesitating-hurried-voiced man, a brilliant
Chinese scholar and with just the right soupçon of snobbery'.

After a week in Tientsin, only three days of it spent out of bed, Steven
impishly described himself to his mother as 'quite learned in Chinese
matters . . . I am acquiring decided views. I think the only solution for
China is to re-establish an Emperor as a constitutional monarch; like all
big Empires they need a figurehead, especially as they have too much
individuality to sink into the useful vice of patriotism.' This optimistic,
Anglicized vision presumably bore some relation to the British policy
imbibed at the Consulate, the heady effects of Johnston's reflected Imperial glory and Steven's own irrepressible monarchical sympathies.
'Living in a consular house is very amusing,' he declared, 'as news
comes through so quickly and confidentially.' Reacting to one such
rumour, of another coup in Peking, and rioters waving red flags, Steven
characterized Chinese Communism as a simple import of Russian Bolshevism, unlikely to take root in its own right, and dangerous mainly in
that it might provoke an exaggeratedly militaristic response from Japan.

Early December found Steven still blithe enough about the harmlessness of the war, despite a fortnight of theoretical subsistence under siege, but his original confidence and excitement were fading. From day to day he hoped in vain for his progress to Xanadu, though matters sounded still more disordered at Peking. 'We live in the midst of civil wars,' he wrote in leisurely and languid spirit to his grandmother,

> ... but you never notice them, except for headlines in the newspapers; they don't affect one's comfort or safety in the very least. In a few days I'm going up to Peking, which sounds the most interesting town in the world. There, there are apt to be occasional riots, but Europeans never come into contact with them unless they want to be reckless. Even the Chinese themselves are fairly untroubled by their civil wars!

To Kitty he more mischievously played up his possible peril:

> There were bright little riots [at Peking] over the weekend – literally bright; they burnt quite a lot of cabinet ministers' houses; and they spat at Europeans in malice; but as they do that anyway from carelessness, it doesn't make much difference. (I have never seen such haphazard spitters as the Chinese – no idea of aiming and making clean shots.) But all the colonels at Tientsin shake their heads warningly and order me to mark their words, Peking is a nest of Bolsheviks; they seem quite relieved (kind gentlemen) when I say that I have made my will ... perhaps you will come into your inheritance before long: all my London furniture ...

But to his mother he was by now complaining that Tientsin was 'hideous to look at', and bemoaning the unreliability of even the Consulate's tittle-tattle: 'rumours come rushing here before anywhere else, and an air of omniscience hangs over the place. Unfortunately facts never live up to the rumours; the impending battles never take place, and the riots are decidedly stingy. However one hopes ... ' Sometimes the stories seemed picturesque enough to be taken on trust: 'Statesmen and generals pay visits in disguise; Chang Tso Lin's son* spent a night this week at our chicest hotel dressed as an American's

---

* Steven alludes here to the 'Old Marshal', Chang Tso-lin (or, in modern Pinyin transliteration, Zhang Zuolin), who in 1925–6 was allied to the Japanese; and his

body-servant, in an attempt to find and pacify his former friend the rebellious general.' Amid the siege's anxiety and boredom, unlikely stories could fructify and persist. One such was to become part of Steven's cumulative legend, gleefully invoked for the rest of the century.

It seems that the chief reason for Reginald Johnston's rapid ascent in Steven's esteem was that he suggested he might easily arrange for Steven to meet his Imperial pupil. The story of this meeting was often related by Steven as the first and most exalted of his many monarchical encounters abroad; he gives a fairly full account of it in his *Alphabet*. There it is not Johnston, but 'his understudy, I think an Australian', who called on the Kers some time in November ('I cannot, alas, give the actual date') and, upon finding there Steven, a young, cultivated Briton of no immediate occupation, asked him without preamble if he could play the piano. Steven had enjoyed musical exercises with Puffin and Margot Asquith in his Summer Fields days, and at Eton had proudly kept his hand in and even dabbled in composition, while at Cambridge he had maintained his dulcitone. He answered modestly that he could play a little. The understudy expressed delighted relief: 'the Emperor had just started to learn the instrument and what he liked most was to play duets. All that he could manage so far was very simple music, like nursery rhymes, with both hands playing the same tune; and he wanted someone to go thump-thump in the base. Would I come and supply the need?'

Two visits to the Imperial Residence in the Japanese concession followed, 'a large villa, full of rather showy occidental furniture, with an upright piano in the drawing-room'. Pu-Yi was Western-inclined in many of his tastes, habits and interests; a decade later, when the Japanese installed him as the puppet-Emperor of Manchukuo, he would insist on becoming the first Chinese Emperor to be acclaimed in military uniform. Steven described himself as impressed by the young Emperor's appearance and bearing, 'a frail etiolated youth, not at all good-looking but with an air of race suitable for the last head of an

---

scapegrace, opium-addicted son and heir, 'the Young Marshal', Chang Hsueh-liang (or Zhang Xueliang).

old dynasty'. The duets 'sadly revealed that he would never be a pianist', but they proved to be a pretext for settling down to more general conversation over jasmine tea. Pu-Yi seemed interested in history – especially as it concerned his own dignity; he questioned Steven carefully in 'adequate English' on court rituals of the past, but never quite got the difference between Byzantine Emperors and Ottoman Sultans straight. On Steven's second visit, he recalls the Emperor growing more confidential about English history and its bearing upon his marriages:

> He called himself Henry because of his admiration for King Henry VIII. His chief wife, of whom he was clearly not fond, he called Mary, after Bloody Mary, but his chief concubine was Elizabeth. I never was privileged to meet the Imperial ladies, so I cannot tell how appropriate the names may have been. But certainly he bore little resemblance to Bluff King Hal.

In fact 'Elizabeth' was Wanrong, the primary Empress; the Western names Henry and Elizabeth, bestowed by Johnston and Miss Ingram, were common knowledge, but the identification of Pu-Yi's less loved wife Wenxiu as 'Bloody Mary' appears to be a fresh refinement of Steven's.

Alas, Steven's surviving family correspondence casts doubt on the whole Imperial interlude. In the *Alphabet* he underplays the extent of his acquaintanceship with Johnston, whom he says he met only in February 1926, months after his interviews with Pu-Yi. But his engagement diaries and letters show he already knew Johnston perfectly well by mid-November 1925. Of the Australian understudy's existence there appears no trace in Steven's letters and diaries or the details of the Imperial Household. While Steven admits in the *Alphabet* that a third appointment was planned, for February with both Johnston and his pupil, and cancelled on account of Pu-Yi's sudden illness, his letters home from that month – his last in Tientsin – state all but outright that this meeting was the only one ever contemplated, and, accordingly, that Steven never met the Emperor Henry Pu-Yi at all: 'I left China with one so bitter disappointment. The tea party was all arranged at which I was to meet the Emperor and Empress, but that very morning the tiresome brat developed influenza.' Musing on the same setback, Steven declared to Leslie that, such was the degree of his annoyance, 'I feel republican!' Combined with the lack of any mention of the Emperor (unlike the frequently referenced Johnston) in Steven's engagement diaries apart from the cancelled tea-party, all this leaves the conscientious reader with the gloomy impression that the entire Pu-Yi story is a distracting flight of Runcimanian hocus-pocus.

False coin or not, the story became part of the heritage Steven continually purveyed throughout his life. In 1994, on learning that a new young acquaintance, Guy Black, had a casual proficiency as a pianist, Steven insisted that they stand up to play a duet. Black was puzzled by this insistence, as no music was at hand, so that any harmonious duet seemed impracticable. But all Steven seemed to want of him was the repetition of four chords as a base; the same service he claims in the *Alphabet* to have provided for young Pu-Yi. After a minute or two, Steven explained to his startled accompanist that he had now played with a man who had played with the last Emperor of China. All his life, Steven delighted in these historical chains, unexpected apostolic successions; he opens his unpublished memoirs with a consideration of some examples:

> Links with the past are ... comfortable to contemplate, and give us some reassurance about the continuity of human history. My Runciman great-grandmother was born in 1812; and I remember being taken to see her when I was two, not long before her death in 1905 ... There was a Cabinet colleague of my father's, Sir Charles Hobhouse, who did not die till 1941, who told me one day that his godfather had been born a British citizen in New England, that is to say, before 1776 ... One evening in June, 1931, I was dining with the novelist E. F. Benson, and was seated next to an elegant and lively old lady, Violet, Lady Greville. In the course of the conversation she boasted to me that she had danced herself with the Prince Consort ... she suggested that we should take the floor together ... after a few rather stately steps, we retired ... I shall always be grateful to her for this link with Albert the Good.

It is a little disillusioning that, in his eagerness to thread such chronological patterns, Steven seems to have been willing not just to exaggerate but to invent. Then again, there was something peculiar to late and post-Imperial China that played to the fantastic in Steven, Harold Acton and other writers before and since. One of Steven and Acton's first intoxicating sips of chinoiserie might have come from their school library's copies of *China under the Empress Dowager* and *Annals and Memoirs of the Court of Peking*, by J. O. P. Bland and Sir Edmund Backhouse. Backhouse was eventually to be exposed by Hugh Trevor-Roper as the most audacious of Sinophile fantasists. The *kind* of fantasy which the Pu-Yi episode most likely forms, a broadly accessible historical joke with a risqué tinge, was to recur throughout Steven's spoken and written repertoire. Finally, it is a curiosity worth noticing that, while placing his factually dubious yet temptingly plausible version of the young Emperor in the foreground, Steven deliberately obscured the extent of his genuine contact with Reginald Johnston.

With or without those Imperial audiences, Steven's time in Tientsin proved eventful. Further dinner guests at the Consulate included an American explorer, Owen Lattimore. Lattimore, like Steven, was edging towards Peking, but after that he had planned a camel caravan across Mongolia and the Gobi Desert. Steven was astonished to be invited, offhand, on to the expedition – 'a tempting idea, but hardly practicable while my health was insecure'. But he accepted the proposal of another visitor, a Japanese dealer in cameos, Ken Isawa, to accompany him back to Japan at the beginning of February. Steven did not particularly care for his guide-to-be, disapproving of his business practices, 'importing antiques from Japan and selling them to tourists as being Chinese'; but Lucy Ker persuaded her young guest that the offer presented 'a wonderful opportunity for seeing Japan from a Japanese angle'. The arrangement left him with another two months of adventure in China; and Steven looked forward to Japan coming next. 'I am to be taken to Nikko and Kyoto by a Japanese artist [thus were laundered Mr Isawa's cameos and curios], to live in Japanese inns, and move in Japanese circles. It is all very clean and hygienic. The Japanese even wash their trees.'

As the siege proceeded, Steven developed an anthropological interest in the Chinese troops, execrably equipped as they were, and often, it seemed to him, largely indifferent to the causes of their generals:

'wars consist of looting rather than fighting, as one doesn't need arms for the former, and arms are such a nuisance to carry about; besides the Japanese always sell you ammunition which proves to be blank.' He still found it hard, from the safety of the Consulate, to believe in the reality of combat and casualties, but he began to feel empathy both for the rank-and-file combatants and for the civilian population on grounds of economic subsistence:

They are fighting on the line now; all night I could hear the guns, poor old guns that made a noise more like a hiccough than the proper thunderous roll of modern warfare . . . life in the foreign concessions goes on quite unconcerned. Nor need the guns make one feel sorry for the Chinese; the guns are fired to show that it is a battle, but the less numerous side has already run away before they begin. It is when the looting begins that one feels sorry for the Chinese; the victors loot because they are the victors, the vanquished because they won't get any other pay.

Even the Consulate now began to feel privations:

I am in a beleaguered city. Think of that, now! The siege of Tientsin has lasted nearly a fortnight (though at a considerable distance); but today the guns are nearer, and they say that the city may fall tonight. Nous verons. Hitherto the siege has affected us very little; but food and coal are growing a little short (at Peking they're very short), and today there's an atmosphere of crisis and anxiety – the wires are all cut, so one can't telegraph to the outside world . . . no boats have come up the river for 24 hours. And if you walk in the Native City (one mass of panic) or in the Chinese ex-foreign Concessions, you are liable to have rifles suddenly pointed at your head. I'm afraid – really very glad – that I won't have to witness a battle. The incorrigible Chinese will go on killing each other and looting each other's goods: while I remain uninterestingly here, living on corned beef, or even pony's meat, and – oh dear! – rice.

One of the foremost lures of China to Steven had undoubtedly been silk, and though he was still hoping to find the best treasures at Peking, he had made a start among the traders of the port; but now he was frustrated to discover that 'the shopkeepers in the native city have cautiously (and very annoyingly) buried their best wares underground':

> I went down into the heart of the native city this afternoon, with a Chinese-speaking Americaine [probably Isabel Ingram], to the Women's Temple and the one really old part of Tientsin; and we went into several native curio-shops, in the hope that [through] fear of being looted (a fate that is almost certain to befall them) they would sell treasures cheap. But alas, by now they have hidden away all their good stuff, out of the looters' reach, and the shops were filled with trash. The smarter shops in the Concessions are more worthwhile, as the rich Chinese sell their things there. The native city was full of panic; you could see whole families leaving their houses, with basketfuls of clothes and bales of bedding – motorcars ostentatiously flying Japanese flags – red cross vehicles (mostly springless carts, poor wounded) ambling out to the Front. But it seems that Li Ching-lin, the governor of Tientsin, is really and sincerely having little victories – he of course controls all the news that comes from the battlefield – ; and so the Christian General may not take Tientsin after all: which is a nuisance, as it means more battles on the railway.

On Christmas Eve, after a day of spirited resistance, the garrison at Tientsin surrendered to Feng's army. Steven watched the Christian forces enter the city, saddened that they marched by, contrary to report, without any hymns or even carols, 'shuffling along in silence in the bitter cold'. Back at the Consulate, he ran into one of Feng's much bemedalled officers, informing the Kers 'solemnly and courteously, that his Commander was now master of the city'. It was the first but not last time that Steven would witness a victorious invasion. 'I am undergoing the experience of being in a fallen city,' he wrote to his father in a more sombre tone than his mother or Kitty usually received:

> . . . one isn't sorry that it's over. The guns had been growing closer and closer; and at last this afternoon, the defeated troops of Li Ching-lin, after a magnificent recovery yesterday, fell back in disorder through the city, forcing poor Chinese civilians to give up their clothes, which they put on, and looting Chinese houses and shops, killing those who

had nothing to provide ... just across the river, in the ex-Russian concession, you could see soldiers scurrying and turning into civilians, while the Kers' poor washerman had his house burnt over his aged parents' head – they are now in refuge in the stables here.

But the fall of Tientsin, however frightening, was not without advantage for Steven. As the Christian warlord now held both Peking and Tientsin, its neighbouring port, Steven could at last continue by train to the ancient capital of the Chinese Empire, the place he anticipated to be 'the most interesting town in the world' – 'I'm glad the war is over; the next one won't break out for either a fortnight or for three months, so a learned Japanese told us. I was growing so bored and tired of gun-fire.'

On 4 January 1926, after another spell in bed with flu, lying still and practising Russian exercises to keep his grammar fresh, Steven at last exchanged Tientsin for Peking, still confident that Communism had little chance of prevailing in China. 'The sensationally minded talk alarmingly of the stealthy approach of Bolshevism; but one avoids them, as they are almost always bores and fools. But one cannot prophesy here.' Steven's account of his train journey on the Blue Express and arrival at Peking exchanges dystopian gloom for disorientating brightness:

At last, at last! Dear angel Peking, divine ducky delicious Peking! I set out from Tientsin at 9 this morning, and travelled slowly in a hot savoury train, over 80 miles of flat – dead flat – brown earth. The train joggled along on its single line past shell-holes first and trenches that wound round the graves – graves are just little mounds of earth; the richer ones are rather bigger, – and then miles of bare treeless flats ...

... at last the Western Hills came in sight, jagged on the horizon, and you began to see the two-humped camels that bring merchandise and coal from the West; and the train starts bumping through wall after wall, into the fields and gardens that live in the heart of Peking ... the most marvellous city that I have ever seen.

It is a wonderful place, full of atmosphere – dusty and very highly scented, immensely overpowering, physically and figuratively. I have shopped in richly filthy shops, and have wandered through the various cities; the impression is chaos – of traffic, noise and colour.

He spent his first night in the capital at the Grand Hôtel de Pékin, 'the wickedest and smartest establishment (on dit) in all the East' – a five-storey red-brick paean to international plutocracy, built in 1915–17, looking on to the superseded glory of the Forbidden City. Among the louche Western tourists the Grand Hôtel had lately entertained were a young Italian diplomat, Galeazzo Ciano, and an increasingly impecunious American divorcee, Wallis Warfield Spencer.* That night, partly because of a persistently ominous fortune-teller, Steven had a dream-premonition of his grandfather's death. It was more than a decade out, which is perhaps worth bearing in mind given that in 1937, and ever afterwards, he would claim accurately to have foreseen the real thing.

Steven would recall his four weeks in Peking in January 1926 as 'among the most enjoyable in my life'. For the Tientsin Consulate he now exchanged a Chinese-style house in the Legation Quarter, where his *Patroclus* shipmates, the Edwardeses, made good their offer of hospitality. Arthur Edwardes had the larger house of the head of Customs at his disposal, but avoided it as it was said to be 'badly, even unpleasantly, haunted'. If Steven had been disappointed in the murkiness of the Yellow Sea, he now received full recompense in the ambered atmosphere of the Peking winter:

> The great walls that surrounded the various rectangular quarters of the city were still all extant, massive and mustard coloured, pierced by occasional gates over which were built pagodas with turquoise and green tiled roofs . . . The weather was icily cold but clear. The sky was almost always cloudless, pale lemon-coloured rather than blue. The earth outside the city was bare and yellow . . . The canals round the city were frozen stiff and provided a splendid means of transport . . . Adept young Chinese took charge of ice-punting and could soon reach enormous speeds . . .

The first visit Steven paid on one of these punts was to the British Legation, under the charge of Sir Ronald and Lady Macleay. Sir

* The future Duchess of Windsor was even more determined than Steven to reach Peking on the then bandit-ridden Blue Express: 'Having come so far, I did not propose to be stopped by a mere Civil War' (Wallis Simpson quoted in Anne Sebba, *That Woman* (Weidenfeld & Nicolson, 2011), p. 52).

Ronald Steven found ineffectual in person, 'a pathetic figure, kind and liked, but abused in China for whatever he does in obedience to His Majesty's Government'. Macleay had attracted particular opprobrium from his American counterpart, John MacMurray, who considered him a backward Tory imperialist, predisposed alike against 'liberal ideas' and 'American rebels'. Steven considered Lady Macleay 'a passée beauty, amusing, spoilt and scandalous'. His first exchange with her set the tone; he made a polite remark about the kindness he had received from the Kers, the Edwardeses and now the Macleays, to which Lady Macleay snapped: 'You need not think that it is due to your beaux yeux. It is just that we like new tea in the teapot.'*

Acidulated though she might be, Lady Macleay was playing host to a cousin by marriage whom Steven found much easier company, Lady Delia Peel, 'eager, well-informed, full of humour and almost too energetic'. A friend of Lady Elizabeth Bowes-Lyon, who had become Duchess of York in 1923, she was able to supply Steven with exalted gossip alongside their rapid progresses around the Imperial City. The first monument to which she escorted him was the Temple of Heaven, built in the fifteenth century by the Yongle Emperor. Steven was stirred into a melancholy excitement by this forlorn temple complex, abandoned by both worshippers and subjects: 'The vast park is almost deserted, and no priests look after the temples; and everything is falling into ruin. You feel cut off from all the world and suspended in time, at the close of a great civilisation ... the size, not of the buildings but of the design of their placing, the colour, and the deadness of it all.' On their next outing Lady Delia accompanied Steven into the Forbidden City, whose beauties, gloriously outré by the staid standards of Doxford, Steven lingered upon with glee in one letter to his father:

> inside the Imperial City is the Forbidden City, the huge imperial palace, in its way more impressive than Versailles – courtyard after courtyard, all beautifully proportioned and in perfect symmetry,

---

* In her *Times* obituary Lady Macleay was praised for her 'wit, intelligence and forthright charm' (*The Times*, 27 August 1960).

fortress-like entrances, and tall ceremonial halls – all roofed with imperial yellow tiles – white marble steps and bridges, and (you will be horrified but really it is successful) pink walls.

On the whole Steven considered the Legation society, Lady Macleay and Lady Delia not excepted, to be exhaustingly fast. 'Social life is very intense out here; and Peking is famed for its gossip and scandals. It is also famed for the dreams one has here – they say that the dryness affects the brain!'

In this respect Steven found a new Chinese acquaintance more sympathetic and helpful, 'a dear old man' whose existence he excises from his engagement diaries while mentioning him, unnamed, in the *Alphabet*. Steven had encountered this elderly silk-merchant on one of his trawls of the Peking stalls, searching for presents which would be priceless at home. He makes it plain in his family correspondence that he was not above buying looted property on these raids, and, indeed, sought out looted articles for reasons of economy and, still more, provenance:

> One object which I know I've got cheap – though it is very difficult to know now how to employ it – is the whole set of trappings of the marriage chair of the bride of the late Emperor Kuang Hsu. The story of how they were sold is scandalous. When the present ex-Emperor [Pu-Yi] was married, he sent them out to be copied. The eunuch in charge said that he couldn't get them copied, but did have it done, and sent the copy back to the ex-Emperor (who is notoriously ignorant about such things), and sold the original to a silk-merchant, who was only too glad to sell it again: as if such a tale came out, the government would use it as a chance of squeezing exorbitant fines.

The silk-merchant implicated in the story of this depredation was Steven's new acquaintance, 'who seemed to have taken a fancy to me'. After Steven had bought the magnificent Imperial chair-trappings, the merchant invited his new Western customer to accompany him to the Lama Temple, and then to the Temple of Confucius.

> The latter was a large high rectangular hall with frescoes round the walls, not, I thought, of very good quality. A rickety wooden staircase led up to an equally rickety wooden gallery from which more frescoes

were to be seen. It all looked so unsafe that when my kind friend asked me if I wanted to climb up to inspect them I said no. He seemed to be inordinately pleased. It was only much later that I learnt that those frescoes on the upper level were all of them pornographic ... My unwillingness to see them proved to him that I was well brought up and clean-minded.

The flirtatious element to this vignette is consistent with other hints about Steven's exploits while in Peking. He felt transformed by his time in the city, 'a strange place, not particularly oriental – it isn't brightly glamorous ... just entirely different to any place that one has seen or imagined', for reasons quite apart from its geography, even its history.

In this new world and new mode, Steven could – as his parents had, in quite a different context, hoped – forget his shyness and become enterprising, explorative, even wild. His position as the guest of a well-connected couple within the Legation Quarter offered independence, safety, propriety and opportunity. Decades later he remarked off-hand, on the evidence of this youthful expedition, that the Chinese were better lovers the further north a traveller proceeded.

The person who most impressed Steven in his knowledge of Chinese culture and politics was neither Chinese nor British, but an Australian, W. H. Donald, writing in 1926 for the *Manchester Guardian*. Unlike most Westerners in Peking, Donald was strictly teetotal; his maxim was that 'He travels fastest who travels dry.' Steven felt that Donald's was fittingly the clearest head in the city; he was 'the man I think most interesting and politically wisest'. Donald seemed to be 'an intimate friend of every Chinese, and yet liked and respected by the most imperialistic British' (such as the Macleays). Bespectacled and balding, he had a severe, headmasterly appearance but a warm smile; his conversation was as easy-going as it was enlightening. Although exceptionally well connected in Chinese political circles, Donald had consciously avoided learning any Chinese languages over a twenty-year career (unlike the supposedly sealed-off high Tory Lady Macleay, who spoke Mandarin well and practised calligraphy daily). He was thus, rumour had it, allowed deeper into Chinese friendships, as China's contending politicians did not fear that he might betray their confidences. His most famous and influential days, as 'Donald of China', still lay ahead of him.*

It was at supper with Donald, on 26 January, that Steven met the Chinese Foreign Minister, Dr C. T. Wang. With V. K. Wellington Koo, Wang had represented Chinese interests at the Treaty of Versailles; alone among the delegates they had refused to sign it, in protest at concessions to Japan. Yale-educated, Wang spoke fluent American English and carried himself with urbane slipperiness. In the early 1920s he had briefly served as premier of China; now, as Foreign Minister, he was considered 'so indispensable that, no matter who might be ruling in Peking, he never lost his post'. Steven, who enjoyed putting foreign politics in perspective by comparison to the Liberal ministries and oppositions in which his parents had struggled, dubbed Wang 'the Lloyd George of China, a bland opportunist, brilliantly dishonest ... officially very anti English, but genial. Mrs Wang was homely and comfortable (like Dame Margaret [Lloyd George]) and spoke little English.' The next night Steven met a second, concurrent Mrs Wang (presumably the Chinese answer to Frances Stevenson), 'an elegant and lively lady, very ready to talk about the Chinese way of life' – 'As his first wife disliked parties it was she who accompanied him everywhere. There was nothing derogatory in being a second wife, she said. It was, she thought, like marrying a younger son in England. You were not the chief lady in the family, but you enjoyed a perfectly respectable position.' The second Mrs Wang went on to instruct Steven in 'the finer points of Mah Jongg; such expertise as I acquired was unfortunately wasted, as once I had left Peking I never played it again.'

On Steven's last weekend in Peking, Donald insisted that he must see such of the Chinese countryside as remained untouched by the war. Steven had hoped to take the chance to reach the Great Wall, but did not receive the necessary permit; 'the Wall was in bandit country,

---

* Donald's feats would include weaning the Young Marshal, Zhang Xueliang, off opium, organizing the release of the kidnapped leader of the nationalist Kuomintang, Chiang Kai-shek, and surviving for three years in a Japanese prison camp while concealing his true identity.

and the government did not want the embarrassment of having visitors robbed or held for ransom.' Donald's expedition, west into mountainous terrain, promised to make up for this exclusion. 'Suddenly the foothills appeared and behind them higher mountains, with the fantastic shape that one sees in Chinese paintings. This was where in older days the Emperors had gone to hunt deer and to shoot game-birds.' Donald had the lease of a former Imperial pavilion, 'the Ladder to the Cloud Mountains, built by the Emperor K'ang-si, c. 1690, and beloved of the Empress Dowager . . . I found it primitive but comfortable.' Better still, Donald drove Steven and his other companions, an Irish peer, Lord Gosford, and his countess, to a promontory 'from which one could see in the clear winter air, some twenty miles away, a long section of the Wall, climbing up and down the mountainsides'.

'I might have liked Japan better', Steven speculated in the *Alphabet*, 'had I not come there straight from China . . . After such monumental splendour even the prettiest things in Japan seemed . . . so twee.' If Peking had been 'just entirely different to any place that one has seen or imagined', Japan immediately seemed the reverse; 'one had seen it all before in numerous books and pictures.' What was ancient in Japan left Steven cold after China (he is distinctly tart about the 'erroneous belief' that Japanese civilization is older than Chinese), while what was modern struck him as ignoble imitation; 'they were determined to show us their skill in adopting Western technologies . . . their successes were remarkable, but that did not make them more attractive.'

From Kobe Steven and Ken Isawa, 'my bear-leader', took the train to the greater city of Kyoto, where they were lodged at a small hotel whose proprietress was one of the curio-dealer's old friends. Steven accorded Ken Isawa the unlikely accolade of being 'just like a Cook's guide', while his new hostess was, he suspected, 'an ex-Geisha girl' (physically she reminded him vaguely of one of his Stevenson girl-cousins). Worse was to come:

> In the evening Geisha girls came to play and sing to us (not very well)
> while we had another meal – this I found considerably unattractive;
> they have a passion for raw fish; and the amount of rice they eat! . . .

We changed into a series of kimonos on top of each other; mine were provided by the chatelaine, which seemed a quite usual habit. Going to bed I was highly embarrassed . . . as the chatelaine turned down the sheet and waited; but I was relieved to find that I was supposed only to take off my top kimono, and to sleep in the rest. My other great embarrassment is the way that when one goes to the WC females rush to open the door and bow you in, and then they stand watch outside – really a useful precaution, as there are no locks in Japanese houses.

While Steven resisted the attractions of the hostess and her handmaids in the evenings, vainly encouraging them to leave his side with repeated sayonaras, he became aware that Ken Isawa was fleecing him by day, marking up the bills for travel and fare whenever Steven asked his advice. In the company of his 'bear-leader' Steven witnessed the ceremony marking the 2,586th anniversary of the Japanese Empire, amid the Buddhist temples of Nara; he thought this 'a wonderful place . . . It has the feeling of being very old, and deer wander fearlessly through the streets and parks.' The eating-houses were all filled with pilgrims, so to Steven's relief he and his guide resorted to a Western hotel, and he was liberated at least for an evening from sushi.

'I am enjoying Japan immensely,' Steven assured his mother, quickly adding an important qualification – 'not the Japanese very much; they are like the French, individually charming, but as a nation officious and touchy – but they love tourists (rare nowadays) and so I am popular.' He was worn down by the lack of English-speakers and the food he found so unspeakable, though he had happily taken to wearing a kimono before luncheon. During a brief period off Ken Isawa's leash, he found two more likeable Japanese acquaintances. One, indeed, was a business rival of his 'bear-leader':

> the leading *antiquaire* here (and in all Japan, so I have several times been told), a clever faced little gentleman called Mr Shiba – I call him the Queen, so as to remember his name . . .
>
> . . . He insisted on paying for everything himself . . . and hinted very delicately that he did not think highly of [Ken Isawa], and hoped that I was not being exploited.

After a taciturn week getting by on his very limited Japanese, Steven was charmed by Mr Shiba's 'old-fashioned English . . . derived from his reading of Shakespeare, from whose works he made frequent apt quotations'. The other Japanese remembered with affection was the 'personable young son' of another hotelier, who, with greater success than the Geisha girls, 'determined to see that I enjoyed myself . . . He insisted on accompanying me to the public bath . . . to make sure that I learnt the proper technique.'

Watching Noh theatre at Tokyo, Steven took a dislike equally to the form and the city. Conversely at Osaka, when taken to see the more popular Ningyo Joruri – puppet theatre – something within him concentrated, and responded:

> Being a foreigner, I was given a chair, high and out of place. The stalls and circle, in the old Japanese style, were divided into pens, where the audience crouched singly, drinking the pale tea provided or buying long drawn out dinners.
>
> . . . We came in for the last act of an obscure tragedy: when a Samurai, whose daughter is the wife of a rebel, commits hari-kari to atone for the lies that they told, to save her life and her husband's . . .
>
> . . . Here again, to an uncomprehending alien, it was the minor details that made the strongest impression – the little procession of countrymen across the stage, and how one of them shook the snow from his umbrella – the way that the son gazing drearily from the windows thrummed his hands on the sill. And I think it was right to notice the details, the commonplaces, the homeliness; for these were the features with which the great Popular drama of Japan made its appeal, the features that have kept it alive and dynamic: while the rigid aristocratic No-drama stayed as magnificently static as the feudalism that was its patron.
>
> . . . the audience clapped and settled down again to their dinners, until the next drama should begin. But we had to leave, to go out past the dark Shinto shrine and the old right-angled streets and the huge foreign-style offices, to catch the evening train to Kyoto.

It is perhaps unexpected that Steven rebelled against Japanese feudalism in its theatrical incarnation, finding Noh to be 'the slow progress of an uninteresting story'. He had greatly enjoyed the first two volumes that had emerged by 1925 of Arthur Waley's translated *Tale of Genji*, Japan's supreme chivalric romance, which he considered 'one of the greatest novels in the world's history'. He was also won over readily enough by the mountain city of Nikko, which he associated with the world of *Genji*'s original author, Lady Murasaki: 'It seemed to be on a larger scale than the other old Japanese cities, with an unself-conscious serenity.' Unselfconsciousness: this was the quality Steven sought and missed, in Japan as in himself.

# 9
# The World

*Bulgaria, 1928–34; Roumania, 1934*

> it is perhaps more especially a story of the past, referring to
> that day when all was declared to be good, when the morning
> stars sang together and all the Sons of God shouted for joy.
>
> Arthur Waite, *The Key to the Tarot*, 1920

> It seemed a happy world, but a world that has vanished
> forever.
>
> Steven Runciman, 'Roumania',
> *A Traveller's Alphabet*, 1991

During his last term as an undergraduate in the summer of 1924, Steven
had taken a weekend trip to London and glimpsed the Queen of Roumania at Wembley. 'She has painted lips, painted eyes and dyed hair, but
is rather beautiful,' he coolly informed Ruth. In the *Alphabet*, for all this
sangfroid, Steven declares that 'I had fallen a distant victim to her glamour many years previously, while I was still a schoolboy.' In 1997 he
reviewed a biography of Marthe Bibesco, and attested that this Roumanian princess – a far closer acquaintance of his – 'was not as classically
beautiful as her friend Queen Marie'. Towards Queen Marie he displayed
the gallant, stylized devotion he was to offer several female royals –
Queen Mary, Princess Marina and eventually the Queen Mother.

Queen Marie was born into the British royal family, eldest daughter
of Queen Victoria's second son, Prince Alfred, Duke of Edinburgh,
who called her 'Missy'. She had been courted by the future King George
V, but, though not averse, was forbidden to respond in kind, and in
1893 at the age of eighteen was married instead to Ferdinand, nephew

and adopted Crown Prince to Carol I of Roumania. Ferdinand was being extricated from an attachment to a Roumanian lady-in-waiting, Elena Văcărescu, who was thought to be insufficiently royal and worryingly intelligent. Although the marriage was unhappy, Marie managed to convince her husband to support the Allied powers in the First World War. When she represented Roumania at the Paris Peace Conference, Steven thought: 'She acted her role like a first-class Hollywood star . . . It was due to her . . . that Roumania emerged from the peace-making at Versailles with her territory doubled in size.'

But it was Marthe Bibesco, Marie's friend and subject, whom Steven first came to know, when, in March 1934, he called in to see the Baroness d'Erlanger at 139 Piccadilly, once the town-house of Lord Byron:

> I was shown straight up to the Baroness's bathroom . . . in which she was painting the portrait of a glamorous lady, introduced to me as Princess Bibesco. I was delighted to meet her. In 1919, as a schoolboy, I had attended the wedding of Elizabeth Asquith to Prince Antoine Bibesco and had noticed this splendid lady who seemed to be the bridegroom's leading female relative . . .

Elizabeth Asquith, the daughter of the Prime Minister by Margot and the elder sister of Steven's friend Puffin, had married the cousin of Marthe's husband, Prince George Bibesco. The Bibesco were a superseded Roumanian royal house, having produced the last Hospodar of Wallachia; while Marthe, born to the Roumanian branch of the Mavrogordato family, claimed descent from Othello. Neither Marthe nor Elizabeth Bibesco was destined for a happy marriage; no Bibesco prince was capable of fidelity. Elizabeth Bibesco, pinioned between the world wars, fell victim, like her father, to the bottle, and, heartbroken at separation from her native country and her only daughter, died in 1945.* Marthe, Steven indicated after her death, having endured marital assault before the birth of *her* only daughter, later fell in love with (among an extraordinary variety of other

---

* Rebecca West was to give it as her opinion that Elizabeth Bibesco turned to drink because she was intuitive and well informed enough to foresee something of the fate of Eastern Europe.

distinguished men)* a third Bibesco, Antoine's brother Emmanuel, the friend of Proust: 'but he was homosexual and gently repulsed her.'

Marthe had been thirty-three when Steven first glimpsed her at Elizabeth Asquith's wedding; she was now forty-eight. He described her personal appearance with detached appreciation: 'She had huge green eyes, a perfect complexion, neat features and splendid gold-brown hair; and when dressed in the flowing garments that suited her she must have been a glamorous vision, well suited to the brush of Boldini.' Steven's interest in the Princess was, however, chiefly cultural. He had arranged to go as the Cambridge representative to the fourth International Byzantine Congress, to be held at Sofia that September; as he already knew Bulgaria well, he was also planning to visit Roumania, which had an increasingly important place in his conception of the Byzantine heritage.

A month after they had met in Piccadilly he wrote to Princess Bibesco, ' . . . I know that to see Roumania with your help would be to see it far more significantly . . . I am a very promising convert to a *culte* for Roumanian church architecture . . . I cherish a list that you gave me of all the churches that I ought to see.' The eagerness in his tone was not merely climbing fervour. He had enjoyed *Izvor*, the Princess's book on Roumanian folklore and scenery, and he hoped to make as much use of Marthe's knowledge as of her introductions. For Steven the best people always included Clio, the Muse of History. He did not bother to conceal from Princess Bibesco his innocent delight when she told him that, though she could not herself be present for his Roumanian visit, he should have the company of her husband's nephew, Prince George Cantacuzene, bearer, Steven thought, of 'the most romantic of all the surnames that survive'. Before leaving for the Congress and Roumania, Steven wrote to Marthe to tease her about the mission that had kept her from chaperoning him: 'I hope that you have an enjoyable visit to America. I

---

* Her name was connected to the Crown Prince of Prussia (Kaiser Wilhelm II's heir); the French prince Charles-Louis de Beauvau-Craon; her confessor, the Abbé Mugnier; Alfonso XIII of Spain; Henry de Jouvenel (the ill-fated husband of Colette); the Labour Secretary for Air, Lord Thomson, and his superior, Ramsay MacDonald; the Duke of Devonshire; and, oddest of all, the regally homosexual Sir Philip Sassoon.

must confess that I feel I am luckier in visiting Roumania.' Marthe was visiting the recently elected President of the United States, Franklin D. Roosevelt.

The presence of the International Byzantine Congress at Sofia was a happy circumstance for Steven, who by 1934 was probably better connected within Bulgaria than within any other foreign country. His first visit, in the spring of 1928, had sufficed to gain him entrée both into the academic establishment and into the diplomatic and political elite, especially as represented by one particular Bulgarian family. The Stancioffs were educated, cosmopolitan, influential, Catholic and abidingly Anglophile. Like the Bibesco, they entered circles familiar to the Runcimans through an Anglo-Balkan marriage: that in 1924 of Nadejda Stancioff, who would become Bulgaria's first female diplomat, to Sir Kay Muir, a Stirling tea and jute millionaire. Steven obtained an introduction to 'the Bulgar Lady Muir' from Charlotte Bonham Carter, and would afterwards refer to Charlotte and Marthe Bibesco as his 'lovely pair of Balkan godmothers'. In 1925 Nadejda's brother Ivan Stancioff married an American heiress, Marion Mitchell; and in 1928 Ivan and Marion accommodated Steven during his first substantial stop at Sofia, in the company of Ruth. Marion Stancioff distinguished herself when Ruth's handbag went missing, rustling up the town-crier of Radomir to orchestrate its retrieval.

The Bulgarian monarchy, like the Roumanian one, was an artificial German import without any historical connection to the land and people who had invited its rule. But while the Bibesco, with their old claim on Wallachia, were implicit rivals to the Hohenzollern Roumanian kings, the Stancioffs had thrived by offering their talents to the Coburg Bulgarian tsars. They were professionals, not princes, of a class in some ways closer to the Runcimans. When Bulgaria was still an Ottoman province the Stancioffs were Stamboulu, indicating a Constantinopolitan origin. A banker uncle in Vienna put a particularly conscientious young offshoot, Dmitri, through its University. Prince Ferdinand of Saxe-Coburg-Gotha, with his formidable mother Princess Clementine of Orléans, passed through Vienna in 1887 on his way to take over Bulgaria, a project which was near-universally derided, as Ferdinand was widely considered, to quote Queen Victoria, 'totally unfit . . . delicate, eccentric and effeminate'. But 'Foxy' Ferdinand had an eye for useful, as well as handsome, young men. He recruited Dmitri as a confidential *homme d'affaires*; Dmitri married the Savoyard countess who served as Princess Clementine's lady-in-waiting and converted to Catholicism; and from then on, as diplomats, confidants, playmates and courtiers, the Stancioffs flourished like the spreading vine.

It was through the good offices of the Stancioffs that Steven was able, upon his next visit to Sofia in April 1930, to be presented to Tsar Boris III, the childhood companion of Ivan and his siblings. Steven's trepidation about this occasion belies the impression he tended to give in his later decades that he had been intimately acquainted with all manner of royalties since the cradle.* He was full of gratitude and admiration for his host: 'I liked Ivan enormously – he's very good company, entertaining, cynical and full of information. He's also extraordinarily sympathique – for instance he saw that I was in a dither before going to see the King, though I tried to hide it, and he dealt with me very well.' As for the young Tsar Boris himself, during this first exchange Steven was blushingly won over:

> I thought that he was really rather a charming man – not just quite pleasant, but he literally did put me at my ease! He asked me a lot of questions about what I'd seen in Greece and was going to see here and generally talked about Bulgar history – he knew quite a lot – ; he said his sister had been very much impressed by my *Romanus Lecapenus*. It was altogether very easy. He is serious and obviously good, but I was able to raise quite a lot of smiles. At the end I asked if I might dedicate my Bulgar book to him. He blushed and said he would be most honoured 'si cela vous fait plaisir'. He was most cordial when I left and hoped to see me soon again in Bulgaria. His secretary told Ivan that HM had found me most refreshing after the people to whom he usually gave audiences and that I had a 'charming and interesting personality'. So there!

* Steven's degree of apprehension about an audience with the relatively minor Balkan monarch Boris in 1930 is another flaw in the story of his encounter with the Emperor of China in 1925.

Steven inscribed another copy of *The First Bulgarian Empire* to Ivan and Marion Stancioff, the seal on a lasting friendship with them and their children; but the crownstruck dedication he had offered to Boris III would not, in the long run, prove so auspicious. In the meantime, he was soon inured enough to the majesty that hedged Boris to start gossiping about the Bulgarian dynasty. Boris's father Ferdinand had abdicated in his son's favour because of his opportunistic, short-sighted support for the Central powers in the First World War, and was still happily living out his days between ornithological and botanical pursuits in his native Coburg, and more frankly hedonistic spells on Capri. But Foxy Ferdinand had a reputation as a *coureur des femmes* in addition to his widely noised penchant for blond, blue-eyed, Teutonic youths, and Steven began to speculate with relish on which of the Stancioff siblings the ex-Tsar might have fathered. 'I don't think Lady Muir can be King Ferdinand's daughter – she looks very like Ivan and not at all like HM. But Feo, the unmarried sister, is different – she is fairer and more aquiline, so perhaps it is her!'

Two other episodes enlivened Steven's second Bulgarian sojourn, a slight diplomatic incident and a minor act of cultural larceny. One night Steven supped at the British Legation. He described the British Minister, Sir Sydney Waterlow, as 'an apoplectic looking bon viveur with intellectual tastes and fine moustaches'. It happened that Waterlow was that evening trying to mediate between the Bulgarians and the Greeks, as the Greeks had accused the Bulgarians of opening their diplomatic bag. Lady Waterlow took a direct approach, turning to the Greek Minister and shouting at him, 'Tell me, is it your people who have been prying into Bulgarian secrets, or the other way round?' As Steven recalls, 'There was a pause; then, fortunately, someone burst into laughter, in which even the protagonists joined, but not the British Minister, who looked as though he could have killed his wife.'

Later Steven explored archaeological remnants at Preslav, where the local schoolmaster was so struck by his youthful appearance that he offered him any object that took his fancy in the small museum there. Steven confined himself to abstracting a small, plain fragment of painted ceramic, 'which I thought it could well spare'. At the larger Sofia museum, Steven had a fateful encounter with 'a Bulgarian savant, a charming man called Filov who is an authority on old Bulgar art'. Europe would hear again from the charming Professor Bogdan Filov before too long.

In the summer of 1933, Steven had confirmed his intimacy with both the Stancioffs and their royal patrons when he joined Ivan and Marion at their house between Varna and the royal summer palace at Evskinograd.* Their son, Johnny Stancioff, explains that this house above all was responsible for the continuing social ease between the younger Stancioffs and the Coburg princes and princesses: 'when the royal children grew, they'd flip over to my grandfather's house, while my father and his three sisters played tennis at the royal tennis court. Feo and Ivan were sort of the same age as Boris and Cyril, and the King's sisters as Eudocia and Nadejna.'

Tsar Boris's younger brother Cyril already had a reputation as a libertine almost equal to their father Ferdinand's, and at Evskinograd his was the only bedroom to lead into the garden, facilitating his adventures. Steven faithfully, and gleefully, reported to his mother all that he saw of the palace and its surroundings:

> I saw all the royal gardens, a vast affair, run by only 7 gardeners (the Bulgars are an industrious race) ... The Palace at Evskinograd is in the best Coburg style (which is rather like the Rothschild style in England), grandiose but a trifle mixed. The furnishings were done by Maple's in 1890 – round seats with palm trees growing from their midst, tassels everywhere, built in divans at the corners of the rooms with an over mantle [sic] effect of mirrors and shelves supporting insignificant knick-knacks, enlarged photographs posed on wicker easels, a cheap mahogany hat-rack and umbrella-stand in the hall. From the brass and wood chandelier in the inner hall hangs a stuffed pelican (that touch made me think of the gun room at Eigg). The Royal Family adore it. If a piece of stamped velvet is worn or yellow silk fades, all Europe is scoured to match it exactly. A homely scene was being enacted before the front door; the dirty Royal linen was being sorted on the ground. Sheets and pillow-cases lay all around. The Royal bathing beach was unpretentious but pleasant.

---

* Slavicized Euxinograd – that is, city on the Black Sea.

A train-ride away from this domestic scene so reminiscent of the opening of Penelope Fitzgerald's *The Blue Flower* lay an ancient and abandoned Bulgar capital, Trnovo, in which Steven was much interested. At the suggestion of no less eminent a pair than the Prime Minister, the 'tall, upright, gentlemanly' Nicholas Moushanoff, and the mysteriously giggly Tsar Boris, Steven agreed to accept accommodation there at the Arbanassi monastery, despite the protests of the Prime Minister's wife. On arrival Steven discovered that not only was the place wretchedly uncomfortable, with a stream running through it that sufficed for all hygienic demands, but it was regarded as a 'lady's monastery' of a certain sort. The Abbess, 'still a handsome lady who spoke excellent French', had certainly, Steven gathered, enjoyed the Prime Minister's patronage and was on at least friendly terms with the Tsar as well. Looks could be most deceptive in the Land of the Roses.

On his 1934 visit Steven barely paused at Sofia before revisiting his friends at Varna, enjoying the last of their summer idyll. The Stancioffs took him to pay his respects to a neighbouring landowner, General Savoff, one of the architects of Foxy Ferdinand's ephemeral successes in the Balkan Wars, and together they wandered through his 'acres of grapes, all exquisite'. The Tsar and Prince Cyril were occasionally of the company. But on returning to the capital for the Congress, Steven received a disagreeable surprise. He was not, as he had thought, the sole and official representative of Cambridge and Britain; his much slighted Cambridge contemporary, Roger Hinks had supplanted him:

> I have only one English colleague, a youngish man from the British Museum, of whom I'm not passionately fond; so it was slightly to my chagrin that I discovered that the Foreign Office has appointed him official representative of England, the more so as he's not really a Byzantinologue. But in revenge I receive far more attention, being better known amongst these gentlemen, so I can't complain.

In fact they were both granted similar perquisites, and were presented with autographed photographs of Boris III after the British Legation tiresomely blocked a generous Bulgarian suggestion that

Steven and Hinks be both gazetted Knights of SS Cyril and Methodius. The first evening was spent, to Steven's weary dudgeon, in splendid gourmandizing:

> a banquet that lasted 2½ hours, with a speech in Latin from our Bulgar president [the mayor of Sofia] (who clearly doesn't know Latin) . . .
> It was a fatiguing occasion, but I was highly entertained – I was sitting next a Greek professor, a malicious little man whom I knew before, who knows everyone in the Balkan learned world and all their innumerable feuds and idiosyncrasies.*

Steven's mock-modest protestations about his lionization barely hid his satisfaction and amusement:

> My week in Sofia, though utterly exhausting, was wildly enjoyable. I'm very glad I went – not that my Byzantine knowledge has been increased, but it has been very useful and interesting meeting all the Byzantinologues, and all so terribly funny . . . I *did* find it pleasant being in circles where everyone knew me by name.
>     Then the parties were such fun. The banquets . . . were almost too much; one was always still eating at midnight . . .

This mild vice of gratified vanity was one to which Steven would become increasingly accustomed. The 'Byzantinologues' whose acquaintance he made with such efficiency would have continued importance in Steven's life and career. Those who survived the coming war would many of them end up transplanted to British or American universities; others would vanish under Communism. Franz Dölger, Professor of Byzantine Diplomatics at Munich (not, that is, diplomacy, but the critical analysis of historical documents), maintained his tenure, despite a post-war brush with dismissal, until 1963; Francis Dvornik, on the other hand, a Czech priest and expert on the Patriarch Photius, would emerge at the richly endowed Byzantinist institution of Dumbarton Oaks, outside Washington DC; Gheorghe Brătianu, son of the National Liberal Roumanian Prime Minister, would succumb mysteriously to his country's post-war secret police, the Securitate. Steven's chief friend in the

---

* This was Professor Michael Lascaris, from Thessalonica, an expert in the Frankish occupation of Greece, who was ill disposed to his Bulgar colleagues.

Bulgar academy, Vasil Zlatarski, the begetter of the whole Congress, did not long outlast it.

Brought closer by their mutual disappointment in Bulgarian knighthoods, Steven and Hinks were by now largely reconciled to each other's company. They enjoyed paying a joint call on the Metropolitan of Sofia: 'His Eminence spent most of the time mimicking Americans talking English (a language of which he does not know a word) and the rest in uttering pious sentiments about the union of the Orthodox and Anglican churches.' They both regretted the absence from the Congress of the greatest historical authority in the region, with the possible exception of Zlatarski – Professor Nicolae Iorga, the doyen of the Roumanian academy, sometime tutor to King Carol II, who had boycotted the Sofia affair over a territorial controversy with the Bulgarian nationalist historians. This concerned the province of southern Dobrudja, awarded to Roumania after the First World War in recognition of the country's loyalty to the Allies, but, as Steven quietly agreed, historically and ethnically Bulgarian. Though he sided with his friend Zlatarski on this question, Steven made up his mind to pay his respects to Professor Iorga during his Roumanian visit.

Thomas Whittemore, the American representative to the Congress, was better known than Steven or Hinks. Steven would later write of him:

> He was a man whom professional archaeologists and scholars dismissed as a pretentious amateur; and, indeed, he had a gift for making himself appear to be a charlatan ... His persuasive powers enabled him to raise money from rich American ladies, whom he handled with superb artifice ... I first met him in Istanbul in 1928, and always enjoyed his rather eccentric company.

This is, granted, a double-edged sort of tribute, but it is truly mixed rather than essentially catty.* Whittemore's career had been moulded

---

* After enduring perhaps too long a spell of Whittemore's self-aggrandizing company in post-war Athens, Steven later wrote to Hilda of 'that old American fraud, the mosaic-cleaner of St Sophia, who impresses them all enormously here, to my mingled amusement and irritation' (SR to HR, 24 March 1946, Elshieshields).

under the influence of Matthew Prichard, another somewhat suspect enthusiast for the Byzantine aesthetic, equally foreign to conventional scholarship. A friend of Matisse, Prichard was the aesthetic and spiritual guru to David Tennant's Gargoyle Club, described by Hilary Spurling as an 'eccentric English dream of Bohemian Montparnasse'.* Whittemore's great achievement was at Istanbul, where he indubitably rescued Hagia Sofia from the complications of its history. According to Patrick Kinross, the story Whittemore liked to tell involved a single conversation with Kemal Atatürk, after which the Turkish Founder-President had caused a sign to be hung on the doors into the then mosque: 'This museum is closed for repairs.' In fact the process was more gradually – and skilfully – accomplished; Whittemore first persuaded Atatürk to let him uncover the Byzantine frescoes which had been hidden by the Italian restorers working for the Ottomans in the late nineteenth century.

One evening in the Bulgaria Hotel – a resort rather different in atmosphere from the Gargoyle Club – Steven and Hinks joined Whittemore and a British Legation attaché, Jock Balfour, later to be described by Isaiah Berlin as 'very wholly mad', given to taciturn impersonations of William the Silent. What Steven called 'the most memorable moment of the Congress' then occurred, as 'a young man looking like a grubby Lord Byron' propelled his way into their circle and, upon finding out which one was Whittemore, handed him a letter of introduction. The grubby boy's name was Patrick – Paddy – Leigh Fermor; he was in the tenth month of a walk across Europe, from the Hook of Holland to (as he unhesitatingly thought of it) Constantinople; he was nineteen years old. In Steven's eyes, indeed, Leigh

* Prichard's other favourite disciples were Georges Duthuit, the Byzantine art historian, son-in-law of Matisse and lover of Georgia Sitwell, and the learned but irascible John Pope-Hennessy. The fashionable David Tennant's attraction to Byzantine art was one of several signals that interest in Byzantium was emerging in the 1920s (comfortably before any of Steven's widely circulated work, contrary to the credit he would now and then claim); another was the success of the Russian artist Boris Anrep, who was taken up by Ethel Sands and Bloomsbury after the war and whose mosaics for Mrs Jowitt, the wife of a lawyer and MP, Steven thought 'very beautiful' (SR to KR, 9 October 1924, Elshieshields). These showed Lesley Jowitt telephoning from her bath and from bed, and dancing at the Gargoyle Club. Anrep had based his designs loosely upon the mosaics of Ravenna.

Fermor would never become any older, and in 2000 he would dispatch a birthday letter wryly declaring as much: 'anyone gifted with
eternal youth has no need of birthdays – but when I reflect that some
65, or more, years have passed since first you burst into my life at
Sofia, I realise your rare ability to defy time, whose winged chariot
seems to have lost its way in pursuing you . . . '

Leigh Fermor's louche good looks might have brought to mind one
of Steven's favourite and least reputable pupils, Guy Burgess, if in a
less spoilt and generally better-wearing model. For his part Leigh
Fermor was already forming lasting mental images of his new and
distinguished Byzantinologue acquaintances. Whittemore struck him
as 'the dead spit of Holbein's Erasmus', his conversation 'erudite and
shrewish'. Steven and Hinks he placed in the same category:

> both of them impeccable in panama hats and white suits of the won-
> derful Athenian raw silk . . . their bi-coloured shoes were spotlessly
> blancoed and polished; and they both belonged far more aptly to the
> deck of an Edith Wharton yacht or to the cypress alley of a palazzo in
> a novel by Henry James than to this hot little Balkan capital. As I had
> just been scrambling about the Rhodope mountains and sleeping
> out on the way to Rila monastery, I must have been even filthier than
> usual.

Leigh Fermor found Hinks, for all his opinionated plastering and
slightly over-emphatic urbanity, warm and amusing, but was made
nervous by Steven at this first meeting. In *The Broken Road*, the
posthumously worked-up third volume of his transcontinental travel
diaries, he calls Hinks 'kind, under his provisos and reservations and
diverting regional prejudices', while Steven, less obviously extrovert
than Hinks or Leigh Fermor himself, he simply but accurately notes
was 'pleasantly feline'.

When the Congress's allotted week had passed, Roger Hinks departed
to stay at a Tuscan villa, as he told Leigh Fermor, 'with one of those
beautiful Italian gardens. You know, solid mud all winter and in
summer, nothing but dust.' Leigh Fermor's Bulgarian adventure continued into the deeper rural obscurity of Bulgar Macedonia, where he
soon fell in with a party of gypsies and a 'pretty, fair-haired,

frowning girl called Nadejda, studying French literature at the University of Sofia: a nimble *hora* dancer endowed with unquenchable high spirits'. And Steven could at last access the long-anticipated delights of Roumania.

In Sofia, which Steven called 'a market town with a few of the trappings of a capital added', Ivan Stancioff might complain with justice of a shortage in cultivated conversation. Despite such gatherings as the recent Congress, the local intelligentsia was restricted. Neither the scarce native aristocracy nor the court possessed grandeur, riches or much in the way of bohemian glamour. Education among the agrarian population was not advanced, though neither was their poverty as deep as that of much of the Roumanian peasantry. Bulgaria was relatively united in resenting the humiliation and loss of territory inflicted in recent military misfortunes. It was partly Bulgaria's sealed-off, mournful mystery that lent it freshness from the scholarly perspectives of Bury and of Steven himself. Roumania was a different proposition, larger, richer, more diverse and more divided than Bulgaria. Victorious in war by happenstance and in diplomacy by strenuous publicity, its royalty were embedded in global gossip columns and prone to world tours, its European veneer arduously burnished, its social declivities stark. The Roumanian aristocracy had a good case to represent one of the oldest veins of nobility in Europe, even going back, as Steven felt with particular conviction, to Byzantium itself.

'Bucharest', Steven wrote in the *Alphabet*, 'was at that time eager to think of itself as the Paris of the Balkans':

> It was not a particularly beautiful city, most of it having been built in the later nineteenth century, but it was full of glittering shops and elegant houses, and here and there churches and monasteries from the seventeenth and eighteenth centuries, in a style that was basically Byzantine but with strong Italian influences. There was a prosperous middle class . . . and a lively aristocracy . . . they all spoke French, only using Roumanian when they had to deal with the lower orders.
>
> . . . I enjoyed moving among this bright and not uncultured society, with its rather simple sophistication and its easy-going attitude. Divorce was frequent and obtained without difficulty. It was sometimes hard to remember who was now married to whom.

Steven was especially amused to be introduced to the new second wife of Prince Dimitri Soutzo, Clara-Thérèse, née Hughes, an American Frenchwoman of nineteen already on her third marriage, with 'green lacquered toe-nails, such as I had never seen before'. Soutzo's first Princess, Hélène, had been a close friend of Proust and was now married to her old lover, the darling of the French literary right, Paul Morand. Leigh Fermor reproduced a memorable flavour of the conversation and coincidences of these polished Bucharest salons: 'It was exciting and impressive to hear the name Marcel dropped so easily ... that Anna, who seemed to be everyone's cousin, was the Comtesse de Noailles* that Paul, if not Morand, was Valéry; that Jean was Cocteau and that Léon-Paul was Fargue: clues scattered in a paperchase that could be followed later.'†

Steven's own pleasure and manoeuvrability in these contexts were unalloyed. Though Princess Bibesco was still in Washington, he could rely on the aid of her nephew George Cantacuzene, a distinguished architect and traveller who had just returned from Persia, and of her daughter, Princess Ghika, who gained Steven ingress to the Bibesco palace at Mogoşoea, 'ornately splendid, but not garish or vulgar'. One banquet there persisted in Steven's memory for its archaic majesty if not its edibility:

> A young peacock had somehow fallen out of a great cedar in front of the house and had broken his leg and had to be put out of his misery; he was served up for dinner ... in the proper manner, on a golden platter with his head sewn on to his body and the long tail feathers stuck in to trail behind the dish. It was, I thought, macabre; and he tasted like a tough, coarse old turkey.

Steven always viewed the enigmatic otherness of birds and reptiles with greater sympathy that he could summon for the sentimental,

---

* The poet – not to be confused with the vicomtesse, Marie-Laure, Steven's occasional French hostess.
† Leigh Fermor also left impressions of interest about Marthe Bibesco's cousin by marriage, Antoine Bibesco, and his daughter by Elizabeth Asquith, Priscilla: the one 'an aloof, Germanesque, leonine, sardonic figure, even ... a slightly sinister one'; the other 'an omniscient, piercing-eyed prodigy' (Patrick Leigh Fermor, *The Broken Road*, ed. Artemis Cooper and Colin Thubron (John Murray, 2013), p. 188).

anthropomorphic kinship many Britons have with domesticated mammals. Both turkeys and peacocks had had their place in his inner mythology since childhood. Writing to Marthe Bibesco later of the image he would retain as the essence of Roumania, he described 'a vision of Mogoşoea, with a peacock on the balustrade, all looking as though it might suddenly vanish in the golden evening light'.

The most exalted Roumanian introduction Steven obtained came, however, from outside the Bibesco affinity. In London, at supper with his Eton contemporary George Wansbrough and his new wife Elizabeth, Steven had met a Spanish-born employee of the Ford Motor Company, Mr Orleans, along with his wife. The true identities of this cosmopolitan pair were the Infante Alfonso of Spain and his wife Beatrice, who happened to be the youngest of Queen Marie of Roumania's three sisters ('Baby Bee'). Steven thought the difference between these sisters was that 'Queen Marie always struck me as being a beautiful actress playing the part of a Queen; the Infanta was by birth a beautiful princess.' Her friendship gained Steven a summons to tea with his schoolboy 'pin up', the now widowed and powerless but still popular Roumanian Queen, at the Palace of Cotroceni (today, in a drastically altered form, the presidential palace of Romania), 'a palace built out of a monastery – the church and the side-buildings are old; the palace is 1890, but decorated by Her Majesty herself.'

Steven wrote an account of tea with Queen Marie to his grandfather, old Walter Runciman:

> I feel that I must write to you at once to tell you that I have come out unscathed from my interview with the Queen of Roumania! I went to tea with her today; and it is true that I was shown over her bedroom! but I was taken by her lady-in-waiting there, to see her Byzantine pictures and carvings. She was very gracious and kind and I thought her a beautiful and rather charming woman.

Queen Marie was rumoured to have developed a long-term attachment to a faithful courtier, Prince Barbu Stirbey. She certainly heeded his sensible advice on foreign policy, and he might have fathered one or two of her younger children. But her scholarly admirer was excited not so much by her marital conduct as by his privy glimpse of her taste in decoration and her extraordinarily constituted bed:

We waited in a room all of gilt. The furniture was gilt but in early XXth Century art shapes; the walls were gilt lincrusta on a turquoise ground – magnificent is an inadequate word. There an aide-de-camp talked to us, till a lady-in-waiting summoned us to the Presence. HM received us in a long arcaded room, done in the oriental style, cushions and divans and little low tables. She herself was draped in white crepe-de-chine and hung with ropes of pearls – looking really very beautiful. She was most affable and gracious and talked quite intelligently while we ate red caviare sandwiches and drank rather nasty tea. Then she told her lady-in-waiting to take me up to her bedroom, to show me her icons there. Some of them were very good. Her bed is made from an iconostasis – which I think perhaps a wee bit blasphemous. Apart from the icons the bedroom was incredible – lavish carved woodwork everywhere, shelves, alcoves, niches on all sides. Restraint is not the keynote of Her Majesty's taste in decoration.

I adored it all, of course . . .

At Steven's side was his latest host, the civilized but rather by-the-book British Minister, Michael Palairet. As he was presented, Palairet whispered in Steven's ear a reminder that British gentlemen do not kiss the hands of foreign royalty. Steven disobeyed him, shrugging off an old-fashioned glance. His boyhood reverie had been gloriously realized: 'The palace was redolent with the scent of frangipani and stephanotis . . . She was still beautiful. Her golden hair may have been helped to retain its colour, but her complexion was still wonderfully fresh and her eyes deep blue.' Marie's actual conversation was mainly on the topic of her own autobiography, and on the theory and practice of that art: she declared herself 'in favour of frankness, unless it was really hurtful'. Steven quietly noticed that the collection of icons was in fact a medley of sharply varying quality, adulterated with 'poor nineteenth century specimens'. He wasted little time asking Palairet where the Queen had acquired the shoddier examples, and was entertained to hear that they were recent British booty, plundered from Cyprus and presented to the Queen by Sir Ronald Storrs in the late 1920s.

Queen Marie's memoirs, 'the best of all royal memoirs', as Steven, a comprehensive judge of the genre, declares, were published in three volumes the month after Steven's return home. They stopped at the end of the Great War, understandably, for the complications of the inter-war period weighed heavily upon the Queen. The greatest difficulty of her life was her eldest child, King Carol II of Roumania. As Steven once put it, Carol II made Edward VIII look uncontroversial. He had renounced his claim to the throne when his father refused to recognize his marriage to a minor Roumanian noblewoman, Zizi Lambrino, before changing his mind and repudiating this unfortunate first wife. Then he had left his royal second wife, a popular princess of Greece, for a hated mistress, Elena Tampeanu. Magda Lupescu, as she was better known – that surname the wonderfully sinister Romanicization of her maiden name, Wolff – was 'a handsome, voluptuous lady with flaming red-gold hair', the daughter of a pharmacist, the widow of an army captain and, crucially, Jewish. The ire Carol caused by abandoning his Greek royal consort for such a woman forced him to abandon his rights once again, in favour of Michael, his son by his second marriage, and the only heir acceptable to his parents and people. But in 1930 Carol usurped his own son in a coup with backing from the British press baron Lord Rothermere and the Roumanian anti-Semitic right – even though Madame Lupescu remained at his side.

Steven would later claim to have met King Carol as well as Queen Marie on that first trip to Roumania. In certain company, he went further and claimed that the King had proved amenable to indiscretions with men as well as women, hinting with his characteristic mixture of decorum and subversion, at privy knowledge of the King's 'over-large needs'. Alas, there is no sign in his engagement diaries that they ever met before the war, though they later had rich and racy mutual friends in Portugal, where Carol II was to spend his exile. By 1934 Queen Marie was on such bad terms with her son that it seems unlikely that Steven was received by both. A more plausible form of connection between the visiting historian and King would have been the police informers who were instructed to monitor any guests of Queen Marie at the Cotroceni Palace, however apparently innocuous.

After the royal excitement came a return to academic investigation: Steven had an appointment with old Professor Iorga, who had disdained to attend the Byzantine proceedings at Sofia. The great national historian of the Roumanians, as Zlatarski was of the

Bulgarians, Iorga had served as the young Carol's tutor and then, not long before Steven met him, had briefly served as the King's third Prime Minister in 1931–2. Steven respected Iorga's historical standing without thinking anything much of either the tutor or the pupil's political powers. He states that Carol II's 'energy as king . . . seems mostly to have been spent in changing prime ministers almost yearly, with little regard to the votes of the electorate', while to his mother he wrote that Iorga had been 'a very bad [Prime Minister]; his one memorable decree was to forbid government employees to wear lipstick or powder; he also made his own books obligatory in every school' (the first of these innovations does indeed seem a peculiar ordinance in a country whose army officers were almost proverbially famous for their painted faces). Iorga had an impressively biblical appearance, his eyes sunken, his beard long, silver and forked, his frame gaunt. To Steven's consternation, he seemed worried that his visitor was suffering from jaundice; only later did the younger historian realize that while deciphering the Professor's thickly accented French he had confused *jeune* and *jaune*. For all this teasing Steven regarded the book Iorga had just published, *Byzance après Byzance*, as a work of critical importance and influence: 'it was [Iorga] who inspired me to interest myself in a subject about which I wrote a book many years later, the fate of the Christian heirs to Byzantium under Ottoman rule.'

Although Iorga's own political philosophy at times incorporated both authoritarian and anti-Semitic elements, he was to be identified as a dangerous rival by the Nazi-aligned, anti-monarchist Roumanian fascists, the Iron Guard, though these latter had learnt several tricks from the high-handed ministries and the cult of personality around Carol II. In the late 1930s King Carol paid several British writers to visit his country, uneasily aware of his own unpopularity with the British public after the disfavour shown to his British-born mother. One such interested pen belonged to Sacheverell Sitwell, who visited Roumania for four weeks towards the end of 1937, drawn, by his own admission, by his total prior ignorance of the country:

> At the first mention of going to Roumania, a great many persons, as did myself, would take down their atlas and open the map . . . I was

more than delighted at the prospect ... largely because I had no knowledge whatever of what lay in store for me ... I made up my mind not to read any book about Roumania before going there, in order to let it come as a surprise ...

Among the surprises in Sitwell's account was the alleged popularity and ability of the country's monarch:

Roumania has never before known such prosperity, and this, it is immediately obvious, is the result of wise rule. Every Roumanian will tell you that King Carol is their ideal ruler ... The resemblance of King Carol to the Hanoverian family is striking and, if I may say so, of comfort to an Englishman. After a few moments it was borne in upon me that this is the ablest man in his country and, after Kemal Ataturk, perhaps the person of most ability in Eastern Europe.

Also pressed into Carol's service was the New Zealand-born royal biographer Hector Bolitho, who had achieved some prominence in 1932 with his work on the Prince Consort, *Albert the Good*, much admired by Steven. Bolitho arrived in a comically comfortless Bucharest in the January of 1938; 'all I asked of Roumania was two boiled eggs. They offered me theatres, music, libraries, but the eggs did not appear.' He, too, was initially taken in by Carol's superficial resemblance to a serious-minded British prince of Teutonic ancestry and constitutional propriety, rapidly comparing the King to his ancestor: 'The abiding good in him – the wish to improve the world, the liking for supervision and organized progress, and his deep mistrust of the mysterious – came from his great-grandfather, the Prince Consort.' But Bolitho (who, it is not entirely incidental to note, was homosexual) was, like Steven, enchanted over tea with Queen Marie; from the by now mortally ill Queen he learnt to regard her son with caution. His account of his first meeting with the Queen shows a similar stripe of *amour courtois* to Steven's, under less constraint: 'She had the rare qualities and talent that stir men to immediate chivalry ... To this day I can visualize the oval of her face, the warming sympathy of her eyes ... a string of big, creamy pearls that lost themselves in a foam of shell-pink silk ... ' Bolitho records that Queen Marie was troubled by the abdication of Edward VIII ('such a tragedy, all that charm and love and devotion thrown away'), on whom he happened to have written a hatchet-job, and he preserves a notably despairing maternal judgement on Carol: 'I tried to describe my pleasure over King Carol's educational schemes, his eagerness for improvement, and his interest in the peasants. The Queen answered, with curious coldness, '"I wonder if time will prove that it is only froth and bubble."'

Steven, less gullible or venal than Sitwell, was not taken in by Carol, judging him 'unkind, unreliable, and a bit unbalanced'. Queen Marie died of cirrhosis of the liver in July 1938, spared the worst that was to come. In September 1940 Carol named an ally of the Iron Guard, Marshal Ion Antonescu, his latest Prime Minister; the very next day he and Madame Lupescu were packed off into exile. That November, amid a spiralling purge, Carol's old tutor and one-time Prime Minister, Iorga, was kidnapped by Guardists acting on their own initiative and shot dead among the ruins of the medieval town of Târgşor. Pondering Iorga's fate and that of the Nazi puppet in Bulgaria, Bogdan Filov, executed by a Communist firing squad after the war, Steven reflected, 'It is, it seems, a mistake for Byzantine professors to become Prime Ministers.'

One of the historical sites of Roumania about which Sachie Sitwell was most enthusiastic was the monastery – transformed into a convent in the nineteenth century – at Horez, with its 'white walls and red towers'. Once again he felt his ignorance to be a positive advantage – 'I can frankly confess I had never heard of it until the day before we visited it . . . a sensation hardly to be obtained in any other country in Europe.' Though he had heard reports of a Venetian architect's involvement in its construction, in the end he brushed them aside: 'On the contrary Horez would seem to be the perfect pattern of itself, a convincing example of the Roumanian native style, displaying this at its best and pushed to the highest degree of beauty of which it is capable.' To Steven, better briefed by Princess Bibesco, it was the Italianate and Byzantine effects that explained Horez's distinction, and that drew his own narrative, organic, accretive interest. Whatever the truth of its genesis, the convent was the scene of an odd adventure. Steven had planned to spend the night in a guest-room there, and was at first shown into a very fine one; but, all of a sudden, 'a flustered nun came into the room . . . and hurried me across a courtyard and up a tower, leaving me in a far more austere chamber.' She then locked him in and left him alone, 'with nothing to do except look out of the window onto the neighbouring countryside'. It was an anxious moment, and perhaps of little comfort that the scenery around Horez possessed much picturesque charm. Sitwell described it as:

> Tuscan Roumania . . . the same blue hills which might be above Pistoia . . . with that amount in it, too, of Provence . . . The roads, happily, were slow and winding . . . There was no hurry, for there could be no speed . . . in the midst of this country . . . are the dwellings of the fifteenth century, in type: equivalent to the Border towers of the Lowlands.

Well acquainted with Guelphs and Ghibellines, with Albigensian wars and with the ballads of northern reivers, Steven could only hope impotently for rescue from his ecclesiastical kidnappers. Relief came after an hour. It transpired that the local bishop had arrived unexpectedly, and the nuns had been obliged instantly to conceal any traces of another male visitor until their superior had departed.

After a week in the capital, Steven responded to Princess Bibesco's tip, and her nephew Prince Cantacuzene's willingness to act as cicerone, and set off for the distant rural province of Bukovina, to stay at Crasna, the seat of Marthe's princely, Othellan kin, the Mavrogordato. Bukovina had been a Habsburg province until the dissolution of that Empire after the First World War; Steven was surprised to find that in the smart circles there 'the atmosphere was entirely Austrian.' The servants were straight from Vienna, while the right-hand man and estate manager of Steven's latest host, Prince Nicholas Mavrogordato, was himself 'a Russian prince of German origin, Peter Wittgenstein', whose ancestor and namesake had led an army into Wallachia and Moldavia in the Russo-Turkish War of the early nineteenth century. It was this figure of fallen splendour who now served as Steven's chauffeur; on a trip to the ruins of a Genoese fortress at Hotin, they stopped for a picnic and, as a result of Steven's eager photography, were menaced by Soviet riflemen across the Bessarabian border.

On his return to London, Steven sent Marthe Bibesco a long and heartfelt thank-you letter:

This is going to be a difficult letter to write, because I do not see how I can find words strong enough ... particularly in the English language with its taste for understatement. I owe to you three weeks of enjoyment and interest such as I have never experienced before ... and what I appreciated almost most, Prince George Cantacuzene answered a lot of stupid questions of mine and ... set my mind going along what I believe to be the right lines about the Roumanian past.

This is a subject that fascinates me and I think it is very important for every would-be Byzantinologue. For Roumania is the chief heir of Byzantium. The very name is surely significant – not as the land of Trajan's Romans but as Roum, the land of the Romaioi, Byzantium. And thus – though the churches of Bukovina in their forest valleys are amongst the loveliest things that I've seen – I was almost more interested by the great buildings of the seventeenth and eighteenth centuries, by Horez or Vacaresti or Mogoşoea itself. There I think you see how Byzantium would have developed had she remained free, in those splendid Baroque monasteries or Mogoşoea the doubly Byzantine: directly so, and with an indirect Byzantinism that had travelled through Venice and the Renaissance – the work of Princes that were the sole survivors of the Byzantine world. I long to write a history of those Princes that kept alive Byzantium in a hostile world, the great native princes, ending with magnificent tragedy in Brancovan,* and then the Phanariots,† passionately preserving this Byzantium away in the north and ruining it with their unwise improvident opportunism, till one comes to the dramatic pathetic anti-climax of Prince Alexander Ypsilanti,‡ and the fading of Byzantium before nineteenth century

---

* Constantine Brancovan, Prince of Wallachia, ancestor of the Bibesco and builder of the Mogoşoea; he was publicly beheaded, with his four sons, at Constantinople, and thereafter regarded as a martyr to the cause of Roumanian independence.
† The Greek merchants of Constantinople increasingly deployed by the Sublime Porte as a viceregal class in Wallachia and Moldavia – families such as the Chiote Mavrogordato.
‡ Alexander Ypsilanti was a Phanariot who served first as a Russian cavalry officer against Napoleon, then as a leader in the Greek War of Independence – a conflict about whose philhellene heroes Runciman tended to be scathing.

nationalism. Forgive me boring you with all this, but I feel so very full of it and I must come back to Roumania ...

In the event he would not do so until 1969, by which time the last traces of 'Roum' had been all but abolished, 'lying in the clutches of a dictator determined to destroy palaces and churches and even villages in order to create an ugly industrialized land for which it was never suited'. But just before that drabber, sadder visit, Steven's earlier Roumanian travels bore their grandest fruit, *The Great Church in Captivity*. In that book Runciman would finally pursue the Balkan track of *Byzance après Byzance* that he had scented more than three decades earlier.

# 10

# Sailing to Bulgaria

A History of the First Bulgarian Empire *(written 1928–9, published 1930)*; Byzantine Civilization *(written 1932–3, published 1933)*; The Medieval Manichee *(written 1936–40, published 1947)*

The first shadows of evening were terrible amid the Russian storms; but the sunset was lit with splendour before the night came at last. But the tragedy is not perfect. Bulgaria did not bear within herself all the seeds of her decline and fall. Bulgarian history must always be read with Constantinople in sight.

Steven Runciman, *The First Bulgarian Empire*, 1930

The only Occultist product of Christian Dualism may lie ... in the symbolism of the Tarot Pack. These strange cards, which are first found in the fourteenth century, have never been seriously studied by a non-occultist scholar ... There seems to me to be a trace of Dualism in the pack, but it has long since been overlaid with debased Kabalistic lore ... the *Tower Struck by Lightning*, or *Maison Dieu*, which suggests the heretics' view of a Catholic church ...

Steven Runciman, *The Medieval Manichee*, 1947

While researching his fourth book, *The Medieval Manichee*, in the spring of 1936, Steven described its conception to his grandfather, old Lord Runciman, with the sort of placidly insincere self-deprecation that maddened professionals like Norman Baynes: 'I am busy over the question of medieval heresies and the heretical connections between Eastern and Western Europe. I find it immensely interesting, but I fear that it is all very obscure.' Steven's academic imp of the perverse had compelled him to put the history of the Byzantine Empire to one side just as Byzantium was solidifying in the consciousness of the general reading public. He now traversed murkier waters.

*The Medieval Manichee* sounded almost as odd to scholars as to laymen. Even the title, as its author unashamedly explained, was wilfully misleading:

> To the ordinary Medieval churchman, in the East as well as the West, all dualists were Manichaean; and I have used a name that they would have found intelligible and natural ... I hope therefore that the inaccuracy will be forgiven me, and that no one will open this book hoping to find in it an exhaustive account of those true Manichaeans who lingered on into the Middle Ages in the far-off recesses of Turkestan.

Manichaeanism was the religion of the prophet Mani, who, though born within the dominions of the Zoroastrian Empire of Sassanid Persia, always, as Runciman emphasizes, described himself as an 'Apostle of Jesus Christ'. Poised somewhere between Christian revelation, Zoroastrian dualism and possibly even Buddhism, Mani's creed long survived its founder's execution at Persian hands. Runciman's point in his title is that 'Manichaean' was even more important as a label for hostile orthodox invective than it was as a substantial influence on Christian heresies. 'In future the average orthodox Christian, when faced with any sign of dualism, would cry out "Manichaean" and everyone would know that there was rank heresy. Ideas that were Gnostic ... or crudely Zoroastrian were swept up into this all embracing epithet.'

Steven finished the new book in 1940, but its publication was delayed for seven years by the war. In an essay he offered to an anthology edited by Norman Baynes, also published in 1947, Steven condensed his argument, describing 'Bulgaria's most curious contribution to the religious thought of Europe': 'The Cathars and the Albigensians talked darkly of their Black Pope in Bulgaria ... The connexion between the Bogomils and the Albigensians is sometimes doubted, but to anyone who compares Slavonic Bogomil literature with Albigensian it is obvious.'

It was to him. The odour of brimstone and mystery might always have drawn the study of heresy to Steven's attention and his taste. But the interests and principles which he displayed in *The Medieval*

*Manichee* are consistent and revealing. Runciman thought the Bogomils and 'Albigensians' (or 'Cathars') both represented versions of Christian dualism. Dualism attempts to solve the problem of evil under an omnipotent and benevolent deity. Its Christian variant divides God and the world of the spirit and the Devil and the world of the flesh into separate, almost equal Powers. Some Christian dualists went so far as to identify the Power of Evil with Jehovah, the vengeful God of the Old Testament.

Runciman argues in *The Medieval Manichee* that all Christian dualist heresies descend from the theories of the early Gnostics, by way of the Paulicians in Armenia and the Bogomils in the Balkans, reaching their apogee with the Cathars of southern France and Italy. Together all these, in Runciman's view, form one 'tradition', even 'religion'. This idea still has academic defenders and popular acceptance, though it is contested by later scholarship arguing for the separate origins of all these 'heresies', and suggesting that in many cases their unorthodoxies were exaggerated by established Church hierarchies for political reasons.* After the Second World War, on the verge of producing the *Crusades* trilogy that would establish him as a truly popular historian, Runciman continued to be preoccupied by Balkan matters, and the strange, little-understood story of Bulgaria, the country that had first made his name.

In the spring of 1924 the yacht *Sunbeam* had wafted Steven into a never-forgotten first view of the city of cities, Tsarigrad, Micklegarth, not yet Istanbul and still, just, Constantinople. The Runciman family spent a week there amid Ottoman grandeur that seemed almost unaltered, even though the Caliph – lately the Sultan's Crown Prince – had been, much to Steven's regret, abolished by Atatürk that February. He was conscious of a great age having just ended – 'I was glad to have a glimpse of the past' – but, if anything, this only intensified the Polis's golden pall. Returning through Bulgaria on the Orient Express made no such impression upon him. But four years later, on another spring voyage, Steven found the position reversed. The newly designated Istanbul was in a distressing state: 'There were no more camels in the streets. The men all wore cloth caps and the women had been

* Cf. R. I. Moore and Mark Gregory Pegg.

ordered to remove their veils ... the weather was cold and grey.'
Bulgaria on the other hand now seemed an abundant *nova terra*, a
beguiling prospect of sunlight, snow and orchards. The country
promised activity as well as beauty, and Steven quickly fulfilled that
promise. Though on the face of it Bulgaria might seem a dourer and
even more difficult stretch of historical territory than Byzantium, it
was, as Bury had hinted on first meeting his last pupil, usefully free
of intruders.

Runciman's first book, *Romanus Lecapenus*, the monograph
resulting from his fellowship dissertation, had been written 'cold',
without much first-hand knowledge of Turkey, Greece or Bulgaria,
and at times, for all its élan, this shows. But his admirers urged the
young Byzantinist to proceed to a fuller work on medieval Bulgaria,
and when the time came Runciman did not disappoint them. William
Miller, the reigning authority on Balkan history, was an unusually
versatile figure even in that age of distinguished amateurs. The Balkan and Italian correspondent for the *Morning Post*, he had lived in
Rome until he could no longer put up with Mussolini, and afterwards
based himself at Athens, where he tinkered slyly in liberal, Venizelist
intrigues. Having praised *Romanus* in moderation, a year later he
unbent to hail *The First Bulgarian Empire* as 'the fruit of much
research, a knowledge of Bulgarian, and', significantly, 'visits to
Bulgaria'.

Steven was remarkable to his new peers for his youthful qualities,
actual, apparent and affected. He was, at twenty-five, unusually
young to be undertaking such radical and mobile academic research;
his smooth complexion and delicate style of dress – and address –
served to heighten this effect; and in his prose and his method, his
was the attitude of the young pretender, the insurgent and the
explorer. The established savants he found in Sofia differed in their
reactions to the novelty he presented. Professor Petar Mutafcieff, tall,
dressy and bald, with an intense, astringent stare, was widely regarded
as the second-best historian in the Bulgarian academy. He took
against Runciman immediately, on grounds of youth but, more
importantly, of origin: 'it was absurd for a young man from Western
Europe to think that he could understand Balkan history. When
eventually my book appeared he repeated this view,' Steven recalls

blithely in his *Alphabet*, 'though graciously saying that I had done better than might have been expected. As I knew that he did not read English, I was not greatly worried.' There was more to this antipathy, though, than a joking difference over international rank, age and linguistic ability. Mutafchieff's *History of the Bulgarian People* showed him as a nationalist in Bulgarian terms, an idealist in historical ones. To him the incursion of this smart young Englishman was just the latest of various baneful interferences from the overweening West.

Steven ignored this line of attack both because he was in fact more in sympathy with independent, Orthodox, Slavonic Bulgar culture than Mutafchieff imagined, and because he knew he had on his side not the second but the first among Bulgarian historians. Vasil Zlatarski was the founder of medieval Bulgarian history. Sixty-two in 1928, with his full beard and curling whiskers he bore some resemblance to his contemporary, King George V. A professor at Sofia for twenty years, he had picked over all the exiguous Slavonic evidence for the early life of his country. In the process he had provided his young, unconfident nation with a background it sorely needed. Bulgaria had been one of several ad hoc Balkan Ruritanias with a foreign monarchy, an unstable future and an opaque, barbarous past, a mere rebellious nuisance to Greeks, Russians and Turks, lacking even the mythical prestige of Serbia's epic cycle. Now it stood revealed as an ancient former power, an empire that had twice flourished, and was now being reborn to a prosperous destiny.

Zlatarski's discoveries, and his imperial terminology, played an important part in Ferdinand of Saxe-Coburg-Gotha's elevation from Prince of Bulgaria to Tsar, in 1908, after the country declared full independence from the Ottoman Empire. Even King, or Tsar, Boris III, the beneficiary of the post-war stitch-up that exiled his father, Foxy Ferdinand, back to the family seat in Coburg, could be recast into continuity with the great Tsar Boris I who brought Christianity to Bulgaria. Zlatarski – whom Steven addressed, as he did Mutafcieff, in French, receiving German replies – welcomed this precocious new British contributor to his field with none of the other Professor's suspicion. Here the reputation of having been the great Bury's last pupil and successor, and the continuing support of William Miller at Athens, both served Steven well. He was guided towards out-of-the-way Slavonic sources to which only their discoverer, Zlatarski himself, usually had access.

Runciman's second book, *The First Bulgarian Empire*, holds an independent line. Often the beneficiary and usually the ally of his Bulgarian predecessor, the young British newcomer never allows himself to become Zlatarski's tame apologist. The historians of the Balkans are taken to task with confident candour. In his preface Runciman reminds his readers and his new Bulgarian friends alike that 'to belittle your enemies is the least effective way of magnifying yourself.' Byzantium and Bulgaria emerge from his book elevated in concert; but the tone can verge upon what Mutafcieff, for one, might have considered typically British complacency. Sometimes the young pretender's remonstrances are undeniably about to be outstripped as events unfold. Runciman declares that 'In Western Europe, where national rivalries are less unendingly acute, and so learning has freed itself from patriotism, the words of Balkan historians no longer carry conviction.' Here spoke the child of Asquith Cabinets, and the youth accustomed to Baldwinite compromise, convinced by the world view of his serious-minded, authoritative father, so cosmopolitan in theory, so local, specific and even parochial in practice. The year was 1930; Action Française was on the rise in France; the National Socialists had become the second largest party in the Reichstag; old Lord Runciman did not trouble to moderate his enthusiasm for the Duce. The reasonable internationalism the younger Walter Runciman had instilled in his own sons was already looking sadly dated.

A son more loyal than affectionate, Steven thought and cared about contemporary politics more than many of his friends in Cambridge or London assumed. Unlike the historian-journalist Miller, however, he professed a nice-minded sort of constitutionalism that kept his duty to the past separate from and supreme over his preferences in the present: 'It is not for the historian to meddle in modern politics . . . But, if its history can arouse any interest in and sympathy with the country that is its modern heir, I shall be well pleased; for that result is, I think, within the legitimate aspirations of the historian.' He concludes his preface by warning against unthinking Balkan patriotism, and explaining how such propaganda can exploit the sparse sources of medieval history – 'lacunae are excellent playgrounds for the

1. (*top left*) Walter Runciman the Elder, 1st Baronet and Baron Runciman of Shoreston, SR's grandfather, 'from whom our material blessings flowed', on board one of his supplementary yachts in the mid-1920s.

2. (*top right*) SR's parents, Walter Runciman, later 1st Viscount Runciman of Doxford, and Hilda Runciman, née Stevenson. This picture was taken after the 1928 election in which Hilda joined her husband in the Commons, the first wife so to do.

3. (*bottom*) The Runciman siblings sitting together in birth order, in the grounds of Doxford in the early 1910s, from Leslie (born 1900), through to Margaret or Margie (born 1901), Steven (born 1903), Ruth or Ruie (born 1907) and Kitty (born 1909).

4. (*top*) Collegers at Eton after swimming at 'Athens', a bathing-spot on the Thames, in 1918. SR, who had grown so tall so rapidly as to unsettle his constitution, is second from the left, Eric Blair, the future George Orwell, on the far right.

5. and 6. (*bottom*) Two photographs of SR by Cecil Beaton at Cambridge, 1922. On sighting Steven at a lecture Beaton immediately declared, 'I should adore to model him.'

7. (*above*) Gaillard Lapsley, Fellow in history at Trinity, Cambridge, an expert on the English medieval constitution and a close friend of both Henry James and Edith Wharton, in his rooms in 1923.

8. (*below*) The Runciman children, minus Margie and plus two outsiders, performing a play at Doxford in 1924. The entire cast has undergone Saturnalian gender reversal. Leslie and Steven are fashionable and statuesque beauties in the back row; Jacques Laparra, whose mother gave Margie board and lodging in Paris, is the fetching maid on the left; on the right Leslie's new wife, Rosamond Lehmann, makes an arrestingly heroic classical soldier.

9. (*above*) A Cecil Beaton shot from 1927 of goings-on at Stephen Tennant's house in Wiltshire. From left to right, the dangling heads belong to SR, Zita Jungman, Teresa 'Baby' Jungman, Stephen Tennant, Dolly Wilde, Oscar's niece and doppelgänger, and Borden Harriman, a slightly bemused American visitor of diplomatic stock and theatrical profession.

10. (*below left*) SR with the novelist Edith Wharton, her irascible Pekinese, Linky, the American Byzantine historian Royall Tyler and Tyler's wife and child, taken in the early 1930s.

11. (*below right*) SR photographed by Cecil Beaton in 1927, wearing one of the Chinese silks he looted during his Chinese adventure in 1925–6 in his new rooms at Cambridge.

12. (*top*) The residence of the Stancioff family, SR's Anglophile Bulgarian friends, in the country by Varna, on the Black Sea.

13. (*bottom left*) George 'Dadie' Rylands, by now a Fellow of King's, Cambridge, had fallen out with Steven over his friendship with Rosamond Lehmann in 1927, but was back in favour by the 1930s. Here, in about 1934, he is photographed by Steven walking in King's gardens with Eddie Bates, a promising Trinity pupil, and Anne Barnes, a semi-detached Cambridge wife who was not alone in nursing unrealistic feelings for Dadie himself.

14. (*bottom right*) Douglas Davidson, arguably Steven's closest and most loyal Cambridge friend, possibly a brief lover and certainly a moral preceptor, on the Isle of Eigg in 1932, practising his art. Although Steven admired Davidson as a man more than almost anyone else, he was patronising about his friend's limited though 'charming' talent as a painter.

15. (*right*) SR in his new rooms at Nevile's Court, 1932, decorated with grisaille Napoleon III wallpaper acquired in Paris, depicting the legend of Cupid and Psyche.

16. (*above left*) 'The sweetheart of Eigg': SR on Eigg in 1932. Steven's father acquired the Hebridean Small Isle, much to his younger son's satisfaction, at the end of 1925; here Steven is photographed during his first large-scale independent house-party there.

17. (*above right*) One of the first pupils Steven invited to Eigg, 'the undergraduate whom I find most intelligent and sympathique at the moment, though his teeth are too far apart', was Guy Burgess, pictured here setting out for a swim from the island Lodge in 1932. Burgess was recovering from a nervous breakdown that had prevented his taking final examinations, possibly brought on by alcohol and benzedrine.

18. (*above left*) Another unhappy younger Cambridge friend encouraged to recover at Eigg, in 1933, was the good-looking, heartbroken, heavy-drinking Corpus Christi student Robert Hamer.

19. (*above right*) Eddie Bates at the window of Dadie Rylands's rooms in King's, 1934.

20. (*below*) One of Dadie's most brilliant favourites was Noel Annan, photographed here in the early 1930s, who wrote of Steven that 'whatever it was fashionable to dislike, he praised, and he opened one's eyes. He would tease and gossip and uncover vistas of experience and pleasure ahead.'

21. (*top*) SR in Syria, 1938, with Count Stanislas 'Stas' Ostrorog (*centre*), a Constantinopolitan-born exiled Polish aristocrat living off a slice of an arms fortune, who acted as the French Resident in Damascus.

22. (*bottom*) In 1938–9 Steven took a disgraced and blackmailed Eddie Bates with him on a tour of the Far East, a chance to experiment with travel journalism, dabble in diplomatic intrigue, experience a new part of the world and witness another young Cambridge friend, Prince Chula of Siam, pictured here in 1938, in his ancestral setting.

Chauvinists, where their imaginations can play the most riotous games.' But in this book, far more than in his stylish but essentially sober, precise, school-of-Bury first outing *Romanus Lecapenus*, Runciman learnt to frolic in the evidential void with abandon, originality and plausibility.

Even in *Romanus* Runciman had proved himself a master of the soaring rhetorical opening; but *The First Bulgarian Empire* ascends into a still higher flight. The book begins with what the author claims is a plain retelling of a Byzantine account, in fact the most romantic sort of paraphrase: 'Once upon a time, when Constans was Emperor in Byzantium, there lived a king called Kubrat on the shores of the Sea of Asov. In due course he died, leaving five sons behind him, whom he bade live in concord together. But the brothers in a short time quarrelled, as princes often do ... ' Runciman is making the point that the earliest Greek accounts of the Bulgar people savour of fairy tale. But at the same time he has no compunction about letting his own prose complement that savour. Examining the origins of an invading barbarian horde, he puts forward the following hypotheses, drawing on his knack for sudden discomfiture: 'Some say they were the Hiung-Nu, the race that was the terror of China; but the Goths, who knew them best, thought otherwise. They told of the wicked sorceresses that King Filimer the Goth banished from his Scythian kingdom, who mingled on their wanderings with the evil spirits of the desert; and from that union were born the Huns.'

Runciman delights in differentiating himself from the Bulgarian historians in the same breath as sagely narrated jokes:

> The first monarch mentioned was Avitokhol, of the house of Dulo, who reigned for the portentous period of three centuries ... His successor, Irnik, did not compete with such tenacity of life; a mere century and a half was all that he could manage ...
>
> Even allowing for the lengthy lives that their excellent sour milk is said to grant the Bulgarians, the matter remains unconvincing ...

Runciman insinuates a comic overlap between the modern Bulgarians and their distant antecedents. Zlatarski – as we have seen, a substantial, pioneering national historian who offered the young foreigner every possible assistance – is implicitly compared to a beaten

Bulgar peasant, sullen and superstitious in the face of an enlightened Byzantine enemy's victory: 'The Bulgars were deeply ashamed by their defeat. The hill where Leo lay in ambush was long called Leo's hill, and Bulgars passing by would point at it and sadly shake their heads . . . For discussion of this campaign, whose existence Zlatarski and others deny, see Appendix VII.'

Runciman also develops the habit of quietly slipping himself into a Byzantine chronicler's place. He reproves the Byzantines gently for their enterprising but imprecise accounts of the Bulgars: 'They made their attempts at ethnographical elucidation, but often it was easier to give up and seek instead a literary flavour, calling every oncoming tribe the Scythians or the Cimmerians.' But this remark scarcely covers Runciman's own tracks in instilling into an almost sourceless, lost national history some of that same 'literary flavour'. He can hardly ever conceal his glee at the Byzantine scholars' thought processes and aesthetic direction – 'There was a king of the Crimean Huns called Grod – Theophanes euphonized his name into Gordas, and John of Antioch even more mellifluously into Gordian . . . ' Twenty-five years after the publication of *The First Bulgarian Empire*, the Greek diplomat-poet George Seferis would make a perceptive comment about Runciman's chameleonic power of sliding into purple-born prose: 'the primary significance that Runciman's work has, for me at least, is that it is written by a Byzantine, an imperial Byzantine, not a national Byzantine.'

Practically the only evidence for the identities and reigns of the early Bulgar khans, or *knyaz*, comes from a Slavonic king list originally unearthed by Bury and forced into some kind of order by Zlatarski. But it took Runciman's quick glances and quicker sentences, his insight into the personal alongside the political, to make of these grimly disinterred names with their generic similarities to the Book of Genesis a legible pattern of royal families rising, falling and squabbling. Every bit as keen as the most patriotic Bulgar authority to embrace the direct descent of these earliest khans from none other than Attila the Hun, Runciman decides upon a particular dynasty – mainly on the grounds of its sporadic and persistent returns to power – as representing the Hunnic royal descent. This he describes as the 'House of Dulo', fitting this ancient and obscure warrior clan neatly into the world of the *Almanach de Gotha* and the Saxe-Coburgs. At the same time he retains a worldly consciousness of the propagandistic significance in invoking Attila. He is sensitive to the nationalistic tendencies of his own time, and healthily sceptical about them, but does not quite grasp their malignity or permanence: 'Not long ago a wave of militarism swept over Europe, and an awful ancestry became the boast of any bellicose nation; Attila was proudly called cousin, if not grandfather, by them all.' That wave had scarcely begun to rise, let alone pass, by 1930.

Steven's interest in the history of his own country had been on the wane since his childhood, though he was always to retain some fondness for the picturesque internecine wranglings of Scotland, and some admiration for the continental and flamboyant Plantagenets. In depicting early Bulgaria he occasionally leans on an image of Britain that owes much to Walter Scott, Macaulay and *Our Island Story*. Hasty as he is to acquaint his almost universally ignorant British readership with a complex ethnic situation, Runciman makes much of the dichotomy between the 'Bulgars' – a Hunnic class of warrior-nobility who spoke an all-but-lost Old Bulgar tongue – and the Slavs, 'a gentle race', natural agrarian subjects occasionally brightened by talented priests and courtiers, but prone to the sullen faults of heresy and apathy. An easy, crowd-pleasing parallel occurs to him: '[the Bulgars] were only the landowning, organizing aristocracy, similar no doubt to the Normans that three centuries later were to order the backward Anglo-Saxons.' This seems great nonsense to anyone interested in the Norman Conquest today; the documentary evidence of charters, witnesses and chronicles all show that the Normans inherited a sophisticated, centralized system of law and administration from the Anglo-Saxons, and retained English prelates and clerks to help them understand and implement it. But in its time this comparison won the particular approval of Miller, for one, and it illustrates two of Runciman's rhetorical strengths. He was quick to show political rivalry with a pure and binary clarity; and when considering whether a historical period should be understood in terms of its uncompromising peculiarities alone, or compared with profit to others, however separated by time and space, he was consistently to choose and to defend the second method.

Runciman readily demonstrated the freshness of his interpretation. He startled his predecessors and his contemporaries in his adjudication both of a notorious Bulgar Khan and of an infamous Byzantine Empress, Krum and Irene. Krum's military prowess made him a Bulgarian founder-hero of sorts, but his paganism, his grisly reputation – he whittled a Byzantine emperor's skull into a drinking-vessel – and even his name, tended to calcify his memory as that of an archetypal, unrepentant barbarian warlord, worthy of his inevitable if uncontemporaneous surname, 'The Fearsome'. In *The First Bulgarian Empire*, Runciman puts the case for Krum as a measured and visionary ruler, possessor of 'a caution and forbearance rare in a barbarian conqueror', a general proceeding with defensive, Fabian care and a politician as willing as any Byzantine to resort to diplomacy and subterfuge when recourse to arms seemed unpromising. Runciman reveals the Bulgar warrior as the mastermind behind Byzantine infighting: 'Theophanes's conclusion, that Leo was guilty but too clever to be definitely compromised, is, I think, absolutely convincing. But it seems to me that, to make the story credible, Krum must be implicated in the plot.'

To the astonishment of the increasingly impressed Miller, Runciman did not hesitate to apply the most approving term of his own era's political discourse to the skull-swigging Khan's achievements: 'Barbarian that he was, with his ostentation and craft and cruelty, his concubines, his human sacrifices, and his cup that was an Emperor's head, the Sublime Khan Krum was a very great statesman.' At the same time, Runciman remains more than tolerant of the not unnaturally perturbed Byzantines, and the desperate methods to which they resorted to neutralize this dangerous opponent. 'The episode that followed', he writes of a Greek attempt to have Krum stabbed during a parley,

> is deeply distressing to our modern sense of honour, and patriotic Balkan writers have long seen in it an example of the perfidy and degradation of Byzantium. But we live now in a godless age. In the ninth century every true and devoted Christian saw the heathen either as animals or as devils, according to their capacity for inflicting evil on the faithful.

The author's worldly and wry sense of humour hangs on those two discordant words, 'modern' and 'honour', not so very long after the

Great War seemed to render their harmony so much hypocritical cant. To these high- and empty-sounding values he opposes heartfelt religious piety, and it is with the help of piety, too, that he embarks on the rehabilitation of the Byzantine Empress, villainess, latter-day Medea and quasi-saint, Irene of Athens.

Irene is a marginally better-known figure in Western historiography than Khan Krum. Her reputation as a patroness of the arts and her unofficial aura of sanctity in the Orthodox tradition barely impinge upon more enduring infamy. Her sex and, subordinately, her notoriety led the Pope to crown Charlemagne as a rival Roman emperor; she is then said to have proposed to marry her involuntary new Western colleague. She outdid all that by blinding her incompetent and petulant son, Constantine VI, who did not long survive the operation. But Runciman's line on her is clear from her first introduction – it is, in a word, Orthodox:

> The Empress-Regent Irene, of blessed memory, spent the spring of 784 in touring her northern frontier. It was a felicitous time ... Thrace ... was being refilled with a busy population transported from the East, Armenians – heretics indeed, but politically harmless so far away from their kindred. And so the Empress, with music playing, made her Imperial progress along to the town of Berrhoea ... rechristening it Irenupolis ...

She is one of several historical characters who captured Runciman's gamesome sympathy at least partly on visual grounds. Her fall elicits one of his tersely heartfelt, almost Homeric threnodies: 'her white horses no longer drove through the streets of Constantinople.' He liked her panache and her outrageousness, and on to her policy of relentless persecution of iconoclasts and heretics he projected his own ornate, 'iconodule' artistic and religious feelings. Writing for an American readership in the mid-1970s, he would mischievously claim the Empress for the cause of Women's Liberation.

Runciman advocated an interpretation mostly amenable to Zlatarski, and indeed to King Boris himself, who became the *First Bulgarian Empire*'s dedicatee. Runciman aimed to demonstrate that Bulgaria had been best served by those among her rulers who built up her independence and distinctiveness, rather than those in thrall to an alien, if more sophisticated, dream of Greek culture and power. The two great exemplars in this argument were the Khan, or Knyaz, Boris, who brought Bulgaria into the Christian fold and haggled her Church towards its Slavonic liturgy and national identity; and on the other hand the Tsar Symeon, Boris's son, who spent his ambitious and bloody career in a semi-successful pursuit of imperial dignity. While Boris was confident and consistent in his strategy, Symeon, Runciman suggests, suffered from the effects of a conflicted upbringing, educated at Constantinople and known as 'Hemiargus', or half-Greek. Runciman sums up the two rulers' strategies with novelistic flair:

> . . . [Symeon] realized now that he could never be more than half-Greek or half-Imperial. The other half was ineradicably Bulgarian, newly risen from barbarous heathendom. Boris had been wiser and more fortunate . . . his aims were utterly opposite to Symeon's, national, not international. In his dealings with the Empire he was like a child, but an un-selfconscious child who hopes to grow up soon . . . Symeon was like a clever, naughty child, who knows what a nuisance he makes himself and how gladly the adults would like to keep him quiet, who sees through their devices and understands their weaknesses and thoroughly enjoys annoying them, but who all the while is conscious that he is a child and they are adult, with something about them far beyond his grasp; and so he feels foiled and cheated and resentful.

It is a comparison that feels confessional, tempting its reader to see the young Steven, as an undecided 'Hemiargus', too aware of his surroundings and of his elders' falsities to rest entirely content within them.

In Runciman's first book the authorial tone had owed much to Bury and so ultimately, despite its author's disavowals, to Gibbon. Religious motivation was treated with polite, detached scepticism. But in *The First Bulgarian Empire* the young Byzantinist embraced a new rhetorical position, one whose playful ambiguity would intrigue and puzzle his readers for the seventy years of his subsequent career. This position had three tenets – near-total identification with the interests of the Orthodox Church; a keen interest, scientific rather than supportive, in dualist heresy; and a tantalizingly factual approach to black magic. The third of these tenets is most crisply embodied in Runciman's assessment of the career of Benjamin, a younger son of Symeon:

> Benjamin's life was given over to a study of the Black Arts; and he became so clever a magician that at will he could turn himself into a wolf or any other animal you pleased. Many of his fellow Bulgars took too great an interest in fortune-telling and in demon powers, but few could hope to acquire a proficiency such as his; and so, though in himself he might be actively unpleasant, he never attracted a large following.

Heresy, as opposed to magical lycanthropy, Runciman already handles with sympathy and understanding. 'Dualism has always been an attractive and natural religion,' he insists at the outset of his moderately expressed, if eventually uncompromising, verdict on the Bogomils. To 'Pope Bogomil', the shadowy founder of the sect, Runciman does not hesitate to attribute the qualities of 'genius', praising the adaptability of the creed he started: 'this intricate Armenian religion', expertly tailored 'to suit the needs of the European peasantry . . . so suited to its purpose that before two centuries were over it had spread to the mountains of Spain'.

Indeed, Runciman's attention is so caught both by Bogomil's intellectual origins and by his legacy that Bogomil's followers – mostly illiterate, agrarian Slavs – receive unusually sustained coverage in his work. Partly this is because the effects of the Bogomil creed – 'equally but passively opposed to all Governments' – seem to reinforce the role that medieval, rural populations usually occupy in Runciman, sullen bystanders to the belligerent manoeuvres of rulers with larger concerns in play. But Runciman also allows for the radical potential in such a heresy: 'A faith that teaches that all matter is evil is bound to have serious social consequences.' He never quite tires of the Bogomils, and their brooding background dissension lends to *The First Bulgarian Empire* an incidental societal breadth unusual in his writing.

In *The Medieval Manichee*, the full work Runciman devoted to the Bogomils and their theological cousins a decade later, Runciman expands in puckish vein on another source of fascination these heretics hold for him. It was a game he had commenced in the earlier book with an allusion less learned than coy – 'their abstention from women was so marked that among their later disciples in France, often called the Bougres . . . it aroused the prurient suspicions of the Orthodox; and their name in English still preserves the meaning of an alternative form of vice.' By the time of the *Manichee* Runciman, bolstered by a more established reputation and a distinguished, professorial war record, was willing to be more expansive, to enjoy himself by producing smoke and then, in a leisurely but plausible manner, avouching fires. Dualism 'was associated with orgiastic obscenity', he warns, adding, ' . . . the regularity of the charges makes some investigation necessary.' Each rumour about the dualists' sexual conduct is detailed gravely, keeping up Runciman's impartial demeanour, and then, with cautious regret, justified.

> certain of the Gnostics indulged in organized orgies . . .
>
> Casual promiscuity and unnatural vice were not discountenanced by the religious authorities . . . there was definitely an easy-going attitude about sexual morals, an attitude peculiarly agreeable to the people of Southern France . . . we can understand how the name of 'Bougre' . . . acquired its later sinister significance.

'Natural religion' and 'unnatural vice' are, Runciman seems at pains to convey, inevitable bedfellows. He goes on gleefully to cross-fertilize the more lubricious accusations with the various magical rumours that relate to dualism and, in particular, to the Cathars of the Languedoc: 'Was there some Secret Tradition amongst the Dualists that might support the dark suspicions of the Orthodox? . . . It may be that the secret practices of the Templars, with their cult of evil and unnatural vice, were partly based on Dualist ideas and usages.' Sometimes such questions remain safely rhetorical; at others Runciman gladly lends his support in some very rum quarters. By invoking 'the somewhat inarticulate tradition of the Witch-Cult . . . the remnant of an older nature worship', he gave cheerful credence to the sincerely held but, historically speaking, wildly heterodox theories of his acquaintance Margaret Murray. Murray believed in the perseverance of an organized pagan religion, extant at the highest (royal) levels, and lasting in Britain, at least, well into the seventeenth century. Runciman's scrupulous inclusion of her oeuvre in his bibliographies would never cease to baffle and annoy staider contemporaries and successors.

This teasing vein provoked Lynn White of the *Journal of Bible and Religion* to complain that 'if Runciman's learning is great, it is capricious.' The epithet was well chosen, but caprice is not the whole story; part of the power behind *The First Bulgarian Empire* and *The Medieval Manichee* is provided by Runciman's willingness and ability to manipulate history as self-portraiture. It is a profoundly personal sympathy and identity, too, that animates his treatment of the Orthodox Churches (whether Greek or Slavonic). Without ever formally belonging to the Orthodox Church – the freedom afforded by his more-than-semi-detachment from one of his great subjects would always be of use to him – he could assimilate himself with ease into defending the lofty mysteries of its art, hierarchy and theology. In *The First Bulgarian Empire* the most typically Runcimanian figure is Photius, Patriarch of Constantinople, who is accorded a word-portrait of the kind that Runciman reserves for his most rewarding sources: 'Photius was prodigiously learned – too learned, some said, whispering of sorcery; he was as determined and courageous as the Roman [Pope], and far more subtle, far more imaginative, with far more knowledge of his audiences.'

Knowledge of the audience was to Runciman among the most crucial and versatile of virtues, whether in writing or lecturing. The true authority must know when to enlighten and when to bamboozle. Photius had certainly mastered the second talent in his elaborate theologizing to the converted Boris of Bulgaria:

Historians ever since have gaped at this torrent of patronizing culture and metaphysical sensibility that was poured over a simple barbarian, who sought only to have far simpler problems solved for him – whether trousers were indecent and turbans counted as hats. But Photius knew his business ... It showed the Khan better the relative status of his country and the Emperor's, that he should understand not one word of those subjects that were apparently the common talk of Constantinople. Photius took a long view; he kept his dignity intact even at the expense of the needs of the moment.

Runciman – who also took a long view, and kept his dignity intact – generally preferred, as a historian, elucidation to obfuscation. But that does not stop him from admiring the wily Patriarch's thornier methods: methods he would himself put to good use in *The Medieval Manichee*, a work which does not shrink from extended, if elegant, theological choreography.

The book Runciman produced between these two, *Byzantine Civilization* (1933), which he himself would readily come to admit was one of his weakest, was the result of suppressing his personality and cultivating instead a thinly spread, objective comprehensiveness. Its composition gave him little pleasure and he rushed it into wholeness, betraying himself into several errors which attracted unfavourable comparison with, and delighted attention from, the ever-vigilant Argus of British Byzantinism, Norman Baynes, 'who ever afterwards treated me with contempt'. A reviewer at the *Oxford Magazine* condescended to remark that 'whatever the defects of the book, it is very good for Mr. Runciman to have written it at this stage.' But any satisfaction the emerging Byzantinist might be able to derive from another step trodden on the *cursus honorum* was cancelled out by the opprobrium of a rival who in some ways was Runciman's Oxonian counterpart, Robert Byron. Byron levelled at his acquaintance – they had met, uneasily, in the circles of Adrian Bishop and Maurice Bowra – the sort of barbs Runciman would rarely have to face again:

> Mr. Runciman lacks the capacity for narrative . . . he carries the fear of over-statement to the point of mania . . .
>
> One is led to feel . . . throughout the whole book, that while he is dealing with actual written evidence he is happy and brilliant, and his judgment sure; but that when broad perspectives are concerned he grows puzzled and diffident, and the intuition of the historian forsakes him.

Runciman spent most of his career affecting – and, indeed, probably enjoying – superb indifference to his critics among academic specialists, those he regarded as the smaller, more specific Bayneses of later eras. But behind each such splendid retort – as when he gaily reminded an increasingly frustrated Jonathan Riley-Smith that he, by comparison to his interlocutor, wrote literature – should be traced far earlier injuries that were able to hit home. Contrary to what – like many another successful but sensitive writer – he claimed, Runciman collected and read reviews of his work assiduously, sometimes going as far as to stick the cuttings into scrapbooks. The charges of failing in style, 'readability' or grandeur and originality of conceit were far more wounding to him than technical controversy about factual detail or historiographical method. As a still-young man, his ideal reader was not a fellow Byzantinist, but a worldlier figure, Lytton Strachey, for example, who might be ignorant enough about the Eastern Roman Empire to make a puerile quip about the name 'Lecapenus', but knew proper writing when he saw it. From now on he would give the Byrons or Bowras as slender excuse as possible to pin him down as a merely dry, pedantic exemplar of that order from which he was already hoping to escape, the 'puzzled and diffident' professional dons.

*Byzantine Civilization* may have impressed only those readers relatively ignorant of its period, but among these less learned enthusiasts were some of the grandest and smartest of Steven's acquaintances. Not long after its publication, Lady Ottoline Morrell, who had taken a shine to Steven while they were recuperating at the same spa, thought it would be amusing to introduce the coming expert on Byzantium to the great poet lately associated with that city's name. Just before he approached Yeats, Steven later recalled, he was buttonholed by another, less celebrated poet, Thomas Sturge Moore. Sturge Moore, although long a friend of Yeats, had become envious of his fame and frustrated by his style. 'That man Yeats is obsessed by gold,' he hissed in Steven's ear. 'All he ever writes about is gold. Ask him what he means by it, why don't you.' Wearily willing to placate one bard by posing an innocent question to the other, Steven enquired what exactly was the significance of gold in the master's oeuvre. Yeats recoiled, fixing the young Cambridge don with a cold, contemptuous stare. 'Gold is beauty,' he snapped and, turning away, would say no more.*

---

* Professor Robin Cormack, on hearing this story, wryly remarked that Yeats's curt explanation was not so very different from Runciman's own attitude to the specialist study of Byzantine art.

When the *Manichee* finally appeared, old Lord Runciman, Yeats, Sturge Moore, Lady Ottoline and King Boris III and his Third Bulgarian Empire had all had their day. In certain respects it proved to be Runciman's own *Sailing to Byzantium* – a supremely characteristic, memorable, riddling work. It possessed enough uncanniness to do honour to the Order of the Golden Dawn, while keeping its narrative, good order and confident sense of time and place. Between two wide-ranging essays with resonant, abstract-sounding titles – 'The Gnostic Background' and 'The Dualist Tradition' – the heresies come forward neatly under sharply delineated names, like barbarian invasions: the Paulicians, Bogomils, Patarenes and Cathars. Yet Runciman's case depends on the thread running through all their blurring and overlapping of doctrine, of geography, even, at times, of personnel:

> So it was that one great confederate Dualist Church arose, stretching from the Black Sea to Biscay. In all the countries into which it spread, its successes were made sure by political conditions, by circumstances of racial politics, of class politics, and of personal politics . . . But the political impulse was not everything. Behind it there was a steady spiritual teaching, a definite religion, that developed and declined as most religions do, but that embodied a constant Tradition . . .

Runciman quoted a hostile Armenian prelate, John of Otzun, on the Paulicians of Armenia: 'They thought, he added, that they had found something great and new, whereas it was really old and out-of-date.' Many authorities in the field of Christian heresies would today apply that same charge to Runciman. The substance of his portrayal of the Bogomils strongly resembled the thesis of his younger friend, Prince Dimitri Obolensky; and his almost ideological adherence to the principle that 'Heresies, like civilisation itself, are apt to spread Westward from the East' had been anticipated in the work of the French Dominican scholar Antoine Dondaine. It is true that the Second World War (as Runciman coolly put it, 'the recent circumstances of the world') had prevented his access to much vital recent scholarship, whether cut off in Occupied Europe or even at home. But when he came to revise the *Manichee* in the early 1950s, he added only a few oddments to its bibliography, scarcely altering the text at all, conscious that this short book had more to offer than fresh information or evidence. It was in its organic but ordered structure, its interpretation, imagination and narration, that *The Mediaeval Manichee*'s novelty shone clear.

Runciman begins by setting out a position worthy of a great prelate, or high official, of the Orthodox (or, for that matter, unusually for him, even the Catholic) Church. The liberal, secular values of Gibbon and the Enlightenment are, for the present, driven out by a remorseless and logical piety. 'Tolerance is a social rather than a religious virtue,' the unbending narrator declares. This is a voice to be understood as a rhetorical, even poetic persona, quite distinct from the opinions of its author, a devoted and practical ecumenist, who would always denounce intolerance as itself a mortal sin. But at this moment Runciman takes evident delight in constructing for intolerance, even persecution, a cast-iron, coherent intellectual case. In so doing he takes the fight to complacently elastic solutions:

> orthodox doctrine is complex and difficult, and it is tempting to make some simplification here or there – tempting, but not to be endured. For the vast superstructure that orthodox theologians have built over the fundamental Christian revelation is not the baroque expression of the whims of a few pedants and eccentrics, but the attempt of the best brains of a great intellectual era to display all the implications of that revelation. Sceptical historians might mock at the passion with which early Christian ecclesiastics would fight over some tiny doctrinal delicacy; but even an iota might clarify or might mar an essential aspect of the Faith . . . The Church was narrow-minded because the true Path is narrow . . .

Runciman's admiration for at least the scholarship and the style of the Church Fathers was sincere; he once grandly informed Stewart Perowne that Tertullian 'created medieval Latin as a literary vehicle'.* But the misleading clarity of his homily's concluding, curt sentence,

---

* Runciman's equally well-read and open-minded near-contemporary William Empson lacked this ability to forgive Tertullian's often ghoulish *Schadenfreude* on aesthetic grounds, dismissing his writings with a shudder as 'gloating over torture' (William Empson, *Milton's God* (Chatto & Windus, 1961), p. 247).

with its striking present tense, is not for a moment to be accepted without inflection. 'Beware', writes Anthony Bryer, who first encountered Runciman during his own wartime childhood in Jerusalem, 'of Steven Runciman when he is laying a false trail.' At one level he is doing just that to his readers here; yet at the same time he is providing them with a clear and worryingly unanswerable vision of the truth as the early and medieval Christian hierarchies perceived it.

In one important respect his sympathy with the ecclesiastical powers was unfeigned. Runciman was irritated by the inconsistency of the Whig tradition, which blamed any sin of ignorance, bigotry and backwardness upon religion, lauded the triumph of state over Church, and caricatured powerful divines as worldly, corrupt intriguers. He was quick to point out that it was the support of the state that had transformed the Church into a uniform system with the power and volition to persecute; that it had been in the state's interest and with its encouragement that it had embraced that power; and that the active work of enforcement still ultimately lay with the state. In consequence, 'it is the State, not the Church, which persecutes, and the State that should be blamed for the cruelties of persecution . . . when a sect is persecuted it is because the State is convinced that that sect is undesirable.'

Admittedly, the question seems to become more than a little blurred during the period Runciman covers, especially given the bellicose, mercenary and ambitious character of the Western higher clergy, which he fully accepts. It is hard to absolve on the grounds of his cloth a figure such as Arnold-Amalric, Abbot of Cîteaux and Archbishop of Narbonne, the experienced politician and military commander who reputedly declared, when asked what was to be done with the population of the captured town of Béziers, 'Kill them all. God will know his own.' The political record of Byzantine prelates, who were in any case both more separate from and more subservient to their secular arm, is, if chequered, tangibly less disgraceful; and it is worth noting the reply Steven gave in his last ever interview, with *Pemptousia*, the magazine of Mount Athos, to the question of which Byzantine figure he most admired: 'I am interested in so many personalities. But mostly I admire certain religious men. Generally, the non-spiritual but important characters of Byzantium are not, for me, worthy of admiration.'

In his pithy account of the origins of Gnosticism, Runciman sets out from an unusually unsentimental position vis-à-vis the Roman Empire. While many Englishmen of his class had been conditioned by two kinds of imperial historiography, classical and British, and especially by the popularity and clarity of Gibbon, to admire the antique splendours of the pagan Roman Empire, Steven had, from his very earliest youth under the tutelage of Torby, learnt to prefer the Greek language and culture, and he refused to glorify the pre-Christian Roman world: 'sin was a very real thing to the Early Christians. The world that they knew, the cruel, luxurious, uncertain world of the Roman Empire, was undoubtedly a wicked place.'

It is worth lingering on that triad of adjectives, 'cruel, luxurious, uncertain'. Together they represent something like the antithesis of the life Steven desired; but he was fascinated at the same time by their recurrence in history. He carried this contradiction in his own personality; he loathed violence, bullying and discourtesy, but was himself capable of coldly psychological cruelty, casual, deliberate and not infrequently both. He lived a frugal but a particular life, its privations and its adornments carefully selected. He required routine and stability in his personal habits, but rarely missed a chance for strange, far-flung travels, and delighted in springing the unexpected upon others.

Runciman's reading of the earliest heresies is passionate and engaging, but its emphasis on spectacular curiosities conveys an impression of sleight-of-hand, stronger on verve than quantifiable value, like the esoteric encyclicals of the Patriarch Photius to his barbarian convert Boris of Bulgaria, rigged up to startle rather than enlighten. He received wide if ambivalent praise for his 'careful and mildly cynical exposition' and his 'light, bemused style'. These reviews contain a germ of the same assumption – that Runciman was not entirely serious. It may be salutary to consider instead the possibility that he was. With the leisurely air of one who knows, he states that the origin of Gnosticism 'is to be sought in the age-long magical tradition'. He shows a capacious (or, as the *Journal of Bible and Religion* had it, capricious) grasp of the oddest and smallest offshoots of the general movement:

Sects arose that gave reverence to Cain, to the Sodomites and to the Egyptians. Above all, the Serpent was applauded . . . under the name of the Ophites, the Serpent-worshippers; and dark stories were told of their practices. Nor . . . were the stories entirely unjustified . . . certain of the sects were frankly licentious . . .

. . . Moreover, the tendency towards magic, fashionable at the time, had a strong effect.

Part of Runciman's case for the connection between Gnosticism and the later heresies on the one hand and magical processes on the other was indeed a rational point about the workings of the heretical hierarchies. Gnosticism and its successors preserved from the earliest forms of Christianity an adult ceremony of baptism, of vastly greater spiritual importance than the orthodox, infantile variety. It was typically administered either at the deathbed of a rank-and-file believer, or in order to create an exalted, exemplary form of priesthood, a 'spiritual aristocracy'. The powers thought to be conveyed by this ceremony were hardly distinguishable from magic, and so 'the initiate became to some degree a magician.'

From the various 'Gnostic extravagancies' with their 'taste for fairy stories', Runciman now proceeded in the *Manichee* to tell a story that, like that of medieval Bulgaria, was his to trace afresh for a lay English public. In treating the Paulicians of Armenia, he relied, as with Bulgaria and Zlatarski, on older work, while confronting it with flagrant but persuasive ingratitude. The previous English authority on the Paulicians was the lately deceased Frederick Cornwallis Conybeare, a Dreyfusard, pacifist Oxford don who, in Runciman's estimation, was 'as an Armenist . . . excellent, and careful as a theologian. But his use of historical evidence sometimes betrays more hasty enthusiasm than judgment.' By faulting Conybeare's knack of interpretation while gracefully acknowledging his linguistic competence, Runciman could incorporate the marrow of his work, the Armenian texts he had discovered, translated and edited, while preferring his own view of their significance. 'I disagree with almost all [Conybeare's] conclusions,' he explained cheerfully, 'but every student of the Armenian Church must be grateful to his memory.'

Conybeare had in 1891 unearthed, from the library of the Holy Synod at Edjmiatzin (modern-day Vagharshapat), in Armenia, the main text which casts light on the theology of the Paulicians, *The*

*Key of Truth.* The preface he wrote to its translation, seven years later, is a breathless story of gradual realization:

> My first impression on looking into it afresh was one of disappointment. I had expected to find in it . . . at least a Manichean book; but, beyond the extremely sparse use made in it of the Old Testament, I found nothing that savoured of these ancient heresies . . .
>
> . . . now at last I understood who the Paulicians really were. All who had written about them had been misread by the calumnies of Photius . . . and other Greek writers, who describe them as Manicheans. I now realized that I had stumbled on the monument of a phase of the Christian Church so old and so out-worn, that the very memory of it was well-nigh lost.

Runciman's Byzantinophile pen naturally writes the 'calumnies' of his admired Patriarch Photius and the other Greek authorities firmly back into the narrative. He will have none of Conybeare's romantic and delighted certainty that these are Christian 'Old Believers' rather than just another link in his interlocking chain of dualist heresies.

Conybeare admitted that he had first been drawn to the Paulicians by Gibbon, whose brief account of the sect in *The Decline and Fall of the Roman Empire* is even more admiring and romantic. With scarcely a pinch of his usual detachment, Gibbon declared that the Paulicians 'investigated the creed of primitive Christianity; and whatever might be the success, a Protestant reader will applaud the spirit of the enquiry.' He also saw them as both reformers against theocracy ('their liberty was enlarged, as they reduced the number of masters at whose voice profane reason must bow to mystery and miracle') and justified rebels against tyranny ('It is not unpleasing to observe the triumph of rebellion over the same despotism which has disdained the prayers of an injured people'); and, all in all, incorporates them into the victorious progress towards Western Enlightenment ('the seeds of reformation'). Gibbon claims and sentimentalizes the Paulicians very much as Milton had done the Waldensians of Piedmont in his sonnet of 1655 ('Even them who kept thy truth so pure of old, / When all our fathers worshipped stocks and stones').

Runciman set himself the task of briefly sketching a more disinterested and truly sceptical version, which might also capture more detail, theological, political and personal. More important than a Protestant future to his evocation of the Paulicians was a complex Armenian past, the story of a territory contested militarily and intellectually, proud to regard itself as the Cradle of Mankind, at Mount Ararat after the Flood, but regularly subjected to the campaigning seasons of Roman and Persian armies, and the vying of the great religions they brought with them. Even leaving dualism aside, the ecclesiastic situation, Runciman made clear, was ticklish. 'The Armenian Church, from injured pride and petty patriotism rather than from deep theological sentiment', had lapsed from formal Orthodox uniformity and control; yet he notes an Armenian canon against employing heretical housekeepers, and many of the bitterest sources on the Paulicians he uses come from the Armenian clergy. The very name of the Paulicians is parsed by Runciman in a more local, specific fashion. Where Gibbon and Conybeare accept the idea of its alluding to a purer reading of St Paul's epistles, he eventually decides on an obscurer, Armenian Paul, not neglecting mischievously to emphasize that Paulicians, literally translated, 'must be either the followers of some contemptible Paul or the contemptible followers of Paul'. With his invariable flair for the utterly unexpected witness, he cites the travels of Lady Mary Wortley Montagu as evidence that, by at least the eighteenth century, the remaining Paulicians had entirely forgotten their origin and the purpose or nature of their distinctness from Orthodoxy. 'The history of the Paulicians contains many definite facts. Their doctrines must remain largely a matter of conjecture.'

Having established to his own and the bamboozled reader's satisfaction that, although we do not know what the Paulicians thought, it was almost certainly very peculiar, Runciman takes us through a streamlined performance that he will repeat in the cases of the Patarenes in Bosnia and the Cathars of France, a process of which he had already proved his mastery in *The First Bulgarian Empire*. Thus the story of the Paulicians becomes in his hands the brisk political biography of 'a free-booting state under Arab suzerainty', holding out on the fringes of Armenia, and sustaining itself 'in happy anarchy, raiding the Empire and collecting slaves to sell to the infidel'. The heretic leaders are notable for military ability, nepotism, treachery and euphony. 'Chrysocheir came of a good Greek family,' yet turned his back on his smart Constantinopolitan relations, which 'justifiably annoyed' the Emperor. Runciman notes approvingly that Chrysocheir and his uncle and predecessor, Carbeas, 'remained merely military leaders and were never admitted into the ranks of the Initiate'; he has an ironist's appreciation for a dualist sect that 'had sufficient truck with matter to use material things in self-defence'. The Bogomils, on the other hand, who according to his thesis carried on the Paulician tradition, 'found it a more useful weapon to adopt a practice fully consistent with their doctrines, that of passive resistance'. Runciman is tempted to associate Bogomilism with the Marxist drift of historiography from which he recoils in his own day. 'Their struggle was visibly one of class ... and in class-warfare the strike rather than active hostility is the weaker side's better policy.'

Bogomilism is most lively in Runciman's eyes (and prose) when it has settled in a specific geographical and social structure, and become a sort of 'state religion' in Bosnia, complete with a dynasty of rulers and a hierarchical local church. This is the phase mostly covered in his discussion of the 'Patarenes' (a term more usually employed, for example by Marco Polo, as a vague and generic term for heretics in northern Italy). An ill-fated papal attempt to deal with Bosnian heresy extracts from Runciman *en passant* a paragraph-long anecdote that sounds like the premise of an historical novel:

> There happened to be at that moment in Hungary an impoverished Byzantine prince, John Angelus, son of the Emperor Isaac Angelus and of King Andrew's sister Margaret. He was to command the Crusade, and was advanced 200 silver marks by the Archbishop. But, together with the money, John Angelus disappears from history, despite an angry letter from the Pope.

Runciman's notionally central argument in the *Manichee*, that 'the political impulse is not everything', is contradicted by the drift of his style. He remarks that, after the Ottoman conquest of Bosnia, Bogomilism was 'a national dress that could easily be taken off and forgotten'. 'Weak and evanescent' the Bosnian monarchy may have shown itself in the end to be, but with its kingly names, Ninoslav or Dragutin, its conversions, bastardies and dissensions, it cannot help leaving a more vivid impression than Runciman's impishly mysterious account of the religion behind it. It is no coincidence that in *The First Bulgarian Empire*, Runciman unstintingly enjoys himself at the rebellious mountain court, 'land of high lakes and valleys', of the Tsar Samuel and his bickering successors:

> Comforts might be crude, but there was romance too in the Bulgarian Court. The Tsar, by his wife Agatha Chryselia, had several children whose wild passions brought love into Bulgarian history . . .
>
> . . . There was at the court of Ochrida a slave called Irene, who had been captured as a child at the fall of Larissa, a creature of marvellous beauty. The Princess, probably all too well endowed with the looks of her father's race, the race that gave its name to ogres, could never hope to rival the radiant Greek captive . . .

There is much more of this: a genial but naive prince intercedes for his cousin's life, only to be, in the end, murdered by that cousin; a wife pleads with her husband not to attend a parley, only to witness miracles by the side of his slaughtered but sanctified corpse; a proud and ambitious old general is blinded in the privacy of his own orchard. But during all these dramatic goings-on the Bogomils have been respectably but firmly shunted out of any role of active importance. They merely 'made no complaint against [Samuel's] rule, either from indifference or from terror'. In the *Manichee* Runciman goes so far as to opine, with that occasional weakness for teleology which he had absorbed from G. M. Trevelyan, that 'Their passivity was not in tune with the time.'

At last Runciman comes to rest upon the Cathars, the aspect of his subject best known to his Western readership. The story of the Cathars still attracts regular attempts at revisionism. As the scholarly view of heresy in the Languedoc has shifted from proto-Protestantism to *sub rosa* dualism to home-grown anti-clericalism, and frequently back again, the popular version, with all its absurdities of conjecture and taste – involving Mary Magdalene, the Holy Grail, the Priory of Sion, the Templars and, not uncommonly, the Freemasons – outrides the specialists' theories, its shadow looming as vastly as the crag of Montségur where the heretics made their final stand. Runciman, too, had to confront this rock, not least because it was connected to an entire, fervid occultist passion for which he held more than a sneaking sympathy. But he refused to allow personal considerations to interfere with the force of his case:

> Modern occultists have liked to see themselves as the heirs of Cathar martyrs and to take Montségur as the Mt. Thabor of their magical tradition . . .
>
> There has been so much loose thinking, fostered in particular by the Theosophists and the Neo-Occultists, of the connection of the Dualist Tradition with Eastern religion on the one hand, and with the Occult Tradition on the other . . .
>
> The Cathars certainly gave Montségur, as their one physical place of refuge, high-sounding titles – but such names should never be taken literally. The castle had no spiritual significance for them. Catharism had nothing to do with Magic, Black or White. The idea that the treasure smuggled out of Montségur on the eve of its fall was the Grail itself is picturesque but untrue. The treasure may have included sacred books but was chiefly material treasure, money, a worldly commodity but one very necessary to a church.

The unaccustomed sobriety of this judgement yet leaves a trace of doubt. How can the historian dissever with such surgical confidence the knot of intractable heresies – whose contradictions and obscurities he has so lovingly illustrated – from Magic, Black or White, without more compendious knowledge of those queerer arts than he acknowledges here?

Yeats's second Byzantium poem is alive to this uncertainty:

> Before me floats an image, man or shade,
> Shade more than man, more image than a shade.

# 11

# Death

*Eigg, 1932; Cambridge, 1932–7; Spain, 1936;*
*Trebizond and Istanbul, 1937*

> . . . the passage into a state to which ordinary death is neither
> the path nor gate.
>
> Arthur Waite, *The Key to the Tarot*, 1920

> Best cut out all the talk of renewing
> And wordy philosophies of destroying –
> Easiest by far to tell them straight
> We don't do this for fun, and, joking apart
> We mean what we say, and don't care if we hurt,
> For there's plenty to do, and no time to wait.
>
> John Cornford, poem written at Cambridge, 1933

As Steven's young donhood progressed, he found that the familiar position in which he stood to his more agreeable pupils was shifting. 'When first I returned to Cambridge, I was very little older than the undergraduates; and my relationship to my friends amongst them was more or less that of an older brother.' In real life Steven was, all importantly, a younger brother. His bond with Leslie, after the difficulties over Steven's antipathy to Rosamond Lehmann had ceased to apply, was one of broad, bemused harmony; and it must have been exciting and pleasurable for Steven adopting his own brother's kindly protectiveness towards successive undergraduate cohorts at Trinity. But the convenient replaceability of these smart young men came to involve inevitable changes. Even a young don is not forever young, while 'undergraduates remain the same age, so that the relationship became more that of an uncle'. Steven found to his surprise that this change lent him social confidence. He made surer progress in undergraduate circles throughout the 1930s, even as his own undergraduate days had been dominated by charismatic dons such as Maynard Keynes, Frank Birch, Dennis Robertson and Gaillard Lapsley.

In the summer of 1932, Steven was for the first time in the enviable situation of having the laird's Lodge on the island of Eigg at his disposal, and that of his chosen guests. In the early 1920s his father had conceived a passion for Eigg, one of the Small Isles, with Rum and Muck, in the north of the Inner Hebrides. He had taken the chance to purchase it late in 1925 from the heiresses of a deceased rival shipowner, Sir William Petersen. Steven received news of the acquisition 'with delight' while he was still in China. Initially he always accompanied his family there, helping his parents to entertain various Liberal relics, would-be candidates and Whig offshoots, including Gerald France, Ida Swinburne and Janet Trevelyan. The first time his father let Steven bring a friend of his own, in 1929, he played safe by inviting a respectable Trinity scientist, Maurice Black, best known for his comprehensive collection of rocks, although they had relatively little common ground. In fact Steven found the company of an undergraduate named Donald, a son of family friends invited by the Runciman parents, the Macleans, definitely more engaging.

Steven's initial caution paid off. By 1932, while his father, now President of the Board of Trade under Baldwin, and Hilda were away at the Lausanne Conference, Steven was left in possession of the island in its most glorious summer months. He could offer as many and as remarkable friends as he liked the run of a house and gardens in whose design he had himself dabbled. This time the Trinity cast was more diverse. Outram Evennett and Norman de Bruyne were young Fellows, like Steven himself; Evennett was a Catholic, a 'first-class pianist' and another historian, specializing on the Council of Trent; de Bruyne, Trinity's Junior Bursar, 'a wonderful purveyor of all the College gossip', would later make his name and fortune as an aeronautical engineer. The presence of the older artist Douglas Davidson, who amid the ongoing froideur between Steven and Dadie Rylands over Dadie's fondness for Rosamond Lehmann was indisputably Steven's closest friend, was only to be expected. Oswald Balfour, a favourite nephew of the one-time Prime Minister, Steven teasingly described as one of a circle of 'middle-aged bachelors' (Balfour was thirty-eight, nine years older than Steven), 'where one will best find a husband for darling Ruie'. In the event he decided Balfour 'is not suitable, I think (drinks a bit too much) . . . from the generation which was just all through the war, and they've never got over it – perhaps naturally'.* Then there was Wake Thring, a blond Achilles more athletic than intellectual in his interests, who had held and won a private Cambridge undergraduate Olympics during the spring just past. With rank and beauty thus represented, it was left to one of Steven's most original and startling pupils to exemplify the youthful life of the mind. This was an irrepressibly charming though revoltingly unhygienic Etonian eccentric of twenty-one, Guy Burgess.

Steven was already an enthusiastic photographer, and during this first of his personal Eigg house-parties it is Burgess (not the more conventionally good-looking Thring) who draws the most attention from his lens. Bearing in mind Steven's high standards, both physical and moral, it is on the face of it a bizarre anomaly that he should have tolerated, let alone favoured, a boy like Guy Burgess. But Burgess tended in his dealings with his many friends to prove an exception to every kind of rule. Steven recalls that 'I quite often, when he came to see me, either for supervision or a social call, had to send him away to clean his fingernails.' Yet Guy became a favourite pupil, whom Steven urged to stay on for further study at Cambridge, repeatedly invited to his rooms and even, at this first opportunity, to Eigg. Steven's strictures seem to have been in equal measure theoretical and flirtatious. To Kitty Steven mentioned Guy as 'the undergraduate whom I find most intelligent and sympathique at the moment, though his teeth are too far apart'.

Burgess had arrived at Trinity to read history in 1930. His background was comfortably military; his father, an elderly naval officer, had, as Guy liked to inform his friends with some relish, expired *in flagrante* with his mother before his small son's inquisitive eyes. The

---

* Arthur Balfour had himself, as he related in a letter to Walter Runciman, spent blissful summers birds'-nesting on Eigg while his own Prime Ministerial uncle, Lord Salisbury, was proprietor of its neighbouring island, Rum.

boy dropped out of Eton to attend the Royal Naval College at Dartmouth, but, his father's ghost apparently unlaid, he dropped back in again and garnered a scholarship to Trinity. He would later claim to have been committed to Marxism even at school, but when Steven knew him as an undergraduate Burgess appeared to be, if anything, a High Tory. He was devoted to the memory of the great imperialist Prime Minister Lord Salisbury, and admired above all other passages of English prose the romantic threnody of Lord Justice Crewe to the old nobility of the realm:

> And yet Time hath his revolutions: there must be an end to all temporal things, finis rerum, – an end of names and dignities, and whatsoever is terrene; and why not of De Vere? For where is De Bohun? – where is Mowbray? – where is Mortimer? Nay, what is more and most of all, where is Plantagenet? They are entombed in the urns and sepulchres of mortality.

A slightly later lover of Burgess's, Micky Burn, remembered him describing these as 'the most moving sentences there are'. This nostalgic *cri de coeur* in praise of Crewe's peroration was overheard as Burgess's habitual setpiece both before and after his conversion to Communism, during his first year of postgraduate life in 1933. Contradictory in his attitudes, he was, at least, consistent in his contradictions. Physically Burgess looked confident and luscious, but almost prematurely depraved, his high complexion arranged in both dimples and jowls. He had the body of a keen amateur cricketer with a hearty appetite. In fact his favourite delectations, leaving aside voracious carnal exercise, were cloves of garlic taken raw and equally unadulterated liquor. His breath was often compared to that of a dragon, but his smile, smugly wicked, was nonetheless part of the exceptionally persuasive arsenal of his personality. Burgess was said by a close heterosexual friend, Goronwy Rees, to have obtained conspiratorial intimacy with so many of his contemporaries partly because of his worldly, uninhibited sexual expertise. This was perhaps acquired during his schooling, which, for all the 'eccentric Etonian' label, had been formed as much of amphibious racketiness as grand conventionality. Rees, who had himself resisted Guy's amiably immediate advances at their first meeting, continued:

He was gross and even brutal in his treatment of his lovers, but his sexual behaviour had a generous aspect. He . . . had none of the inhibitions which were then common to young men of his age, class, and education. He regarded sex as a useful machine for the manufacture of pleasure . . . Guy had the faculty of retaining the affection of those he went to bed with, and also, in a curious way, of maintaining a kind of permanent domination over them . . .

Steven was older than most of the connections to whom Rees alludes here, and less shockable; he would doubtless have approved of Guy's no-nonsense, unsentimental Epicureanism, at least in theory. But it is certainly the case that Guy 'retained his affection', and as to 'permanent domination', if theirs was a 'master–pupil relationship' (as Rees fleetingly alludes to Burgess's relation to Steven) it would over the next decade come close to reversal.

At any rate Steven describes the Guy Burgess of June 1932 as no more than 'a bit grubby' (already lenient) and not remotely Communistic, 'showing no wish to abandon the pleasures of traditional good living'. At some point Guy gave a pair of bronze French Empire candlesticks to Steven, in return, as Steven later told it, for his having prevented Trinity from sending Guy down over an unspecified disgrace. Though Guy was a promising, rewarding pupil with powers of articulacy that seemed both original and plausible, before his final examinations he seemed to suffer from some kind of nervous lapse (it has been suggested that this 'breakdown' was brought on by alcohol and benzedrine). Burgess's Part I papers at the end of his first year at Trinity had gained him an airy First. Now Steven found himself in the mildly embarrassing position of having to vouch for this star pupil meriting an *aegrotat* (or automatic pass degree necessitated by illness), as Burgess announced himself too thrown by his mental state to take any final papers at all. That Steven responded to this apparent disappointment by inviting Guy to the wholesome atmosphere of Eigg indicates both Steven's solicitude for pupils who had won his affection and the extent of his liking for Guy in particular. It also speaks of Burgess's genuine talent, potential and originality. Steven was joined in his efforts to keep Guy at Trinity by his old family friend G. M. Trevelyan, the great narrative historian of his day.

Steven and Trevelyan were not merely bending the rules to oblige a pet, but recruiting to their college what they considered a remarkable mind. Rees is, once again, an observant witness of Guy's abilities when it came to historical structure, insight and imagination:

> The truth is that Guy, in his sober moments, had a power of historical generalization which is one of the rarest intellectual faculties, and which gave conversation with him on political subjects a unique charm and fascination. It was a power which was, I think, completely native and instinctive to him. It might have made him a great historian; instead it made him a communist. He saw historical events as following rational and intelligible principles and as developing according to general laws . . . In all Guy's comments on history and politics, illuminating though they often were . . . there was a myth-making element which belonged to art rather than sober fact.

Guy, then, had a tendency towards teleology which must have thrilled the old-style Whig Trevelyan, and which Steven, though he disagreed in principle, found compelling in this particular guise. Guy's mythomaniac plausibility also happened to cohere with Steven's convictions on Clio, Muse and snob.

Another favourite undergraduate whom Steven invited to Eigg in the aftermath of a disastrous Cambridge downfall was Robert Hamer, who would find a measure of fame as a director of post-war Ealing comedies, notably *Kind Hearts and Coronets*. Steven had him to stay at the Lodge in the summer of 1933, the year after Burgess, after Hamer had scraped a third-class degree. A close mutual friend of both Hamer and Steven, the future composer Geoffrey Wright, at Corpus with Hamer, explained in an interview with the film historian Charles Drazin that Hamer had been betrayed by a contemporary with whom he was deeply in love, had been sent down for a year as a consequence of the ensuing scandal and had never afterwards recovered his intellectual *esprit*. Hamer now joined the very select company of Steven and Douglas Davidson; and judging by Steven's array of photographs of this then entirely obscure young man sunbathing in near-total undress, his host took a strong interest in him. Hamer shared with Steven's early schoolfriend Anthony 'Puffin' Asquith real directorial brilliance and a destructive relationship with drink. He married an actress and lived with the daughter of one of his producers, but his closest friend, the screenwriter Diana Morgan, thought he would have been happier had he accepted his homosexual inclinations.

Even as he exhorted Guy Burgess under the bright Hebridean sky to remain at Trinity, Steven had made the same decision for himself, with an access of relief, a vague sense of destiny fulfilled and a more definite knowledge of practical improvement in his position. At first his somewhat precarious four-year prize fellowship, with its emoluments of £300 a year (equivalent to about £15,000 today), had obliged his ornate taste to yield to ancestral caution. Irritated by the costs of his first book's printing in 1929, Steven confessed himself 'altogether rather bitter on the subject of subsidized Presses run by semi-Dons'.* But in the summer of 1930 his old tutor and patron upon the academic *cursus honorum*, Lapsley, hinted that better times would not be long in coming; Lapsley was to retire in two years, and had persuaded the college that Steven should be his successor, a full and permanent Fellow in history at Trinity. Typically Steven reacted to the good news with sudden, private doubt:

> If I'm going in for an academic teaching career, here is the best offer which it is possible to get – even the pay for an academic post isn't bad – rising from about £450 I think with the perquisites of a Fellow. But teaching here now is a full time job in term-time; what research one wants to do must be done in the vacation when one has finished writing one's lectures . . .
>
> But the question really is: do I want to side-track my life by staying, settled and fully occupied in teaching youths Medieval European & English Economic history, in this pleasant but rather unreal atmosphere – which will I think seem less pleasant the older I get? I have a feeling that I ought

---

* After Cambridge University Press had sent him their final invoice, Steven had to pay £100 more than he expected for his publishers' 'not sufficiently business-like' services (SR to WR, 16 October 1929, Elshieshields). Since his father had lately bought him a car, which he detested, he felt inadequate and dependent in applying for more help, but Walter Runciman insisted on paying the supplementary sum and Steven could salvage his dignity only by handing over the £47 17 shillings that *Romanus Lecapenus* earned in its first year's royalties.

to be able to lead a fuller and more interesting life elsewhere – though where, I don't know. A semi-academic life is rather unstable and may well be unsatisfactory; there is a lot to be said for settling down properly to the academic career – particularly as I have got a sentiment for this place and feel pride in actually being a Fellow.

Altogether I'm still in a slight muddle as to what I really do think.

By 1932, when the decision had to be made or missed, the muddle had given way to radiant clarity. Steven's initial uncertainty and his later resolution share an origin. He was surely remembering the advice and the warning that Trevelyan had given him on that first evening in 1927 when, freshly returned from the French hospitality of Edith Wharton, he dined at Trinity as a Prize Fellow:

> the most distinguished of the new Fellows, Trevelyan, had been a Prize Fellow in his younger days and then had left Cambridge in order to be free to write his books without the distraction of a University career. Now . . . newly appointed to the Regius Chair of History at Cambridge, he was re-admitted . . . After the dinner he took me aside and advised me to follow his example . . . to take full advantage of my Prize Fellowship for the opportunities that it would give me for research . . . But if I wanted to concentrate on writing I ought to escape from Cambridge . . .

Trevelyan's tactfully implied warning about the burden of teaching, lecturing and, increasingly, administration that a full fellowship would involve, and its adverse effect on literary fecundity, had already by 1932 come partially true. In early 1930 Steven was planning a popular biography of the German Emperor Otto III, which might have brought him to the attention of the general reading public twenty-five years before *A History of the Crusades* and *The Sicilian Vespers*:

> I am being filled with enthusiasm for my book on Otto III, which I shall write next term. It will be really a biography, but the biography of an Emperor always involves a lot else, and of this Emperor involves most of the fundamental theories of the Middle Ages. It won't be a monument of profound erudition, but I'm finding that a certain amount of original research has to be done.

But no biography or monument, profound or not, came to pass. The work Steven ended up rushing out instead in 1933, *Byzantine Civilization*, was drily disappointing. Only in his last two years as a don did Steven settle to the more characteristic *Medieval Manichee*, whose publication was then stymied by war. All the same, by 1932 Trevelyan had come round to the idea of young Runciman as a proper Fellow of Trinity, as Steven recounts:

> I received a letter from the Master . . . offering me a Fellowship and an Assistant Lectureship in History, and a letter from [Jim] Butler saying on behalf of the History staff how much they hoped I would accept – a very nice letter, though the History staff would naturally hope it, as otherwise they'd all have more work to do! And while I was drowsily contemplating these letters, lying in bed – it was 8.10 AM – I heard someone in my sitting-room ask for me, and emerged to find George Trevelyan, who had come to make sure that I was going to accept.\* I have accepted . . . [Trevelyan] talked a lot about it – certain from the point of view of a career etc. that I ought to accept, particularly if I could manage to leave after 5 or 10 years. The appointment is a five yearly one, and is always renewed except in cases of gross misconduct – though even so I should always be able to appeal to the King . . .

That early-morning consultation was a product of circumstances that also helped Steven to decide; he was still living in his old undergraduate rooms in the Great Court. A permanent fellowship entailed translation to the more secluded Nevile's Court, where an accessible and private lavatory and kitchenette were the most mundane, if not the least essential, of the benefits to be considered: 'I no longer had to walk across a court in my dressing-gown to take a bath.' Here Steven was more sparing with his furniture than he had been as an excitable, newly semi-independent undergraduate, and

---

\* When Steven was an undergraduate and a young don, his elders seem to have been by convention remarkably free with imposing their advice on uneasily grateful younger protégés. Steven himself carried on this tradition into a less deferential age; some pupils appreciated these uninvited interventions more than others: Noel Annan, for instance, was prickly, Donald Nicol appreciative. Steven was less typical of his generation in himself accepting professional help from pupils such as Guy Burgess and Michael Grant.

Benedict the parakeet did not follow him. During Steven's absence in China the bird had become inseparably attached to the college servant with whom his master had deposited him, and by her was rechristened and resexed as Polly; she would only be returned in time for the taxidermist. The dulcitone tinkled on regardless. When Stewart Perowne called by the new rooms to offer Steven his congratulations, he was titillated by a mounted letter to Princess Alexandrina, the future Queen Victoria, from her Aunt Adelaide, Queen Consort to William IV. In what was to become the most famous touch of all, Steven 'proceeded to embellish the room with a French grisaille wallpaper of the 1820s which I had discovered, illustrating the legend of Cupid and Psyche'. The adjacent rooms offered 'a celebrated study in contrast' – starkly functional, they were inhabited by a brilliant but unclubbable twenty-two-year-old Fellow in Classics, Enoch Powell.

Steven tended to be popular with the mothers and aunts of his pupils, who thought of him as a reliable source of entertaining yet reassuring gossip on the wild, well-born boys they had dispatched to Cambridge but feared they might have lost to Newmarket. Two of his most admired charges, in particular, came to him burdened with anxious maternal recommendations and advice. There was George Jellicoe, 'the son and heir of the Admiral', John, 1st Earl Jellicoe, victor of the Battle of Jutland, and well disposed to Walter Runciman. His mother, the Admiral's widow, instructed Steven to introduce George to 'all the right people', and was irked when Steven not very innocently reported that her son was working hard and consorting with all Cambridge's best scholars. Steven and George Jellicoe's friendship would be lasting and opportune, but for the moment a still more important catch was Peter Montgomery, a handsome and musical boy from an Ascendancy family in County Tyrone, whose aunt, a friend of Hilda Runciman's, had urged Steven to safeguard his morals. Peter Montgomery's circle of friends and lovers brought Steven into a number of fateful dramas. Montgomery's future was to be a sad one, oppressed by the division of his native island, the increasing irreconcilability of tenants and friends, into an alcoholic detachment alien to his real temperament. But in the late 1920s and early 1930s he was untouched by history, on or off the Cambridge course, and was exceedingly attractive in appearance and behaviour. Steven was far from the only young don with an interest in this bewitching and leisurely young man. His leading competitor was a slightly younger Prize Fellow, Anthony Blunt.

Three years younger than Steven, Blunt already ranked highly in this college of prodigies. Steven could not fault 'his knowledge and genuine care for works of art', nor quite articulate his dislike of Blunt's coldly accurate sense of humour. Superficially these two young Trinity Fellows had much in common, in specific questions of circumstance and taste quite as much as in their shared sexuality. Like Steven, Blunt had a stern, God-fearing mother named Hilda, to whom he remained emotionally close, but whose standards and strictures he was delighted to have evaded. His rooms, their walls half covered with enormous prints of Poussins, were almost as splendid as Steven's. Blunt remained always formally courteous and friendly; but Steven felt disapproved of, even teased, and withheld his own friendship as best he could, despite their increasing number of connections in and out of Trinity.

Blunt was a precociously recruited Apostle, and Steven, though friendly with individual members of the Society, always thought the Apostles collectively absurd. When they began with something close to unanimity to espouse Marxism he concluded that the group was losing even its capacity to be amusing in company. Guy Burgess at some point gossiped that Steven himself 'had been proposed as a member, but was, rightly, turned down as being politically incorrect'. Steven would in any case have avoided such a doubtful entrance to a circle unlikely to appeal to his real interests, offered by the hands of juniors he considered beneath him, whether Guy, whom he couldn't help liking, or Blunt, whom he equally involuntarily detested. In an interview for a biography of Blunt Steven remembered him as 'pleased with himself' and 'supercilious'; in his 'Footnotes to a Long Life' he approached the nub of the matter more closely: 'His manner towards me was definitely somewhat patronizing; and one does not enjoy being patronized by one's juniors.' As a Prize Fellow Blunt in theory held equal rank at Trinity to Steven, but Steven would never acknowledge him as much more than a sharp-tongued schoolboy. On learning of Blunt's lifelong treason in the service of the Soviets in 1979, Steven would splutter, 'I never fully realized why I disliked him. Now I do.'

One of the rare occasions when Steven let Blunt see that he had felt any substantial slight occurred on an evening in November 1934, when Blunt collaborated in a practical joke with Guy Burgess and Dadie Rylands (himself only just back in favour with Steven). They had all been invited, along with several others including Victor Rothschild and his new wife Barbara, to a party under the benevolent aegis of Cupid and Psyche. Blunt had earned his admission as an ever-more inseparable friend of Guy, and even Steven now and then admitted to finding his company interesting. Blunt, the Rothschilds, Guy and Dadie all connived in smuggling in a supplementary guest, Lady Mary Dunn, disguised as a youthful undergraduate with the aid of a severe Eton bob and a capacious dinner-jacket. Steven was visibly annoyed and the story was subsequently told against him by Lady Mary, as the caricature of a misogynistic, precious queen. She implies that Steven resented the pollution of his rooms by a female presence after hours, in contradiction to college regulations. Steven's engagement diaries, which clearly show the presence of Barbara Rothschild at the party, belie an already unlikely story – Steven was not, leaving aside his odd and inconsistent prejudice against lesbians, misogynistic, and often enough entertained women – for instance Fredegond Shove and Elinor Wylie – in the evening.

Steven's irritation was real, but had different causes. Both Victor Rothschild and Mary Dunn were recently married; Anthony Blunt had briefly acted as Lady Mary's acknowledged suitor in 1930; the arrangement that evening seems more likely to have been that Blunt was adopting his old pose of *cavaliere servente* in order to assist the resumption of an existing, on-off romance between Rothschild and Lady Mary. This sort of charade was positively enjoyable to, for example, Dadie Rylands, but to Steven, though it might entertain him in the form of gossip, in closer proximity it possessed a depressing staleness. His sympathies would have lain with Barbara Rothschild and her mother, Mary Hutchinson, a kindly Bloomsbury hostess of his.* Besides, he had a less altruistic but quite understandable

* For her part Barbara Rothschild neither liked nor trusted Blunt by instinct, while her sister-in-law, Miriam Rothschild, skewered him by complaining that he had 'iced coffee in his veins instead of blood'. Barbara was herself unfaithful to Victor,

grievance. Blunt, as Steven well knew, was by now enjoying the attention of Peter Montgomery, whose attractions Steven also felt keenly;
it was, then, additionally galling to have to put up with Blunt acting
the heterosexual roué while shielding a genuine rake. Besides, with
his comic-opera stratagem of the disguised boy-bride, Blunt had
teased Steven in front of Dadie, a very old friend on delicate, newly
re-established terms with his host after the Rosamond rift, and Guy,
for whose moral and intellectual, if not physical, delectation Blunt
and Steven were now increasingly competing. These were not easily
forgivable infractions.

Steven's renewed friendship with Dadie, however, proved resilient.
The pair who, with their friends and votaries, had as undergraduates
elicited the half-scornful, half-envious sobriquet of the 'Tea Party
Cats' from Frank Birch, now pooled their preferred undergraduates
and companions again, forming the nub of another, longer-lasting
set. Dadie was the acknowledged chieftain of all theatrical goings-on
in the University, and gave it as his opinion that the best student actor
was by some distance not the dignified Michael Redgrave, born to
the purple of silent movies, but an emergent comedian, the son of an
electrician, famous for his 'almost sylphlike' transvestite turns,
Arthur Marshall. Academically, as opposed to histrionically, Dadie
identified his brightest talent as a quondam head boy from Stowe,
Noel Annan. The new inner ring demonstrated its catholicity by
incorporating as a member one who was neither an undergraduate,
nor even a man, Anne Barnes. Her husband worked for Cambridge
University Press, Steven's already loathed publisher, and their son
was a baby, but Mrs Barnes rarely missed a gathering at Dadie's or at
Steven's rooms, unencumbered by her dependent males. She could
match Arthur Marshall bottle for bottle, but was overtaken in dissi-
pation by a young Trinity historian adopted by the group at Steven's
pressing suggestion, Edward Bates.

The short story of Eddie Bates's life bears a weird kinship to the
long promenade of Steven's. Steven was always an advocate of
employing counterfactual thought in his historical narratives, and

---

and earned the distinction of being called 'a bad girl' by Dadie Rylands. (Miranda
Carter, *Anthony Blunt: His Lives* (Macmillan, 2001), pp. 99, 183.)

Eddie Bates's floundering, hedonistic, charming career provides a succession of might-have-been glosses upon Steven's career and private life. The younger man illustrates the obverse of the good luck of which Steven was always conscious and the self-protective qualities which he instilled in himself from an early age. Eddie was born in 1913 into a much longer-established family than that of the Runcimans, notable in the identical domains of shipping and of politics, the fiercely Tory Bateses. Eddie's father, Sir Percy Bates, 4th Baronet, of Hinderton Hall, a sandstone early Waterhouse redoubt in the north of Cheshire, became Chairman of the mightily merged White Star-Cunard line in 1930. Upon Eddie had fallen the misfortune which Steven was always thankful to have escaped – he was his father's only son and heir. Sir Percy, according to his entry in the *Oxford Dictionary of National Biography*, 'was terse in speech and judgement: he never encumbered his talk with platitudes, or troubled to obscure the directness of his thought. Such characteristics [were] allied with a determined jaw, and, on occasion, an emphatic manner.' He was a father more like the older Walter Runciman, that proverbial family ogre, than the younger, with his principles, his dignity, his distant, high standard of public service and his never quite exorcized shadow of hesitation.

Eddie's mother, Mary Ann, daughter of a Dean of Norwich, nurtured religiosity of a Low persuasion less open-minded than the Scots Enlightenment ecumenism of the Runcimans. Hellfire warmed the sometimes striking images of her parental counsel. At Radley more hellfire followed for Eddie. The young man who reached Trinity in 1933, sick of the flames' lick, was lissom, stylishly tailored, his slightly pointed, puckish face displaying a debonair contempt as if in direct, reactive relation to his father's craggy solidity. He was thoroughly determined to have a good time in the more subversively fashionable aesthetic faction of undergraduate life. A direct Trinity contemporary of the Communist poet and ideologue John Cornford, Eddie was oddly – to Steven, attractively – untouched by the grimly iron age in which he had chanced to mature. About his every third word, spoken or written, tended to infectious cod-French. Noel Annan on his first acquaintance with Eddie was intimidated by his good looks and outrageous manners; but to his delighted surprise Eddie easily accepted and advanced him into the higher echelons of Dadie's and Steven's evenings, and was soon, indeed, giving him worldly love advice on the perils of 'naïf youths'.

Candidates who had distinguished themselves by their scholarship papers, their interviews or their genealogies were gossiped about and eagerly anticipated by the dons who formed their prospective supervisors before they had even materialized at Cambridge. John Cornford, in consequence, had already by the time he arrived at Trinity in 1934 been proclaimed 'the cleverest boy of his generation'. Certainly he turned out to be one of the best looking, with thick black curls and etched cheekbones worthy of some melancholy Russian princess, though Steven somewhat unconvincingly professed to find him physically 'very unattractive' from the start. John's parents were a professor of Latin and a poet, Frances Cornford, née Darwin, the childhood companion charmingly captured in Gwen Raverat's illustrated memoir *Period Piece*. Steven admitted Mrs Cornford to be 'intelligent and not unfriendly', but still *au fond* thought her 'grim and disagreeable'. But, 'having looked forward to teaching this paragon' John, he regretfully declared his supervisions with Cornford 'a disappointing experience'. Cornford dismissed him as a superannuated intellectual relic with a peremptory arrogance that might have called Steven's own disdain for the legendary Eton history master Tuppy Headlam, twelve years previously, ruefully back to his memory. Cornford had, quite literally, no time for Steven's general remit, medieval history, let alone the more specific and unusual course his supervisor was now offering on Eastern Europe. His mind was thorough and unswerving in its training:

> The essays that [Cornford] brought to me, whatever the subject, were full of the Marxist interpretation of history. While our interviews resulted in my acquiring a fuller knowledge of Marxist doctrine, he learnt nothing from me, brushing aside rather curtly any interpretation that I might attempt to give to, for example, early medieval politics. He was not, I thought, the cleverest youth that I had to try to teach that year. There was an extremely bright one, whom actually I found almost as irritating owing to his right-wing views; but he was prepared to listen to what I had to say and even admitted sometimes that he might have been wrong.

This second and more ultimately assimilable pest was Eddie Bates, though Steven was the only authority to vouch for his intellect, rather than his more evident looks and lovable disposition. Neither Bates nor Cornford would live to fulfil their promise as undergraduates in 1933. Cornford would undergo a form of leftist canonization that extended even to the body of formally conventional Rupert Brooke-like poems he left behind, but Bates, for quite deliberate reasons, would fade into obscurity.

Steven diagnosed both his would-be-protégé, Guy, and his hardening rival, Blunt, as being 'absolutely glamorised' by John Cornford. This was for Steven a convenient turn of phrase that allowed him to privilege the natural explanation of his eyes over the baffling evidence of his ears, that intelligent scholars, one an actual Fellow of Trinity and the other with hopes of becoming one, were offering their blind obedience to a callow and fanatical undergraduate. It was a question of the discipline and of the sexuality that they shared. Rather than accept that two men he had judged to be historically sensitive thinkers had embraced a counter-historical doctrine, a path he could scarcely understand, let alone emulate, he chose to see an old, comprehensible story – two Uranian pleasure-seekers hankering after a cold, narcissistic and unavailable heterosexual youth. John Cornford, indeed, soon fathered a son by a working-class Welsh girl, Ray Peters, with whom he lived in his Cambridge digs; at her he directed a small collection of mediocre verse that fused sexual with political excitement. It suited Steven to believe that this latter-day Puritan was couching his 'relentless' recruitment to Marxism in terms of insincere flirtation, and that the friend and foe he knew well were fools for love, not ideology.

Yet Steven had to admit that the ideology itself, so unappealingly rigid when its source was the zealous Cornford, sounded much more persuasive, organic and ductile when enlarged upon by Guy. Guy's Marxism was attractive in that it could not possibly be taken seriously; it seemed to run in such contradiction to his unvarying hedonism, and was otherwise a beast of many colours. To some Burgess would declare sympathy with Russia against America in continuation of Lord Salisbury's High Tory, imperialist diplomacy. To others, when oiled, he bragged of connections at the Soviet Embassy. Steven remained, politics aside, cautious about his former favourite's direction. Guy shifted his postgraduate thesis blithely from the causes of the seventeenth-century revolution in England to those of the Indian Mutiny of 1857; incidentally, the materialist, Marxist bent he brought to both subjects indicates that Guy was truthful about his sympathies all along, and that Steven, in attributing so much malign influence to John Cornford, was once again exercising wishful thinking.

Steven would claim to David Plante that about a year into Guy's research a definite correlation became noticeable: 'In his early days, Burgess was bright and had charm. As he grew older, the charm got murkier, and after he became a Communist he never washed.' This is probably unfairly tricked up for the punchline; Guy's hygiene had never approached the passable; that was almost part of his magnetism. In any case, Steven had to realize that he had been wrong to persuade Guy to stay on at Trinity; never a very convincing don, Burgess left Cambridge early in 1935, to pursue a picaresque temporary career that encompassed the Anglo-German Fellowship, the wilder reaches of the Conservative Party and the very first *Week in Westminster* broadcasts at the BBC. He remained a frequent and welcome visitor to Trinity, sometimes as Steven's guest and sometimes as Blunt's.

Another young Trinity historian was Courtenay Young, a cousin of Elinor Wylie's soldier inamorato Clifford Woodhouse; Steven also knew and admired two of Courtenay's uncles, Geoffrey Winthrop Young, the mountaineer, and Hilton Young, a Lloyd George Liberal politician, a close friend of Trevelyan and, through Thoby Stephen, Vanessa Bell and Virginia Woolf's brother, a Bloomsbury connection. Courtenay, with the encouragement of Steven, who lent him the translations from the Chinese of his own older friend Arthur Waley (also being devoured at this time by Michael Redgrave), switched from history to Chinese for the second half of his tripos. His future would lie with MI5. The Young family, of Formosa Place, a villa on the Thames named for the distant island eventually to become Taiwan, was headed by Sir George Young, 4th Baronet, the most mysterious and interesting of the family to Steven. Sir George was the wonder of the baronetage, a Communist polyglot, late of the Foreign Service, especially learned in Turkish and Portuguese. Steven was delighted when Courtenay invited him to his father's house in the south of Spain, near Torremolinos, Málaga, in the spring of 1936.

This was Steven's first visit to Spain. He had met Queen Ena of Spain through Baba Brougham, her one-time lady-in-waiting; she had confided in him her abhorrence of bullfights. He had glimpsed Ena's philandering and vacillating husband, King Alfonso XIII, with Marthe Bibesco, to whose favours the exiled King at least aspired; and most recently he had befriended the Infante Alfonso and his British Infanta Beatrice, as Mr and Mrs Orleans, at the dinner-table of his Eton contemporary George Wansbrough. With the Infanta Beatrice, Zita Jungman and Kathleen Alington, he had stood godparent to the Wansbroughs' son, Joseph. But of Spain and its increasingly eventful political circumstances he knew little, and the atmosphere in which he now arrived shocked him. The Orleanses had equipped him with a letter of introduction to the Duke of Alba to be proffered on his way through Madrid. Steven was thus armed with a passport to a world that was all but abolished.

Spain had been a moderate republic of doubtful stability since 1931, after the collapse of the military dictator Miguel Primo de Rivera, who had enjoyed King Alfonso's for once consistent support. But only recently had this state of affairs had much direct effect on the Spanish aristocrats Steven came across now and again in London; in February 1936 the Spanish left had assumed a febrile air of unity and triumphed electorally as the Popular Front. The result for Steven's entrée at Madrid was unfortunate:

> I don't like Madrid much – an ugly town and at its worst in wet weather. There's a curious unfriendly nervy excitable yet devitalized atmosphere – perhaps it is due to the height. The riots seem to have stopped; I suppose it's discouraging to be riotous in the rain, one still sees however churches smouldering on. My introduction to the Duke of Alba isn't much use, as he is in Paris, but I shall see his house. Titles are all firmly abolished in Spain; the nobility have all to use their family surnames – and as they all have dozens it is difficult to discover what they are now called. Everyone of course knows who the Duke of Alba is, but it took the concierge of this hotel and me hours poring over the telephone book before I, with my superior Almanach de

Gotha knowledge, identified him as Jacobo Stuart y Falco, and his house, the former Palacio de Liria, as 12 av. I. B. Ibanez.

The Duke's brother, Hernando Stuart y Falcó, was in residence to admit Steven's letter and show him about the neo-classical palace. Steven was fortunate to catch both the guide and the residence when he did; Hernando was among somewhere between one and two thousand civilians in the environs of Madrid suspected of Francoist sympathies to be rounded up and executed by firing squad in November, while the palace would be hit by seventeen fire-bombs dropped by Franco's air force early in 1937. Only the façades and a couple of particularly fine bathrooms survived, though many of the remarkable contents were rescued by Republican soldiers acting alongside ducal servants.

Steven now intermixed with a knot of moody, agitated, politically homogeneous young men, lounging aggressively in the city squares:

> They are all vehement royalists – the youth indeed seems to be royalist, the University so much so that it has been almost perpetually closed since the General Election that brought in the Left. The young men that I know are violently political, but otherwise seem to have no occupation. I gather they live on their estates, producing wine or cork. They all live with their parents, but one is never invited to the home; all their hospitality is done in cafés or restaurants. The women seem really still to live in a kind of purdah.

It must have all been an educative contrast to the young men of Cambridge, whose politics leaned with like inevitability in the opposite direction. It was back to this world that Steven now continued, to his Communist host Sir George at Torremolinos, paradoxically situated in Andalusia, a region which would stand firmly for Franco. After the tangible unease he had found in his fleeting encounter with the doomed youth of Madrid, Steven arrived at a more familiar and often absurd scene of English paradox:

> The house-party consists of Sir George and Lady Young and the son [Courtenay] whom I know at Cambridge: H A L Fisher, recovering from a nervous breakdown, and Mrs Fisher (Lady Young's sister) – and really if I had gone abroad from a nervous breakdown I should

have left Mrs Fisher behind – and their daughter Mary, a clever pleasant very un-got-up girl (no powder, no perm) of the First in Greats type: Mrs George Kennedy, wife of an architect whose Vandal hand is much seen at Cambridge (Keynes admires him) . . . with 2 sons, one a first-year Cambridge undergraduate, the other a bedridden cripple of 15 – and finally Miss Lim, a Chinese lady from Girton who had nowhere else to go for vacation. She is smart and dashing and I believe a great success at Cambridge. Sir George seems almost ga-ga and they half treat him as such.

H. A. L. Fisher, Warden of New College, a Napoleonic historian and Liberal statesman of splendidly martial appearance and portentous repute, was the cousin of Virginia and Vanessa Stephen, the brother-in-law of Ralph Vaughan Williams, and the uncle of Steven's poetical friend Fredegond Shove. More to the point, like Hilton Young, he was an adherent of Lloyd George* and so a political opponent of Walter and Hilda Runciman, for whose benefit Steven is guying him and his wife, the economist and suffragist Lettice Ilbert. Steven's analysis of their daughter was tart but not unfair; she rose to become Principal of St Hilda's College. Fisher himself was fatally hit by a lorry in 1940, and three years later his underclothes, found lying neatly folded in a drawer at New College, were arrayed on the dummy corpse used to decoy German intelligence in Operation Mincemeat.

Sir George insisted on showing Steven, against his protestations, the Málaga bull-ring. Lady Young and her brother-in-law, Fisher, both seemed averse to the idea for reasons that went beyond kind-hearted distaste for bloodsport; but Sir George was ungainsayable. When his guest reached the ring, he found it occupied not by bulls or fighters but by a seated circle of sand-spattered human beings, for the most part scowling, down-at-heel Spanish men, salted with 'two or three other equally eccentric English residents'. It proved that, as the matadors and picadors had in a body removed themselves and joined the rebel army in Morocco, the otherwise unoccupied bull-ring had become the

---

* The economist Lionel Robbins commented that the presence of Fisher in a Lloyd George coalition Cabinet had its similarity to 'a good man who had inadvertently entered a brothel – and rather enjoyed it' (Lionel Robbins quoted in Alan Ryan, 'Fisher, Herbert Albert Laurens', *ODNB*).

headquarters of the Málaga Communist Party, of which Sir George was honorary treasurer. Steven was thus once again caught in a claustrophobically unvaried political climate. After pondering the bellicose youths of Madrid and the idealists of Málaga (who included, for one meeting, Duncan Grant, on his way down to visit the Bloomsbury Hispanophile Gerald Brenan) Steven felt he could offer his grandfather, who believed, not altogether without prescience, that a Mussolini-figure was called for, a précis of the Spanish outlook:

> I think Spain is in a very unhappy state at the moment. The Communists are very strong and have managed to fuse the left-wing socialists with them; and they will soon get hold of the government. But I doubt if they will keep it – their communism is very childish and unpractical; and the right wing parties, monarchists and clericals, are uniting with the fascists, who are growing in numbers. Whatever happens, I am sure Spain is going to pass through a period of chaos, perhaps even civil war. I must say I am glad I am not a Spaniard.

At the same time he tweaked the older Walter with his passion for Mussolini's Blackshirts by observing that, despite the troubled atmosphere, English tourists abounded. 'Everywhere I met people that I knew, holidaying like myself. I suppose it is because no one wants to visit Italy now.'

Steven left Spain after nearly a month; three months after that, in July 1936, General Franco landed in Spanish Morocco, spirited from the Canaries with the aid of two plucky British aeronauts (one of them an intelligence agent), and the Civil War began. Just after Christmas, it would claim the life of one of the youngest and earliest British volunteers, John Cornford, killed at the age of twenty-one during the long and successful defence of Madrid against the Nationalists at the end of the year. The strangely logical fusion of Jingoism and Marxism in the verses for which he had been famous at Cambridge had, by the time he died, been developed by the experience of war and separation from his homeland and his two lovers, Ray Peters and Margot Heinemann, into a sudden and surprising vein of genuineness:

> Heart of the heartless world,
> Dear heart, the thought of you

Is the pain at my side,
The shadow that chills my view.

The wind rises in the evening,
Reminds that autumn is near.
I am afraid to lose you,
I am afraid of my fear.

Blunt, for one, could not entirely regret the death of the inflexible young beauty whom Steven had mocked as his and Guy's 'guru'. 'He was the stuff martyrs are made of, and I do not at all know what would have happened to him if he had survived. He was a highly emotional character and I strongly suspect that he might have gone back on his Marxist doctrine, and if so I think he would have suffered acutely.' Blunt, who had led his life in disloyal allegiance to a creed that reflected Cornford's youthful nature far more closely than his own mature one, felt more comfortable with the idea of the red star of Trinity as a fallen demi-god than as a disillusioned human being, in the pattern of, say, Orwell. Steven, who never brought himself to observe Cornford so closely, could not really accept the young idealist as an emotional being at all, any more, indeed, than he had accepted his old schoolfriend Eric Blair as one. Just as he considered that the novels of Orwell revealed 'inhuman detachment', and that Blair even as a boy had showed 'pity for the human condition rather than for the individual human', so his last word on Cornford would label him 'strange', 'extremely clever' (as he had not at first especially acknowledged), 'forceful, merciless, rather inhuman'. His anger with Cornford outlasted the boy's death, because he continued to care about and resent the effects of his legend on Guy, and even, to some degree, on the despised Blunt. It is salutary, perhaps, to remember that from the Cambridge Marxist perspective Steven, Dadie and their old-fashioned aestheticism were 'inhuman' too, as the highly flavoured rhetoric of Goronwy Rees has it:

Love of the arts, sexual experiment, personal relationships, delight in the many-coloured surface of life, seemed a poor and inhuman response to the sufferings of millions of men and women. Pleasure gave way to politics; aesthetes and homosexuals suddenly turned revolutionaries, political agitation took the place of dinner parties and conversation gave way to polemics.

A much less untimely death than Cornford's, but one of greater practical import from Steven's perspective, took place in the summer of 1937. That June Steven had set out on his first pilgrimage to Mount Athos – the same where on his return to Thessalonica he ended up becoming an unexpected assistant midwife – and then, in the company of one of his most drily efficient former pupils, the numismatist Michael Grant, he went on to Trebizond, once seat of its own independent Empire, and later to be immortalized in the last novel of Steven's old friend Rose Macaulay. He found Grant, the unflappable son of a Boer War veteran, reassuringly unobtrusive as a travelling companion, but also easy, when necessary, conversationally.

The youngish don and his ex-pupil enjoyed themselves bathing at the enchanted springs of ancient Bursa in Turkey, whose virtues were 'particularly recommended for sterile women, so it may have been rather wasted on us. But it may have other uses, as there certainly was a large gentleman's section in the public baths.' They stopped for lunch on the lusciously wooded summit of the Zigana Pass, 'above the bleak valleys of Eastern Anatolia . . . as we ate by the roadside . . . a detachment of the Turkish army went by, on its way, as it was politely expressed, to "assimilate" the Kurds. The men in their thick uniforms had been marching for hours uphill in the summer heat. The aroma that they left behind somewhat ruined our picnic.'

After separating from Grant, Steven paused for a rest at Istanbul, planning to look in next on the Stancioffs at Sofia. As was his usual habit when in the locale, he called on the British Embassy at Ankara; its current resident was a starchy baronet, 'Pompous Percy' Loraine, 'a silly man . . . and I gather not a great personal success here. Lady L. is a niece of Black Lily's [Lily Stuart-Wortley-Mackenzie, a daughter of the 2nd Earl of Wharncliffe of supposedly mixed descent] and has something of her manner (not suited to an embassy) – and with her too you are conscious of a coal-black Mammy lurking in the background.' Steven noted the presence of a young man called Alastair Graham attached to the Embassy, though Graham, characteristically, left no great impression; his self-effacing form of literary immortality, as the model for Sebastian Flyte, lay eight years and a world war ahead. Sir Percy Loraine, blissfully oblivious to his guest's harsh opinion of himself and his wife, took the greatest satisfaction in arranging for Steven the most exalted introduction in the country, to Atatürk himself.

> There, amid the sugar-cake fantasy of that nineteenth-century baroque palace [Dolmabahçe, in the Beşiktaş district of Istanbul], I was privileged to meet the great man. He was stocky and upright but obviously sick, with a complexion that was pale olive-green.* His eyes, however, were unforgettable. They were steely blue in colour, and they seemed to pierce right through you.

The President behaved with great grace, remembering, or tactfully affecting to remember, Steven's father. Atatürk spoke with sincere approval, Steven thought, of the restoration being undertaken by Thomas Whittemore and Ernest Hawkins at Hagia Sofia. This Steven found particularly entertaining as he had lately had to endure many tirades from Whittemore's great rival, J. H. Baxter, excavator of the Great Palace of the Emperors, about what a fraud, charlatan and vandal Whittemore was. It was pleasing to find so much more enlightened liberality of opinion in the Dictator of Turkey; Steven also noted that Atatürk seemed to be the last Turk left in Istanbul who expressed thorough scepticism of his own pan-Turkic racial theories. Darryl Pinckney recalls Steven late in life describing the great leader offhand as a skilfully covert Jewish homosexual.

Pompous Percy, like Steven's father and grandfather, was a devoted yachtsman. It was aboard Loraine's vessel, floating up the Bosphorus, enjoying further hospitality in a somewhat ungrateful spirit, dreaming of 'how enjoyable life must have been for visitors to Ottoman Constantinople who had the right contacts in the easy-going days of the nineteenth century; before the austere reign of Abdul Hamid', that Steven suddenly had a presentiment of some unsettling, but unspecific, revolution. He cancelled the next leg of his adventure, with the Stancioffs, writing an insincere but plausible letter about his ninety-year-old grandfather's troubled health, and returned

---

* Steven described André Gide's colouring in remarkably similar terms.

home on the Orient Express. When he reached Doxford, he found all four of his siblings had arrived ahead of him, hastily assembled from their own holidays at Vienna, Paris and Bern. It was a presentiment they had all shared – a form of the Runciman 'knack' for the uncanny, supposedly inherited from their sorcerous old monster of a grandfather, with his knowledge of the curse that killed in a year and a day.

No news or summons had reached the five siblings as yet, but they all now hurried in a body into their native county of Northumberland, leaving non-Runciman spouses behind. They found their parents at Doxford preparing, with earnest countenances, to go over to Shoreston House, where the elder Lord Runciman lived, to the whole family's scandalized acquiescence, with his adopted niece and common-law wife, Mary. The doctors were already present and did not recommend that his lordship be disturbed. One phase of recovery in that stubborn constitution was reported on the second day; but on the third all struggle ceased.

Steven reported that Mary Runciman, the de facto widow, whom no one in the family liked and to whom only Leslie was even minimally polite, was left 'comfortably endowed'; in fact, though she had the use of Shoreston for her lifetime, she could not afford to keep it up. Her last years were spent unavailingly trying to ingratiate herself with her common-law step-descendants, on one occasion rather poignantly recommending to Steven where he might find cheap sandals in southern Spain (by then the war was on and Steven was busy in the neutral power further east, Turkey), a glimpse of her gayer days yachting with her baronial ogre. Walter the younger was encumbered with a second unhelpful peerage and, at that, a baronetcy, and Hilda in a mixture of mischief, dominion and barely masked snobbery took to calling him simply 'Lord', as in 'Dearest Lellie, I think, and Lord quite agrees … '. Poor Lord soon had weightier concerns to confront abroad, recalled to the front line of public duty by the latest Conservative Prime Minister Neville Chamberlain (who had kicked him upstairs in the first place), to investigate one of the most delicate international controversies the fearful century had yet produced.

Steven himself inherited a farmhouse which he put out to let at once: 'The building was not unattractive, but the view from it was

not interesting.' He did not have to set foot in it, let alone turn countryman, for the legacy to alter the manner of his life. He was rich, or
anyway rich enough; if he wished, he could now take Trevelyan's
never-forgotten advice and leave Trinity. Guy Burgess had some
intriguing ideas as to where Steven might go next. But it was, in a
roundabout sort of way, love rather than war that would end up
determining that course.

# 12

# The Devil

*London, 1937–8; the Far East, 1938*

> The figures are tailed, to signify the animal nature, but there
> is human intelligence in the faces . . .
>
> Arthur Waite, *The Key to the Tarot*, 1920

On leaving Cambridge in 1937, Eddie Bates was puzzled, as Steven had been before him, by the problem of how to adopt a career that was outwardly palatable to his parents and privately sympathetic to himself. Steven at this point in his life, a decade previously, had not seriously desired any profession outside Cambridge, or even Trinity. The acquisition of his prize fellowship was far more important than he admitted even to as close and old a friend as Dadie, to whom he had claimed in 1927 that 'I shouldn't really be sorry not to get it.' His real feelings were not at all blasé:

> I suppose that I just could not face up to thinking what my life would be if I failed to win a Fellowship. I vaguely wondered if I might be offered a teaching job at some other Cambridge College. But it was for Trinity that I felt loyalty and affection. I did not want to make do with something that, snobbishly perhaps, I would regard as second-best. I never cared for my parents' idea that I might try a post in the Foreign Office . . . My father still wondered if I would like to go into publishing . . . Sir John Murray might perhaps be helpful. But I wanted to write my own books, not to be a midwife for others'. I wondered about the Museum world; but I would have in that case to acquire some serious specialist knowledge. Wisely perhaps, I decided not to worry about a possibly grim future until it should become necessary.

Eddie Bates did not have the temperament or the circumstances to avoid such worries. Unlike Steven, he was his father's heir, under pressure to enter the family shipping firm; he was already drinking to a notorious and derailing extent, and his degree was not respectable enough to offer any chance of academic escape, even were the rules to be bent for him as they had been for Burgess. So, unlike Steven, he decided in favour of the 'Museum world'. Steven had been put off this path by his opinion of the Director of the Fitzwilliam Museum at Cambridge, Sir Sydney Cockerell, 'distinguished and ridiculous'. Eddie's patron was, instead, none other than Roger Hinks at the British Museum.

Among Eddie's confidants was Dadie Rylands, to whom he described, in September 1937, his first immersion in the Italian Drawings Department:

> Well the plunge is taken, and here I am swimming for dear life in the strange grey sea of the B. M. I can't pretend I *like* work (who could), but it might be a great deal worse, and I suppose it's good for me. No time to mope, no time to do anything in fact. So far I have no idea of how it all works, & where my little bit of reshuffling helps to serve the world's knowledge, but that will doubtless come. Anyhow they are very gentlemanly people on the staff, not to say Courtly. And I do appreciate the Courtly, in this rude century. Talking of that I had a very rude evening yesterday, with a Bookie's clerk, and maybe that is why I feel so tired.

With the help of his limited, accessible, regular income, an understanding and incestuous social milieu and freedom of action in the form of an automobile named Aubrey, Eddie was initially able to lead precisely the life for which he had hoped – a continuation of his undergraduate days. His dipsomania and sexual libertinage remained cheerfully unhindered. He was a difficult friend to keep, and Steven, for one, did not at this time retain him. To Dadie that October Eddie was obliged to write a frank and self-aware apology after a row he had needlessly begun: 'I know when I am sober what these things are to you, and when I am drunk nothing of that passes my mind.' The next year Eddie rallied Anne Barnes, after an unsatisfactory trip back to the University to see her and recoup their old adventures with

Arthur Marshall, with a vigour that verged on the desperate. 'Don't take Cambridge too ill; soon the whole thing will be a speck of dust on our impossibly glorious horizon.' To Dadie he complained more bleakly: 'Life seems to consist entirely of painful partings which do their best to prevent one from enjoying the present.'

Eddie began to suffer from a season of predictable romantic adversity. Though he claimed immunity to emotional as opposed to physical passion, his guard relaxed in favour of another former Trinity man, Kit Nicholl. Eddie laughingly blamed this new access of sentimentality on the malign influence of reading too many of Topsy Lucas's novels. But he continued to insist that his problem was 'not love in any way': 'I think I nearly always despise anyone I think is attractive, & certainly all who think me so, that's the worst of living like a Tarte Maison.' To Dadie's justified alarm, this increasingly chaotic young man, who tried his patience both by stealing promising partners and by comporting himself with ever-diminishing discretion, was by the summer of 1938 professing himself eager to move in with him. After a dose of lazy flattery comparing Dadie to Byron and to Napoleon's Polish mistress Marie Walewska – not a sign of historical erudition: la Walewska incarnated by Greta Garbo had just stormed the screen – Eddie launched into an ornate suggestion:

> I am not supposed to propose to you until the holiday. But still you must admit that the monstrous birth is being brought at a good speed to the world's light. Mama said at one juncture that only a Good Woman's Love and/or Christ could save me [presumably from drink – as yet Sir Percy and Lady Bates remained carefully blind to their son's other unorthodoxies]. So you see, my dearest heart and Hope of heaven, what it's all been like . . .

Uncertain whether to take Eddie even to the slightest extent seriously, Dadie kept his distance, and his role of confessor. Eddie proved the least repining of penitents: 'I believe even cryptic remarks are better than silence, though I suppose it's part of the disease to think anything preferable to what is actually happening. But I won't weary you with my reflection on l'amour le merrier.' This disavowal of further confidences was, however, strictly rhetorical, as in the same letter Eddie goes on to detail his hankerings after a twenty-one-year-old cousin, 'Pud', a stranger glimpsed in the street and a burly young street pick-up called Amos.

Eddie had scant liking for Hinks, his Museum superior (he told Dadie that he much preferred Anthony Blunt), but he had little objection to dining and indeed carousing with him – he was now quite indiscriminate about company, so long as there was some. He described an evening in late July with Hinks and others:

> Dinner with Roger H was of course disgusting, though not tête-à-tête; it included a shy German boy, & a rather odious Norwegian, also Boy [Le Bas] I think . . . I'm sorry my writing shakes so much, but I have just had what is now a most usual kind of shock. I had what I thought was a most agreeable experience after Simon [Morrison, another Trinity man, liked but mocked by Steven] & *son russe* had retired, & now I find my stud box & cheque book are gone . . . a bit disheartening.

The enigmatic pick-up Amos had revealed himself as a pickpocket; in itself this would not have seriously discomposed Eddie – as his letter indicates, it had happened more than once before – but six weeks later it was clear that Amos aimed for the more ambitious and disarming feat of extortion. Dadie received the 'long, involved, and unabridged' account on 11 September:

> And now, I must try to tell you about the catastrophe . . . It appears that my father was indirectly warned . . . that my *train de vie* was about to plunge me into a whirl of blackmail. I have had to admit to frequenting Hyde Park Corner and knowing a lot of guards & other male whores. I have denied any suggestion of having taken them home, paying them or fucking them. This has been believed. I have had to admit to being homosexual and to having had men. So you see that *cela a été très jolie*. My parents have been wonderful, & of course, have suffered terribly since the information first arrived . . . They have been a little comforted by my denial of the London picking-up charge, & my vague explainings and palliations of Cambridge days; I have also denied your knowledge of anything but my *proclivities*. They are now agreed, and so am I, that I must leave London, & there is talk of my going round the world . . . There is now nothing to worry about. My parents are wounded but not poisoned. I myself suffer from surgical shock, but that's all.

Steven renders this fraught drama in the *Alphabet* in the following tactful words: 'A young man just down from Cambridge . . . had been promised by his parents a trip round the world before he settled down to a serious career; and they asked me if I would let him set out with me.'

Eddie's debacle had finally decided Steven in favour of a trip he had in any case been contemplating, now that, after old Lord Runciman's death, and his own subsequent resignation from Trinity, he had the time and the funds.* Through Peter Montgomery, Steven had befriended several other young Harrovians. Henry Maxwell was the son of one novelist, William Babington Maxwell, and the grandson of another, Mrs Braddon, author of *Lady Audley's Secret*; but Steven took as yet only limited notice of him, partly because he was 'no beauty, looking rather like a human daddy-long-legs', and partly because his best friend was an object of much more obvious interest, aesthetically and socially. This was Prince Chula Chakrabongse of Siam, later Thailand. Chula's father, Chakrabongse, was the favoured son of King Chulalongkorn, 'The Great Beloved', by his half-sister and senior wife; he was thus a likely candidate to succeed to the Siamese throne. But, returning from his education at the court of Tsar Nicholas II, Chakrabongse had fallen in love with a noblewoman in the Ukraine and married her; and Thai law debarred from succession to the throne a prince of mixed descent. Chula thus stood in close proximity to a crown he could never attain. His father died, predeceasing the King his grandfather, in 1920, when Chula was twelve, and the adored, exceptionally pretty child was sent to England for his education, where, with scarce interludes, he would remain for the rest of his life. He retained a fresh, youthful appearance through all his relatively few fifty-five years; he had a slim build, a wide, pale, delicate face and large, richly lashed dark eyes. His principal interest was motor-car racing; when invited to watch Chula and his cousins Bira-

---

* Steven resigned his fellowship early in 1938. His successor in the set of rooms in Nevile's Court was 'a philistine mathematician' who had Cupid and Psyche banished from the walls; as Noel Annan recalled it, 'A malediction was uttered. Shortly afterwards he died' (Noel Annan, review of SR, *A Traveller's Alphabet*, *London Review of Books*, 4 April 1991).

bongse ('Bira') and Abhas compete, Steven found the experience 'interesting rather than enjoyable'.

Not especially privately, Steven hoped that his princely young friend might still have a chance of claiming his throne, or at least its regency; that Chula might defy his father's example and marry a suitably royal Siamese cousin, both because Steven felt that Chula would make 'a good Regent, if a trifle autocratic', and because he anticipated the luxurious and fascinating expeditions that might in this case result. That autumn of 1938, Chula disappointed Steven by marrying an Englishwoman, Lisba Hunter, thereby destroying the political capital and hereditary claim he had left in Siam and effectively committing himself to life as an exotic sort of English gentleman. In so doing Chula was emulating not only his father's adventurous Russian romance, but, even more closely, the marriage of his younger cousin and ward, Prince Bira, who had that year married an English fellow art-student, Ceril Heycock – against Chula's own initial disapproval. Steven was unmoved by the neatness of this Anglo-Siamese arrangement, and he did not take to Lisba (though he did not at all mind Ceril, who was a more venturesome character, and married to a prince for whom Steven cared less intensely).

Though he had not attended Chula's English wedding, Steven was much more tantalized by the invitation that followed to Bangkok itself – a chance to see his charming young friend not only in the unfamiliar and somewhat unwelcome guise of a husband, but as a prince in his native country, among his notional people. Prince Bira had jocularly, and inaccurately, warned Steven that 'I fear after you have visited our land of dreams you would never enjoy any other part of Asia!' Besides this natural curiosity and the sharper personal spur of Eddie's predicament, Steven had some larger motives to turn to a second Far Eastern tour. The Munich agreement had come and gone, and despite the Prime Minister's famous reassurances, most informed onlookers still saw much to fear in the international situation. Such onlookers included Steven, whose father was back in the Cabinet as a reward for an ill-starred diplomatic mission to Czechoslovakia. Accordingly 'before I settled down to my writing, I wanted to go right away for a few months to see distant parts of the world. With war looming on the horizon I might never have another chance.' Steven was also, for the present, without a clear professional direction. When he received an approach from *The Times* for a series of dispatches from French Indochina and the Dutch East Indies, he was pleased to accept, on the off-chance that this might prove a promising start to a new vocation.

Steven spent the evening before his and Eddie's departure supping in Cambridge with Anne Barnes and Eddie's recent lust-object Kit Nicholl, but on the voyage out he was cautious about being seen in company with the partially exposed, vulnerable and unpredictable younger man. He relaxed his carefully assumed sense of distance only when they reached Paris. Eddie was also entertaining mixed feelings about the expedition. He had borrowed a sum of money from Dadie, sufficient to supplement his parents' cautious allowance and irritate its donor; in his thank-you letter he put on a brave face ('all is for the best à la longue ... a long tour is just what you had recommended; I can face it with pleasure'), but in fact his chief anticipated consolation seems to be that, after he and Steven had separated at Java, he might be able to take up with somebody else. But Eddie's emotions on this point would not prove lasting or lucid.

Proceeding on their outward journey by *Chitral*, a P&O liner out of Marseilles, that set sail on Armistice Day, Steven and Eddie paused at Malta. They were personally conducted about 'the old and lovely city of Mdina' by the tubby and moustachioed figure of General Gerald Strickland, Lord Strickland and Count of Catena, an Anglo-Maltese institution, the island's 'Grand Old Man', Prime Minister of Malta from 1927 to 1932. As their tour continued into evening, Strickland explained to Steven's occult satisfaction that 'every other person you see in the streets after dark really is not there.'

They reached the Far East proper on 1 December 1938, at Penang, of which Steven had happy memories from 1925, and were treated to lunch by agents of the Cunard Line called Noakes and Watson, Eddie's shipping connections on this occasion trumping Steven's. They sat near the topmost peak of the island, and Eddie confessed that 'though not really one for Nature, I must allow she could hardly have done better.' His opinion of his hosts was more guarded:

We went to the Watson *palais* for drinks. [Mrs Watson] was a hard vulgar woman with a zest for life ... Carnivorous is the only word I can think of ... my dear, *ce qu'ils boivent*. I am nowhere. You will be pleased to hear that I am being very cautious with the drink. I feel it is quite the wrong company to get even *égayé* in. There is something *déclassé* about the atmosphere ... the rather low commercial class sets the tone and not the Government people as in India ... all very Somerset Maugham, and left the same nasty taste which some of his characters do.

Steven's own remaining letters to Dadie, though they were written later on, do not in the least support the image Eddie here projects of a reformed character, quite as sober as Steven, passing sophisticated comment on colonial company. It is also notable that Eddie dissociates himself – exactly as Steven would have done – from his family's commercial tradition, instead identifying himself with the 'government' class of professional diplomats and administrators. Eddie is attempting to reproduce the pattern set by Steven, but the effort does not convince. It certainly did not convince Steven:

Eddie was very good all the time ... never drunk so that it showed; hot weather fortunately tones down his amorous ambitions – there was no trouble of that sort – and he was really making an effort to be considerate, and unselfish. Occasionally his ladylike poses and gestures were embarrassing ... he is not at his best in the early morning – it rather shocks one to see how dependent he is on the demon alcohol ... he won't always make the effort about talking to the tiresome people that one has to talk to when travelling ... I do find it rather unsatisfactory to deal with someone who cannot see the necessity for such a thing as self-discipline.

This portrait struggles unsuccessfully to be fair-minded verging on lenient rather than fractious edging towards judgemental. In so doing it reveals the mental energy both men were expending on putting up with each other in close and prolonged proximity.

One momentary incident after that lunch, lastingly recalled by both men, encapsulates the essential difference between them. As they were descending from the peak by funicular, Steven pointed out a sleek-looking cobra, about 6 feet long, enjoying a luxurious sleep in the sun. Eddie reacted with such panic that Noakes of the Cunard Company dispatched two local servant boys armed with sticks, to destroy the offending animal. Eddie was in a ferment as he watched the cobra's reaction: 'it got underneath & lashed at a really horrifying speed down the line . . . God the horror.' Steven was coldly furious that the royal beast's siesta had been disturbed, outraged by the boys' assaults and inwardly cheered when the cobra vanished from the scene unharmed. 'It was beautiful . . . I have never minded snakes.'

Not long afterwards Steven and Eddie parted for the first time in the venture; in the *Alphabet* Steven mentions that his friend simply wished to stay for a couple more days at Penang while he continued to Bangkok, but Eddie complained to Dadie of feeling low about his old supervisor and friend's abandonment of him. Steven clearly enjoyed this short interlude of independence; he was thrilled when Prince Chula received him at Bangkok in full-dress uniform, accompanied by an aide de camp.* Though he considered Chula's palace, Ta Tien, to be in fact 'a rather ugly seaside villa, with large reception-rooms and very few bedrooms', Steven was soon impressed by the company. The Prime Minister and quasi-dictator, Field Marshal Phibun, arrived late to supper having just been saved from a gunman while scrambling into his dinner-jacket. The young King Ananda Mahidol, his mother and his siblings called in, as did Princess Lakhshami, the discarded fiancée of one of the boy-King's predecessors, whom Steven imagined had been demoted for her high spirits. Chula soon took Steven to visit the British Minister Sir Josiah Crosby, after whom Chula had named his pet mynah bird for the tentative but regular manner in which Crosby jerked his neck. Steven had heard good reports of Crosby, who was thought to be genuinely popular in Bangkok or to have gone native there, according to perspective. Crosby was to be implicated three years later in the defective advice that led to Singapore's capture by Japan. His homosexuality was frequently if irrelevantly raked

* A Malaysian newspaper reported that 'Mr. Steven Runciman, a former Cambridge don and historian with a taste for distant travel, in tribute to his father, Lord Runciman's fame, was received at Bangkok with semi-regal honours' (*Straits Times*, Kuala Lumpur, 4 December 1938).

up by detractors. Steven could take pleasure, at least initially, in all these introductions without the irritation of simultaneously having to superintend Eddie Bates. But after Eddie's delayed arrival, further introductions continued; the two visitors dined with Phibun in private; Steven was amused to note that the Field Marshal employed a taster before sampling his iced soda. They next met Pridi, Phibun's Finance Minister and rival, with an Education Secretary whom Steven thought pleasingly presentable. On these visits they generally travelled through Bangkok by boat, over canals called *klongs*; 'nearly all the market stalls were floating . . . unlike the canals of Venice, the *klongs* were remarkably clean. There were no speed-boats on them, only a few slow motor-boats; for the most part punts were used.'

Steven and Eddie were shown over the royal menagerie by the French Minister, Paul Lepissier; Steven especially remembered the pair of 'royal white elephants . . . coloured a rather unattractive beige . . . each bore a title that was the equivalent of Duke.' Before long the unfortunate M. Lepissier would be representing the shaky authority of Vichy France, and as such would be quite powerless to shield the French colony of Indochina from Phibun's ambitions. Throughout the month of December Bangkok was celebrating the Constitutional Fair, celebrating the powers conceded, under duress, by the boy-King's immediate predecessor, Prajadhipok; and Chula both teased and flattered Steven by calling upon his services to act as as judge, alongside Chula himself and an elderly Cabinet minister, in the Fair's beauty contest. Steven felt himself to be unqualified in adjudicating between 'charming and elegant young ladies, all very respectably dressed'; but when it was made clear to him that he would have to make a decision, he picked one who seemed to be flirting with him. Chula and his colleague burst into dignified giggles; Steven had chosen the pretty Minister for Education, whom he had earlier met in his formal capacity, now tricked up in tasteful drag. Once more Eddie seems to have been excluded from the epicentre of these high-jinks – he was evidently not, for instance, invited to pass judgement on the Thai beauties – and his tone about the Bangkok tour in general is grudging: 'really we have not had a moment's peace, and only a few of exhausted coma.'

Steven, by contrast, was relishing both the experience of this far-off, seductive kingdom and the transformation it wrought on his young royal host's character: 'Chula is terrific in Siam, very princely all the time . . . One moves about with a terrific entourage of cousins & secretaries & servants, all of high rank. The head cook is a Marchioness.' Chula's wife Lisba, however, had not, despite or even owing to her best efforts, won him over. '[Chula's] English wife is just *slightly* common; I don't find her an attractive character, but she's clever and made herself extremely pleasant to me.' Steven reserved a more detailed and patronizing evisceration for the benefit of his sister Ruth:

I am rather sorry for Mrs Chula. She has certainly bitten off more than she can chew. She is trying to fill her role with dignity, which makes her very self-conscious. The Siamese clearly prefer Mrs Bira [Ceril, who was in turn complimentary about Steven in her memoirs], who is more of a lady and smiles more readily. Mrs. C. is saying to herself all the time 'I am now a Princess.' I don't dislike her, but I just rather regret her. But I quite understand after seeing them how C. would never have been satisfied with a Siamese girl as a wife – the only worthwhile Siamese women belong to an older generation [Steven was thinking here chiefly of Princess Lakhshami]. C. however is very much somebody in Siam because of his vast wealth, and I have the distinct impression that many of the Siamese authorities are pleased that he has made a marriage that has so entirely ruined his chances of the throne or of any great political influence, and are therefore disposed to be cordial to Mrs C., which she attributes to her charm.

Steven felt flatteringly close to real power, and conscious of his own father's renewed status on his return to the British Cabinet, during his one private audience with the King's cousin and Regent, Prince Aditya. He wrote to his father in a vein of contented intrigue:

When I had talks with the Prince Regent in Siam, he so obviously hoped that I would report to you what he said – that I would prove to be, in fact, a back door to the Government – that I have thought it worthwhile to note down the gist of it, in case it might amuse you or anyone else. He was quite frankly indiscreet in what he said – but I think it was very calculated indiscretion!

Steven had correctly interpreted the Regent's friendliness; but he was also indulging a certain *folie de grandeur*, his own, his father's, who though back in the Chamberlain administration since the Czech-oslovakia crisis was hardly a power within it, and indeed the Regent's, who was an insubstantial figure compared to Field Marshal Phibun, as subsequent events would prove. Nevertheless, this intimate exchange with a high-level foreign potentate, Steven's interpretation of its significance and his relaying of it back via his father to the British Cabinet was not without result: Foreign Office records show that, owing to Steven's observations, British decorations were bestowed upon both Phibun and Pridi. These politicians loathed each other, so the counterbalancing initiative presumably came from the Regent. The boy-King's possible education in Britain was also discussed, and Prince Aditya issued a warning, through Steven, against the meddling of the Thai Edward VIII, the arbitrary and abdicated ex-King Prajadhipok in London, whom Prince Bira nicknamed 'the old owl'. Steven would converse similarly with the Sultan of Johore and the Governor of the Dutch East Indies, in both cases reporting scrupulously back to Lord Runciman. These moments provide interesting prototypes for Steven's later activities during the Second World War. They also show why Steven deliberately left Eddie out of interviews with high-level dignitaries, inducing predictable resentment in his younger companion.

On 15 December, Steven and Eddie proceeded, according to a prior plan, on a Christmas visit to French Indochina; they intended to spend the New Year at Singapore and then to explore Malaysia, finally to part at Java, from where Eddie would fly to Hong Kong while Steven lingered to research his articles for *The Times*. They boarded a 'clean, unhurrying train' to a border town, Aranya, where a car awaited them, the first of many conveniences secured by Steven's somewhat theoretical new position as a roving correspondent. As they penetrated into Indochina's lusher, thicker jungle, their route was almost embarrassed by the profusion of wild peacocks, and Steven observed that 'Malay peacocks are much more splendid than their Indian cousins ... their wives, too, dressed in blue and green.' For five days they would drive out every morning into the forest to explore the splayed ruins of Angkor, with their brightly feathered guardians. Even years later, Steven struggled to articulate his feelings in his *Alphabet*: 'I can only record how awed one is to see these grand edifices with their towers and statues and the huge stone-carved faces of the gods twisted and toppled by the relentless force of the jungle, trees now centuries old, growing in their midst.' At the time he expressed himself with a poem of gentle, ludic ominousness:

> Where the superb Khmer Emperors
> Offered disdainful prayer
> To Shiva the Destroyer,
> Amongst the vast destruction
> Of all the works of Khmer.
>
> The peacock of the jungle
> Struts out and spreads his train,
> Where the imperial elephants
> And princesses in palanquins
> Will never pass again.
>
> O proud peacock,
> Will the day never come
> When there will be no more peacocks
> In the Cambodian jungle
> And your harsh voice be dumb?

Steven was proud enough of this poem half a century later to reproduce it in *A Traveller's Alphabet*, commenting with sage sadness that in view of the jungle's devastation by war it turned out to be prophetic all too soon. He did not similarly broadcast the other poem he wrote at the same time, under the label 'Angkor: Jungle Poems'. It is a less successful piece formally speaking, but decidedly more revealing:

> Love is a terrible tiger
> Prowling in the dark green night
> Of the jungle. Love is a tiger
> Whose teeth have a deathly light.
>
> A little love is a tiger cub
> With pretty velvet paws.
> But a tiger cub is treacherous
> And soon shoots out its claws

And a big love is a tiger
Ruthless and terrible,
And your bones will bleach in the jungle
And your soul will burn in Hell.

This poem's whole force is best discerned in the knowledge that its creator was exploring the jungle and the ruins of Angkor alongside a companion with the temperament and the record of Eddie Bates. As such its strange dangling between flippancy and menace gains definite purpose. In part it echoes Bates's own exaggerated idiom, while also alluding to the non-conformist religion both young men had grown up with, and often against – Eddie more antagonistically and less successfully than Steven. The poem can be read as a rueful, unwilling confession that Steven still, through his exasperation, felt a strong emotional attachment to Eddie (who might be supposed to figure as the charming and deadly cub); or, perhaps more plausibly, as a stern if teasing warning to the younger man against the perils of sentimentality. Eddie, for his part, seems to have been much less moved by or interested in the whole Angkor episode; his account to Dadie skips straight to their visit to Saigon, whose seamy attractions were more in his line.

Over Christmas Steven weathered the experience of being stood up by an oriental emperor for, most probably, the second time in his life. His *Times* assignment had persuaded Bao Dai, Emperor of Annam, later Vietnam, to receive this distinguished pair of visiting British aristocrats and journalists for Christmas lunch at his palace in Hué, capital of Annam. 'On dirait un autre monde,' Eddie wrote of the city, ' . . . a soft blue & green country, moitié chinois moitié écossais . . . enjoying a rainy season, which we didn't enjoy very much.' But it turned out that the Emperor was after all unavailable, having broken his leg playing football the day before, 'not', Steven thought, 'a suitable pastime for an Emperor'. So their Noël feast was passed instead at the French Residency. Steven commented on the kindness of the French in receiving 'two unknown Britishers' at short notice, on the 'memorable deliciousness' of lunch and on the stirringly familiar beauty of Hué: 'The view up the river reminded me of the Thames from Richmond which late eighteenth-century artists loved to paint.

The Palace was Chinese in inspiration but, I thought, simpler and somehow more substantial than the palaces at Peking ... our enjoyment was unalloyed.' Eddie privately conceived a passion for the son of the Resident, M. Grasseuil: 'he was only 13, but whether it is the tropics or what I don't know.' Fortunately a diplomatic incident was averted, as Eddie's attention was quickly distracted. In general he considered the Annamites 'the most *énervant* race, little melting tinies, cringing, fussing and fawning'.

This odd couple, a Samgrass with integrity and a Sebastian without romance, saw in the new year at the Raffles Hotel. Eddie has the more diffuse account of the year's turning:

> Well, dear, somehow I must tell you [Dadie] about New Year's Eve, but frankly my muse has not the epic touch required. We were bidden to a party in the hotel which started with drinks at 8. It consisted of three married couples, of whom one was the Prime Minister of Johore (black) and his wife (white), ourselves and another man ... the table was groaning under crackers, rattles & guns, caps, whistles & coloured balls for throwing, and some wildly amusing little vegetables, which stuck to anything they hit. Au premier abord it was clear that it would be too unfriendly not to join in, and soon Steven & I and the horrified PM of Johore were bedizened in funny hats (Steven contrived to look like la reine Marie de la Roumanie) and were throwing with the best. When inspiration, ammunition or the bubbly faded, the guests just put whistles in their mouths and blew, banging on the table, stamping and whirling rattles ... Conversation was perforce the tiniest bit impeded during this, but when we got at last to the tables round the dance floor, the most charming flirtations sprang up between various couples. I was lucky as there was one woman, a little gayer than the rest, who talked mostly to me or Steven. Vers minuit there was a male ballet impersonating the old year, chased by the strokes of the clock; upon which there was a rending of paper and a huge horse-shoe descended from the ceiling bearing a large plain girl of 11 in electric green who wished us a happy New Year in ringing Australian tones.

Steven adds in curter temper that this 'young lady ... laden with confetti to scatter among us all ... descended head first, screaming, with her skirts falling about her face, leaving her under-knickers all too visible. It was a bad omen for the beginning of 1939.' Exactly a year later, while gloomily waiting to hear from the War Office, Steven would receive a grandly knowing thank-you letter from the deeply gratified, if by then ardently pro-Japanese, Field Marshal Phibun on receiving his Grand Cross of St Michael and St George:

> In receiving the high decoration graciously conferred upon me by His Majesty King George VI, I esteem it a very great honour conferred not upon myself alone but also on my country, Thailand ... [The Field Marshal had just changed its name from Siam by decree.]
>
> ... We crave for nothing more than an everlasting peace and happiness, and our present desire is to see all of our fellow creatures the world over blessed with happiness. We would also like to see the hostilities in Europe come to an end ... I sincerely hope that the year 1940 will bring peace and happiness to all.

# 13

# The Chariot

*London, 1931–40; Piedmont, Stresa, 1935;*
*Baghdad, Syria, Beirut, 1938; Czechoslovakia,*
*Prague, 1938; India, 1939; Sofia, 1940–41;*
*Cairo, 1940–41; Istanbul, 1938, 1940, Pera*
*Palace Hotel, 1941*

M. Court de Gebelin said that it was Osiris Triumphing,
the conquering sun in spring-time having vanquished the
obstacles of winter. We know now that Osiris rising from the
dead is not represented by such obvious symbolism.

Arthur Waite, *The Key to the Tarot*, 1920

The Runciman children had watched every gathering crisis and tentative entente in the years between the wars from a prominent window
seat. After the 1931 general election had produced a bizarre National
Government mainly consisting of Conservative MPs, led by a Labour
Prime Minister, with the support of the anti-Lloyd George faction of
the Liberals, Steven wrote a concise and cheerfully knowing briefing
for his sister Ruth's benefit:

> When [Papa] saw Ramsay on Tuesday, Ramsay said that the Con-
> servatives insisted on Neville C. at the Exchequer, and as that meant
> 457 votes he couldn't go against – But in that case Papa must go to the
> Board of Trade. Papa said no he wouldn't, though he might consider
> the Foreign Office, but Ramsay said that wasn't important, and
> begged Papa to think over the B of T . . . If the Cabinet isn't announced
> tomorrow, John Simon is to have the Foreign Office – no Tory wanted
> it, except Lord Londonderry, who couldn't, because he was naughty
> during the election.

This is typical of the Runciman family view – chattily intimate
about the whole political class whom the children had grown up to
regard in a spirit of wry comedy, as a throng of mildly dysfunctional

honorary uncles: impossible Winston, irrepressible Ramsay, Neville and Austen C., John Simon with his 'legalistic brain', naughty Lord Londonderry and his naughtier-still wife, and always, in the shadows, the jovial, demoniac form of the Welsh Wizard. The Runciman perspective is Liberal leaning but in practice non-partisan. It understandably exaggerates the prominence, standing and ability of their long-suffering father; in truth Walter Runciman never neared the Exchequer or the Foreign Office.

In his capacity as President of the Board of Trade, Walter Runciman was a leading figure in the negotiations of the Stresa Conference, of April 1935, between Ramsay MacDonald's Britain, Laval's France and Mussolini's Italy. The Conference's bad faith and ineffectual decision-making were framed by a setting of ravishing natural and historical beauty, the sixteenth-century Palazzo Borromeo, on the tiny Isola Bella opposite the town of Stresa on Lake Maggiore. One modern guide has called the 'Borromean isles' 'a wedding cake of terraces and greenery floating improbably ... the sense of surrealism enhanced by the symbolic statuary and the flock of white peacocks'. Here the Italians promised to take part in a 'Stresa Front' against Germany in the event of *Anschluss* (union with Austria), in return for a tacit free hand from France and Britain in Abyssinia. Here both of the President of the Board of Trade's sons came to keep their father company, and to satisfy their own international inquisitiveness; for all the Isola Bella's appeal, the company of three Cabinets full of European prevarication could not entirely hold the Runciman brothers' interest.

Leslie drove them further down the lake, first to call on the Villa Taranto at Pallanza, where 'an eccentric millionaire of Australian origin called Neil McEacharn, the widower of a high-born German princess', had caused a house to be built and a garden arranged, neither of which met with Steven's approval. 'The Villa Taranto ... had the air of a municipal park; the food ... was pretentious and almost inedible; the house-guests were a remarkable mixture of the raffish and the highly respectable ... ' It sounds as if McEacharn – actually a retired Scots soldier of means, whose sex life had made unwise his continued residence in the Lowlands – ran an establishment not so very different from others Steven would later frequent, Henry

McIlhenny's at Glenveagh, for example, or Gian Carlo Menotti's at Yester House. Steven reacted against its brand of kitsch partly on his own behalf, with the intermittent distaste he could display for high camp that did not originate with him; and partly, perhaps largely, out of embarrassment on his brother's behalf.

So the brothers motored on to San Remigio, 'a handsome old house with no pretensions to comfort . . . the garden lacking in flower beds but full of old trees and statuary'. Its owners, who remembered Walter Runciman from a trade mission during the First World War and were happy to entertain his sons, rejoiced in the name of Marchese and Marchesa della Valle di Casanova, though the Marchesa was a native of Dublin. The Runciman brothers accepted an invitation to linger at Villa San Remigio throughout the rest of the Conference. Steven suspected his brother, now three years into his second marriage, of intriguing with the Casanovas' daughter Ester; Leslie countered that Ester was more interested in the conspicuously unmarried Steven.

At any rate, the success of the Stresa Conference for Steven and Leslie's social round, if scarcely for European accord, set a precedent. When public affairs called for Walter Runciman to spend extended periods abroad, his children were determined not to pass up the adventure and the gossip. The younger Walter's melancholy elevation to the Lords and out of the Cabinet by Neville Chamberlain in 1937 might at first have seemed to have brought this era of opportunity to a regrettable end. Steven and his siblings must have felt renewed excitement – their parents undoubtedly did – when rumour had it that the wavering Prime Minister had changed his mind about their ageing father's usefulness. Lord Runciman had been recruited for a highly sensitive role, globally prominent but officially hush-hush. He was to act as a British mediator – yet not as the accredited mediator of the British government – in the historically fascinating and topically intractable young country of Czechoslovakia.

The rise to the German Chancellorship of Adolf Hitler had been, at first, slow to affect London society's view of Germany in any serious way. This was in large part due to the high esteem in which the incumbent German Ambassador in 1933, Leopold von Hoesch, was generally held.* Both the British Foreign Secretaries who had dealings with Hoesch counted him as a friend. These were Walter Runciman's old ally Sir John Simon, leader of the anti-Lloyd George faction of the old Liberal Party; and Anthony Eden, who at this point was still inclined to allow the Germans a sympathetic hearing. One of Hoesch's admiring Second Secretaries left a vivid description of his Ambassador's reputation, qualities and foibles:

> [Hoesch was] one of the most brilliant personalities produced by the German Foreign Service between the two World Wars. An elegant and adroit diplomat of worldwide experience, possessed of a keen political intelligence . . . by no means free of snobbishness or of a sizable dose of vanity. Of the social success that he revered and preferred to seek in aristocratic circles, he was assured by his tall, slender figure, his perfect manners and his pleasing personality. Although a bachelor, he knew how to make the German Embassy a centre of social and political life, and under him it was generally considered to be the 'smartest' embassy in London.

Hoesch was even considered to have assisted Anglo-German relations by his taste in 'style and furnishings'; the decoration of his Embassy was adjudged to be a commendable, if doubtfully comfortable, example of British aristocratic restraint. Another of Hoesch's social coups, upon which British counter-intelligence could only gaze with grudging appreciation for 'that ubiquitous fellow', was his intimacy with Wallis Simpson; his flirtations with the American-born London hostess Emerald Cunard were also immaculately timed and professionally rewarding. In sensational segments of the press Hoesch was earning himself the title 'arch-Hitler spy of Europe', one he privately regarded with disgusted mirth. Although a maddeningly effective envoy, Hoesch, with most of his staff, was thought to be

---

* The younger Runcimans had become accustomed to attending dinners and parties at the German Embassy in its Weimar incarnation after 1927, when Leslie befriended the then Ambassador Friedrich Sthamer. Like Hoesch, Sthamer was an adept and cultured host, and the well-born, rich and artistic mingled at his table. One of his best and most talented guests was Adila Fachiri, a virtuoso Hungarian violinist noted for her ordered classicism and her 'altogether un-English attractiveness'. Mrs Fachiri entertained Steven with her lively interest in spiritualism.

'hostile to, or at least unenthusiastic about, the Nazi seizure of power'. For three years after Hitler's arrival at the Chancellorship the German Embassy in London remained practically free of members of the Nazi Party, an acknowledged, and in Berlin highly suspect, lair for intelligent scepticism towards 'the New Germany'.

Beyond his lasting bachelorhood, his record of public *amours courtoises* with rich and intriguingly connected American women and a certain amount of persistent but hazy gossip, there is no solid evidence for the direction of 'Leo' Hoesch's sexual preferences. His British friends accorded him a degree of sympathy that would not have ill befitted a widower on the death of his terrier, Giro, electrocuted in February 1934. Giro remains the only German diplomat in Hitler's employ to be afforded a solemn gravestone in London; it is testament to Britain's love of dogs that the spot survived undesecrated through the Blitz. What is not in question is that the pre-Ribbentrop German Embassy to the Court of St James's was notable, by the standards of diplomatic missions of its day, Nazi or otherwise, for its near-open tolerance of homosexually inclined officials. Its Counsellor was the gigantic and warm-hearted Count Bernstorff, who like Hoesch proved a great success as a ladies' man, attracting the keen-sighted adoration of the playwright Enid Bagnold, but was according to Graham Greene 'a complete homosexual and haunter of homosexual clubs'. There was Wolfgang zu Putlitz, who, though he self-protectively joined the Nazi Party, was to supply information to MI5 and also to Soviet Russia through Guy Burgess; a mutual lover of theirs, Jack Hewit, felt himself to be playing the role of a 'Mata Hari'.

A frequent guest of Steven's at Trinity and of Leslie's in London, twice visiting the Runciman parents at Barton Street, was the German Third Secretary Werner von Fries, another non-Nazi bachelor; after the war he would be involved with the 'Circle of Friends', an association in aid of former German diplomats that explicitly rejected Nazified elements whenever possible. Burgess would name him to his Soviet masters as a usefully homosexual potential contact. Fries, who had also served in Ankara in the late 1920s and so had Constantinopolitan friends in common with Steven, was a friend of Steven's younger acquaintance Geoffrey Wright. Through Fries both

Runciman brothers had entrée to the younger element at the German Embassy, to Leo's increasingly celebrated parties, as lavishly victualled as the Embassy's decoration was chaste. But the fun would soon be over. Hoesch was on the point of being recalled by the Führer when he succumbed to a heart-attack, in April 1936. The talk of poison around his death was no more deeply substantiated, nor more inherently implausible, than the rumours of his homosexuality had been. His replacement was a very new and topical broom, Hitler's thoroughly self-satisfied flatterer Joachim von Ribbentrop; no bachelor he, for his tough wife Annelies was said to be the driving force in their household. It was murmured that Ribbentrop missed the point of Hoesch's strategy – not to mention his good taste – by actually embarking on a physical affair with Mrs Simpson. Fries tried to uphold Hoesch's old, civilized regime by taking the sensitive job of spying on Ribbentrop, on behalf of the German Foreign Minister, Baron von Neurath, who, in common with many other German higher officials, loathed the new Ambassador in London. Fries was dismissed for his pains, and would spend the war in the relative safety of the Wehrmacht; he was replaced by the young, thoroughly Nazi Prince Otto von Bismarck.

In 1935, during Hoesch's last year at the Embassy, the Anglo-German Fellowship had been formed, at the suggestion of a group of Conservative MPs and businessmen who purported to be interpreting the will of the Prince of Wales, soon and briefly to be Edward VIII. The Fellowship's predominant and British half had theoretically noble intentions, rejecting any connection to Nazism or anti-Semitism and claiming to represent businesslike, internationalist, pacific mainstream opinion. But from the Fellowship's inception there were signs that differentiated it from the cultured ambiguity of a man like Leo Hoesch, in service to a Nazi government purely by malign circumstance. The Fellowship's British Secretary, Ernest Tennant, a cousin of Margot Asquith, was unusual among Britons and Germans in his degree of affection for the oleaginous Ribbentrop, and the chilly true believer who replaced Fries, Prince von Bismarck, was a German founder member. Walter Runciman was offered membership and a false story later went about that he had accepted; in fact he prevaricated long enough to be technically, if not quite reputationally, in the clear, and before he had made up his mind the Fellowship's cause had been rendered untenable by events. Leslie gladly joined, as did, to the shared bafflement of Steven and Cyril Connolly, two of their most professedly Marxist friends, Guy Burgess and Kim Philby. It was not so much the leap from one totalitarianism to another that puzzled Steven and Connolly as the bizarre spectacle of these disciples of Cornford sprinting to incorporate themselves into a solidly bourgeois movement, its origins on the Tory backbenches, its appeal and its organization very largely aimed at entrepreneurs rather than intellectuals. The idea of joining the Fellowship was unthinkable to Steven more because of its milieu than because of its convictions or its unstable allegiance. For him, involvement with the ponderous Anglo-Germans would have been tantamount to running for Parliament, or joining the family shipping firm.

At the very end of Hoesch's tenancy of the Embassy, and against his urgent and unavailing advice, Hitler had retaken the Rhineland, demilitarized according to the terms of the Treaty of Versailles. In March 1938, with the Stresa Front's impotence proven, Germany accomplished the very result that the unprincipled entente of Britain, France and Italy had vowed to prevent, the *Anschluss* with Austria. The news found Steven passing Istanbul by train, on the way to Baghdad. He had just given his last lecture as a Cambridge don; he was some distance into the writing of *The Medieval Manichee*; and he had planned with satisfaction a month in the Near East and Levant, with a variety of old friends, rival authorities and new dignitaries. Steven was not expecting to be disturbed by contemporary politics, but when the news caught up with him his powers of composure and observation did not desert him:

> The conductor woke me in great excitement on Saturday morning to tell me of the German coup in Austria. I didn't at first know whether to believe him as he was a very volatile man, a Bulgar, but not as phlegmatic as most Bulgars. Indeed, he told me, he had had to leave Bulgaria because he once spat in the face of the Minister of Communications. However the Italian papers, rather cool in their language, proved him right. I feel a truly British longing for a British newspaper.

Steven soon fell in with Sir Maurice Peterson, the new British Ambassador to Baghdad, travelling from his previous post in Sofia. Peterson, a Scot of stern bearing and sudden frankness, with an enormous pipe clamped in the corner of his mouth, complained of Steven's acquaintance Bogdan Filov, soon to be the Bulgarian Prime Minister and apparently a notoriously bad-tempered cheat at bridge. Steven considered Peterson 'not very ambassadorial', and noted that he seemed uninterested in the history or even the scenery of Asia Minor, though he brightened up considerably when Steven lent him 'a risqué French novel'.

At any rate, Steven and the Ambassador disembarked at Baghdad firm if dissimilar friends, united by their nationality in the midst of crisis. At Peterson's first party, Steven was introduced to an even more powerful figure, the head of the British Council, Lord Lloyd. Peterson himself had previously worked under this increasingly omnipresent and ambitious character when Lloyd was High Commissioner to Egypt and the Sudan, and has left a revealing portrait of him:

> Small, dark, overflowing with nervous energy, he possessed a driving power which left but little respite either for himself or those who worked for him. He had a keen, almost feminine intuition . . . a real asset in the East where most things happened underground . . . one of the few in official position to find favour with Lawrence of Arabia. His courage, both physical and moral, was of a high order.
>
> . . . But his great qualities were not without counter-balancing defects. His mind was, above everything, suspicious . . . He had, too, a sense of the Vice-regal which led him to an exaggerated insistence on pomp and circumstance . . . he was actuated, not by any mere taste for ostentation, but by a conviction that in the East it was not well to relax even for a moment . . . the bugles and the outriders which must mark the coming and going of the British representative . . .

Peterson shared the assumption of much of the Foreign Service that Lloyd was homosexual, an assumption that Lloyd's marriage to Blanche Lascelles in 1911 did little to shift and his appointment of James Lees-Milne as his secretary in 1931 much to confirm. Steven found Lloyd unsympathetic. His perceptive support of T. E. Lawrence was no great recommendation. Steven had met that hero early in 1935, shortly before Lawrence's fatal motor-bicycle accident, at a party given in his honour by the colonial grandee Sir Ronald Storrs: '[Lawrence] gave me a feeling of mistrust and almost physical repulsion.' Steven was now equally unconvinced by Lloyd himself: '[Lloyd] as president of the British Council of Cultural Relations is touring the Near East, and taking charge of the various embassies he visits, making himself thoroughly at home and ordering about the poor diplomats as though they were his footmen. What an odious man – merely getting away with it because he has energy and self-confidence, but utterly bogus really.' Little did Steven know how decisive a part Lloyd's great legacy, the British Council, would before long play in his own life.

From Baghdad Steven passed to Damascus, where his host was the French Resident, Count Stanislas 'Stas' Ostrorog. Stas and his elder brother, Jean, who maintained a splendid wooden *yali* on the Asiatic strait of the Bosphorus where the boys had both grown up, were exiled Poles with an unusual relationship to the most exotic of the Runciman family's Liberal connections. One of the most generous financial supporters of the Liberal cause in general, and the Asquith family in particular, was the fabulously successful and enigmatic international arms dealer Sir Basil Zaharoff. He remained loyal to the Asquiths with overwhelming munificence long after the fall of the Asquith ministry; at her wedding to Prince Antoine Bibesco, Elizabeth Asquith, for example, was given by Sir Basil a silver box containing white lilies and a cheque for £1,000. Hilda Runciman, as a loyal wife and fixer of the Asquith faction, could rely upon a more discreet but equally reliable form of floral bounty; she used to invite Zaharoff to lunch before throwing her dinners, in the full knowledge that she would be able to decorate Barton Street free of charge with the flowers he sent in recompense. Steven remembered as a small boy having his auburn hair tousled by 'the modern Monte Cristo', and would joke late in life that he had been puzzled and disappointed not to have received any substantial billets-doux from Sir Basil.

'Zedzed' (Zaharoff's real first name was Zacharias) was in fact the marrying kind, on occasion bigamously. He put this to the proof for the last time in his mid-seventies, by his union in 1924 with his long-time Spanish mistress, Marie de Muguiro y Beruete, Duchess of

Marchena, whose previous husband, a Spanish Prince of the Blood and violent lunatic, had only just died. Marie's two daughters were notionally royal Bourbons, though almost universally assumed by experts in the field of royal legitimacy, such as Steven and Stewart Perowne, to be Zaharoff's. One married the prodigal heir of the Walfords, a shipping family not entirely unlike the Runcimans; the other married Jean Ostrorog. The elder Ostrorog brother, from Polish penury and virtual statelessness, suddenly became an independent magnate. As to his new countess, 'it was a happy marriage so long as they seldom saw each other . . . she stayed in Paris, where Jean would occasionally visit her; and she was very generous in subsidizing the upkeep of the *yali* in Turkey.' Jean could enjoy his own pursuits and support his younger brother Stas's adventurous diplomatic career.

The Ostrorogs did not, as Zaharoff had done, adorn London galas and trouble to impersonate international respectability. Their step-, or blood-, father and uncle-in-law had been a brilliant and unscrupulous meritocrat; the Ostrorog brothers, whose own father had been one of Zaharoff's tame accountants, were *racé* leftovers, last scions untroubled by dynastic responsibilities. They had certainly been unknown to Walter and Hilda, and Steven probably located them in the first instance using a copy of the *Almanach de Gotha* and his ear for the gossip of the Golden Horn. Jean Ostrorog was Zaharoff's second choice for his younger 'step' daughter, Angèle de Bourbon; during the Great War Zaharoff had tried to entice his favourite aeronautical inventor, Sir Dennistoun Burney, to take her hand for a retainer named, a little wildly, at £100,000. Jean was not so good a catch and his prize was lesser, but still carried eminent practical advantages. At the death of the old Duchess, only eighteen months into her second marriage, in 1926, Zaharoff protected her legacies by obliging both quasi-Bourbons-in-law to undergo divorces of convenience; but his own amiability and financial support within unusually elastic reason seamlessly continued. Jean, presumably for the sake of *amour-propre*, misrepresented this solution of mutual consent to his guest, telling Steven with scant gratitude that his former wife was 'frightful'.

By 1938, when Steven looked up Stas in Damascus and then Jean in Istanbul, Zedzed was no more; and both his ex-maybe-sons-in-law were, though to a lesser extent than their erstwhile wives, among his heirs. It is tempting to wonder how gilded an offer Zaharoff might have extended for the second son of a shipping family, whose hair he had so often ruffled – though it might have taken untold ballrooms of flowers to win over Hilda. Steven preferred Stas of the brothers, 'a splendid host, highly intelligent, very well-read and witty, with a gift for making friends wherever he was posted'. After the second war Steven visited Stas at the French Embassies of Dublin and Delhi; and during it he obtained from the younger Ostrorog a bizarre and unlooked-for personal favour. For the present he gloried in his first true sight of Damascus:

> suddenly there was a bright green line on the horizon . . . abruptly, we left the desert and were winding through lush greenery, with fruit trees in blossom, water everywhere, and the city walls rising ahead, and a background of mountains. It was easy to understand why to the Arabs of the desert Damascus was the pearl of cities, and why the Prophet himself was said to have refused to visit it because no one had the right to go to Paradise till he was dead.

This Damascene visit was one of startling intellectual as well as aesthetic cohesion, and would, as will be detailed later, provide general and specific direction for *A History of the Crusades*.

After three days' further enjoyment of 'the pearl of cities', Stas and Steven proceeded to Beirut. The society here was entirely French; Stas confided that the residence of the High Commissioner, the comte de Martel, had quite lately been converted from a casino, and Steven wrote to Margie that its atmosphere had been little changed by its new function. Also visiting the Martels was the novelist Jean Schlumberger, who with Gide and Roger Martin du Gard dominated Parisian literary life between the wars. He was the father-in-law of Steven's friend Robert Francillon, sometime French Lector at Cambridge. Though Steven respected Schlumberger (as he did not Gide), he considered his daughter Sabine, now Madame Francillon, 'lacking in sparkle', and was not slow to insinuate that Francillon had married against his usual preferences, in pursuit of social and intellectual advancement.

Afterwards, the Crusades fructifying in his thoughts, Steven took his chance for a fortnight's tour of the Frankish remains in Syria. His instinctive distaste for T. E. Lawrence was bolstered when, at Sah-youn, Saône to the Franks, a French expert, Jean Lassus, showed him evidence that Lawrence had fabricated the architectural measure-ments for his Oxford thesis, just published to wild acclaim as *Crusader Castles*. Traversing inconvenient routes and steep terrain, Steven had, with a thrill of pleasure at his own occasional but real physical enterprise, to turn horseman, an experience he was pleased to describe to his centaurian elder sister:

> I've visited innumerable sites and Crusaders' castles. You should have seen me going to the castle of Sahyoun in a gorge in the mountains – on horseback, escorted by a Captain in the French military police! The horse gave me hay fever for two days afterwards . . . The castles, espe-cially Krak des Chevaliers, Mayab and Sahyoun, are fantastic places of vast size (Bamburgh is tiny in comparison) and all perched on top of huge steep lonely mountains.

It was typical of Steven to keep their Northumbrian childhood in mind as a point of reference when describing his travels to his siblings; decades later, he would explain in a lecture for the benefit of a Turkish audience the resemblance between the mountains of Lesser Armenia and the Border of the ballads. In his consciously comic choice of Bam-burgh for his comparison, he was perhaps slyly alluding to Hilda's pageant for the Duke of Northumberland there, so much enjoyed by Stephen Tennant, Rosamond Lehmann, then Runciman, and her lover Wogan. Margie herself had just resolved a long phase of marital diffi-culty, and was newly divorced, free to marry a man who shared her and Leslie's love of aviation, Douglas Fairweather. Embarrassedly affectionate, and demob-happy, Steven assured her, 'I'm terribly glad everything is tidied up (though it may be conventional to set store by that) . . . I'm longing to see you . . . I'd like Douglas to see my Cam-bridge rooms before I leave them forever.'

Shortly before reaching Belgrade on his journey home, on 16 April, Steven reported a snippet of international hearsay to his mother:

> I have been interested, listening to [his fellow passengers'] conversa-tions on politics, to hear them all praise N. Chamberlain's policy – I heard one, a Yugoslav, I think, say that N. C. was the man who was

going to preserve peace in Europe. I slightly resent all this lauding, but I suppose it is justified. A charming old Turkish general to whom I talked at dinner last night said practically the same thing.

That summer, Chamberlain's plan for the preservation of peace in Europe would lead him to call for the very man he had dismissed the previous year, Walter Runciman, now Viscount Runciman of Doxford.

The most comprehensive historian of the Runciman Mission to Czechoslovakia of 1938, Paul Vyšný, has stated that the party chosen by Chamberlain to deal with the emergent crisis between Germany and Czechoslovakia 'did not contain a single person with any detailed knowledge or understanding of the complex issues that had given rise to the conflict between the [Czech] government and the Sudeten German Party'. While, no doubt, an unfortunate state of affairs, this was scarcely surprising, or even avoidable. But the situation in the majority German-speaking Sudetenland bore a certain resemblance to the question that had helped above all others to divide and demoralize the British Liberal Party, that of Ireland. The settlements after the Great War had resulted in the foundation of new countries founded on the doctrine of national self-determination. This state of affairs left the young post-war nations vulnerable to the very arguments by which they had been set up.

There had been a strong German element in the historic lands of the Bohemian Crown since the twelfth century. Under the Habsburgs the German-speaking population had become concentrated on the borders of the old kingdom – the strategically crucial, mountainous Sudetenland – and had enjoyed traditional advantages, linguistic, economic and political, to the benefit of both the German aristocracy and the middle classes. The reversal of these advantages, precipitated by the outcome of the world war, and a new order in which the Czech majority, with the particular support of France, enjoyed official primacy for the first time, left inevitable resentment among the supplanted German 'ascendancy'. An international problem had come into being which had the capacity to transform the most impartial onlookers into violent partisans.

Britain was not in fact bare of knowledge or sympathy about the place Chamberlain called with tactless euphony 'a far-away country' with 'people of whom we know nothing'. Several of the names invoked as the Foreign Office planned the shape of the British mediation were firmly pro-Czech experts. The first President of Czechoslovakia, Thomas Masaryk, had acquired the unqualified respect of Steven's new diplomatic acquaintance, Sir Maurice Peterson. Sir Horace Rumbold, who had retired from the Embassy at Berlin in 1933, was profoundly suspicious of the Nazis and so instinctively inclined to hear out the Prague government; his was among the first three names cited by the recently appointed Foreign Secretary Lord Halifax, though civil servants complained that Rumbold 'lacked practical experience of administration . . . in the face of racial or religious hatreds and jealousies'. The greatest journalistic British authority on Central Europe, the writer, spy and adventurer Sir Robert Bruce Lockhart, and the leading academic authority on the Balkans, Professor Robert Seton-Watson, were both Czech-friendly, and both were enthusiastically proposed in the press. But neither Robert found the Foreign Office's favour. Seton-Watson's old tutor, H. A. L. Fisher, was thought a safer choice, but was too ill to travel. But there was plenty of sentiment in favour of the Sudeten Germans, too, among British diplomats. The Sudeten leader Konrad Henlein, who had only recently sworn loyalty to Hitler after half a decade of seeming to drag his feet, was assumed to be relatively reasonable; a diplomat whom Steven would later know well, Clifford Norton, deemed the Sudeten 'führer' to exude 'a strong impression of sincerity and honesty'. The outgoing British Minister at Prague, Sir Joseph Addison, considered the nation to which he was accredited 'a fictitious country founded on several injustices and maintained by the continuance of injustice'; on being once asked whether he had any Czech friends, Addison had expostulated 'Friends? They eat in their kitchens!' For every romantic drawn to Bohemia several practical men could be found to avouch that Czechs were, as a rule, fanciful and uncouth Ruritanians.

It was not in any case such experts of either camp whom Chamberlain or Halifax now required. They needed a discreet figure with the appearance, but not too much of the inconvenient actuality, of substance. The envoy they began to envisage should be independent of

Her Majesty's Government, but amenable to its desires, and should be public but unspecific in his mission, uncommitted to any extreme, even that of moderation, a manoeuvrable mirror to murky realities. Sir Horace Wilson, Chamberlain's favourite Talleyrand, first suggested that Walter Runciman was to be recommended for his 'record that would impress ... an ex-Cabinet Minister of wide and varied experience ... known internationally ... A puzzling demeanour which might, in certain circumstances, be of advantage.' The mission, it is implied if not admitted, is that the Prime Minister and Foreign Secretary wanted a name, not a voice, a reputation, not an agenda, an actor in the theatrical, not the functional sense. Lord Runciman, suspecting much of this game, delayed, refused and worried through the first half of July. But the Prime Minister, whom Walter Runciman did not greatly like or respect, deployed the more persuasive Halifax to urge the retired statesman where his duty lay.* Politics, not shipping, had truly been the younger Walter's career and identity, his means of justifying himself to, and differentiating himself from, an overpowering father. In the honourable guise of indispensable public service, it possessed a call he found it impossible to ignore.

Lord Runciman was also, as his family could well discern, increasingly interested in what the Czechoslovakian venture might entail. His jibe to Halifax – 'I quite understand: you are setting me adrift in a small dinghy in the mid-Atlantic' – had more jaunty pride about it than complaint, though it also perhaps hinted at Walter's private regret that he would now miss that year's late-summer yachting season. To Chamberlain he sent a more historically grounded, but equally unperturbed, expression of pessimism: 'what a cockpit Bohemia has always been! For 800 years they have quarrelled and fought: only one king kept them at peace, Charles IV, and he was a Frenchman!' In the event, Walter and Hilda Runciman spent six weeks in

---

* In the First World War coalition Cabinet Walter had judged Chamberlain to be 'insignificant and unsuggestive', borrowing the words of a nineteenth-century Scots Presbyterian minister, the anti-Catholic rabble-rouser John Cumming (Charles Hobhouse, *Inside Asquith's Cabinet*, ed. Edward David (John Murray, 1977), p. 249, 22 June 1915).

Czechoslovakia, through August and the first half of September. There they were visited by their three elder children, first Margie, for a week during which she attracted wild attention from the Czech press as a celebrated 'Flying Lady', then Leslie, who going one better arrived in his own aeroplane, and finally Steven, who came out for the mission's last five days. Steven paused at Brussels to accept the hospitality of the Dutch Legation. Its occupants, Baron and Baroness Harinxma, were friends made in Istanbul, and Steven was especially fond of the Baroness's aged English mother, who had, he liked to remind mutual acquaintances, once been a *fille de joie* known as 'Newmarket Nell'. On arrival at Prague, he was met by the First Secretary to the British Legation, Jack Troutbeck, who was privately sceptical about the mediation's usefulness. Among the Foreign Office choices attached to the mission two were already known to Steven, the banker Robert Stopford and the diplomat, linguist, balletomane and pseudonymous novelist Frank Ashton-Gwatkin.

Ashton-Gwatkin was a clever and irreverent intriguer who, though extremely serviceable to Lord Runciman and referring to him as a 'delightful chief', was not remotely his sort of person and had been obtruded upon him through the intervention of another mandarin, Lord Tyrrell. Ashton-Gwatkin had a complicated but intense emotional relation to the Empire of Japan, his first posting in 1913, and was reputed to be one of the few Englishmen to regard the Japanese Emperor as a genuine divinity. His 1921 novel *Kimono*, written as 'John Paris', is as frank and forward-looking on both racial and sexual matters for its day as it is unsettling for a later age. The character most analogous to the author displays a worldly, epicurean strain of uninhibited bisexuality. A prodigious but ultimately flippant figure, Ashton-Gwatkin was immovably confident that Europe ought to be realigned towards an economically and politically stable German hegemony, of whatever political complexion. The parodic ballads he wrote about the negotiations initially come as something of a relief, varying the mission's dry history of incrementally justified compromise. But they shock by their cavalier vein and blindness to imminent horrors:

> Good Lord Runciman looked out
> On the street of Stephen;

Nobody was round about,
Not a p'liceman even.
He was thinking how he might
This and that determine,
When a poor man came in sight,
A Sudeten German . . .

Ashton-Gwatkin's role in fixing his boss's meetings with Henlein, often by way of a range of pro-Sudeten German Party aristocrats, has been emphasized by Vyšný, from whose account Ashton-Gwatkin emerges as the mission's most proactive personality, superficially attractive in his ingenuity, fatally complacent in his vanity – the quintessential younger man who 'would have to accompany [Lord Runciman] and do most of the work'. With hindsight, the only thoroughly praiseworthy and substantially successful member of Walter Runciman's staff was the less noticeable Bobby Stopford, a protégé of Sir John Simon, who later arranged passports out of Czechoslovakia for as many Sudeten Jews as could be managed. He would remain a friend of Steven and his siblings after the war.

At the mission's ad hoc base in Prague, the best suite in the Hotel Alcron, comfortable, neutral and efficient, Steven found his mother in residence, but his father and brother away at Schloss Rothenhaus, the fifteenth-century palace of the House of Hohenlohe-Langenburg. Hilda warned him that his father had been wearied by the last difficult few days in the Sudetenland. She had recently committed to her journal her hunch that Hitler 'doesn't sound like a man who is eager to take over Europe, which so many people here believe'. Vyšný, with wintry irony, arraigns Lord and Lady Runciman for their social round during the mission: 'It could, of course, be argued that the fault lay with the Czech nation for having the carelessness to lose most of its aristocracy following the Battle of the White Mountain in 1620, and that a British peer, wishing to associate with his social equals, had little choice but to seek the only suitable company available, which happened to be German.'

The accusation that Lord Runciman chose to spend most of his energy in both his social and negotiating capacities with Sudeten German-leaning Bohemian nobles is substantially, but not completely, fair. Visiting in this last stage of the mission, Steven encountered several pro-Czech figures and situations. To be sure, the Hohenlohes, with whom Walter and Leslie had been dining on the night of Steven's arrival, would not emerge from the affair with much credit: Prince Max Hohenlohe, Lord Runciman's frequent host and an old acquaintance of Ashton-Gwatkin's, was a tireless conduit from the British mediator to Henlein (whom Ashton-Gwatkin and his chief code-named 'Chicken'); and the preposterous Princess Stephanie Hohenlohe, though by birth Viennese Jewish, was Hitler's 'favourite princess' and one of his most farcically conspicuous spies. But the Runciman parents and their sons spent the next evening in unimpeachably Czech society. News that depressed Walter, in particular, had just come out; Chamberlain had made clear his intention to meet Hitler and discuss the Czech problem in person, a course which Lord Runciman, despite Ashton-Gwatkin's and the Prime Minister's urgings, had throughout refused to contemplate.

Realizing the extent to which his own role was now otiose, Walter prepared to return to London, leaving Bobby Stopford and his former Parliamentary Private Secretary, Geoffrey Peto, to finish the mission's details, and his family to find hospitality in circles fully as Czech as they pleased. Walter's last night in Prague was passed with Hilda and their sons at the Philharmonic Orchestra, listening to a concert in commemoration of Thomas Masaryk. The Runcimans then dined at the French Embassy, whose government was more firmly committed than Britain's to the integrity of Czechoslovakia. Steven was placed between Count Eugen Czernin and Franz Schwarzenberg, two of the German-speaking aristocrats who formed part of the class that Czech observers, journalists and historians were to find so suspect. In fact both were declared supporters of the Czechoslovakian Republic, though Czernin, Steven noted with approval, preferred to describe himself as 'Bohemian'. Czernin had a slight connection with the fading world of Bloomsbury: his cousin Otto had been married, miserably, to Lucy Beckett, the half-sister of Violet Trefusis. Their English-educated son Manfred took the name of Beckett, and in the coming war would distinguish himself in both the RAF and SOE.

The Schwarzenbergs, one of the great Protestant families which had contrived to survive the Battle of the White Mountain, now played host to Hilda, Leslie and Steven over the weekend. There Prince Max Lobkowicz was also in attendance, proprietor of thirteen castles and innumerable Old Master paintings. None of these Bohemian gentlemen had much time for Henlein or any for Hitler. Prince Adolph Schwarzenberg had flown black flags at the *Anschluss* and opened the gardens of his Vienna palace to the city's Jews; his adopted son Heinrich would be consigned to Buchenwald after the invasion of Czechoslovakia. But even so, these men were German by language, culture and social background, and lived on estates in the Sudetenland among tenantry that now overwhelmingly supported Henlein and absorption into Germany. The princely families were as complex as they were affluent and sophisticated; many, including the Schwarzenbergs, the Kinskys, the Czernins and the Lobkowiczs, signed a declaration of loyalty to Czechoslovakia that would ensure troubles for their families until the Berlin Wall fell.

In a fair if literal-minded manner, Lord Runciman tried to ensure that, for every Sudeten German-friendly noble who welcomed him, he also met one of this more nuanced and nostalgic 'Bohemian' party. Vyšný's point undoubtedly has weight – in a polarizing universe lurching in the direction of war, the impression given by Lord Runciman's weekend visits was of a British mediator as aloof as he was bamboozled, in the hands of a single, compromised oppositional elite. But there is reason as well as loyalty in Steven's description more than fifty years later of his father's efforts as 'a fruitless diplomatic mission, the subject of much subsequent criticism, not all of it well-informed'. Steven would relate a story that Bobby Stopford had confided in him regarding his father's many doubts about the results of their mission, when events had already rendered second thoughts and qualifications useless. It was characteristic, filial and right, if not very fashionable, for Steven to keep pointing out the situation's lack of ready clarity.

One interested onlooker, Halifax's Private Secretary Oliver Harvey, was shocked at the physical and even mental state of Walter Runciman after his return from Prague:

> I was horrified at his appearance. He looks ten years older and ashen and very anxious to keep out of any row over Czechoslovakia at any cost!

... The old man says one thing to the Cabinet and another to Gwat-
kin who is drawing up his letter ... Runciman is quite broken down
and is now rather pathetic. I am afraid we were mistaken as to his
sticking powers ...

These remarks seem cold-blooded coming from the assistant to the
Foreign Secretary who had striven to ensure Lord Runciman's acceptance of the job. But they have a certain uncharitable force. Lord
Runciman clearly put across several distinct versions of his exhausting
and troubling exploits, with their various international ramifications,
to different audiences. In Cabinet Harvey found him pro-Sudeten
German to a positively defeatist extent, while outside it Stopford and
Steven sensed misgivings. Steven's father was soon, to his own satisfaction, to the despair of Harvey ('this is making way for older men,
with a vengeance') and the disgust of the anti-appeasement Church-
illians Brendan Bracken and Lord Beaverbrook, rewarded by a return
to the Cabinet as Lord President of the Council. He enjoyed, for all
that it was worth, the confidence of the King, who told a lord-in-waiting
that he considered Runciman one of the few men around Chamberlain who was not 'vacillating and weak'. A more perceptive and
malicious vision, that of Steven's mischievous friend Rose Macaulay,
approached nearer the mark: 'We don't listen much to wireless news.
We feel, probably, like the landlord of an inn I stayed in in France,
who told me he did not want to hear of "tous ces hommes terribles,
Stalin, Hitler, Mussolini, Runciman" – he preferred Beethoven and
Mozart. Poor mild little Runciman has got into fearful company!'

No doubt the auditors of the Masaryk memorial concert would
have agreed with that readily enough. Walter Runciman the younger,
once described by a Liberal Cabinet colleague, Sir Charles Hobhouse,
as 'able, honest, hard-working, courageous' and worthy of 'high
office, but never the highest', had been persuaded, against his own
wavering better judgement, to launch his dinghy into deep and icy
sounds. He had proceeded to prove his unfitness for the challenge,
not in fact by his choice of aristocratic weekend companions, but by
the line of least resistance he allowed himself to accept from a section
among them. For all his qualities, his ideals, his conscientiousness
and sense of duty, at the most crucial episode of his respectable

political career he left the rising name of Runciman dimmed. He would probably have been much surprised had he lived to see the extent to which his younger son was to recoup the setback.

'For all its beauty, I do not find India sympathetic,' Steven was one day to write in *A Traveller's Alphabet*. This was an understandable but ungrateful sentiment. The severe amoebic dysentery he contracted on his first trip to the subcontinent, in 1939, ruined his appreciation of India and almost claimed his life; but it may also have saved it. His efficient guardian angel arranged matters doubly well. A treatment developed in Germany and first marketed in Britain only a month before the outbreak of war proved effective, but the disease left Steven manifestly unfit for military service, at least in the short term.

Though no physical or moral coward, Steven was well aware that his particular talents would best serve the Allies far from the front line. Fortunately the War Office, in the main, agreed. In early 1940 they had at first blundered, offering him a cheerless combination of danger and tedium, redeemed only by a hint of farce: field service in France censoring the modern Greek homeward letters of Cypriot muleteers. 'Rather to my relief my doctor told me to refuse the offer'; Steven's doctors had something of a flair for conveniently pessimistic advice. The next official was markedly more sympathetic, urging a considered convalescence.

One friend who veered between fly-by-night acquaintance and daily intimacy was much in evidence at this juncture. Guy Burgess had, to all appearances, left Cambridge and Communism for journalism and a less ascetic political position. His tutors' references describe him variously as 'advanced', 'somewhat towards the left' and a proponent of 'left-wing conservatism'. Burgess's career had taken him to the BBC by way of a stint working for the Tory MP Captain Jack Macnamara, a rumoured fascist sympathizer and, probably more to the point, homosexual. None of these guises appealed to Steven, who was saddened by Burgess's habitual drunkenness. But his old pupil's charm was impossible to gainsay, and Burgess was also a surprisingly fecund source of sensible life advice. Burgess, no less than Trevelyan, seems to have urged Steven's escape from the academy, but with public service abroad rather than a literary career in mind. As Steven waited in War Office limbo, keen to be of use but anxious to avoid the muleteers, he found himself more and more in Burgess's company. The War Office was now Burgess's ostensible place of work. Towards the end of the year he was charged with crashing one of its vehicles while under even more influences than usual, but was exonerated on the grounds of 'hush-hush' national employment. Steven appreciated advice from his rackety but stylish ex-pupil, recognizing the amusing paradox of their role reversal. Burgess, who had helped to lure him out of Cambridge back into the world, would now, in the midst of war, help him find his place there.

The place Burgess arranged was to be, after all, a familiar one to Steven: Sofia, capital of Bulgaria, five years earlier the site of the fourth International Byzantine Conference. At this stage of Steven's life Bulgaria, not Greece, was the foreign country in which he had most friends and expertise; but in wartime it presented a different and less welcoming atmosphere. Steven depended for his pleasure and stimulation on satisfying hard work mixed with glamorous social mingling; in his previous Balkan adventures he had found Bulgaria a rich source of both, but now both the nature of his employment and the changed sympathies of Bulgarian high society gave him cause for discouragement.

He was attached to the British Legation at Sofia as Press Attaché, a role whose ad hoc informality and raffish overtones Burgess might have relished, but to which Steven felt innately ill suited. He set off on the *Durham Castle* from Southampton, seen off by Leslie, Kitty and her husband Oliver Farrer. With the Mediterranean, the sea with most natural historical appeal to Steven, closed off by war, the ship rounded South Africa, putting in at Cape Town, and arrived in Cairo after a voyage of three weeks. Steven imparts little of this preliminary wartime visit to Cairo in the *Alphabet*, claiming to have stayed only a week and to have spent most of that bedbound. In fact it was a fairly social fortnight, in which Steven was reunited with some old acquaintances and met some important new ones.

As was Steven's habit in war or peace, he soon became acquainted with the British diplomatic mission, in this case the Ambassador Sir Miles Lampson and his much younger, distinctly dictatorial Florentine-Yorkshirewoman wife, Jacqueline. The Lampsons wielded almost viceregal power in Egypt.* A younger Cambridge favourite, Robin Fedden, was teaching at the University of Cairo; with him Steven met Tom Boase, a genial, languid, tubby art historian with an interest in the Crusader States, and a short, dumpy English spinster, in her late forties, her face disfigured by an accident in childhood, who was already reported to be the coming talent in British propaganda, or 'persuasion', in the Middle East – Freya Stark. The *Durham Castle*'s next port of call was neutral Istanbul, a stop about which Steven is once again oddly reticent. Here he briefly saw Professor Whittemore, whom he still regarded with an uneasy mixture of irritation and admiration. Christopher Glenconner, Stephen Tennant's eldest surviving brother, looked in. More often than any of these, indeed for a week daily while the ship loitered in Turkey, Steven dined with his formidable contemporary the Roman historian Ronald Syme, long acknowledged to have been part of the world of intelligence, without ever being identified with a specific duty.†

Steven disembarked at Sofia in mid-September. After barely a month there, his new work seems to have demoralized him, and he was writing to his new Cairene acquaintance Miss Stark, already exploring the possibility of new employ in the Middle East after a sudden deterioration in the international situation. It was 28 October 1940, and the latest development had been the οχι of the Greek dictator, Metaxas, to the ultimatum of his Italian counterpart. Greece

---

* Jacqueline Lampson's father, Sir Aldo Castellani, had served as physician to King Umberto, Rudolph Valentino, Elsa Schiaparelli and Mussolini. He was now Chief Medical Officer in the Italian Army. Jacqueline's husband Sir Miles frequently quarrelled with his notional host, King Farouk of Egypt, especially about the King's preference for Italian servants and friends. Farouk is supposed to have snapped back: 'I'll get rid of my Italians when you get rid of yours' (quoted in Artemis Cooper, *Cairo in the War 1939–1945* (Hamish Hamilton, 1989), p. 60). The young King liked to step on Lady Lampson's feet at public occasions. Sir Miles could only respond by deriding Farouk as 'the boy' and emphasizing his political impotence compared to the British Embassy (Michael Haag, *Alexandria: City of Memory* (Yale University Press, 2004), p. 159).

† Syme, like Steven, occupied the official position of Press Attaché, at Belgrade and then at Ankara. This title sometimes functioned as a cover for a more covert role, as will be seen later in this chapter. There is a theory afoot that Syme's eventual Order of Merit was granted in part for wartime services.

was now the British Empire's sole unconquered, combatant ally, an alliance in which both parties privately feared they had more to risk than to gain. To Freya Stark, Steven's tone combined the pessimistic and the stoic:

> It certainly looks as though we shan't be here much longer – though the reaction of the ordinary Bulgarian to this morning's news was quite genuine panic lest he now would be involved. But the authorities are German-bought; and we must wait to see what the Germans decide.
>
> So I suppose we shall meet in Cairo soon. There was talk of a centre at Jerusalem for broadcasting to the Balkans – an admirable idea, which I hope they'll pursue. Have you heard anything of it?
>
> I must confess I rather long to be out of a country which is full of Germans and where the Press is so outrageous that a German told a Bulgar that he had no idea how badly England was doing till he left Germany for Bulgaria.

Evidently Steven could not rid himself of the suspicion that he was wasting time and energy. At the beginning of 1941, after six months in the job, he confided as much in a letter to his middle sister Ruth: 'A lot of my work is, I think, quite needless, but it wins me the approval of my Minister, a lot is rather dull routine and some is really quite interesting. It's all a bit depressing, as the Bulg. govt is rather hostile to us and very stupid, and the Bulg. press most lowering to read, as it's chock-a-block with German propaganda.'

Steven had left his civilian academic work, as he thought at this point, for ever, and he was, with the encouragement of Burgess, considering the Foreign Service as a permanent career beyond the war. His exposure to the footling quality of so much diplomatic activity was therefore as enlightening as it was dispiriting. 'I'll always be glad of having had this experience of diplomatic life,' he continued, ambiguously enough, to Ruth. The British Minister, George Rendel, a deeply conscientious public servant of whom it was remarked that 'Nobody could really be so worried about his work as George always looks,' seems to have had no doubt about the calibre of his Press Attaché's output. He recalls in his memoirs that Runciman 'did a great deal of useful work in making the true facts known and in counteracting the more outrageous forms of German propaganda'.

Guilt was part of Steven's problem; not that he regretted his exemption from military service, but his relative safety in neutral Bulgaria while friends and family were bombed at home chafed at his conscience. On this subject his letter to Ruth is at once callow and moving, frivolous and earnest:

> I wonder if we would have minded the last war as much as this one, had we been the same age. I rather think it was more hysterical but gayer and less grey and grim. Still, I can't complain about my fate. The only things that I mind for myself are, first, being so far away and out of touch, and, secondly, the thought that I'm missing all the bombing and strain that everyone else has had. When I come back to England I'll be like a youth who has never been to school!

In the First World War officers in the trenches had regularly dismissed the ordeal of the trenches as a new iteration of public school; Steven was playing at adapting the truism for the blitzed generation. It may seem odd that such a practised and enthusiastic traveller as Steven should complain of being 'so far away and out of touch', but in fact the loneliness of wartime Sofia was an even sorer trial to him than his professional unease.

A memo from late June 1951 adds a layer of explanation, and of complication, to the awkward match between Steven and his duties; it accounts too for his sense of separateness in a country he had known well for twelve years. After Guy Burgess's defection to Moscow with another of Steven's younger Cambridge acquaintances, Donald Maclean, Steven's former pupil Courtenay Young – by now an MI5 officer of a decade's standing – was tasked by his superior J. C. Robertson, head of the service's counter-espionage division, with retailing everything he knew personally about the renegade. Young professed himself ignorant of his Cambridge contemporary's pattern of life to a scarcely plausible degree, but the name of their old supervisor, and the remembrance of an obsolete and forgotten mission, surfaced in his report:

> I have been racking my brains but I really have very little to give you . . .
> [I saw] a certain amount of [Burgess] after the end of the war, almost invariably in the Reform Club . . . occasionally, of course, with BLUNT.

Our conversations were almost entirely social, and I cannot remember politics being touched upon at all. The nearest approach was a series of rather scathing remarks made upon some despatches of Steven RUNCIMAN's, when the latter was sent out on a rather foolish mission to King Maurice [corrected to Boris] of Bulgaria, in order to attempt to keep Maurice [corrected again] out of the war. His despatches had got delayed in transit, and only reached the Foreign Office four years after the event, via Tehran, and like so many Foreign Office despatches read dispassionately, and in the knowledge of subsequent events, read very silly. BURGESS was somewhat malicious regarding RUNCIMAN's activities ... RUNCIMAN was not, I think, a friend of BURGESS, as BURGESS belonged to rather a different set who had a hate against RUNCIMAN's particular milieu.

While no evidence suggests Steven was a salaried or official operative of MI5 or MI6/SIS, this note is the most substantial proof that he was sent to Sofia with both an overt and a covert task in mind. His press job was not only a 'cover'. The role involved genuine, vital, onerous and often exasperating work to assist the Minister. But Steven also had instructions to make use of his highest-level connections; his social life in Cairo, Istanbul and Sofia itself, so gently effaced from the *Alphabet*, had not after all been idle or incidental.

It is overwhelmingly likely that Steven continued to perform such unremunerated but not unimportant functions auxiliary to the intelligence services throughout the war, at least. He continued to be consulted occasionally and informally by MI5 in the 1950s. Steven had personal links with MI6 through, among others, Nigel Clive and Nick Elliott, as will be seen, and was able to gain places at the Joint Services School for Linguists, regarded by the Soviets as a 'spy school' pure and simple, for his niece Ann and her husband Harold Shukman, also in the 1950s. But in wartime the practical ramifications of this probably undefined connection were that, though Steven had cognizance of the British intelligence connections to whom he might bring useful 'tidbits', he did not necessarily possess any reciprocal official secrets.

That Guy Burgess appears first to have planned the Sofia mission and recruited his supervisor and friend to perform it, then afterwards to have dismissed and denigrated Steven's efforts to Young, is wholly typical of this charming and repellent man, who once in a fit of panic asked his Russian puppeteers actually to liquidate another close friend, Goronwy Rees.* As for Young's denial of Steven and Burgess's whole friendship, this seems to be either a misunderstanding of the breach caused between them by Anthony Blunt and John Cornford, or possibly represents Young feigning extreme obtuseness in an attempt to shield his old history supervisor (and himself) from further annoying enquiries put by MI5 top brass. But a subsequent memo, to be detailed later, indicates that Young's limited appreciation of social and humorous niceties was perfectly genuine.

Burgess's idea that Steven might have influence with the King and other exalted members of the Bulgarian political elite was, in principle, sound; Steven had shown himself to be on good terms in the past with King Boris, Prime Minister Filov and members of the political and diplomatic class such as Ivan Stancioff. But by 1940–41 the situation was altered. Hospitality to the British, from the Bulgarian point of view, was now a matter not of politeness but of considerable bravery. Filov, the agreeable art historian turned Prime Minister, revealed himself to be a German stooge. Steven had initially been favourably impressed by this curious statesman who, as the Soviets were to jeer after his execution, 'preferred making history to teaching it', but his superior Rendel had small patience with the professor-politician, 'a stupid man who had never counted very much anyhow'. Filov's anti-British manoeuvres could be petty. He forced the Bulgarian Queen to dismiss an Anglophile lady-in-waiting, and was to make a particular nuisance of himself after Bulgaria joined the Axis powers, resisting the efforts of various Allied diplomats to be evacuated to Britain rather than their occupied countries of origin. Under his Prime Minister's influence, King Boris's ogreish bonhomie turned nasty; Rendel was wont to refer to the Bulgarian monarch at this time as 'King Jekyll and King Hyde'.

---

* The Mitrokhin Archive, material on Russian intelligence supplied by a KGB defector to Britain, shows that the NKVD (forerunner of the KGB) rejected Burgess's request for Rees's assassination with contempt, though their disdain was directed against his jitteriness and incompetence rather than his human duplicity.

To Rendel, who complained that 'almost everyone in Bulgaria was a peasant or the child of a peasant', among the 'very few' families in the country with 'any inherited tradition of cultivation' were the Stancioffs, who remained stoutly pro-British. But Steven felt that the imminent threat of war, as much as or more than war itself might have done, loomed over their friendliness. What had once seemed spontaneous Stancioff generosity was becoming, perforce, a political position, and a dangerous one at that. 'I felt embarrassed to see much of my Bulgarian friends,' Steven admitted, 'lest they should get into trouble later on.' Thus deprived of so much of the sophisticated continental society which had formed for him Bulgaria's chief charm, Steven fell back on Legation company. Greece provided him, now as it would later, with many friends, and he was always welcome at the table of the Greek Minister, Panagiotis Pipinelis. The American Minister, George Howard Earle III, had a reputation for colour, a Bulgarian concubine, an occasional Hungarian mistress and a pet melanistic leopard, which last he was said to resemble in his habits.* All the same, Steven felt stifled; as he told Ruth, 'I do rather feel the lack of intimate friends. The Legation people are all very pleasant and up to a point we're all quite intimate. Considering the smallness of the society there's remarkably little friction though one or two people are danger points . . . '

Among this tight and watchful society was Norman Davis, another 'press attaché': like Ronald Syme a New Zealander, of 'undistinguished appearance', but gregarious, gourmandizing and an exceptional linguist. Alongside Magdalene 'Lena' Bone, whom he married towards the end of the war, he represented the British Secret Service at Sofia, with the official rank of Steven's assistant. Most of Davis's real work involved liaison not with journalists but with underground anti-fascists. Davis stayed in the Balkans even after the Germans had entered Bulgaria, until his capture by the Italians. After the war he would edit the fifteenth-century letters of the Paston family of

---

* When the Americans belatedly withdrew their own Ministry in June 1942, Earle was rumoured to have left a briefcase of their confidential papers at the residence of one of his latest conquests.

Norfolk, before succeeding J. R. R. Tolkien as Merton Professor of English Language and Literature at Oxford.

It was Davis who arranged a welcome excursion for several members of the Legation staff, including Lena Bone and Steven, who spent a week at Istanbul shortly before Christmas 1940. Steven extracted every opportunity he could during this brisk sabbatical to widen his lately straitened circle, dining with diplomats exiled and substantive, Allied, neutral or complicated, their powers ranging from Iran to Belgium. He met the Irish fantasy novelist Lord Dunsany, soon to occupy the Byron Chair of English Literature at Athens, and to be pilloried in the novels of Olivia Manning as Professor Lord Pinkrose. Without overmuch nicety Steven looked up his Constantinople-reared Franco-Polish friend Jean Ostrorog, who was a French diplomat as he had been before the war, but who, unlike his brother Stas, recognized and worked for the Vichy government. Steven lunched Michael Grant, and enjoyed a gossip with the elderly Lady Gilmour, the elder sister of the exiled Lord Beauchamp. It is difficult not to wonder precisely what Davis and Miss Bone were doing during this pleasant interlude.

The other regular 'Legation people', apart from Rendel, his daughter and their staff, were the men with whom Steven now had to deal professionally: a select, hardened group of Anglophone journalists committed to favourable coverage of the Allied cause (essentially, at this stage, the British cause, supported by Greece). Some were British, some American, and there was even one Bulgarian, accredited to *The Times*. The most experienced reporter on hand, and the journalistic knot's acknowledged leader, was Bobby St John, a Chicago-born former classmate of Ernest Hemingway's who had made his name in the 1920s. St John had so irked Al Capone with a series of editorials exposing his brothels that Capone rather gamely bought the proprietorship of his newspaper. Since he had begun as Balkans correspondent for the Associated Press in 1939, St John had been especially stirred to action by the rise of pogroms under parties such as the Iron Guard. The other reporters were all a little in awe of him, even David Walker of the *Mirror* and Reuters and Cedric Salter of the *Daily Mail*, who were, in fact, SOE agents themselves.

But Steven's favourite among the press lobby was the sympathetic, darkly good-looking and cultivated Bulgarian Michael 'Misho' Padeff, whose American mother and British education had left him with cosmopolitan, polyglot talents and Allied allegiances which *The Times* was quick to exploit. Steven frequently dined with Misho, sometimes with the Padeff parents in attendance, sometimes with Padeff's closest friends among the other reporters, Mr and Mrs Cedric Salter, but by preference alone. The younger Bulgarian was in turn perceptive about his new British friend:

> Dining with Steven was a real rest . . . one of the friendliest Englishmen I have ever met . . . Not a professional diplomat but a historian . . . one of the most thorough students of Balkan and Bulgarian history in the English-speaking world. He speaks and writes Bulgarian to perfection, although he is too modest to admit it. A shy person altogether, his usual place at big official parties in some corner of the room where, undisturbed by anyone, he can observe with interest the pictures or the furniture . . . too modest even to admit to his knowledge of Balkan affairs and Bulgarian history . . . only those of his friends who knew him intimately were aware of how much he really knew.

Like Rendel, Padeff rated Steven's application and success in the role of press officer that Steven himself found so unlikely very highly, in part *because* of Steven's apparently untainted, impartial, slightly incongruous air in fulfilling his duties. Both Rendel's and Padeff's testimonies are entirely at odds with Steven's no doubt sincerely felt attitude of inertia, futility and reprehensible amateurishness. Padeff felt Steven was managing a thoroughly polished performance against nigh-on impossible numerical odds:

> in dealing with people, especially with journalists, Steven was successful, for we were all charmed by his sincerity and his simplicity. From a journalistic point of view, he ran the Press Office of the Legation, which, during the few months preceding the arrival of the Germans, had developed into a big news agency, with great skill and efficiency. One thing only could be regretted about Steven's appointment; it had come too late! Before the war, the British Legation in Sofia had no Press Attaché or propaganda service whatsoever . . . whereas Goebbels had despatched to Bulgaria over two hundred Press and publicity

experts, both official and unofficial, to pave the way for the benefits of the New Order. The situation in the other Balkan countries was much the same.

Padeff was working in perhaps the most precarious situation of all the various journalists at the Embassy, even the secret agents; as a Bulgarian citizen, he continued to be subject to Bulgarian law, even as Boris III and Filov's administration became more and more panicked by Russia and subservient to Germany.* By continuing his employment for *The Times* and his attendance at the Legation – where he and Ann Rendel's Bulgarian young man, Sveto Radeff, were now the only Bulgarians to be found at table – Padeff made himself vulnerable, as his friends were anxiously aware. Now and then they tried insistently to warn him.

On 27 February, the reporters were called in for an urgent morning briefing by Rendel and Steven. A White Russian and naturalized Briton, Mr Greenevich, employed by the British Legation at least ostensibly as a passport control assistant, had been snatched off the Orient Express on his way to Istanbul, disappearing at the Bulgarian town of Svilengrad, near the Greek border. The Bulgarian Foreign Office denied all knowledge of this outrage; Rendel was inclined gloomily to identify it as the first direct act of the Gestapo against his mission. The correspondents were arrayed in a semi-circle around the Minister and his Press Attaché; St John led the questioning, anxiously seconded by Salter. Padeff noticed that Rendel was more than usually exhausted and worried, and that even Steven, to whom he attributed a serene ability to float above the world crisis, this time seemed affected. Salter asked if the British Legation intended to stay on in the event of German occupation, as had occurred in the case of Sir Reginald Hoare's mission in Roumania.† Rendel replied that 'I do

---

* When Bulgaria finally publicly joined the Axis powers, and Rendel broke off Britain's diplomatic relations with the kingdom, Bobby St John asked the British Minister to speculate why the Bulgarians had given in to Germany. Rendel's peremptory answer, 'Fear of Russia' (Sir George Rendel, *The Sword and the Olive* (John Murray, 1957), p. 183), was misinterpreted by the expectant journalists as the even more enigmatic and ominous 'fear of pressure'.

† This episode is detailed minutely in Olivia Manning's *Balkan Trilogy*.

not know the reasons for the British Legation remaining in Bucharest after the arrival of German troops there. I myself am not prepared to stay here in such a humiliating position.'

When the meeting broke up, Padeff found himself confidentially approached first by his senior colleague and friend, the *Mail* correspondent Salter, then by the Press Attaché, Steven. Salter in a lowered voice told him that 'It's getting rather hot here ... I have a strange feeling,' and urged him to leave Bulgaria as soon as possible, preferably that very day – Salter himself intended to depart on the next. 'He couldn't have made a better or a truer prophecy,' Padeff later meditated; he was unaware at the time, and may have remained so, that Salter was among the Legation's SOE contacts. Steven, for his part, merely reminded Padeff mildly that they had a dinner engagement. Padeff brushed off Salter's warning and later went off blithely to an excellent supper, where, not for the first time, he admired Steven's ability to provide an escape from the all-encompassing mugginess of looming invasion: 'Like the perfect host that he was, Steven, during dinner, never spoke of the situation, and I enjoyed this short respite from reality ... my last happy recollection of Sofia and of Bulgaria.'

The very next day, as Salter had implicitly warned, Padeff was arrested (along with Sveto Radeff, whose courtship of Ann Rendel was thus permanently interrupted). The episode began in farce, as the Bulgarian policeman seized upon an old batch of Oxford love-letters written in English as evidence of political disaffection; it would proceed after the occupation to bouts of torture under Gestapo supervision.

Padeff survived the process with a steelier spirit and a bellicose commitment to pan-Balkan, left-leaning resistance. He later became a BBC writer, a partisan and biographer of Marshal Tito, and briefly the husband of Priscilla Bibesco, whose father Prince Antoine, no lover of Bulgarians, ambiguously called him 'the most charming man of his race'. Steven, who may have felt partially responsible for his younger friend's imprisonment, soberly noted 'Misho's arrest' down among his engagements for 28 February.

The irony was, Steven came to realize, that only the German entry into Bulgaria – that inevitable event which he was in principle employed to avert – would resolve the claustrophobic tension that had so darkened the fascinating country he remembered. When, on 5 March 1941 the Wehrmacht marched in, 'magnificent specimens, obviously hand-picked to make an impression, all with the faces and expressions of robots', it 'was almost a relief'. Now the grinding work of the deadlock would have to evolve itself into some kind of progress. As he boarded the diplomatic train for Istanbul, seen off, despite the threat of German reprisals, by the dauntless Ivan Stancioff, Steven could not know that with this change of scene would come his most immediate brush with physical danger in the whole war.

Even as King Hyde admitted German troops into his country and allowed his Prime Minister to make difficulties about the exact meaning of diplomatic immunity, King Jekyll, never entirely absent from the mercurial disposition of Boris III, had offered Rendel and his departing staff the use of the German-built Korona Express, his own royal steam engine. The King was himself trained in driving this beloved toy, and had in happier years taken his Germano-British cousins, the Earl and Countess of Athlone, on a spin in it. The Legation staff was instructed to pack a night in advance, leave its luggage at the station and collect it the next morning. Two suitcases were unrecognized, but this presented no great puzzle, as the Air and Military Attachés had gone on ahead. Their clerks assumed responsibility for these strays. The Military Attaché's clerk, Stanley Embury, opened the suitcase in his charge and found there some old newspapers, even older clothes, and a spare wireless battery. He had heard such devices were cheaper to come by in Bulgaria than Turkey, and thought no more of it. The journey went more than smoothly, as the Turks, friendlier than had been expected, supplied two supplementary engines at their border. The Korona Express reached Istanbul an hour in advance. As the British Embassy was quite unprepared for such efficiency, no cars had as yet arrived, but an American journalist recognized Steven from a Sofia party. Under these benevolently transatlantic auspices, he was conducted to the Pera Palace Hotel well ahead of his colleagues.

Steven retired to his room for a rest; Rendel and the others, now joined by Embassy officials, about fifty people all in all, reached the hotel around twenty minutes later. Rendel now also repaired upstairs, not from weariness but industry: only in his own room could he look over in sedate security such secret documents as had not already been laboriously burnt in Sofia. The Embassy Chaplain and the Vice-Consul milled about in the Palace lobby, welcoming the new arrivals from Bulgaria, especially the few women. Ann Rendel was the Minister's daughter and thus until lately the Legation hostess (Mrs Rendel, a famous traveller, was back in Britain, in poor health). Gertrude Ellis was the Minister's private secretary; Eleanor Armstrong, a Dumfriesshire girl, had been stenographer to the Legation at large. The war effort was already having an effect upon such distinctions. The Chaplain, Mr Oakley, was especially attentive to Miss Armstrong. The Vice-Consul, Mr Page, gave the Turkish porters assistance with the luggage. He would be very lucky to survive this act of chivalry.

Steven's punctual habits and delicate health left him a light sleeper. He was still awake and feeling a little feverish when the bomb went off. To its report more organic sources of disturbance soon added themselves; the next-door bedroom proved to contain two children, but no parents. Steven's first response was to try to reassure them, but after meeting with little success, he hurried downstairs. The lobby, 'a ghastly shambles', had been entirely destroyed. Mr Page was shouting at Mr Oakley to help him carry a screaming girl, Miss Armstrong, out of the scene. The Chaplain shouted back, what Steven could plainly see, 'Her legs are gone,' though Mr Page could not at first take this in. The other secretary, Miss Ellis, had lost an arm. The Legation First Secretary was badly but not mortally hurt. The immediate fatalities, all in Steven's direct view, were Turkish – three Pera Palace servants, two plain-clothes policemen escorting the British, and a taxi-driver.

Rendel came down now, to find his daughter unconscious from shock but uninjured. He made brave but muddled arrangements for the treatment of the two dying secretaries. Gertrude Ellis was accidentally taken to the German hospital; she was well treated there, generously dosed with precious morphine. It was perhaps not yet the time to apportion blame. But Steven in his account of the incident praises the initiative shown by Stanley Embury, the Military Attaché's clerk, who realized at once what had happened and rushed to find the second malignant suitcase. The Turkish police, Steven notes in *A Traveller's Alphabet*, 'had time to see the bomb was of German manufacture before they threw it into a convenient pit nearby'.

Other accounts had no such certainty as yet. It may have been routine diplomatic obfuscation that led Rendel's staff initially to insist that the idea of Nazi involvement was 'fantastic', but it does seem that the Minister privately supposed Bulgarian terrorists to be the more likely culprits. A German atrocity, however, made for much better propaganda, and after Berlin had commented that the British had probably blown themselves up through incompetence, it was no doubt felt that the Nazis generally deserved the blame; the report to Eden, the Foreign Secretary, proceeded accordingly.* There the enemy's motive was said to be the general belief 'that H. M. Legation was the centre of a widespread system of espionage'.

Thus Steven arrived back in the city that constituted the crossroads and *omphalos* of so many of his past, present and future preoccupations. As far as he knew, he was there by chance, expecting neither to stay nor to return. But in its dramatic suddenness and longer-term ambiguity, his arrival in 1941 was to prefigure his later, longer residence in Istanbul. The bomb in the Pera Palace showed that luxury was no shield against pain; the act of terrorism, the Turkish reaction, even Miss Ellis dying in German care, revealed the complexity of an enemy who apparently stooped to any depth, but was not lacking in an unpredictable instinct for chivalry. For now, though, the bombing was simply the violent bookend to the Sofia position, and Steven was bound elsewhere, for Cairo, well known as the listless Field of Asphodel for British operatives of every kind.

---

* Back in Bulgaria, even the pro-British Stancioffs believed the German theory of a self-inflicted British disaster; as did, by implication, the Turks, whose government permitted the Pera Palace to sue Britain, George Rendel and Stanley Embury for damages. The Bulgarians may have been motivated by an unwillingness to blame terrorists of their own, the Turks by pecuniary interest. Or Her Majesty's Secret Service could, not for the first or last time, have been as maladept as its enemies alleged.

# 14

# The Wheel of Fortune

*Cairo, 1941; Jerusalem, 1931, 1941; Istanbul,*
*1942–4; Syria and Transjordan, 1944*

> The symbolism is, of course, not exclusively Egyptian ... in
> the design itself, the symbolic picture stands for the perpetual
> motion of a fluidic universe and for the flux of human life.
>
> Arthur Waite, *The Key to the Tarot*, 1920

In Olivia Manning's *Balkan Trilogy*, her protagonists Guy and Harriet Pringle disobey the British Council's orders sending them to Cairo, preferring to stay in Athens rather than proceed to the indecision and unemployment which they have heard is all there is to be found in Egypt. 'Cairo had become a limbo for Organization [British Council] employees thrown out of Europe by the German advance ... a workless muddle.' Like their fictional counterparts, Manning and her husband Reggie Smith were driven to Cairo in the end all the same. They got on the last boat from the Piraeus and arrived there in April 1941. Steven reached Cairo at precisely the same fraught time. Two years later, Manning recalled her first reaction to Cairo's disconcertingly provisional atmosphere: 'We did not suppose for a minute that we would remain there. We felt the town at once crowded and empty, for temporary use, like a railway station. Yet we had to stay. We had to try and settle down in spite of our restlessness. In the end we acquired rather a taste for it.'

Steven found the surroundings of wartime Cairo as demoralizing as Sofia. His problem was not lack of employment. His linguistic abilities had been recognized at a high level, and he was faced with a difficult task: the production of radio bulletins in Bulgarian, Roumanian, Serbian and Greek. But his new superiors at the British

Embassy in Cairo were less to his taste than Rendel. Steven felt that they interfered with his work, underrated its results and, what especially annoyed him, meddled with his choice of personnel for private reasons – 'Members of the Embassy regarded it all as an opportunity for finding jobs for the boys or, rather, for the girls, some of whom were far from suitable.'

Manning, as sharp-tongued as Steven but less subtle, her gaze hardened by habitual jealousy, expatiated on sexual relations in Cairo with less delicacy: 'None of the men on leave wanted to resort to the brothel quarter, but in the end there was not much else for them. The belly dancers, rolling white velvet flesh in the roof restaurants, were "protected". The local girls were chaperoned. The English girls were booked up for weeks ahead by staff officers.' She also, as Steven would never have done, committed to print a vicious perspective on Cairene queer life: 'These people would do anything, but only for money. European homosexuals were soon complaining of the boys, who could not be persuaded to put up even a pretence of wanting anything but to be paid, and quickly. The level of intelligence was too low for a more complex interest.'

But Cairo in the war was also famous for a more glamorous social round. For Guy Crouchback in Evelyn Waugh's *Officers and Gentlemen*, the Cairo of Julia Stitch and Ivor Claire is a kind of Spenserian House of Pride, a court of almost allegorical splendour thinly stretched over mortal corruption. A bitter outsider's angle upon this soiled high society can be perceived in Manning's barb about English girls and staff officers, neither categories that recurred much in the circles frequented by her husband, a boisterous Communist. In Anthony Powell's *The Military Philosophers* Pamela Flitton leads the infatuated Widmerpool to the point of madness in Cairo, and is 'stuffed . . . against a shed in the back parts of Cairo airport' by Bob Duport.

Amid Powell's source material for Pamela the figure of Barbara Skelton slouches; she became King Farouk's lover the year after Steven and the Smiths arrived in Cairo. Steven's new chief, the British Ambassador Sir Miles Lampson, was continually irritated by the King, who ignored any suggestion that the blackout applied to his Alexandrian palace's many windows. In other circumstances all this might have been Steven's sort of scene; he could easily have out-charmed the aggrieved Sir Miles, and become an ornament of the Farouche entourage. The diarist, epicure and MP Henry 'Chips' Channon took the view that 'the Cairene scene is just my affair, easy, elegant, pleasure-loving, trivial, worldly; me, in fact . . . ' But Steven's situation as well as his taste led him to avoid this particular royal-hunt. He never met Farouk, though years later he was to befriend the King's beautiful and better-behaved sister, Princess Faiza.

Steven was in Cairo from late April to early July 1941, a period of industry and increasing disaffection which corroborates Manning's account to a surprising extent. He was proverbially well connected; she groused about her perceived exclusion from the beau monde, from her husband's friends on the left, from the literary world, from Egyptian life, from English expatriate life, from military society and from the British Council. Steven was discreetly but evidently homosexual; Manning found it hard, though she maintained certain exceptions, to suppress her disgust and suspicion at such patterns of life. It might be tempting to suppose that some of her monsters of privilege and effeminacy were modelled in part on Steven, were it not on record that she had other targets in mind. Feeling unwanted at the fringes of a party, left out by a trio of flirtatious males, Manning shows little inclination towards sexual broad-mindedness: 'There was a sense of union between the three who seemed to be hinting at a game that was not played out in public.' But despite what might be taken to be essential and tribal differences, Manning got on with Steven as well as she did with anyone. Steven's own feelings about that depressing, overworked spring-to-summer Cairene spell come to a similar conclusion on that artificial, wasted period. 'It had an unreal glitter about it.'

Steven had a tendency to become unwell whenever he verged on being unhappy. Mid-July found him practically prostrate, though his mission was more or less accomplished; the Serbian bulletin was up and running, even if many dissolute Embassy girlfriends persisted on its staff. On his way to Cairo, with his usual grasp of diplomatic trickery, Steven had been careful to leave much of his luggage at Government House, Jerusalem, and this enabled him to spend some leave from Cairo over the summer cultivating friends in the Holy City. One of these new connections, to Owen Tweedy, British Director of

Publicity at Jerusalem, now paid off handsomely. The moment medical advice suggested Steven be moved to a more temperate climate, Tweedy invited him on to his section. When it came to picking subordinates Tweedy's criteria were more humane than stringent (in this respect he differed markedly from Steven).

Tweedy did not last long as Director at Jerusalem, but his replacement, Christopher Holme, had an equally tolerant disposition. A friend of Robert Graves and Louis MacNeice, Holme had written poetry and produced works, both translated and original, on comparative religion in antiquity. He now found himself in his ideal post, the Holy City, but saddled with a demanding job. The Ministry of Information's tasks in the Middle East could be wearyingly monotone. Everything, as Tweedy had earlier emphasized to his subordinate war photographer, Cecil Beaton, depended on conveying the impression of British might. Neither Holme nor Steven felt entirely suited to this duty, which so often involved obfuscation rather than elucidation. Film censorship fell within Steven's purview, and he soon tired of the bottles of Hierusalemite whisky pressed on him by cinema proprietors of both Arab and Jewish extraction.

Steven had first visited Syria and Palestine in 1931, as a guest of the High Commissioner of Palestine and the Transjordan, Sir John Chancellor, whose son Christopher Chancellor was a friend from undergraduate days. Another friend of the same vintage, Stewart Perowne, was also attached to the British administration and gladly showed Steven around the Holy City. Steven's vantage point rose to a still more exalted level after the arrival of the Earl and Countess of Athlone, respectively Queen Mary's brother and Queen Victoria's youngest granddaughter Princess Alice, with their own daughter Lady May. 'Royalty is most amiable,' he wrote to his father:

> Princess Alice is quite a lady (rather unique among princesses, I should imagine), very good at being gracious, very friendly and quite intelligent. Like all royalty, she is very strong, indefatigable at sightseeing and never sits down. Old Athlone is a lovely old man, sensible, with the Hanoverian trick of repeating every sentence, very genial with an extremely simple sense of fun. The daughter is incredibly common, rather bumptious but good company.

Steven attached himself to the Princess, whose progress was more historically rewarding than her husband's round of 'military camps, installations and municipal improvements', as 'an informal aide de camp'. He soon thought Jerusalem 'a wonderful place, with a greater variety of people and things than anywhere in the world'; Steven and the Athlones speedboated and swam in the Dead Sea, visited a Russian abbess 'dignified, and of Imperial birth' on the Mount of Olives, and were shown about the Dome of the Rock and the al-Aqsa mosque by the Grand Mufti, 'a sinister red-bearded Arab who was rather over-affable', of whom history was to record much more.

A still more prominent protagonist of the iron epoch to come was the butt of Steven and Princess Alice's horseplay a week later, during Easter. The Colonel of the Warwickshires was in charge of the garrison of Jerusalem; he seemed to Steven and the Athlones ill bred and puritanical. While holding candles during the Miracle of the Holy Fire, 'the most sensational of the Easter ceremonies', Steven, Stewart Perowne and Princess Alice competed to drip wax on the colonel's bald spot; only Perowne missed. 'Several years later, when I met Princess Alice for the first time after the war, she said to me "Do you remember what fun we had dropping wax on Field-Marshal Montgomery?"'

On Steven's second, wartime stint at Jerusalem a decade after the Athlone merriment, Stewart Perowne was stationed at the British Embassy at Baghdad, but during one of his visits to Jerusalem Steven found another source of religious divertissement. They took a day-trip to Bethlehem, where a local urchin became their self-appointed guide. This boy showed an engaging mixture of cynicism and faith. He demonstrated the falsity of various relics, before introducing Steven and Perowne to a young girl whom he addressed as 'Saint Helen'. Helen's healing powers, it transpired, were vouched for not only by the unscrupulous up-and-coming cicerone, but by three Scotswomen turned Greek Orthodox nuns. Naturally, Steven soon professed himself convinced. 'I am glad to have known a saint,' he would later declare of this episode. 'St' Helen's physical appearance had also proved to be of some professional interest to him – 'a fair-haired, fair-skinned girl who must, I think, have had Crusader blood'.

Steven's *History* was still a tentative project, voiced only to a few friends and informed grandees like General Wavell; but he was now in the ideal city to let it solidify in his imagination. He felt the tension between Jews, Arabs and all the city's many other denominations to be a potentially destructive force, but one wisely channelled into a force for competitive ingenuity: 'It was a great asset to have an excellent Hebrew orchestra established in Jerusalem.' Religion was a cause not so much for division as for educative variety. 'What I most enjoyed doing was going to see the heads of the various religious communities and attending their services. It was a very ecumenical life.'

It was certainly a more settled one than the snatched spell in Sofia waiting for Bulgarian neutrality to lapse, or the artificial jollity of Cairo, close enough to the front for the Desert Fox to boast he'd turn up in time for cocktails at Groppi's. Steven now lived close to his friendly chief Christopher Holme, in a handsome house of respectable age and Arabic architecture near Herod's Gate. It was an inexpensive quarter owing to the murder of a British archaeologist in the 1930s, not far from what was now Steven's threshold; Holme had been the first British subject to return to the area, and Steven was the second. The landlord, Mr Husseini, was held to subscribe to 'the more unyielding sort of Arab nationalism'. A motherly Armenian housekeeper, Sima, who preferred bachelor tenants, being too 'masterful' to put up with young wives, waited upon Steven. He had collected pictures and furniture to his satisfaction (his successor described the house's decor as possessing 'a certain sumptuous austerity'), and was still living easily within his wages. In retrospect, Steven was to consider the Jerusalem post as both the happiest and most interesting period of his war work. All the same, his reaction to the next situation that came his way reveals that the Ministry of Information round was palling enough to make him welcome a change of function.

After three months in Jerusalem, Steven received a letter from Michael Grant. Grant was among the most learned of the young men who had entered the orbit of Steven and Dadie Rylands during the 'Tea Party Cats' days, a fine classical scholar and an especially distinguished numismatist. Like Guy Burgess (with whom he had little else in common) Grant had at first entered the War Office as a cover for work in military intelligence. By 1941 he had been transferred to the British Council in neutral Turkey, on account of a copybook attractively blotted when he tried to prevent the internment of a German friend. Grant found Istanbul life more stimulating than the army and the spooks, but his role's most difficult aspect was assuaging the increasingly monarchical whims of İsmet İnönü, Atatürk's successor as President. During one of their first exchanges İnönü abruptly asked, 'Queen Mary I came after Queen Elizabeth I, did she not?' The Minister for Education, Hasan Âli, frantically signalled to Grant that he should agree. 'And so, by remaining silent, I falsified history.' According to Steven, his own chair at Istanbul University had its origin in another such loaded presidential query. 'İnönü . . . had been driving round Istanbul and had noticed a building that he did not recognize. He made enquiries; and at last someone said that it was probably Byzantine, but no one could tell him anything more. He was angry to find that none of his officials knew a thing about Byzantium. It was, he said, all part of the history of the city and the country. It was disgraceful that Byzantine studies were not taught at the university.' The irate President summoned Hasan Âli, who appealed to Grant, who recommended Steven.

In Grant's memoirs he represents himself as obedient, not to any presidential diktat, but to the British Council chief in London, Lord Lloyd. Lloyd wanted to capture several professorial chairs in Turkey for Britain, to counterbalance the many German refugees who had acquired tenure there (anti-Nazi Germans being regarded with exaggerated suspicion by the Council, in part owing to Lloyd's own anti-Semitism). Grant, like Tweedy before him, wanted a reliable and entertaining friend at hand, and thought of Steven. He knew his man well, and his approach was at once flattering, urgent and cautious.

> the post has very remarkable possibilities, both academic and propagandist. In the first place it is intended to have an 'advisory interest' in all monuments, museums, and excavations in the city, and the mind reels at the possibilities of influence that this will entail . . . On the more academic side I feel you will appreciate the glamour of being the leading Byzantinist at Byzantium . . .

'Glamour' was a touchstone Steven could hardly resist, especially in the name of national importance. He was a Scot, a classicist, an occultist, alive to the word's several allurements. Throughout his life he expressly held that to be 'glamorous' was a kind of social duty, though in his historical writing glamour often accompanies tragic flaws such as indolence, superficiality and complacency. Steven thought over Grant's appeal long and seriously, but he felt, and was, destined to succumb.

Grant was offering to negotiate for him double the usual professorial wage out of British Council funds. Steven might have felt rich enough to leave Trinity in 1938, but the hectic arrangements of war were leaving him, more and more, logistically and financially marooned. Jerusalem was a cheaper place to live than Istanbul, and to leave it would be to sacrifice comforts built up at a cost, from the large Armenian landlady to a small collection of furniture as exquisite as it was serviceable; Grant had to make this change worth Steven's while. In February 1942, Steven wrote Ruth a letter under whose sarcastic bravado his conflicted feelings bristle: 'I may of course have to flee from Turkey at short notice and lose everything there, but one gets so indifferent about that sort of thing these days. Despite all the risks I'm very pleased to be going. It will be funny to be a Professor, but I think it may come easier to me than to be a Publicity Officer.'

He was far from indifferent about 'that sort of thing', and he did not really think his imminent Chair of Byzantine Studies 'funny'. He would indeed be the leading Byzantinist in Byzantium, and (after a good six months of prevarication) not even his furniture could stand in his way. His replacement at the house by Herod's Gate, the journalist John Connell, recalled looking over his predecessor's garden: 'there were, in amongst the stone paving of some earlier tenant's gardening efforts, the cyclamen which Runciman had planted; these flourished, delicate, trembling, indestructible, spring after spring, fragile in appearance, extremely tough in reality.'

For parting gifts, Steven had testimonials and tips from the Hierusalemite Patriarchs of various Eastern Churches; for transport, he was soon back, for all the ominous precedent, to the diplomatic train. The journey took him straight through the former Crusader States in Syria, which had passed from Vichy to Free French control after heavy fighting only the previous year. Steven's last train to Istanbul might have led to tragedy, but this one was characterized by farce; at one point he found himself called upon to protect the British Ambassadress to Ankara, Lady Knatchbull-Hugessen, from 'the lecherous advances of a drunken wagon-lit attendant'. He arrived in the city on 1 March and was asked to begin at once, in mid-term.

For the moment Steven was lodged, not very auspiciously, in a room in the Pera Palace Hotel, 'which had recovered from the effects of the bomb'. The question of Steven's salary from the University was a vexing one, and, though he did not discover this until later, the answer involved a cut to the pay of many German Jewish professors, refugees from Nazi Germany and Austria without any embassies to stand up for them. Several of these talented men (who included the great critic Erich Auerbach, then at work on his masterpiece *Mimesis*) not unreasonably took against the British interloper.

After Lord Dunsany had been appointed to the Byron Chair of English at Athens in 1940, he was asked by a well-wisher what, exactly, this chair was. 'I don't know,' he is supposed to have replied, 'but I am paid to sit in it, and it is very comfortable.'* Runciman's Chair of Byzantine Studies at Istanbul was much more than a sinecure, involving regular lectures on history, and classes on art and archaeology. In *Byzantine Civilization*, Runciman is pithy about Byzantine art to the point of being perfunctory, and his greatest powers are undoubtedly revealed instead in the grand concepts and elegant shapes of his narrative history; but in these Istanbul years he found the classes on art more rewarding to give than the historical lectures. He felt distant from his audiences, relying heavily on his Turkish interpreter. He disliked the method of examination in history, where students repeated his arguments back to him by rote. The make-up of these students, too, depressed him: Turks, but not Greeks or Jews, were permitted to attend, and Steven doubted the ability of several of the boys, in particular, rich Turkish youths who were sent to the University 'as a matter of course'. The classes, by contrast, were open to any race or denomination, and, being optional, attracted

---

* This probably apocryphal quip was repeated against Dunsany by, among others, Steven and Olivia Manning, implying that Dunsany had later tried to make heroic capital out of a soft war career.

more enthusiastic acolytes. Most of the best, Steven observed, were female.

So was Steven's interpreter; he found her both a skilful assistant and a refreshing companion. Münire Çelebi enabled his lectures to proceed alongside near-simultaneous translations, making up for his then ropey Turkish. She was a witty conversationalist and, it soon emerged, a fit object for Steven's social curiosity. In the aftermath of Atatürk's supremacy, Turkey had enjoyed an enlightened season for women's education; Münire benefited from this, studying at the American College for Girls. She was the most prodigious child of an old Turkish clan, the Karacalarli, who, Steven discovered, were the more sophisticated city connections of the Kings of Egypt. As an undergraduate Münire had insisted to Atatürk – a family friend – that the ancient Hittite language was closer to Armenian than to Turkish, to the President's exasperated amusement. Not long before Steven's arrival, she had become the second wife of Bakir Çelebi, hereditary head of the Mevlevi Order, better known in the West as the Whirling Dervishes. Bakir, a corpulent, handsome divorcee with wary eyes and a moustache of contained, curling panache, wagered his hookah that Steven could not smoke it all evening without emetic effect. The splendid hookah in question would long adorn Steven's future residence in far off Dumfriesshire.

Steven was among eight British scholars Grant had succeeded in luring to Istanbul by March 1942. Other than Grant, he once again saw a lot of Ronald Syme. Whether or not Syme was a spy, it is hard to see him resisting a job which allowed him authority over and input into every historical excavation in Turkey. The head of the archaeological faculty, however, under whose remit Steven as well as Syme occasionally came, was one of the official, Nazi-sanctioned German representatives, rather than a stateless refugee; 'a good scholar', Steven remembered, 'but not a lovable man'. The excellent German Institute was barred to academics from the Allied powers, a tangible hindrance to intellectual co-operation.

Steven's living arrangements became increasingly out of kilter with the demands of his widening circle. The Pera Palace with its 'high, old-fashioned splendour' and its sanguinary associations was a necessary evil for two months; after that Steven moved into a flat not far off, attracted by its majestic view of the Bosphorus and the Beyoğlu quarter, but soon found it too pinched and vertiginous for ease of entertainment. His guests were of British, Turkish and miscellaneous extraction. There was Halide Edib, Atatürk's famous female cavalry commander, who now led the University's English Department. Derek Patmore, a travel-writer who had become a war correspondent, dropped by to dispense or gather stray stories. 'The leading young lawyer in Istanbul', Süreyya Ağaoğlu, was one of the few people intelligent and forceful enough to intimidate Steven, who invited her all the same. Even Marthe Bibesco often called to expatiate on her 'vague and unreal idea that through her international connections she might somehow inaugurate a peace movement'.

Grant, Steven's fellow Trinity don, might at first have been surprised to find that another frequent visitor was one of Steven's least favourite ex-pupils, Nicholas Elliott, who as a Trinity undergraduate had been an idle and unruly young historian. But there was a ready explanation: Elliott was MI6's man in Istanbul, as Grant, himself not long out of the Secret Service, soon learnt. Steven was clearly aware, too, of Elliott's real position. 'When a former Cambridge pupil of mine came to Istanbul to work in the Embassy special service, I warned my friends at the University that I intended to see him,' he wrote in his memoirs; 'but as I had no secrets to tell him, no one need worry.' The Turks seem to have accepted this not very watertight assurance, *faute de mieux*, but it hardly explains Steven's sudden change of attitude.

Elliott was one of several connections between Steven and an even more perfervid diplomatic scene than Istanbul, Turkey's capital, Ankara. There a tense, though courteous, wrangle for Turkish support played out between two Ambassadors with a certain amount in common, Franz von Papen and Sir Hughe Knatchbull-Hugessen (whose wife Steven had delivered from the drunken railway attendant). Both Papen and Sir Hughe were out of favour with their governments; both placed higher value on peace than on victory; both believed in keeping up appearances, but were willing to exploit any advantage espionage could provide. Steven found this atmosphere amusing and imaginatively stimulating. Papen himself remembered Lord Runciman's younger son from pre-war diplomatic parties, and,

Steven says, used to wink at him in the Ankara bazaar. Drawn by the climate as much as the gossip, Steven began to slip off to Ankara as regularly as he could, sometimes using an excavation or authentication as his excuse, a trick Grant had imparted. In September 1943 he received a permit to investigate the remains of antiquity around Konya, or Iconium; he wrote to his mother about 'the richest expedition, from the sightseeing point of view, that I have ever made':

> We motored ... through miles of impressive and almost untouched classical and medieval ruins, tombs, aqueducts, colonnades, churches, castles, in fantastically rich profusion, and in particular we visited the Corycian Cave, one of the great oracles of Classical times. It is an extraordinary place, a vast gash in the ground on which you come quite suddenly after climbing an old Roman road up a rather featureless hillside ... Vapours in the old days used to rise and inspire the oracle; and the atmosphere is still curiously heavy and damp.

Back at work in Istanbul Steven's circumstances were mellowing. By 1943 he had moved out of his poky top-floor flat, and into 'a large wooden house' in Old Bebek, up the Bosphorus from Beyoğlu and further from the University buildings. This place, rented from a Turkish colonel, was said to be haunted by the ghost of an enormous black hound. It was a mental as well as a geographical withdrawal from close involvement with the disappointments of the University. That September Steven wrote to his mother at Doxford:

> I can't honestly say that life in Turkey grows on one – rather the reverse. It is certainly interesting and, though often maddening, often highly entertaining; and there are a good many individual Turks of whom I am genuinely fond. Moreover I have a nice house and enjoy comforts sadly lacking in most parts of the world today. But from the academic point of view my life is pointless – I can't do any real research myself and I can't achieve any real education of my pupils because the raw material is so raw – their preliminary education is so feeble.
>
> ... I had a flattering if embarrassing tribute the other day when I was unanimously asked by the professors of the Faculty of Letters to arbitrate in a dispute between a Turkish and a German professor – even the German, though Nazi in sympathy, accepted it, chiefly, I

think, because the Turks, who flattered him all right when Germany was powerful, no longer bother to do so as they (rightly) dislike him personally and he thought I might be less ungenerous to a humbled foe.* Indeed I have noticed with interest lately that he has been very anxious to please me; but, for obvious reasons, I see him only when academically necessary to do so and then never alone. My other triumph is that the Academy of Fine Arts (hitherto a German stronghold . . . ) has asked me to give a regular course.

This letter exemplifies two facts about Steven's attitude to his war-work: that he *did* above all think of it as war-work rather than academic endeavour, a series of 'foes' and 'strongholds' to be confronted and infiltrated; and that by 1943 he rightly sensed that his position had turned, with the war itself, in Britain's, and his own, favour.

The chivalry of his German counterparts and rivals was becoming palpably less disinterested, especially at their Ankara Embassy. Franz von Papen, ex-Chancellor of the Weimar Republic, an aristocrat, a Catholic, even a papal chamberlain, had come profoundly to regret his role as the unwitting midwife of Nazi Germany, when, in 1932–3, he had played Lepidus to Hitler's Caesar. He was as charming as he was ineffectual; Hitler continued to regard him with a combination of perverse gratitude and contemptuous affection, the Turks strongly resisted Ribbentrop's occasional attempts to have him recalled, and even Knatchbull-Hugessen had little to say against him. Among Germans, it was becoming more and more widely known that the safest shelter for an anti-Nazi diplomat was Papen's Embassy.

At the same time, this Embassy was experiencing what seemed to be a great coup for the Reich, the acquisition of confidential Allied documents and photographs stolen from Sir Hughe by his Albanian valet, Elyesa Bazna, code-named 'Cicero', in what therefore became known as 'the Cicero affair'. It is another crack in Steven's official account of his neutral, academic indifference to, and ignorance of, British espionage that he happily admits to a remarkable degree of information about Cicero's real movements and motives. 'The story

---

* Professor Norman Stone suggests that the German scholar alluded to by Runciman here is Helmuth Ritter. If so, Steven was greatly mistaken about his Nazi sympathies; Ritter had in fact been blacklisted by the Third Reich after a homosexual scandal.

was told, without overmuch accuracy, in a book which was turned into a film. Long before the time when his activities according to the book were discovered, my former pupil [Nicholas Elliott] . . . hearing that I was going to Ankara to dine at the Embassy, told me to look out for this Albanian-born valet-footman who was known to be trying to sell information to the Germans. But that British Intelligence should have been intelligent for once rather spoilt the story.' It must be added that Michael Grant's memoirs contradict this impression of unshockable complicity; he writes of Bazna that 'One of the reasons why he escaped suspicion, and was thus a useful spy, was because he was so rude.' Subsequent readings of the Cicero affair have suggested that Bazna was a pawn of the British 'Double-Cross' system all along, feeding the German secret service, the Abwehr, false information that ultimately assisted the Allied invasion of Italy; so Grant's apparent gullibility might, in fact, be scrupulous discretion. Either way, the scandal ruined Sir Hughe's public image. He was sent off to liberated Belgium, and replaced in September 1944 by Steven's old travelling acquaintance Sir Maurice Peterson, with a consort whom Steven remembered as endearingly and multilingually foul-mouthed.

In January 1944, Elliott had arranged the first direct defection from the German Embassy at Ankara, that of Erich Vehmehren and his wife, who was Papen's cousin. Elliott met Vehmehren through a secret door in a tea-shop in Beyoğlu, and greeted the German, who had won a Rhodes scholarship before the war, with the line 'Why, I believe you were coming up to Oxford.' In the spring of that year, Steven found himself receiving the implicit overture of another of Papen's subordinates, Reinhard Henschel, who had become the German First Secretary at Ankara. Dining one night at the Swedish Legation, Steven was surprised to be presented with a case of Mumm champagne, one of the best Rheims vintages, which could only have come from the occupied zone in France. This proved to be a gift from Henschel, who fondly recalled the lectures of Mr Runciman of Trinity, from his days as a Cambridge undergraduate. 'In fact,' Steven was wryly to reflect, 'I think that this had not been just a casual friendly gesture.'*

---

* Henschel, a member of an industrial dynasty which owned steelworks and built locomotives (and fighter-bombers), was never a Nazi Party member and had a con-

In the summer of 1943 the German spymaster in Istanbul, Paul Leverkuehn, played host to an aristocratic foreign affairs expert with wide experience of Britain and America, Adam von Trott zu Solz. This was one of several signs that year that anti-Nazi Germans were using Istanbul to communicate covertly with the Allies. Erich Vehmehren, a cousin of Trott married to a cousin of Papen, had indeed been sent out by the head of the Abwehr, Admiral Canaris, to facilitate Papen's scheme for peace negotiations via the Cardinal of New York, 'Franny' Spellman. The Vehmehren defection orchestrated by Elliott put Leverkuehn, Vehmehren's patron and Abwehr superior, under immediate Gestapo suspicion. After the July 1944 plot by Trott and his confederates to assassinate Hitler had failed, Henschel, who had dispatched the case of Mumm to Steven at the Swedish Embassy, was himself dispatched back to Germany in disgrace, as a known associate of many of the Catholic, aristocratic plotters – the faction known to the Gestapo as the Schwarze Kapelle, or Black Orchestra. It was the Third Reich's Guy Fawkes Night, the fruition of a process that had matured in Istanbul. Steven may not have had any active role in these intrigues – though his former pupil Elliott was at their heart – but is unlikely to have been altogether unwitting. David Abulafia summarizes some of the wilder assumptions of Steven's acquaintances in his 2000 memoir:

> The idea was that [Steven] would pose as a disaffected young English aristocrat, the sort of person who might one day be useful to Germany if it found itself ruling Britain and its Empire. As the son of Viscount Runciman, who had negotiated with the Germans at Munich [sic], Runciman was ideally placed. On the other hand, it is doubtful whether he was particularly effective ... Once again we should conclude that he was something more than a professor of Byzantine studies, even if it would be absurd to cast him in the role of James Bond.

But Steven's overt wartime victories were of a less spectacular sort than defections and conspiracies. At the Ankara History Congress of

---

sistently oppositional reputation throughout his precarious wartime diplomatic career.

November 1943, he was particularly satisfied to be the first foreigner in the billing, before both 'non-Aryan and echt Germans', and, in the event, the only non-Turk given time to speak.

> I was audible, which my predecessors had not been, and they were all kind about my accent and diction, so it seemed to have gone well . . .
>
> Now I can enjoy the rest of the proceedings, which I find full of entertainment. By their treatment you can tell exactly who is and who is not in high fashion at the moment; everyone is extremely affable to me, the Minister of Education particularly so, so I must be fairly high.

The ascension of his reputation with the Turks, and the corresponding increase in his workload, both flattered and irritated Steven. Of the various committees on to which he was now promoted, he remarked, 'Like all committees composed of academic persons, they waste an interminable amount of time.' One committee in particular, though, had compensatory comic value: 'It is even one of my tasks to assist in the purification of the Turkish language – a task for which I cannot be said to be qualified.' Steven's social life advanced in harmony with his professional success. He spent the eve of 1944 at a Turkish supper-party, and furnished an arch account of the occasion:

> [The party] was made embarrassing by my hostess's cousin whose wife was expecting a Happy Event at any moment. She came to the party all the same (looking around the guests I was relieved to see that an eminent gynaecologist was present) and her husband, owing to understandable nerves, became excessively overindulgent and hilarious, dancing his native Azerbaijani dances and so on, to the poor wife's deep distress. But it was a nice party – apart from the 'not quite nice' element . . .

By March Steven was acting the bountiful host himself in a particularly enthusiastic gathering at Bebek. He employed one old serving-woman, more garrulous than reliable, and as a result learnt to cook for himself for the first time (a habit he was to maintain in later life). He could be caustic on the subject of his guests' gluttony: ' . . . I gave an enormous party for all my friends on the staff of the University and the Academy of Fine Arts. I also invited, as a *pièce de résistance,* the leading poet of Turkey, a vast and genial old man, distinguished by enormous greed. The refreshments were not so terribly lavish (especially after the poet had passed the buffet) but the merriment was great.'* The poet in question is most likely to have been Faruk Nafiz Çamlıbel, who was also a member of the Turkish Parliament. Steven was sceptical about Turkish politicians in general, especially those who combined their positions with intellectual pursuits; perhaps he had learnt from the perfidy of Bogdan Filov in Sofia. Back at the Ankara History Congress, he had complained: 'Lectures were supposed to take 20 minutes each. Actually the first lecture this morning lasted for 65 minutes, but the lecturer was a member of the Turkish Parliament, so no one liked to stop him – so also was the second lecturer who took merely 35 minutes.'

For all the entertainment his social round and the fortification of his academic status provided, Steven was becoming restless again. As so often with him, inner discontent manifested itself in psychosomatic symptoms, and he developed painful sciatica – a problem he shared with his assistant, Münire. He blamed the melancholy climate of Istanbul: in fact, he was homesick. He had never quite dropped his claim to the second sight; perhaps he sensed that the year of 1944 would be one of many transformations in his family, and in any case, with victory in sight but not concluded, to worry was perfectly rational. Steven had not seen any member of his family since embarking for Sofia at Guy Burgess's suggestion in 1940. Leslie was *en poste* in Persia, and Kitty's husband, Oliver Farrer, was serving in the RAF in the Middle East, but it had so far proved impossible to visit either. Always eager for family news, Steven grew plaintive in late 1943 when he heard that Margie was expecting a child. By 1944 he was determined to acquire leave from the British Council to return to Britain for family reasons. Grant's reaction was, as ever, optimistic, but the international situation remained too unstable to be sure either way: '[Michael Grant] tells me that the idea of my coming home for a

---

* Steven's insistence on doing his own cooking and his resentment when it was received too enthusiastically intensified with the passing of time. In September 1959 he complained to Leslie Perowne (Stewart's younger brother) that 'Much as I like cooking, I do find that one's guests *eat* so much. Then off they go like Ugly Sisters to enjoy themselves, while I stay a Cinderella beside the stove . . . ' (SR to Leslie Perowne, 22 September 1959, Elshieshields).

month or two next summer is fully approved of. Perhaps if things start happening here in the spring (which is very possible) I may get home earlier, as I don't imagine that my present job would continue uninterrupted and it would be an opportunity. However no one seems to have the slightest idea as to what will happen in these parts.'

By 'things happening here', Steven alludes to the prospect of Turkey joining the war on the Allied side. Grant had ruled out the idea that the Turks would support the Axis powers from Hitler's invasion of Russia in June 1941, but especially after the fall of the German-leaning Foreign Minister, Numan Menemencioğlu. Churchill himself had, in January 1943, met President İnönü in a railway carriage outside Adana, and there had attempted to woo him to full commitment to the Allies; but the negotiation had proved frustratingly inconclusive (Grant told Steven that Churchill had lost his temper over the subtlety of the dubitative tense in Turkish). By 1944 matters were no more settled. The great difficulty for Steven about obtaining his leave was that he felt he could not, in good conscience, leave his post unless he could guarantee being able to return to it on time. 'However, a fortune-teller, a very distinguished Turkish lady of the highest birth, whose powers are very remarkable, told me ... that my hand was very lucky, and that if I had a disappointment in the near future, I should discover later that it was all for the best!' This prediction, at least, turned out to be sadly misguided. That April was a month of sudden deaths.

One was completely unexpected. Far from any front, in a neutral country, and only in early middle age, Bakir Çelebi suddenly perished of a heart attack on the 25th, leaving Steven's assistant a young widow at the centre of a complicated succession crisis. It was the sort of dynastic problem on which *A History of the Crusades* was to lavish loving detail. Münire was childless, and the office of Çelebi Effendi of the Mevlevi Order fell to her sixteen-year-old stepson, Celaleddin Çelebi. He had lived with his father and stepmother in Istanbul, but his mother, a cousin whom Bakir had divorced for reasons of political incompatibility, resided in seclusion at Aleppo. Now it was necessary for the boy to travel to her country, as most of the Mevlevi lodges, or *tekke*, whose sworn allegiance Celaleddin required, were in Syria and Lebanon. The Syrians and Lebanese regarded Turks as historic oppressors; the Free French who had overcome the Vichy authorities there in 1941 viewed citizens of a neutral power with a jaundiced eye. It seemed that the new Çelebi Effendi would be deprived of his ancient heritage by the banal, modern requirement for a visa in the middle of world war.

But this was the kind of problem Steven, in the present as in the past, was born to untangle. He wrote at once to an old friend, Stas Ostrorog, who had defected from the Vichy administration of Indochina to join the Free French in Syria. Stas, as a child of both exile and the Bosphorus, had automatic sympathy for a Turkish Çelebi Effendi. He granted a pass to 'Son Altesse le Çelebi Effendi et son entourage entire', covering anywhere in Syria and Lebanon. Celaleddin set out in the company of his stepmother and his late father's well-beloved friend Professor Runciman of Istanbul University. Stas knew Steven was interested in Syria, barred to him first by Vichy and then by the exigencies of his post, for reasons of his own: he had been present at a supper at the British Consulate, in 1938, where Steven admitted to the future General Wavell his eventual aim to write a new history of the Crusades.

The Çelebi Effendi's little party toured every *tekke*. At Aleppo he was reunited with his mother, İzzet Altınanıt, who thanked Steven profusely for his services to her son. What Bakir's two widows made of each other on this occasion cannot be guessed, though Münire seems to have been an affectionate stepmother, which perhaps eased matters. For his part, Steven was growing weary of continual welcoming and whirling ceremonies, at Hama, Homs, Tripoli and Beirut, his mind already perhaps straying on to another era; but he cheered up immensely when young Celaleddin announced that Professor Runciman was to be made an honorary Dervish at once.

Back in Istanbul in early May, Steven received late news by airgraph of a birth and another death, closer to home and only days apart. Margie had given birth to a daughter, Elizabeth, on 8 April, five days after her husband Douglas Fairweather vanished in an Anson transport aircraft on an emergency trip across the squally Irish Sea. His body was found on the Ayrshire coast, at Dunure, not long after the birth of his daughter. Unanimously regarded as a hero, Captain Fairweather did not conventionally look the part. He was fifty-two at his death, far too fat for a Spitfire (preferring the weighty Anson which fitted his build and his temperament), and nicknamed 'Poppa'. He measured long flights in chain-smoked cigarette butts (twenty-three from Belfast to White Waltham, for instance); became renowned, contrary to his surname, for flying undaunted through appalling weather conditions; and was a free spirit, careless of Air Transport Auxiliary regulations.* His affection for his wife had been deep, if at times opaquely expressed. 'I love you better', he once assured her, 'than any dog I ever had . . . or even a pig or a cat.' Steven – who could be an acerbic judge of his siblings' spouses, as in the case of Rosamond Lehmann – had liked and admired Douglas. He felt deep guilt for not having somehow anticipated or responded to this disaster in his sister's life, writing to his mother in May:

> . . . I had for weeks past been thinking of wiring to you to ask for news of Margie, as I felt disquieted at having heard nothing at all about the baby; but then I thought I might have muddled the date and that it would be silly to fuss you with questions. I wish I had, as it is horrible to feel that I failed Margie in sympathy for so long at such a moment.

However much Steven might wish to comfort his widowed sister or meet his newborn niece (though impatient with pregnant women, he behaved well with babies), he resolved not to proceed directly home without official permission and the certainty of returning to Istanbul by autumn. He contented himself with arranging a July based in Cairo, where he could negotiate with the British Council chiefs more directly and be closer to news of the front. It was a decision he would soon regret, but for the moment the long summer vacation, a flight

---

* Giles Whittell delightfully elaborates on Douglas Fairweather's anarchic record: 'Captain "Poppa" Fairweather, too large for a Spitfire and much larger than life, had been tried out as a commanding officer in Prestwick, but was found too disrespect-ful of rules: when the ATA tried to ban smoking in its aircraft he would start taxi flights by handing round a silver cigarette case offering "instant dismissals". When no-one could be found to look after his pet goat, he flew it round the country with him. When White Waltham insisted that taxi pilots use maps, he used one of Roman Britain. He was also known to leave his pocket diary open at the map pages on his knee, but never to refer to it.' (Giles Whittell, *Spitfire Women of World War II* (Harper Press, 2007), p. 222.)

into Egypt and some long-delayed academic research and writing seemed to offer a cheerful prospect.

It is said that Lawrence Durrell set his *Quartet* in Alexandria, rather than Athens, only because he had fewer acquaintances to offend there. Nonetheless, from its raffish founder's day on, the city has possessed a certain reputation. Steven Runciman must have been the only visitor in July 1944 who spent most of his days there locked up reading over the minutiae of medieval theology; he was checking the references for the typescript of *The Medieval Manichee*, a work which had been suspended in almost-readiness since the outbreak of war. The heresies of the past certainly did not blind him, however, to the unorthodoxies of the present – or, in this ancient and modern city, the way past and present met, flirted and did not quite blend:

> Alexandria is an extraordinary place – more Levantine than anywhere that I have seen – Mediterranean with a touch of African fantasy, very amoral – everyone goes to the bad here (but I shan't stay long enough) – and enjoys it very much. It is odd too to be in a place so loaded with historic memories of which not one trace remains – only a misnamed Pompey's Column, a second rate sphinx and a few bare catacombs. But the streets bear proud titles like Alexander the Great Avenue, Anubis Street or Octavian Augustus Street; and even the Pullman Car in which I travelled yesterday was named Cleopatra.

Evidently there was much to enjoy in Egypt. With the front on the move far away, 'the tenseness had gone' from the always miscellaneous atmosphere of smart Cairene society. In these circumstances, combined with the hardening obduracy of the British Council on the matter of leave and likely return journeys, the slackening of Steven's determination to return to Britain seemed reasonable enough. He wrote to his mother, insincerely but understandably, that 'It's all a poor substitute for coming home, but from all I hear I was right not to insist.' In Cairo, Steven renewed his acquaintance with Paddy Leigh Fermor, now a garlanded war hero on account of his exploit on Crete, kidnapping the German commandant, General Kreipe, that May. He also continued his plans for *A History of the Crusades* in ever less nebulous form, interviewing all the Egyptian authorities on the subject he could find. So far, of all his wartime destinations

Steven had been fondest of Jerusalem – of its climate, architecture, history and company – and he decided to move on to the Holy City when his former superior, Christopher Holme, offered him hospitality. This was to be a convenient and congenial stepping-stone in a family visit that would take him east, not west, to see Leslie, who was Air Attaché at the British Embassy in Tehran.

Not long after arriving at Jerusalem in early August, Steven received the news that at last 'things had indeed happened' – Turkey had broken off relations with the Axis powers, though it was not yet clear whether this would lead to a full state of war. Papen and his whole staff, anti-Nazi though they might be, were perforce on their way back to Germany. There were rumours of a Nazi firestorm looming over Istanbul, and the city's many distinguished old wooden houses – such as the one Steven rented in Bebek – were feared to be in particular danger. Michael Grant precipitately married his Swedish fiancée, Anne Sophie Beskow, to avert any separation from her in the event of invasion. Fear was much more plentiful than information.

In *A Traveller's Alphabet* Steven claimed that he found fear in Jerusalem, too, dominant at this point, in a city whose diversity he had three years earlier felt to be a healthily competitive force. He was on the whole inclined to blame the Jewish terrorists of the Stern Gang for the deterioration in the city's harmony, though he admitted that they 'set an example which certain Arab elements were only too willing to copy'. He did not convey any of these forebodings in his letters home at the time, however. Writing to his mother on 9 August he describes with pleasure and nostalgia the resumption of an old and welcome pattern of life:

> I am staying . . . in a lovely old Arab house, not unlike the one which
> I had when I was here, and filled largely with furniture bought from
> me when I left . . . I love being back in Jerusalem. I was given a very
> cordial welcome by all the people in the office . . . and on the streets
> people I barely knew at all greet me as a long lost friend. One can't
> help being gratified.

Stewart Perowne, as ever, was a ready facilitator of amusements. For all his work at the British Embassy in Iraq, he found time easily enough to whisk Steven into Transjordan. Together with the Iraqi

Consul, they dined with the Emir Abdullah, an architect, with T. E. Lawrence, of the Great Arab Revolt against the Ottomans. Steven found this ruler 'though nearly seventy, old for an Arab . . . very vivacious, lecturing us about British policy and full of complaints, some reasonable and some fantastic'. He was also amused to note that this veteran Arab leader preferred to converse in Turkish, and was indeed quick to criticize his visitor's accent (so much for Steven's seat on the Purification of the Turkish Language Committee).

Nineteen-forty-four was a year when Steven paid for his wartime adventures and excursions a cruel price in guilt and grief. Celebrating with the Mevlevi, he had returned to the news of Douglas Fairweather's fatal crash into the Irish Sea. Now, parting company from Perowne, he received back at Holme's house the wire which informed him that Douglas's widow, Steven's beloved sister Margie, had suffered an almost identical fate, after crashlanding an ill-maintained Proctor air transport in Cheshire on 4 August. Steven went to bed and did not emerge for a week.

# 15

# The Star

*Istanbul, 1944–5*

> The summary of several tawdry explanations says that it is a
> card of hope.
>
> Arthur Waite, *The Key to the Tarot*, 1920

Douglas and Margaret Fairweather had been casualties of the war,
but in a way they were not its victims. Flying had been their common
and all-consuming enthusiasm (one Margie also shared with her elder
brother Leslie); their deaths brought to mind Yeats's Irish Airman:

> Nor law, nor duty bade me fight
> Nor public man, nor cheering crowds
> A lonely impulse of delight
> Drove to this tumult in the crowds.

While Lord Runciman, living out the pattern of the 'public man',
had allowed himself to be convinced over the matter of the Sudetenland, Margie and Douglas embarked on secret flights over Germany,
photographing the airfields of the enemy-to-be. Both had recently
decided that Hitler must be confronted, but politics were a tertiary
consideration. The secrecy no doubt excited them, but the flying was
the thing, and, war or no war, they would have taken to the air
anyway.

Douglas was disqualified by age and Margie by sex from action
with the RAF, but the Air Transport Auxiliary offered duties quite as
difficult and indispensable. Douglas's Anson was carrying a wounded
Canadian officer and a nurse; all three were lost off the western Scots
coast. Margie, less foolhardy and unluckier, was on a fairly routine

taxi flight, carrying an official from the Ministry of Aircraft Production and – perhaps to relieve this minor VIP's small talk? – employing her youngest sister Kitty as adjutant. Instantly recognizing the baleful symptoms of engine failure, Margie was unable to switch fuel tanks on account of a vent pipe that had carelessly been painted over. She crashed her light Percival Proctor in a manner that saved her sister from fatal injury, protected the ministry's man, Mr Kendrick, from anything worse than a broken thumb, but doomed herself.

So recently widowed, Margie left a newborn and now orphaned daughter, Elizabeth; but her spirit had been aerial before it was maternal. Her daughter by her first marriage, Ann King-Farlow, had been evacuated to Eigg in the summer of 1940 with her aunt, Ruie, and subsequently spent her holidays from boarding schools in Oxford and Berkshire back on the island. Margie's reticent exterior and determined will left differing impressions on relatives and acquaintances. To Steven, she was the most charming, witty and affectionate of elder sisters. To her first husband, a sensitive man exhausted by tuberculosis, she was not invariably sympathetic. To her ATA colleagues, including the other seven female pilots permitted to transport Spitfires, she embodied aristocratic froideur. While Douglas went by the genially undignified air force nickname of 'Poppa', Margie was known, especially among younger recruits, as 'the Cold Front'. But her brother-in-law, Oliver Farrer, was to find two RAF pilots whom Margie had trained to fly Spitfires visiting the site of her crash, both sobbing where they stood.

A month after Margie's death, her elder and her younger brothers met in Tehran, for the first time since the outbreak of war. Leslie Runciman had been, in his initial wartime incarnation, the founding Director-General of the British Overseas Airways Corporation. In this role, he had been instrumental in the creation of the ATA and, later, in authorizing and encouraging its employment of female pilots. Whether or not Leslie felt responsible for his sister's fate, he was deeply affected, and, like Steven, welcomed the prospect of a little familial comfort so far from home.

Since the previous year he had been Air Attaché at Tehran under Sir Reader Bullard, a British Minister and Ambassador even Churchill found somewhat wearing. Like Leslie and Steven's grandfather,

Bullard was a fearsome, self-made success, and never tired of saying so. He was unsympathetic towards Persians ('blow-flies in their next lives'), and bullied the young Shah, Mohammed Reza. After the previous Persian monarch Reza Shah was adjudged too pro-German in sympathies and deposed, his eldest son had become the figurehead of a Russo-British coup, while the two powers carved up effective control of the vast, ancient nation and its plentiful reserves of oil. Bullard showed little tact in regularly reminding the Shah of his subordinate position, and set the hapless monarch to reading Thucydides. In common with others among the Ambassador's subordinates, Leslie tried to ease the harshness of Bullard's yoke with a gentler approach to the Shah, whom he regarded as 'a pathetic figure, but sympathetic, if one could feel that there was anything solid there'. In the winter of 1943 Bullard's Legation shared the task of hosting the Tehran Conference, the first meeting of Stalin, Churchill, and Roosevelt. Leslie witnessed the presentation to Stalin of the Sword of Stalingrad, the silver-hilted state sword commissioned by King George VI that would eventually lend Evelyn Waugh's trilogy its bleakly ironic title, *The Sword of Honour.*

Now Leslie's younger brother's visit, his sister's death, his Embassy work and his leisure all seemed to stream and combine into a single theme of movement by air. Steven arrived in the Persian capital on 15 September, by a small, hot, unpressurized aircraft which had brought him in stages from Lydda. He had found his views of the western Persian mountains beautiful but alarming. He disembarked green around the gills and unsteady on his feet. The altitude of Tehran itself gave him little chance to recover, and in any case the Builder Shah Reza's city was not especially recuperative to behold. Steven's old acquaintance and rival on Byzantine questions, Robert Byron, had once called Tehran 'that vile stinking intrigue-ridden pretentious vulgar parody of a capital'. Amid his scant luggage Steven carried a sheaf of condolence letters on the death of Margie, which he had requested his mother to forward from Doxford for the brothers' joint consideration.

Though generally discreet to a fault about his private life, Steven was less inhibited about those of his friends, and even, as the brief but mischievous account of his visit to Iran in *A Traveller's Alphabet* demonstrates, of his relatives. After the collapse of his brief marriage to Rosamond Lehmann, Leslie had remarried in 1932 Katherine Schuyler Garrison, an American. This marriage was contented and enduring, producing an only son. All the same, Steven, who evidently resented being dragged out and about in Tehran society while in what he still felt to be a fragile state, slyly intimates in his memoirs that his (by then late) brother had been something of a Don Juan in Persia:

> One evening soon after my arrival [Leslie] took me to a grand dance held in a smart hotel in the mountains, where he planned to have a happy evening with his favourite Persian girl-friend. But after a little while I was in a state of collapse, in terror that I was going to faint. I begged him to take me home. He was most unwilling to have his pleasure interrupted and seemed ready to leave me to my doom. But fortunately the husband of his girl-friend, who, like me but for a different reason, was not finding the party enjoyable, offered to drive me home himself . . .

This sketch in soft colours and sharp lines bears all the usual hallmarks of the Runciman tease. The exaggerated purity of the narrator's diction invites the reader to cast the steamiest of aspersions. The anodyne qualifier 'favourite' suggests a whole seraglio of Persian brides at Leslie's command. Genteel Britannic touches ('grand dance', 'smart hotel', 'girl-friend') only act to emphasize their opposite, the mountainous Persianity, the sordid, gaudy hubris that comes all too easily to the mind when contemplating the Pahlavi era. Husband and punchline alike are procured with expert comic timing. But it is surely, in fact, implausible that a disgruntled Persian husband would have left his wife and his rival alone in order to escort home the latter's valetudinarian little brother.

The letter Steven sent to Doxford about this time implies that Persian life was less glamorous: 'Tehran itself is a rather charmless city, dusty and squalid, with oversize avenues. Society seems gay, though definitely limited ... I've also made contact with the intellectual world, which does not however seem very intellectual.' The leading 'intellectual' at the Shah's court in 1944 was Mirza Mohammed Qazwini, editor of the poet Hafez, an antiquated exquisite who might have been expected to amuse Steven. Perhaps, remembering the portly Turkish laureate who had disturbed the commissariat at his Istanbul supper-party, Steven still had a jaundiced view of widely acclaimed Near Eastern men of letters. In fact he much preferred the young Shah's fearsome new chief of military intelligence, Hasan Arfa. General Arfa was of British diplomatic and Russian aristocratic heritage on his mother's side, had been immaculately educated in Paris, Lausanne and Monte Carlo, and was the husband of Hilda Bewicke, one of Diaghilev's ballerinas and a friend of Vera Bowen's whom Steven remembered well from the late 1920s.

Though Steven had come to Iran with the chief purpose of visiting his brother, he had promised the British Council to deliver a couple of lectures while in the country. His first, in Tehran itself, passed without event or, he thought, inspiration; but the second was at the old Qajar capital, Isfahan. This was a long way from Tehran, except by aeroplane; and Leslie had a light aircraft at his personal disposal for any errand he judged official. Steven's much bemoaned altitude sickness was accordingly tested rather more severely than it had been at Tehran soirées; Leslie displayed the aerial view of the Zagros Mountains to his brother in elaborate, low-flying detail. Steven in turn behaved with exaggerated sangfroid throughout the journey – because, he claims, he trusted Leslie's competence absolutely, though his reader may be left to infer that he was determined not to give his brother the satisfaction of showing fear.* Either way, Leslie rewarded him with a more comfortable, and historically more attractive, return flight, veering off course to swoop over Persepolis.

In the aftermath of a beloved sister's death by plane crash, during a stay engineered in part so that the brothers could mourn her together, this fraternal joshing seems a striking example of the Runciman phlegm. It was a matter of stoicism rather than repression, for Margie still recurred in the brothers' conversation, as well as their thoughts. Later in the week, Leslie listened to his chief, Bullard, who

---

* It seems that daredevil taxi flights were a regular joke of Leslie's. In 1946 he was to give Bullard, who had just retired, a lift to Baghdad; he told his ailing superior in stern tones that his aircraft was designed only to go between Persian mountains, not over them.

had just returned from leave in England, describing the admirable smoothness of his return journey. The Ambassador had particularly enjoyed the picturesque nature of his short flights from Cairo and Haifa to Lydda, in a Percival Proctor. 'Ah,' Leslie interjected, 'the machine that killed my sister.' Steven's reflection on the situation of his motherless nieces, who were both to be brought up by their paternal families, epitomized both their realism and the strength of their feeling: 'One could have wished the arrangements different, but it would only cause more difficulties to try and alter them.'

After a fortnight in Persia, Steven returned to his post at Istanbul by way of a week in Iraq, where Stewart Perowne proved as obliging and hospitable as ever. Steven's romantic attachment to the idea of Ur led only to disappointment, as the Iraqi authorities refused to grant him a permit to visit its ruins, but he did gain an audience with the Prince Regent, Abdullilah. Steven thought him an amiable character, which was an unusual assessment. Norman Daniel, writing immediately after the 1958 revolution, produced a particularly contemptuous account of Iraq's artificial, British-instituted monarchy in general and the Prince Regent in particular:

> To the people he seemed to be totally without thought for public welfare, unscrupulous and ambitious for himself and the fortunes of his family, subject to no law, whether of political or of private behaviour. Of his unsuccessful marriages and private life, doubtless many exaggerated reports were believed; but belief in them was not confined to the political opposition, and to the ordinary man in the street he was the symbol of evil living. Actual acquaintance with him produced no contrary view.

Steven tended to look favourably on royalty of practically any variety, but on this occasion there may have been more to it. Abdullilah was not a straightforward despot, but a flawed man with sporadic good intentions, an ambiguous position and a tendency to compromise. The Regent had just appointed a Prime Minister who reflected his own doubts and hesitations, Hamdi al-Parachi, an elderly, non-partisan, generally respected but somewhat ineffectual choice. It was a court, and a Cabinet, with the kind of atmosphere that Lord

Runciman's son was well placed to understand. In Stewart Perowne Steven had a well-informed and worldly guide to the Regent's complicated and cautious policy; Perowne believed that Iraqi political parties were best compared to 'the Italian combinazione, a transient association of a few interested individuals for a transient material end'.

Steven found that the Iraqi elite – like the Emir of Transjordan – were, for all the tergiversations of their decades of independent monarchy, as culturally close to Turkey as they were politically allied to Britain. In one case this put him to some inconvenience – an Iraqi minister was sending his son to be educated at Robert College in Istanbul, and Steven was enjoined to keep this sheltered seventeen-year-old company on the train. 'I was asked to be kind to him as he had never left home before. He had never seen a mountain before and was excited at the prospect of seeing the sea. Poor boy, he clung rather desperately and his naïveté was a trifle tedious.'

He was back at work soon enough, his first social engagement being dinner with Michael Grant and his Swedish wife – whom Steven had met before at her Embassy, but not since her marriage. Fortunately for her, because Steven could be damning about his friends' choices in love, and rarely reversed a negative verdict, he was enthusiastic about Anne Sophie both in public and in private. At the University and in the conspiratorial surroundings of the British Embassy at Ankara, he found society altered, on the whole for the better. The Germans, whether Papen and his Schwarze Kapelle, Catholic, Nazi-sceptic associates, or those of a less nuanced variety, such as the Nazified head of the Istanbul archaeological faculty, were gone. The many German Jewish refugees among the University staff, of course, remained; they now tended also to be friendlier, and Steven entertained Professor and Frau Auerbach to tea.

Though Steven had liked and respected the previous British Ambassador Sir Hughe Knatchbull-Hugessen, now dispatched to Belgium, Sir Maurice Peterson, his successor, soon proved himself a man of loyalty and principle. In September, Bulgaria, the first posting of Steven's tangled war, had experienced a Communist coup d'état. Steven's old friend Ivan Stancioff, who as a notorious Anglophile had been viewed with suspicion by the pro-Nazi government, was now condemned by the Bulgarian Agrarian National Union as a friend of the royal family. He sought asylum at Peterson's Embassy, remembering the Ambassador's friendship during his earlier Sofia posting; this was at once granted, and Stancioff remained welcome in spite of an irate letter from Eden, who was fearful of offending the Russians and their new Bulgarian client-state. Steven admired Peterson's integrity, if not invariably his table: Lady Peterson had been known to admit dog biscuits to their cheeseboard.

Despite his many friends, as the war drew to a close Steven's patience with his position diminished. His contract committed him to his Chair of Byzantine Studies until March 1946, four years after his original appointment, but he regarded this as months too long. He was still isolated from his bereaved family, and had little real prospect of settling undisturbed to what had become a fully formed conception, *A History of the Crusades*. The unabashedly nepotistic practices involved in marking University examinations annoyed him more than his position as an honorary Turkish dignitary could afford him satisfaction – although it still afforded him quite a lot. He described meeting a new Turkish Cabinet to his mother rather as though he was the Sultan or President who had just appointed them. 'Agriculture', he noted, 'was particularly gracious.'

As so often before, Steven's health began to reflect his disaffection, and to suggest to him the smoothest means of escape. He had complained of sciatica on and off since his arrival in Istanbul. His description of the climate epitomizes his feeling for the whole city of Istanbul – not as wholeheartedly admiring as the Byzantine partisanship of his historical narratives might suggest, but incapable of even grousing about the weather without simultaneously evoking the city's ancient, sophisticated, decayed appeal:

> No city is more splendidly situated than Istanbul; but its setting has one cruel disadvantage. I have often thought that the inherent melancholy and pessimism of the Byzantines was due to the climate of their imperial city, to the cold wind that blows in winter down the funnel of the Bosphorus from the Black Sea and the steppes of Russia beyond it, to the hot enervating wind, the *melteme*, blowing from the south in summer, and to the all-pervading damp.

In the February of 1945 Steven was kept firmly bed-bound by his recurring complaint, stirring only to write plaintive letters to his University superiors, Michael Grant and his mother. At his most dramatic, he even began to suggest that he might not last another Istanbul winter, calling up a vision of another, if rather improbable, Runciman war casualty, a sort of involuntary Missolonghian deathbed. This remained his elective position until the summer, though he exploited two interludes of greater strength and mobility pleasurably enough; not for nothing had he often reminded his friends of the paramount importance of 'enjoying poor health' in the full sense of the verb. In late March he took the waters at Bursa, 'as many Byzantines had done before me', while he spent the whole of that May recuperating, and sightseeing, in Kyrenia, on Cyprus. It was the perfect place for Steven to find himself for the celebration of VE Day: an island which, perhaps even more than Istanbul, defied definition between Europe and Asia, and which was quite as integral to the story of the Crusades.

Back in Bebek, the ailing and widely esteemed Professor was sedulously attended to by a 'young Turk who lives not far off and to whom I give avuncular advice now and then – his parents are good friends of mine.' Steven's lectures were delivered without any hitch by Münire during his absences, and he was back at his post to fulfil the only duty for which his presence was indispensable – a further, and as it was to turn out final, round of undergraduate examinations and marking, marred, as ever, by political considerations. The Examination Board of Letters at Istanbul was tripartite; Steven kept the peace between a pair of Turkish academics who exemplified a divide that persists to this day in Turkey, one a Kemalist of extreme 'pan-Turanian' Turkic racialist tendencies, the other a pious Koranic sage, uninterested in any concerns outwith the scriptural. Hitherto the situation had proved frustrating but surprisingly stable; the balance was upset by the arrest of the Kemalist, who was implicated in an attempt to chloroform the Turkish Cabinet, and was replaced with an undistinguished but ambitious University administrator. Steven now found himself outvoted with regularity, rather than able to intrigue with his conveniently irreconcilable partners. 'I realized then that I was unsuited for oriental academic life. It was time for me to leave.'

By now Michael Grant was ready to accede. Professor Runciman had been a wartime appointment, a necessary check on superior German intellectual firepower, his very presence a *coup de prestige*, quite apart from any useful intelligence Steven may, unofficially, have imparted to his old pupil Nick Elliott. While trying to convince his friend to join him in Istanbul, Grant had emphasized the post-war opportunities that the Byzantine chair might entail; but these were allurements, not real responsibilities. Grant arranged for the University to accept the Professor's resignation – whereupon both Steven's health and his sense of adventure made a swift recovery.

Steven had decided he was not after all looking for a permanent, comfortable retirement back in London, Northumberland or Eigg. He wanted another job, with decent remuneration and new surroundings, that would nonetheless permit him to settle to the book he was now determined to begin. Wisely, he preserved his formal connection to the British Council, which he suspected might soon have such an opportunity at its disposal. In the meantime, well shot of the factions and committees of the University, he readied himself for a new lease of social life.

The Italian Embassy was coming to be regarded as the most diverting scene in post-war Istanbul, with the grand old House of Savoy undergoing a certain rehabilitation in the eyes of the Allies – if not those of its own subjects – after its (eventual) triumph over Mussolini. Two years earlier, when Italy agreed to an Armistice with the Allies after the 25 Luglio coup that overthrew Mussolini, Steven had been much entertained to discover from the disclosure of the Italian Ambassador's papers that he had headed the Italian dossier listing British agents. He would always treasure his description in that file as 'molto intelligente e molto pericoloso'. Now, in less tense circumstances, he indulged a pleasure that the exigencies of international diplomacy had too long denied him – Vatican gossip. The new Papal Legate, a Monsignor Roncalli, exceeded Steven's expectations:

> To look at, he was a short, rotund peasant, but with a quick mind, a wonderful sense of fun and a serene and tolerant benevolence. I have never known anyone else who gave one such a happy feeling of sheer goodness. He was loved in Istanbul, even by the Moslem Turks and by the Orthodox Greeks, whom history has made deeply suspicious of anything emanating from Rome.

Roncalli seems to have approved of Runciman too. Even after his election in 1958 as Pope John XXIII – and after *A History of the*

*Crusades* had provoked the fury of Catholic reviewers – the new Pope asked after Steven with affectionate interest, by way of mutual friends. Steven, for his part, never quite forgave himself for failing to hurry to an audience with *il Papa Buono* before Pope John died in 1963. He thus missed his chance to become a papal favourite in addition to being a defender of Orthodoxy and an honorary Whirling Dervish.

Before long, a new and intriguing possibility for useful work in the Near East had materialized. Back in September 1943, a year and a half into his Istanbul post, and enjoying some leave in Beirut, Steven had run into a celebrated acquaintance from younger days – the explorer Bertram Thomas, sometime Prime Minister of Oman and the first man to cross the Empty Quarter of the Arabian desert.* Thomas was regarded by certain of his colleagues and subordinates, as well as by the rivalrous successors of his feat, Harry St John Philby and Wilfred Thesiger, as something of a cardboard hero. It was alleged that Philby – whose assistant Thomas had once been, and whom Thomas had narrowly pipped to the prize – subsequently made a much harder crossing, while Thomas, as Thesiger put it, 'took the easy way through', 'bundled on his absurd saddle'. Thomas's motives were impugned as mercenary, 'dining out on the Empty Quarter', his writing as workaday, his manner as pompous, his life as pampered and Rolls-Royced beside Thesiger's own ascetic ideal.† Moreover the older explorer's reputation had, along with his health, been irreparably damaged by ever-sharpening dipsomania. All the same, he had

---

* In his late twenties at Cambridge Steven had veered between being glamourized and bored by Bertram Thomas, who in turn seemed to pay him plenty of attention; Steven spent the evening of his twenty-ninth birthday as Thomas's wryly attentive guest at the Royal Central Asian Society. 'Lots of distinguished personages made speeches about Asia and Indian problems and so on. It wasn't a thrill' (SR to KR, 19 July 1932, Elshieshields).

† Steven called Thesiger himself 'a strange creature, not wholly lovable but interesting. He suffered from a monster of a mother' (SR to Guy Black, 2 May 1987, quoted with permission of Lord Black). Steven would quite often draw oedipal inferences about men of his own class and sexual orientation whom he disliked. As for the elder Philby, Steven had respected his reputation while at Cambridge, and thought his son Kim 'a nice, quiet young man' (SR to KR, 13 May 1932, Elshieshields).

shown kindness to Steven from their first meeting, and Steven was in turn loyal and admiring.

Since March 1944, Thomas had been in charge of the Middle East Centre for Arabic Studies (MECAS), an Arabic-language college set up under the aegis of British intelligence, and based, initially, at Jerusalem. Thomas's Chief Instructor, Major Aubrey Eban, was an intelligence officer in touch with both SIS and the Jewish Yishuv militia, who would later become Israel's Foreign Minister. Whatever its source of funding, Thomas insisted that the purpose of MECAS was 'to teach Arabic as a language of modern intercourse. The task . . . is severely practical – the acquisition of a living language . . . a process only feasible in the environment in which the language lives . . . We are here concerned primarily with the street; the sound of the language, the idiom, the current cliché are more vital than the current theory.' Over its first year, MECAS suffered from the deterioration of British popularity, and consequently security, in Palestine, and by the autumn of 1945 Thomas was involved in a diligent search for a new site and additional personnel. His adventures, however cosseted, had left him with a great variety of Levantine friends; but on this occasion the most persuasive community proved to be one of the smallest and most secretive, the Druze. The origin of this sect would six years later be related, elegantly if cavalierly, in *The First Crusade*:

> the Caliph Hakim, the son of a Christian mother and brought up largely by Christians, suddenly reacted against his early influences . . . Hakim became convinced that he was himself divine. This divinity was publicly proclaimed in 1016 by his friend Darazi . . . by now the fury of the Moslems was aroused against the Caliph, who had substituted his own name for that of Allah in the mosque services. Darazi fled to the Lebanon, to found there the sect that is called the Druze, after his name. Hakim himself disappeared in 1021. He was probably murdered by his ambitious sister, Sitt al-Mulk; but his fate remained and still remains a mystery. The Druzes believe that in due course he will come again.

In more recent history, the Druze had turned Anglophile – as opposed to the incurably Francophile Maronite Christians – and Thomas's Druze friends, by invoking this past, convinced him to move MECAS on to Druze territory, to the village of Shemlan in an unspoilt rural area, the Chouf, but still conveniently close to Beirut. Thomas offered Steven the assistant directorship of the new school, a posting on ground contested in the Crusades, superior to Major Eban and answering only to Thomas himself. It must have seemed a most alluring place for Steven to write the book he had in mind.

Yet, after a short consideration, Steven refused. Perhaps the sternness of the syllabus had put him off; he gave as his excuse his lack of fluency in Arabic, despite Thomas's disarming assurance that he could doubtless perfect the language on the job. The undeniable odour of military intelligence that still clung about MECAS may have put him off; Steven still accepted a British Council wage, which theoretically forbade him political partisanship, and he had thus far kept his nose quite clean in this regard. Or possibly he had already received intimation of an even more tempting prospect.

The casualties of war among Steven's friends and acquaintance had been various and unpredictable. Eddie Bates, that lost, hedonistic reprobate, had confounded everyone's expectations with the most orthodox of heroic deaths, shot down over Germany at the beginning of 1945 on a bombing mission. Robert Byron, Steven's Oxford counterpart in Byzantinism, who had sparred with him over style and approach, but whose intellect and passion Steven seldom faulted, died early in 1941, torpedoed en route to Canada as a war correspondent. Adrian Bishop, whom Steven had known through Keynes and Bowra, a heavy-drinking but rarely disoriented wit, had broken his neck, uncharacteristically falling down a Tehran staircase, a mysterious death that rumour connected to his excellent work for SOE. The young Duke of Wellington, whose boorish father and religiose mother Steven had encountered with Stephen Tennant at Wilsford, had been killed in a Commando unit fighting in Salerno under Colonel 'Mad Jack' Churchill, and was succeeded by his uncle Gerry, a one-time attachment of Cecil Beaton's. According to Baba Brougham, the new Duke's show of mourning was hardly convincing. Rex Whistler had fallen in the Normandy campaign, after, according to some accounts, predicting his own death; lamented by everyone, he now approached the symbolic canonization previously accorded to Raymond Asquith.

Two old friends Steven might have reasonably assumed would spend the war in honourable safety had succumbed to the Luftwaffe: Bobbie Longden, the Eton and Oxford love-object of Cyril Connolly, Master of Wellington, had been the school's only victim when a bomb hit the chapel; while Petica Robertson, Topsy Lucas's elder sister, became Cambridge's only casualty from bombing while performing duties as an air-raid warden.

An extraordinarily ungenerous letter Steven wrote to an old protégé, Noel Annan, from Istanbul in early 1945 shows the kind of disillusion evinced by the later stages of Waugh's or Powell's war trilogies – an irrational but understandable conviction that, when so many deserving friends have fallen, there is a taint of dishonour in the successes of the survivors. After expanding on his grief for Margie and the state of his own constitution, Steven turned to the real topic of his letter, Annan's recent election to a fellowship at King's at the age of twenty-nine (fixed by Keynes). This might be considered an example of exactly how a one-time don of Steven's type thought the system ought to work – a well-connected, talented young man, with first-class academic qualifications and practical wartime experience, being manoeuvred into a comfortable and distinguished post-war life by influential friends. Steven had won his own Trinity fellowship and, even more, his Byzantine chair at Istanbul in this fashion; and it was also how he would shortly find himself the Representative of the British Council at Athens.

That Steven's reaction was so extreme is a reflection of his gloom, and the bitterness engendered by the long war – but also of the way in which he did not always conform to the expected pattern. He wrote to Annan:

> They tell me you have become a Fellow of King's: and I send my congratulations, because it is my duty ... but I couldn't disapprove more – not so much of King's for choosing you: that was perhaps natural; but of you for being chosen, for being the sort of person that is chosen ... But who can escape his destiny?
>
> I always feared that you were doomed given your tastes, your admirations, and your type of snobbism; and my fears were confirmed by your bright war career [Annan had achieved rapid promotion in

intelligence partly through the patronage of Bill Bentinck, later Duke of Portland and at this point in charge of the Joint Intelligence Committee] and by those so scintillating reviews in the *New Statesman and Nation*. Well, it is done now ... We must just watch you with affectionate sadness, modelling yourself upon the Provost [still John Sheppard] and trying earnestly to become a Character ...

My disapproval is a measure of my affection. It saddens me to think of you never growing up but remaining, Peter Pan among Peter Pans, floating airily across a stage of tinsel.

Steven's usual elegant good-humour does not quite neutralize this letter's acidity. Noel Annan, conscious that its criticism was in earnest, was moved and injured enough to complain to Dadie Rylands: 'this may give you a pensif cinq minutes.' Yet the third element to which the letter lays claim, affectionate solicitude, is sincere. Steven had escaped his own academic career with relief, and the few elements of conventional academe involved in his Istanbul posting had seemed to him a barren waste of time. In a way, his reproach to Annan is a recapitulation of the advice Trevelyan had given him nearly twenty years earlier. Annan himself seems to have interpreted Steven's homily as an argument for a public career: 'Dear Steven always wished to change me and to make me a better and less vulgar and silly fellow than I am ... I think he wanted to turn me into a talented member of the English upper classes – not a role I can play.' Here, perhaps, the future Provost, Vice-Chancellor and peer protested too much.

But even as Steven regarded Noel Annan's glittering ascent with disfavour, unseen wheels were turning on his own behalf. He was still at the disposal of the British Council, and Michael Grant had ensured that, despite his early departure, his record at Istanbul was excellent. Of all the British Council's post-war centres of operations, none combined theoretical importance and practical disorder to the same extent as Athens. The presence and prestige of the British School at Athens had ensured that the city was one of the longest-established objects of the British Council's attentions. Besides, a mixture of strategic realpolitik and romantic philhellenism – both emanating from Winston Churchill – ensured that Britain had still, for the time being, the dominant hand among the Allies in Greece. At the same time, the British Council had withdrawn for three years under German occupation, and, in the aftermath of Greece's liberation, much of it by Communist aligned resistance movements, its re-establishment was inevitably chaotic.

If the consequences of invasion and liberation were not difficulties enough, it was widely believed that the pre-occupation Athens staff had been institutionally sub-par. The Beaverbrook press, whose opinion, seconded by Churchill, was that the Council was an expensive luxury, encountered in Athens an ideal hunting-ground for profligate and sybaritic intellectuals, described by the *Evening Standard* as 'long-haired, effeminate and ineffectual old school-masters'. Olivia Manning, embittered by her husband's cool reception in Athenian conciliar circles just before the city's evacuation, immortalized the same hostility in her *Balkan Trilogy*. Her Athens is peopled by an exquisite, fabulously rich fake Major, a hypochondriac, eternally youthful yet 'mummified' Director and his beautiful, complacent favourite, a lecturer who has shirked his post through the influence of a father in the Commons, a versatile Kingsman with a mysterious smile, and a 'pretty pair' of malingerers who address each other as 'the old soul'.*

In 1940 C. W. F. Dundas, the British Council chief in Cairo, sent a gloomy memorandum to his London superior, Lord Lloyd:

> I feel very strongly that some of the Council's Greek staff have gained (and a few deserved) a reputation for qualities which make their position untenable in the especially difficult and delicate circumstances of the present time. It is variously said that they are indiscreet, extravagant, lack any serious purpose, do not consider the public effects of their personal behaviour, or are irresponsible in financial matters. It is, too, repeatedly said, however slanderously, that they are 'pansies', 'longhaired' or 'soft'. This unsavoury reputation unhappily found its

---

* Manning's choice of King's as the alma mater of the homosexual Alan Frewen and the selfish, besotted Director, Colin Gracey, is not surprising. She will have been aware of the college's reputation as 'Bloomsbury-on-Cam', which during Steven's undergraduate days made King's as suspect to older bachelor dons as it was alluring to the younger set.

way both to Egypt and to Cyprus this summer, and we still have unwelcome repercussions of it from time to time.

Almost without exception English people evacuated from the Balkans to the Middle East have the same stories to tell ... 1) Maladministration. 2) Public immorality of staff. 3) No efforts made to conciliate British Communities. 4) Failure to limit minorities in our Institutes. 5) Disloyalty of the staff to the Council. 6) Disloyalty of the Staff to each other coupled with internecine quarrels. 7) Financial muddles.

'Flux' Dundas and Lord Lloyd were themselves implicated in the popular strictures against the British Council atmosphere. Dundas was almost certainly the model for Manning's valetudinarian Director Colin Gracey, while Lord Lloyd, who was well known to detest women, had caused astonishment at his marriage. It was evidently time for a shake-up, and in this sense the dissolution of the British Council in Greece during the period of enemy occupation came as a welcome pretext. Kenneth Johnstone, the Council stalwart, soldier, spy and diplomat, was initially responsible for identifying promising new staff, but could not himself stay to oversee their installation. Among his choices for assistant personnel were the novelist Rex Warner and the guerrilla heroes Maurice Cardiff and Patrick Leigh Fermor, but the post of Representative itself came with precise and exacting ideals which proved difficult to satisfy. As the Whitehall official specified to Johnstone, 'We must be particularly careful in our choice of a permanent Representative ... a person of some academic reputation, for preference not a classical scholar, who is a competent administrator, knows the Greeks and can speak modern Greek. In temperament he should be the kind of person to whom people like to take their grievances.' These last two requirements were particularly irreconcilable, as anyone who really knew Greece and the Greeks would be tainted by association with a particular political faction. One way or another, these problems ruled out the first three names considered for the post, Romilly Jenkins, Nicholas Hammond and Steven's now long-established wartime guardian angel, Michael Grant.

So it was that the new broom selected to reconstruct an efficient and influential British cultural centre, in the country considered to be the front line against the spread of Communism, and in the midst of an unpleasant reaction against favouritism, unprofessionalism and aesthetical decadence, was Steven Runciman. In retrospect, it seems a bizarre choice. Olivia Manning's various patently homosexual *bêtes noires*, in their social exclusivity, their perpetual complaints about their health, their fastidious appearances, their brittle witticisms and fluting tones, even in their family and educational backgrounds, bring Steven generically to mind. Yet, during their brief acquaintance in the confusion of wartime Cairo, the novelist had not taken against the historian. More than the sum of his mannerisms, and equipped with his mother's sense of public duty, Steven would prove to be as successful in his new task as, in private, he was candid about its oddities.

# 16

# Justice

## Athens, 1945–7

> the moral principle which deals unto every man according to
> his works ... differs in its essence from the spiritual justice
> which is involved in the idea of election.
>
> Arthur Waite, *The Key to the Tarot*, 1920

After not quite two months in his position, the new Representative to the British Council at Athens felt able to offer his mother a dispassionate, if withering, assessment of the state of Greek politics and British interference: 'We have forced on Greece a government of which a parallel would be if Britain today had forced on her a government of such relics as could be found of the 1906 Liberal administration – excellent, certainly, but a wee bit unreal.' This was an analogy bound to have forcible significance for both Steven and Hilda Runciman. One such 1906 'relic' was Walter Runciman himself, briefly promoted back into the Cabinet and then ruined by association with his report on Czechoslovakia. He had not been in good spirits or sound bodily health since the outbreak of war, and his symptoms had been recognized as Parkinson's disease towards its end; Hilda now took de facto charge of the family. When Steven compared Greece's plight to a hypothetical Britain under unelected and outdated rule, he chose a parallel with historical and domestic force. It was in part this historical sensitivity that enabled Steven to sustain, for eighteen months, a difficult role in an impossible situation.

Athens offered useful if often insoluble work, and life abroad in a climate and country to which Steven was inevitably drawn. His return to Britain had been brief and not very inspiring. As the more caustic of his letters home emphasize, he regarded the new Attlee government as a pack of cack-handed, dreamily ideological ignoramuses, incapable of standing up to Russian pressure. But personal far more than political reasons made his spell at home depressing. His father was a disappointed and a dying man, succumbing to slow, miserable degeneration. His favourite sister had left two daughters, one, orphaned of both her parents, still less than a year old; complicated questions over their custody preoccupied Hilda. It is hardly surprising that Athens was a tempting prospect by contrast, even if Steven preferred, as so often, to plead considerations of health.

Under the unprecedented and pressing post-war circumstances, the usual protocol that the Council keep itself separated from military and intelligence hierarchies was impossible to sustain. In the months before Steven arrived the organization was temporarily in the charge of Prudence Wallace. Her husband, Major David Wallace, an envoy sent by Churchill, had been killed the previous year while observing EDES, the right-wing, British-armed Greek partisans, ambushing a German column in the mountains. Mrs Wallace was reinforced, and then unofficially replaced, by Maurice Cardiff, a young Scots Guards officer who had been seconded to Athens from the Aegean and hastily briefed for the job of Assistant Representative.

In his memoir, *Friends Abroad*, Cardiff remembers finding himself in conversation with 'a charming erudite colonel' (in fact Johnstone of the Council), who was in the process of packing his own suitcase. Cardiff was presented with sudden and novel instructions: 'I had imagined I had only been sent for because my work in the Aegean had come to an end and I was required for other military duties. Now, to my surprise, I found myself being asked to take over the running of an organisation of which I had scarcely heard and which had nothing to do with the army.' The youngest child of an army family, Cardiff was, according to his *Guardian* obituary by Geoffrey Wheatcroft, 'much less conventional than his exterior suggested, and not designed for soldiering'. Before the war Cardiff had revealed his unconventionality in a somewhat conventional manner, by eloping to Gretna Green with an actress, Leonora Freeman. But he had the adventurer's and the travel-writer's knack for languages, and picked up modern Greek for fun during their honeymoon. This fateful skill led him into SOE, and the Aegean. Unlike, for example, David Wallace – who while working with EDES had been instructed to rank Communists, if anything, below Germans – Cardiff had fought alongside Communist partisans in the Aegean.

Cardiff's feelings about his new superior were immediately cautious. A careful, articulate observer, on further acquaintance with Steven he became more cautious still. He was unaware that he had at once deeply impressed the new Representative. The day after their first meeting, Steven wrote to his mother in high spirits: 'I was pleased to find [Cardiff] extremely pleasant and intelligent – a major aged 29, still loaned by the military. He has been struggling alone with the work for some months, but instead of resenting my coming in over him seems genuinely glad. I think he will be excellent to work with.' But Cardiff for his part found Steven, though 'friendly and charming', more than a touch disconcerting. He was less contented than he seemed about his new subordinacy. Along with Johnstone, he had set matters on a new and promising footing with speed and competence, especially by separating out and staffing the British Institute under Rex Warner, a racy and enthusiastic novelist. Now Cardiff and Warner both served at the whim of an outsider with a mysterious air, lately some sort of Byzantine professor, but without military rank or administrative experience. That Steven's reputation as a historian lent him a certain automatic gravitas did not necessarily lessen Cardiff's irritation. Though Steven was genuinely delighted with his assistant, he could be inadvertently patronizing about Cardiff's abilities and achievements. After a glance at the status quo he was writing to Hilda: 'The whole organisation has been chaotic. My excellent Assistant Representative came in after the chaos had started and had neither the time, the experience nor the authority to clear much up; and I am unearthing all sorts of mess. (Alas, the Army tried to run it at first, all too amateurishly.)' An unconventional soldier Cardiff may have been, but he was still part of the army structure which had been forced to do the best it could, during the British Council's trickiest juncture in Greece so far. It cannot have been easy being treated, however genially, as a regrettable stopgap by a civilian, part of whose specific job description was to help to disentangle conciliar arrangements from the military.

These were difficulties inherent in Steven's and Cardiff's respective positions; their personalities led to more serious, if less articulated tensions, particularly on Cardiff's side. Steven liked the company quite as much as the appearance of patrician, heterosexual young men of action; his natural tendency was to treat Cardiff rather as he would have done an amusing pupil, Noel Annan, Guy Burgess, Nick Elliott, even, in the best case, George Jellicoe. But Cardiff was independent-minded and, as Wheatcroft notes, in fact atypical of the British officer class. This made him more hostile than most young men of his milieu might have been to Steven's *haute snobisme* and evident, if well-behaved, sexuality. 'I was prompted to attach a mental label to him; "handle with care" '. No doubt this was not the only label that Cardiff privately attached to his new chief.

Steven had been flown out at the beginning of October 1945, with a stop at Naples, whose dilapidated state after the Allied invasion he found especially demoralizing, bringing as it did happier inter-war days to mind. He had first known the city while sailing with his father on *Sunbeam*, in the early 1920s. With probably more musical than racial prejudice he now observed that 'Naples is shabby and scarred and it seems as if the worst of every army was stationed there. The American troops were nearly all black, and looked much more civilised than the bedraggled British. I hated Naples. It was sad to see it so degraded. They say, however, that the Opera is as good as ever, and much appreciated by the troops . . . '

Steven found Athens, for all the fighting it had lately endured, more reassuring. The Australian-born British Ambassador, Sir Rex Leeper, who had been instrumental in the foundation of the British Council more than a decade earlier, was a natural ally to any protégé of Grant's. Leeper's role was presently, like Lampson's in Egypt, closer to Viceroy than Ambassador. He embodied the paternalism of post-war British policy in Greece (even proposing that Greece should join the Commonwealth), but also identified himself wholeheartedly with the Council's more nuanced cultural aims.

Haughtily confident in his own and British rightness, Leeper was not popular with the Greek or home press, and the previous year the Foreign Office had decided to balance his tough approach with the emollient ministrations of a new and celebrated press attaché, the cartoonist Osbert Lancaster. Lancaster was an instantly conspicuous addition to the Embassy's dramatis personae. Bevis Hillier has remarked of his personal appearance that 'he looked like one of his own cartoon characters and, as he aged, he resembled more and more an effigy of the English gentleman on a French carnival float: bulging eyes, bulbous nose, buffalo-horn moustache, bald head, striped shirt, pinstripe suit from Thresher and Glenny, old-fashioned shoes with rounded toes.' Lancaster, with his famous architect's eye and pencil, found the style and situation of the Embassy bizarrely incongruous. While gunfire scattered about the Athenian streets, the British diplomats resided at a vast holiday villa of vivid pink stucco, 'almost ostentatiously recognisable', as if to resemble the cartographical colour of the Empire. This was the legacy of Leeper's predecessor's wife, Lady Palairet, who had repainted the place immediately before the German invasion on what were allegedly aesthetic, rather than defiant, grounds.*

One unofficial but intense connection between Council and Embassy was the love-affair between Osbert Lancaster's secretary, Joan Rayner, on the run from her husband at the *Daily Express*, and Paddy Leigh Fermor, another of Johnstone's finds. Steven and Paddy, of course, were old and, on the whole, admiring acquaintances, although, penned up in the same office, they were to prove antipathetic types. After meeting the 'grubby boy' in Sofia and the wounded war hero in Cairo, at Athens Steven was to witness a third, not invariably attractive phase in Paddy's development. Like Bonnie Prince Charlie in his middle years, Paddy was a folk hero without an immediate cause. He got on easily with everyone, especially Greeks; but there were rumours that, had he tried to settle in his old Cretan battleground, his life might have been in danger from the locals who had

---

* Lancaster's taste for the absurd had been richly gratified over the Christmas of 1944, when the Embassy received a surprise visit from first Harold Macmillan, then Churchill, while something like a state of siege prevailed outside its front door. Leeper's supply of champagne ran dry, whereupon Macmillan outraged diplomatic practice by breaking into the unfortunate Palairets' abandoned, pre-war cellar, which the more punctilious Germans had spared. After his own period as Prime Minister, Macmillan was to describe this initiative as 'the only thing I'm really proud of in my career' (Harold Macmillan (in 1984), quoted in Richard Boston, *Osbert* (Collins, 1989), p. 139).

suffered German reprisals; not to mention the drinking he would nightly have undertaken with cronies. As it was, he never refused Cretan hospitality, for which he was scarcely, however, in a position to pay. Despite his fervent and deepening love for Joan, his affairs with Greek girls were also myriad. It was not a tone of life designed to endear him to his new superior.

Steven's relations with the British Embassy would vary with its occupants, but his oldest friend in the Athenian diplomatic population was a Greek, Panagiotis Pipinelis, the former Greek Minister at Sofia. During his uncomfortable spell as a press attaché in pre-invasion Sofia, Steven had found the Ministry of Greece, Britain's gallantly singular continental ally, to be an entertaining refuge. Pipinelis and his wife made an amusing pair of national caricatures, he short and swart, she a blonde Swedish giantess, encountered, like Michael Grant's wartime bride, during social rounds with the enviably well-supplied and hospitable neutral powers. Pipinelis's friendship paid off when, in accordance with Churchillian British policy, the King of the Hellenes returned and the former Minister in Sofia was appointed his *chef de cabinet* and the chief conduit to the royal gossip that Steven now regarded as the principal compensation of his job.

As yet, however, the royal return was too dangerous, too openly and widely opposed, to be effected, even though the British General Sir Ronald Scobie, whom Steven admired to an exaggerated degree ('the most popular man in Greece ... more typically a nice, simple British soldier than you could believe possible'), was still roughly in control of the military situation. Leeper allowed the Archbishop of Athens, Damaskinos, to be appointed Regent; London's orders were to exert and exploit pressure upon the Archbishop exactly as if he were indeed the King. Damaskinos had been appointed by the German and quisling authorities, but the spirited and uniquely public resistance he had put up against the deportation of Greek Jews to Poland had won him an unusual combination of popularity with the Athenian populace and with his British patrons. When threatened with the firing squad by an SS commander, Damaskinos had replied with the utmost archepiscopal disdain that it was more usual for prelates of the Greek Orthodox Church to be hanged than shot. The Archbishop's position constituted the sort of organic political irregularity that appealed to Steven, as did Damaskinos himself, though that did not stop the new Representative retailing home semi-salacious inferences about the Regent's private life ('the Regent Archbishop's lady friend . . . looks like a toad but is very intelligent. They say it is all quite Platonic').

By late October 1945, Steven was installed in a conveniently positioned flat with 'very meagre and ugly furniture', which he considered too expensive but, as he gleefully told Hilda, 'Anyhow it is the poor British taxpayer who pays, not I. (How that will shock you.)' He began to entertain as avidly as in Istanbul: 'I am giving a very smart party next week at my office to meet myself – all on the cabinet ministers', ambassadors', generals' and admirals' level. We decided that unless we kept it official and lofty we should cause endless offence.' But there was a middle way between the amusing but airless rites of officialdom and the disordered, poetical carouses until dawn preferred by Paddy Leigh Fermor and Rex Warner. Steven's ideal intellectual company was encapsulated by Georgios Seferiades – better known as the poet George Seferis – 'a large gentle creature who combines enormous culture with a modest kindliness'. A native of Smyrna, who felt and expressed a keen sense of exile, Seferis's lyrical sensibility accompanied a strong sense of patriotic duty; the first would eventually bring him the Nobel Prize, the second diplomatic posts in Beirut and Britain, and a reputation as the laureate who defied the junta of the Colonels. For the moment, he and his wife, Maro, with her arresting features and her classically blonde Hellenic colouring, provided a relatively tranquil bohemian context for Steven's delectation, as set against rowdier characters like Odysseus Elytis and George Katsimbalis.

Maurice Cardiff's memoirs paint an informative portrait of Steven at this time, as naturalistic as it is courteous:

No doubt . . . I must have made blunders enough, grammatical, social, political and of every possible kind to make him wince, but there were two early perceptions on my part which helped to smooth our relationship. Steven was already at work on his great history of the Crusades. When needing to consult him in his office, before entering I would open the door a little just long enough for him to put aside the

'Crusades' and replace it with some workaday file on his blotter. The second was more important. In response to any proposal I might make to him he always said 'yes'. But he had two kinds of yesses, one short, even clipped, was a true affirmative; the other, long drawn out with a dip in the middle, signified 'no'. The distinction was lost on Paddy, who on the strength of the longest of drawn out 'yesses' would set out on a six-week tour of the islands or a trip round the Peloponnese.

It is not quite as clear as Cardiff's account makes out that Steven was already at work on *A History of the Crusades*. Though he had had the project in mind since at least 1938, he cannot have got much of it written, or even researched, in the Athens years. His letters confirm that he was genuinely preoccupied with Council business, began the writing of *The First Crusade* later at Doxford, and completed the body of it in seclusion on Eigg. Cardiff tended to play up Steven's amateur, *fainéant* attitude, and the story of the clandestine 'Crusades' manuscript may, for all its charm, be an example of this. Nor were Paddy Leigh Fermor's admittedly frequent excursions out of Athens such renegade caprices as Cardiff implies. Steven recognized that Paddy was a liability in the office but an asset outside it, and encouraged him to get about, fuddling his stories of Crete and General Kreipe over neat ouzo to enormous Greek audiences.

Cardiff privately thought that Steven surrounded himself with a 'very nasty set' of dubious younger men, especially Ronald Crichton, the Council's Music and Arts Officer, and Bill Barron, the Deputy Director of its Higher Institute. Steven made much of Crichton's 'gentle birth' (his cousin, the Earl of Erne, had been killed in the retreat to Dunkirk) and wide knowledge of opera. Bill Barron he mentions in his letters only to tick him off in characteristic, oblique temper for inadequate table manners. Cardiff clarified but faintly what he had meant by 'nasty', suggesting that Barron in particular performed the offices of a Figaro or Pandarus to the Council's homosexual contingent. Cardiff's obituarist, Wheatcroft, was to reflect some of the same suspicion in commenting that the British Council 'did become something of a system of outdoor relief for unattached aesthetes'.

Another of the aesthetes in question, one whose credentials as a womanizer were well attested, was Rex Warner, the novelist, classical scholar and translator, who as head of the British Institute, under the Council, also now reported to Steven. He too was capable of passing on catty opinions about Steven's favourites, commenting of a fancy-dress dance thrown by the Council that 'we are to have eighty guests, including about eight heterosexuals' (Steven dressed as a fairly convincing Greek sailor, Cardiff remembered). Warner's own private life tended to eventful contours; he had been one of the several lovers of Steven's and Dadie's old Cambridge patroness, Topsy Lucas, and was later to leave his wife for Barbara Rothschild. The Warners fitted most coherently into the raucous crowd congregating around Joan Rayner, Osbert Lancaster and Paddy Leigh Fermor. Their modern Greek was patchy and their Greek acquaintances at first few. Although Rex Warner particularly appreciated Seferis, whom he translated by leaning on his excellent ancient Greek, he knew the poet mainly through Steven. Cardiff and Steven were united in their mixed opinion of Warner's strengths and limitations. Cardiff liked him but had misgivings about his character:

> Quick to spot the comedy in our not infrequently misplaced endeavours, the merest amateurs that we were, to live up to the high ideals in cultural diplomacy set by [Johnstone], he tempered our dismay at the worst of our failures by his deep and reassuring chuckle . . .
>
> It was only gradually that I found it disconcerting that he seemed almost always to agree with anything which was said to him, and was ready to fall in with any proposal so long as it did not involve him in physical or mental exertion.

As for Steven, in the course of his duties he had to rate Warner's various attributes in a report back to Whitehall. The last of these reports, after a year and half of co-operation, allowed the Institute Director 'A for Personality, Initiative, Tact and Zeal and Extra mural activities and relations, B for Accuracy, and C for Judgment, Power of taking responsibility, Power of supervising staff, and Linguistic ability in relation to country.' For his part, even Warner looked down on the capabilities of his deputy and companion in debauch, Paddy: 'though very charming and mad, he does nothing at all.'

Life in Athens was full of incident and accident. One week Steven was called upon to help rig up and attend the national celebration over the anniversary of Greece's repulse of the Italian army: 'one kept seeing long lines of widows and orphans enjoying themselves hugely, or of moustached girl guides . . . a lot of gunfire and sirens (noise for noise's sake, mostly); the Parthenon floodlit and looking far lovelier than ever it does by day;* and no one doing any work at all.' Whisked down to Patras, where the Council was opening a British Academy, Steven found the local dignitaries in varying states of enthusiasm about English literature. The Prefect regaled him with a recitation of 'If', but the Mayor's speech trailed off after the phrase 'all the great English authors whose names we know so well'. Steven was entertained, if somewhat exhausted, by the bibulous Archbishop, who blessed him repeatedly and stood him endlessly replenished cocktails, declaring that as his spiritual father he would take any suggestion of payment as a sin against their filial bond. The ensuing muggishness may go some distance towards explaining Steven's sceptical reaction the next evening to a 'not very good lecture by Harold Nicolson on Byron'.

Steven's gloomy views on both the Greek and British political outlooks increasingly converged:

> The political situation is shocking. The Greeks themselves are to blame, but I doubt if our intervention has improved – partly because no one in authority at home conceives it as possible that any country should want not to be left wing – and partly because our diplomatic theory (so correct in theory) is that only a centre party can see that elections will be fair and only a centre party is possible when the extremes are so bitter. But if *nobody* wants a centre party, what can it do? The Right, which was supporting us, considers that we have let them down badly. The real Left (as opposed to the mild left of the Government) considers that

---

* On Steven's first trip to Greece in the spring of 1924, his father had been much impressed by the 'superb Acropolis' (WR to HR, undated postcard 1924, Elshieshields), but Steven himself resisted this philhellenic piety. In 1930 he informed his mother that 'I have seen all the sights [in Athens] – even gone dutifully round the Classical museums and monuments, though, except for the archaic stuff, I can summon no enthusiasm for it. The Parthenon I find impressive for its size and position, but no more; and as for most of the mess – after letting it lie about for more than 2000 years it is surely time for someone to tidy it away' (SR to HR, 31 March 1930, Elshieshields).

not enough has been done, but that this is a heartening sign that by pressure and agitation more can be acquired . . .

Fortunately politics are right outside my scope, specifically outside, and I can refuse to discuss them.

Steven had upset Leonora Cardiff when her husband, not long after his superior's arrival, returned briefly to the Aegean to wind up some obligations he had contracted among the partisans during the earlier, guerrilla phase of his career. No doubt a little put out at having to do without his capable young deputy so early into the post, Steven joked that 'I don't think you'll be seeing Maurice again.' Whether this barb was aimed at Cardiff's loyalties or his life expectancy, it did not go down well. In December, it was Steven's turn to take a sabbatical to his past, returning to Istanbul via Salonica to sort out the loose ends of his Turkish existence.

When he had finished packing up his icons and the better half of his furniture for dispatch to Athens, Steven emerged into a deluge of entertainment and intrigue. After nine months' absence, he found himself a much missed, fêted figure in Istanbul life:

> I had also to say goodbye to all my Turkish friends, which involved an enormous amount of over-eating (you are liable to be given cold chicken and hot sausages at a tea party). They were all so pleasant that I felt quite sad at leaving – particularly the University where I was given a charming welcome, so that I was really ashamed of having left them a year before I ought.

The British in the city were less welcoming but more ingratiating. Since Grant, as well as Steven, had moved on, the British Council in Turkey was riven by internal enmity. 'Almost all of them took me aside and said, please couldn't they be transferred to Greece? but I wouldn't have any of them.' Whitehall's specification that the new British Council Representative should be 'the kind of person to whom people like to take their grievances' had, much to Steven's chagrin, proved prophetic.

After witnessing a government-staged riot in Istanbul against the Communists ('scarcely commendable . . . the sight of Turkish ladies tearing in their enthusiasm foreign books (that they could not read) with their teeth cannot have been edifying') and changing his Turkish cash into Greek notes at a healthy profit, Steven returned to Salonica in a third-class train, 'like travelling in a stagecoach', overcrowded with Greek officers and poultry. At the University of Salonica, he found himself lecturing to a surprisingly large crowd of some three hundred Thessalonians. 'I gave them a lecture full of moral uplift about the evils of materialism. The Greeks, being more materialistic than most people, love moral uplift.'

Returning to Athens in the first days of 1946, Steven found a capital paralysed by strike action:

> E.A.M., the Communist party of Greece, is thus hoping to obtain power. Yesterday we had no telephone, for two days no trams, last week no taxis (but they reappeared this week), today no electric light, and the water company employees tried to turn off the water supply but they made a mistake and turned the tap the wrong way, so that Athens, which is strictly rationed for water, enjoyed a welcome flood.

Steven, who was close in Leeper's counsels at this time, saw a more fallible and vulnerable side of the Ambassador than other accounts of an adamant, effective operator indicate. 'He was very cordial, but depressed and almost pathetic – not a strong man, physically or otherwise. I don't like the general situation here, but perhaps it's not much worse than in the rest of the world.' This detached, philosophical gloom was typical of Steven, but at heart he still acknowledged that he had 'a liking for Greece, which is a much nicer country than modern England and where I not only feel physically well – extraordinarily well considering the non-stop life I lead – but also believe (conceitedly) I am more of a success and more useful than many of my compatriots'. Presumably the compatriots to whom he was comparing himself favourably were Warner and Leigh Fermor.

By now Steven was, however scrupulously he might emphasize his position as an impartial Council employee, mingling, and meddling, in decidedly political cabals: 'mostly in circles that the left-wing press calls "Monarcho-fascist". Most Greeks disapprove bitterly of our policy, but are still extraordinarily friendly to us personally. I am glad to say I have also my left-wing contacts.' But friendship with the odd left-leaning poet hardly balanced out intriguing, as Steven now happily began to do, with right-wingers of both monarchist and republican persuasions. His letters home were now models of right-wing invective against the tottering Greek Cabinet:

[The Embassy] are determined to keep in office a left-centre government which represents nobody and is a laughing-stock. The Prime Minister, poor man, is 84, the Secretary to the Navy a mere 87. [Here Steven did not exaggerate.] Most of the other ministers are irresponsible left-wing journalists ... The present Prime Minister seems to have accepted office on condition that Britain gives Greece a loan. But I doubt if the loan will be given. He too will be let down.

In fact, he was not; the British loan came through, a bankrupt patron's lifeline to an even less solvent protégé (ultimately, of course, the money was American). To Steven's extreme annoyance the government staggered on until April.

But the immediate effects of the loan were evident and welcome. Prices halved and British popularity in Greece soared. When Steven's collection of icons finally turned up from Istanbul, this proved particularly useful:

a dockers' strike, then a civil servants' strike ... prevented me from getting them through the Customs. I eventually did so in great style. Not being a diplomat I was liable for duty on them all. But by approaching them amicably we eventually had a touching scene when the customs officials protested that it would be a breach of hospitality to charge me anything, while I declared that it would be an *honour* to contribute something to the revenue of so gallant a country as Greece. In the end I paid a nominal sum.

At the same time the Attlee government's attitude to the Greek question was altering in a direction far more favourable to Steven's instincts. The Labour Foreign Secretary, Ernest Bevin, a portly and self-confident trade unionist, enjoyed Attlee's complete confidence. Bevin had a free hand in foreign policy, and turned out to pursue such imperialistic strategies that someone called out in the House 'Hasn't Anthony Eden grown fat?'* After a frank exchange of opin-

---

* A quip attributed to various MPs, both Conservative and Labour, including (not very plausibly) Churchill.

ion with his Russian opposite number, Bevin decided the Greek left was too intransigent to be appeased. A socialist British administration thus supported in power a combination of Greek royalists, the republican right and near-fascist sympathizers, some of whom had actively backed the Germans against the Communists during the war years. It was a strategy of dubious political merit, but its paradoxical nature no doubt appealed to Steven's sense of the absurd.

Steven busied himself with a new round of lecturing, both to British soldiers (he found sergeants asked the best questions afterwards; officers were thick-headed, privates tongue-tied) and to Greek students. On one of these occasions at the University he found an exalted and unexpected audience: 'I had two Orthodox bishops, bearded and black-robed, sitting in the front, both apparently understanding English. They crossed themselves whenever I mentioned the Church. But fortunately I did not slip into heresy and indeed I paid a tribute to the Byzantine church; so they announced their approval and blessed me afterwards.' Off-duty, Steven enjoyed himself at the Opera, 'a praiseworthy institution started by the Germans during their Occupation – but the operas chosen are a bit odd. This time it was Flotow's *Marthe*, a piece of early Victorianism that I never thought to see.' Almost more operatic was an evening spent entertaining a Greek war hero:

> a portentous gentleman called Colonel Gigantes (who was head of the Greek 'Sacred Legion' – their parachute regiment which had a remarkable record for courage, –) in a 'taverna' – a popular restaurant – while all the Heroes of the Resistance at our table sang wild Greek folksongs – very movingly. It's all rather exhausting and often a strain on the digestion.

Gigantes – in fact Christodoulos Tsigantes – was an interesting figure to be found swilling retsina at the British Council. An SAS battle comrade of Wilfred Thesiger and Steven's one-time favourite pupil George Jellicoe, he had purged from his unit any officers with committed leftist tendencies. His tiny but disproportionately effective regiment was variously translated in English, but was named for the Sacred Band, the Theban phalanx of fearless homosexual warriors. The MI6 officer Hugh Seton-Watson described them as 'the private army of the Greek right'. The Sacred Band was disbanded now but, in tippling with their erstwhile commander and his friends, Steven was being either naive or mischievous.

In early March Steven was granted another quick spell of leave and briefly returned to Britain. He took his niece, Ann King-Farlow, who had not seen her uncle since the war, out of school at Downe House for a day of treats in Newbury. Immediately he had heard the news of his sister's death, Steven had written to Ann with uncensored grief and affection: 'Ann darling, I loved your Mummy more than I loved anyone else in the world except my own mother. She was a specially wonderful person, and we'll never see anyone like her again . . . I wish I could come home to see you.' It had taken him another year and a half to make good upon this wish, and he found his niece, to whom he was more than half a stranger, shy and subdued. Perhaps remembering his own shyness at her age, and his favourite pursuit of hunting for furniture, he drew her out as they made a tour of antique shops in Newbury. Ann remembered still feeling the 'state of non-being' which had set in at her mother's death, and panicking that her uncle, who had so adored her mother, 'undoubtedly would find me loathsome'. She softened in his presence a little as she watched how he 'loved spying out things', and he concluded in his letter to Hilda that 'she was not very talkative, but seemed to enjoy it and to like being talked to . . . she showed great interest and asked a lot of questions.'

Both General Scobie and Sir Rex Leeper had been replaced during Steven's trip home; on his return he drily speculated 'what difference the new régimes will make. We are said to be on the verge of an economic crisis; and there will be civil war in early April.' Both predictions came true, but the new ambassadorial pair quickly contributed to Steven's reservoir of gossip. Sir Clifford and Lady Norton disappointed him almost immediately by failing to attend a lecture given by the Rector of Athens University, thus being shown up by 'the Russian Ambassador . . . the French, the Turkish, even the Canadian, the Belgian and the Pole', not to mention Steven himself. 'It was a dreary way, indeed, to spend the first fine Sunday morning of spring – but what is an Ambassador paid for?' Steven enquired, concealing, not quite successfully, his pleasure at settling among the other, more diligent Ambassadors as the only emissary of Britain. Sir

Clifford's pre-war post had been in Poland, and it had been thought in London that his experiences there would encourage him to resist Russian meddling; the war itself he had passed comfortably as British Ambassador to Switzerland. Steven's first judgement of Norton was scarcely complimentary – 'The impression that he gives is of a hen-pecked, kindly half-wit' – but this was pallid stuff indeed compared with what he thought on first meeting Sir Clifford's hen.

'A heavy-built blear-eyed old battle-horse with 1920 Chelsea leanings – not quite eccentric enough to go down well with the Greeks, who like the British to be smart or mad'. Lady Norton, born Noel Hughes, was known to her many friends as 'Peter'. She was at this time, like her husband, in her mid-fifties; she wore her hair short and preferred ambisexual, faintly nautical costume. In the 1930s she had, with the Belgian surrealist E. L. T. Mesens, founded the London Gallery, an avant-garde outlet in Cork Street billed as the first modern art gallery in London. A decade later, the cause and patronage of art was still her paramount concern. Cardiff remembered an early conversation with Peter: 'It was her intention, she announced in her forthright way, to set up, when her husband died, an artists' colony on the island of Poros ... ' It is hardly surprising that Sir Clifford's attitude to Peter's artistic protégés was ambivalent, though he was too rigid a diplomatist to complain of his rivals in public.* Steven delightedly relayed a version of Peter's suspected affair with a war correspondent in his loftiest timbre of public-spirited reproach:

> Lady N. goes about everywhere ... with her new boy friend ... It is not a success here, for the Greeks rightly loathe the sensation-mongering news reporters (particularly just now when they can do so much harm) and also loathe an open flouting of moral conventions (though they don't in the least mind what goes on in private). Lady N. has been implored to be more discreet, from many disinterested sources, but no, she is not going to desert her friends because the Greeks are so silly.

The end of March 1946 saw the first Greek elections for ten years,

---

* Cardiff added with satisfied mordancy that 'if she persisted in her idea of founding the colony, it never came to fruition, since, contrary to expectation, she died long before her husband' (Maurice Cardiff, *Friends Abroad* (Radcliffe Press, 1991), p. 6).

following the dictatorship of Metaxas, the German occupation and the British quasi-protectorate. Whatever their historical significance, these did not attract much enthusiasm. The left, whose defeat was inevitable, boycotted them, and the right, sure of British support, made little effort to secure that of the populace. The previous six Greek Prime Ministers (including the Regent Archbishop) had been appointed by Britain (in the guise of Rex Leeper); to most Greeks, their successor, Constantine Tsaldaris, leader of the centre-right, monarchist Populist Party, was merely the seventh in that line. Steven, sympathetic to the right, interpreted the lack of interest to the new government's advantage, implying that the only real dissent was fomented by left-wing Anglophone journalists:

> the whole campaign has gone off with no serious incident (though the B.B.C. has tried to invent some) and indeed with a general apathy. The result is a foregone conclusion – a right-wing victory. The Left have therefore tried desperately to postpone the elections and having failed are childishly refusing to vote – officially. I believe in fact quite a lot will. A wise objective Greek told me that the whole thing is simply a plebiscite between Britain and Russia (with the British press-correspondents all supporting Russia) and therefore no one is interested in the slanging of personalities that is the usual Greek election fare. The new government will therefore be of the 'Populist' party, mainly but not entirely Royalist, and the next problem will be the King. I should say that a good majority of the Greeks want him back; but unfortunately he isn't very good as a King. The Populist leaders are all acquaintances of mine. Alas, though friendly they are almost all quite exceptionally stupid and I fear will make endless errors and will cause the pendulum to swing back all the quicker.

Steven hardly ever admired elected politicians – perhaps owing to too much enforced and futile Liberal canvassing in his youth – but his scepticism about King George II of Greece at this point, given his usual tendresse for royalty and his support for the Greek right, is remarkable. It must reflect information from Panagiotis Pipinelis, the former diplomat and future courtier. George was tainted by his support for Metaxas, somewhat as in the case of the House of Savoy and Mussolini. Soon Steven was expressing the wish that King

George 'would abdicate in favour of his stupid but more genial brother Paul'.

The new Cabinet offered fresh prospects for lionization of which Steven was quick to take advantage. Prime Minister Tsaldaris's foremost asset, from Steven's point of view, was his wife:

> just the type of woman whom I adore. They say she came off the streets, but a long, long time ago. Actually I believe she was the daughter of King George I of Greece's Dutch housekeeper, but she certainly had a full career before she married Agamemnon Schliemann, the son of the archaeologist, and then passed on to M. Tsaldaris. She is highly decorated and dyed and wears portentous hats.

In sly allusion to Madame Tsaldaris's rumoured past in the *demi-monde*, Steven nicknamed the new Prime Ministerial couple 'the Justinian and Theodora of our time'. Once again, he trumped the Nortons and performed a para-ambassadorial function by being the first British official to gain entry to the Prime Minister's house; he claimed that the Tsaldarises were offended not to have become acquainted with the Nortons already, although as the ambassadorial couple had been *en poste* for only a fortnight, this hardly seems fair. At any rate, he felt 'altogether (unlike the British Embassy) well in with the new government, being on Christian name terms with the Ministers of Labour and of the Police and on bowing terms with most of the others; though unfortunately the Minister of Education, the one most useful to me, is an obscure figure whom no one has ever met.'

Steven's poetic parties grew more ambitious in tandem with his political ones – no doubt because the poets, scenting patronage, made themselves more readily available. To mark the visit to Athens of Raymond Mortimer, literary editor of the *New Statesman*, whom Steven had known and mildly satirized since undergraduate days, he invited half of the contemporary Mount Helicon for an evening at his flat:

> My literary party was very chic – only the accepted great masters were invited, and all except the doyen of Greek poets (M. Sikelianos) accepted – and he invited me instead to visit him on Monday at his

retreat on Salamis.* M. Kazandzakis, the epic poet, who has written the longest poem in all the world's literature, even put off his departure to his country seat to attend. I had eight of them, with wives.

Steven judged the Warners worthy of attendance at this party, but snubbed the Cardiffs and Paddy. Probably he felt that the Cardiffs would not fit in, but Paddy might do so too well. Steven fulfilled his duties on behalf of British culture by treating the poets to a stately recitation from Tennyson's *Maud*.†

At Easter Steven enjoyed skewered Paschal lamb by the sea with Osbert Lancaster and Joan Rayner, and pondered his position. He wrote to Leslie about the relative merits of life in Britain and Greece, freedom and employment:

> though I very much enjoy being here and quite enjoy most of the local work and feel that if you are going to live abroad nowadays you must have a semi-official position, I shan't be sorry to be set free . . . as far as my personal wishes go I should like to stay on here till the spring, as I feel remarkably well here and view a British winter with horror . . . England seems to me such hell now, that I really can't contemplate living in London; and though it would be very delightful to settle at Eigg for several months of the year, it would hardly be a stimulating life. It is shocking to have become so dépaysé and it is doubtless very demoralizing to live in a country where it is much too easy to be Somebody – but it is very agreeable. Indeed I find life in Athens very delicious. The climate is the best in the world, and the country the loveliest. The people, for all their obvious faults, are very sympathique. I have a most desirable and comfortable flat, with a view that is unsurpassed – the Acropolis, the sea, the islands and the Peloponnese. So what more

* Angelos Sikelianos had written, besides a large body of popular nationalist lyric poetry, the protest against Axis deportation of Greek Jews promulgated by Archbishop Damaskinos. Before the war Sikelianos had been married to the American beauty Eva Palmer, a 'bisexual biscuit heiress' with an amateur interest in reviving the Oracle of Delphi (Eleni Sikelianos, *Jacket*, issue 27, April 2005 (http://jacketmagazine.com/27/w-sike.html)); he was now living more sedately with a Greek wife.

† This poetical company included George and Maro Seferiades; Nikos Kazantzakis, epic poet and author of *Zorba the Greek*, whom Steven found disagreeable and vainglorious; and George Katsimbalis, the riotous subject of Henry Miller's *Colossus of Maroussi*.

could one want? There will almost certainly be an economic crisis soon, and a civil war is always round the corner; but anyhow life is never dull here.

Steven, whose intellectual, professional and recreational existence was so dependent upon foreign travel, nonetheless attached moral value to residence in Britain and proximity to his family. But he now thought of his native country as a depressing, socialist mess, and his fondness for Greece was growing – in a moment of aesthetic honesty he even drops his habitually adolescent mockery at the expense of classical architecture and the Acropolis.

Just as in Turkey, Steven regarded expeditions to exquisite sights off the beaten track as one of the prerogatives of his work, and his descriptions of these hidden treasures to his mother bring out his most lyrical note:

> we rowed out to a nearby island overgrown with flowers. An eccentric Englishman had lived there, but his house was bombed in the war and he died soon after, and the whole place has become a romantic ruin with garden flowers run wild.
>
> . . . I spent yesterday afternoon in bed and today (Sunday) went on a delicious drive into the country to a little village on the Gulf of Corinth where there's a curious 4th Century B.C. castle. The scenery was superb and the flowers incredible – huge red and yellow poppies, cystus, mallows, love-in-a-mist, wild roses – everything you could think of.

After his autumn leave Steven attempted to persuade his mother to accompany him back to Athens to join some of these excursions: 'I hope by then you'll have arrangements made so that Papa could be left for 3 weeks or so. You'll be quite comfortable in my flat; and I'm sure the life would amuse you.' But his father's state was worse than he would admit, and Hilda would not leave her husband's side.

At the official opening of the new Parliament, Steven made two new royal conquests, Princess Andrew of Greece and her son: 'She is almost stone deaf but gets over the difficulty talking all the time herself – a wonderful mixture of shrewd sense and the royallest of platitudes. Her son Prince Philip (now in the British Navy) is said to be the man that our Princess Elizabeth wants to marry – he is remarkably good looking and charming.' Steven had previously heard something of Princess Andrew from a new friend, Gerald Green, ADC to General Scobie. During the fighting of December 1944, Green had been landed with responsibility for protecting the Princess and her cousin-by-marriage, Princess Nicholas, both widows of Greek Princes, from possible Communist kidnap. The Princesses loathed each other on grounds of precedence. Princess Nicholas, born a Russian Grand Duchess, scorned Princess Andrew as a 'mere Battenberg' and, worse, a German (in the wake of Greece's occupation by Germany); Princess Andrew, 'as Queen Victoria's favourite great-grand-daughter, had little use for haughty Russians'. Steven clearly preferred Princess Andrew and often gave her lunch at his flat. Afterwards he would write home with thrilled reports on her eccentricities (she had been committed to an asylum in the early 1930s, and at times he wondered how she had got out of it).

Steven's next excursion, at the end of May, was to Rhodes. The Dodecanese Islands were under the direct authority of the British army, 'which governs them not inefficiently but with a minimum of tact. They are people used to administering conquered territories such as Eritrea, and they treat the Greeks like conquered blacks.' He decided, however, not to meddle with the army's heavy-handed educational practice, reserving British Council intervention until Greece proper had been handed back the islands. Instead, he busied himself with ironing out an obscure quarrel between the British command and the Greek Orthodox Church, naturally taking the Church's part: 'all the priests had gone on strike against the collaborationist Italophile Archbishop, who was refusing to recognise his suspension by his ecclesiastical superior the Patriarch of Constantinople. This again was being mismanaged by our authorities who by trying to be neutral gave the impression of supporting the wicked Archbishop.' Exactly as with the German-initiated opera at Athens, Steven showed himself to be humorously aware of Axis contributions to the island's upkeep, which he teasingly criticized on aesthetic rather than political grounds:

> I feel that the Italians have overdone the restoration of the old town,
> but it certainly is very lovely. I thought the countryside incredibly

beautiful, with all the contours of Greece but far greener richer valleys and blindingly white villages with a curious Gothic touch to them, and all the Castles of the Knights dotted about.

The Greek military mission on Rhodes was headed by none other than the veteran reactionary Colonel Tsigantes, 'that colourful old ruffian on a heroic scale', who now hailed Steven as an old friend; Steven in turn found Tsigantes and his suite of officers more entertaining than the grisly British commander, Brigadier Gormley.

Rhodes was also the retreat of the poet and novelist Lawrence Durrell, a good friend of Cardiff's who readily welcomed Steven. Durrell recalled a late-night party where Steven, cheerfully inebriated, 'suddenly launched into a high-pitched warble of "Oh! the Fairy Queen" ', from Purcell's opera of that name. By his own account, Steven rarely drank to excess and scarcely ever sang, but Greece and Durrell had a way of coaxing out the lurking Dionysiac. Later in the year Durrell would lead Paddy, Joan and Paddy's battle-companion Xan Fielding in a makeshift, intoxicated and entirely naked fertility rite 'in the ruins of ancient Camirus'. Neither Tsigantes nor Durrell seems to have egged Steven on quite this far, but it is clear from the account of another British reveller in Greece about this time that Rhodes was a promising spot for pleasure-seeking.

John Craxton was an acquaintance of Peter Norton's through her gallery and a close friend of the artistic and literary patron Peter Watson. Craxton was an impoverished young artist of a nervous disposition that his recent life had tended to exacerbate. Sharing a wartime London flat with Lucian Freud, he found his talents attacked and his life endangered by his mercurial co-resident. Craxton himself, charming, affectionate and without intellectual pretensions, was subject to extreme spells of manic-depression. Unable to put up with Freud and his miasma of semi-criminal melodrama, he had found himself by May 1946 in Switzerland, and a predicament, if anything, still more absurd. The heavily armed Swiss husband of his Scoto-Swiss patroness, Kathleen Bürgi, was certain (operating from mistaken premises) that Craxton was cuckolding him. 'As if by heaven sent', Lady Norton revisited her Swiss stomping-ground on an RAF bomber, looking to buy curtains. She took Craxton with her back to Athens, agreeing to maintain him on a stipend of £30 a month.

Craxton, a generous-hearted young man, fell for Greece more precipitately and lastingly than he would for anyone or anything else in his life. To his main confidante, E. Q. Nicholson (wife of Kit and herself an artist), he poured out his rapture: 'Oh Quee! I can't tell you how delicious this country is & the lovely hot sun, all day and at night Taverna's hot prawns in olive oil. & greek wine & the soft sweet smell of greek pine trees. I shall never come home. how can I?'* Soon he had decided to pay the Dodecanese a visit. 'I have absolutely no permission to land on Rhodes too so that adds a spot of political excitement,' he boasted with adolescent glee. Once landed he distributed 'a nice Anichist [sic] prologue just to let people know I'm not putting across the British Council or any other "Message"'. Small wonder that Steven, who would have been in charge of clearing his permission and keeping him on board with the British Council's strategy, initially agreed with the many Athenian gossips who found Craxton's close association with Peter Norton insufferable: 'I must say our Embassy is a curious place nowadays. What do you think of an Ambassadress who gives a public display of dancing the jitter-bugs with a disreputable young artist as partner in a night club that isn't even the most chic?' Craxton – who almost immediately won over his fellow reprobate Paddy and would eventually prove harmless, friendly and talented enough to reassure Steven – settled down, relatively speaking, on the island of Poros. It is clear from his correspondence that he found the islands not merely aesthetically recuperative but erotically convenient; he also haunted Piraeus, picking up sailors, whether Greek or American.

'  . . . I don't know if you have any experience with Greek boys,' Steven was to write that September, in his capacity as Representative, to one Nigel Logan, an applicant for a post as an assistant master at a Greek private school 'run nominally on British public-school lines':

They are quick and bright and responsive, utterly dishonest and completely amoral. Nothing will stop them cheating, and their private

---

* Craxton's letters in the Tate Archive are remarkable and beautiful objects, written on black or coloured paper and bursting into unpredictable doodles in mid-word.

lives are a disgrace. They are exasperating but very likeable. If they feel that you like them and if they can respect you for being just and for knowing your stuff and for behaving respectably (outwardly at least) – indeed for having all the qualities that they lack – then you do not have much difficulty. It is essential to avoid politics – even the boys are passionate politicians – and to avoid the loose morals that so many Englishmen have in the past thought permissible in Greece. I am sure this advice is superfluous, as you will know the sort of qualities required. The standard of Greek masters is depressingly low. One has to be prepared to face corruption and intrigue.

The school in question, the Anargyrios and Korgialenios College on the island of Spetsai, would later become notorious as the setting for John Fowles's novel *The Magus*. Fowles despised the school and regarded everything it stood for as the antithesis of what was worthwhile and beautiful in the Greek character. Logan, perhaps discouraged by Steven's frank advice, let his application lapse.

Steven had made several friends in the Greek army, whose officers he considered to be:

> very pleasant simple men with beautiful manners and so much more to say for themselves than the equivalent British officer . . . about the best educated class (as regards general education) here, because their school is the only one that is properly disciplined. They are all extremely monarchist and right-wing, saying, with some truth, that only a rather authoritarian government can get anything done in Greece.

He frequently accepted the hospitality of a Greek officer, Karol Sakellariou. The Sakellariou family lived at Xylocastro on the Peloponnesian coast, in what had been 'for Greece, a large and comfortable house but now, after occupation by Italian, German, Communist Greek, and finally British troops, was in a horrible state . . . the family were living in what had been the servants' quarters.' Steven was moved by the hospitality of these genteel Greeks, now 'looking rather shabby' but still keeping an overwhelmingly generous table. The Sakellariou matriarch insisted on his attending Orthodox worship with the rest of the family: 'we had to go and light the lamps in a family chapel in a village where the mother comes from, some miles away inland, up one of the loveliest valleys that I have seen. The chapel was on a cypress-clad hilltop, with the family farmstead perched half way up.'

Friends among families like the Sakellarious – a social group Steven cheerily dubbed 'the good bandit families' – provide a context for Steven's stubborn belief that the Glucksburg dynasty remained popular among Greeks at large. When a plebiscite was held in the August of 1946, the Greeks *did* invite King George II to return, though the vote remained open to the doubts which had tarnished the election.* Steven continued to harbour scepticism about the personality of King George: 'an unalluring figure . . . I doubt if he'll stay long. However the Communists here by their outrages have really killed Republicanism in Greece, at least for the next few years. The present Royalist government, though rather stupid, is not doing so badly.'

King George arrived in Greece at the end of September, a gloomy, diminished-seeming man. 'Marooned in his palace for his own security,' Cardiff recalled in his memoirs, 'bereft of his English mistress and friends and acutely bored by his Greek subjects, he ordered his equerry to round up any British residents whose conversation might be amusing to him.' The English mistress in question was Joyce Brittain-Jones, the divorced wife of a drunken Black Watch officer. Although Eden considered her influence on the King wholly benign, and though she had, unlike Wallis Simpson, acquired the confidence of her lover's family, the Foreign Office considered knowledge of her existence in Greece would be prejudicial to King George.

This most literally Anglophile of Greco-Danish monarchs fell out with Cardiff after the Assistant Representative was rash enough to admit to friendship with 'that terrible fellow Durrell'; but Steven made no such blunder. Introduced at the behest of the much maligned Peter Norton to King George's heir presumptive, Crown Prince Paul, and his wife Princess Frederika, whom he had long suspected might make a better fist of the Greek monarchy, Steven was not altogether disappointed:

---

* About 95 per cent of voters favoured the restoration of the monarchy; multiple voting was rife, and the right-wing Minister of the Interior was even rumoured to have destroyed a number of boxes of royalist votes so as to present a final result that was more plausibly proportionate.

The Crown Prince is very likeable, much more genial than his brother and, though stupider, perhaps less foolish. He talked very soundly about his plans for Greece and seems far fonder of the country than his brother is. The Princess is a bright little thing. They all say that she is the cleverest of the whole Royal family, though I believe rather tyrannical with her staff. They were very cordial and had, I discovered, taken a lot of trouble to find out exactly who we all were.

That night Steven dined late with the Katsimbalises, Warners, Cardiffs and Durrells, along with several other loose-living bohemian acquaintances, an occasion he thought, by contrast to the royal audience, dismally overlong.

In mid-November the British Council, an organization for which Steven had ever less patience, sent out as its latest lecturer an old *bête noire*, John Lehmann, younger brother of Steven's former sister-in-law:

He has grown up very different from Rosamond . . . a pompous, didactic, self-opinionated bore, very competent as a lecturer and, I gather, in his own profession as an editor and a publisher . . . I was amused to see the Greek reaction to him. They can't help admiring him as an impressive and successful young man, and they court and flatter him because he may be useful to them – and he swallows it all – but they all are quite sharp enough to see that he is really a fraud. He used to be very left-wing but now is swinging hard toward the right. He lectured twice, very impressively though he didn't say much, really; and there have been several parties for him, most of which I have avoided . . . He has been very affable to me, and wonderfully patronizing.

In his memoirs John Lehmann politely described the 'worldly-wise, amusing, scholarly personality of Steven who was *persona grata* with the Greek Royal family'. But the visit cannot have been easy on either side, and Lehmann preferred the Embassy set, striking up an immediate friendship with Peter Norton and her pet painter. He left a particularly admiring account of the newly Craxtonified Embassy decor:

Gigantic, brilliantly coloured pictures of young Greek shepherds, in curious perspective with their sheep and the Greek landscape, decorated the august walls of the reception rooms in the British Embassy, where elegant eighteenth century portraits had hung before. Britain was fortunate in having these men and women to represent her at that particular time: if their appointment was not the result of extremely skilful choice by some anonymous genius in the Foreign Office, it was certainly an exceedingly lucky chance.

John Lehmann was just the foretaste of what the Council had in store; at the end of November Steven received three unwelcome visitors: Sir Cameron Badenoch, the Council's Auditor-General, Dr A. E. Morgan, its Educational Director, and H. A. Smith, a Professor of International Law. Smith, 'a dear old man', proved 'no trouble at all', except insofar as he felt obliged to support his baleful colleagues. Badenoch, 'a grim humourless son of the manse of quite incredible meanness, but I think very competent', was an Indian Army stalwart, and a tough proposition. At least Steven could feel respect for the Auditor-General, but Dr Morgan was the incarnation of everything he loathed about post-war Britain. When Steven complained, as was his wont, that 'we have fought this war to make the world safe for bureaucracy', Morgan was precisely the sort of bugbear he had in mind. Steven considered him 'amiable, pompous, boring, personally easy but disastrous for work, as he cannot see that foreign countries can possibly be different from England. His rigid obstinacy is most remarkable. His social ideas are of the half-baked leftishness, so fashionable in England and so utterly inapplicable elsewhere.' A week later into Morgan's visit, Steven would no longer concede even the amiability or personal ease:

> Dr Morgan . . . is about the most unsuitable man for such a post that you could imagine. He knows nothing of foreign countries and refuses to learn – he cannot see why they should [not] be just like the rather sloppy left-wing Britain that he represents. He never listens to anything that he doesn't wish to hear. He is offensive (though I'm sure he means to be genial) out of sheer arrogance; he is tactless to a wonderful degree; he is obstinate, and he is patronizing. Many of his ideas are not unsound, but he leaves us all so angry that it is difficult to do them justice; and most of his ideas seem to me to be nonsense. He has infuriated every member of my staff and is resented by the Greeks that he

meets. He also has a way of mixing himself up at once with all the
most undesirable Greeks, without referring to me, and making plans
of an appallingly unsuitable nature, behind my back.

It sounds distinctly as if Dr Morgan had had the temerity to make
unofficial contacts among the Greek left.

What Morgan had made of the truant, occasional presence of Paddy
Leigh Fermor and his Cretan associates in the British Institute office
has not survived, but he is unlikely to have approved. The much
grander and more urbane figure of Maurice Bowra, the Warden of
Wadham, had drifted through Athens earlier in the year, giving as his
opinion the loftily misspelt and hardly revelatory verdict that 'Mr
Lee-Fermore is . . . unfit for office work'; Steven, who in turn thought
little of Bowra, seems to have used this report as a pretext for allowing
Paddy to undertake the vagrant lecture tours he, in any case, preferred.
But after this latest visit from the London officials, he called Paddy into
his office. Paddy was congratulated on the success of his Kreipe orations, but Steven pointed out that his expenses had been hugely
excessive. He did not mention, but privately had not forgiven, having
had to pay off several of Paddy's 'little irregularities' – Greek
girlfriends – himself. Paddy was fired, a decision Steven represented as
being entirely his own. Initially, Paddy felt both hurt and obscurely
guilty, and their parting was not up to his usual standard of buoyant
sangfroid. The letter Paddy fired off to Larry Durrell mingles tantrum
with intimations of mortality, declaring himself 'older than the rocks
among which I sit'. When Steven seemed willing to renew their friendship a few years later, Paddy was relieved but surprised.

In fact, it seems possible in retrospect that the dismissal of Paddy,
to official eyes a high-living liability, was a sacrifice demanded by the
steely Badenoch and the doctrinaire Morgan. If so, it is understandable that Steven took responsibility for the crushing of this exceptional
butterfly beneath the bureaucratic wheel. To have been seen to act at
the behest of higher functionaries he despised would have been even
less tolerable than assuming a mask of efficiency himself. Perhaps,
given that Paddy was sacked on grounds of expense, the 'quite incredible meanness' of Badenoch supports this theory. Not long after he
had dispensed with Paddy's services, Steven complained to his brother

that the British Council 'is coming all out for the Common Man. I shall leave its service without the slightest regret, though I shall be sorry to leave Greece. The end of May seems the best time to do so for many reasons. I think I can hide from the Greeks till then how awful this organization really is.' The root of Paddy's popularity among Greek acquaintances as well as (later) among British readers, and of his incongruity in the Council's service, was that he was such an Uncommon Man; for all his experience with the Cretan Resistance, he gloriously lacked Steven's long-cultivated facility for civilian adaptability, self-preservation and camouflage.

The spirit of the age notwithstanding, Steven continued to make the most of royal and diplomatic company. King George's sister Princess Katherine, one of Mrs Brittain-Jones's most determined defenders, was herself engaged in a romance with a British com-moner, Richard Brandram, an artillery officer whom Steven had known slightly as a 'charming, gay and disreputable' Cambridge undergraduate. Eager to discover the details of this latest royal *mésal-liance*, Steven invited Princess Katherine to lunch, together with the Cardiffs and Nigel Clive ('a good-looking young man attached to our Embassy – the Princess likes good-looking young men'). The occa-sion was a great success. The Princess told him that life in the palace was very confusing owing to the fact that the butler, an Englishman, was called King; Steven responded by introducing her to his house-maid, who had been born into a republican family and christened Vouli, the Greek for parliament. Afterwards Steven mocked Kather-ine's naivety and her lover's motives with equal relish:

I think there must be something odd in a young man who gets engaged to a really very plain Princess aged 33, without any money. She hasn't even many jewels; for when her mother Queen Sophie (who had inher-ited most of her mother the Empress Frederick's wonderful collection) died she was very young and her elder sisters said to her: 'You were Mother's favourite, so you must have the dear little string of pearls that she always wore', while they made off with the great ceremonial ropes, and 'you must have that sweet little brooch that she was so fond of', while they took the tiaras . . .

Nigel Clive, the young attaché Steven had summoned to act as princess-bait, was more than a pretty face. He was working not just for the Nortons but for SIS, in a secret role analogous to that which Nick Elliott had performed at Ankara. Elliott and Clive, these two young spies, very different men, would later fall out on several occasions, most momentously over the Philby affair. It is interesting that Steven so swiftly befriended both, suggesting that their profession as much as their individual characteristics attracted his interest. Elliott he already knew well as a refractory Trinity pupil; Clive, a school-friend of Noel Annan's, was more innately sympathetic. Together they took to trawling Byzantine churches and, Clive recalled, scouring for 'icons, tanagras, Mycenean and Black Attic pottery, all of which were at that time purchasable from my modest salary'.

It was through Princess Katherine that Steven achieved one of the most rewarding positions of a life bestrewn with honours – that of Astrologer Royal. She had heard of his reputation as an adept in the occult sciences, and naturally asked him to read her tarot. Mindful of the King's disapproval of her proposed marriage to Major Brandram, of Brandram's raffish character and of the romantic idealization with which the Princess regarded her English sweetheart, Steven somehow contrived to predict a carefully optimistic outlook, including a hint that a sudden event might lead to an unexpected gift. Well pleased, Katherine repaid him with family gossip and recommended him to King George. When in due course his audience with the King, or rather the King's with this famous soothsayer, occurred, Steven was amused to find George preoccupied by almost identical concerns to his sister:

> The Princess again honoured me with more and more confidences about all her family all through the meal (which was excellent; the Palace chef is superb). Then afterwards I retired into a separate room with the King and took out my cards. What was interesting was that he didn't want to hear anything about affairs of state – not that I felt I could venture far on that line – but he did want desperately to know about his future private life, a subject on which I felt I had to tread with even more delicate care. It was a fascinating interview. He seemed content with what I told him; and I certainly learnt a lot about him. I hear I am in extremely high favour in Royal circles. Perhaps too high . . .

Steven was not in as well informed a position vis-à-vis Mrs Brittain-Jones as he was in relation to Richard Brandram, but he seems to have found the right tone to satisfy King George, even if his open intimacy and entanglement with Greek royalism by now grated on his superiors. An adverse report against Steven and his staff as compromised by the Greek right seems to have reached Sir Ronald Adam, the Chairman of the British Council in London, by the January of 1947; at the end of that month Adam himself, not very coincidentally, 'descended upon us'.

Steven had initially greeted the appointment of Sir Ronald Forbes Adam, Adjutant-General for the British Forces, as successor to the narcissistically tyrannical Lord Lloyd with enthusiasm. 'If he's a good competent administrator, he may be a godsend to this unhappy organization. Educated at Eton, I note.' But on arrival at Athens Adam proved disappointing:

> He is not difficult to deal with, as he is anxious to please; but I do not like him. He seems to me rather slippery; he has one eye the whole time on the Labour Government, with which he is doing very well. He doesn't like to learn, but to show off ('Mr Bevin himself said to me the other day ... ' or 'Miss [Ellen] Wilkinson [Minister for Education from the 1945 election until her death in February 1947] told me ... ') and especially to boast about having been a delegate to U.N.E.S.C.O. In some ways it is rather nice to see someone who so loves his position; and he is certainly clever. But, I think, no good and not honest.

Increasingly out of kilter with the new British establishment of the post-war consensus, Steven resorted ever more to the company of Greek dignitaries like Prime Minister Tsaldaris with his racy wife and his ropey Cabinet. Tsaldaris fell at the end of January, replaced by a coalition, but Steven found this fractionally more centrist Cabinet to be quite as charming. The new Prime Minister, Dimitrios Maximos, was full of memories and praise of Steven's father, which, with Viscount Runciman disgraced and dying, must have come as an unexpected and moving tribute. Steven impishly continued to usurp the ambassadorial duties of Sir Clifford whenever possible: 'we opened an Exhibition of English Books at our Institute. The Ambassador was to have opened it, but was delayed by bad weather on returning from

England, so I had to do it myself. I am growing quite self-confident about such things.' He had reached a state of settled rapport with King George. The King was by now rumoured to have cancer, but gamely appeared at any British Council arrangement Steven suggested, always in high spirits ('very royal in that he made two jokes about toilet-paper, but otherwise informal and very amiable').

Steven did not regard his own relationship to the House of Glucksburg as one of flattery, but rather of cool-eyed, intense and reciprocal fascination. The scientific extent of his royal-watching brought him pleasure, though it carried its own, sometimes unpredictable, risks. Early in February, the Crown Prince, Paul, a restless and bulky visitor at an overcrowded British Institute reception, stood on his neighbour's foot. Steven's privileged proximity to the Greek monarchy had gained him a broken toe. Princess Katherine soon bustled round to Steven's flat, full of condolences and solicitude, but her lady-in-waiting mischievously informed Steven later that the King himself had 'laughed more heartily than he had for years. It is of course just the sort of joke that Royals really like.' Steven was inclined to attribute to this episode the access of good humour that led King George to consent, at last, to his sister's marriage.

Steven was expecting the last royal entertainment of his posting to be Princess Katherine's wedding; but the King of Kings intervened. 'Our great event here', Steven wrote to his mother on 4 April 1947, 'is the sudden death of the King; which was so unexpected that many people thought it at first an April Fools' Day joke.' The sudden event Steven had innocently predicted to the Princess had come about with a vengeance. King George, after delaying his sister's wedding in life, again postponed it in favour of his funeral. He had not been suffering from cancer after all, and his fatal heart attack took all Athenian society off guard. Steven's account of the dead monarch's reputation was measured: 'He was not a popular man, and one did not see much sign of distress, apart from flags at half mast from almost every house. But he was respected, particularly so recently; and many people, even republicans, were saying it was a tragedy.' Even the constitutionally named housemaid Vouli – whose principles had, Steven suspected, been softened by Princess Katherine's tips – 'snivelled quite sadly'. Steven thought the ceremony 'excellently managed':

I was surprised to see how big the crowds were, and how silent when the cortège passed – very moving . . . all the Court officials on foot, and a good military band, then the clergy with the Archbishop, in splendid robes, then the coffin on a gun-carriage followed by the new King and his 6-year-old son on foot (a touch that produced many sobs from the onlookers) and then the [new] Queen and princesses in cars, and more soldiers. The Greeks, if they choose, can carry out such a ceremony with magnificent dignity.

Steven had seen King George the night before his death, at a British Council-sponsored showing of Laurence Olivier's *Henry V*; there the King 'was very well received, though I thought he looked awful'. George had not been a monarch in any grand Shakespearean mould, neither heroic nor tragic, but Steven did not neglect the touch of romance and fidelity in his life: 'The King's lady friend from London came out and drove discreetly in the funeral in a closed car as a lady-in-waiting. As, so I believe, she had been legally married to him, that was only right.'

'We are still mourning our King here,' he informed Doxford a week later. The British Representative, soon to return home, no longer made any attempt to conceal his Greek colours.

# 17

# The Hermit

*Athens, 1947; Veneto, Venice, Asolo, 1947; Oxford,*
*1954–7; Los Angeles, 1957; London, the*
*Athenaeum, 1950–70*

It is a doctrine of divine parsimony and conservation of
energy, because of the stress, the terror and the manifest
impertinences of this life.

Arthur Waite, *The Key to the Tarot*, 1920

By January 1947, tired of the British Council's unsympathetic principles and frustrating procedural tangles, Steven, for the first time in
almost a decade, felt the appeal of academic life. Yearning for the
time and independence to settle to the *Crusades*, he now heard
through the vagaries of Athenian and conciliar gossip of an older
Byzantinist's retirement. John Mavrogordato had occupied the Bywater and Sotheby Chair of Medieval and Modern Greek at Oxford
since the outbreak of war in 1939, and Runciman was now widely
mentioned as his most qualified replacement.

Mavrogordato's family origins intrigued Steven. He was part of the
Phanariot caste of Greek merchant princes, who had thrived under
Turkish rule, named for the Phanar quarter of Ottoman Constantinople. His immediate family had decamped to London – like the
antecedents of Steven's school contemporary Denis Dannreuther – in
the late nineteenth century. As a scholar Mavrogordato – 'Mavro' to
his colleagues – lacked Runciman's style and self-confidence, but
proved himself to be respectable and original. In 1919 he had been
considered as the inaugural Koraes Professor of Modern Greek at the
University of London, but was rejected in favour of Arnold Toynbee
owing to a general feeling that 'private means and natural indolence'
stood in his way. This assessment was, perhaps, self-fulfilling, for

Mavro remained unemployed, and largely unpublished, until his appointment to the Bywater Chair.

Steven saw the succession to the Bywater Chair in terms of both scholarly efficacy and his personal comfort. The chair covered historical as well as linguistic scholarship, for both the Byzantine and modern eras. Mavro was a Byzantinist, a linguist and (to some degree) a Greek; the choice of Steven would confirm the chair as a Byzantine possession, but in other respects manifest a change. In any case Steven was not quite sure whether he really wanted the prize, or was merely excited by any opportunity to escape the Council:

> If they want a modernist and a philologist they won't choose me; if they want a Byzantinist they probably will. I shall certainly accept if offered it, but I shall be rather relieved if they don't, as I don't really want to live in Oxford. I should prefer to have my headquarters in London ... I feel I do want somewhere less restricted than College rooms in which to keep my belongings. However I had better wait till I know whether I'll be offered the Chair or not before fussing about the disadvantages.

Hilda and her younger son agreed that one advantage of the Oxford scheme would be to keep a beneficent eye on his niece, Ann King-Farlow, who was on the point of applying to be an undergraduate. Steven averred that 'I don't like Greats for anyone who is naturally superficial and slack; for them the discipline of a Cambridge tripos is better. But I think Ann wouldn't be superficial.'

By the end of February Steven had been informed that the Bywater Chair would go elsewhere, to Constantine Trypanis, a modern Greek poet and translator already *in situ* at Oxford as Mavro's assistant. The force of Steven's objection to the successful candidate hints that he had come genuinely to desire the job:

> I can't say I mind at all, except for a feeling of indignation that it has been given to a Greek, a philologist, an oily unpleasant man with not a very good record in the war (he managed to grow sleek and fat and prosperous when most Greeks were starving) and a scholar who is considered bogus even by Athenian standards. It brings out all one's worst prejudices against Oxford to see how he has taken them in

there; which again is a consolation – it makes me realize how specious-
ness always triumphs there. I remain more loyal to Cambridge than
ever! My real embarrassment is that when I write to my backers to
thank them I simply cannot make the proper gentlemanly remarks
about what a good choice has been made.

Maurice Cardiff also recalled that Steven's interest in the Bywater
Chair had been palpable, and that Steven repeated with indignation
Maurice Bowra's opinion that Trypanis 'would be very good at
tea-parties and with dons' wives'. When no less a figure than Isaiah
Berlin, not a habitual ally of Steven's, complained of the decision,
calling Trypanis 'some worthless British Council Greek', Bowra
returned that Steven was 'a worthless Cambridge queen', whereas
Trypanis 'knew how to treat great men' (by which Bowra very likely
alluded to himself). Steven's invective against Trypanis's war record
and academic credentials, which was groundless, may have originated from the bitterly disposed first Mrs Trypanis, who ran an
Athenian nightclub which Steven had occasionally visited with
Osbert Lancaster and Joan Rayner. Steven's acrimony did not persist. Trypanis would be among the most admiring reviewers of the
*Crusades* trilogy and *The Eastern Schism*. By 1976, when, as Minister for Culture, he escorted Steven around Mistra, Steven had come
to regard him as a friend of long standing.*

In the meantime Steven still craved a smooth exit from the Council. Along with Nigel Clive, he had plotted to secure Freya Stark as a
visiting lecturer in the spring of 1947. Her credentials for inspiring
Anglophile sentiment were impressive. Through her 'persuasion'
work alongside Adrian Bishop, Jack Connell, Christopher Holme
and Stewart Perowne, she had become a heroine in the Hester Stan-
hope or Gertrude Bell mould to Arabs in Syria and Palestine. More
importantly, both Steven and Clive found her sympathetic and entertaining company. But Steven's recommendation of her was shelved
for a period of 'dallying' that he found infuriating, before Miss Stark
was finally turned down on grounds of expense. Steven pointed out

---

* Steven's correspondence with Donald Nicol does however indicate that he held
Trypanis in low regard academically, if not personally, as late as 1970.

that another candidate for a lecture series had fallen through and so inviting his choice would be perfectly economical; the Council preferred to make a further saving. To Steven's intense annoyance, after he had announced that he would leave Athens in the summer Freya Stark was invited after all, for the subsequent autumn. He showed his exasperation in a letter to her in late February, about the same time he learnt the discouraging news about the Bywater Chair:

> ... I'm terribly shocked at the way the British Council has behaved. You liken it to a charmless woman, I more positively (and not for the first time) to a bitch ... It is tragic for me, as I am resigning at the end of May – and can you blame me when the BC plays games like this? It is no consolation to *me* that October is, as regards weather; the best of all months in Greece and that Nigel [Clive] will still be in Athens to welcome you. I should prefer you to come with the Easter processions and the asphodel.

A few months after his arrival in Athens, Steven had written to Marthe Bibesco of the lowering effect of seeing Greece in ruins: 'I love this country, but there is so much misery and demoralisation here that it is a melancholy task to try to work in it.' By 1947 his melancholy had turned to anger: against the Communist forces he blamed for the country's misfortunes, the vacillating and ill-informed Labour government at home and British left-wingers in the press and Parliament who expressed support for the Communist 'brigands'. There is a detachment born of gloom and experience rather than indifference in his description to his mother of the appalling state of health among Greek children: 'I believe it is true that the vast majority of children in Greece have tubercular tendencies owing to malnutrition – this was the case even before the war and naturally has been worse since.' In similarly unsentimental vein he was shocked to see in *The Times* 'a letter pleading for the life of a 15-year-old boy condemned to death by the Greek courts. The letter should have added that the boy had committed more than one murder and had been trained to become a murderer. Is it in anyone's real interest (apart from the brigands' and the communists') to keep such a boy alive?' The Labour MP Ivor Thomas, an eccentric, adventurer and linguist, drew Steven's particular ire: 'The escapades of Mr Thomas M. P. with the brigands were particularly disgraceful,' he complained,

> as he visited and publicly praised the most notorious of all, who had just murdered the young daughter of a Greek M.P. and tortured the wife of another so that she died. Mr Thomas had also got into difficulties about his transport and the Greek Government (which he so reviles) sent a special plane to enable him to return in comfort to Athens.

But for all his distaste Steven continued to consider Greece itself 'the most beautiful of countries', and professed himself to Freya Stark 'heart-broken to leave Greece but delighted to leave the BC. Will you help me to make a wax image of a personified BC and stick pins in it?'

In the last months of his posting, Steven's vein of subversion could be discerned in official lectures:

> I gave a lecture at our Institute on Tuesday on 'Barbarian Invasions' – not so much historical as a theory of history, ending up with a plea for better education than modern educationalists provide. It went down quite well – the more intelligent Greeks saw that I was attacking modern Greek education (which is deplorable): the less intelligent thought that I was attacking either the Americans or the Russians, while the American wife of the Swedish Minister thought my peroration so beautiful and so true that to my embarrassment I had to dictate it to her all over again.

Steven had wartime form on making friends at neutral and comfortable Swedish embassies. With more controversial disregard for the advice of his colleagues and the sentiments of his Greek hosts, he also mingled happily with the Italian diplomatic contingent. This was a continuation of his Istanbul and Ankara practice; after Italy's change of allegiance he had readily enjoyed the new range of acquaintances to be found among the Italian and Vatican representatives, including, most prominently, Cardinal Roncalli. But Turkey had in practice been neutral whereas Greece had at one stage been Britain's only ally. For Steven to sup with the Italian representative at Athens was cosmopolitan but not prudent. Though aware that it offended the Greeks, he considered sympathy for the Italian Minister a higher duty: 'the poor man has a miserable life as the Greeks, with few exceptions, won't receive him. Actually he is doing well, being extremely tactful and self-effacing though dignified.' Six years later, Steven's forgiving attitude would prove to have been far-sighted when Italy included among its war reparations to Greece a Greek-run Byzantine Institute, to be based, for reasons of historical resonance and architectural integrity, at Venice: 'a very civilized form of reparation'.

Steven's genial relations with Italian diplomats formed part of a deeper nostalgia for pre-war Italy, where his family had in former days been so picturesquely entertained. Having arranged his release from the Council, he now proposed an enjoyable return to Italy.

Steven was leaving a country, a city and a British Council fundamentally altered by the President of the United States' new, more proactive policy in the region:

> Truman's declaration on Greece and Turkey has been widely welcomed here, and rightly. It is perhaps a little galling for us to find all the time-serving Greeks at once neglecting us in favour of the Americans, and minor Government officials (always an unpleasant race) have been rather chillier to us lately – I notice it in my official relations with them. But most Greeks tell us frankly that after a few months of American occupation all Greece will so love the British that Britain could not have made a cleverer move! Meanwhile there has already been a scandal as it has been found out that American business-men have secretly (through undoubted corruption) bought up a majority of shares in the one Greek air-line ... One can't help enjoying it – but still I hope that the Americans won't make too much of a mess, as their presence is really necessary to keep the Russians out.

In 1945 Steven had arrived in what amounted to a British protectorate, its archepiscopal, Anglophile Regent supported by British troops. Now it was acknowledged – by no one more eagerly than the government in London – that, as Greece spiralled into civil war, it had become America's responsibility.

Steven still wrote of the 'war in the north' and the 'brigands' as vague, remote acts of criminal atrocity, as if they were taking place in some far-off country and state of mind. From his point of view, for the most part, they were. Avoiding political engagement, as opposed to gossip, Steven amused himself in these last Athenian months by

toying with the idea of writing a short biography of George II of
Greece, a project in which he was encouraged by the late King's secretary and best friend, the ceremoniously amiable Colonel Levidis:

> He took up the idea enthusiastically, and rang me up this morning to
> tell me that the present King was very keen that I should, and so was
> the late King's political adviser, M. Pipinelis [Steven's old friend from
> his Sofia days] ... So I am more or less committed to it. I have said
> that it must be clear that it is not official but my views are my own and
> that I want as far as possible to avoid controversial political issues;
> and that it must be short and human. It is rather a formidable task, but
> interesting. It gives me a wonderful excuse for coming out to Greece
> for a month next spring! There are certain difficult passages to
> consider – not least the question of Mrs Britten Jones.

This never fulfilled project illustrates Steven's continuing feeling of
attraction to Greece and the sometimes paradoxical firmness of his
loyalty to the Greek royal family, though he reserved the right to be
personally sceptical about them. The new King, George's brother
Paul, was the bulky Crown Prince who had broken Steven's toe. His
wife, Queen Frederika, a Hanoverian princess by birth, was already
suspected of autocratic tendencies. Steven found her more impressive
than her corpulent husband, but scarcely a safe bet: 'She is extremely
clever, dangerously clever for a Queen, a little hard ... not much
humour – the King has more – but bright and quick. They obviously
love being King and Queen – fortunately – though they rightly hate
their politicians.' Steven's hunch that Queen Frederika's temperament
was ill suited to a constitutional monarchy would be amply justified
during the reign of her son.

Steven now underwent a conversion in his attitude to another
powerful woman. He had previously been censorious about the British Ambassadress's escapades with young artists like John Craxton,
but she won his approval at the party after Princess Katherine's wedding to the scapegrace Richard Brandram:

> Though mad and rather bad [Lady Norton] is no fool and can be most
> entertaining. She poured into my willing ears, most indiscreetly, the
> full account of the visit of the late King's lady friend [Joyce

Brittain-Jones] to Greece for the funeral. The lady had stayed at the Embassy. Contrary to the usual situation in such cases, his family were furious with her for not having been with him all the time and for not having returned here with him. She, poor woman, had been kept in England first by her own illness and then by the death of her father. (I had said this when reading his cards but hadn't known that it was true.) There were several painful scenes of hysteria, it seems. He died intestate and she gets nothing. The house that he bought for her in London goes to Katherine. But I believe that the family will be generous. Lady Norton made me promise to see her when I go to London. I shall.

It is not clear whether Steven ever fulfilled this good intention, but he did remain friendly with Lady Norton and John Craxton.

As a final Athenian tease at the Embassy circle, Steven disseminated a rumour that the dour, domestically long-suffering Sir Clifford had secretly expired, leaving his racy widow to usurp his duties. The Ambassador himself got wind of the story and was noticeably cold – if not actually moribund – at Steven's farewell party. Steven's departure was regretted by his staff, who regarded him as fair, competent, courteous, discreet and greatly preferable to the successor the Council had chosen, a pompous former Eton beak, Wilfrid Tatham, who came with a wife known for her good looks and bad temper. Among the wider British community Steven was more suspect; and to the Greeks he was not yet the byword for philhellenism he was later to become. His greatest admirers came from other foreign delegations; the Belgian Minister told him that 'you are the only official working in Greece of whom I have never heard any criticism.' As Steven smoothly admitted to his mother, 'I do like diplomats and courtiers; they flatter one so well.'

Steven spent his last days in Greece holidaying on the island of Andros. Though his visit was largely sedentary, he made one long excursion to a convent, 'which I was incorrectly told had treasures. The nuns gave me a chilly reception at first . . . because they thought I was Russian. On discovering their error they entertained me hospitably with a large and nauseating glass of warm sweet goat's milk.' The most prosperous of the Andriots were former sailors and present shipowners, so Steven felt himself atavistically at home – usefully so amid ongoing anti-Communist panic:

> The officer of gendarmerie, an officious and odious man . . . at first was suspicious and ordered me to report at his office. I was very haughty, so then he asked me to come and drink a cup of coffee with him and later in the evening invited me to join his table at the restaurant, where he was with the headmaster of the Lycée, the local lawyer and three charming retired sea captains, to one of whom our surname was very familiar as he had frequently come across our ships. I think that that reassured the gendarme that I was on the side of the rich and not a Communist agent.

After a last weekend in Athens during which he lay low at Ronald Crichton's flat, but was discovered by the ever-hospitable Swedish Minister, Steven could at last, in mid-June, contemplate his Italian tour. He wrote excitedly to Freya Stark urging her to accompany him on a pilgrimage to the Byzantine basilica on Torcello: 'That Madonna is one of the loveliest things in the world.'

Steven's first stop was at Rome, where he stayed for three days with the head of the British Institute, his once despised Cambridge contemporary Roger Hinks. Feeling the climate to be 'too hot for a really *mondain* life', or for much sightseeing, Steven spent most of his energy on rejuvenating what he felt had become a rather drab and professional wardrobe. He was delighted by what he saw of:

> the excellent and not wildly expensive shops – though it was almost impossible to buy a pair of shoes that was not fantastically dago – the discreet pair that at last I did find at once developed a shameless squeak. I enjoyed Rome immensely . . . a most seductive city, and in spite of increasing inflation and eternal political crises it is in a flourishing condition.

Steven's next stop, Venice, involved a shorter stay but a far grander billet, staying at the beautiful and cursed Palazzo Dario. Its temporary inhabitant, Bill Wilson, 'a pale, gentle young man with a much older, semi-invalid, but rather intelligent wife, Sylvia', was the local head of the British Information Service. Wilson was busy reporting to his London superiors, but his wife was delighted to show Steven over their inauspicious palace.* The weather was humid and stormy, as befitted a place under a shadow. But Steven found one aspect of the Venetian social scene particularly reassuring:

> We are chaperoned by an English spinster of uncertain age, a friend of the wife's, who has come out here to paint. Indeed, one of the most consoling sights of nowadays is the reappearance of English spinsters sitting on camp stools in front of their easels in all the picturesque corners of Venice. You feel at last that peace has come again.

After a solitary visit to Torcello, Steven proceeded into the Veneto, and the more salubrious breeze of Asolo.

In Freya Stark's first volume of memoirs, *Traveller's Prelude*, she describes the aesthetic and historical circumstances that have lent their unique charm to this quiet provincial town in the Veneto:

> The place has scarcely changed [since her father arrived there in the 1890s] ... Many little towns are seated on blossoming slopes of the foothills, with a line of snow behind them and the wash of the plain in front; but there is a distinction about Asolo which dates back through centuries, ever since the last Queen of Cyprus [Catherine Cornaro] received it from Venice in exchange for her island, and kept a gay and learned country court, and was painted by Titian and praised by Bembo, her cardinal, whose villa half fallen to decay is in the plain below, and whose invented verb, *asolare*, describes something that scarcely exists – the purposeless, leisurely, agreeable passing of time.

This elusive something had rarely felt further away from existence than in the weary, insolvent, hectic post-war world; and although Steven had found Athens exciting (and inexpensive), the Greek

---

* Though the Wilsons would escape their makeshift wartime tenancy of the Palazzo Dario without setbacks, it had already ruined its eponymous Dario clan of Venetian officials, an Armenian diamond dealer and a succession of eminent but ill-fated homosexual exiles. In 1981 the curse was implicated in the decline and death of Kit Lambert, manager of the Who and son of Steven's 1920s acquaintance Constant. Lambert *fils* adopted the style of Barone Lamberti, veered into abandoned drug addiction and took up with Peggy Guggenheim, to whom he left the palace; but she prudently elected never to reside there. A more suitable and satisfying way-station for a traveller of Steven's temperament can hardly be conceived.

situation had never offered much in the way of *dolce far niente*. Asolo was the perfect remedy. Steven wrote of its mild routine to Hilda with tangible relief: 'we made one or two excursions to the exquisite villas in the neighbourhood; otherwise it was a quiet life of reading and talking.'

It was less relaxing, perhaps, for their hostess; Freya complained to her favourite correspondent, Sir Sydney Cockerell, of the 'stream of people', remarking in particular that 'a quiet little female party . . . is being broken into by Steven Runciman.' Steven had narrowly missed Paddy Leigh Fermor and Joan Rayner, but the 'females' with whom he now coincided, besides Freya herself, were of independent interest.

Steven already knew Pamela Hore-Ruthven, who had been one of Freya's assistants in wartime Cairo. She and her 'war boss' were close and undeviating friends, but they made a piquant composition: Freya, for all her queenliness, dumpy, diminutive, facially disfigured and self-conscious; Pamela slender and blonde, her beauty unconventional only in the vastness of the blue eyes that earned her the sobriquet 'Frog'. Steven had reliably got on with Pamela and her dashing, impecunious husband Patrick, in Cairo and then in Jerusalem, and enjoyed lavishing the occasional boiled chicken on this glamorous, revitalizing couple. Patrick had been wounded and captured on a Commando raid late in 1942, and died in an Italian-run hospital, leaving Pamela with two sons, Greysteil and Malise. The boys had been born and brought up in Ireland, and she now took them to Asolo for their first excursion abroad. Eight and five years old, respectively to become a Conservative minister and a historian of Islam, the Ruthven boys cheerfully absorbed Steven into the games they played beneath Freya's ilex tree, setting great store by his claims to possess magical powers and accordingly dubbing him 'the witch-man'. Juliette Huxley, 'a very amiable and pretty Swiss woman whom I used to know long ago who has been ruined by becoming consciously the wife of the head of UNESCO', had first met Steven at Hyères, while she and her husband were calling on Edith Wharton and Marie-Laure de Noailles. She had been amusing, if indiscreet, about how traumatized her brother-in-law Aldous had been during his unhappy teaching post at Eton, warning Steven never to allude in Aldous's presence to those bygone, chaotic French lessons.

More intriguing to Steven than Mrs Huxley in this too official incarnation were two very different soldiers, both of them middle-aged veterans of the First World War. Gerald de Gaury was a British officer of Huguenot descent, who became the political adviser to King Ibn Saud; in the recent war he had undertaken a mysterious mission with the assistance of Robert Heber-Percy, the lover of Lord Berners. De Gaury may have become infatuated with Heber-Percy, and certainly took a number of stylish and revealing photographs of him. The other ageing warrior was a more poignantly comic presence. As a young woman Freya Stark had been pressed by her mother and a local Asolese baronessa, Clothilde 'Clot' de Bottini Sant'Agnese, to marry Clot's brother Gabriele, an artillery officer. But Gabriele had been insufficiently enthusiastic; when he did eventually propose, Freya refused him. The young barone took his disappointment philosophically. He entered the employ of the Count of Turin, a dashing cadet of the House of Savoy, who had in 1897 achieved brief European celebrity by wounding a sharp-tongued Orleanist pretender in a duel over the courage of the Italian army. The Italian monarchy was abolished in June 1946, and the Count expired that October, leaving his equerry, who had risen to the rank of general in his service, existentially rudderless. Steven, who might have been expected to find this passé Italian courtier picturesque, instead thought him 'pathetic'; 'with his minor royalty dead and the royal family in exile, [Bottini] has no more purpose in life. I have never seen anyone so utterly defeated.'

Steven soon learnt of General Bottini's rejected suit from Freya, and teased her about ambitions the Italian might still entertain in this direction. 'My visit to Asolo was delicious,' he wrote soon after his return to the bleakness of post-war London. 'I don't think I've ever enjoyed one more. Even the melancholy of the poor General helped as chiaroscuro to show up how heavenly everything was.' When Steven was told in September of Freya's engagement to Stewart Perowne, he admitted that 'I can't help thinking a little wistfully of General Bottini.' Had Freya chosen her old suitor, the results might have been happier. Perowne, who was also present on that Asolo week in the summer of 1947, had a weakness for esoteric uniforms of ranks both high and low that General Bottini might have satisfied.

Passing through Paris on the final leg of his journey home, Steven was soon in a position to compare its atmosphere: 'Of the two I really found London the less depressing town. Paris was gloom itself, the French demoralized, bitter and drab; whereas in London, dreary though life is, people in general seem less rude and disagreeable . . . but dreadfully tired . . . I am fleeing as quickly as possible to the Hebrides . . . Italy is certainly the land in which to live at present.' His London flat at Norfolk Road, St John's Wood, had been slightly bombed and extensively burgled, and was still mostly uninhabitable; Steven was, in any case, happy to adopt a secluded life on Eigg as he began writing the *Crusades* trilogy at last, after the requisite raid on the London Library.

Steven admitted no visitors outside his family in that summer into autumn 1947, and scarcely any from within it; a hesitant, friendly attempt by his sister-in-law Kay, Leslie's second wife, to provide him with a few domestic amenities and keep him company on the island, was interpreted as a hostile incursion. Steven was enjoying the material as well as intellectual self-reliance that, always latent in his character, had been moulded by the war and would harden through the rest of his life. He relieved his background reading with satisfying experiments from the larder as much as the library. 'I am doing my own cooking, which I love – the process I mean. The results sometimes disappoint me – and further am plunged into making apple and blackberry jelly, to say nothing of butter and cheese . . . The great work on the Crusades moves slowly . . . I have barely reached the birth of Mahomet!' He reported this limited progress to Freya Stark, one of the few friends he trusted on matters of prose style. He admired her compromise between plainness and porphyry more than the efficient Mandarin of her wartime superior and now, briefly, husband Stewart Perowne, or the excitable magniloquence of Patrick Leigh Fermor.

The publication of *A History of the Crusades*, whose three volumes first appeared for Cambridge University Press in 1951, 1952 and 1954, marked the height of Steven's reputation and celebrity, a height from which he would not so much decline as gradually be transfigured. In 1951 *The First Crusade* was broadcast in an abridged form on the BBC's Third Programme. In 1955 Isaiah Berlin – usually restrained in his praise for Steven – nominated the whole trilogy for the inaugural Duff Cooper prize, on the grounds that it 'would start the whole thing off in a very respectable way'. Such 'respectability' in the eyes of the world was a new accolade for Steven, and presented a new opportunity.

Before the *Crusades* trilogy he had been read, admired or reprimanded within a small circle with specific qualifications of knowledge, geography, taste, language and acquaintance – the savants of the Balkans and of Byzantium, joined with more courage than comprehension by the most adventurous of educated lay readers. Now Runciman was on the standard curriculum, and on the mind of the bureaucrats whose business it was to make intellectuals public. Steven still presented a puzzling portrait to outsiders; he rarely invoked his wartime professorship. American reviewers sometimes described him as a 'diplomat', hoping with a half-remembrance of Sofia to veil the anomaly of this already rare specimen, so very independent a scholar. Steven himself did not regard his Istanbul post as having conferred any proper emeritus status, any more than he thought of himself as even a quondam diplomatist, press officer, film censor or cultural administrator. Accounts of his wartime career were often assumed to be circumscribed by the Official Secrets Act; this evidently amused him, and he took care that his denials should be as insubstantial as his hints. In fact he regarded his current position as primarily that of 'a quiet literary life'.

Nine years after losing the Bywater Chair to Constantine Trypanis, Steven was a frequent guest at Oxford. He directed at the University the traditional tribal mockery of a product of Trinity, grandest of Cambridge's colleges, while privately admitting that he was coming to feel more intellectual and personal attachment to the study of history at Oxford. A by-product of the trilogy's success was that in 1954 Steven was invited to give the Waynflete Lectures at Magdalen College, later published as *The Eastern Schism*. While the book does not entirely escape its original medium, Steven evidently enjoyed the occasion for an extended tease against, especially, his Roman Catholic acquaintances. He viewed his hosts at Magdalen with quiet satire. Typical of his ambivalent attitude towards friends and acquaintances at Oxford high tables is an aside scribbled to his fellow Cantab Stewart Perowne:

> I am much enjoying my Oxford visits. Apart from Tom Boase himself and Albert [Hourani, an Arabist], I find the Magdalen High Table a little dull; but I much enjoy the visits that I have made up to All Souls, where the talk is really up to its reputation; and there are many other good friends like Nevill Coghill, David Cecil, etc., who are all worth seeing.

Tom Boase, President of Magdalen since 1947, had invited Steven in the first place. His appeal to Steven was exemplified by an essay Boase wrote in 1939, when Director of the Courtauld, on 'The Arts in the Latin Kingdom of Jerusalem'. Like Steven and Dadie Rylands, as a young don Boase had involved himself wholeheartedly in student theatricals. They had in common, too, a fondness for the socially soigné, and a love of the Middle East and of travel, to which the Second World War had amply catered. Boase was another veteran of the schools of propaganda at Cairo, an admirer of Freya Stark and a teasing friend of Stewart Perowne. In his Courtauld days, Boase had cultivated a close friendship and professional alliance with Steven's younger rival from 1930s Cambridge, Anthony Blunt. Not everyone found Boase so charming; the young Betjeman ridiculed him as a fat sycophant and a staggeringly boring speaker.

Both Nevill Coghill and Lord David Cecil were more thoroughly and naturally appealing to Steven than Boase. Nevill Coghill was a civilized Anglo-Irish gentleman, a skilful translator of Middle English poetry and the director of many inspired Oxford productions. These included *The Masque of Hope*, one of the last of its kind in English literature, produced in 1948 to honour a visit to Oxford by Princess Elizabeth, and a famous *Tempest*, in which Ariel seemed to glide across the surface of the lake at Worcester College. Lord David, a critic who exemplified the distinguished belleletrist, was an older friend of Steven's, another non-institutionalized Etonian, happily married to Rachel MacCarthy, a daughter of Bloomsbury. But a closer, more difficult friend to Steven than either of these was the great intriguer Trevor-Roper.

Amid the plots, counter-plots, intrigues, stalking horses and cat's-paws of 1950s Oxford, in no faculty was the scheming so endemic as that of history. The legacy of war no doubt played its part in this febrile, merciless atmosphere. Almost all the history dons had served in at least one of the world wars, whether as soldiers or as spies. For some, like Karl Leyser, the senior history tutor at Magdalen, a German-born internee turned naturalized British war hero, soldiering had, perforce, preceded the academic life. Others, like the Christ Church stalwart, Provost of Worcester and ubiquitous fixer J. C. Masterman, had surprised the establishment of military intelligence with the usefulness of their hitherto donnish talents. 'Can you write the King's English?' an SIS superior of Masterman's once demanded. 'That', J. C. replied mildly, 'is almost my only qualification.'

Hugh Trevor-Roper, another Christ Church man, had been a protégé, colleague and friend of J. C.'s in both peace and war. He was candid and acidic about most of the other men with whom they had had to deal in SIS, MI5, Special Branch and Bletchley Park. 'Very limited intelligence,' he pronounced, evidently relishing the pun, ' . . . by and large pretty stupid, some of them very stupid'. The baroquely named Major Valentine Vivian, to Trevor-Roper 'a serpentine character reminiscent of Uriah Heep', had confidentially, and baselessly, accused Trevor-Roper, his junior officer, of treasonable communication with the Abwehr during a hunting holiday to neutral Ireland, a charge that could have led to Trevor-Roper's execution. The end of the war had brought Trevor-Roper great professional success with his popular book *The Last Days of Hitler*, the fruit of an investigation ordered by SIS; but peace also left him restless, questing after new enemies to belittle as mediocrity incarnate. In peace as in war, his bitterest foe was called Vivian.

Trevor-Roper's peacetime Vivian, a foe of higher calibre, was V. H. Galbraith, since 1947 the Regius Professor of Modern History. Galbraith's background was tough, and his style, whether as a historian, writer or University politician, austere, thorough and territorial. At the Universities of Manchester and then Oxford, his career was bookended by Firsts in history, the products of energetic and minute archival research, but blemished by his lack of classical style. During the First World War Galbraith displayed enough ferocity to gain the admiration – and the Croix de Guerre – of the French. In 1928 he became a Fellow in history at Balliol, and his first book, *Introduction to the Use of Public Records* (1934), was clear, functional and dry. To the venerable Regius Professor Maurice Powicke, who sought to gather around himself a Praetorian retinue of competent medievalists, Galbraith was a godsend. When Powicke retired he ensured that Galbraith, his spiritual heir, would succeed him.

To J. C. and Trevor-Roper, this was a gloomy portent, sealing the triumph of 'unambitious archivists', parochial, narrow English medieval studies, over their beloved faculty. Trevor-Roper saw Galbraith as the very antithesis of the liberal, humane style, writing to J. C. in December 1956 that 'our present Regius Professor would say that any historian who writes well must be a bad historian.' He also sneered at the Professor's *novus homo* extraction; in a letter to Bernard Berenson, of March 1957, Trevor-Roper called Galbraith 'a plebeian character who seeks to divert attention from his historical failings by low buffoonery'. Galbraith in turn had an aversion to Trevor-Roper rooted quite as much in personal as in intellectual antipathy. Bound by the inflexible code of a man who had made his own way in both army and academy, he considered Trevor-Roper 'as clever as a monkey', but, at bottom, 'no gentleman'.

This sanguinary academic world was a sphere from which Steven Runciman had been blessedly liberated by his grandfather's death in 1938. Besides, he was by disposition as much as education a Cambridge rather than Oxford man. Though an exact contemporary of Evelyn Waugh, Harold Acton, Brian Howard and the rest of the Hypocrites Club who lived fast but, thanks to *Brideshead Revisited* and *A Dance to the Music of Time*, never quite died, Steven's social overlap with this assemblage was slight. He had known Cyril Connolly and Anthony Powell slightly at Eton and continued to do so in adult life; but his closest Oxford undergraduate friend was the economist Roy Harrod, whom he had met with Keynes. Steven's pleasures were more sophisticated and less raucous than those of that delinquent Oxford generation and Harrod was respectable, public-spirited and congenial to the Runciman parents. Steven told Harrod, 'I fear I should never be a success at Oxford . . . I should never talk or drink enough.' However, by the post-war period, Cambridge was beginning to develop a reputation – unfortunate in Steven's view – for narrower professionalization. Trevor-Roper diagnosed signs of the same disease at Oxford, and was determined to lead the alliance that would purge it.

Like many of its earliest reviewers and readers, Trevor-Roper felt that in *A History of the Crusades* he could sense the presence of the Zeitgeist. With the chameleonic facility of a great stylist, he illustrated the lucid quality of Runciman's prose in the phrasing of his review: 'Mr. Runciman's learning is deep, his presentation clear, his style firm and graceful. He has the gift of occasional irony.' For Trevor-Roper *The First Crusade* embodied his argument for wider range, accomplishment and breadth of conceit in historical writing:

> A great movement, disconcerting three cosmopolitan civilisations, and leaving its evidence in Slavonic and Arabic, Armenian and Syriac records, is obviously beyond the scope of those narrow medievalists who crouch, in devout but rigid and uncommunicative postures, before their national repositories. But Mr Steven Runciman is a scholar who can study such sources, and – what is almost as rare – an historian who can use, a writer who can express, their evidence.

The 'narrow medievalists', cast elsewhere in Trevor-Roper's correspondence and gossip as 'Medieval Manchester Mice', had names: Powicke, Galbraith and Galbraith's own leading pupil and preferred successor, Richard Southern. By setting up Runciman as their antitype and extolling his superiority in both learning and style, Trevor-Roper was simultaneously advertising his own. Five years later, with a more specific agenda in mind, he wrote to Masterman:

> For mere interest, give me an obscure Bogomil heretic enlivened by the wit and scholarship of Runciman rather than the most outrageous Angevin adventurer reduced . . . even by Powicke, to prim and spinsterish conformity. Of course I know that history doesn't consist of style only, and our present Regius Professor [Galbraith] would say that any historian who writes well must be a bad historian; but, in fact, if one looks at the admittedly great historians, one finds that they all had style as well. It goes with the character, as the banquet goes with the wine, inseparable if the substance be good.

This encomium was far from disinterested, but it does show that Trevor-Roper's interest in Runciman's work had not begun with or been limited to *A History of the Crusades*, and that, while he admitted some respect for Powicke, he was avid for a change of air in the history faculty.

A surer proof of his sincere enthusiasm for Runciman's work, but also a trace of their less harmonious personal assessments of each other, can be found in a 1951 letter from Trevor-Roper to Bernard Berenson, the correspondent he most of all respected and strove to impress: 'there is one English book [*The First Crusade*] that I have just read with pleasure, by a rather spiky Northumbrian neighbour of mine, Steven Runciman (son of that disastrous Northern shipping magnate who, in 1938, went to Prague for Neville Chamberlain to diddle Hitler).' Steven and Trevor-Roper's bond flourished best on paper. This was not unusual for Hugh Trevor-Roper, who could be chilly and combative in person, but whose written idiom, in his sporadic books, his masterful essays and most elegantly of all in his barrages of letters, was irresistible. Trevor-Roper's correspondence seduced its recipients even as it implicated them deep within his conspiracies. One of Steven's special interests, the Greek Orthodox Church, overlapped with Trevor-Roper's profound learning in early Anglican theology, and Trevor-Roper never hesitated to write picking Steven up on points of fact, with all the glee of a generalist correcting a specialist. Each had real respect for the other and they maintained a lifelong outward sympathy, but there were reasons why Steven usually managed not to visit the Melrose lair of the Trevor-Ropers when travelling between London and Scotland. Steven's admiration was tinged with wariness, and Trevor-Roper's good will was never entirely disinterested. Steven read the witty dispatches of the '*Mercurius Oxoniensis*'* with delight, but remained on his guard.

In July 1956, Steven received a letter that fully justified such wariness. Trevor-Roper wrote to enquire whether Steven would accept the Regius Chair of Modern History at Oxford, if the Prime Minister should offer it to him upon the imminent retirement of the despised Galbraith. It was one of the most difficult dilemmas Steven had yet encountered. Since 1938 he had accepted only one academic job, his

---

* Trevor-Roper's alias as a mischievously gossip-mongering seventeenth-century don; under this *nom de guerre* he gleefully prosecuted Senior Common Room feuds in Aubreyesque prose in the letters pages of the *Spectator*.

Istanbul Chair of Byzantine Studies, and even that under the exceptional circumstances of war work. Michael Grant, his old pupil and friend, had pleaded with him on the grounds of increased pay, national importance and 'the glamour of being the leading Byzantinist in Byzantium', well knowing that after years outside the academy Steven would be most unwilling to be confined there. For all the distinction, influence and uniqueness of the Istanbul role, Steven had come to regret it, finding in it an exhausting distraction from real research and writing, and a millstone on his mobility, liberty and health. If this was the eventual consequence of a chair that had been practically designed for him, how much more onerous would be Trevor-Roper's proposal – a job that carried with it charge of the fractious history faculty, and a sentence to residence in Oxford, surrounded by the dons he could doubtfully endure for a single evening at Magdalen High Table.

But Steven was generously endowed with senses of both duty and vanity. Though he was almost certain he would come to hate such elevation, neither his principles nor his pride permitted him to refuse the Regius Chair out of hand. His reply on 21 July to this Mephistophelean offer shows his reaction – he dreaded the burden of work the chair implied; he felt it was his duty to accept it once properly proffered to him; but, no naïf in academic or worldly politics, he suspected Trevor-Roper's unacknowledged motive in proposing him:

Having once escaped from academic life I have no personal wish to return to it. All the University Boards and committees, all that futile administrative paraphernalia that now seems to fill academic life, are horrifying to me. But, quite apart from liking flattery – and your letter is something that I find dangerously flattering, – I do seriously feel that we should all do what we can to get the History Schools of our Universities out of the present morass. (Cambridge is every bit as bad as Oxford, probably worse; I would rank [David] Knowles higher than Galbraith, but Cambridge has no modern historians with the least idea of what history means, while Oxford at least has you and one or two others.) So I think I can truly promise that if I were offered the Chair I would not refuse. I should accept rather diffidently and rather unhappily; and, for both reasons, do please consider whether there is not someone more suitable academically and more impressive in the eyes of a P.M.; and please don't consider yourself in any way bound by an undertaking to me should you have a better idea.

Steven in feline fettle accepts Trevor-Roper's claim that there is a higher historical cause he ought to put ahead of his own comfort, and also hints that Oxford might be preferable to Cambridge. The 'one or two other' historians he was prepared to praise alongside Trevor-Roper included above all Dimitri Obolensky, a Byzantinist and, even more excitingly from Steven's perspective, a prince. Steven's dutiful language – 'we should all do what we can' – is both sincere and a knowing post-war pastiche of the old spirit of national unity. His reference to the fact that the chair was in the gift of the government indicates a further source of reluctance. Family Liberalism had set Steven firmly against Anthony Eden, who was now Prime Minister, while family gossip denigrated still more fiercely the Prime Minister's wife, Clarissa. Steven told Stewart Perowne that the eight-year-old Clarissa Churchill had briefly been in the charge of his own Nannie Laight, who had only disagreeable memories of the job. By his canny evocation of a candidate 'more impressive in the eyes of a P.M.', his pre-emptive absolution of his correspondent from any promise and his teasingly vague 'better idea', Steven revealed that he had detected Trevor-Roper's game.

Ambitious and Tory-leaning, Trevor-Roper had enlisted Runciman as his stalking horse while he gauged the support necessary to take the chair for himself. The detailed letter he had written to Masterman purported to be a manifesto in Steven's favour; but the quality Trevor-Roper chiefly recommended applied as evidently to himself: ' . . . [Runciman] can write. There is a liberalism, an elevation, a vitality about his work which makes that of our own local antiquaries, nibbling away in their narrow sectors, look mean and stale.' 'My suspicion is that J. C. might want to run me,' he had warned his wife Lady Xandra – herself Trevor-Roper's least enthusiastic backer, worried that the chair would upset their domestic arrangements and involve tedious social obligations. The new year of 1957 brought developments that bolstered Trevor-Roper's not very secret designs on the chair: J. C., his old tutor, became Vice-Chancellor of Oxford, and his publisher, Harold Macmillan, Prime Minister of Great Britain, in whose personal gift the chair lay.

Rumour of what was going on spread from Oxford to Doxford and reached Leslie, who had become with their father's death in 1949 the 2nd Viscount Runciman. He seems to have written to his brother warning him that Trevor-Roper's offer was not to be trusted. Steven's reply on 12 February reveals much of what he has truly thought all along about both the temptation and the tempter:

> ... I'm interested in what you say about the Regius Professorship ... I had written to Trevor-Roper before I left to say that there seemed to be so many suitable candidates in the field that he should indicate through his channels of intrigue that I should be dropped. He sent me a very entertaining and indiscreet answer about all the agitations and goings-on but said that his friends still thought that I was the candidate to push. I gather that my 'election agent' is a Fellow of Christ Church whom I don't know and don't think I should like, named Blake ... I think – and hope – that this sort of press-publicity doesn't do any good. I *know* that I don't want the job – shades of the prison-house – but I know that if offered it I'll really have to accept.

Steven's reluctance to get involved is further illuminated by his misgivings about Trevor-Roper's ally Robert Blake. Once again, the subtext is a matter of wartime history and political disharmony. Blake crossed the divide among the war veterans in the academy, the soldiers and the spies – he had been both a heroic officer on the Italian front and an MI6 operative until 1947. Steven was aware of the intelligence connection, but his distaste for Blake related to the Christ Church don's brand of fierce Toryism. The biographer of Disraeli, Blake continued to write and research on Toryism above all other topics, and was active on the contemporary Conservative Party's behalf in the Oxford student association and at large. Such a man might indeed be a perfectly qualified 'agent', but his conversation was hardly likely to allure Steven – who, though basically apolitical, remained at least residually Liberal. Trevor-Roper was himself eventually to become Master of Peterhouse as a result of a similar political mismatch; the dons there mistook him for a High Tory who would resist the entry of female undergraduates. On this occasion, the mistake was his.

'Runciman is my man,' Trevor-Roper wrote to J. C. Masterman, but neither he nor Blake were entirely Steven's sort of man.

Not only Steven's letter to Leslie, had the Oxford plotters seen it, but its very postmark could have told them as much – he was writing from Los Angeles. 'I love this city,' he enthused to his brother, 'the sheerest fantasy, except for the movie circles which are cosy and sedate.' Steven was the guest of the director George Cukor, and of Metro-Goldwyn-Mayer Studios, Inc. Even as he contemplated the Regius Chair, Steven entertained the idea of a lucrative job as a historical consultant on a new film about the Byzantine Empress Theodora, to be called (he laughingly explained to all his correspondents) *The Female*. It was a gilded and a mobile hermitage Steven had fashioned for himself, and he received the news that he would not after all be obliged to relinquish it happily enough. 'I learn from yesterday's *Observer* that you are likely to be the next Regius Professor,' he wrote cheerfully to the ascendant Trevor-Roper. 'A very good appointment, I thought – and what a relief it would be to me' – thus pre-empting by several months the official announcement. After his election, Trevor-Roper, for his part, maintained his graceful, but not entirely convincing, professions of unworthiness and astonishment. To Wallace Notestein at Yale he wrote: 'If [A. J. P.] Taylor is, as it seems, simply not *papabile*, and if my other candidate, Steven Runciman, is disqualified as a Cambridge man and a medievalist (but how different from Oxford medievalists!), then who am I to spurn this unexpected crown?'* Subsequently, J. C. Masterman liked to clear himself of the charge of fixing his old pupil's appointment by putting it about that Runciman had definitively refused to be considered. This was not exactly the case. The retiring Regius Professor, Galbraith, was undeceived. Furious on behalf of his own favourites, Taylor and Richard Southern, he fumed that 'Macmillan and Masterman deserve both to be sacked for what they've done!'

In 1950 Steven, still free of any official academic post, at work on *The First Crusade*, and living between Norfolk Road and Eigg, was rather

---

* Trevor-Roper's implication here that he approved of the candidature of Taylor, his most credible likely rival, is even more devious than his use of Steven as a stalking horse.

to his surprise asked by Cambridge to take on a new pupil. To his own even greater astonishment, he accepted him. The doctoral student in question was, like Steven, a Scot who had grown up in England, a connoisseur of monasteries and a genealogist of forensic, even dotty, commitment; but, as in the case of Steven and Bury, many attributes of their characters and philosophies diverged.

Donald Nicol was a Church of Scotland minister's son, born in Portsmouth and educated at St Paul's. Twenty years Steven's junior, he maintained a trace of a Scots accent all his life; he had a drily humorous speaking voice, was tall and, in a dour way, good-looking. Nicol came of age in the Second World War; following strict pacifist family principles, he joined a Friends' Ambulance Unit. In 1944, he was ordered to Greece. By the time Steven arrived at the British Council Nicol had returned home, but he came back for another stint as an employee of the British School of Athens in 1949, after completing his deferred undergraduate degree. Nicol thus witnessed both the Dekemvriana street-fights, British soldiers against leftist rioters, in Athens at the end of 1944, and the last, weary months of the Greek Civil War which had blazed up during Steven's last year in the Council.

Nicol's Greek experiences left him embittered against British and American policy, broadly holding the opinion, as a colleague recalled, that 'the only people who could run this country are those we have locked up in the prisons', though he also deplored the unscrupulous brutality of the ELAS fighters towards the civil population. But Greece had a more lasting and forgiving vision to impart to him: though personally a determined rationalist, he developed an impressive insight into Orthodoxy, both Greek and Slavonic. Like Steven in the 1930s, he visited the monasteries of the Meteora and the Holy Mountain of Athos, and he surpassed Steven by exploring and growing to love the monasteries and ruins of Ioannina in Epirus, where Lord Byron had once met Ali Pasha, and where, long before that, the Despots of Epirus had ruled an enterprising if ephemeral Byzantine breakaway principality.

It was to the Despotate of Epirus that, once returned home and promptly married, Nicol decided to devote his doctorate. The subject left the Cambridge historians baffled, till someone thought of Runciman and wondered where he might now be found. So it was that, with uncharacteristic trepidation, Nicol made his way to the Athenaeum Club, the traditional pasture of the Anglican higher clergy, and, since 1928, the metropolitan oasis of Steven Runciman. The older Byzantinist with his mysterious war record, his magic ring and that faint but just discernible touch of make-up, took his new pupil's measure with some reminiscences about his own Athenian spell, complimenting in particular the strategy and personality of the British commander from 1944 to 1946, Sir Ronald Scobie. 'Something prevented me', ran Nicol's wry memory of this first exchange, 'from saying that Scobie had blundered.'

Fortunately, the further away from recent history Runciman and Nicol journeyed, the more they found in common in allegiance and technique. Like Steven, Nicol enjoyed and valued narrative structure above recondite detail, and he had acquired Steven as a supervisor at the very moment when *The First Crusade* had turned Runciman into one of the most famous and commercially successful narrative historians in the country. Although Steven remained hard at work on his second and third volumes throughout Nicol's doctorate (completed in 1952), their unorthodox Athenaeum conferrals – a marked improvement in efficiency and comfort on Bury's quick-fire interrogations beside the Cambridge backs – gave the student no impression of scattered attention. Steven was more successful as a doctoral supervisor than he had been with the gilded youth of Trinity in the 1930s; very likely he found Nicol's esoteric, later Byzantine material a welcome relief from the epic, ethical stumblings of the Latin Crusaders.

Steven was free with useful information on the present as well as the past: the limited, enclosed and eccentric circle of Byzantinists among whom Nicol must now learn to operate. They made up a chamber of horrors he enjoyed guying, whether to amuse, to panic or to profit the younger man. There was Joan Hussey, a loyal pupil of the inexorable Baynes, secretly Catholic, prolific, competitive, grudging with her regard; Steven always called her 'the Hussey'. She was one of Nicol's examiners, and he quickly admitted to Steven how alarming he found her. After Nicol had endured a viva with punishing moments but a generally encouraging air, Steven wrote to reassure him: 'Thank you for letting me know about your inquisition . . . I ought to have remembered that the Hussey's love of her own voice detracts from her formidability. But she's a good conscientious examiner; so if she approves, it means something.'

Then there was Franz Dölger, Bavarian doyen of Byzantine Diplomatics. Steven admitted his competence ('fairly business-like'), but attacked his character with a prejudice that was predictable so soon after the war: 'Dölger . . . is very anxious to live down his Nazi past by being nice to the British.' Steven tended to avoid the Munich conferences under Dölger's superintendence – 'to be ordered about by him in his best Nazi manner is an unattractive prospect, nor is Munich so very interesting a city' – though his respectful acknowledgement of Dölger in his bibliographies to some degree gives the lie to this show of true-born British bravado.

Probably the oddest of all the great post-war Byzantinists, and the one upon whom Steven most loved to lavish his faux-bemused satirical eye, was Professor Henri Grégoire of Brussels, 'a man of intense vitality and learning, some of whose ideas trembled on the edge of fantasy'. Steven applied to this ancient and peculiar authority with increasing persistence on his pupil's behalf, but was reliably entertained by Grégoire's lackadaisical disinclination to co-operate:

Yesterday I saw Prof. Grégoire to whom I spoke of your publishing part of your thesis in *Byzantion* [the journal of Belgian Byzantinists]. (I had written to him twice and he said airily that he had lost the first letter and the second arrived when he was ill – or was it the other way round?)

Grégoire moves in a mysterious way, but in the end the results are usually all right.

. . . you must surely realise by now that the only way to get an answer from [Grégoire] is to go in person to Brussels; which is not always easy. It may be a bit better now that Marguerite Mathieu [Grégoire's pupil and, Steven liked to imply, devoted lover] is back. She, though hysterical, is slightly less unbusinesslike than the rest and sometimes can induce Grégoire to answer letters . . . On the other hand Mme. Grégoire, who is jealous of Grégoire's work and of Mlle. Mathieu in particular, not infrequently destroys all his correspondence just to annoy him. The whole place is a mad-house.

One of Steven's favourite historical fancies was that the Byzantine chronicler Gregoras must have resembled his Belgian namesake – 'a fussy and incurably verbose little man and not always very accurate'.

When the leading French Byzantinist Paul Lemerle gave *The Despotate of Epirus*, the book that had emerged from Nicol's thesis in 1957, a harsh review, Steven was quick to reassure and defend his protégé:

> Lemerle's effusion . . . is the sort of review which is most irritating. First he criticizes you for not having written the book that he thinks you should have written – and how he thinks that one can venture on culture and social life, etc, until one has got the political part clear puzzles me; but that is the modern fashion. Narrative history is 'out', so I have been informed; one's friends call one 'traditional' if one tries to write it, and one's foes 'out-of-date'.
>
> Then he talks of errors without specifying what they are, apart from your not having consulted certain articles – and who has ever the time to read all the articles that are poured out on every subject nowadays. It seems to me so much more important to have read the original sources . . .
>
> . . . I am disappointed in Lemerle, whom I have always rather liked. Is there some article of his own that you have neglected? that is so often the cause of a bad review. Or have you just cut the ground from under one of his pupils' feet?

Once again Steven marks out Nicol as more than a disciple – an ally and possibly an heir, in the cause of narrative history. In fact, he is extending on Nicol's behalf the same sort of proprietorial patronage of which he accuses Lemerle. Steven was becoming proud of Nicol, his work, his interests and his potential; and that pride led him for the first time in his career to diverge from his careful academic policy of aloofness towards both rivals and allies. Personally, his affection for Nicol was touched with the filial; he got on with his pupil's devout, cautious, hospitable Scots Catholic wife, Jane Mary, and happily twitted Nicol, in short order the father of three sons: 'It's very impressive and Patriarchal to go on producing sons like that.' In terms of professional prospects, the academic career of this talented, serious-minded, impecunious Scots scholar was developing into something close to a vicarious shadow of what might have been Steven's own.

By the beginning of the 1960s Nicol was working as a lecturer at University College Dublin, while Steven's renown had, with his knighthood in 1958 and the publication of *The Sicilian Vespers* later the same year, reached its peak. It was at this point that Steven was, for the third and final time, considered for a British professorial chair. This was the Koraes Chair of Modern Greek and Byzantine History at King's College London, named, unfortunately in the view of Steven among others, after the nineteenth-century Greek republican ideologue, inventor of the 'purified' *katharevousa* form of the Greek language, Adamantios Koraes, whom Steven considered to have been a 'remarkable man' but also a 'monster'.

This was the chair for which John Mavrogordato, in 1919, had been narrowly ruled out as too *fainéant* in favour of the ill-fated Arnold Toynbee. From 1946 to the early 1960s it was held by Romilly Jenkins, a great Byzantinist who attracted something close to loathing in Greece because of his contention that modern Greeks had inherited no classical Greek blood and little Byzantine (in private Steven was disposed to agree, but thought it irrelevant compared with their Hellenic linguistic and cultural heritage). Jenkins had just been lured to the best-endowed post-war nucleus of Byzantine Studies, Dumbarton Oaks at Washington, DC, in receipt of a salary Steven speculated was about five times London's; and King's College London seemed in no particular hurry to find a replacement. When Steven, as Chairman of the Anglo-Hellenic League, enquired into the matter, concerned at the prevailing inertia over the organization of the library, he was taken aback by the response, as he confided to Nicol: 'I was offered the Chair with the suggestion that I could treat it as being purely honorary and needn't do anything. I was shocked and told them so, telling them that it was their duty to get someone young and active. Would you take it on if it were offered to you? I'm prepared to start an intrigue.'

This 'intrigue' would take another eight years to effect; King's College offered the chair next to Cyril Mango in early 1963, and though

Steven had expected this, he was surprised that Mango accepted. Mango, for his part, regarded Steven as an old-fashioned amateur. When Nicol eventually became Koraes Professor in 1970, Steven considered it his most gratifying triumph in the field of academic politics.

# 18

# The Trilogy

A History of the Crusades: The First Crusade, The
Kingdom of Jerusalem, The Kingdom of Acre
*(planned from 1938; written 1947–53; published
1951, 1952, 1954)*

... he that increaseth knowledge increaseth sorrow.

Ecclesiastes 1: 18 (quoted by Steven Runciman as epigraph
to the final chapter of *A History of the Crusades*)


Steven Runciman's great three-volume classic, *A History of the Cru-sades*, is a paradoxical work: both introductory and climactic in its qualities. Its sales remain high and steady because it is still the most seductive introduction to its subject in English. Yet, as an introduction to its author, it is hardly representative. Runciman had never before written, and would never write again, on so monumental a scale. The trilogy involved a new departure, too, in its intended audience, for while Runciman's prose was always jargon-free, clear and accessible, his subject matter – Byzantium, Bulgaria and Bogomils – had hitherto been firmly directed towards a small circle of specialists. While the Crusades had never been treated in English in the detail Runciman now delivered, they were nonetheless episodes familiar to the general reading public, in part due to Walter Scott's version, which Steven derided.* They were also, then as now, topical. The British and French Mandates in Palestine and Syria had recently elapsed. Egypt was still a client-kingdom yoked to Britain, when Runciman's second volume,

---

* Bernard Swithinbank recalled their cursory presence on the Eton history syllabus early in the twentieth century: 'We heard of the Crusades vaguely, because some English princes took the cross, and we knew the names of two or three Popes who gave trouble to England, and that was all we knew of European history from 100 AD to 1453 AD' (quoted in Richard Davenport-Hines, *Universal Man: The Lives of John Maynard Keynes* (HarperCollins, 2015), p. 45).

*The Kingdom of Jerusalem*, which recounted earlier Western incursions on the Nile, was published. A generation earlier in 1917 General Allenby had entered Jerusalem quietly on foot, but this had not stopped the British press from falsely ascribing to him the boast that 'the wars of the Crusaders are completed'. Steven was conscious that he was shifting from specialist territory to a subject widely, if often erroneously, imagined and invoked. This consciousness affected his style. While in previous work his idiosyncratic personality had expressed itself in drily witty asides, he was now prepared to be bolder and more sententious. The ringing judgements and lyrical homilies in *A History of the Crusades* might lead the reader to wonder if Steven would have made an excellent bishop. The trilogy was the climax of his career; he knew it, and did not hold back.

Written over about seven years – from Steven's departure from Athens in 1947 until the completion of the third volume, *The Kingdom of Acre*, in 1953 – *A History of the Crusades* had been gestated and researched over a much longer span. He had kept the subject in mind at all of his relevant foreign posts in the Second World War – Cairo, Jerusalem and Istanbul – and visited Syria as often as he could. The relatively short-lived Frankish colonies in the area had not at first particularly interested him, but over the 1930s this changed. In October 1935, he touched on the topic of the Crusades in an article in the *English Historical Review*, discussing Charlemagne's relations, real and legendary, with Palestine. The piece shows wide reading outside of Byzantine matters and close contact with W. B. Stevenson, then the leading British expert on the Crusader States. But Runciman's wit and understated comic timing are what really stand out:

> Isaac and the elephant, Abbu'l-Abbas, arrived ... in Aachen that spring; where the latter had a considerable influence on Carolingian art before succumbing to the rigours of the North. What was the purpose of Charles's embassy? ... it is unlikely that even the desire of possessing an elephant could by itself induce Charles to fit out an embassy for Baghdad. The elephant must have been a subsidiary object, the main object being political.

Steven's second trip to Syria, in 1938, crucially involved that useful diplomatic host Stas Ostrorog. Over supper at the British Consulate,

Steven and Stas met an old comrade of General Allenby, full of nos-talgic memories of the 1917 Jerusalem campaign, Brigadier Archibald Wavell. Steven confided to the future General, Viceroy and antholo-gist that he was 'hoping to write a book on the Crusades'. Wavell suggested that Steven 'come and see him some day, as he had studied their history when he was helping Allenby plan his invasion'. That day took eleven years to arrive; it occurred through the good offices of Freya Stark in the spring of 1949, halfway through the writing of *The First Crusade*. '[Wavell] kindly had me to lunch and gave me a fascinating account of Allenby's campaign. It was not wholly relevant to my work, as Allenby invaded Palestine from Egypt, while the Cru-saders came down from the north. But it gave me a good lesson in military strategy.'

When he first met Wavell in March 1938, Steven had been finan-cially independent for only a short while, following the death of his grandfather the previous August. He had been master of his own time as well as money for an even shorter period, resigning his Trinity fellowship earlier that year. Steven was torn between two very differ-ent counsellors – G. M. Trevelyan urging him to write and Guy Burgess urging diplomatic work abroad. The intention he volunteered to Wavell seems to imply that, by that Damascus spring, Steven had decided to spend his liberty and his legacy writing, after the Trev-elyan model. In fact, the Second World War intervened and the next few years fell out more according to the Burgess pattern. But Steven was determined enough not to let his plan – tentatively expressed, but inwardly resolved – slide altogether, no matter where the chaos of war-work might lead him. Indeed it is notable that, in the event, his wartime journeys followed a similar trail to those of the Crusaders. Guy Crouchback in Evelyn Waugh's *Sword of Honour* trilogy volun-teers for service in Italy and finds himself seconded to Yugoslavia. Steven, for all his endearing protestations of naivety, was no such innocent in the workings of British bureaucracy.

The Second World War produced remarkable fictional trilogies, by Waugh, Anthony Powell and Olivia Manning, the last two both acquaintances of Steven. It might not be altogether mistaken to consider *A History of the Crusades* as an exercise in a closely related genre. Like the Guy Crouchback novels, the three wartime instalments of *A Dance to the Music of Time*, *The Balkan Trilogy* and *The Levant Trilogy*, Runciman's trilogy, though actually written years after the war, is obviously formed, and informed, by the experiences, losses and expectations of the war years. Like the trilogies of Waugh, Powell and Manning, Runciman's seems to hark back to an older kind of extended fiction, more romance than novel, in the manner of Malory or Spenser; its scenes wild, wide and careless of Aristotelian unity, replete with an enormous, shifting cast that manages to be both intricately recurring and shockingly mortal. If it be objected that *A History of the Crusades* is based on fact, that rather literal-minded contention has been disputed, with varying degrees of politeness, by authorities as various as Jonathan Riley-Smith, David Abulafia, Christopher Tyerman and Robert Irwin. *The Sword of Honour* closely follows the structure of the diary Waugh kept covertly during active service; it would scarcely need a medieval scholar to find the result less fictional than the unforgettable scene with which Runciman opens *A History of the Crusades*, of the Caliph Omar receiving the homage and the keys of Jerusalem from the lofty height of his white camel.

'Their enterprise itself was no novelty,' W. B. Stevenson had wearily written in *Crusaders in the East* (1907). 'Syria is a stage which waits from century to century for a repetition of the same drama.' Runciman brought freshness to this repetitive cycle through his gift of expression as much as his methodology. He was far from the first narrator of what Gibbon had called 'the World's Debate' to make a serious effort to include the Muslim perspective, or to stress the importance of Arabic sources; his great French predecessors, especially René Grousset, had done the same. Runciman's learning was wider but scarcely deeper than that of Grousset or Jean Richard. Where he excelled was in his ability to display and adorn that learning. His enterprise might be no novelty, but he intended it to read like a novel.

Runciman's narrative voice assumes confident possession of every conceivable item of general interest or intimate detail. For example, the defeated Patriarch of Jerusalem, Sophronius – the second character we meet in *The First Crusade* – is rapidly fleshed out with discreet, authoritative ease. Steven came to know several Patriarchs well; Sophronius, from the seventh century AD, is treated as a close and gossip-worthy acquaintance. John Moschus, a Byzantine monk who is in fact at this moment Runciman's source, is name-dropped, rather than cited, as if he were some mutual social connection, a minor character rather than an authority. The Patriarch's career is related as pithily as if Runciman has already discussed it at length, or else it is common knowledge. Two more of Runciman's favourite devices come into play at this early juncture. The historian's hindsight is transformed into a sympathetic character's foresight – 'he had fought steadfastly against the heresies and nascent nationalism that he foresaw would dismember the Empire.' And, without either ostentation or shame, the most romantic conclusion is drawn. Sophronius, we are confidently informed, 'died of a broken heart'. The essence of the technique lies in the distance between the authorial voice – informed, tasteful, imaginative but plausible – and the lay reader's position of indebted ignorance.

But though he was aware of a larger congregation of laity than he had previously addressed, Runciman also sustained a conversation with fellow scholars, whether friends who would appreciate his obscurest jokes or rivals to be corrected and teased. For this more rarefied audience, the same Olympian distance that serves both to bamboozle and to reassure the general reader operates as a different sort of game, indeed as a dare. The real experts substantially knew both the primary and the secondary material upon which Runciman drew. Where most contemporary scholars would seek to differentiate their work by citing new material, Runciman preferred to astonish, and sometimes outrage, the historians among his readers by treating long-established sources with high-handed boldness. Old standbys among the chronicles are dismissed with urbane discrimination as distorted by prejudice or hearsay, while obscure and incomplete evidence is moulded with insight and imagination into a coherent interpretation, with gaps in time and in evidence gracefully repaired. This process, systematic but largely implicit in the text, is gamely revealed in the appendices Runciman provides on his sources. Radulph of Caen, the author of the *Gesta Tancredi*, is quietly eviscerated: 'His style is that of an ignorant but very pretentious man.' Anna Comnena receives a more gallant verdict: 'modern historians are too ready to belittle her. She was an intelligent and very well-educated woman; and she was a conscientious historian, who tried to verify her sources.' Even Anna, a Byzantine princess, cannot verify her sources with so much *de haut en bas* decisiveness as Runciman.

Runciman is able and willing to find larger significance in anecdotes which, though picturesque, have generally been ignored as too elaborate and tangential to make any exemplary point. He gives full attention, in what Robert Irwin half admiringly calls his '*Beau Geste*' idiom, to the rackety careers of figures such as Roussel de Ballieul, a Norman adventurer in Byzantine employ. Roussel's story is certainly of interest in itself. It was to catch the eye of the historical novelist Alfred Duggan, who retold it as *Lady for Ransom* not long after *The First Crusade*'s publication. Roussel was the commander of the mercenary detachment of Norman knights at the Battle of Manzikert. He and his contingent treacherously deserted the field, contributing to the catastrophic defeat of the Byzantine army by the Seljuk Turks. Despite this, the Byzantines could not afford to do without him, and he was dispatched back to Asia Minor to retake territory lost to the victorious Turkish nomads. Roussel managed to capture Ankara – but then, following the example of his cousins in Sicily, held it himself as an independent mini-state. When the Greek Emperor sent another army led by his uncle against the Norman rebel, Roussel defeated it, took the uncle prisoner and then declared him Emperor, giving himself legal cover to advance on Constantinople itself. He was eventually tricked into surrender by Alexius Comnenus – later Emperor Alexius I – but he had been so popular with his Asiatic subjects that they could be convinced to abandon his cause only when news emerged of his blinding. 'In truth,' Runciman reveals, 'Alexius could not bring himself so to mutilate him; and such was his charm that even the Emperor was glad to hear that he had not suffered that indignity.' But Runciman characteristically does not let the matter rest there: 'Roussel disappears from history. But the episode left its mark on the Byzantines. It taught them that the Normans were not to be trusted . . . ' Thus Roussel becomes a literary prototype for the unscrupulous Normans, Bohemond and Tancred, who figure later in the narrative.

Another technique which Runciman uses to entertain both the lay and the learned reader – if on slightly separate planes – is in his memorable paraphrases of primary sources. He employs several tones for this purpose. There is the acidic, all-but-explicit judgement, which might fairly be called Gibbonian (though Runciman would have jibbed at the comparison): '[Peter the Hermit] was a man of short stature, swarthy and with a long, lean face, horribly like the donkey that he always rode and that was revered almost as much as himself.' The sources obligingly supply the ugliness and the donkey, but the artful juxtaposition is pure Runciman. His carefully arranged selections can instil solemnity, however, quite as well as humour. Some lyrical passages seem to approach fairy tale and folk myth:

> The brothers formed a striking contrast. Baldwin was even taller than Godfrey. His hair was as dark as the other's was fair; but his skin was very white. While Godfrey was gracious in manner, Baldwin was haughty and cold. Godfrey's tastes were simple, but Baldwin, though he could endure great hardships, loved pomp and luxury. Godfrey's private life was chaste; Baldwin's given over to venery.

Runciman has extracted two distinct physical descriptions in different chronicles and related them to each other to compose a novel picture, an almost suspiciously lucid contrast of a blond, bluff, pious brother and a dark, worldly, scheming one. Effective as this willingness to edit in a novelistic direction undoubtedly is in descriptive passages, when it is applied to action and causation it becomes even headier – and even more provocative to the more scholarly, professional segment of Runciman's readership. Here is his reinterpretation of the Old French Chronicle of Ernoul, the passage leading up to the news of the Christian defeat at Cresson:

> About the middle of that morning Balian and his company arrived at La Fève. From afar they had seen tents of the Templars dressed below the walls; but when they drew near they found that they were empty; and in the castle itself there was silence. Balian's groom Ernoul entered the building and wandered from room to room. There was no one there, except two soldiers lying in one of the upper galleries, sick to death and unable to speak. Balian was perplexed and worried ... Suddenly a Templar knight galloped up dishevelled and bleeding, shouting out of a great disaster.

Once again we see the primary chronicler, Ernoul, subsumed into Runciman's overriding prose and dramatic timing, as a minor character within a larger scene. It is a scene that seems as impartial as good history and yet as involving as good fiction because it contains perspectives of which no mere historian can really be sure. Runciman leaves Ernoul as a shadowy bit-part, while he seems to claim direct access to the inner thoughts of the groom's master, Balian.

To incorporate and to overwhelm the primary historians, Runciman reveals them as interested parties and players. He rises above the uncertainties of lost, incomplete or competing manuscripts; he is thoroughly decided about his sources' identities, characters, social circles and political interests. He is a master of the quick pen-portrait, but very few even of his epic's protagonists receive as memorable depictions as the memoirist Usama ibn-Munqidh or the historian William of Tyre:

> Though an utter intriguer to whom personal loyalty meant nothing, [Usama] was a man of great charm and intelligence, a soldier, a sportsman and a man of letters. His reminiscences . . . have no chronological order and are the unverified recollections of an old man, but they give an extraordinarily vivid picture of life amongst the Arab and Frankish aristocrats of his time.

> William . . . is one of the greatest of medieval historians. He had his prejudices, such as his dislike of lay-control of the Church, but he is temperate in his words about his personal enemies, such as the Patriarch Heraclius and Agnes of Courtenay, who both deserved his censure . . . he had a broad vision; he understood the significance of great events of his time and the sequence of cause and effect in history. His style is straightforward and not without humour. His work leaves the impression that he was himself a wise, honourable, and likeable man.

It is not completely fanciful to catch a strain of identification in both of these portraits. Usama ibn-Munqidh was an unconventional, semi-detached but extremely well-connected scion of the princely Arab dynasty that ruled Shaizar. Steven shared his love of travel and gossip, and of social, if not actual, lion-hunts. Despite the 1924 prediction of an Istanbul gypsy that Steven would live to a ripe old age, he cannot have known, as we do, that he would join Usama in the select ranks of nonagenarian autobiographers. Steven's sympathy for William, Archbishop of Tyre in the latter twelfth century, is still more obvious – indeed William is very rare among Latin clergy in Runciman's work in being presented almost entirely favourably. In listing the virtues of William's historical approach, literary practice, high standards and humane character, Steven comes close to stating his own ideals. At the same time, he buries both Usama and William by praising them; they are attractive but subordinate voices, while he remains the sole chronicler. This is another tactic reminiscent of fiction. T. H. White, a contemporary of Steven's who shared several of his Bloomsbury acquaintances, incorporated into yet another war-time trilogy – *The Once and Future King* – the authorial figure of Sir Thomas Malory, presented as one of King Arthur's young pages. In recent times the protagonist of *Baudolino*, Umberto Eco's 2000 novel, imparts his life story to the Byzantine historian Nicetas Choniates – incidentally described by Runciman as 'accurate and reliable . . . in spite of an over-rhetorical style and a tendency to moralize'.

The tendency of Runciman's own rhetoric to moralize – reined in for the most part in his work prior to *A History of the Crusades* – develops more decidedly as the trilogy advances. Even at the time, this perturbed some readers. R. C. Smail, a historian of a more characteristically Cantabrigian and technical kind, published an article in the *Cambridge Historical Gazette* entitled *Crusader Castles of the Twelfth Century* in 1951, the same year as *The First Crusade*. Smail regarded Steven with measured respect, which was readily returned. But, in a broadcast that year for the BBC's Third Programme, Smail felt himself bound to express reservations about what he saw as *The First Crusade*'s simplistic moral dichotomy: 'It seems to me that Mr. Runciman does less than justice to this tragic situation, this clash of two justifiable but mutually exclusive points of view.' Steven, as his *magnum opus* progressed and its themes emerged more consistently, became impatient with this mannerly even-handedness. His own world had just endured a traumatic struggle, where, as Steven saw it, the uneasy, ambiguous virtues of an elderly civilization in imperial decline had confronted the potent, single-minded malice of nationalist fanaticism. Victorious but exhausted, the Allies now found themselves in a position of fearful responsibility; if history contained lessons for them, this was no time to be shy about declaring them. The left-wing critic Bruce Bain came nearer than Smail in comprehending Runciman's mission, when he wrote in 1954, reviewing the second volume, of its 'blend of scholarly sobriety, poetic imagination, and compassionate indignation'. Runciman, Bain goes on, 'provides, indirectly, a terrible warning to all those, in America, England or the U.S.S.R., who want to wipe unbelievers off the face of the earth'. Steven's delicate exterior as an *arbiter elegantiarum* made him a surprising evangelist, even in the cause of tolerance, but the war had left him with a certain sense of mission.

His sermon is not hard to decode. 'All over the Empire there had fallen that atmosphere of lassitude and pessimism that so often after a long bitter war assails the victors no less than the conquered,' Runciman declares in the first, background chapter of *The First Crusade*. The Empire is the seventh-century Byzantium of Heraclius, a pyrrhic victor over Persia; but it could easily be cash-strapped, weary Britain. The description is a useful breath of empathy as Runciman prepares the war-worn reader of 1951 for what will, essentially, be a military saga. It is also a fine example of his unembarrassed appeal to universal parallels, across history and geography. The same first chapter contains one of Runciman's most quotable and, by the same token, most elusive of aphorisms: 'Unlike Christianity, which preached a peace that it never achieved, Islam unashamedly came with a sword.' This misleadingly pellucid statement incorporates in a more literal sense the memory of one of Christ's most disturbing announcements: 'I came not to send peace, but a sword.' It expresses a more Gibbonian sentiment than is usual with Runciman: distrustful alike of the hypocrisy of Christianity and the brazenness of Islam. Over the action of the trilogy the uncontrolled martial spirit signified by 'the sword' swings from the conquering Caliphs to the unruly Franks, back to the severity of the Mameluks. Applied to Steven's own time, the comparison is implicitly critical of all extremes – the moral void entailed by militaristic fanaticism, as well as the unrealistic hopes of pacifism and appeasement which had so fatally embroiled his own father.

Steven's personal attitude to the war effort, in the context of his immediate family as well as the country at large, was at first ambiguous. His conveniently poor health kept him from active service. He maintained a hesitant loyalty to the Chamberlain policy of appeasement which his father supported; it was left to his closest sister, Margie, and her second husband, Douglas Fairweather, to become bellicose rebels within the family. Steven felt less certain of where he stood, or ought to stand. He loathed the tone of the German regime, an exaggeration of everything he found vulgar and oppressive in Western culture (he had always hated the music of Wagner, describing *Parsifal* in particular as 'a disastrous and evil opera'). But he offered his father support and admiration in private and public. While Steven was sceptical about the extent of Neville Chamberlain's ability and suspicious of the Prime Minister's brief popularity after the Munich Crisis, this was more out of a sense that his father had received insufficient credit than a product of doubts about appeasement. He continued to hope for peace, and even after the outbreak of war wrote to Leslie Perowne, brother of Stewart, that he 'didn't really approve' of it. But his war-work during and after the conflict, especially in Athens where he had his longest true exposure to a country at war, developed his attitude and his principles. By the writing of *The First Crusade* Steven was deeply affected both by pacifist preferences and by an almost professional aversion to totalitarianism, whether of fascist or Marxist origin.

'The Christian citizen', Runciman observes at the outset of the first volume, 'has a fundamental problem to face: is he entitled to fight for his country?' Entitled, not obliged: this question is some way ahead of the celebrated 1933 Oxford Union motion, 'That this House will in no circumstances fight for its King and Country'. For Steven, a great glory of Byzantine civilization was its advanced humanity over questions of bloodshed. 'The Byzantine soldier was not in fact treated as a murderer. But his profession brought him no glamour.' Runciman himself, though in principle eager to identify with Byzantine urbanity, would reveal himself throughout *A History of the Crusades* to be subject to less enlightened feelings. Try as he might, he could hardly help the fact that his favourite sister was Margie Fairweather, the heroic female Spitfire pilot, and he himself the product of a

Western tradition that valued prowess in arms. Had it been otherwise, he could hardly have written his lapidary epitaph on Richard the Lionheart – 'He was a bad son, a bad husband and a bad king, but a gallant and splendid soldier.' This ambivalence surfaces again in Runciman's observation in *The First Crusade* that 'The code of chivalry that was developing, supported by popular epics, gave prestige to the military hero; and the pacifist acquired an ill repute from which he has never recovered.' For all his rational and sometimes sermonizing inclination towards Byzantium, with its professional army and civil service, and its preference for diplomacy and intrigue over arms, Steven recognized the attraction and the value of the warrior spirit, recognized, too, that he personally cut an anticlimactic figure in the wake of the Crusaders. Even horses gave him hay fever.

To the Princess Anna Comnena, 'one of the most typical of Byzantines', war was, Runciman says, 'a shameful thing, a last resort when all else had failed, indeed in itself a confession of failure'. But those months in Czechoslovakia had convinced Steven that all else had, indeed, failed. His account of the German Crusade of 1095 in *The First Crusade* is suffused with distasteful memories, suggestive of the anti-Jewish feeling running high alongside Nazi propaganda, which Steven must have observed in the Sudetenland. Runciman's dominant note here is one of disgust. The great Crusading hero Godfrey of Bouillon, claimed for German nationalism by way of an epic tradition that described him as a saintly swan knight, is shown no quarter by Runciman's understated but withering contempt:

> Godfrey of Bouillon ... appears in later legend as the perfect Christian knight, the peerless hero of the whole Crusading epic. A scrupulous study of history must modify the verdict.
>
> ... His administration of Lorraine was not very efficient. There seems to have been some doubt whether [the German Emperor] Henry would continue to employ him. It was therefore partly from despondency about his future in Lorraine, partly from uneasiness over his religious loyalties, and partly from genuine enthusiasm that he answered the call to the Crusade.

This unexpected portrait of an undistinguished thug, dim in all senses, is affirmed when Runciman accuses him of extorting a sum, uncompromisingly labelled 'blackmail', from defenceless, rich Jews, at the mercy of the fanatical German Crusaders in Godfrey's army and even less organized sympathizers throughout his domain of Lower Lorraine. Lesser German leaders and anti-Semitic religious enthusiasts come in for sharper criticism. There is 'a certain Volkmar, of whose antecedents we know nothing'; Runciman allows this rare admission of genealogical ignorance to form an implicit reproach. There is – a lighter note within this grim account – 'a multitude of simple enthusiastic pilgrims . . . some of them following a goose that had been inspired by God'. Runciman even refuses these persecutors the doubtful respect due to competence in evil. 'It was not a very impressive attack,' he sneers of one episode, while emphasizing that this in no way diminishes the responsibility, the sin or the malevolent legacy of the attackers: 'Small as was the massacre at Spier, it whetted the appetite.'*

After the war, a broad historiographical controversy emerged over the nature of Nazism – whether it was a coherent creed, and Hitler's an organized, infernal intelligence (the argument put forward in, for example, Hugh Trevor-Roper's 1953 edition of *Hitler's Table Talk*), or merely a haphazard set of ancient prejudices under a lucky mountebank, grown to monstrous proportions (the view that would emerge in A. J. P. Taylor's *Origins of the Second World War* (1961)). The consistent relationship Runciman draws between rusticity, ignorance and evil implies he held the second view. This hangover of wartime contempt can lead to some eccentric generalizations. Describing the aftermath of the death of the Emperor Frederick Barbarossa, Runciman declares that 'the Germans, with their strange longing to worship a leader, are usually demoralized when the leader disappears.' This may now seem practically as prejudiced as the Crusaders' antipathy for the Jews, but it was hardly a surprising attitude

---

* Tyerman considers this judgement of Runciman's to be 'rather astonishing' (Christopher Tyerman, *God's War* (Penguin, 2006), p. 101), but the dozen murders and one forced suicide at Spier are surely a relatively gentle horror by the standards of the period and of the whole First Crusade. Runciman can sound blasé and he is not immune to the casual anti-Semitism of his class at this period, but in this instance he is firmly on the side of the victims, denigrating, rather than defending, the perpetrators.

in the British post-war landscape, even at cultured and cosmopolitan levels. In 1969, nearly two decades on from *The First Crusade*, Kenneth Clark (an old acquaintance of Steven's) sounds similar, when, in his sixth *Civilisation* programme 'Protest and Communication', he all but equates Martin Luther and Hitler, claiming – with H. G. Wells as his authority – that the German people are uniquely susceptible to forming 'communities of will', congregations united under the potent sway of a charismatic individual.

In the story of the First Crusade as Runciman tells it, the charismatic and dangerous figure at the heart of the Crusaders' 'community of will' was Bohemond de Hauteville, Prince of Taranto and then Antioch. Bohemond, born Mark, was the eldest son of the Norman adventurer Robert Guiscard ('The Wily'), Duke of Apulia. Such was the promise of his burly size as an infant that he was quickly renamed after Buamundus Gigas, a giant from a passing jongleur's fable which had amused his father. Bohemond was everything a Norman noble desired in a son and heir: tall, good-looking, fierce and cunning. He was less blessed in his mother, not because she lacked personal qualities, but because she could only confer a modest alliance with another Norman baron. The Guiscard accordingly repudiated her in favour of a more exalted match with Sichelgaita, a Lombard princess and southern Italian Valkyrie who fought beside her husband in the front line. Her son by Robert was soon named as the Guiscard's heir, leaving Bohemond unsatisfied and ambitious. What followed is the part of Bohemond's background which made him represent for Runciman the beginning of an important historical trend, the antagonism of barbarous Franks towards cultivated Greeks. Robert Guiscard attacked the Byzantine Empire, and Bohemond, hoping to replace the heritage his half-brother had taken from him with a new kingdom over the Adriatic, was his father's chief commander.

All this had played out a decade before the First Crusade, but for Runciman Bohemond's past history with the Greeks is the key to his whole importance, character and behaviour, to the 'vastness of his unscrupulous ambition'. Just as Byzantium is the lodestar that directs Runciman's outline of the story of the Crusades, envy of Byzantium becomes the unifying motive that characterizes his Frankish villains. The reader is at once shown Bohemond in *The First Crusade* as a

Machiavellian stage antagonist. The chronicle sources show him as joining the Crusade in a moment of spontaneous religiosity, on watching a band of pilgrims wearing the cross go by; he is supposed to have taken off his cloak and ordered it to be cut into crosses for his own men. For Runciman, this episode simply implies a respect for big battalions – 'it was only the arrival in Italy of enthusiastic armies of Crusaders from France that made Bohemond realise the importance of the movement. He saw then that it could be used for his advantage.'

Bearing in mind Bohemond's past, Runciman can make even his attempts at diplomacy seem insincere – 'His policy was to behave perfectly correctly towards the Emperor.' Bohemond was one of the most successful of the First Crusade's leaders, its best general, and has left the strongest personal imprint on the chronicles (he may have commissioned the most famous, the *Gesta Francorum*). Runciman uses quasi-novelistic instinct, and the insight into the rivalries of high politics attained in part by watching his own father's career, in part by his British Council experiences at Athens in 1945–7. He displays Bohemond, for all his posthumous reputation and sympathetic biographers, as a controversial, difficult man loathed in his own day. This account of Bohemond helps to clarify mysteries about other important leaders. Historians had long been puzzled by the behaviour of Raymond, Count of Toulouse, a Crusader leader who underwent a strange volte-face, from stubborn resistance to the Byzantine Emperor Alexius to becoming his most loyal friend. Explanations prior to Runciman ranged from inconsistencies in the chronicles to bribery by Alexius. But having once portrayed Bohemond as the root of the trouble, Runciman can interpret the affair in purely personal terms: 'it is probable that Bohemond's departure was of greater assistance [in satisfying Raymond of Toulouse]. The Emperor was able to see Raymond in private and explain to him that he too had no love for the Normans and that Bohemond would never in fact receive an imperial command.' There is no documentary evidence for so conversational a solution. But Runciman's proposal is compellingly psychological.

One of Runciman's most characteristic passages is his retelling of Anna Comnena's physical description of Bohemond. Christopher Tyerman, whose full-length study of the Crusades eventually succeeded and at least technically supplanted Runciman's, has pointed out his predecessor's unscrupulous adjustment of chronology from 1108 to 1097 so as to appear to be an erotically charged memory from the Princess's teenage years:

> His person was very impressive. Anna Comnena, who knew him and hated him passionately, could not but admit his charm and wrote enthusiastically of his good looks. He was immensely tall; and though he was already over forty years of age, he had the figure and complexion of a young man, broad-shouldered and narrow-waisted, with a clear skin and ruddy cheeks. He wore his yellow hair shorter than was the fashion with western knights and was clean shaven. He had stooped slightly from childhood, but without impairing his air of health and strength. There was, says Anna, something hard in his expression and sinister in his smile; but being, like Greeks down the ages, susceptible to human beauty, she could not withhold her admiration.

To Tyerman, this 'not so suppressed eroticism' is typical of Runciman's 'mischievous' prose. Tyerman interprets the phraseology as a signal from a man, and a time, that instinctively combined discretion with flirtation: 'That remark about the Greek love of beauty lifts the curtain on Runciman's own sexuality just that little bit – and quite deliberately, as it seems to me.' In fact Runciman was following the lead of an earlier biographer of Anna Comnena, Georgina Buckler, an old Girton friend of his mother's, who in 1929 had drawn out the same innuendo with less subtlety. 'If Anna admired noble birth, hardly less did she admire beauty; like a true Greek she almost makes a god of a handsome face and a well-made form ... Her portrait of Bohemund has been construed by her critics into an unconscious revelation of her love for him.' Runciman's originality here lies in his trick of effortlessly inhabiting these historical characters' interior lives, in a manner inaccessible to any stricter historical propriety. As lacking in scruple as the Norman he depicts, Runciman does not hesitate to assure his readers that Anna 'knew Bohemond and hated him passionately'. His assertion that Anna perceived 'something hard in his expression and sinister in his smile', far from being a literal translation of her Greek, is a flash of film noir, seeming to grant the reader momentary access to Bohemond's secret thoughts.

Throughout the trilogy, Runciman obeys above all one rule that is especially attractive to the lay reader – he never omits anything interesting on the grounds of mere unreliability. *A History of the Crusades* is a near-comprehensive compendium of its era's intrigues, rumours, hearsay and speculation. This contributes to its lively feeling of being itself a chronicle history, by some uniquely well-informed contemporary of the people and events it describes. 'I have followed the example of the old chroniclers, who knew their business,' Runciman claims in the introduction to *The Kingdom of Jerusalem*. One trick of this trade was for the writer to retail the wildest tittle-tattle while distancing himself from it, to protect his work from any charge of too much credulity. At this dissociation Runciman is a master; he employs a rough but discernible hierarchy of detachment. Details he vouches for without hesitation, however unverifiable they might seem on reflection, are told in the main text as straightforwardly, even nonchalantly, as possible: 'Even in the private intimacy of their bedchamber she would nag at him to go and redeem his reputation. He could not claim he was needed at home; for his wife had always been the real ruler of the county. So, wearily and with foreboding, he set out again . . . '

This third-person narration, at once omniscient and intimate, is the mannerism most likely to infuriate succeeding historians, especially when he uses it to develop a theory derived from his own fast-moving and speculative mind rather than from any primary document. To the general reader it is an implicit and absolute promise of safety, like the confidence of the chauffeur who is offended if his passenger reaches for a seatbelt. Though Runciman loves this register, his temperament is too complicated and his historical curiosity too mobile to employ it exclusively. Sometimes he wishes to draw attention to the originality of his answers to difficult, unpromising questions. In this temper, his voice becomes more conditional, self-aware and scientific: 'It is probable that Alexius himself never took his ambitious Italian scheme very seriously'; or 'It may be that Queen Melisende's influence was exerted in favour of a policy that would justify her sister Alice and humiliate the man who had tricked her.'

This tone sounds measured and qualified, but provides cover for particularly adventurous supposition. Nowhere is this more the case than when the narrative approaches one of Steven's favourite pursuits, that of counterfactual history. It is not surprising that a man so diverted by fortune-telling should have found the tracing of alternative outcomes an appealing pastime. Runciman does at one point, in the third volume, issue a disclaimer, but only as an afterthought to a particularly skilful piece of counterfactual gambolling: 'Had the Mongols penetrated into Egypt there would have been no great Moslem state left in the world east of Morocco ... It is idle to speculate about the things that might have happened then. The historian can only relate what did in fact occur.' But when he encounters a good story that he cannot even pretend to entertain, Runciman will include it with a side-swipe at its origins. In cases of extreme unlikelihood or irrelevance, it may even be banished to a footnote; but very rarely is it joylessly suppressed: 'There they killed one of the Emperor's pet lions ... Orderic Vitalis muddles the story and says that the Emperor used lions against the Crusaders'; or 'The fate of the Margravine of Austria is unknown. Later legends said that she ended her days a captive in a far-off harem, where she gave birth to the Moslem hero Zengi. More probably she was thrown from her litter in the panic and trampled to death'; or 'Rudel seems certainly to have visited the East ... but his love-affair with *La Princesse Lointaine*, Melisende of Tripoli, must be regarded as being at least half-legendary. Peter Vidal is said to have gone as far as Cyprus on the Third Crusade, but there he married a Greek girl and decided that she was heiress to Constantinople.'

The episode where Runciman is most cavalier with the truth is undoubtedly the bizarre story, told at far greater length in the third volume than its doubtful relevance justifies, of the Children's Crusade. Widely and variously recounted, with scarcely a name, date or place in common between dozens of sources, its tale seems to belong not to history as Runciman understood the discipline, but to anthropology with its flexible study of past societies' collective subconscious, as explored in Eugene Backman's account of the Dancing Plague in 1518, or Robert Darnton's *The Great Cat Massacre*. In, or around, the year 1212, a shepherd boy called Stephen or Nicholas, in France or Germany, roused a movement of children – though many young priests were among them – to follow him on the basis of his visions. They were to win back Jerusalem from the heathen by miraculous armed victory – or perhaps by missionary conversion. They believed the Mediterranean Sea would part for them, yet happily hired ships when it did not. They ended up in Genoa and accepted the republic's offer of citizenship – or in Rome, where the Pope told them to go home – or in Egypt, or Baghdad, after villainous Marseilles merchants had sold them into slavery. Somehow their story found its way back to the West, but always in a different version.

Almost every stage of the Children's Crusade had, by the time Steven wrote *The Kingdom of Acre*, been dismantled by sceptical scholars; it was an etymological quibble away from passing into myth. Historians including Dana C. Munro and H. E. Mayer stripped away bit by bit the visionary shepherd boy, the betrayal and enslavement, and increasingly the children themselves. There *had* been two demographic movements with an apocalyptic ambience, one French and one German, at about the right time, the new consensus set about deciding, but they cannot have contained, much less been led by, children. It was all a misunderstood metaphor; these wanderers must have dubbed themselves children because God's children, the Gospel tells us, are the poor. Runciman cites Munro's sobering essay without demur in his footnotes – but the story he actually uses, with remarkable powers of compilation, is an extraordinary patchwork of the traditional version, incorporating almost all its divergences and alternatives. A later authority on the subject, Gary Dickson, contradicts Munro by deciding that the Children *were* actual children after all. Runciman's telling cannot be disposed of one way or the other so easily; as so often, its essential grandeur rises above the controversy. 'It was not the little children that would rescue Jerusalem.'

In 1977, the Dutch historian Peter Raedts complained with more condescension than comprehension that, although Runciman 'cites Munro's article in his notes, his narrative is so wild that even the unsophisticated reader might wonder if he had really understood it.' Such po-faced literalism would have amused its target. The Children's Crusade, as Runciman tells it, in all its accumulative, extravagant and unknowable oddity, is the most extended joke within his tragic saga. Two recent critics of the Runciman approach consider that 'Comedy militates against complexity, whereas historical scholarship embraces it.' Runciman would have taken this pompous syllogism as a depressing vindication of his sincerely held view that a light touch need not preclude sophisticated vision, and that professional scholars who scorn the first risk blindness to the second. Runciman's aversion to the more dour academic conventions contributed to a disinclination to fall himself victim to younger biographers, 'scrupulous in their study of sources, but . . . insensitive to the atmosphere of the past and unaware of that transient element, its humour'.

If *A History of the Crusades* is on occasion gossipy in its allusions to romantic intrigue, it is at the same time a discreet account – elite and encoded. This too is part of Steven Runciman's persona – no sensationalist scandalmonger but the eternal insider, and a reliable and mannerly courtier. 'Romance', or to use Runciman's preferred word, 'glamour', is more usually applied in the trilogy to brilliant politicians, good-looking and spendthrift princes and heroic, risk-taking soldiers than to erotic matters. Yet Runciman is interested in amatory gossip and persistent in tracing its (usually unfortunate) political consequences. He exploits romantic episodes more for their comic potential than as passionate tragedy:

> There, at the end of the month, Fulk and Melisende were married amid great festivities and rejoicing. The arrangement had the approval of the whole country, with perhaps one exception. The Princess Melisende herself was unmoved by the short, wiry, red-haired, middle-aged man whom political advantages had forced upon her.

> In choosing a husband for Constance, Manuel showed greater ingenuity than sense . . . He forgot about Constance herself. John Roger was frankly middle-aged and had lost all his youthful charm. The young Princess, whose first husband had been famed for his beauty, would not consider so unromantic a mate . . .

> . . . Andronicus, though already aged forty-six, was more interested in adventure than administration. He soon had occasion to visit Antioch. There he was struck by the beauty of the young Princess Philippa . . . Forgetful of his governmental duties he stayed on in Antioch wooing Philippa in a series of romantic serenades until she was dazzled and could refuse him nothing.

An unsentimental scepticism unites these vignettes. They concern male vanity and female shallowness. Runciman's men are not always old roués, no more than his women are all susceptible ingénues. The roles are reversed in the case of the ambitious, vain, thirty-something Princess Alice of Antioch; she thought she was being wooed for herself by a handsome young adventurer, who then married her daughter instead.

A different kind of discretion is at work when same-sex liaisons impinge upon the action of the trilogy. This is perhaps a more interesting subject to today's reader, both because it concerns Steven himself more personally and because it displays so clearly the difference between his time and ours. None of Runciman's work came close to provoking the censor. But period considerations and sensitivities are undoubtedly at play, in a way that justifies Tyerman's suspicion that he is being propositioned by the prose, or Robert Irwin's allegation that a 1920s rather than medieval cultural conflict is being enacted.* When Runciman writes of homosexual activity among the Muslim aristocracy, his authorial stance is completely unflustered:

Mohammed in his turn was murdered by a former page of Qaraja's, called Jawali, with whom he had rashly become intimate . . .

He was succeeded by his son, Alp Arslan, a weak, vicious and cruel boy of sixteen, completely in the hands of his favourite eunuch, Lulu.

Since the loss of Ascalon there had been increasing chaos at the Caliph's Court. The vizier Abbas survived the disaster for a year. His son Nasr was the favourite of the young Caliph al-Zafir; and their intimacy gave rise to scandalous gossip. This infuriated Abbas, not for

---

* 'In particular, Runciman had presented the internal history of the Kingdom of Jerusalem . . . as being dominated by the rivalry between two aristocratic factions: on the one hand, the sophisticated, orientalized settlers, on the other the fire-breathing, gung-ho, strategically inept newcomers to the East. One can perhaps see it as a kind of prefiguration of the hostility between arties and hearties in Cambridge in the 1920s, and there can be no doubt which side Runciman thought he was on' (Robert Irwin, review of Christopher Tyerman, *God's War*, *Times Literary Supplement*, 8 September 2006).

moral reasons but because he rightly suspected that al-Zafir intended to play off the son against the father. Usama, who was still at the Court, learnt that Nasr had indeed agreed to murder Abbas. He hastened to reconcile them and soon persuaded Nasr that it would be better to murder the Caliph instead. Nasr invited his benefactor to a midnight orgy at his house and there stabbed him.

Steven had plenty of aesthetic sympathy for medieval Islam, but his works would hardly pass unreproached through the later severities of Edward Said. To Runciman, as to practically all his contemporaries who were drawn to the culture of the 'Near East', the attraction of Islamic civilization was bound up with the legacy of Edward FitzGerald, 'translator' of the *Rubáiyát of Omar Khayyám*. A midnight orgy here and there was practically *de rigueur*. When it came to homosexual innuendo among the Franks, Runciman adopted a subtler and more knowing manner. There was the famous example of England's chief representative in the Crusades, Richard the Lionheart:

> A more delicate problem concerned King Philip's sister Alice. This unfortunate princess had been sent as a child, years before, to the English court to marry Richard ... Soon there had been ugly rumours that Henry II was too intimate with her himself. Richard, whose own tastes did not lie in the direction of marriage, refused to carry out his father's arrangement ...

This was an easy enough case, as another historian, John Harvey, had just taken the controversy upon himself in a popular 1948 study, *The Plantagenets*, where he denounced 'a conspiracy of silence' around Richard's sexual inclinations. In the early 1950s Steven could in passing refer to the great warrior-King as a 'bad husband', and be fairly certain of being understood.

A much more obscure instance was the sexuality of King Baldwin I of Jerusalem, and here Runciman indulged in a midnight orgy of his own, a festival of ambiguity and nuance. On introducing Baldwin – whose abilities he admires throughout – Runciman comments that his private life was 'given over to venery', but supplies no details. His return to this subject opens the door just a crack wider: 'Baldwin was fond of amorous adventures; but he was discreet and the presence of a queen at the court prevented him from indulging in his tastes. The Queen also had a reputation for gaiety and had even, it was said, bestowed her favours upon Moslem pirates when she was voyaging down from Antioch to take over her throne ... ' When the pirate-friendly Queen has been safely divorced, Baldwin makes a much more expedient marriage, to the wonderfully named Countess Adelaide del Vasto, mother of King Roger II of Sicily. Here Runciman embarks on a spirited Shakespearean pastiche:

> The Countess set out from Sicily in such splendour as had not been seen on the Mediterranean since Cleopatra sailed from Cydnus to meet Mark Antony. She lay on a carpet of golden thread in her galley, whose prow was plated with silver and with gold. Two other triremes accompanied her, their prows equally ornate, bearing her military escort, prominent amongst whom were the Arab soldiers of her son's own bodyguard, their dark faces shining against the spotless white of their robes.

Runciman hints at a covert enjoyment in structuring the scene through King Baldwin's eyes: very interested in the display of riches; more than a little in the Saracen guards; less so in their queenly cargo. That Baldwin and Adelaide were middle-aged pleasure-seekers Runciman uses to vivid effect in his parody of Cleopatra's barge; but while sexual attraction flares into view, it does not connect the principal pair. By a Frazerian identity of king with kingdom, Runciman delivers a neat summary of the situation – 'All the country rejoiced, but not so much at the coming of its new, ageing mistress as at the wealth that she brought in her train.' Meanwhile the most likely object, according to the chronicles, of Baldwin's actual affections, is mentioned *en passant* as 'a renegade Moslem in Baldwin's personal service'. On this delicate matter, as on others, Runciman's account offers separate levels of enjoyment for readers at various stages of learning – and of human perceptiveness.

The insider's gossip, however, is never permitted to distract from or deflect the trilogy's grand, and consistent, moral themes. By *The Kingdom of Acre*, Runciman's imperative ethical standards build up to two particular, climactic moments of denunciation, both now legendary in the historiography of the Crusades. The first is

Runciman's view of the Fourth Crusade's sack of Christian Constantinople in 1204:

> There was never a greater crime against humanity than the Fourth Crusade. Not only did it cause the destruction or dispersal of all the treasures of the past that Byzantium had devotedly stored, and the mortal wounding of a civilisation that was still active and great; but it was also an act of gigantic political folly ... In the wide sweep of world history the effects were wholly disastrous.

The most prominent early use of the phrase 'crime against humanity' was by Abraham Lincoln in 1860, referring to the 're-opening of the African slave trade, under the cover of our national flag, aided by perversions of judicial power'. From the very first, then, it was a term with forceful but imprecise legal implications. The Allied powers after the First World War used the formula to condemn the Armenian massacre, but were still unable to agree exactly why. This ambiguity was first codified in August 1945, in the run-up to the Nuremberg Trials. When *The Kingdom of Acre* was published in 1954, 'crimes against humanity' had possessed a formal definition for less than a decade. Runciman's use of the term so soon after the Holocaust and the Nuremberg judgements should not be considered a lapse in taste by a recondite scholar more interested in medieval than in recent history. His allusion was deliberate, and his words were meant to be provocative. Writing decades later in *A Traveller's Alphabet*, Steven wisely avoided the stale repetition of shock value and employed the language of the dramatist rather than the prosecutor – 'There is no greater tragedy in history than the Fourth Crusade.' But *A History of the Crusades*, conceived and researched in the Second World War's shadow and written in its immediate aftermath, was intended to draw as drastic and spectacular parallels as possible. Impact was, in this case, more important than tact. In this homily Runciman both presented to a wider Western audience the long-inherited grievance of the Greek Orthodox Church, and himself helped to shape and harden that sense of injustice. Had Steven lived to see Pope John Paul II's apology in 2004 for the sack of Constantinople, he would have felt vindicated, while still regarding the Holy See's contrition as coming eight centuries too late. An admirer of the political abilities of Pope

Innocent III, Runciman is careful to emphasize that this great medieval Pope's immediate instinct was to repudiate the atrocity: 'He was profoundly shocked as a Christian, and he was disquieted as a statesman.' His portrayal of the way in which the Pope disappointed history, by deciding against his better judgement to ignore all but the most convenient aspects of the conquest, is a fine study of evil in its passive, complicit form, and a masterful counterpoint to the violence of the siege as he retells it. By consciously setting his parable beside (even beyond) such recent innovations as the Nuremberg Trials, he ensures its timelessness, at the price of some notoriety.

Another subject in which the trilogy exploited, rather than evaded, its significance to the post-war landscape was the conceptual relationship between the Crusader States and the State of Israel, founded in 1948, just three years before the publication of *The First Crusade*. Runciman soon attracted an involved Israeli readership. One young Israeli soldier and writer, Uri Avnery, was struck on reading the first volume by the remarkable geographical overlap between the outposts around the Gaza Strip he had just helped to erect and the castles built similarly to contain the Egyptians after the First Crusade. After reading the whole trilogy, Avnery wrote to Steven with a simple question:

> Did you ever think about the similarity between them and us?
>
> The answer arrived within days. Not only did he think about it, Runciman wrote, but he thought about it all the time. Indeed, he wanted to subtitle the book 'A guide for the Zionists on how not to do it'. However, he added, 'my Jewish friends advised against it.' If I ever chanced to pass through London, he added, he would be glad if I called on him.

Avnery was certainly at the wrong end of a Runciman tease in the matter of the subtitle, but he accepted Steven's invitation with enthusiasm and took his chance to get to London as soon as he could. Steven's surname had vaguely baleful implications for him – Walter Runciman's record in Prague still hung faintly over his son – but Avnery was soon charmed by the historian's reality. They sported over sherry with a conversation half of crucial topical import, half of parlour-game indulgence: was Ben-Gurion the ruthlessly able conqueror Baldwin of Boulogne? Moshe Dayan the irreconcilable warmonger Reynald de Chatillon? Avnery himself the subtle peace-maker Raymond of Tripoli? Avnery emerged from the encounter convinced that if Israel were to avoid the Crusader States' unhappy example, it must become an integral part of its region, not 'a fortified ghetto'. In 1982 he crossed the lines of the siege of Beirut, becoming the first Israeli to meet Yasser Arafat in person.

Runciman's wording on the 'greatest crime' of the Fourth Crusade may be unsettling for the general reader, but his conclusions about that disgraceful affair are not on the whole called into question by fellow historians. A more controversial challenge to other scholars is contained in his almost mystically eloquent conclusion to the third volume, in which the whole crusading movement is bitterly arraigned and found wanting:

> The triumphs of the Crusade were the triumphs of faith. But faith without wisdom is a dangerous thing. By the inexorable laws of history the whole world pays for the crimes and follies of each of its citizens. In the long sequence of interaction and fusion between Orient and Occident out of which our civilization has grown, the Crusades were a tragic and destructive episode. The historian as he gazes back across the centuries at their gallant story must find his admiration overcast by sorrow at the witness that it bears to the limitations of human nature. There was so much courage and so little honour, so much devotion and so little understanding. High ideals were besmirched by cruelty and greed, enterprise and endurance by a blind and narrow self-righteousness; and the Holy War itself was nothing more than a long act of intolerance in the name of God, which is the sin against the Holy Ghost.

This lightning seizure of the moral and theological high ground has proved especially annoying to Catholic historians, from *The Kingdom of Acre*'s original reviewer in the *Tablet* to Jonathan Riley-Smith. Runciman's peroration is almost impossible to dismiss – another, more highly coloured manifestation of the paradox, to which he had initially drawn attention in *The First Crusade*, of the contradictory Christian attitude to warfare. His adversaries can only splutter at its anachronism, which, after all, it wears proudly. Again prefiguring the broadcasting style of Kenneth Clark, on his last page Runciman embraces his role as 'the historian', and strides openly before the reader through the ruins of his scene, glancing to left and right, 'gazing back across the centuries', with enlightened sorrow. At the same time, it is easy to make too much of Runciman's conclusion. The final verdict is so memorable that it occludes the balance of earlier sentences ('There was so much courage and so little honour, so much devotion and so little understanding'). Even some of Runciman's friends were baffled; the Portugal-based epicurean Peter Pitt-Millward wrote a deeply moved, almost hysterical letter, enquiring why, given that the Crusaders emerged as so self-evidently dreadful in his masterpiece, Steven had wasted so many of his years and pages on them.* It was a query that missed the point entirely. The trilogy was not only an essay in adjusting the historical record; it was also a great story, albeit, like many of the greatest, a tragedy. No moral consideration should allow its readers to underestimate the writerly pleasure Runciman evidently felt, and widely transmitted, in the composition of *A History of the Crusades*. A lecture Steven delivered in 1959, based on the 'Life in Outremer' chapter in *The Kingdom of Jerusalem* but further elaborated in detail and tone, forms a revealing postscript which somewhat redresses the balance:

> we cannot withhold all sympathy from the great families of Outremer. They were selfish and short sighted politically. They showed a vulgar taste for parading their wealth, a deplorable love of intrigue, a blithe disregard of the sterner moral virtues. But these languid lords who seemed only to bestir themselves when there was a plot to be launched, a commercial deal to be arranged or a sumptuous entertainment to be given, and their painted and perfumed ladies who married and re-married so easily, clinging onto their dowries the while, were not without courage or enterprise. Their lives were precarious; and they knew it.

---

* 'Admiration at what you've achieved is hopelessly bound up with amazement that you should ever, in the teeth of your loathing for the subject on which you've spent years, and spent what for anyone else would have been a whole lifetime of hard work, have tackled it at all' (Peter Pitt-Millward to SR, 7 December 1954, Elshieshields).

... At any moment the lord might have to rise from his couch to ride out against enemy raiders. At any moment his lady might find herself in charge of the defence of her castle. At any moment the festivities might be interrupted by the sound of the infidel mangonels pounding against the walls. Life was merry, but it was short; and when the crisis came there was no lack of gallantry among the lords and ladies of Outremer. They had tasted with relish the gracious things of life; and they faced their doom with pride and resolution.

This is also a fairer distillation of how the trilogy should be read. Though Steven would indeed have made an admirable bishop, he would have done better still as a novelist.

# 19

# Strength

*Isle of Eigg, 1949–66; 1997*

The card has nothing to do with self-confidence in the ordinary sense ...

Arthur Waite, *The Key to the Tarot*, 1920

'Upon the earth I am a man,
A silkie in the sounding sea;
And when I am far away from land
My hame it is on Sule Skerrie.'

'The Ballad of the Great Silkie of Sule Skerrie', as
rendered by Steven Runciman to Charles Turner, 1961

In November 1949 Walter Runciman succumbed to the Parkinson's
disease that had debilitated him over the preceding decade. He had
left politics for the last time at the onset of his undiagnosed condition
and the Second World War. His last post, the Lord Presidency of the
Council, had been a reward for his labours in Czechoslovakia. As one
of the smattering of National Liberals in Chamberlain's Cabinet he
had lasted in it for under a year. Now he was accorded a memorial
service at Westminster Abbey; the post-war mood was generous, even
nostalgic, towards the almost obliterated 'Victorian' breed of politician he had represented. The *Times* obituary was tactful. Lord
Runciman was hailed as a 'LIBERAL ELDER STATESMAN':

one of those who lent ability and strength to the great Liberal administrations before the war of 1914 ... now an almost vanished band,
but of that goodly company none could rival Runciman for fairness,

integrity and mastery of his subject ... Runciman was regarded as possibly one of the eventual successors to the premiership and the sudden eclipse of the Liberal Party was a great personal misfortune to him, stoically borne but none the less deeply felt ... he stuck gamely to the failing fortunes of his party and sacrificed to the chances and high risks of politics the certainty of eminence in business.

A decade had served to soften attitudes to the mission to Czechoslovakia: 'at best a thankless task, and in the circumstances an impossible one. Events pushed Runciman and his mission into the background ... he returned to this country physically worn out by his efforts and by disillusionment at their failure.'

Steven had served as the obituarist's chief informant, although the notice made mention among Lord Runciman's children only of his elder son and heir and his eldest daughter, 'killed flying in the last war'. Not yet the best-selling author of *A History of the Crusades*, Steven neither merited nor sought the paper's attention. But his influence lay heavy over its reticence on Czechoslovakia. It is not clear – though Steven helped to make it appear so in retrospect – that Lord Runciman was unhappy with the consequences of his report at Munich. He seemed rather to veer between unsettled pessimism and feeling that the Sudeten Germans deserved even greater concessions, inconsistencies that might be attributed to his draining degenerative illness.

If Steven had helped to upholster his father's memory, though, he was franker in private about his reasons for so doing. To Freya Stark he wrote with open, self-analytical nostalgia:

My father's death, after long years of failing body and mind, was a happy thing, easy and peaceful; yet it was impossible not to mind when it happened, largely, I suppose, because death in its graciousness wipes out the later pathetic memories and restores him to what he was, and so, unreasonably, we feel hurt and cheated by its finality.

Steven had admitted to Leslie three years before their father's death that he dreaded his occasional returns to the parents at Doxford, but felt obliged to drag them out for as long he could bear: 'Mamma's life being what it is, I feel it is the least that I can do.' Hilda was now to remove to London; Leslie inherited the house with the family titles, Viscount, Baron and 'the embarrassment of the baronetcy', though he did not intend to stay at Doxford long. Steven found himself pre-emptively mournful about the large, slightly ominous old north-country house whose discomforts and peculiarities he had for so long lampooned: 'I never much cared for it, but all the same I mind leaving it.'

The younger Walter left, apart from land, property and the shipping firm, just short of a million pounds (now equivalent to more like a hundred million). The division of this among his four surviving children left Steven, even as a second son, entirely liberated from financial concerns at almost the precise moment in his life when he was best situated to enjoy that freedom. The death of his grandfather, the elder Walter, had encouraged Steven to unshackle himself from Trinity – only for the Second World War and then ongoing national service for the British Council to determine the location, practicalities and purpose of his life for the ensuing decade. Since his return from Greece, Steven had brought out *The Medieval Manichee*, a substantially pre-war work, and then settled to writing the first volume of his trilogy. He had found himself most productive while staying at his father's secondary property, the Isle of Eigg, of which he was now, jointly with his brother, left as proprietor and laird.

Steven always enjoyed recounting to visitors the story of the first episode in which Eigg had assumed historical prominence. This was the massacre in AD 617 of St Donnan, a lesser-known proselyte in the tradition of, and perhaps in rivalry with, St Columba. Along with one hundred and fifty of his monks, according to the *Annals of Ulster*, he was burnt alive on a beach as a mass offering to the pagan pantheon by a local Pictish queen, whose own name, much to Steven's regret, was nowhere firmly recorded or remembered. The island endured another frightful massacre when, in the sixteenth century, the population of some four hundred MacDonalds, having taken refuge from MacLeod raiders in a great cave, were discovered and smoked into suffocation. Eigg remained in the possession of the Clanranald branch of the MacDonalds until 1827. Its first external purchaser was Hugh Macpherson, a college principal and Professor of Hebrew at Aberdeen University. He and his son Norman, a Professor of Scots

Law, remained absentee proprietors whose fondness for their island retreat proved an inadequate stay against famine and stagnation; the population sank from over 500 to 233 by the close of the nineteenth century.

The next sale delivered Eigg to Robert Thomson, an English journalist and gunrunner, who had some success prior to the Great War in promoting his acquisition as a destination for sportsmen and other tourists. Thomson won the affection of the Catholic islanders by building them a new church, fitted out with some seventeenth-century silver candlesticks and an altarpiece adventurously attributed to Zurbarán. The island found its next owner midway through the war in Sir William Petersen, an extrovert shipowner of Danish origin, who was rumoured to have perpetrated an act of arson on the laird's Lodge left by Thomson in order to achieve a more economical purchasing price. That rumour was typical of the attention Petersen drew to himself; he was recalled as a ready but imprudent showman, throwing a Christmas party for the island children dressed up as a robust Santa Claus with a Norse fir for a walking-stick. Gaelic was still the native language of the Eiggeach islanders, and in the resilient bardic tradition Petersen figured as a rather incompetent and vainglorious Viking giant. His several daughters were better liked, but the situation seemed to offer small promise of permanence, since they were too addicted to horses to contemplate marriage.

One of Petersen's creditors, a shipping scion playing in a larger league, was the younger Walter Runciman, defenestrated from the Commons in 1918 and now left at a loose end by the Liberal civil war. At a house-party early in the 1920s in the newly rebuilt timber-and-steel laird's Lodge, Walter Runciman told another guest that in the event of their host's bankruptcy, which he thought more than likely, he would himself be interested in the island. Petersen died early in 1925 and was grandly interred, with the aid of a winch, at Castle Island, the grassy islet that shelters Eigg's harbour. His eccentrically braced and crenellated wooden Lodge did not survive him, burning down just as Thomson's before it had done. Petersen's daughters, discovering quite how few were their resources for bloodstock and flutters, proved Walter Runciman as good as his word. Steven was pleased to hear of his father's new Hebridean investment while stopping at the Grand Hôtel de Pékin in early 1926. His excitement would not be disappointed; many aspects of Eigg, the life to be found there and the traditions of its people naturally endeared themselves to him. Steven was more unusual as a landlord in finding this affection before very long returned.

Strictly speaking, Leslie was the island's sole legal proprietor while Steven was left in full possession of the Lodge, the eccentric laird's residence erected at the closing of the 1920s by the family architect, Robert Mauchlen of Newcastle, to replace the two Lodges destroyed by fire at the bookends of the Petersen period. The new Lodge's structure, Italianate in inspiration and imperfectly suited to the Hebrides, owed something to Steven's amateur interest. He was also almost entirely responsible for the planning of the garden, and his father's bequest of the Lodge recognized these contributions. In fact, as was the only practicable way, the brothers acted together as both lairds and householders, often, if usually separately, staying at the Lodge with, in Leslie's case, his family and a shooting party, or, in Steven's, a rather different sort of party. Leslie and Steven kept each other punctually informed of goings-on in island society, and helped each other and their chief minister, the factor, over minute questions of employment, livestock, repairs and the various, persistent paternalistic responsibilities that went with a solvent lairdship.

Steven's pre-war house-parties on Eigg had been frequent enough for him already to possess an affectionately outré reputation among the islanders. In the years 1932–9, he had entertained every summer, inviting mainly male and almost entirely Cantabrigian casts, with occasional sympathetic spouses included. In the first years after his return from Athens, with his trilogy on the go, Steven came to the island more frequently, but less often accompanied. In Walter Runciman's last years, with the proprietor incapacitated and the highly capable Hilda preoccupied in seeing to his demanding comforts, the factor, Campbell, had persuaded his employers to let the island to one of its few inhabitants of means outside the Runciman family, an Eton-educated gentleman farmer. Robin Gowans had large-scale plans to improve on the Runcimans' existing strategy for a self-sustaining farming island; he was equipped with 120 Galloway cattle, a brand-new tractor and the first pair of Wellington boots the island had seen. Steven visited the island under Gowans's stewardship in the summer of 1948 with his first post-war contingent of any strength – two younger Trinity friends, Kit Nicholl and Philip Hay, with their wives, and Steven's eldest godson John Chancellor, the son of Christopher Chancellor and Sylvia Paget. Steven took against Gowans during this overlap, and after the brothers' inheritance he advised Leslie with confidence and some anticipation that they could manage the island by themselves.

A few glimpses of Steven emerge at this time, just before the beginning of his own spell as co-laird. In a brisk letter to Freya Stark from December 1948, Steven speaks of an enjoyable luncheon with the Catholic priest. The Runciman parents had always impressed upon their children the importance and rectitude of treating the island's religious representatives with parity, but despite their Methodist and Presbyterian origins, and Steven's enthusiasm for recreational Papist-baiting, all the Runciman proprietors preferred the company of the priests to the ministers. Steven laments the interruption of ten days of peace by 'my mother and brother, arriving tomorrow to discuss the whole running of the island'. It seems that Hilda and her sons were already preparing for the structural changes that would follow the death of the infirm and now incapable head of the family. Presumably the question of Gowans's tenancy and innovations came up during this period. Less informed but more detailed views are provided by several guests to the island. Miriam James, daughter of Steven's school contemporary George Wansbrough, remembers that her mother Elizabeth, who was now separated from George and whom Steven had come to prefer of the two, rented a cottage on Eigg in the summer of 1948. Mrs James recalls her mother teasing her old friend about his island sobriquet, 'the sweetheart of Eigg', a line of oblique mockery to which Steven did not take. Philip Hay wrote in early 1949 at his pleasure in finding the island (for all the effects of the brief Gowans regency) quite unaltered from his pre-war memories. Hay had endured a cruel war as a prisoner of the Japanese, forced to work on the construction of the bridge over the Kwai, and confided to Steven with unusual emotion that his reminiscences of Eigg had helped to keep up his own and other captives' spirits.

The dissenting eye was that of young John Chancellor, the godson whose parents' marriage Steven claimed to have abetted. He was twenty-one years old, about to go up to a place at Trinity, Cambridge, that conscription had kept out of reach. He had never thought his godfather's company conducive to his entertainment or comfort, an aversion Steven felt and returned. 'There was an evil fairy at John's christening,' Steven would often joke. 'I hope it wasn't me.' John was staying at the Lodge and tried to keep out of his host's way, but still found their temporary cohabitation difficult: 'we didn't get on . . . he thought I was rather a failure, slapdash . . . I thought him punctilious, shy, self-conscious and mannered.' Nor did the young National Serviceman relish the company of the Hays. Less conscious or forgiving than Steven of Philip Hay's dreadful war, John found Hay an intolerable bore and was amused at the exaggerated servility he displayed during frequent phone-calls from Princess Marina, to whom Hay was equerry and his wife lady-in-waiting. On the other hand, when Steven privately retailed to his godson gossip that the Princess and her equerry were intimately connected, while casually suggesting that she had maintained her Danish-Greek parents in their Parisian exile through 'immoral earnings', John bridled at this hostly betrayal of confidence, which he thought an unsuccessful attempt to impress him.*

John Chancellor did also recall that Steven, just beginning to compose the text of *The First Crusade*, would try out its opening sentence on the assembled house-party. It ended up as follows, its cadences and glimmer of visual delicacy carefully weighted: 'On a February day in the year A.D. 638 the Caliph Omar entered Jerusalem, riding upon a white camel.' While drafting the second volume, *The Kingdom of Jerusalem*, two years later, Steven would write to Stewart

---

* The more usual object of such scurrilous rumours was Princess Marina's late husband, Prince George, Duke of Kent, a bisexual morphine and cocaine addict, who was reported by the security services to have been spotted soliciting in drag along with Noël Coward on the blacked-out streets of wartime Soho. Steven's allusions to Marina's 'immorality' were probably a camp exaggeration of her brief spell as a model.

Perowne from Eigg of 'sitting in solitude here, like Marius among the ruins of Carthage, except that my ruins are text books of mine and quite half the London Library. With a mountain range of them around me I am ... trying vainly to find justification for statements about which I have been and still feel quite positive.' For all the accusations of charlatanry Steven attracted throughout his career from Norman Baynes onwards, he was actually as conscientious about his sources as about his cadences – though perhaps not more so.

While still in Athens, and disinclined towards the austerity of London under the Attlee government, Steven happily contemplated spending many months annually on Eigg, though he admitted he might miss 'a more stimulating existence'. His father's death and the reclamation of the island's husbandry from Robin Gowans provided a chance to put into practice the regime of which he had dreamed. Leslie and Steven had, since the younger brother's return in 1947, spent each Christmas and New Year at Eigg, with Leslie's family and usually the Holts, another shipping dynasty with whom Leslie was on excellent terms. But over the Christmas of 1949 the two brothers spent Christmas alone on Eigg. There was much to plan, although neither would consider permanent residence on the island, so that the experienced factor Campbell still maintained day-to-day control. Campbell was honest and competent, but neither young nor especially popular. Though an islander, his sympathies were almost inexpediently wedded to the continuation of unimpaired lairdly prerogative.

In some ways the situation on the island when the Runciman brothers took over was similar to that at the start of the Petersen reign; in both cases there were the lingering abnormalities of a world war to be remedied. But Eigg in 1949 was, if anything, bleaker than it had been in the 1920s. Far fewer of the islanders who had volunteered or been conscripted into the war returned this time, not because more had been killed but because, separated from each other to avoid the local tragedies of the first war's Pals' Battalions, most of the young men had found jobs, and most of the young women husbands, in very different worlds. Eigg's reduced population, already under a hundred, was evidence of this absent generation. The average

age among the adult crofters was sixty-five. It was an island of children brought up by grandparents. This was even true of the Runcimans; Margie's elder daughter Ann King-Farlow had grown up partly in the formidable care of Hilda. But in these circumstances the continuity that two well-respected, financially liquid lairds in their late forties represented, with the succession apparently secured by way of Leslie's son Garry, was more reassuring than the sudden irruption of Petersen with his fleeting extravagances.

Steven, in particular, made the most of this advantage. He used his genuine skills and bruited reputation as a prodigious linguist both to pick up a little Gaelic and to make out that he understood a great deal more. He was knowledgeable about the island's history and, especially, its folklore and superstitions, in some of which he came to believe. In particular he adopted the warily devotional attitude of the Eiggeach towards the appearance of the New Moon. He noted with interest the persistence of a Gaelic anthem to its rising, rendered into English by the folklorist Alexander Carmichael thus:

> Hail to thee, thou new lit moon,
> I bend the knee, thou queen so fair
> Through the dark clouds thine the way be,
> Thine who leadest all the stars
> Put thy flow-tide on the flood,
> Send thy flow-tide on the flood.

Only by the 1930s, when his family had owned Eigg for some years, did Steven begin frequently to allude to a thereafter besetting fear of seeing the New Moon through glass.* He also much enjoyed

---

* Steven's first invocation of this lunar premonition of disaster comes in a letter to Kitty, written from a Spartan roadside in April 1930: 'Pity me, oh pity me. I have just seen the New Moon through glass. Such a pretty and new New Moon too. I know that means that I shall be killed or anyhow maimed when travelling in the postal motorcar tomorrow, from here to Tripolitsa – 3 hours of the most awful roads, overhanging precipices, and the Greeks are such dashing drivers. The postal chauffeur always turns round to talk vivaciously to the passengers behind at the tricky bits – I just prayed all the way coming here. Once a car overtook us and our chauffeur lost his temper. So off we raced down the mountain-side; we won easily . . . I won't post this till I get to Athens, so you'll know if I am safe' (SR to KR, 2 April 1930, Elshieshields).

the Hebridean legends of selkies – shapeshifting seal-men and women of flirtatious and philoprogenitive tendencies. He copied out 'The Ballad of the Great Silkie of Sule Skerrie', telling of 'a lady who was seduced by a seal', for a New York admirer, the composer Charles Turner. Steven showed an atypical but amiable face to the Eiggeach, in contrast to the more ever-present and resented factor, and even to his harder-headed elder brother, the senior laird. Steven took the surprising step of reviving the children's Christmas party that Petersen had inaugurated; but while Petersen had mainly attracted mockery, Steven began to receive a rare amalgam of good will and respect. Soon he had also fixed the euphonious Eiggeach Easter Egg Hunt as an inflexible date in his engagement diary; small presents for every child on the island were hidden inside the large and handsome wooden globe in the Lodge's library. Steven's always unexpected flair for entertaining the young, whether the dozens of rowdy children on board the *Patroclus* cruise ship to China in 1925 or the young Ruthven boys at Asolo in 1947, was a consistent faculty that had some qualities in common with the attraction of his prose.

One respect in which Steven, unlike his brother, was detached from island life and procedure was in his attitude to the sporting estate on Eigg, begun by Thomson, expanded by Petersen, perfected by the first Viscount Runciman and still relished by Leslie. Walter Runciman had found the island, although promoted by Thomson and Petersen as unequalled shooting territory, scarce of game but for woodcock, snipe and the ineluctable rabbit. He tried and failed to introduce the grey partridge, but achieved spectacular success with an imported pheasant population in the early 1930s. Petersen's and now Walter's gamekeeper, Donald Archie MacLeod, whose father had been gamekeeper to Thomson, the first holder of such office on the island, became in many incarnations Walter Runciman's right hand, though he found his employer's habitual teetotalism puzzling and, on the one occasion when he was caught secretly tippling at the laird's redundant hip-flask, embarrassing. By 1949 Donald Archie was himself an old man, but Steven persuaded Leslie to retain him. In so doing he may have been motivated by concern less for the old keeper than for his avian stocks. Steven had always felt a distaste for shooting and had avoided joining the guns ever since his years of discretion. On his very first visit to Eigg in the autumn of 1926, he had written plaintively to Kitty, who was now being educated at Gernrode in the German Harz forests, from a small shoot his father had organized in honour of Lady Currie, a family friend who owned land on neighbouring Rum: 'Papa, Uncle Jack [one of Hilda's brothers-in-law] and Lellie were here ... Today they shot – all the poor trusting pheasants were so surprised and shocked, and sat in reproachful rows around the shooters ... so I went on a long walk, and climbed back over the lochs' neighbouring hills.' This youthful identification with the pheasantry never faded. In 1946 he wrote satirically from Athens to Leslie on Eigg asking after his 'lovely days of slaughter'. When Donald Archie died in the late 1950s, Steven persuaded his brother not to hire a replacement, and the shooting at Eigg was given up, as it would turn out for good.*

Steven had looked forward to the Lodge's potential for house-parties and now he could experiment summer by summer with varying dramatis personae of unrestricted distinction, bohemianism and internationalism. The islanders came to appreciate that they were unexpectedly living on a magnet for musical distinction. Steven invited many celebrated musicians, timing his summonses so as to serve performances at the village hall (erected in Walter Runciman's day) as well as the Lodge. These included Clive Lythgoe, a pianist noised about as 'the British Liberace'; a favourite Greek cellist, Eleftherios Papastavrou, whose musical studies were completed partly at Steven's expense; and Yehudi and Diana Menuhin (Sir Yehudi being memorably described by Dugald MacKinnon, the ferryman, as 'a handy man for a ceilidh'). Steven was by now no mean hand on the Bechstein he had installed on Eigg to replace the 1790 grand piano he

---

* Steven's feelings about blood sports were not, however, consistent. Although not much of a rider on account of hay fever and general delicacy, he approved of hunting for its romance, irrationality, atavism and, not least, costume; as a young man he frequently attended and dressed for, but did not ride at, Nothumbrian meets. In July 1997 he fell into conversation with James Lees-Milne on the subject of the recently elected New Labour administration: 'We agreed that hunting can't be justified, any more than hereditary peers, or for that matter religion – yet they are all good things' (James Lees-Milne, *Diaries 1984–1997*, ed. Michael Bloch (Hachette, 2011), p. 496).

had too precipitately sold in 1946. The frivolous dulcitone-rattler of Trinity had, it seems, matured

An invitation to Eigg from Steven was a Janus-faced privilege. It could be either a mark of great favour and intimacy, or a test unfairly rigged against an object of disapproval. The actual conduct of the host would not outwardly vary a great deal between these two categories. Ever since his wartime Istanbul days Steven had kept firm and interested control over his own cooking, and this gave him total, sometimes capricious, power over his guests, reinforced by the nature of the island, linked to the mainland only by a twice-weekly ferry and the *Dido*, a boat reserved for Eigg's proprietors. Steven's regime was exact and regular: he would take three meals a day with his visitors (never permitting them into the kitchen to witness his processes, regardless of their dignity of rank or forcefulness of temperament), go on a solitary walk after breakfast, stay undisturbed in collation and composition in his library (in which even fellow scholars were infrequently welcome) and instigate a collective night-walk in the evening. He was deliberately free with invitations to the island, but he assumed, and preferred, that very few of them should be accepted. When lecturing abroad – especially in America and Canada – Steven preferred to give out his Eigg address rather than particulars of his more accessible house in St John's Wood. New acquaintances high in Steven's favour, such as Charles Turner, the attractive young composer he encountered in the early 1960s, were invited in the first instance to his London address. They would then be summoned to Eigg as a special further favour.

Steven enjoyed telling carefully selected young friends of 'my Hebridean isle'. To such acolytes he would boast that Eigg's scenery was far more exotic, if its amenities were less luxurious, than Glenveagh Castle, the rival fairyland in Donegal belonging to Henry McIlhenny, also a connoisseur of Celtic surroundings, beautiful objects and handsome young men. The moral seriousness of Scots, as opposed to Irish, romance was a theme upon which Steven would happily dilate:

> You may talk of the Celtic Twilight. But this is not the fey whimsy of Ireland. There are no mischievous leprechauns or hysterical banshees.

The ghosts and fairies of Western Scotland are of sterner stuff. The woman sitting in the waterfall is washing your shroud. In that dark loch there lurks a water-horse, who emerges as a fine young man to lure unwary maidens to their death. He will devour them in the depths, leaving only the lungs to float on the surface.

Simon Elliot, a younger cousin of John Chancellor whom Steven preferred to his official godson, remembers an instance when Steven failed to reckon with transatlantic social and professional determination, and in his annoyance resorted to an elaborate and childish series of slights. Elliot knew of Steven as a legendary parental figment of 'velvet caps, parakeets on shoulders and rouged cheeks', but they first actually met when Steven thought to look him up in 1960, during a Canadian lecture tour at McGill University, Montreal, where the nineteen-year-old Elliot was an undergraduate. They got on sufficiently well that, when Elliot withdrew from McGill the next year and needed a scholarly retreat in order to cram for entrance to another university, his parents thought of packing him off to Steven on Eigg. Elliot was obedient but ambivalent about this plan:

> Before I knew it, it was arranged – not by me – that I would go up and stay with Steven for a minimum of a month on Eigg.
>
> It was quite a daunting thought, what with his reputation . . . I went up very nervously. We met at Euston, and went up to Fort William on the sleeper. One or two friends said 'you'd better watch out.' I was slightly in awe about going to stay with someone I didn't know very well for a month on an island at the best of times . . . well, we got to Eigg. Not the most promising house, so austere and Scottish . . .

Robert Mauchlen's modern and Mediterranean intentions for the Runciman Lodge were often lost on visitors to whom it seemed appropriately spare and comfortless, part of an undifferentiated Hebridean scene.* But when the usual routine was put into practice,

---

* The writer Andro Linklater, visiting the Lodge under the ownership of the most infamous of post-Runciman lairds, Keith Schellenberg, in the mid-1970s, used that recurrent adjective 'austere' of the house: 'so like a colonial officer's bungalow, verandah, cane chairs, wooden floors . . . '. Having heard that Steven Runciman, whose career he admired, had had a hand in the Lodge's design, Linklater puzzled

Elliot found it to be, after all, surprisingly workable, easy-going and gratifying. His host, who was at work on *The Fall of Constantinople*, was largely inaccessible, but during the exceptions over meals Elliot began to appreciate the value as well as the oddity of the situation: 'to have conversation for a month at every meal with somebody who had such an enormous range of stories was the most huge gift that a young man could ever have had.' For his part Steven was evidently pleased with his young guest. Elliot never felt, then or later, any suggestion of impropriety: 'he was a kind elderly friend.' A photograph of this good-looking, conversationally receptive boy fast asleep is preserved in Steven's albums.

It was then that Steven received a telegram which, as he did not trouble to conceal from Elliot, reduced him to 'towering, incandescent rage'. John Dillingham, a Kentucky doctoral student in his early thirties, one of the many American academics who had been insincerely bidden to Eigg, was now on the mainland at Mallaig awaiting the next boat. 'This young professor from Idaho, or wherever it may be in the Mid-West,' Steven complained, 'looks as if he has contrived to interrupt our whole summer.' He could not now turn the young academic back, but Elliot remembers his host's expression when he met Dillingham at the jetty:

> [Steven's] mood did not improve when eventually the ferry arrived . . . he could have the most awful sort of sinister smile. If he liked you it lit up the world, but if he was out for you it was demonic. This thirty-something professor appeared, absolutely thrilled, here was the great man, absolutely 'Dr Livingstone I presume'. He appeared perfectly harmless, perfectly nice, but it didn't make any difference to Steven, who wasn't having any of it.

At his first supper on Eigg the unfortunate American scholar was treated to a display of knowledge not of Byzantium or the Crusades, but of a subject he found infinitely more recondite. 'How well are you

---

over the character of a man who could combine such austerity with 'a fine style, striking work, and a harlequin life', and speculated about the 'locked away consciousness that drove him to such diversity' (Andro Linklater to author, 9 October 2013).

acquainted', Steven suddenly enquired after an uncomfortable lull in the conversation, 'with the English order of precedence?'

As he listened to Steven enlightening the newcomer, it dawned on the young Englishman that the information being imparted varied, as it ran through royalty, nobility, clergy and judiciary, between 'the deeply obscure and the definitely made up'. When Steven affected uncertainty and asked Elliot to jog his memory on a fine point relating to a second lieutenant of Guards sitting next to a canon of Salisbury Cathedral, Elliot played his allotted part in the game. For the next four days the enterprising American was tormented at every meal by implausible problems presented by phantom dinner-parties. When Steven began vestigially to bore even himself, on the fourth day, he demanded that the hapless Dillingham recite to him the Presidents of the United States in reverse order. On the next day, the American's last, having interpreted Dillingham's too-rapid salting of his food as a slur against his cooking, Steven half poisoned the poor man with grotesque quantities of pepper and salt applied in advance. Elliot felt some pity for the outsider, but 'he certainly could not have said that Steven had not entertained him.'

'He was a snob of course, as are we all,' Elliot forgivingly concludes, showing a certain familiarity with the rules of the game: 'He had a tongue like a viper if he wanted to use it. He selected his targets with care.' Steven would not have been so infantile and high-handed had the American visitor been, say, Gore Vidal. He responded strongly to birth, upbringing, good looks and reputation, all reliable fences against his devilry. But Elliot, who readily admits that his intellectual common ground with Steven was limited, found him a remarkably democratic companion: 'He didn't talk down to one at all . . . I'd never read anything about the Crusades, but he didn't get bored, he took trouble to be interesting and never patronising.' Once his guard had lifted, the benefits of Steven's friendship continued and fructified – he gave this young friend an Edward Lear sketch purchased in his Cambridge days, and furnished him with an introduction to George Cukor (a contingency which led to Elliot meeting Marilyn Monroe, 'one of the great occasions of my life').

Two of the most fêted, and in turn appreciative, summer visitors to Eigg were the covertly slandered Princess Marina, Duchess of Kent, in 1955 and 1958, and, in 1960, Steven's most eminent Greek friend from British Council days, George Seferis. Princess Marina's first visit, by helicopter, occasioned a great deal of excited preparation, and though Steven groused about this, especially the royal Duchess's presumptuous attempt to infiltrate his kitchen, it obviously pleased him exceedingly. On her next visit Steven arranged for Marina to launch two lifeboats that would shortly serve Eigg.

George and Maro Seferiades arrived on the island as a treat for George shortly before his retirement as Greek Ambassador to the Court of St James's. In a tribute to Seferis published in 1983, twelve years after the poet's death, Steven described their 'arduous passage' to Eigg, a descent to a jettiless rocky shore on the mainland, 'trying not to slip upon the sea-weed', before they could board the *Dido*, 'a boat designed to convey sheep rather than ambassadors'. The grey waves of their voyage were unforgiving, but 'hardly had they arrived when the sun broke through ... thenceforward for the rest of their visit it shone almost daily in a cloudless sky.' If Steven felt George and Maro had proved a fortunate meteorological talisman, Seferis for his part thought Steven's company thrillingly unnerving. 'The strange thing is that when this man talks about ghosts and creatures from the world of faery, his eyes light up.' Steven's eyes must have been almost permanently alit, as he kept the Seferiadeses busily discomfited with ghost stories and examples of the second sight. Steven often thought in years to come of the poet's impressions both of the Hebrides and of their inhabitants; he claims that Seferis praised the Hebrides above even the isles of the Aegean, as well as remarking a little opaquely that 'Celts are the Romans of the North.' That the Greek islands and the Western Isles of Scotland were at least comparable, and even similar, in their degree and style of beauty was a consistent theme of Steven's: 'the west coast of Scotland and the coast of Greece . . . were designed by the same architect, though the colourist was different.' The idea of Seferis contemplating the Hebrides appealed to a later poet, Edwin Morgan, who in a 1984 collection imagined Seferis's state of mind on the island, with an inevitable parallel to the famous philhellene rallying-cry of Byron:

> The isles of Scotland! the isles of Scotland!
> But Byron sang elsewhere; love, died elsewhere.

Seferis stiffly cupped warm blue May air
and slowly sifted it from hand to hand.
It was good and Greek. Amazed to find it,
he thought the dancing sea, the larks, the boats
spoke out as clear as from Aegean throats.

Steven would have approved Morgan's description of Sir Walter Scott in the same poem as a 'tawdry Ulysses'.

Certainly Steven recruited and cultivated unusual and distinctive people in whom he was interested, and snubbed a sizeable number in whom he was not; but the islanders of Eigg, both in general and individually, always counted as members of the first group. He felt a specific and personal interest in their existence, as well as a sense of paternalistic, more or less feudal responsibility, which might be considered unfashionable today but was well received by the Eiggeach at the time. Though most of Leslie's as well as Steven's concerns as lairds were deputed to the factor, the brothers took great care to recruit competent and reasonable men to this position, allowing considerable interregna while they examined possible candidates. In the summer of 1955 Leslie hired the man who would turn out to be the last Runciman-employed factor at Eigg, Rutherford; of this appointment Steven wrote to Stewart Perowne, 'After interviewing a number of crooks and drunkards we at last found a man who was honest and sober.' Though neither Runciman brother had much professional experience of farming, they believed in the importance of overseeing their factor's decisions, and preferred to accompany him, for instance, while he was selecting livestock on the mainland; three years would pass before Rutherford was permitted, if necessary, to undertake this task on his own initiative.* Indeed Rutherford seems to have had at first a reputation for being tentative about asserting his authority, and one shepherd, McIsaac, patriarch of a numerous family, was reported to Steven as boasting that he 'ran Rutherford'. This 'insolent son of Eli' (Steven's sobriquet) was replaced as soon as could be contrived

---

* Steven wrote to Marthe Bibesco of sending lambs to market – 'though I am no farmer, my acte de présence is advisable when they are dispatched – otherwise the shepherds quarrel over precedence!' (SR to Princess Bibesco, undated, before 1964, Harry Ransom Center, University of Texas, Austin).

with the more amiable and co-operative Duncan Ferguson, whose way with a fiddle Steven had noted.

By way of Rutherford the brothers were careful to match their properties with conscientious tenants, who were permitted substantial leeway in the old Runciman family tradition of laissez-faire Liberalism; some were encouraged to take in lodgers of their own. The Runcimans made concerted attempts, too, to lure back and retain the young Eiggeach lost to the economic realities of the mainland. Donnie Kirk, for example, a young boatman with the Clyde Coaster steamboats in Glasgow, was given the choice with his city-born wife of coming back to live at either Galmisdale (a fine old farmhouse which had served as the laird's residence between Petersen's burnt Lodges) or the more practical and comfortable croft of Laig. The Kirks accepted Laig and soon single-handedly revived the island's capacity for lobster-fishing. The main shortcoming of the Runciman brothers' management arguably came in the field of technological advancement, in which neither of the ageing lairds had any interest, and which stagnated, compared with Walter and Hilda's time, for lack of financial backing. A neighbouring Hebridean proprietor thought the brothers irresponsible for installing an electrical generator for the Lodge, while not exerting themselves to provide electricity for the whole island. But complaints of this nature rarely came from the islanders themselves, who did not think of their lairds as leading significantly softer lives than themselves.

It is clear from Steven's letters to Leslie that he derived a human and intellectual reward from concentrating on the problems of the islanders, problems he retailed in a style neither more nor less serious or gossipy than much of his historical writing. There were continual cases of contumacious sheepdogs:

> The situation over the dog-slain lambs is not satisfactory, though rather entertaining. Johnnie Kirk who had sworn to Rutherford that he saw Dugald's dog chasing them has been got at by Dugald and says that after all it might have been only another dog looking like Dugald's. The only dog that does look like it is one of Hugh MacKinnon's; and Hugh is therefore not on speaking terms with Dugald. Dugald is not on speaking terms with Rutherford, after an angry scene when he

accused Rutherford of trying to reduce his wife and children to the gutter. (Dugald recently, just before all this, bought for about £200 a tractor from Hugh MacKinnon, who had paid £230 for it but couldn't somehow get round to learning to drive it. So neither seems very near the gutter.) Rutherford is not much perturbed, but is a bit distressed, chiefly because he doesn't know what to do next. Nor, I confess, do I. We can't bring an action, because no one would come forward and bear witness; and the fact that Dugald guiltily shot his dog is not positive evidence. Rutherford is now sorry that I didn't have him bring the Mallaig police across. At least, he says, that would have revealed that none of the crofters has bothered to take out a dog-licence. But I am sure that wouldn't have done. It would have been terribly resented had we called in an outsider; whereas so long as the dispute remains within the island, there won't be permanent ill-feeling . . . Hugh clearly feels guilty, having two notorious killer-dogs himself, and won't summon a meeting. I think we may have to say that we shall let the matter drop if the crofters jointly guarantee that it won't happen again and that they'll compensate us if it does.

Leslie, like Rutherford – who as factor, under the terms of Walter Runciman's will, was strictly speaking employed by the elder Runciman alone – tended to be quicker to advocate police involvement whenever matters got seriously out of hand than Steven, who had a strong, romantic sense of isolated *omertà*. Describing the experience of lairdship in a casual telephone conversation with Duncan Fallowell in 1996, thirty years after the Runcimans had sold the island and seventy after they had arrived there, Steven summarized the occasional wrinkles he and Leslie had encountered with the islanders in breezily affectionate terms. 'There were no real difficulties. Now and again they tried to pull a fast one, but we made light of it and all got on rather well.' By comparison, Eigg's spectacularly less successful later laird, Keith Schellenberg (in Steven's distant view likeable enough in his way but 'a mixed-up kid'), would in 1994 endure the arson of his Rolls-Royce by islanders he denounced as 'dangerous, rotten, barmy revolutionaries'. Schellenberg called the police without hesitation, but to no avail, finding his culprit firmly protected by a populace united in stony disdain.

In 1960, on Leslie Runciman's sixtieth birthday, Steven wrote to his brother to congratulate him on the successful exercise of a difficult duty:

> I hope you will be looking back on your past decades with satisfaction. You have the right to be pleased with what you have achieved, especially as you have had to enjoy the horribly two-edged advantage of inheritance: which, for all its benefits, makes it so much harder to be someone in your own right. But you have fully attained to that – And, as one of your relatives, I'd like now to say how grateful we all are to you for having at the same time accepted your hereditary role and been such a helpful and considerate head of the family.

The family in question had endured further troubles over the previous decade, some more expected than others. Hilda fell into a noticeable decline after a heart attack in September 1954; at the time Steven had thought her 'recovering remarkably well; but we have been warned that when she is up and about and again, she had better stay far more quiet than I think she will.' The beginning of that year had seen a more shocking disaster, what Steven described without exaggeration as a 'ghastly family tragedy'. This was the suicide of his brother-in-law and younger Trinity contemporary Oliver Farrer, whose happy marriage to Kitty, youngest of the Runciman siblings, Steven had encouraged with as much zeal as he had deprecated Leslie's to Rosamond Lehmann:

> Oliver shot himself . . . rather than face prosecution for having been drunk while driving and causing an accident which may involve a life. My sister was in hospital with a badly broken leg, and he was lonely and worried and began to drink, with this horrible result. I think he killed himself feeling that he would otherwise be utterly disgraced – his life was all public work – and it was kinder to my sister (whom he adored) to make an abrupt end . . . He was a very lovable creature, a friend of mine since our undergraduate days, but he was always a little nervy and unstable, and I had always feared that he might take to drink.

Hilda finally died in 1956, 'after eighty-seven years of vigorous life, a serene and contented end'; but as in the case of his father – indeed, probably, given his much greater closeness to Hilda, more so – Steven found her loss hard to rationalize: 'There should have been no sorrow, but we are all too human . . . I find myself feeling lost and bleak.'

Eigg was the reverse of a refuge from death, a place so suffused with and accustomed to the duties and customs of mortality that Steven could analyse and observe (in both senses) the rites of death more sharply there. One strangely lasting quasi-familial relationship from the days of Leslie's first marriage was the continuing fondness of both Leslie and Steven for Honor Philipps, cousin of Rosamond's lover Wogan, and briefly herself at least admired by Leslie (Rosamond, an interested party, loudly claimed that Leslie and Honor's affair had been entire and flagrant). Honor had led an unusual married life. Her relentlessly ambitious mother, Lady Kylsant, more or less obliged her to espouse an almost equally unwilling party, Gavin Henderson, later, as the 2nd Baron Faringdon, infamous as the Labour peer whose maiden speech addressed the Upper House as 'My dears' instead of 'My lords'.* A sailor attended the wedding night; the marriage lasted only four weeks de facto, during which Honor would lie awake and alone at night, fantasizing that her husband might have hanged himself. Honor's second husband, Vere Pilkington, was a skilful sportsman, a prodigious harpsichordist, friend of Poulenc and Chairman of Sotheby's. His sexual preferences were ambivalent, but he was more tactful about them and the marriage became a true love-match. To the Runciman brothers the Pilkingtons were a relatively rare couple who were integral to both brothers' sets of friends. They were frequent and welcome guests at Eigg who stayed, unusually, at the same time as both brothers.

After one such visit, in the summer of 1961, the Pilkingtons had repaired to a holiday house in Portugal and Leslie to England. Steven wrote to his brother from the aftermath of an island funeral which had itself had mortal consequences:

---

* As Lord Faringdon, Gavin Henderson had his house, Buscot Park, redesigned to increase its fidelity to the eighteenth century by Geddes 'Paul' Hyslop, a fashionable if derivative architect, at one point the lover of Raymond Mortimer and a friend of both Steven and Dadie Rylands. In 1959 Steven quietly and unfavourably compared Faringdon's looks and wits to those of Bryan Guinness.

You will want to know the details about John Angus. It seems that he went out to lay some lobster pots yesterday evening, about 8 p.m., in that fibre bottomed boat that they have [the same boat acquired by the returned Glaswegian, Donnie Kirk]. It may be that as a result of Mrs J. D. Campbell's funeral that afternoon, which was followed, I understand, by a party where whiskey flowed (I didn't feel obliged to attend it), he was feeling a little reckless, though he was never a heavy drinker . . . it anyhow wouldn't be decent to dwell on it now. It is a very unsafe boat, and he seems to have capsized it . . . Two youths on a yacht had seen the accident and were putting out in their dinghy . . . Gordon Campbell was able to drag him ashore . . . the youths were extremely competent (I saw them today and was able to express our appreciation); they landed and started working on him, while Gordon ran up to the Rutherfords to telephone for the doctor. But for once the Rutherfords were out, at the school house; so Gordon came on here . . . Eventually I got through to Dr Maclean who went down there at once. But apparently nothing could be done. They worked at him for hours, thinking there was just a sign of life, but he was probably dead when they got him ashore. Dr Maclean says it was drowning, but Rutherford tells me that no water came out of his lungs, so probably the shock and cold of the water was too much for his heart.

I went to see Archie [the dead man's brother] this morning, who was calm and very dignified about it, though he had been hysterical the previous night, clinging to Rutherford when he arrived as the one person who could help – not to the doctor (this I got from Mrs R) . . . The body was laid out . . . and I had to go in and see it. The widow is said to be taking it well – probably not quite realizing it yet. They've kept her a bit doped today, so I was recommended to wait till tomorrow before calling on her. Archie is taking Dido over to Mallaig tomorrow to fetch the coffin (he wanted to do it himself.) The widow wants to have the first part of the funeral at her home on the mainland (near Knoydart, isn't it?) and then to bury him here. It seems rather silly to have all that going to and fro, but I'm all for it if it will give her distraction.

What ought we to do for her? I wonder about a life-pension, as she is so much younger than we are – Garry might have to go on paying it for decades. Do you think maybe a sum down and an annuity till the boys have all left school. The youngest is only 1 year old.

. . . It also affects our whole labour problem. Of all the men on the island he was the one that we could least spare.

Before posting this letter, Steven received a phone-call from the Pilkingtons' twenty-four-year-old son, Hector. Honor and Vere had been caught in a Lisbon car-crash; Honor was killed outright, and Steven hoped, in vain, that Vere would die of his injuries: 'one cannot honestly hope for him to survive as he was entirely dependent on her. I'm desperately sorry for their child, a very nice boy.' The death (as he assumed) of two close friends did not distract Steven from the immediate plight of the late John Angus's family: 'Mrs John Angus very calm on the whole, with just one outburst – "Oh, Sir Steven, tell me that it is a wild nightmare, and then I'll soon awaken." They do reach a sort of poetry on these occasions – Archie, on showing me the body yesterday, said: "And this was John Angus." ' Leslie arranged a pension of 30 shillings weekly (now about £50) for the bereaved family, payable from the Eigg Estate.

As Steven's planning for the maintenance of Mrs John Angus indicates, he was in the early 1960s still assuming that Eigg would remain in the family for at least another generation, through Leslie's son Garry. In 1955 a twenty-first-birthday party was thrown for Garry on the island, at which he was implicitly displayed to the islanders as heir, and presented with a fishing-rod by the assembled Eiggeach. But over the next decade, to Steven's frequently expressed disapproval (for academic as well as family reasons), his nephew seemed increasingly committed to an American life. After Garry had married in 1963, Steven complained to Leslie about what he felt to be the heir apparent's lack of proper family piety: 'Garry seems to want to stay in America as long as possible and showed no sign of intending to visit either Doxford or Eigg before going to Liverpool. I hope that you will get him to do his duty in both places. Doxford's not my business at all; but I feel strongly that he should present Ruth as his wife at Eigg.'

Steven was well aware that island properties were expensive and impractical, and that Eigg would not suit him or Leslie as they grew older. But, though Eigg was not an ancient family property, only in truth a benign side-effect of his father's love of yachting, Steven felt bound to it with an attachment he himself mocked as 'sentimental' but could not ignore. During discussions with Leslie and Rutherford over the island's farming he was aware of a tendency in himself towards the romantic over the prudent and the natural over the cultivated, though he was careful to rein himself in and defer to Leslie and the more expert factor: 'I am a little alarmed for ecological reasons at the proposal to cut the whole of the manse wood (the main home of the gold-crest and various other birds): but ecology and good forestry don't go hand in hand . . . ' The human intricacy of the island's small kingdom, the gossip, the divisions, the religious politics and the bargaining, appealed to him almost as much as Eigg's natural beauty. In contrast to this involuntary connection Steven found his nephew's polite, distant attitude to the island (for whose responsibilities Garry had, after all, never asked) puzzling, even disloyal. 'Though nominally fond of it,' Steven complained to Elizabeth Wansbrough, 'he says he would never be here much, and doesn't really care for it.' When Rutherford confessed his intention to retire early in 1966, rather than face another exhausting search for a freshly adequate regent, the brothers, Leslie with more phlegm than Steven (his wife Kay did not much care for Eigg either), faced the inevitable and put the estate up for sale again. As Steven told Mrs Wansbrough,

> I shall have to break the news to the islanders. Leslie gets here very little now . . . I, much as I love it, am beginning, with increasing old age and rheumatism and arthritis, to dread the journey. Being ill here is no fun, and soon we'll have no domestic help at all . . . [The daily at the Lodge, Mrs Lachie, was now in extreme old age and was alarmed by the hoover, which Steven wielded himself before the arrival of especially fastidious guests; she too handed in her notice that year.] It will be an awful wrench for me, but I have persuaded myself that it is wise.

A contributing element to Steven's surrender was that he had found with surprising speed what seemed to be a more than suitable replacement, in Scotticity, in picturesqueness and even in its domestic arrangements: 'a Border tower, with medieval walls and turrets built around 1600, with a little and comfortable late 18th century house attached to it – a willing gardener and wife, ex-housemaid, living in its lodge . . . '. Elshieshields Tower, by Lochmaben, also constituted a far superior rookery for Steven's books to the inevitable dampness of the Eigg library. Steven spent his last house-party on Eigg playing host to two splendid specimens, James Jewell and Bill Riley, a sharp-tongued set-designer and a brawny Australian befriended in Los Angeles. The transition once effected, Steven was soon making spirited jokes about its relative convenience – 'after Eigg, [the tower] is almost like living in Hampstead.'

As a laird of sorts Steven had belonged to perhaps the oddest elite of his whole studiedly *distingué* life, a category and a community understood only within itself. His station on Eigg was more aristocratic in practice than in theory; but the world to which he belonged in the Isles was also intimately communitarian. It was a seascape of shared frustrations, jokes and vulnerabilities. The Catholic MacNeil of Barra, the next best thing to a surviving Celtic sovereign, liked to send friendly, inquisitive and only faintly rivalrous letters over to 'my next-door neighbour of Eigg', rather as Louis XIV addressed Charles II as *monsieur mon frère*. Notorious absentees like Dr Green ('Dr No' to his tenants) of Raasay were frankly disapproved of as putting the landowning caste to shame; the scholarly socialist laird John Lorne Campbell of Canna was thought of with cautious awe by Steven as 'that admirable Campbell'; and the MacEwens of Muck were suspected of being 'Arts and Crafty'. Other imported lairds like the aboriginally Canadian Howards on Colonsay admired and envied the Runcimans for their smooth, successful and popular example, passing on with astonishment the rumour that the brothers were pawky enough to turn an occasional profit from islanding.

In times of mishap help was always near at hand. Steven would often arrive on his island as a sole passenger by ferry, a suitcase of books and another of clothes being stowed among Eigg's groceries, bread and letters. On one chaotic occasion in January 1962, a timorous captain ('a temporary man whom no one knows', Steven added with a local's disdain, 'as Captain Mackinnon is away after a nervous breakdown') refused to try a landing on the south harbour of Eigg, which he had never performed before. The ferry proceeded to Rum; with only one passenger to inconvenience, the captain felt one Small Isle was as good as another. Rutherford swung into action and made the requisite phone-calls. Rum had since the late 1950s belonged to the Nature Conservancy Council, whose representative now found himself in the ancient position of Gaelic chieftain offering hospitality to a sudden visitor. Steven described his makeshift reception with irreverent relish:

> Peter Wormell of the Nature Conservancy gave me a very pleasant welcome ... a very amiable young man, a good naturalist ... His wife, as you know, was the post-mistress (and no one could understand why he needed to marry her – no one else had needed to –) She's a bit rough, older than he, I should think, but intelligent ... he's obviously much in the hands of her family – her brother is the stockman, her sister-in-law the present post-mistress ...

In a sense what mattered in the succession to Eigg was that a proprietor, whether singular, corporate or charitable, now be located who would fit seamlessly into this background of specific peculiarities, difficulties and humours – absentee as little as possible in body, and not at all in spirit. The leading candidate, certainly in his own eyes, was a frequent visitor and friend of Steven, George Scott-Moncrieff.

A nephew of the translator of Proust, Scott-Moncrieff resembled his uncle in linguistic and literary ability and interest, and in his attraction to the Roman Catholic Church. Unlike C. K. Scott Moncrieff (the nephew but not the uncle employed a hyphen), George was heterosexual, devotedly married to an Orcadian contemporary of the poet George Mackay Brown, and his own poetic inclination led him into the fringes of his native country rather than to continental culture. But he argued with reason that there persisted in the Gaelic a grand tradition of unitive European civilization. The most comprehensive recent historian of Eigg, Camille Dressler, connects Scott-Moncrieff by blood or affinity to 'a sort of Highland Bloomsbury set': '... George Orwell in Jura, Gavin Maxwell near Skye, Compton Mackenzie in Barra, John Lorne Campbell and Margaret Fay-Shaw in Canna and George Macdonald bringing Iona out of obscurity ...'.* It was at Campbell's recommendation that

---

* Blair/Orwell was at Jura from May 1946 until his death in January 1950; unlike Cyril Connolly, Anthony Powell and even their grim old tutor A. S. F. Gow, Steven

Scott-Moncrieff first came to Eigg, desolately widowed, in 1945. He lived at the island's main village of Cleadale for six years, before returning to the accustomed gregariousness of Edinburgh pubs, but would often be enticed back as Steven's guest, one of the few considered hardy enough to be welcomed over Christmas and the New Year. Though really an Edinburgh man not innately rural in his qualities or expectations, Scott-Moncrieff was enchanted by the island's peace, its spirituality, in which he discerned a deal of pagan syncretism, and its people, whom he thought mischaracterized by Lowlands prejudice as work-shy rather than contemplative. He could well imagine himself as Eigg's benevolent protector; but he was a clergyman's son, Gaelicist and playwright, not a shipping scion who wrote best-sellers. Even using as a front two richer and more realistic kinsmen, Neil Usher and Gavin Scott-Moncrieff, while petitioning the lately inaugurated Highlands and Islands Development Board through Usher for funding, Scott-Moncrieff proved, both then and subsequently, unable to solidify his scheme.

Instead Leslie and Steven sold Eigg for £66,000 (today around £1,000,000), about what they had expected, to Robert Evans, an elderly, courtly seeming Welshman who, like Fluellen, stubbornly invoked his captaincy. Steven took the old Captain's measure during his final stay, when the island had already been sold, in September 1966, and found himself cautiously in favour of the new proprietor's personality, while stabbed with aesthetic regret:

> It is very melancholy tidying up the house here – and really even more melancholy still going round the island and feeling that it is not for me to prune back the rhododendrons or to mind seeing so many rabbits

---

made no attempt to renew, let alone maintain, this schoolday friendship; he was probably not aware of Orwell's decline from tuberculosis. Gavin Maxwell he knew fairly well through Wilfred Thesiger and Kathleen Raine, a Cambridge contemporary who was Maxwell's close friend, spurned lover and, in Steven's view, sorcerous nemesis – 'she cut down his tree of life, burnt down his house and killed his otter' (SR quoted in David Plante, *Worlds Apart* (Bloomsbury, 2015)). For John Lorne Campbell he felt careful respect rather than friendship. If this Highland, or Island, Bloomsbury Set is to be accepted, then, as with its urban prototype, Steven was at its edges. Of this loose assortment of Hebridean bohemians only George Scott-Moncrieff was regularly received at Eigg.

now in the glebe. I rather wish I hadn't allowed so much time for this last visit . . .

I don't mind leaving Eigg records, such as my list of birds, as [Evans] is interested and eager to have such things. He looks very old but is I believe under 60 – though only just – a tough gentleman farmer type but civilized. I had been rather prejudiced against him because he was supposed to have said that he didn't want any 'antique' furniture. But actually he had a good eye for the best pieces and was rather cross that I was now going to take them away. All the same it was a melancholy task – and yesterday was such a lovely day – grey with glimmerings of sun and the mainland changing perpetually and so still that the voices of the curlews and the sandpipers seemed the only noise except for seals playing about splashingly in the harbour – and I felt what fools we are to be leaving all this.

Evans soon engaged an especially well-liked factor, Graham Murray, a keen Gaelic scholar, but was soon disappointed at the impossibility of maintaining the legendary Runciman surpluses, which, Steven's correspondence suggests, were more occasional than had been reputed. Five years later Evans sold Eigg on for a profit the Runcimans considered ungentlemanly. He never lived at the Lodge for more than a month, and left the old laird's boat *Dido*, to the fury of his tenants, to rot on the strand. From then on things would become progressively more dysfunctional, as the Eigg Estate wobbled from charity to dreamer to outright fraud.

In the initially successful years of what would become Keith Schellenberg's exceptionally turbulent stewardship of Eigg, a new injection of cash and enterprise encouraged a process which altered the island's population – in Steven's terms, practically beyond recognition. The Gaelic-speaking Eiggeach were dying of old age or dispersing to the mainland. The 'crofters' were becoming well-intentioned, romantic outsiders, who had 'fallen in love' with the island just as Walter Runciman once had. When Duncan Fallowell visited Eigg in 1997, to follow the scandal of its sale to its last laird, the German artist and fantasist Professor Maruma, he found there only one family, the MacEwens, who still spoke Gaelic and were not, in his view, 'New Age' imports. Steven felt he had outlived the Eigg he had loved quite as much as he had outlasted, for example, the royal Roumania of the 1930s. He felt no loyalty and little affection towards the new islanders: 'I don't really feel very sorry for the islanders' present plight. Only two families who were there in our time are still there. The rest all came in during the last 20 years, lured by the possibility of leasing crofters' cottages at a tiny rent – none of them with any previous connection to the island.'

When the Eigg population achieved a community buy-out, a handover that took effect just after the 1997 general election and was fêted as part of the same wider change of air, Steven looked on with benign, faintly puzzled indifference:

> I wish the new purchasers well, but I wonder how they will manage. None of them (with two exceptions) is a native; none of them knows about crofting; and how they will make a living is a mystery. The only solution for the future of these smaller Scottish islands is that they should be acquired by some benevolent millionaire. But few millionaires are benevolent these days.

Steven himself never returned to Eigg after 1966, sticking to his lifelong principle that it is unwise to return to a place where one has been perfectly happy.

# 20

# A Wide Canvas

The Sicilian Vespers *(written 1954–7, published 1958)*, The Fall of Constantinople 1453 *(written 1961–4, published 1965)*

The canvas is wide; it has to stretch from England to Palestine, from Constantinople to Tunis. It is also crowded with characters; but a historical canvas is necessarily crowded, and readers who are afraid of crowds should keep to the better-ordered lanes of fiction.

Steven Runciman, *The Sicilian Vespers*, 1958

Throughout the period when his name was in the ring for professorial preferment at Oxford, Steven, flushed by the success of the *Crusades* trilogy, was at work on a fresh book.* It would come to be regarded as that trilogy's natural sequel; but in its structure and tone it represented a delicate, perfected development. 'That was an unfortunate work,' Steven wrote of Verdi's opera *I vespri siciliani*. *The Sicilian Vespers* under his hand would be, arguably, his most fortunate. Steven began planning it in the autumn of 1954, just before the release of *The Kingdom of Acre*, 'largely', as he claimed disarmingly to Freya Stark, 'because I like the title'. His declared frivolity of motive was transparently misleading. Already he had arrived at the

---

* Claude Cahen, a Marxist authority on medieval Islam based at Strasbourg, expressed astonishment at Runciman's facility: 'The author of this work [*The Sicilian Vespers*] has the remarkable ability to publish yearly a new book, always endowed with the same qualities: a subject on which an up-to-date general assessment is lacking, in English or in any other language; great clarity of presentation, including all that is useful and omitting all that is not; a calm, scientific detachment in dealing with problems liable to an emotional interpretation; and a wide geographical canvas' (Claude Cahen, *Past & Present*, No. 14, November 1958).

grand conceit, structure and purpose of his next subject, 'the whole history of the Mediterranean world in the late 13th century, built round a dramatic central theme'.

In the 1950s, no serious historical thinker – even one sedulously disguised as a litterateur and dilettante – could invoke 'the whole history of the Mediterranean world' without either offering allegiance or issuing a challenge to the great historian of the *Annales* school, Fernand Braudel, whose most famous work, *La Méditerranée et le monde méditerranéen à l'époque de Philippe II*, as sprawling as its title and considerably more complex, had been published in 1949. Braudel and the other *Annalistes* (notably Emmanuel Le Roy Ladurie, who became a very different kind of Cathar expert from Runciman) were greatly admired by Hugh Trevor-Roper, who, though generally an ally of Runciman's in historiographical terms, was more conceptually experimental. Steven, for his part, had no taste for the *Annalistes'* solemn, interdisciplinary, indigestible comprehensiveness. His answer to the hauteur of the French school's central concept of *longue durée*, the supremacy of inevitable and multifarious forces upon history, combined with lofty disdain for the power of individuals or the very reality of narrative event, was precise, practical, no-nonsense and light. Decades later Steven damned Braudel to an admiring if slightly baffled William Dalrymple. He had of course, he explained, begun to read *La Méditerranée*, but 'within three pages I realised that Braudel didn't know what a dromedary was; and as dromedaries were the great racing camels of the Mediterranean I felt I need not bother to read any further.'

The *Vespers* was a more substantial riposte to Braudel – a history covering the same sea three centuries earlier, its narrative shaped by political protagonists with almost Aristotelian unity, cause and effect. All the inclusiveness of the *longue durée* could not, Steven felt, make up for its shortcomings in terms of vitality, and even veracity. As to his own qualifications as a chronicler of Mediterranean history, Steven was in equal parts confident and game. 'I know the eastern part already, but it will mean hard work on Italian and Catalan material.'

Steven settled to the *Vespers* with a delight that had in it some of the satisfaction of infidelity – he was supposed to be concentrating his powers on 'a chapter for the nightmarish and composite American History of the Crusades'.* He was looking forward to the field research ; Steven had last visited southern Italy, in low spirits, on his way to his British Council post at Athens, and had not seen Sicily for a quarter of a century. The actors in the *Vespers* – the Norman kings, the Hohenstaufen Emperors, the Popes and, above all, the hubristic French conqueror Charles of Anjou – are in Runciman's telling participants in a saga rich in both dramatic incident and idiosyncratic characterization. Steven felt the appeal and the difficulty of doing justice to an exceptional narrative that had never quite penetrated the Anglophone consciousness; as he wrote to Stewart Perowne, 'It's such a good *story* but very intricate and will be difficult to reduce to intelligibility.'

Intricate the sources indeed were, but they were also scarce over long stretches of Runciman's intended scope. In his published preface, he would remark with lapidary composure that 'some of the Hohenstaufen and Angevin archives of Naples perished in the course of the last war', while crediting 'the recently published work by E. G. Léonard . . . which, though necessarily a little summary, is invaluable for its learning and its good sense'. This is an exemplary case of Runciman's proximity to recent history inclining him to understatement. At a greater distance of time, later scholars of the Angevin dynasty in southern Italy have referred more baldly to the archives' 'entire' and 'wanton' destruction.

At the outset of the Second World War a Neapolitan official called Count Riccardo Filangieri, whose ancestor of the same name earns a couple of mentions in *The Sicilian Vespers*, arranged for the State Archives of Naples to be sent for their protection to a secluded villa, Montesano, belonging to a relative. This historical trove of incalculable importance was thus preserved from Allied bombing. But as the German occupying forces prepared for the Allied invasion in the autumn of 1943, lacking supplies and harassed by partisans, their discipline broke down. Alarmed by the increasingly vandalistic

* The multi-volume Wisconsin *History of the Crusades*, edited by Robert Wolff and Kenneth Sutton and published between 1969 and 1989, to which Runciman did contribute, while patronizing it as 'the massed typewriters of the United States' (SR, *The First Crusade* (Cambridge University Press, 1951), p. xii).

comportment of successive Teutonic foraging parties, Filangieri applied for protection to the nearest Commandant. He was, alas, too late; beyond control or malignly obedient, the last squad to arrive pronounced in contemptuously staccato Italian, 'Commandant know everything; order burn.' Among the losses were the last documentary traces of the reign of the Emperor Frederick II (1194–1250), King of Sicily and Germany, destroyed by a system that showed such complexities no mercy. Filangieri wrote in a 1944 report to the *American Archivist* of 'an immense void in the historical sources of Europe . . . which nothing will ever be able to fill'. Léonard, cited in measured terms by Runciman, had been the last scholar to see the archives before the war. His oeuvre instantly became a unique, quasi-primary source.

Runciman had never relied in the first instance on density of archival research for the effect of his writings. In some ways he had always thrived on gaps. In the early stages of composing *The Sicilian Vespers*, he was more concerned about his story's style and spirit than its precise content. A year after deciding to start the book, Runciman was still dissatisfied with its prologue. His first draft survives in the form of a lecture, entitled simply 'Sicily: An Introduction', delivered during his second American tour, early in 1957. Runciman's modest declared aim, 'to give some account of that extraordinary island', at first, he felt, eluded his powers. Goethe weighed on his mind, with his judgement that 'Italy without Sicily leaves no picture on the soul.' Runciman now emphasized the strategic as well as poetic centrality of the island: 'In the whole history of the Mediterranean world, where our western civilization had its origins, Sicily has always played an all-important role . . . Any power that wishes to dominate the Mediterranean must have control of the island.'

In a quick sketch of Sicilian prehistory and legend, Runciman already aimed to discomfit the *Annalistes* by limited, unscrupulous and finely balanced raids on their theoretical territory. By lingering upon trade, agriculture and soil erosion before any named individual or political crisis was available; by invoking as his main primary evidence for such desiccated subject matter the pastoral poetry of Theocritus; and by quickly relinquishing all such approaches upon the arrival of the Romans, with their endemic and notorious high political scheming, Runciman quickly demonstrated the dominance of his firmly traditional plot, characters and event. The first three persons named (not counting Theocritus) are Hannibal, Sextus Pompey and Verres. The two men of action are leavened with the corrupt Governor, whose dubious record was immortalized in the expansively gossipy denunciations of Cicero. The pattern is now set; and the parade of invaders and intriguers continues, in strict chronology, through Byzantines, Arabs, Normans and Angevins, down at last to the Second World War. Yet this lecture is curiously lacking in the individuality on whose historical importance it insists. The speed is breathless, the effect often generalizing; and any real effort to 'give some account' of Sicily itself comes too late, with a jarringly peevish topicality:

> It is not surprising that the Sicilians have sought salvation in secret societies, but it is tragic that the indifference or the incompetence of their official rulers should have allowed the secret societies to flourish with an unscrupulous ruthlessness that seems to be almost impossible to overcome. Despite ... the proliferation of tourist monstrosities along much of its coastline, the island is still beautiful ... Let us hope that the future will restore to it the peace and prosperity that it deserves.

Steven had only just revisited Sicily, and had been distressed by elements of what he found there; this jolt of disappointed romance and modern disillusion hampers the idiom and detail, if not the structure, of Runciman's first attempt on the subject.

C. V. Wedgwood, in comparing *The Sicilian Vespers* to Runciman's 'more leisurely and massive *Crusades*', misjudged the pace of the newer work; although compact and eventful, the real strength of the *Vespers* lies in its comparative leisureliness. Peter Green, writing for the *Times Literary Supplement*, was more perceptive: 'This book demonstrates, in sharper focus than [Runciman's] monumental trilogy on the Crusades, the exact qualities of mind which he brings to his subject ... he is a dynamic, as opposed to a static, historian; his approach is organic rather than fragmentative.' The published preface, seamless, specific yet profuse, shows that this ease was an achievement Runciman arrived at by painstaking rewriting (more so than he cared to admit to most of his friends). Part of the development is rhythmic; he cared how his sentences sounded, and would practise them under his breath during long country walks. Rather than putting his case, Runciman seems to become it. Though he keeps the Goethe epigraph, instead of interrogating it he makes his own point about Sicily's importance, in his own way. He draws upon his unerring talent for naturalistic vistas:

> Few islands have been better favoured by nature. Its climate is mild and its scenery beautiful, with rugged mountains and smiling valleys and plains. Even the frequency of earthquakes and the ever-present menace of Mount Etna, though they have borne constant witness to the caprice of natural forces, have in compensation added to the richness of the soil.

This unhurried lyricism increases, by force of contrast, the impact, as the enchanted scene is interrupted by the true subject of the book. 'Man has been less kindly to the island ... Its story is one of invasions, wars and tumults.'

The timbre Runciman had succeeded in cultivating by the time he published the *Vespers* was not only more resonant, but much funnier, than his first attempt (and, indeed, than much of the *Crusades*). The lusher imagery matches the drier wit; and both combine to form the queenly persona which Runciman allows himself to relish. From conceding that 'very little is known about the autochthonous Sicani or the Siculi,' he exalts his stance from the apologetic to the aloof: 'Who the Siculi were, and whether they ... displaced the older autochthonous Sicani, is a matter for prehistorians to dispute.' An *Annaliste* would not have ceded a centimetre of this interdisciplinary debatable land; Runciman abandons the field with palpable relish. The 'petty wars and petty revolutions' of the Greek city-states are economically dismissed as an 'endemic pastime'. A pastoral digression benefits from Runciman's relaxation into the romance of names along with his deadpan treatment of the numinous, all consummated in a mellifluous punchline:

> now and then a Tyrant of Syracuse, a Hieron or a Dionysius, would establish a rule that for a few years kept peace and order. Despite the

troubles it was a happy time ... Cornfields covered the great central plain, from whose meadows the God of the Underworld carried off the daughter of the Corn-Goddess ... The gay and innocent lives of the peasants have been immortalized in the idylls of Theocritus. Yet, even so, man was beginning to rob the island of its wealth ... And while Corydon sported with Amaryllis in the shade, their goats devoured the saplings that might have renewed the forests.

In his lecture, referring to the murder of the Byzantine Emperor Constans II at Syracuse, Runciman had uncharacteristically omitted the manner of the killing; this he now remedied – 'when he was taking a bath, a courtier struck him fatally on the head with a soap-dish.' Similarly he did not this time miss the opportunity to sketch in the birth of the Emperor Frederick II, which his mother – considered, at forty, too old for childbirth – verified by securing nineteen prelates and the populace of a small town as witnesses. To Theocritus Runciman now added another distinguished literary source, Dante: ' ... William II [Norman King of Sicily, 1155–89], after a difficult minority ... was honoured with the surname of "the Good" and, according to Dante, a place in Paradise after his death.' Dante's presence would suffuse the *Vespers*, and colour the book's reception. Anglophone reviewers unversed alike in the period and the poet expressed astonishment at their unsuspected capacity for mutual elucidation. The book attracted bedazzled praise as 'something like a *Who's Who* of those whom Dante hated and the few whom he admired'.

Like *A History of the Crusades*, *The Sicilian Vespers* at its heart dealt with the competing activities of a number of ruling dynasties – the Hohenstaufen of Germany, the Capetians of France with their 'Angevin' offshoot, even, in one of Runciman's few ventures into the history of his own country, the Plantagenets of England.* The most exciting and dangerous of these royal houses was the Hohenstaufen, termed by its perennial enemy, the Papacy, 'the race of vipers'. Frederick II of Hohenstaufen, King of Sicily, Holy Roman Emperor,

---

* The Plantagenet or Angevin dynasty of England should not be confused with the descendants of the French royal house, also called Angevins. It is mainly the French Angevins who enter into *The Sicilian Vespers*, though its action also touches on the English dynasty in passing.

known as *Stupor Mundi*, had already played his part in the *Crusades* trilogy, and Steven had confessed to Freya Stark that he felt 'rather stuck . . . unable to decide about that fascinating, witty, yet obviously odious man'.

In *The Kingdom of Acre* Runciman provides a stern but fair-minded portrait of Frederick:

> His conversation, when he chose, was fascinating. But for all his brilliance, he was not likeable. He was cruel, selfish and sly, unreliable as a friend and unforgiving as an enemy. His indulgence in erotic pleasures of every sort shocked even the easy standards of Outremer. He loved to outrage contemporaries with scandalous comments on religion and morals. In fact he was not irreligious; but his Christianity was rather that of some Byzantine Emperor . . . To the average Westerner he was almost incomprehensible.

The American poet and critic Kenneth Rexroth, dubbed 'Father of the Beats', an unexpected admirer of Runciman's work, had a keen amateur interest in medieval history, and regarded Frederick II with approval as an enlightened despot and patron of letters. He felt that Runciman (whose *Vespers* he otherwise praised) had been guilty in his assessment of the Hohenstaufen of some form of old-fashioned and insular caste prejudice, dashed with prurience:

> Runciman is now not quite as down on Frederick II as he was when he wrote the Crusade book, but he doesn't like him or his bastard, Manfred, either. You feel that this is for no bona fide historical, social or political reason, but the result of a residual British prudery. Both of them just might have made it at lurid Balliol, but never at Cambridge. They were frank atheists and practically wallowed in what Dr. Kinsey used to call extramarital sexual outlets. That Frederick II was the only civilized ruler in the West between classical and modern times is beside the point for Steven Runciman. He is awed by his magnificent appetites and the splendor of his mind, but he isn't going to be pleased if he can help it.

Rexroth's insinuations can be profitably compared to Robert Irwin's later jibe about Runciman's *Kingdom of Jerusalem* reflecting the Cambridge undergraduate 'arties and hearties' declivity. Both

Rexroth and Irwin were absorbed by Runciman's subject matter and bewitched by his style and narrative gift, but also inclined to view him as himself a historical figure, inseparable from a certain context, even legend. In their reactions to his writing they treated him rather as he himself treated his primary sources, with respectful caution, fringed with irreverence.

David Abulafia, Frederick II's 1988 biographer, acknowledges the 'readable' quality of *The Sicilian Vespers* while openly dissenting from its portrayal of the Emperor. Abulafia argues that Frederick was, after all, no *stupor mundi* but a 'thorough-going conservative' and 'man of his time'. Runciman's Frederick is too close to the various sensational accounts of the infidel Emperor for Abulafia's taste. In fact, Runciman's reading is more geographically nuanced than Abulafia allows: 'Though [Frederick] was by blood half-German, half-Norman, he was essentially a Sicilian by upbringing, the child of an island that was half-Greek and half-Arab. As a ruler in Constantinople or in Cairo he would have been eminent but not eccentric. As King of Germany and Western Emperor he was a terrifying marvel.' 'Eminent but not eccentric' comes quite close to Abulafia's reading. In judging Frederick by the diverse cultural standards which his circumstances and power warranted, Runciman performs what C. V. Wedgwood saw as the greatest feat of the *Vespers*: '[Runciman] is quietly and effectively working against the insular and Nordic view of European history, which sees the Channel as the centre, overemphasizes Anglo-French and Anglo-German relations, and puts the Mediterranean as the southern limit.'

In positing, however, that Frederick's heterogeneous character stemmed from its formation in and by Sicily, Runciman again draws Abulafia's disapprobation. Abulafia insists that Frederick was 'not a Sicilian, nor a Roman, nor a German, nor a *mélange* of Teuton and Latin, still less a semi-Muslim: he was a Hohenstaufen and a Hauteville.' Indeed the *Vespers* marks a paradoxical yet persuasive instance of Runciman, exegete of the *Almanach de Gotha*, and lifelong opponent to nationalism and demagoguery, transferring his sympathy from dynastic arrangements to the popular will. His increasingly fervent and romantic partisanship in the Sicilian cause – showing the influence, another scholar has suggested, of too assiduous a perusal of the idealistic southern Italian philosopher-historian Benedetto Croce – seemed to Abulafia to verge upon unsubtle caricature. All the same, when approached by a publisher to help 're-do the history of the Vespers', Abulafia chose to concentrate on a slightly later period on the grounds that 'one does not impudently replace a classic'.

The chess kings who dominate the board of *The Sicilian Vespers* – though, like chess kings, they are often distant from the centre of the game – are Manfred of Hohenstaufen (1232–66), Frederick II's bastard son, and Charles of Anjou (1227–85), younger brother of Louis IX of France, St Louis. Manfred, who usurped the throne of Sicily from his legitimate nephew, Conrad V (known as little Conrad, Conradin or Corradino), was, in Runciman's words, 'a brilliant and glamorous figure'. Runciman's intellectual and aesthetic penchant for the adjective 'glamorous', with its overlapping connotations of ancient Scottishness, uncanny feyness and high camp, has already been noted. 'Brilliant', Runciman's second favourite Homeric epithet, represented the other, cerebral side of his currency of praise; in his view women are rarely glamorous or brilliant, though they may be 'lovely' and 'wise'. As a lost idol of kingly authority, Manfred won a sort of secular canonization from Dante; much later, by way of Horace Walpole, he helped to shape one of Lord Byron's defiant shadow-selves in the poem that bears his name.

In *The Sicilian Vespers* Manfred is portrayed with a vividness not in strict proportion to his active importance, as his career, though dynamic, was cut very short. His real significance, as Runciman would come to show, lay in his reputation and memory. Runciman was capable enough of maintaining scepticism when confronted with the most alluring myths of generosity, ability and even physical attractiveness; his reader need look no further than his cool-headed response to the legend of Richard the Lionheart in *The Kingdom of Acre*. But in the case of Manfred (*pace* Kenneth Rexroth), it is as if Runciman, worn out by the impressive but appalling nature of Frederick II, aware that the meat of *The Sicilian Vespers* will concern the masterful but unlikeable Charles of Anjou, and unavoidably moved by the gleaming testimony of *il Sommo Poeta*, decides to relax and indulge himself, as much as the reader, with an exciting temporary king, a handsome, able anti-hero to admire while he lasts. Runciman lays out clearly in his endnotes the contradictory, partial traditions from which he extracts his portrait:

> Dante describes [Manfred] as 'blond and handsome and gentle of aspect', and calls him an illustrious hero and patron of letters. The Guelf chronicles all accuse him of every possible vice, but the troubadour Raymond Tors, who was a friend of Charles of Anjou, praises him for his probity, justice and elegance, while an anonymous troubadour, after his fall, when nothing was to be gained by praising him, calls him a valorous, joyous and virtuous prince. Modern historians judge him more severely. To Previté-Orton he was 'indolent and undecided', 'a child of the harem', 'loving the imagination of his own greatness', and showing an 'oriental mixture of self-confidence and enervation'. The summing-up of Léonard is temperate and just.

In his great work *Les Angevins de Naples* Léonard, the fortuitous saviour of a portion of the Angevin record, had referred to Manfred's 'belles qualités, affabilité qui, unie à la beauté, lui attachait les coeurs, ouverture et curiosité d'esprit, culture, activité indefatigable, courage et de remarquables dons de diplomate', moderating all this careful praise with a curt pronouncement of Manfred's 'manque de scruples'. Runciman's line is not dissimilar, but he spices schoolmasterly criticism with political speculation, of both counterfactual and psychological varieties:

> [Manfred] had already shown himself to be unscrupulous, treacherous and cruel; but his defects were forgotten in the charm of his personality. He inherited his father's love of learning and interest in the sciences, and the same gift of fascination in his talk, while lacking Frederick's uncomfortable taste for shocking the conventional. In addition he was unusually good-looking. But he was not as great a man as his father. For all his energy in war and in diplomacy, he had a certain indolence over the daily details of administration. He was ready to let his friends and, in particular, his Lancia kinsfolk, do his work for him and soon found himself swayed by them into directions it would have been wiser to avoid. Had he been content to copy his Norman ancestors and reign in Sicily, keeping control of the southern mainland and restricting his further activities to schemes that would benefit his

subjects, he might have founded a lasting dynasty. The Papacy might have reconciled itself to its existence and let him be. But the Lancias came from the north and they had acquired lands in Lombardy. They urged him on to be king not only of Sicily but of all Italy; and Manfred himself, conscious of his Hohenstaufen blood, could never quite forget that his father had been Emperor.

In his endnotes Runciman adds his most original contribution to Manfred's legacy – that this young bastard Hohenstaufen, an unregenerate excommunicate and self-made king, aimed at 'embarrassing papal opposition to his rule by appearing as the champion of Latin Christianity'. By 'Latin Christianity', Runciman principally means the Latin Empire, the dysfunctional Frankish successor state that ruled Constantinople for sixty-odd years after the Fourth Crusade. Like *A History of the Crusades*, *The Sicilian Vespers* points firmly and freshly to Byzantium, and this emphasis also stands behind Runciman's reading of Manfred's successor and nemesis, Charles of Anjou.

While Manfred's beauty and demeanour as much as his character and patronage made him the darling of the poets from the troubadours down to Dante, Charles of Anjou, according to all available evidence, looked like a chess king and behaved like a chess queen. Runciman's first description of him alludes to Shakespeare's Richard, Duke of Gloucester, who in *Henry VI Part 3* declares, 'I am myself alone':

With little family affection to soften him, Charles began as a young man to rely on himself alone. He grew up tall and muscular, with a dark olive skin inherited from his Castilian ancestors and the long nose of the Capetians [Dante, no friend to Charles, also mentions with some relish his 'maschio naso']. He had a healthy well-disciplined body, with all his mother's energy. He had received a good education and never lost his respect for learning or his personal liking for poetry and the arts. But he had his share of his family's austerity and would always abandon his personal pleasures in pursuit of some higher aim; though, while King Louis's austerity came from his genuine piety, Charles's was an instrument to gratify his longing for power. His piety was in its way genuine, but it chiefly took the form of a belief that he was the chosen instrument of God.

Runciman permits himself daring insight into Charles's obscure childhood and family relations as the (probably) posthumous youngest son of Louis VIII of France. At one point he suggests that the leniency shown by Charles's eldest brother, Louis IX, in allowing Charles to invade Sicily for a cause about which the saintly Louis had private doubts, may be explained by the King's 'guilt at loving Charles less than his other brothers'. Runciman's interpretation of Charles's religious disposition is different from his cynical opinion of, for example, Bohemond in the *Crusades* trilogy. He explicitly clears Charles of Machiavellianism, lightly laundered by faith or otherwise, but in Charles's true belief he sees instead fanaticism, megalomania and poverty of imagination: 'His personal ambition was too crude and obvious. His piety was its servant.' Jean Dunbabin, a subsequent biographer of Charles, called Runciman's charge on this point 'unkind', while rebutting it less than convincingly. Dunbabin calls Charles 'too occupied with rescuing the Church to spend time contemplating his soul' and admits that 'his contemporaries do not appear to have perceived him as a particularly religious man.' Geoffrey Barraclough, a younger historian of medieval Germany, was particularly chilled by Charles's record as Runciman presented it. Reviewing the *Vespers* he compared Charles, unsurprisingly, to Napoleon and, more wildly but with more proximate horror, even to Hitler.

Runciman works upon, as so often, a near void of evidence to depict in Charles a coherent protagonist, whose career exemplifies his parable of hubris. From the first Runciman employs the very lack of hard information as itself an insight into Charles as an individual: 'The new king seemed austere and unapproachable. He had none of the gay affability with which the Hohenstaufen had been able to charm their Italian subjects. Though he liked his Provençal troubadours and though he showed a sincere interest in learning and the arts, the impression he made was cold and inhuman.' The Francophile Dunbabin objects that Runciman is arguing speciously from absence, and cannot know that Charles was so dourly unknowable a figure to his true intimates. But Runciman's chosen evidence stands up for his purposes. He cites an exasperated complaint from Charles's first sponsor for the crown of Sicily, Pope Clement IV, that this steely French prince was proving himself to be 'neither visible nor audible nor affable nor amiable'. Paradoxically, Charles as an efficient enigma leaves an increasingly firm imprint on the reader's consciousness. An appalled but compelled Peter Green wrote that Charles's cold-hearted austerity reminded him of 'nothing so much as the late Sir Stafford Cripps'.

Charles may be a historical personage who can be discerned only at a distance, but there is still a lot to discern, and under Runciman's handling this quintessentially ambitious potentate's career assumes a magnetic decisiveness of purpose. At first Runciman lays out Charles's motives as almost trivially high political, a traditional case of Lady Macbeth conjugality: 'Gossip attributed his acceptance [of Sicily] to the influence of his wife.' Charles's sisters-in-law were the Queens of France, England and (on paper) Germany, and his wife was rumoured to be irritated by his dilatoriness in catching up with his brother and brothers-in-law. Runciman entertains the old story, only to undercut it: 'When last they had all met together she had been placed, as a mere countess, at a lower table for banquets, and she bitterly resented it. She, too, would be a queen. But Charles was not a man to concern himself with a woman's whims. His desire for a throne was even greater than hers.'

Once Charles has, in short order, acquired Sicily over the excommunicate corpse of the luckless Manfred, Runciman wastes no time in arguing that the victorious King soon went on to seek a throne even greater than Sicily's. Manfred, a consummate political opportunist, had acquired a few ad hoc Balkan territories – hard by the stomping ground of Steven's academic infancy – by a series of marriage treaties and petty wars. These concerns Charles now took over, but, Runciman is quick to add, ' . . . Charles's ambition was not to be satisfied merely with a few islands and cities along the Albanian coast. He aimed at Constantinople.' *The Sicilian Vespers* initially appeared to many of Runciman's readers to be a foray into the familiar sphere of Western European power play, England, France, Germany, even Spain and Italy at a stretch. In fact it was in some ways Runciman's Byzantine book par excellence; a perfect illustration of Western avarice and Byzantine diplomacy, which Runciman says in the *Vespers* was 'still the best in the world'.

Runciman uses the consistent Byzantine drift of his career to provide the potentially opaque Charles of Anjou with unwavering motivation. In so doing, he delivers a clear portrait and a convincing story. His fondness for what other historians dismiss as historical culs-de-sac can put him in a better position than more teleological thinkers to understand the mentality of historical actors. In the Latin Empire of Constantinople, an inorganic failed experiment that sputtered along for fifty-seven years, he identifies an all-important background, a cause which both Manfred and Charles tried to use for their own advantage. Runciman points out that Western rulers and Popes – especially French ones – never truly reconciled themselves to their toy empire's ignominious failure: 'Its fall was an insult to them. They could not quite understand it, for it never occurred to them that to the Byzantines, as to the Arabs in the East, they did not represent the finest flower of civilisation but were savage intruders with a liking for religious persecution.' The defenders of Charles of Anjou since Runciman's day have argued that the ulterior motives which Runciman attributed to Charles were, in fact, both impracticable and irreconcilable. If Charles aimed at taking the Imperial crown of the East for himself, why did he fund the Latin Emperors in exile, and even intermarry his children with them? If Constantinople was his aim, why did he persuade his saintly brother Louis IX to go on crusade in quite the opposite direction, to Tunis? Runciman's account leaves such objections looking both over-literal and under-worldly. Charles was careful to see that the inheritances of his imperial pawns would revert to him in the case of their untimely deaths; and this is a king who quite possibly had Thomas Aquinas poisoned. As for Tunis,

> Charles was put in a quandary. He had a genuine admiration and respect for his brother, and he was well aware of the force of public opinion that Louis commanded . . . But he was unwilling to abandon his personal eastern venture . . . he decided that if he was to join in a crusade against the Muslims, it would be against Muslims whose conquest would be of direct advantage to him . . .
>
> To the last minute Charles still hoped that Louis might cancel the whole crusade . . . It was only when the French army actually set out that he gave up his preparations for his expedition against Constantinople.

For Runciman Byzantium completes the pattern not only of the biography of Charles of Anjou, but of the island and people of Sicily itself. He never loses sight of the cultural complexity of the Sicilians, with their Greek and Arab legacies, and of Sicily's persistent Greekness he asserts that 'The Greek element in the island was still strong and kept some sympathy with the Greeks of Byzantium.' If the high colour of Runciman's support for the oppressed but stubborn Sicilians – in his own present as in his book's period – on occasion seems simplistic, at least it illustrates his deeply held sense of justice. But though he calls the Sicilians 'of all the peoples of Europe . . . the most adept at conspiracy', Runciman proposes that their armed rebellion was planned, funded and timed by exterior powers – by Aragon and, even more to the point, Byzantium.

> It is remarkable that one of the first actions of the Messinese after they had risen was to send a message to Constantinople, long before they made any contact with Aragon . . .
>
> The main credit, if a massacre deserves credit, should go to the Sicilians themselves . . . The organization of the conspiracy and the alliances that enabled it to succeed was chiefly due to John of Procida [a Neapolitan physician, in Aragonese employ, who became a Sicilian folk hero]; but the financing and the dating were the work of the Emperor at Constantinople.

'If a massacre deserves credit' – although Runciman approves of the Sicilian cause, he keeps his own humane values robustly intact. 'Bloodshed is an evil thing and good seldom comes of it. But the blood shed on that evening not only rescued a gallant people from oppression. It altered fundamentally the history of Christendom.' As in the *Crusades* trilogy, Runciman is torn between glamourized, romantic awe at the military exploits of the medieval Western Europeans, his own ancestors, and a purer admiration for the Byzantine ability to arrive at political achievements by less crude methods. He quotes with approval a boast from the autobiography of Michael VIII Palaeologus: 'Should I dare to claim that I was God's instrument in bringing freedom to the Sicilians, I should only be stating the truth.' An Emperor, Autocrator and Equal to the Apostles laying claim, with some veracity, to the role of a democratic liberator was just the sort of piquancy Runciman liked to pick out.

*The Sicilian Vespers* covered a period and a sequence of events that, for all its historical significance, had come to be remembered and preserved more in the form of folk tradition than formal scholarship. Part of Runciman's apparent volte-face from his usual genial, well-placed internationalism to romantic, and even at times belligerent, Sicilian nationalism can be put down to his gratitude to the Sicilians for bequeathing to him such a rewarding and fitting subject. Accretive Sicilian and southern Italian folklore helps to frame and adorn two of his most vivid narratives within the *Vespers*: his versions of the sudden rise and tragic death of the boy-King Conradin, and of the climactic story of the eponymous massacre itself.

Conradin's dramatic trajectory represented territory of which Runciman had proved himself to be master, sad stories of the death of kings. Recognized as King of Jerusalem and Sicily, and widely regarded as rightful King of Germany, from his father's death when he was two, Conradin grew up under the care of his Bavarian maternal uncles, while his bastard uncle Manfred stole his Sicilian inheritance and the mantle of the Hohenstaufen cause. Runciman, always wryly interested in the legalistic procedures of the Crusader barons, does not forget Conradin's legal but powerless lifelong status in the Levant: 'The barons of Outremer acknowledged him as King of Jerusalem; but had he ever visited his kingdom he would have found his power there strictly circumscribed.' After the death of his usurping uncle Manfred in 1266, Conradin was at last persuaded to reclaim his Sicilian kingdom. Runciman revels in this young pretender's timing, which was at first opportune: 'On 15th September 1267 [the Pope] wrote to Charles to say that he did not believe now that Conradin would invade Italy. At that moment Conradin's army was already marching through the Tyrolean valleys towards the Brenner Pass.'

Pope Clement IV lives up to all the villainy with which Runciman gleefully credits the Papacy, watching the fifteen-year-old King's army from a high window in Viterbo, rubbing his hands, 'muttering hopefully that the lamb was being led to the slaughter'. Conradin's rapturous reception at Rome is lavishly rendered. Though proud of his Protestant Lowland stock and never as captivated as many Scots children by the Stuarts and Bonnie Prince Charlie, Steven had absorbed enough sentiment from the fiercely Jacobite Torby for Conradin's arrival to evoke that later Young Chevalier being adored in Edinburgh:

> Crowds met him singing hymns of praise and flinging flowers before his path. The streets were hung with silks and satins. Everyone was in gala dress. There were games in the Campus Martius and torchlight processions by night. The boy-King, with his beauty and charm, was treated almost as a god. If the great Guelf nobles were absent, watching cautiously from behind the walls of their castles in the Campagna, no one noticed or cared . . .

Conradin's fate, and that of the Hohenstaufen dynasty, was decided at a long, unpredictable, closely fought battle near Tagliacozzo, in the Abruzzo. In the October of 1957, late into the writing of the *Vespers*, Steven embarked on a concerted effort to locate the exact site of the battlefield, as he was later to recall in the *Alphabet*: 'It is often impossible to understand the course of a battle if one has not examined the actual terrain. Sometimes one goes there too late. I once made a long journey through central Italy to look at the site of the battle of Tagliacozzo . . . only to find that the plain had long since been drained and the water-courses moved.' But this disappointment did not in the end diminish the fervour or exactitude with which Runciman described the tergiversations of the battle. After a deceptively total rout of his Angevin enemies, Conradin, who wrongly thought Charles of Anjou dead and the field won, fatally relaxed his discipline. At this point Charles, who had been hiding 'behind the fold of a hill' with his reserve cavalry and a wily adviser, the veteran Crusader Erard of Saint-Valéry, counterattacked. Conradin's knights were mostly killed, many of his nobles captured and he himself put to flight – 'After a disastrous opening Charles had won a complete and unequivocal victory.' Once again prefiguring Bonnie Prince Charlie, Conradin had miserable weeks of disguises and safe-houses ahead of him, but his flight ended less happily in capture.

It was only now that the outcome that crystallized Conradin's historical importance took place. Charles of Anjou, acting with clean-cut political logic ('Conradin's boyish charm made him all the more dangerous') but a disregard for the usual rules of conduct between princes, put the young Hohenstaufen and his inseparable companion Frederick of Baden on trial and had both sixteen-year-old princes beheaded in public at Naples. Runciman does not dilute the repercussions – nostalgic, patriotic, folkloric, even literary – of this cold act of realpolitik:

> It was the only glimpse that the Neapolitans had of the lovely sixteen-year-old boy who might have been their king. They never forgot him.
>
> Conradin's trial and death shocked the conscience of Europe . . . To this day Charles is generally condemned, even by Frenchmen eager to excuse one of the ablest of the Sons of France. To the Germans it has always been the greatest crime in history. Centuries later the poet Heine wrote of it with bitterness.

This evocation of Heine is a fine although somewhat finessed touch. In fact Heine, writing in *Religion and Philosophy in Germany*, had marvelled at a bigoted Junker's remembrance of Conradin, as an axiomatic instance of irrational German grudge-bearing against France: 'What you [that is, the French nation] are really accused of I could never understand. Once in a beer-cellar at Göttingen I heard a young Old-German assert that it was necessary to be revenged on France for Conradin of Hohenstaufen, whom you had beheaded at Naples. Doubtless you have long since forgotten that: we, however, forget nothing.' Runciman's provocative statement that 'to the Germans it has always been the greatest crime in history' recalls his similarly breathtaking, apparently sincere verdict on the Fourth Crusade. Like that earlier judgement, it does not ignore the facts of the Second World War and the Holocaust, but rather unsettlingly alludes to them. Almost as much as the *Crusades* trilogy, *The Sicilian Vespers* is a self-confessed, conscious child of the war just past, as when Runciman declares that 'The rebellion in Sicily was now a European war.' After narrating the splendid farce of a proposed arranged mêlée of champions between Charles of Anjou and Peter of Aragon, which, due to much dragging of spurs on both sides, was never actually fought, Runciman explains with ominous grandeur that 'The real duel was to be fought on a wider tilting-place'; he means the known world.

Steven's sometime crony Tom Boase, the President of Magdalen, cattily opined that 'It is not till the Vespers themselves that Sir Steven warms to his task.' While *The Sicilian Vespers* can hardly be said to lack such warmth as a whole, and it is part of the book's conceptual seductiveness that its story encompasses so much more than its title, it is true that in describing the massacre of the French occupiers in 1282 Runciman surpassed himself. Beginning with a local scene he had himself witnessed on a visit in the already far-away 1920s, Steven offers up the Easter atmosphere in the vicinity of Palermo:

> Easter fell early in the year ... on 29th March. Throughout Holy Week the island of Sicily was outwardly calm ... None of the French officials ... noticed more than the habitual unfriendliness shown them by the subject race. But amongst the Sicilians themselves as they celebrated the resurrection of Christ with their traditional songs and dancing in the streets, the atmosphere was tense and explosive.
>
> The Church of the Holy Spirit lies about half a mile to the south-east beyond the old city-wall of Palermo, on the edge of the little gorge of the river Oreto. It is an austere building, without and within. Its foundation-stone was laid in 1177 by Walter Ophamil, the English-born Archbishop of Palermo, on a day made sinister by an eclipse of the sun ...
>
> There was gossiping and singing in the square as everyone waited for the services to begin. Suddenly a group of French officials appeared ... They were greeted with cold, unfriendly looks, but they insisted on mingling with the crowd. They had drunk well and were carefree; and soon they treated the younger women with a familiarity that outraged the Sicilians.

This is one of the clearest examples of Runciman's sudden, clear, novelistic flights of empathic imagination. Although as a historian his sympathy clearly lies with the Sicilians, to whose dedicated and courageous conspiracy he has devoted the previous chapter, suddenly author and reader alike are positioned firmly among the unsuspecting French soldiers, alien visitors among sacred, insular rites. The incomprehensible words of the Sicilian-dialect folk songs, the looming, ill-omened, stark church building, the Dionysiac mixture of rejoicing and pent-up aggression, all combine to transfer, at the last minute, a mysterious rush of pity towards the French victims. Then that pathos is overturned. The grand hubris of the French occupation is encapsulated in a small, personal, unforgivable last straw, and the bloody Paschal sacrifice begins:

> Among them was a sergeant called Drouet, who dragged a young married woman from the crowd and pestered her with his attentions. It was more than her husband could bear. He drew his knife and fell on Drouet, and stabbed him to death. The Frenchmen rushed up to avenge their comrade and suddenly found themselves surrounded by a host of furious Sicilians, all armed with daggers and swords. Not one of the Frenchmen survived. At that moment the bell of the Church of the Holy Spirit and of all the churches of the city began to ring for Vespers.

Steven had come to know, during and after the war, several countries veined with divided allegiances and complicated moral compromises: Bulgaria, Romania, Egypt, Palestine, Turkey, Cyprus and, pre-eminently, Greece. He was also aware of and grimly interested in the Sicilian Mafia, and the extent to which the Allied invasion of Sicily had toppled the great gangster, Mussolini, by way of cutting deals with many more insidious criminal bosses. Runciman makes sure to display the ugly complications entailed by the Sicilians' moment of bloody heroism. 'Sicilian girls who had married Frenchmen perished with their husbands.'

Yet for all that it follows revolutions, some of them tragic, with profound effects upon Church and state, with unfading resonance for Europe's past and for Runciman's present, the tenor of *The Sicilian Vespers* is lighter, more relaxed and less grandly ecclesiastical than that of *A History of the Crusades*. Peter Green compared Runciman's perspective and prose in this work, usefully though to some extent critically, to that of Strachey:

> the lesson of the Vespers is one which has considerable relevance for our own times . . . the moral dangers of calling in a champion to fight one's righteous wars . . . These large questions Sir Steven, perhaps wisely, avoids: when his dry, elegant prose does flash into emotional life it is most often in a way that hints at the influence (ridden, it is

true, on a very close rein) of Lytton Strachey . . . The danger inherent in Strachey's kind of mentality is that, not being equipped by nature to comprehend vast fields of valid human experience, it is inevitably tempted to treat them as though they were either illusory or derisible or both . . . Now in this respect Sir Steven is far more subtle and sensitive to spiritual issues than either Strachey or [Bertrand] Russell. *The Medieval Manichee* proved that beyond a doubt . . . his position is not so much that of Gibbon or Voltaire as of a sympathizer with Byzantium against the barbarous inroads of bigotry and wanton destruction.

Runciman certainly does not dismiss ancient values and motivations, even when they are far distant from his own position. Never attracted to what he thought of as Roman Catholic intellectual authoritarianism (despite his personal esteem for Pope John XXIII), he nonetheless calls the theory of the universal papal monarchy 'the grandest conception of the Middle Ages', and 'no mean ideal'; its 'gradual suicide' by debasement in local power-play is presented as the central tragedy of *The Sicilian Vespers*. But the elevated promontory from which his narrative voice operates can leave him open to the charge of reasoning from hindsight. Palmer A. Throop, a Texan historian of the Crusades and Papacy, complained tetchily but fairly: 'Runciman intersperses his account with sage advice to Charles of Anjou, Manfred, and an impressive array of popes. Unfortunately, how sage the advice may be cannot be determined without running four decades of the thirteenth century through their paces according to the commands of Runciman.'

But Runciman's writing resembled Strachey's more in its manoeuvrable style than in an occasionally complacent attitude. Where Green's comparison bears most fruit is in Runciman's compact, often comic inclusion of characters and vignettes that, if strictly speaking dispensable, prove more than memorable enough to justify their relevance. Perhaps the most striking example comes with his attention to Machalda Scaletta, an ambitious Sicilian baroness: 'The Lady Machalda . . . had decided that the post of Royal Mistress would suit her and now tried to put her scheme into effect. King Peter had an acutely embarrassing evening. He only escaped by talking at immense length of his loyalty to Queen Constance. It was not an argument that the Lady Machalda found attractive.' Nor does Runciman fail to satisfy his readers as to the fates of such fleeting but involving bit-players. The final appearance of Machalda is especially well turned: 'The emir [of Jerba], Margam ibn Sebir, was imprisoned in the castle of Mategriffon at Messina, where he soon had the Lady Machalda for company. She shocked her gaolers by her gay and immodest dress when she went to play chess with him.' Hélène Wieruszowski, an expert in medieval Germany and Italy understandably furious at being elided from Runciman's snappy bibliography, quite missed the point of this technique – 'It would have helped the reader if Runciman had concentrated on the results rather than every phase and detail of earlier developments.' Runciman, far from being the smug and partial Bloomsbury-tinged Byzantinist some of his critics willed into existence the better to attack, took care about people and possibilities regardless of their ultimate importance.

In his preface to *The Sicilian Vespers*, Runciman had warned his readers that they would need a high tolerance for complexity, as he navigated them through messy historical truth, rather than tidy fictional artifice: 'a historical canvas is necessarily crowded, and readers who are afraid of crowds should keep to the better-ordered lanes of fiction.' In some ways this challenge was typical of the disingenuous, teasing side to his mentality; and elsewhere he could be perfectly ready to declare something like the opposite – that good history relies on the same imaginative and structural power that sustains great fiction. In December 1962 Steven delivered a lecture to the Royal Society of Literature, with another great, Northumberland-born narrative historian, C. V. Wedgwood, presiding in the chair. Its theme was 'Medieval History and the Romantic Imagination'.

Veronica Wedgwood was a friend of Steven's of long, if rarely easy, standing. A scion of the pottery dynasty, she had taken a First in history at Lady Margaret Hall, Oxford, under the tutelage of A. L. Rowse, who called her 'my first outstanding pupil'. The Runcimans were well acquainted with the Wedgwoods, by way of the social and political common ground between the younger Walter Runciman and Veronica's uncle, Josiah Wedgwood, later 1st Baron Wedgwood.

After the rupture of his marriage to his cousin Ethel, Josiah Wedgwood had stayed with the Runcimans at Doxford for some months of 1913; Steven remembered meeting him and his son, another Josiah, 'rather priggish and self-righteous', on holiday from Summer Fields.* For all this shared background of non-conforming, serious-minded, well-to-do Northumbrian gentry, Steven only properly met Veronica Wedgwood in 1936, when his youngest sister Kitty invited him to her first marital home to meet his fellow historian. Wedgwood had just brought out her first book, on the Earl of Strafford, and was a contributor to the *Times Literary Supplement* and *Time and Tide*. They realized that they had many historical attitudes, and the influence of G. M. Trevelyan, to unite them; but though Wedgwood was a consistent, public admirer of Steven's writing, he never quite acknowledged her talent in return. Probably Wedgwood's appearance told against her; her countenance was as stern and plain as her prose and her protagonists were sprightly and romantic. Steven rarely felt much kinship with lesbian intellectuals even of Wedgwood's grand, respectable, classically minded calibre. Among his many women friends he preferred more forceful, well-turned-out and worldly wives, such as Charlotte Bonham Carter and, later, Robin Dalton.

In January 1956 Wedgwood had laid out for the *Times Literary Supplement* a condensation of her own historical creed, 'History as Literature'. In this piece she predicted the onset of a golden period for the practice of history as an art, compared to the more scientific consensus of the discipline earlier in the century (as upheld by authorities such as J. B. Bury). At one time, she regretted, 'although the understanding and appreciation of literary form, and the practice of literary style, had never quite left the universities and was slowly creeping back into them, the academic world in general continued to be suspicious of any historian who aimed too openly at literary or, still worse, at popular reputation.' Now she thought the auguries better, among them the high sales and enthusiastic reviews Runciman had attracted since the war:

---

* It seems that the Runciman parents held up young Josiah – in part surely kindly, given the then socially embarrassing fact of his parents' divorce proceedings – as a role model for Steven, a suggestion Steven resented. 'Children are apt to dislike anyone that they are told to admire' (SR to C. V. Wedgwood, 22 May 1950, Elshieshields).

'Steven Runciman's wise, urbane and learned volumes on the Crusades found a wider appreciation in this decade than they could have done had they appeared twenty-five years ago.'

One informed and interested reader of both Runciman and Wedgwood was the increasingly successful historical novelist Alfred Duggan. Writing in the *Tablet* in December 1960, he compared both historians, to what would have been Steven's squared irritation, to Gibbon, and detected in all three a weakness which Steven would have emphatically denied: the tendency to determinism.

> *The Decline and Fall of the Roman Empire* tells us that the Empire declined steadily for twelve hundred years. Miss Wedgwood's brilliant retelling of *The King's War* shows that King Charles never had a chance of victory; Sir Steven Runciman's *History of the Crusades* assumes from the outset, not only that the Crusaders will be beaten, but that it was a pity they ever embarked on such a crazy enterprise.

Duggan goes on to suggest that he and his novelistic profession possess an innate advantage of imaginative leeway, denied even to the greatest historical narratives:

> The historical novelist will show the part that chance can play in human affairs ... The most prudent staff officer would not base his plans on the supposition that the Rhine will cease to be a military obstacle. It happened. The novelist must show men who do not expect it to happen ... The questions are endless, and history cannot answer them for lack of trustworthy material. But sometimes the historical novelist can guess at a plausible answer.

In fact Steven was fascinatedly attentive to the role of chance and coincidence in history, was (sometimes scathingly) aware that historical personages were ignorant of what would befall them, and was rarely above a little fleshed-out speculation. As to his attitude towards the historical novel (he enjoyed Duggan's books, while finding their naively partial Catholicism rather quaint) it would lie at the heart of his Royal Society of Literature lecture in 1962.*

---

* One of the most scathing comments on Duggan, when in 1964 he tried his hand at a straight, simplified short history of the Crusades, came from René Hague, a stable-

'Most historians, I suspect,' Steven artfully generalizes, 'have at some time longed to write an historical novel.' He goes on, with one of his enjoyably atavistic bursts of Border balladry, to describe the historical novel as 'the braid, braid road that leads across the lily leven'. The allusion is to the ballad of Thomas the Rymer, wherein the seer Thomas is conducted by the Queen of Elfland to a crossroads with three paths:

> 'O see ye not yon narrow road,
> So thick beset wi' thorns and briers?
> That is the Path of Righteousness,
> Though after it but few inquires.
>
> 'And see ye not yon braid, braid road,
> That lies across the lily leven?
> That is the Path of Wickedness,
> Though some call it the Road to Heaven.
>
> 'And see ye not yon bonny road
> That winds about the fernie brae?
> That is the Road to fair Elfland,
> Where thou and I this night maun gae.'

If the historical novel, then, was the luscious but delusive road to Hell (with Duggan presumably among those who mistook it for Heaven), Steven, by implication, identified himself not with the first, strict and narrow way (where we might place Bury, Baynes and the historical scientists), but with the tricky compromise of the third path into Fairyland. Smoothly he insists that 'the chief lesson in history which the historian himself learns is modesty,' and accordingly announces, 'For myself, I am no seer who can interpret and foretell the rhythm of the universe.' The disavowal has about it a touch of Caesar refusing the crown.

The historical novelists for whom Steven had the greatest respect

---

mate at the *Tablet*: 'It is as though Mr. Duggan had voluntarily adopted the narrow outlook of the men of whom he writes: as though the novelist had taken control, as often the historian does in his novels' (*Tablet*, 18 January 1964).

were Tolstoy and, in his own day, Mary Renault and Zoé Oldenbourg. To this last, a Russian émigrée and French novelist and historian who felt about the Cathars of the Languedoc approximately as Steven felt about the Byzantines, he referred in the 1962 lecture with special awe: 'the novels of Mme Oldenbourg seem to me to illustrate the squalor, the turgidity and the faith of medieval France in a manner that is very nearly perfect and . . . a superb aid to history.' In Oldenbourg's masterpiece, *Argiles et cendres* (published in English as *The World is Not Enough*), she is sufficiently relaxed about dating to bring forward the Second Crusade thirty years, the better to persecute her unfortunate characters. In his appreciation of her work Steven proved himself, as ever, no pedant, concerned with essential truth over literal fact and delighted wherever he found it. He thought that the sense of romance from which he derived such satisfaction in the best historical fiction was at its fullest in the novels of Proust,

> that most romantic of 20th century novelists . . . one knows all the time that he would have preferred to use the real names that reverberate down the annals of France . . . he was never more pleased, so Sir Harold Nicolson has told us, than when he came upon the name of the Duke of Northumberland (the county in which both our distinguished Chairman [Wedgwood] and myself first saw the light of day!).

It was a typical eccentricity for Steven thus to attribute to Proust frustrated biographical urges, just as he foists novelistic ones upon the whole historical academy.

Even as Fairyland, whatever its charms, lies a good deal nearer to Hell than to Heaven, Steven's means of historiographical compromise lay, he revealed without contrition, decisively towards art rather than science: 'History is an art, but an art with its technical rules, such as, for instance, architecture follows.' It is easy to lose sight of the architectural rules he prescribes, amid the strong flavour of his lecture's stated main theme, romance; but such rules are present, and important. Indeed Runciman sees romance itself in architectural terms: 'the language of the Gothic world, that world of spires and turrets and the horns of elfland faintly blowing'. He goes so far as to accept that the scientific model has value as well as the artistic and architectural ones, only to qualify this concession at once: 'The great scientist has always relied upon flashes of insight that depend upon lucky accidents or inspired guesses.' Above all, he argues for the reconciliation of the various historical duties and dispositions into an organic and pleasing whole: 'We should be careful in drawing an antithesis between the romantic and the classical. They are not mutually exclusive. They exist happily side by side; they can invade each other's territory.' The invasion analogy is philosophically clear, personally characteristic and stylistically apt. After all, much of Runciman's writing – and more of it to come – dealt with the consequences of the overlap and incursion of 'romantic' Westerners upon 'classical' Byzantines. Frankish culture, 'alien to the sparkling Mediterranean', was 'never more terrible and yet never more romantic than when its children invaded those bright southern lands'.

This quality of unrepentant romance displayed within a frame of stable architecture is what makes *The Sicilian Vespers* in some ways Runciman's most exemplary book, as well as one of his most exciting.* In the 1962 lecture Steven confesses that, despite the Byzantine emphasis of his pre-war career and his unfading sympathy for Greek civilization, he had first been attracted to historical study by the medieval history of his birth-culture, Western Europe, rather than by his adopted Eastern one:

> I feel a certain disloyalty to the Byzantines and to the whole civilized world of the Christian East when I have to confess that for me those barbarous names [he has cited four great anapaests, Bohemond, Melisende, Cunigunde, Esclarmonde] have a magic that is lacking in the great names of Byzantium. The latter often have a majesty about them and a ceremonial magnificence; they sometimes have glamour, but they never quite have glamourie . . . it was the lure of the Western Middle Ages that drew me in my childhood to history.

---

* Steven himself was a little surprised at the popularity of *The Sicilan Vespers*. When the Greek academic Pascalis Kitronilides complimented him on it in 1993, Steven at first, disingenuously, scoffed that 'Greeks only ever read the Byzantine ones,' then laughed heartily and without any rancour when Kitronilides added that he enjoyed it much as he would a novel (Pascalis Kitronilides, Runciman Lecture, King's College London, February 2015).

As a Cambridge undergraduate and even as a clever schoolboy, Steven had seemed bored by domestic British history; but by the time of the *Vespers* he preferred to remember an earlier, perhaps more innocent picturesque source of inspiration. In the *Vespers* he had accomplished, more tidily than in the *Crusades* trilogy, the writing of a self-contained, shapely epic; and epic, Steven firmly believed, was 'a form of history', 'more than just an old historical novel'.

In 1961 Steven was delighted to be asked by Cambridge University Press to write a short book on the last stand of Constantinople in 1453, to be delivered by the end of the next year. His sixtieth birthday in July 1963, however, found him still at work on it, and he surrendered the manuscript only the year after that. It was not a heavy book, nor in terms of content an especially original one, but it was nonetheless the product of considerable artistry. Not long after the appearance in June 1965 of *The Fall of Constantinople 1453* Steven could boast with suavity: 'To my surprise (and to my publishers' – they were tactless enough to tell me so!) it has been on the London best-seller list for 3 weeks – only beaten by a book written by one of the Beatles!' (This was John Lennon's second free-association story collection, *A Spaniard in the Works*.) Steven's extended actual residence at Istanbul during the war had been an affecting experience, though an ambiguous one. But in his 1965 threnody to the Byzantine capital, he distilled the best of what he knew of Istanbul's modern, as well as Constantinople's medieval, shortcomings, disillusionments and discomforts, and rendered them into some of his most evocative, calculatedly judged passages and sentences.

After the publication of the third volume of the *Crusades* trilogy in 1954, Steven felt that only one reader, the Greek poet George Seferis, had even recognized one of his principal stylistic objectives, let alone proved fit to judge it: 'What gave me real pleasure were your words about the rhythm of my style. It is my ambition to get the rhythm of the prose right at the significant points . . . it is so difficult to know if one has succeeded, especially as it is a thing that critics never seem to notice, or at least never mention.' Steven's perambulatory exercises in mental composition were greatly assisted by a reader of taste, with a poet's perceptive ear, whatever the geographical and linguistic gulf between Steven and Seferis, though that gulf was real.* Seferis admired Steven's lecture to the Royal Society of Literature in 1962 because 'it is the first of your papers that I see with so much personal touch in it.' On receipt of the offprint of Steven's 1966 lecture at Athens, 'Byzantine Art and Western Medieval Taste', Seferis commented: 'What a splendid writer you are. I was going to say: apart from the historian; but this of course is not right. All your qualities, including the honesty and the precision of the historian, contribute in making this freshness, which always attracts me.' This later lecture, too, had a strong element of personal idiosyncrasy, containing as it did Steven's beloved anecdote about Lady Ottoline Morrell, Yeats, gold, beauty and the envious Sturge Moore.

Seferis's influence upon Steven would appear, then, to have acted as a liberating, almost candid tendency when it came to Steven's substance and the individuality of his argument, while the poet encouraged Steven's consistent inward preference for a sonorous, plain but rhetorical style. *The Fall of Constantinople 1453* remains popular with a wide lay readership because it calls a tangible and vulnerable world into being. The atmosphere of the book's most visual sketches depends upon a combination of well-excerpted details provided by a startling medley of far-ranging travellers and well-positioned witnesses, and, more unusually, a shrewd and collusive deployment of the second person, in an almost direct address to the reader's senses:

> In many districts you would have thought that you were in the open countryside, with wild roses blooming in the hedgerows in spring and nightingales singing in the copses.

> ... Nearby the Hippodrome was crumbling; the young men of the nobility used the arena as a polo-ground ...

---

* Steven's spoken modern Greek was never as good as he liked to imply, and 'so demotic as to be ungrammatical' when written (SR to Nikos Stangos, 9 October 1993, Firestone Library, Princeton), while Seferis's written English was clear and individual rather than correct in its charm. Yet theirs was a friendship that came to be conducted largely, and after the advent of the Colonels' regime entirely, on paper (in English).

... You might still see richly clad lords and ladies riding or carried in litters through the city ...

This evocation both of the look and the feeling of the city's last days is also assisted by an unembarrassed plunge towards poetic assonance. 'The splendid civilization of Byzantium had already played its part in civilizing the world, and it was now dying with the dying city.' This is not altogether, in substance, what Runciman goes on to argue – he is fresher and more forceful when he points out that Byzantine learning, art and philosophy were never more brilliant, sophisticated and influential than during the Empire's political death-throes. But he has not resisted the balance of the sentence, and its sentiment, at least, rings true. Runciman is on firmer ground when he dwells in an identically structured phrase on the *Golden Bough*-like identification of the last Emperor with his city, and their studiedly impressive mutual downfall. Constantine XII, the last reigning Palaeologus, is called 'fallen with his fallen city', his body lost to a soldier's common grave, 'with the Empire as his winding-sheet'.

That is the grand culmination of Runciman's openly artistic and narrative shape: 'In this story the Greek people is the tragic hero.' But the action begins far away from the city, unusually for this historian, in Britain, the England of Henry IV, with Shakespeare's wearied usurper waiting at his palace of Eltham upon 'a distinguished guest', one who 'for all his high titles ... had come as a beggar'. This is Manuel II, 'lawful heir of Augustus and of Constantine', 'Emperor of the Greeks, as most Westerners called him, though some remembered that he was the true Emperor of the Romans', a wise, realistic, scholarly man, father of the doomed eleventh and last Constantine of the city's fall. Although *The Fall of Constantinople* is a book that undisputedly belongs to its eponymous city, Runciman's handling of such distant corners of the wider scene as his own homeland is not diminished, rushed or overshadowed as a result. His rare excursion into late medieval England is illuminated by the skilfully extracted voice of Adam of Usk, a lawyer in Lancastrian service and a commentator who, like Runciman himself, operates through historical and geographical reach of imagination: 'I reflected how grievous it was that this great Christian prince should be driven by the Saracens from the furthest East to these furthest Western isles to seek aid against them ... O God, what dost thou now, ancient glory of Rome?' Runciman was always conscious of his own origin and perspective from those far Western isles, and exploited the humorous, ironical advantage of detachment they lent him.*

In *The Sicilian Vespers*, written almost a decade before *The Fall of Constantinople*, Runciman had taken a half-forgotten, obscure, regional-sounding narrative and represented it instead as the central tragic spiral of high medieval Europe, of the Holy Roman Empire and the Papacy. In the preface to this later book, similar in its style, structure, remit and dimensions, he takes the opposite course, with a fresh purpose in mind. He writes in the knowledge that his readership has at least heard of the fall of the great Imperial city, and probably ascribes to it some epochal significance: 'In the days when historians were simple folk ... 1453 was held to mark the close of the Middle Ages.' But Runciman sets about thoroughly to undermine this expectation:

> The stream of history flows on relentlessly and there is never a barrier across it ... Long before 1453 the movement that is called the Renaissance was under way ... The Ottoman conquest of Egypt was more disastrous to Venice than the Ottoman conquest of Constantinople ... the tragedy in no way changed [Western] policy, or rather lack of policy ... in the wide political field the fall of Constantinople changed very little.

With the *Vespers* Runciman had been concerned to show the continuing reverberations of a conflict that sounded marginal; but by

---

* In *The Fall of Constantinople* Runciman's 'domestic' perspective manifests itself a few more times after his brief treatment of the Lancastrian court. He mentions in passing the 'saintly but half-imbecile' Henry VI, the founder of Steven's old school, along with the even more distant King of Scotland; he has a theory that the Emperor Constantine's chief engineer, hitherto identified as a German, was a Scotsman named John Grant; and most rewardingly he quotes the King of Georgia's impression of the British Isles: 'His Majesty went on to say there is no accounting for the habits of different races. After all, in Britain, he pointed out, one woman often has several husbands ... ' (SR, *The Fall of Constantinople 1453* (Cambridge University Press, 1965), p. 62, 54).

protesting that the end of Constantinople *was* genuinely marginal, he could liberate its story from generalizations of culture or of period, and illustrate it in its specific circumstances, as 'vitally important' for 'two peoples', the Turks and the Greeks. In so doing he could begin to lay out a theory of Greekness that was after all truly novel, as well as personal, and quite of a pattern with the directions in which Seferis had, sometimes consciously, sometimes implicitly and sometimes all unwitting, led him to develop.

While still at work on the *Crusades* – whose telling in his hands pointed so unwaveringly and convincingly towards Byzantium – Steven had produced several slight but original contributions to Byzantine study. One of the most peculiarly characteristic of these products of the early 1950s was a lecture he delivered at Thessalonica in 1951, on the concept of Hellenism in fourteenth- and fifteenth-century Byzantium under the Palaeologi. It was a subject well chosen for an audience in modern Greece's second city, without the fame of Athens or Istanbul but in some regards better preserved, and with a proud and odd history of its own. Steven – who had often previously stressed, and would do again, the value and vigour of Byzantine civilization independent from classical antiquity – now appeared to modify that position:

> The history of Byzantine civilization is to a large extent the history of a series of Classical revivals. Of these revivals the most remarkable is that of the era of the Palaeologi [1261–1453] ... it was self-conscious ... and inspired less from Constantinople than from the great provincial city of Thessalonica. It appeared in many forms: in art, where there was an extraordinary strengthening of the humanistic element, which threatened to displace the intrinsic mysticism of the Byzantine artistic vision ... even in politics, where the idea of the old Greek city-state was recalled to mind ...

Steven saw this evolution of self-aware cultural Greekness, this consciousness of 'Hellenic blood and tradition', as gathering particular intensity in 'the last decades of the Empire'.

Steven now posited that 'The history of the last century of Byzantium was occupied by one main party struggle, which took various forms ... but which was fundamentally a struggle between East and

West.' His next bold, and unprecedented, step was to aver that 'The advocates of Hellenism ... represent the party that leaned to the West.' An emerging sense of Greek nationality, as opposed to 'Roman' citizenship of the Empire, was born, Steven suggested to his sympathetic Thessalonian hearers, out of an ultimately defeated but intellectually vital political persuasion. He would put it more rhetorically in *The Fall of Constantinople*: 'To the humanists ... working eagerly and devotedly in Italy to obtain help for their compatriots, the atmosphere at Constantinople seemed strange and foolish and narrow. They were convinced that union with the West would bring such new cultural and political vigour that Byzantium could yet rise again. Who can say if they were wrong?'

In fact he had all but declared them wrong himself, in this Thessalonica lecture fourteen years earlier. There he refers to the fall of Constantinople as 'that epic story, which typifies the wild instinctive courage of the Greeks in the face of an invader'. This was a flattering reference to the martial valour of Greece, the British Empire's only combatant ally in the Second World War for the year between the fall of France and Greece's own capitulation, after a far more prolonged struggle. Steven's praise also alludes to his own detailed, personal knowledge of the Greek Civil War obtained while working for the British Council, a conflict whose outcome he regarded as a national victory over alien Russian and Yugoslav interests. But Steven also invokes a form of national characterization, generalization, even somewhat narrow romanticism, of which he was usually more wary. It was philhellenism for public consumption. But, more fortunately, it was wedded to a subtle and hitherto untold interpretation, of how Byzantines (or Thessalonians) had quite deliberately set out to present themselves as Hellenes, or Greeks, to attract a practical Western alliance.

> Hellas meant something by now to Western Europe. The Renaissance, helped on by Byzantine scholars, had taught Westerners to appreciate ancient Greek civilization; and those Byzantines who emphasized their own Hellenism could thereby win sympathy in the West and hope for concrete help. The West might not intervene to save Byzantium, but it would feel an obligation to save Hellas.

There was much to be said for this point of view. Hellas was essentially part of Europe, and the centre of European civilisation was moving westward. But there would be a price to pay . . .

The price Steven referred to was, specifically, the fifteenth-century experiment with Church union between Rome and Constantinople attempted by the last Palaeologan Emperors; but, in the longer term, the question of whether Greek nationalism and the cultural legacy of the Orthodox Church were truly consistent with each other.

In his final, Athonite interview, Steven was to opine that Orthodoxy was the most resilient form of Christianity because 'it offers a very nice solution to the problem of the unity of peoples . . . it doesn't display ethnicism. And it allows for much wider and freer opinions than the Roman Catholic Church.' This argument that Orthodoxy attracts and endures because of its universality, its ecumenism and the tolerance entailed in the principle of Economy, rather than because of any specific national rallying culture, whether Greek or Slavonic, overlaps precisely with what Seferis once wrote approvingly of the *Crusades* trilogy in an unpublished review (translated from his Greek): 'the primary significance that Runciman's work has, for me at least, is that it is written by a Byzantine, an imperial Byzantine, not a national Byzantine.' In the Thessalonica lecture, Steven makes this wider implication of his allegiance to Greekness above Greece itself with reference to another great modern Greek poet: 'The Greek world, as the poet Kafavis [Cavafy] saw, is something bigger than the land of Greece, something wider than Hellas, for all the glories of the Hellene name.' This wider Greekness included the appeal of Orthodoxy, but was not exclusively bound up with it. It had historical, geographical and even political significance, connected to the Greek legacy in Asia Minor and the Levant, in the south of Italy and in Sicily, even in Cavafy's Egypt. It was 'the old, lay Christian empire', and *The Fall of Constantinople* is the story of how it passed from a doomed worldly remnant to a potent memory and dream.

Runciman proposed that 'in its last decades Constantinople was consciously a Greek city'. He caught that city's final temper by means of his narrative's acute visual detail and clear temporal evolution. *The Fall of Constantinople* is briskly chronological. The action begins one Christmas and ends in high summer; it is framed, like a series of medieval tapestries, or perhaps Byzantine mosaics, by panoramas of the city, its gardens and its seasons. The reader is shown an Easter of great natural beauty and unusual joylessness among the faithful: 'In the orchards throughout the city, the fruit-trees were bursting into flower. The nightingales were returning to sing in the copses . . . the storks to build their nests on the rooftops. The sky was streaked with long lines of migratory birds flying to their summer homes away in the north. But Thrace was rumbling with the sounds of a great army on the move . . . ' Even the logistical difficulties of the ensuing siege serve to colour the portrait – 'the gardens in the city produced little at that season, and fishing boats could no longer put out safely to sea . . . ' Later Runciman quite deliberately integrates the dimming of the light in quicker-gathering dusks with the defenders' diminishing morale, in a chapter simply entitled 'Fading Hope'. In describing the ever more disheartening omens witnessed in the beleaguered city, he alludes to an episode in Plutarch and in Shakespeare's *Antony and Cleopatra*, transformed into a famous poem by Cavafy:

> Next day . . . the whole city was blotted out by a thick fog, a phenom-enon unknown in those lands in the month of May. The Divine Presence was veiling itself in cloud, to conceal its departure from the city. That night, when the fog had lifted, it was noticed that a strange light played about the dome of the great Church of the Holy Wisdom . . . Lights, too, could be seen from the walls, glimmering in the distant country-side beyond the Turkish camp, where no lights should be . . . The strange lights were never explained.

Runciman himself certainly does not explain them, but he com-bines his powers of concrete observation and his far-seeing awareness of the poetic mood, both in high literary and more demotic and trad-itional forms. He shows the practical impact on the despairing Christians of the unusual weather for the time of year, but he also means to leave a resonance, for readers alive to it, both of fairy-lights and of the god Hercules abandoning Antony, 'the exquisite music of that strange procession'. Time continues to pass and the historian's eye still does not neglect the useful barometer of the garden-city's greenness. 'The month of May was drawing to a close, and in the gardens and the hedgerows the roses were now in bloom. But the moon was waning.' The last of these enframed visions comes after the city's sack, 'half in ruins, emptied and deserted and blackened as though by fire, and strangely silent'.

In his preface Runciman had recast the 1453 capture of Constantinople; from its traditional significance as a mark of the end of the medieval era, it became the creation myth of 'two peoples', the modern Greeks and the Turks. This argument involved showing that the two nations, both dear to Steven even if Greece might fairly be called a little dearer, had more in common with each other than either might quite expect. Mehmet the Conqueror had ostentatiously taken the ancient Imperial capital for Islam, not just for his Empire, and he had faced a disparate, painstakingly assembled collection of Venetian, Genoese and Greek Christians, with other miscellaneous mercenaries and volunteers, united in a religious cause. But Runciman emphasized at every opportunity that the true picture was more ambiguous than the narrative of one empire and faith overcoming another might imply. His method in so doing was intricately personal.

'A frontier divides,' Steven, that child of the Border, declared during a lecture at the University of Peshawar, in the historic frontier country of north-west Pakistan, given in 1965, the same year that *The Fall of Constantinople* was published, 'but in a curious way, it also unites.' Accordingly, he places much significance upon the cultural interplay on the Anatolian border, between the lawless Byzantine border barons, or *akritai*, and the Turkish *ghazi*, nomadic warriors theoretically fighting to expand the borders of Islam. 'But', Steven insists, ' . . . none of them took religion seriously. Christian lords would become Muslim and Muslim lords Christian, heretics of either faith would join the Orthodox branch, with remarkable lack of conscience if it seemed suitable politically.'

It is amid this fluidity, both religious and military, of the *ghazi* that Runciman locates in *The Fall of Constantinople* the true beginnings of the Ottoman dynasty, speculating that they descended not from established tribal royalty but from 'an able *ghazi* commander of unknown origin'. But at the same time he is careful to display the more illustrious and convenient connections advertised by Mehmet II, the Conquering Sultan of Constantinople, who 'sought to impress both his Turkish and his Greek subjects by supporting a theory that his family was descended from the imperial house of Comnenus'. In fact Mehmet, Runciman shows, was the son of a Turkish slave-girl whom 'later legend, not entirely discouraged by Mehmet himself, transformed into a high-born Frankish lady'. Crucially in Runciman's version Mehmet was looked down upon by his father, Sultan Murad II, for his relatively obscure and Turkic heritage and his consequently neglected education. The last few Ottoman Sultans before Mehmet had tended to have Greeks as both their mothers and their favoured wives, paragons of the harem with names such as Nilufer (Water-lily) or Gulchichek (Rose-flower). Even Mehmet the Conqueror was thus, through the mothers on his paternal side, at least a quarter Greek by blood, and, in Runciman's view, felt towards Greek learning and standards of beauty a complicated, emulous attraction.

Although he professed to find his Turkish sources by and large 'peculiarly disappointing', Runciman is able to build up a convincing and detailed counterpart to his portrait of the Christian defence in his description of the Sultan's court and camp. As in the case of the rift among the Greeks, between those 'Hellenes' who accepted Church union and the devout and politically pessimistic medley who held firm to uncompromising Orthodoxy, Runciman identified yet another party struggle. On the one hand there were 'Moslems of the old school', the court officials associated with the former Sultan Murad II, 'a man of peace by temperament' who 'longed to retire to lead a life of meditation'. The outstanding example of these tolerant, old-fashioned statesmen was Halil Pasha, Murad's 'old and trusted friend' and his son's Grand Vizier. Halil 'had always been a kindly friend to the Christians', and may or may not have actually been 'a pensioner of the Greeks'; in any case he was a familiar type, often encountered during Steven's own far-flung wanderings: 'even the most highly revered of Oriental statesmen are apt to be fond of receiving gifts.' Opposed to this experienced, faintly Walter Runcimanesque, character, with his tolerance for exterior Christian enemies and his distaste for internal Islamic heretics, Runciman depicted an unsavoury collection of 'upstart renegades'. These advisers, men such as Zaganos and Mahmud Pasha, were younger and more bellicose. They included a disciple of a heretical Persian dervish, and a strategically gifted eunuch; they were personally closer to the twenty-one-year-old Sultan and, most notably, were almost all of them recent 'aggressive converts to Islam', of Greek or Slav extraction, 'without vested interests and wholly dependent on the Sultan's favour'.

This characterization was typical of Steven's generally jaundiced view of converts throughout his life, especially those to Catholicism. Here Runciman even ends up proposing an ingenious connection, at least of sympathy and possibly of actual intrigue, between the political moderates on both sides; he suggests that Mehmet's eventual execution of Halil related to the similarly timed killing of the Emperor Constantine's former chief minister Lucas Notaras: 'Notaras sent [Halil] bribes: money hidden inside a fish. They were certainly on good terms with each other.' The traditional account is that Notaras was put to death when he refused to let his son be sent to the Sultan as a catamite, so this argument represents a relatively rare instance of Runciman privileging political likelihood above even the most enticing gossip.

On the walls, in the camp and in the fleets, still more than in the Emperor and the Sultan's councils, Runciman showed matters to be more nuanced than the clash of the 'two peoples', Greek and Turk, might imply. Quite apart from the Greeks divided along theological lines, and the intensely rivalrous allied contingents from the sea-republics of Genoa and Venice, who detested each other even more than they distrusted their hosts, part of the defence of Constantinople was actually made up of Turks, the retinue of an exiled Ottoman prince and hostage, Orhan. Knowing what his fate would be if he fell into his cousin the Sultan's hands, Orhan fought with great bravery before attempting to flee the city's fall in the guise of a Greek monk, 'hoping that his perfect knowledge of Greek might save him from suspicion'. (It did not.) As for the Sultan's army, its leading gunsmith, Urban, deviser of a monstrous cannon that could fire only seven times a day, to infernal effect, was a Hungarian Catholic, while Runciman gives the besiegers' notorious irregulars a sketch that fully illuminates their colourfulness: 'the Bashi-bazouks ... many thousands of them, adventurers from every country and race, many of them Turks but many more from Christian countries, Slavs, Hungarians, Germans, Italians and even Greeks, all of them ready enough to fight against their fellow-Christians in view of the pay that the Sultan gave them and the booty that he promised'. The defence's numerically vastly outnumbered naval arm had remarkable success against the Sultan's fleet during the siege's first weeks; Runciman points out that very few of the Ottoman sailors were Turkish, or even Muslim, and that their morale was readily sapped by a fierce resistance.

The spirits of the besiegers as well as the defenders, indeed, form a mechanism of taut suspense throughout Runciman's narrative. Despite the deep shadow of the book's title, nothing seems inevitable. So many variables are ushered into play, and yet, Runciman does not quail from repeating, 'little would have changed in the long run':

> If Sultan Mehmet had been less determined or Halil Pasha more persuasive . . . if the Venetian armada had set sail a fortnight earlier, or, at the last crisis, had . . . the postern-gate of the Kerkoporta not been left ajar . . . Byzantium might have lingered on by another decade.

Runciman has no patience with the traditional, Gibbonian assumption of any connection between the fall of the city and the Italian Renaissance; and in several subsequent books he would return to the detail of how Greek scholarship flourished at home and percolated to Europe long before 1453. Once again his most forcible counter-argument is personal: 'of the two great intellectual figures amongst the Greeks . . . Bessarion was already in Italy and Gennadius remained on at Constantinople.' In an entertainingly damning and comprehensive pursuit of the last exiled Palaeologi, he makes use of the same dichotomy: 'Mehmet Pasha [a convert, né Andrew Palaeologus] in Constantinople and the feckless Constantine in Rome'. The symbolism appears to be clear – submission to the *Tourkokratia* or dilution into the Catholic West in its cultural pomp was, for a time, to be Greece's fate: 'the end of an old song', as Runciman has it, another Scotticism serving as a lament for Byzantium.

Although an immediate popular success, *The Fall of Constantinople* attracted at first a mixed reception from professional historians. Hugh Trevor-Roper, still Regius Professor at Oxford, usually as stalwart an ally in public as he was pedantically competitive in private, did not see how an imperial remnant so plunged into decadence as Byzantium merited an elegy, and felt inclined to welcome the advent of the Ottomans. John W. Barker of Wisconsin University was disarmed by Runciman's admission, one of unusually genuine modesty, in his preface that Sir Edwin Pears's 1903 work, *The Destruction of the Greek Empire*, 'remains the best account of the events of 1453' – but he was inclined to agree with it, calling *The Fall of Constantinople* by comparison with Pears 'a seriously flawed book'. Eminent admirers, however, soon emerged; oddly enough, two of the most notable were Roman Catholic clergy.

Gervase Mathew was a Dominican friar as well as an expert on Byzantine art and one of the so-called 'Inklings' around C. S. Lewis, J. R. R. Tolkien and Charles Williams. He had known Steven for decades; they sometimes disagreed on academic questions but shared a mischievous scepticism about Maurice Bowra.* On the strength of *The Fall of Constantinople*, Father Mathew now hailed Runciman as 'the greatest of living historians; in an age of miniaturists he retains the power to paint on a wide canvas but he does so with a miniaturist skill and precision of detail; his only parallel is Dom David Knowles.'

David Knowles, a quasi-disaffected Benedictine monk, was a medievalist of exceptional quality with a knotty, conflicted character. When asked whom *he* considered the greatest living British historian, Steven consistently and unhesitatingly named Knowles. While Mathew praised Runciman to the heavens but went on to dissent interestingly from the burden of his latest book (Mathew had a greater romantic certainty that Byzantium could and should have lasted for at least another generation), Knowles accepted that Runciman 'shows, perhaps more clearly than any previous English writer, that the final catastrophe was inevitable'. Knowles was alive to the influence of his and Runciman's own times on the tense structure and sombre parables of the book: 'as we read of the promises, the debates, the haverings and the final delays and refusals in the western countries, our old wounds of the past sixty years feel the chill of winter.' Himself a passionate and urgent stylist, Knowles produces a

---

* There is an unconfirmed story in circulation that Steven and Father Mathew once corrupted a Wadham scout to acquire some of Bowra's nail-clippings, for the purposes of placing a demoniac curse upon him.

depiction of Runciman's prose at its most compelling in *The Fall of Constantinople* that goes beyond even Seferis in accurate insight: 'For almost half his short book Sir Steven moves slowly through the last century of Byzantine history. Then, for some sixty pages, his narrative breaks into flame. There is no over-writing, no purple patch, but the reader is held.'

For all his professional respect for Knowles, it was another response to *The Fall of Constantinople* that Steven professed to appreciate most of all. Late in the 1950s, at one of the composer Samuel Barber's dinners in New York, he had encountered the youthful, bumptious and rich jack-of-all-letters Gore Vidal. Vidal recalled that he parlayed through his introductory conversation with Steven 'on equal terms', with reference to *The Crusades*, the 1935 Cecil B. DeMille screen epic in which Saladin kidnaps Richard the Lionheart's queen, Berengaria. By 1965 Vidal regarded himself as much more historically aware, having the previous year published an historical novel, *Julian*, that drew enthusiastically on primary material from early Byzantium. He declared in a piece for the *Reporter* that *The Fall of Constantinople* had convinced him of the best historical writing's quality and necessity:

> To read an historian like Sir Steven is to be reminded that history is a literary art quite equal to that of the novel. The historian must be a master not only of general narrative but of particular detail. He must understand human character. He must be able to describe physical action, a difficult task for any writer . . . he must be, in the best sense, a moralist.
>
> Yet today the historian is not accorded the same artistic rank as the 'serious' novelist. I suspect that much of this is due to the high value we place on 'creativity', a vague activity that somehow has got mixed up with the idea of procreation.
>
> . . . But the art of a Runciman is certainly as creative as the art of the sort of novelist who tells us how his wife betrayed him with his best friend last summer.
>
> . . . I consider it a sad commentary on our period that in the literary arts we tend to prefer gossip to analysis, personality to character, 'creative writing' even at its worst to historical writing at its best.

Vidal was being, as usual, unnecessarily provocative. After years blacklisted by the *New York Times* because of the candidly homosexual and evidently autobiographical theme of his third novel, *The City and the Pillar*, he must have derived particular satisfaction from standing alongside Runciman against the 'procreative' norm; but he himself had certainly written the kind of novel he condemns here. Steven would not have seriously accepted many of the conflicts Vidal stirs up, such as the implausibly puritanical opposition of 'gossip to analysis'.

Besides, like Mathew, Vidal occasionally appeared to admire a different book from the one Runciman had actually written. He enters the breach to defend Runciman against his sometime ally Trevor-Roper with a peculiar if memorable analogy:

> in nature there can be no action without reaction. This law also appears to hold true in human nature ... Evoke once too often a vision of golden youths listening to wise old men in the green shade of Academe and someone will snarl that those Athenian youths were a dreary lot taught by self-serving proto-fascists of whom Plato was the worst. Depict Byzantium as the last custodian of the Greek heritage, destroyed by barbarous Turks, and Professor H. Trevor-Roper will promptly ask the readers of the New Statesman: 'As a living political system was the Byzantine Empire, at least in its decline, really better than the Ottoman Empire in its heyday?'

This comparison involves exactly the sort of post-Wildean sentimentality about classical Greece that Steven deplored; Vidal's description of the Platonists as a 'dreary lot' of 'self-serving proto-fascists' could easily have come from Runciman, who had described Plato's great fifteenth-century Byzantine disciple Plethon as advocating a 'national socialist dictatorship'. Vidal thinks Runciman persuades his reader of 'the traditional view that the fall of the city was indeed a great and significant event, and not merely a minor happening in some vast cyclic drama'. This is precisely the tradition that Runciman spends a great deal of space revising, refining and playing down.

Despite these oddities Steven told Anthony Bryer, a younger Byzantinist and the child of wartime friends, that he thought Vidal was on this occasion 'his most perceptive reviewer', not just of *The Fall of*

*Constantinople* but of any of his work. In part this was a teasing declaration that Steven was proud to stand well beyond the academy and
ally himself with Vidal's high-camp grandeur, just as Evelyn Waugh's
Catholic tribalism would lead him to insist that *Helena* was his greatest novel. But Steven also recognized that Vidal had, in his
self-promoting, associative, interested way, seen him much as he
wished to be seen. Vidal draws a line between Steven and a later
school of historians who fell short of his high standards:

> historians, not content with telling what happened, now reveal exactly
> why it happened, ordering events in history in such a way as to fit
> some overall and to them entirely satisfying theory of history. Along-
> side the publicists and grand designers, Sir Steven looks to be curiously
> demure. He tells his story plain. Since God has not revealed any master
> plan to him, he does not feel impelled to preach 'truth' to us. He does
> make judgments but only after he has made his case. He likes a fact
> and distrusts a theory. He is always pleasurable to read . . .

Some of these observations are shrewd – Runciman's chaste or
'demure' turn of phrase, his lack of metaphor or purple indulgence
(as noted by Knowles), itself an effective colour in the end, is his most
deliberate tool. But much of Vidal's eulogy is naive. Runciman did
not lack a theory, a plan, a sermon or a verdict; instead those he implicitly offered were highly congenial to Vidal. Steven would have been
amused as well as pleased by Vidal's chivalrous intervention, though he
still had more in common with the sharp-quilled Trevor-Roper, the
ferociously impressive Knowles and above all Seferis, with his mournful, contradictory patriotism and his liberal historical conscience.

# 21

# The Fool

*The White Rajahs (written 1957–60, published 1960); Sarawak 1957, 1959; California, Los Angeles, 1957–8; the Philippines, Manila, 1957; Pakistan, Lahore, 1957–8; Australia, Tasmania, Sydney, 1959*

> His countenance is full of intelligence and expectant dream. He has a rose in one hand and in the other a costly wand, from which depends over his right shoulder a wallet curiously embroidered. He is a prince of the other world on his travels through this one . . . He is the spirit in search of experience.
>
> Arthur Waite, *The Key to the Tarot*, 1920

> An historian dealing with characters long dead may legitimately assign motives, speculate on rumours and even indulge in a little scandal-mongering. It is neither courteous nor helpful nor wise for him to do so when he is dealing with the fringes of the present.
>
> Steven Runciman, *The White Rajahs*, 1960

Late in 1956, while still researching and writing *The Sicilian Vespers*, Steven accepted the most outlandish commission of his literary career. Sir Anthony Abell, Governor of Sarawak, was a man burdened with the nightmarish responsibility of ruling a brand-new Crown Colony in a post-colonial world. Sarawak had for a century after 1841 been under the rule of independent British adventurers, the 'White Rajahs' of the Brooke dynasty. Over the years several attempts by the Brookes to bestow the territory upon Britain had been rebuffed by an indifferent, even embarrassed, Foreign Office. But the third Rajah's fickle experiments with constitutional monarchy, combined with the impact of Japanese occupation during the Second World War, made Sarawak's cession to Britain overwhelmingly desirable, both to post-war Britain and to the Rajah, Vyner Brooke. The move was resisted, however, by the Rajah's nephew and heir pre-sumptive, Anthony Brooke, with the support of a sizeable proportion both of Sarawak's official class and of its population, especially the comparatively rich, content and confident Muslim Malays. It would not be entirely misleading to compare the predicament of the twentieth-century Sarawakians to that of the thirteenth-century Sicilians.

In any case, Sarawak's union with the British Empire – at a time when most colonies were already headed in the opposite direction – was effected, after a bitingly narrow vote of the Kingdom's Council, in 1946. Two and a half years later, the new Crown Colony's second Governor, Duncan Stewart, was greeted on arrival by a young Malay apparently eager to take a photograph, then stabbed to death by an accomplice. The assassins, who were thought to be sympathetic to the return of the Brookes, dealt a fatal propaganda blow to the anti-cessionist cause. In fact the Foreign Office was covering up a far less convenient motive: the seventeen-year-old attackers were anti-colonialists acting on behalf of neighbouring Indonesia, itself newly independent from the Netherlands. This was the unenviable landscape to which Abell, described by his superior, Malcolm Mac-Donald, as having 'a genius for friendship [and a] capacity for fun, coupled with a sincere respect for native beliefs', was dispatched. It is in this context that his commission for Runciman to write the official history of Sarawak, from the Brooke acquisition to the controversial cession, should be viewed.

Steven accepted the job, out of curiosity and a desire for an unan-ticipated, exotic holiday. In his *Alphabet* he attributes to the shock of his mother's death his longing for a sudden and total change of scene. To Donald Nicol he wrote from Sarawak in the spring of 1957 that 'With Greece and now, the whole Middle East being more or less put out of bounds by the policy of our Government, I rather liked the idea of switching into fresh Far Eastern fields.' Steven alludes here to Anglo-Greek relations over Cyprus, where his friendship with Seferis had influenced him towards a philhellene line; and to the Suez Crisis, which had confirmed his existing, Liberal doubts about Anthony Eden, whom he and Hugh Trevor-Roper now ridiculed as 'that ineffectual Man of Blood'. It was to Marthe Bibesco that he revealed more of the positive excitement that Sarawak held for him, 'jungle-covered mountains floating on the sea . . . Borneo and the last strongholds of the British Raj . . . with the strange story of the White Rajahs of Sarawak, the Brookes, behind them . . . '.

As ever, it was the subject's landscape *and* portrait that attracted his notice. But this was not the whole story. Though intensely relieved at his escape from the British Council, Steven still felt the appeal of public service, especially when mingled with pleasure. He was leaving for an official task that he intended conscientiously to fulfil. The closest comparison is to his last trip to the same region, his tour of the Far Eastern archipelago just before the Second World War, filing articles for *The Times*, sending confidential letters back to his father and the Chamberlain Cabinet, all the while offering his occasional lover Eddie Bates a means of escape from public exposure *and*, last and far from least, satisfying his own wish to see a new part of the world.

The more pertinent question is not why Steven accepted Abell's offer, but why Abell should have chosen a famous exponent of narrative medieval history, expert in Eastern Europe and the Mediterranean, to investigate the recent history of a Far Eastern colonial possession. Steven felt this incongruity and was apprehensive about his qualifications for the role. 'I never wanted to be commissioned to write a book, and I wondered whether I would be efficient or happy in dealing with modern history.' The job would also involve more archival scrabbling than his usual, grandly intuitive engagements with published sources, even some interviews with living persons. On reflection he decided that the change of locale would be refreshing, while the story of Sarawak would not be altogether unfamiliar. 'From what I already knew about them, the Rajahs were not dissimilar to the Crusader knights . . . while the Ranees showed a kinship to some of the more colourful Empresses of Byzantium.'

In fact the explanation of Steven's selection was entirely personal. The Governor's Director of Information, Philip Jones, was a friend, and put Steven's name forward, since there was doubt 'whether a hack Colonial Office historian would do justice to a government with which the Office had usually been on unfriendly terms'. It was a case of Michael Grant-style patronage all over again. Jones had been deeply affected as a young man when his best friend, John Philips, was killed by pirates in China in May 1926, not long after Steven's own adventures there. A solicitor before the war, Jones emerged from it, by way of the Ministry of Information and the RAF, as a diplomat; after the independence of Sarawak he was to be ordained as a clergyman. Photographs suggest an ungainly, somewhat diffident figure, but a later friend and younger protégé of Jones's, Gordon Gardiner, remembers his striking good looks and charm. As Steven wrote after Jones's death in 1983: 'He was a wonderfully loyal friend, with the great gift of making one feel good and kind and valuable (none of which I am.) He could be a bit foolish as times, due to a vulnerable sensitivity, but he was very good himself and very kind, and unique. And I am grateful to him for having brought into my life some of my dearest friends.' Jones's proposal that his distinguished historian friend should take on Sarawak did not, however, go down well in various quarters of British society in the colony.

In his biography of Sir James Brooke, the first Brooke Rajah of Sarawak, Nigel Barley states that it was 'seriously suggested in 1960 that the choice of Sir Steven Runciman to compile an official history of Sarawak, including a life of Sir James Brooke, was compromised by the writer's own alleged homosexuality'. This complaint apparently originated from 'some of the ladies of the Sarawak Association', the London-based body for old Sarawak hands and their families. James Brooke never married, had courtly friendships with women but seems to have been more passionately affected by certain among his many youthful, adventurous male protégés. The first Rajah's most ardent admirers now worried that the predilections of the historian might somehow infect the reputation of his subject.

A related objection to Runciman's selection was expressed in more trenchant form by one of Sarawak's most important, best-informed and most remarkable inhabitants, Major Tom Harrisson, Curator of the Sarawak Museum. Harrisson, a highly skilled ornithologist, had, prior to the war, founded with Humphrey Jennings the Mass Observation project to survey the British population, applying experience he had gained while carrying out a census of the Great Crested Grebe. During the war he had distinguished himself in guerrilla exploits against the Japanese, and had become the paramount British expert on the intricacies of Sarawak's jungle, fauna and tribal customs. 'He was not an easy man,' Steven would recall with deliberate understatement. Harrisson held himself aloof, kept his colleagues to his own exceptional standards and veered between chilly detachment and choleric roaring. His pathologically orderly cast of mind might well today be associated with Asperger's Syndrome; he subscribed to a coarser, less qualified form of snobbery than Steven; and his recreations lay in the bottle. He was acquainted slightly with Steven; his son's godfather was Admiral Sir Charles Lambe, First Sea Lord, and Steven's favourite maternal cousin. When Harrisson heard that Abell had approved Steven to write the Sarawak history, he was already far gone at his favourite oasis, the Aurora Bar, Kuching. He apparently hectored its other patrons, 'as part of a long diatribe', demanding to know 'Why, of all people, they should have chosen that mincing little queen!'*

Harrisson's biographer argues that 'Tom's real objection to Runciman was not the historian's sexual orientation but his unfamiliarity with the terrain.' Certainly Harrisson later came round, somewhat grudgingly, proving both helpful and judicious. But Steven was evidently perceived at first as an unqualified outsider imposed by 'the Homintern', as represented by Philip Jones.†

On his first trip out to Sarawak, Steven chose to journey by way of Hollywood, where he was to be the guest of the film director George Cukor, and the Philippines, at the urging of their London ambassadorial couple. The Hollywood adventure had a curious background. In early 1955 Steven had received through a mutual friend a summons to meet George Cukor at the Savoy; Mr Cukor, the intermediary explained, was interested in recruiting Steven as Artistic Adviser for an MGM film called *The Female*. Steven joked that he 'felt greatly flattered to be considered a specialist on such an important subject'

---

* It does seem odd that Harrisson, who had met Steven, should describe his tall, bony, slightly stooped frame as 'little'.
† After he had witnessed Jones at work in Sarawak over three visits, Steven judged that his friend was thought to be 'a bit of an old maid, and rather mocked at by the Europeans, but loved by the natives' (SR to RR, 1 February 1959, Elshieshields).

till he 'remembered that there had appeared recently a book under that name which concerned the life of the great Byzantine Empress Theodora'.

Steven and Cukor's common acquaintance, the photographer George Hoyningen-Huene, patron and lover of Horst P. Horst, conducted the historian to the director's hotel suite for a dinner-party where Cukor 'received us in black silk pyjamas, which made me feel a trifle over-dressed'. In other respects, Cukor was a model of professionalism and formality. He explained that the role of the Empress was to be taken by Miss Ava Gardner. Constantinople was to be represented by old Rome; Steven would only have to spend some two or three months there dispensing his advice on set. Steven asked for a short while to think about an offer he was already quite determined to accept. He took great pleasure in consulting those among his friends and family most inclined to disapprove; cross, widowed Hilda, equally averse to empresses and actresses; Leslie, burdened with the family firm; and the most serious-minded of Steven's academic friends. As he had anticipated, the verdict was one of universal shock. It would be 'prostitution . . . My name would be associated with a vulgar and unhistorical production, and what reputation I had as a serious historian would be ruined forever.' Thus forearmed, Steven gave Cukor his cautious acceptance, downplaying his actual enthusiasm:

> I rather liked the idea. To be paid – and, I gathered, well-paid – to spend some months in Rome would not be disagreeable. I knew that the last thing wanted from an Advisor was that he should be about the place all the time advising. He should merely look in from time to time to correct any really blatant anachronism or . . . to insist on the leading lady having a hair-style proper to the period. So I said that I was not uninterested . . .

A year passed without Steven hearing any more. Then he was summoned back to the Savoy, where Cukor was now in despair. The problem lay with Ava Gardner and her innate Southern sense of taste. She refused to tarnish her good name by involvement with such a 'lousy' script. The historian, after all, had shown less scruple than the star (when Steven eventually read the proposed script he saw Miss Gardner's point).

A subordinate of Cukor's at Metro-Goldwyn-Mayer, Dora Levine Hovey, subsequently tried to lure Steven into the studio's employ as a scriptwriter for short historical films, intended to compete with the rising force of television. Steven accepted her self-extended invitation to tea with him, but was disdainful of her historical range; when he asked which famous figures interested her, she alluded vaguely to Joan of Arc and Elizabeth I, and 'I did not think that I could tell many stories just about those two ladies.' Already offended at being handed down to a film producer of lesser distinction, Steven's mood did not improve when he gathered that the budget of any such short films would be tight. To Cukor he wrote testily that 'I was not prepared . . . to have my lovely stories dressed in butter-muslin.' In reply Cukor proposed a fortnight's visit to Los Angeles in February 1957, which coincided happily with the first excursion necessary for the Sarawak commission.

George Cukor had been born in 1899 on 7 July, on the same date as both Steven and another mutual acquaintance, the Italian composer Gian Carlo Menotti. Cukor, a firm believer in astrology (if not well versed in Steven's more esoteric slant on the occult), claimed an innate and intuitive bond with his fellow Cancerians. In some ways the story of Cukor's achievements, his social world, his choices and habits bears some, perhaps star-entwined, comparison with the facts of Steven's own life; but, for all that, their characters, abilities, personal attributes and backgrounds were almost comically dissimilar. Steven was quietly spoken, his courtesy veined with an arch irony, aimed at the appreciation of deserving insiders. Cukor projected his power without compunction or, sometimes, control. Both men had tempers, but Steven's inclined to curtness in the presence of adversaries, or carefully aimed gossip in their absence, whereas Cukor's anger lashed its objects with passionate storms of coarseness. Both believed in high standards and elaborate codes of behaviour, but Steven kept sternly to his own rules; Cukor, in practice, objected only to vulgarity and obscenity in others.

In taking up Cukor's invitation, Steven could peer into a supremely old-fashioned and gleefully elitist social institution, a Hollywood equivalent to the circles in which Steven already moved at home. Since the mid-1930s, Cukor and his set had represented the apex of Hollywood salon existence. Cukor attracted both foreign visitors and local legends; his biographer describes a scene whose appeal for Steven is evident:

> At Cukor's house would be gathered literary titans such as Sinclair Lewis, Theodore Dreiser, Aldous Huxley. There were foreign film personalities passing through Hollywood. British ladies of vague royal derivation seemed to be abundant. There were often illustrious theater people, such as Fanny Brice, Lucile Watson, or Mrs. Patrick Campbell, in Los Angeles for the climate or the vague prospects of work (often prospects nurtured by Cukor). There was the faithful cadre of famous actresses who were friends: Bankhead, Garbo, Hepburn.*
>
> ... Part of the cachet of the house, implicitly and explicitly, was homosexuality. That was part of what made it unique: There was a flow of distinguished homosexual guests from around the globe, and particularly from England: Somerset Maugham, Noël Coward, George Hoyningen-Huene, Cecil Beaton ... and many others.
>
> ... they knew they could find a haven at Cukor's – in a place (the figurative as well as literal Hollywood) that otherwise has confused, alienated, or betrayed many an intellectual, many an artist, and certainly many a homosexual.

Cukor's attitude to his own homosexuality was conspicuously conflicted. By turns he railed against fairies and pansies, whispered into selected ears exaggerated, if sometimes genuine, insinuations of conquests, or adopted a pose of shockable, auntly staidness. He loathed his enduring reputation as a 'woman's director'. During the war he had been denied the officer's commission that was the prerogative of so many of his rival directors, such as Frank Capra and John Ford. He had formed his own view of the reasons behind this slight, and it left him harsher and grander. His favourite adjectives in passing conversation were 'distinguished' and 'distinctive', but his favourite nouns were profane. Steven's first glimpse of him in his black

---

* Though Cukor would direct Audrey Hepburn in *My Fair Lady*, Katharine, the well-born, polished and beady Connecticut icon, was infinitely more to his taste.

pyjamas encapsulated the whole man: physically unattractive, especially to himself; painstakingly, powerfully idiosyncratic in his personal style; wounded, charming, ever willing to exercise attack as the best form of defence.

Steven found his accommodation at Beverly Hills equally impressive and oppressive. Cukor was 'the kindest of hosts'; Steven suspected that the director had somehow found time to read a good proportion of his vast library, and he thought well of Cukor's taste in paintings, especially Impressionists. But he was foxed by the decor of his own quarters, especially the bathroom, which 'presented a problem, as the bath-tub was L-shaped, or, rather, it was a square with a corner filled in. To judge from the salts and essences provided, it was meant for use; but I never learnt how to fit into it.' Steven took to slipping off for secret washes chez Hoyningen-Huene, instead. Hoyningen-Huene, a genuine if dispossessed Baltic baron, who on the rare occasions when he was caught by as opposed to wielding a camera looks fleshy, kindly and rather weary, functioned as a necessary channel between Cukor and Beaton, who respected and disliked each other. Cukor's present project, the musical comedy *Les Girls* (Steven called it 'a not very noteworthy production', but it won a Golden Globe), involved unrelenting, if often unspoken, feuds with the film's composer and lyricist, Cole Porter. Cukor had no greater social adversary than Porter, who competed with him for the attentions of any attractive, talented or otherwise noteworthy male additions to Beverly Hills society. In this instance too, the invaluable Hoyningen-Huene was obliged to settle daily diplomatic intricacies.

Steven was bothered little by Cukor's moodier side. His host was almost always busy filming by day; Steven was astonished by the Hollywood work ethic, writing to Leslie that 'the whole film world is too hard at work to think of social life,' while to Marthe Bibesco he complained, 'Film circles themselves are tout ce qu'il y a de plus respectable – *everyone* works too hard.' The honoured guest was not, however, left unattended; Cukor lent him a Daimler with a handsome young film student, David Peck, at its wheel; its destinations were various and spectacular. Inevitably there was Disneyland, 'the archest funfair you can imagine'; Malibu Beach followed, populated by reassuring numbers of Englishmen. The gardens at Pasadena were enlivened by the passage of an occasional ostrich; and with an access of boyishness Steven told Leslie the Aquarium of the Pacific was 'the biggest ever'. Most intriguing of all was the sprawling thanatomane hubris of Forest Lawn Memorial Park, the celebrity cemetery brought to the attention of the post-war British reading public by Evelyn Waugh's 'Anglo-American tragedy', *The Loved One* (1948). Steven tactlessly, or more likely mischievously, remarked to Cukor that he felt Waugh had scarcely exaggerated its 'hilariously horrifying' kitsch. 'I was soon made aware of the social form . . . I was sharply reminded that [Forest Lawn] had brought comfort to numbers of sorrowing relatives and it was not for me to mock at it.'

Social form was the order of the fortnight; Steven met the two duennas of Hollywood etiquette, the rival Beverly Hills gossip columnists Louella Parsons and Cobina Wright, on carefully distinct occasions. It was refreshing to adapt to the rules of a society so different in personnel, heritage and conduct from the British elite to which Steven was accustomed, yet to find the scene still, fundamentally, familiar. 'Just as in England the best families came over with the Conqueror, so in Hollywood the best people had come over with the Goldwyns and the Mayers,' Steven observed, in an aphorism not devoid of the casual anti-Semitism that he never altogether dropped. 'If, like George Cukor, you belonged to that select group, you did not mix with the riff-raff of the movie world but only with actors and actresses who came from respectable backgrounds. In consequence I spent much of my time, very happily, with Katharine Hepburn.'

Steven's teasing 'in consequence' presents this complicated and sometimes contradictory milieu as if a lucid – though ludic – syllogism can cut through its mystery. He is not saying anything so crude or banal as that the Hollywood of the day was dominated by Jews; but there is an unmistakable hint of something of that kind in his inclusion of Cukor with the Goldwyns and Mayers in a 'select group' (Cukor's early circumstances had in fact been far more challenging than those of the great studio families, his ascent more precarious and meritocratic). Steven's suavely automatic inclusion of Katharine Hepburn in the same category or set shifts his tone to another kind of inference, based not on religion, race, gender or sexuality, but rather on the alchemy between fame, talent and money on the one hand and upbringing, education and shared old-fashioned values on the other – ideals that would have been familiar to Steven's pre-war friend Mrs Wharton.

This was a sort of test that, in Steven's view, Katharine Hepburn and the star of *Les Girls*, Kay Kendall (bride-to-be of Rex Harrison), passed without effort. So, with certain reservations, did Ava Gardner and, later, Sophia Loren. Those who fell short included Clark Cable and Gene Kelly. An inescapable impression emerges that Steven was affected by his increasingly amiable host, Cukor the 'woman's director', in greatly preferring the leading ladies to the male stars. Aware of the attraction they exerted, the leading men – many themselves not without sexual ambiguity – could be bullying and boorish towards those they could get away with labelling as 'fairies'. The great actresses, by contrast, for all their own often difficult temperaments, engaged beautifully with the game of courtliness. In some cases – Ava Gardner, Tallulah Bankhead, possibly Katharine Hepburn – their own sexual multivalence manifested itself in an understanding and entertaining, rather than aggressive, fashion.

According to Steven, his particular protectress soon became the immaculately secure, socially connected Miss Hepburn, who took what she saw as Steven's underdeveloped cinematic education in hand. For this purpose she borrowed the private home cinema of David O. Selznick, Cukor's regular producer and the son-in-law of Louis B. Mayer, the monstrous potentate of MGM. Here, to the accompaniment of champagne, caviar and the jealous, boozy grunts of Hepburn's lover, Spencer Tracy, Steven was introduced first to *Anastasia*, starring Ingrid Bergman, a sympathetic portrayal of Anna Anderson's attempt to impersonate the lost Russian Princess. Steven did not rate this beginning very highly; his allegiance was firmly with the stiff-necked old White Russian Grand Duchesses, unconvinced by the would-be tragic heroine's pretensions. Miss Hepburn next showed Fellini's comedy *I vitelloni*, which went down a trifle better. For this second viewing Georges Cukor and Hoyningen-Huene both put in an appearance, their strenuous filming schedule offering a fleeting hiatus. Miss Hepburn also brought along Lauren Bacall, or, as she was then generally known, Betty Bogart (she had been married, Steven felt unhappily, to Humphrey, her first co-star, since 1945). Steven thought her a sensible girl, persuasive on the illiberal terror of the

Committee for Un-American Activities. He had previously written to Stewart Perowne that 'The MacArthy [sic] probe into private lives is terrifying and shocking everyone – if your aunt's houseboy was a Communist you're doomed . . . this great Democracy is really something of a police-state, especially at Washington.'

But the Hollywood company Steven most enjoyed, and to whose ambit he would return consistently on subsequent adventures in Los Angeles, was less famous, and by its nature carefully self-selecting. At its reins was Clifton Webb, in his prime a Broadway stalwart, versatile in acting, song, dance and social aptitude. As Hoyningen-Huene navigated the tricky shallows between Cukor and Cole Porter, so Webb shimmied as the rainbow messenger between 'the women's director' and Noël Coward, for whom he starred in *Blithe Spirit* and *Present Laughter*. Now, at the end of his dramatic and musical career, Webb remained to Cukor a constant friend, confidant and sexual facilitator. Steven writes proudly to his siblings, with a less than convincing show of indifference, of his flourishing relations with Katharine Hepburn and Kay Kendall. But it is Clifton Webb, whom he leaves quite unmentioned, whose name recurs most tellingly in his engagement diaries for the fortnight.

Webb invited Steven to tea along with two well-known British intellectuals – Christopher Isherwood and Gerald Heard. Steven mentions meeting Isherwood that February to his sister as part of a generalized British Hollywood celebrity *mélange*, including Rex Harrison, Merle Oberon and Terence Rattigan – 'none of them wildly exciting'. As far as Isherwood was concerned, this dismissive opinion was broadly sincere; Steven did not care for that circle, whose members he had known and deprecated in his early years as a Cambridge don; he never respected Auden or Stephen Spender, nor was he in turn much liked by them. Gerald Heard was a different matter and to Steven a more exciting and amiable social catch, a friend of Aldous and Julian Huxley, admired by both Steven and Stewart Perowne.

'Grand historical spectacles', Steven lamented to Marthe Bibesco with more sincerity than he admitted, 'are no longer chic in Hollywood.' By the time he passed on to the Philippines on his way to Sarawak, none of his cinematic schemes had come to anything, but he had much enjoyed himself and he left with a standing invitation back to Cukor's court. 'I wouldn't mind staying here for some time,' he admitted to his brother. 'In spite of all the fantasy life is much less frantic here than in New York, and there are enough Europeans settled here for there to be some sane company conscious of the joke of it all.' This enthusiasm had, of course, its limits. Steven would always proclaim himself to be irremediably of the Old World rather than the New, and more drawn to the East than the West:

> It is from the East that all the fundamental elements of our civilization came, and it is to the East that anyone with an interest in the past must turn. The West should have remained, as it was long ago, a vast area of mystery, bounded by an impenetrable ocean, beyond which there was, perhaps, the rim of the world, the great cliff that led to nothingness, or perhaps the Happy Isles, where the ghosts of past heroes survived. The realms beyond the sunset had, maybe, their allure; but they were alarming and better avoided. 'Comrade, look not to the West. / 'Twill have your heart out of your breast,' said the poet Housman. I feel that I know what he meant . . . Columbus spoilt it all . . .
>
> Byzantine superstition was not all of it ill-based . . . even some of the wisest philosophers believed that the world would last for seven thousand years and that it had been created in 5508 BC. If you do your sums correctly, that brings us to the dreadful date of 1492.

Accordingly he proceeded now from the furthest West to the Far East in pursuit of the Brookes of Sarawak, with their disconcertingly recent past.

In Steven's opinion, the best-looking diplomatic pair in mid-1950s London – and he was a thorough and exacting judge – were Ambassador and Madame Guerrero of the Philippines. Physical beauty alone did not recommend the Guerreros; they were enterprising hosts and well-informed, vigorous conversationalists, 'especially interested in the theatre and the arts'. León María Guerrero was the grandson and namesake of a famous Filipino nationalist and botanist; he would eventually cap his diplomatic career by producing several novels. Steven was not the only formidable *arbiter elegantiarum* to frequent the Philippine Embassy; the ballerina Margot Fonteyn and the American illustrator Fleur Cowles were among the Guerreros' other favourites.

For all his unconventional glamour of personal appearance and his cultural liberality and reach, Guerrero was an establishment man in his own country (he was to prove a firm ally of Ferdinand and Imelda Marcos), and above all a smooth and seductive Ambassador. He was only the second fully accredited representative of his country to Britain, and, as Steven's reputation and fame remained at their peak following the *Crusades* trilogy, by persuading his new friend to linger in the Philippines on his way to Sarawak Guerrero pulled off a magnificent *succès d'estime*. Steven, not for the first time, accepted both the pleasures and the duties of the venture without much troubling himself as to what precise advantages he would confer on his hosts. Some of the results of this sanguine acceptance would surprise him.

The Guerreros' suggestion was also highly convenient to Steven because Guerrero's counterpart, the British Ambassador in Manila, happened to be an old connection whom Steven was delighted to look up, and who offered in turn indefinite hospitality. George Clutton was half a dozen years Steven's junior, though his grizzled, awkward bulk and 'austere and astigmatic' stare made him look about a decade older. He had first made Steven's acquaintance as a colleague at the British Museum of Roger Hinks, Steven's long-time rival but, withal, a resilient, infuriating old friend. Clutton had left the Museum at the same time as Hinks had retired in disgrace over the too-zealous cleaning of the Elgin Marbles. His war, on a desk job for the Foreign Office before a 1944 posting to the Stockholm Embassy, had been sedate but well informed; and with peace he had briefly been dispatched beyond the Iron Curtain as First Secretary at Belgrade. From 1950 to 1952 Clutton headed the British liaison effort regarding the ruin and reconstruction of the Empire of Japan; it was at some point during this stint, if not indeed earlier, that he entered the good graces of MI6. Upon his return to London Clutton was chosen to act as the principal conduit between the Foreign Office and the Secret Service; and in this capacity he played, in 1953, his most historically significant part. As Anthony Eden, then Foreign Secretary, vacillated over the Persian Question, it was Clutton who authorized the overthrow of the elected Prime Minister of Iran, Mohammed Mossadeq. He remained in the MI6 liaison role for another two years, before receiving promotion in rank, if not influence, to the Philippine Embassy.

How much Steven knew or discerned about the covert aspects behind Clutton's public career is impossible to establish. He had enjoyed, in all senses, privileged access to Cabinet policy during his father's days of power in the Baldwin and Chamberlain administrations, and liked in a quiet way to keep up a habit of unexpected knowledge. The air of elite insight that lends to his historical narratives such persuasiveness and confidence was one Steven also cultivated in his social life. In part, this projection of unparalleled sources for the gossip of international power-play was competitive bravado, of the sort that animates his relentless exchanges of royal gossip with Stewart Perowne. It recalls the strategically calculated boasting of Olivia Manning's Russian-Irish émigré Prince Yakimov, ignorant of the international situation to the point of disastrous naivety, but determined to pose as an agent. What Steven certainly did know about Clutton was his sexual orientation, which he held in common with many of Steven's most far-flung hosts. Clutton's homosexuality, well after Steven's 1956 visit to Manila, was to lead him into trouble.

Though Clutton was younger than Steven, an experienced, effective diplomat (and, in truth, spy) at the peak of his career, Steven's own references to his host are protective and solicitous, as if describing a forlorn, even dotty, but much beloved old man, to be offered courtesy, assistance and entertainment. They had not met since before the war, and Steven was shocked by the rapid deterioration of the one-time British Museum Assistant's eyesight, as well as by the undisciplined expansion of his girth (Steven himself always maintained a trim figure). Steven described Clutton to Ruth as a 'very quiet middle-aged bachelor' 'who is tragically going blind', intimating that for this reason Clutton could not possibly remain long at his post. This was not really accurate. After two more years at Manila Clutton was to be promoted in 1960 to the crucial Eastern Bloc Embassy in Warsaw, where he lasted six years before MI6 became aware he was passing information to a Soviet-run former lover. In the *Alphabet* Steven sticks to his blithely doddery characterization of Clutton as a 'rather frail and lonely bachelor' (again that crucial noun, signifier of what Steven called 'innocence') 'who seemed glad to have an old friend staying with him'. It may be that Clutton employed his severe astigmatism and dubious health as a screen by which Steven was at least in part taken in.

Steven's stop in the Philippines was a matter more of industry than of curiosity, particularly for a man of private habits who, though generally gregarious and interested, found enduring continual hospitality exhausting and required occasional isolation for calm and composition. Banqueted by Clutton, his staff, the British expatriate community, the American colony and the leading citizenry of Manila in a manner he thought 'unending', Steven acknowledged a serious debt to his hosts, to be repaid in the form of lecturing consecutively at a bewildering variety of universities. These institutions, he told Marthe Bibesco with little reservation, were 'each worse than the last, except for those run by the Church – and even they keep up a losing fight against low standards of education and spectacular standards of corruption. Yet the islands are lovely ... ' His grousing to Leslie was more specific:

> I was worked to death in the Philippines. There are more, and worse, universities there than anywhere in the world and they all *love* lectures. I gave 5 lectures in Manila – at one (where the ambassador was made to inspect a guard of honour before we began) my audience was over 4500 – none of them really understanding a word.* I lectured ... to the assembled schoolchildren and students of Zamboanga in the island of Mindanao, to a Jesuit seminary at Cebu (my one really intelligent audience) and twice to an American missionary-run University on the island of Negros – very austere, no drinking, no smoking and grace even before breakfast, but a serious attempt at a teaching establishment.

Wherever he travelled over the increasingly globalized world of the second half of the twentieth century, Steven tended to imply he was driven by obligation, a sense of moral duty combining with government pressure in a sort of extension of his wartime and post-war national service in cultural propaganda and administration. Some of

---

* Both Steven and Clutton enjoyed the guard of honour, 'youths in a picturesque uniform who looked endearingly like toy soldiers' (SR, *A Traveller's Alphabet* (Thames & Hudson, 1991), p. 114).

his closest friends took these expressions of frustration and weariness fully at their word; his last and most loyal pupil, Donald Nicol, would wonder in a letter to Anthony Bryer 'whether the Great Man really enjoyed all his travelling and lecturing'. But to believe this line from Steven was, in general, to be bamboozled by it. The odder, the more extreme and story-worthy and certainly the more inconvenient the destination, the higher was its value for parlay in some later exchange of anecdotes or one-upmanship of honours with Hugh Trevor-Roper or Stewart Perowne. As for the adventures themselves, Steven would always be sustained by his wry humour and natural inquisitiveness.

Steven found himself billed – possibly on account of Ambassador Guerrero's novelistic touch – as 'Britain's cultural ambassador', and as such was enthusiastically tracked by the Filipino press. To Ruth he admitted cheerfully that 'after giving nine lectures in a fortnight, I rather thought I had indeed earnt the title,' and in a way his talents and enthusiasms did belong to the diplomatic sphere, if perhaps that of another age, when Sir Thomas Wyatt or Sir Henry Wotton, earlier literary knights, roamed over France, Italy and Spain as Ambassadors Extraordinary. Steven's mischievous pleasure in the confected title is of a piece with his attempts to usurp Sir Clifford and Lady Norton's more amusing ambassadorial duties during his last year at the British Council in Athens. His favourite interlude during this first Manila excursion came when the 'cultural' and accredited British ambassadors were alike invited to see a production of *Macbeth* at the Ateneo, a Jesuit school:

> I have never seen that difficult play better performed. [The cast] spoke their lines admirably, with a faint but attractive accent. The youth who played Macbeth did so with an authority that was very impressive, while the much younger boy who was Lady Macbeth showed a quality of sinister ambition that was rather disquieting.

Two years later, when Steven returned to Manila, Clutton took him back to the Ateneo to see *Julius Caesar*; but the divine spark, incarnated in that particular Philippine Macbeth marriage, had gone. Steven kept for his albums a photograph of himself and Clutton in the front row of *Macbeth*. The Jesuit teachers sitting beside them, gleaming and serene in white, look more wizardly than priestly.

George Clutton stoops and sinks inelegantly in his seat, his ill-functioning eyes almost entirely closed, as if they are giving him pain, or, worse still, he has fallen half asleep and is troubled by agonizing dreams. Whichever it is, it has not escaped Steven, who looks sidelong across the row of clergy towards his host, a slight smile not marring the alert dignity of his posture.

Steven first touched down on his flight from Manila at the small arrowhead-shaped island of Labuan. In the days of the first Brooke Rajah, the place had been thought to be vastly rich in coal; its potential had proved much exaggerated, but even so it could boast the most advanced aerodrome in the archipelago. Air travel would be a constant of the whole venture, not in the languorous new airliners to which Steven was already becoming accustomed, but in ad hoc, manoeuvrable, juddering little machines with all the comfort of Leslie's wartime transports in Iran but even less assurance of arrival. Steven wrote of travel within Borneo that there was 'nothing between aeroplanes and canoes', and he was often to be in equal parts charmed and dismayed by the apparent youth of his pilots. At Labuan he was received by Philip Jones, a heavily affectionate figure, eager to be of use and to ensure the success of the commission he had masterminded. Together they flew on to Brunei and the first excitement Steven had been anticipating, an audience with its Sultan.

Sultan Omar Ali Saifuddien III was by 1957 in the sixth year of his reign over his diminutive but, since the discovery of oil there in 1929, spectacularly rich protectorate. Steven reported breezily to Ruth that although 'said to be difficult' with visiting Britons, whose Empire's enduring control over his statelet he resented intensely, the Sultan had seemed 'perfectly affable to me'. To Leslie Steven described the forty-two-year-old Sultan as a 'tiny, whispering man whose only interest is speedboats'. Thirty-five years later, he was to detail the careful tactics he had employed in keeping the conversation neutral verging on cordial:

> The Sultan was not greatly pleased to learn that I had come out to write about the Brookes. He told me, rather sternly, not to believe all the accusations that the Brookes had levelled against his ancestors. I

tried to appease him by remarking that the Brooke dynasty had come and gone, while his ancient family was still in possession of its throne.

The Sultan seemed satisfied by this diplomatic finesse, though *The White Rajahs* would in the end be candidly critical of the Brunei dynasty, and quietly sceptical of the continuous tradition to which Steven had so flatteringly alluded. Privately Steven considered Brunei 'an absurd little state', and its ruler 'outwardly meek but actually difficult, obstinate and ambitious', 'a very corrupt type of Malay', 'his insults covered with a thin veneer'. Steven foresaw that such seedy beauty and down-at-heel antiquity as the town of Brunei possessed would be unlikely to survive its recent access of cash, though for the moment he quite enjoyed the incongruous architectural juxtaposition: 'The Sultan's increasing wealth was being demonstrated in the building of a number of grandiosely ornate public offices and mosques, which added a bizarre effect that was rather endearing.'

The same adjective occurred to Steven as he passed on to Kuching, the capital of the Brookes, and especially the Astana Palace, from which the White Rajahs had lived and ruled (though they really preferred their modest Devon holiday house, Burrator). Kuching itself Steven thought 'an unpretentious town'; the country around it disappointed him:

> One's vision of the tropics as having cloudless blue skies and great forests full of exotic birds and butterflies and brilliant flowers was not confirmed by Sarawak. There the sky was almost always overcast; the rivers were sluggish and muddy; the forests were thick and impenetrable with overgrown scrub . . . Occasionally, going along the roads and path hacked through the undergrowth one might see a turkey-crow, a large unattractive bird, scuttling away.

But the Astana with its disregard for period fidelity appealed to his senses both of humour and of slightly perverse aesthetic excitement: 'a most eclectic building with a Gothic keep with great tropic-bungalow style wings supported on Gothic cloisters, and full inside of Chinoiserie decoration and Ionic columns . . . not unsuccessful'.

Here Steven was the guest of the Governor, Sir Anthony Abell, lauded in the *Alphabet* for 'his tact and geniality, obvious fair-mindedness and integrity'. Steven's impression of the Governor's entourage was more mixed:

> The set-up is interesting – the old Brooke-appointed officials jealous of the Colonial Office men, whom they think brash and ignorant of local conditions, and are thought in turn reactionary and unadaptable . . . There's quite a bit of tension; but mercifully they all admire the Governor – rightly as he is I think a most admirable and likeable man, a bachelor of 50 or so, and very good company and obviously intelligent and quite tough. The Chief Secretary [Hugh Ellis] is a clever Welshman, hated by the *ancien régime* – I personally would say he is very able and good at it all, but he has that Welsh slickness.

Lloyd George's perfidy was evidently still unforgotten in the Runciman family consciousness. But in essence Steven found himself in friendly, if not very comfortable, circumstances. He attributed some of Abell's success, whether or not revealingly, to his bachelor status – 'the wives of British Governors have all too often behaved like governesses' – and enjoyed accompanying his host on gubernatorial progresses, 'basking in the warm glow of his popularity'. This popularity was all the more impressive given that their destinations included a leper colony and, 'much less melancholy', a prison. The great shortcoming of life at the Astana was the grim, miserly cooking. Abell had endured during his previous service in Africa an ascetic outdoorsman's existence, and was too indifferent to comfort even for Steven's sparing taste. But Steven's appetite for the paranormal, at least, was satisfied when he learnt that the Astana's library had been built over an ancient Malay cemetery. From then on he never felt quite alone in his researches through the archives, experiencing a tingle that was 'eerie but not actually sinister'.

In fact the records at the Astana were so patchy (and its hospitality, perhaps, so uninviting) that Steven moved on after only four days, staying for the next five with none other than the slick Chief Secretary Ellis before settling down with Philip Jones (who employed a passable cook) at some distance from the town. Steven's morning duties now concerned the papers at the Sarawak Museum, and the difficult task of proving himself to the haughty, moody, ill-disposed Tom Harrisson. Fortunately Harrisson was as direct as Steven was game, and a challenge was soon issued and accepted that decided their relationship. Harrisson invited Steven – who correctly interpreted the offer to be more in the nature of a summons – to meet him at an archaeological dig up-country north of Kuching, in the Great Caves at Niah. Steven evenly recalled Harrisson's later confession that he had invited Steven 'in the hope that I would find the discomfort there too much for me and would be deterred from continuing in my commission'.

The journey itself was difficult, dependent on the lone available step between aeroplanes and canoes: a motor-launch at the disposal of a hugely fat Australian-born Police Commissioner and his wife. Steven, with his lifelong immunity to seasickness, was contemptuous of this constabularial couple's drugged, stertorous nights below deck, and he felt himself to be 'rather like a registered parcel', as he was subsequently 'decanted into a speed-boat and whisked up a river'. On landing Steven was met by Harrisson's German wife, Barbara. She guided him along an ever more precarious path:

> I walked four miles through the jungle (which is rather like the rhododendron walk, out of season, in the grounds of a decayed Scottish castle) . . . along single slippery planks poised precariously on piles over endless swamp: then up still more slippery notched tree trunks into a series of fantastic caves, of which the largest – huge, with entrances over precipices on all sides, as though the whole mountain were hollowed out – contains roughly 1,000,000 bats and 2,000,000 swifts, the latter making nests for soup.

The comparison of the outlandish tropical scene with the familiar Scottish one is a typical Runciman device; similarly, on his first trip to Australia early in 1959, Steven was to describe Tasmania for his siblings' benefit as 'terribly like Ireland – decayed houses in romantic scenery and an inbred gentry talking endlessly of horses . . . and making off with one another's wives'. His teasingly round estimates for the wildlife rested on a pleasing social coincidence: when he reached the inmost cave, Steven found there the twenty-four-year-old Lord Medway, working as Harrisson's assistant and laboriously attempting a census of bats and birds. Harrisson caused embarrassment to everyone concerned by his elaborate and uncharacteristic courtesy to his aristocratic underling. Steven knew young Medway already, for all Harrisson's painfully insistent introduction, as a schoolfriend of his nephew Garry, and a nephew of Robert and Eddie Gathorne-Hardy, acquaintances made in more louche, if hardly odder, contexts. At this point, however, pure chance settled Harrisson in Steven's favour. Until then the dig had been irritatingly unproductive; but 'I had hardly been up there an hour before they turned up some "tampan" stones, which showed signs of human workmanship. Tom Harrisson at once regarded me as a *porte-bonheur*; and from thenceforward our relations were of the most cordial.' Steven was initially rewarded for his perseverance and good luck by being put on to the bat-counting team with the eager but overworked Medway. 'It had a sort of mesmeric effect on one, almost like a mystical exercise to attain enlightenment. But I achieved no enlightenment, merely a feeling of relief when it became too dark to continue the exercise.'

As for the Museum papers back in Kuching, they turned out to be a 'scrappy, curious collection', disproportionately related to the reign of the highly effective, autocratic and punctilious second Rajah, Charles Brooke, who had not suffered the setbacks of his uncle James (an archivally destructive rising by the Chinese population) or his son Vyner (the Japanese occupation of Sarawak in the Second World War). Steven realized with some trepidation that for the first time in his already thirty-year-long, distinguished career he would have to rely upon the testimony of the living. Compared to that inconvenient prospect, the elusive mysteries of the Museum archive were positively inviting. 'I'm enjoying my spadework at the history. But it's not going to be an easy book to write,' Steven accurately predicted to Leslie. Yet at the same time he confided to Ruth that 'I think I'm going to enjoy writing about this country. At first I thought the subject altogether too remote from my sort of thing; but it's beginning to mean something now . . . '

Another curious manifestation of Steven's quasi-public sense of duty, persisting at a period of his life which was, in fact, the most independent he had yet experienced, came with his decision to pass the New Year of 1958 in Pakistan, at the International Islamic Colloquium at Lahore. Steven was all his life strangely proof against the appeal of the Indian subcontinent (rather as he was left cold by Japan). After the war, though, his old friend Stas Ostrorog had become the French Ambassador in Delhi, where he now lived with his elder brother Jean – an arrangement that suited everybody, as Jean had served the wrong French government in the Far East during the war, and was not particularly welcome in post-war France. Steven gave in to curiosity and looked up Jean in the spring of 1955, on the way back from visiting Charles Lambe at his naval post in Singapore ('how delicious it is staying in naval establishments – everything is so smooth and mannerly'). But despite Jean's persuasions during various forays through India's landscape and its monuments, Steven remained obdurate:

> Jean indefatigably took me to see all the sights. There isn't a single Moghul monument that I haven't inspected from top to bottom – and to tell the truth, though I didn't dare confess it to Jean, I thought them all remarkably ugly, and the Taj Mahal the worst of the lot. Nor did I find the Indians an attractive race. I much preferred the gayer more smiling peoples of the further east . . .
>
> . . . Moghul monuments are much like Persian, without the charm . . .

The jibe at the Taj Mahal, especially, feels of a piece with Steven's wilfully perverse dismissal of the Parthenon; and the whole begrudging tone would be somewhat moderated by the time of the *Alphabet*, for which, however, Steven reserved his more serious misgivings about Indian culture:

> I am full of admiration for the great buildings of the Moghul Emperors. I was charmed by Goa, with its churches that blend Portugal with the Orient. But . . . the grim poverty of the cities and even in the villages is all too visible. And I cannot like the Hindu attitude that combines an aggressively self-righteous holiness with a tolerance of the caste system. Nor can I believe in any Indian guru.

Such gurus, in Steven's view, undoubtedly included Gandhi, whom he had met and found disappointing in the 1930s. Pakistan presented a slightly different case, however.

Steven was regarded by certain of his most unwary and enchanted lay readers as a genuine expert of the first rank in Arabic and Islamic history; it was partly on this basis, for example, that Philip Jones had presented his friend's suitability to write the history of the Brookes in Sarawak, with its large Muslim population. Steven himself laid claim to 'a certain understanding of Islam, at least until it lapses into fundamentalism'. As a new-born Muslim state, Pakistan intrigued him, and he was flattered and struck by his invitation to the enigmatic Colloquium, whose grand designation he began to mock the moment he accepted the proposal ('an Islamic Colloquium, whatever that may mean'). He also, in some way, felt his acceptance as a duty: 'One ought, when invited, not refuse . . . it may all do good (though probably a waste of time scholastically.)' To Stewart Perowne, alluding to the latter's long and difficult service in Iraq, he added, 'As you know better than I, these Orientals can so easily feel snubbed, while friendliness can do so much good.'

And so, in late December 1957, Steven arrived at the University of the Punjab, Lahore, on his way to his next Sarawak field-trip. He formed part of a British delegation to the Colloquium which also included two younger, rising scholars from SOAS: Nancy Lambton, recently appointed Professor of Persian at London University, whose recommendations had had a hand in the fall of Mossadeq in Iran; and Bernard Lewis, who had just published *The Arabs in History*. Steven was not very impressed by either for reasons that do him small credit: he thought that Lambton, 'like most women-lecturers, cannot make her voice sound anything but monotonous', while he harped on Lewis's extraction in a manner that bluntly anticipated some of the later, baleful insinuations by Edward Said: 'to have a Jew present is a pity at a Muslim gathering.' More to Steven's taste was 'the doyen of Orientalists in London', the aged Petersburg exile Professor Vladimir Minorsky. But soon enough national solidarity brushed aside any reservations Steven privately maintained about his compatriots (and the naturalized British White Russian): 'The Colloquium itself is rather a mess – many of the Muslims objected to Christians attending, and the Syrian and Egyptian delegates use every opportunity for attacking the West in their orations, while the Americans manage to be wonderfully tactless at giving them opportunities. We are rather more tactful . . . ' Steven's attitude to social life in Lahore was mixed ('conversation with the Pakistanis is apt to be repetitive, though they seem to love it if one makes jokes and teases them'), and to the Colloquium itself more absolute – he thought the 'crazy Islamic Congress' an entire waste of effort, a succession of 'dull and elementary papers'.

Two developments ruffled the programme's piously unremitting tedium: the fatal heart attack of an Egyptian delegate, and the New Year's Honours of 1958, including Steven's knighthood. Steven saw that his new title went down well with his hosts, especially the numerous contingent of Cambridge-educated Pakistanis at the University of the Punjab. His own delight was, at least outwardly, moderate – 'when I read in the press that thirty-six knights have been created, I am less impressed'. To Leslie Perowne, Stewart's younger brother, Steven expanded on the nature of this surprise: 'You could have knocked me down with a feather when they said they wanted to make me a Knight, and I still don't think it quite my line – so middle-aged, so associated with Welsh aldermen and failing jockeys. I suppose I'll get used to it. The dear Queen is to do her stuff on me on Feb 11th . . . ' Steven attached considerable importance to the physical act of the dubbing, warning Donald Nicol that 'I oughtn't to assume the title until the Queen actually dubs me . . . but everyone seems to ignore that nicety.' When the great day arrived, the dear Queen having done her stuff, Steven chanced to encounter her mother on his way out of the Ballroom at Buckingham Palace.

In time the Queen Mother and Steven were to become as close friends as a monarch, dowager or not, and a subject ever can be; they had in common high, unpretentious, vigilantly Caledonian standards. But it had not always been thus. At the time of the Abdication Crisis, Steven flirted with the worldly glamour of Mrs Simpson. To Ottoline Morrell Steven had referred to the then Duchess of York as 'that blousy woman, if I may speak so disrespectfully of your Royal cousin', and later, in his correspondence with the Perowne brothers, wherein all three men build up a sort of competitive cult of devotion towards old Queen Mary, the Queen Mother figures as 'the Middle Queen', or 'grinning Lizzie', a derisive portrait in steely, vulgar ambition. Lucullan perfectionists in matters of courtliness, Steven and the Perownes were inclined to mock the Queen Mother for those very attributes that had given rise to her immense wartime popularity. For some years after his Athenian spell, Steven's favourite members of the House of Windsor were its Hellenic spouses, Prince Philip and, especially, Princess Marina, partly because it was about them that he knew the best stories. In any case, the Queen Mother was not best pleased with the brief conversation that succeeded Steven's dubbing. The elder Elizabeth politely asked Steven how it felt to be a knight. 'Now I know, for the first time,' Steven replied at once, 'what it is to be both middle-aged and middle-class.'

Whatever dowdiness he professed to feel about his new title, Steven soon felt its tangible advantages. He set out for his second venture to Sarawak, in the spring of 1959, by way of Australia, 'a country about which I have great curiosity, as I nearly always find Australians extremely sympathetic'. His post-war life in London featured several Australian friends, foremost among them a young beauty, Robin Spencer, lately married to Steven's personable and charming Irish doctor, Emmet Dalton. Secondarily, Steven had arranged to interview a diplomat, R. G. Aikman, who remembered service under the Brookes, and now lived in a suburb of Perth. Aikman 'gave me lunch and a mass of useful information, some of which was too indiscreet for me to be able to use'; he had endured imprisonment by the Japanese and kept up radio communication with the outside world in secret throughout the occupation. He was undaunted by the prescribed code of conduct of the Colonial Office, and vociferous in his loyalty to the ousted Brooke heir, Anthony. Steven made his escape with some relief. He was coming round slowly and uneasily to his new identity, as he wrote to Ruth: ' . . . I don't like being "Sir Steven". For one thing, being unused to the sound of it, I never hear the Sir and think that people are being far too familiar. But here where an Hon. means nothing – a Lord might, but they have little regard for hereditary titles – to be a Sir does undoubtedly add to my prestige, and I ought to be grateful.'

His next two Australian experiences provided an exception to the rule that Australians were unimpressed by noble birth, and an unexpected perk of knighthood. First Steven visited the Tasmanian estate of an Irish acquaintance, Lord Talbot de Malahide, who had inherited the domain there of a 'somewhat delinquent' great-great-

great-uncle. He thought that Tasmanian architecture possessed a ghostly, incongruous elegance that combined startlingly with the wildlife: 'I suppose that no one remembered to tell the Tasmanians that Regency had long since gone out of date in Britain ... In the course of a country walk I saw kangaroos and echidnas (armadillos which look like porcupines) and masses of parrots, though the climate is no warmer than England's.' Back in the urban sophistication of Sydney, a city Steven deemed 'hideous, except in a few decaying slums', he got an even closer exposure to the antipodean fauna. As a knightly VIP, Steven was invited on a special, individual tour of the Zoo: 'I spent a heavenly afternoon being taken round by one of the Head Keepers ... hugging Koala bears and being hugged by Kangaroos.' He later elaborated on both hugs in the *Alphabet*:

> We went first into the koala bear enclosure, where I was handed one of those toy-like animals to cuddle. I asked if they were all as tame. All, answered the keeper, except for one ... sitting on the branch of a small tree. It thereupon climbed down from the tree, walked across and climbed up me. The keeper was greatly impressed ... even allowing me to handle that most shy and delicate of animals, the duckbilled platypus. Finally ... a huge buck kangaroo came bounding up towards me. 'Take care,' cried the keeper as he dragged me away; 'He can become excited.' Two days later I read in a Sydney newspaper that the big kangaroo enclosure was to be closed to all visitors, as a VIP had nearly suffered death or worse at the hands of its largest male.

Before his first arrival in Sarawak Steven had visited Brunei on his way to Kuching to take in a little context and variation; now for his second excursion he travelled by way of British North Borneo, an anomalous chunk of territory that had originally been prized from the Brunei Sultans by the British Crown, rather than the Brookes. His first proposed host there, the British Governor, Roland Turnbull, was an old Cambridge crony, but Steven had never liked him, associating him with the chill, inimical influence of Anthony Blunt. Now he observed that Turnbull harangued his ADCs, and damned his private character: 'very odd, clever, amusing and slightly sinister. I much prefer Abell – cosier and really wiser ... [Turnbull is] a great one for etiquette and ceremony . . . his wife has more or less left him . . . ' The loaded adjective 'sinister' implies another colonial homosexual official enjoying comfortable isolation, one less to Steven's liking than George Clutton. Steven had most likely been briefed against Turnbull by Abell already; the two had fallen out over how to handle the Sultan of Brunei, to whom Turnbull was closer. Steven strove to achieve even-handedness in his exploration of Borneo's political complications, but often the happenstance of whose personality he found to be most attractive ended up encumbering him with a side after all.

Evading Turnbull, Steven now sought the hospitality of the unofficial leader of the North Borneo British colony, a Scottish tycoon, James Mitchell, director of the local branch of Harrisons & Crosfield, merchants in tea and subsequently variously other goods, who had had dealings in the past with the Runciman Line. Steven did not know Mitchell personally, but to his delighted surprise he recognized Mrs Mitchell, who, twenty-seven years earlier, had been a governess in the employ of a very different British official to Turnbull, none other than Sir John Chancellor at Jerusalem. What followed would appear to have made the coincidence as uncanny as it was welcome:

> She reminded me that I had told her fortune then [in 1931] and had been puzzled because there was to be a blank period later in her life when she seemed to be dead and she afterwards would turn to life. She had married soon afterwards, and had gone out to live in Borneo, very happily, till the Japanese invasion at the end of 1941. She had then spent nearly four years of misery in a concentration camp, with nothing to do except to try to keep herself and her young son alive. All that time, she told me, she was sustained by my prophecy that she would come back to life.

Steven lingered with the Mitchells for a couple of days to explore the chief towns of North Borneo, Sandakan and the capital Jesselton, which, he later bizarrely observed, is 'the only capital city to be called after a Jew [Sir Charles Jessel], unless we count St Petersburg as such; but both cities have had to change their names.'

Probably the most notorious aspect of the subject peoples acquired by the Brookes were the head-hunting practices of the Dyak tribes in Sarawak's interior. In *The White Rajahs* Runciman postulates that the custom of taking and preserving the heads of enemies was a relatively novel one, having reached Borneo only in the eighteenth century, and interestingly attributes its persistence to Dyak women, to whom the head-hunts had central importance as tokens of courtship. In tracing the decline of the head-hunters he attributes much of the credit to the Brookes, with their careful, impartial, paternalistic deployment of missionaries from various denominations (as Steven later quipped, 'rather to the puzzlement of the Dyaks, who found that in some districts the holy men married but would not drink alcohol, while in others they drank alcohol but would not marry'). Finally Runciman claims that this gory form of ritual killing and desecration had undergone a minor revival in the twentieth century, in the exceptional circumstances of the Second World War:

> The Japanese concentrated themselves in the towns and among the coast. Not many of them penetrated far up-country. There the indigenous tribes were left very much to themselves; and it was not long before they were assailed with the temptation to go head-hunting again . . . Japanese officials or soldiers who strayed away on their own were seldom heard of again; and several longhouses received the adornment of a Japanese head or two. One Kayan house can boast of the head of a rash Director of Education, complete with his gold-rimmed spectacles, which are still lovingly polished every day.

This seems like one of Runciman's most characteristic, unreliable flourishes. The lip-smacking relish with which it is recounted is slightly disagreeable but comprehensible; the passage follows a brief, bald account of the conditions and atrocities in Japanese prison-camps on Sarawak.

But Steven was also well positioned to have extracted trustworthy details for this grisly vignette. He kept up his surprisingly friendly relations with Tom Harrisson, who had led the guerrilla resistance to the occupiers; he had spoken to the Brooke-era ex-Chief Secretary Aikman, who had survived the war as a Japanese prisoner; and, after his stop in North Borneo, he did indeed undertake a still more difficult investigation into the interior of Sarawak than his visit to the Great Caves. His guide here was Dennis White, the new British Resident at Brunei, a stiff, by-the-book colonial officer who was also a realistic diplomat and a capable adventurer. Steven was amused by the gossip (presumably gleaned from Philip Jones, Hugh Ellis or Abell himself) that behind his pompous, ponderous kindliness White hid an old-fashioned secret – a Malay mistress and a family of unseen half-caste children. At any rate, White put himself entirely at Steven's disposal, and took him to visit a Dyak longhouse (Steven's second; he had seen another with Harrisson on the Niah River). Steven, already ailing from a milder variant of dengue fever, felt that he ought to do his duty and asked to see the longhouse's head collection. He does not say whether any of the relics were Japanese, let alone bespectacled, but certainly he found the experience overpowering: 'Two dried heads grinned down from the roof. I hope that I behaved with adequate courtesy. They were all immensely friendly; and the head-man begged for us to stay the night in his house ... To my relief Dennis White, who by now realized that I was far from well, said that we had to go back ... '

*The White Rajahs*, the book that emerged in 1960 from these travels, amply fulfilled its purpose in the eyes of those who had commissioned it. Abell expressed his delight: 'It showed me very forcibly how little the tactics of the Brunei Junto have changed over the years and I got much amusement from the skill with which you assessed the 3rd Rajah's contribution to Sarawak history – it was masterly and should be studied by all budding diplomats.' But, although conceived by the Colonial Office, *The White Rajahs* was not supposed to be a training manual for British officials. It is subtitled 'A History of Sarawak from 1841 to 1946', and several reviewers – especially transatlantic ones – mutinously pointed out that it seemed to be little more than a family chronicle of the Brookes of Sarawak. This is a fair charge; though Runciman devotes a chapter to Borneo's pre-European history and another to the three centuries of pre-Brooke European involvement in the archipelago, both chapters are mere scenery, foreshadowing the White Rajahs of the title. Runciman had repeatedly proved himself to be something like the supreme master in Britain of dynastic narrative history. He can hardly be blamed, at the height of his eminence, in his mid-fifties, working in an unfamiliar sphere to an unusual commission, for playing to his strengths. The question should be whether, given that *The White Rajahs* is a history of the Brooke family, it succeeds in meeting Runciman's regular standards.

Preparing to savage his Cambridge rival in Byzantinism in 1933, Robert Byron had damned Runciman with the faint praise that 'while he is dealing with actual written evidence he is happy and brilliant.' In relation to *The White Rajahs*, Runciman's first book which required extensive original archival and oral research, this early criticism both does and does not stand up. The overwhelming bulk of the written evidence, as Steven had discovered at the Astana's haunted library and at the Museum of Sarawak under Harrisson's idiosyncratic guardianship, concerned the second Rajah, Charles Brooke, 'the most monstrous autocrat but remarkably shrewd', as Steven summed him up to Leslie. For the ad hoc, personal rule of the founder-Rajah, Sir James Brooke, hardly any written sources remained. For the controversial and chaotic reign of his great-nephew, Vyner Brooke, the third and last Rajah, abundant information existed, but much of it was withheld by the competing interests of the Brooke family, itself divided into two factions, and the Colonial Office. Steven himself did not relish the prospect either of expending energy on exhaustive interrogations or of defending himself in the libel courts from the wrath of the Ranee Sylvia on the one hand and that of the disinherited Anthony Brooke on the other. It might, then, be expected that *The White Rajahs* contains a nourishing kernel between scrappy early and late sections. This is not the case. Rather, it begins as an exceptional and vivid short biography, but slowly declines into a cagey and limited work of history. In the eventful story of Sir James Brooke, Runciman located one of his great subjects, one of his most subtly yet fully realized protagonists. But after that he could only muster ever-diminishing enthusiasm for the great man's less inspiring descendants.

The frankest biography of Sir James Brooke is Nigel Barley's *White Rajah*, published in 2002, while the fullest treatment of the Ranee, Philip Eade's *Sylvia, Queen of the Headhunters*, appeared in 2008. Runciman operated under hindrances from which these later writers were free: the continuing position of homosexuality as a serious crime, and the surviving presence of the famously litigious Ranee. It is of a piece with his character and his career that he leapt over the first obstacle while remaining chained by the second. The work Runciman produced could not be faulted by the most bigoted and jingoistic Brooke hagiographer in its approach to Sir James; but at the same time its implications are perfectly clear to a sensitive reader. Runciman suggests his view quite clearly, without approaching as closely as Barley does to the reefs of speculation. Most interesting for the purposes of Runciman's own story is a slight but perceptible sense of identity with the first Rajah.

'It is likely that his prolonged Indian childhood gave him a sense that his life belonged to the East,' Runciman wrote of James Brooke, thus expressing not only his own predisposition in favour of the Middle and Far East, but also his theory about his schoolfriend Eric Blair, who had, it seemed to him, for atavistic reasons rejected university for the Burmese Police. Runciman's summary of James's schooling contains a generalized memory of the distastefully militaristic experience Steven and Blair had endured: 'The great advantage of the education traditionally given to the British Upper Classes is that anyone who has been through it knows that he is unlikely ever to be so miserably uncomfortable again . . . Like most boys [James] was only ready to work on the subjects that interested him.' Finessing the story of James's mysterious Burmese war wound (used by some admirers to explain the Rajah's lifelong bachelorhood), Runciman quietly shows that it was probably in the lung, and that James was more likely to have stayed unmarried from choice than from physical necessity. He is subsequently judicious about James's emotional attachments to younger men and boys:

> [James] had long discussions about the future . . . with Kennedy [Brooke's ship's surgeon], whom he visited in Ireland, and a younger boy, Stonhouse, who saddened him by refusing to write to him but whom he visited happily in Scotland . . .

> He was at his best with the young. When at Oxford . . . he frequently slipped away to see undergraduate friends, and he had many friends among midshipmen whom he met in naval circles. He was always on the lookout for promising young men who would come and work in Borneo.

Such allusions may seem thin next to the meatier assertions of Barley ('there is little doubt that at this period of his life [James] was carnally involved with the rough trade of Totnes'), but they possess a pre-Wolfenden dignity, even pathos, truer to their subject. When Runciman rises to defend James Brooke's policy, he is implicitly defending the first Rajah's personal as well as public life:

> The British Liberal conscience is a remarkable phenomenon. It is often unattractive . . . characterised by smugness, narrowness, and a certain lack of scruple . . . with regard to Borneo it showed itself at its worst. In fact James Brooke's temperament . . . though liberal in a broad sense, was not akin to that of most Victorian Liberals, with its pious Puritan background . . . It is not surprising that many honest philanthropists in England found him incomprehensible and even a little outrageous.

Such a well-informed analysis could only come from a historian who had practically grown up at Asquith's Cabinet table, who had witnessed the Strange Death of Liberal England, who had taken in, with both loyalty and scepticism, the reasons for the political misfortunes of his father: for Walter Runciman had been nothing if not an old-fashioned, honourable, Puritan Victorian laissez-faire Liberal. Steven appreciated the qualities of that tradition, but he found it stifling and inflexible if maintained in isolation. Among non-conformists, he supremely refused to conform; and in James Brooke he discovered, rather to his own surprise, a long-lost predecessor.

# 22

## The Hanged Man

*Cambridge, 1921–34; London, Islington, 1951–
2000; Oklahoma, Tulsa, 1981; New York State,
Mount Kisco, New York City, 1957–95; Spoleto,
1959; Devon; Edinburgh; Dumfriesshire; various*

He who can understand that the story of his higher nature is
imbedded in this symbolism will receive intimations concerning a great awakening . . .

Arthur Waite, *The Key to the Tarot*, 1920

In the summer of 1953 the youngest peer in England, Lord Montagu
of Beaulieu, was arrested on a charge of indecent behaviour towards
a fourteen-year-old Boy Scout. Lord Montagu, who gave his first
interview about the affair in 2007, utterly denied this accusation (of
which he was indeed soon cleared), attributing its origin to a
'witch-hunt' aimed at prominent, affluent homosexual targets. Steven's old Cambridge protégé Guy Burgess had fled with Donald
Maclean to the Soviet Union in 1951. Both in Britain and in the
United States, under the respective influences of Sir David Maxwell
Fyfe, then Home Secretary, and of Senator Joe McCarthy, the 'Red
Scare' proceeded hand in hand with a 'Lavender Scare', an obsession –
to which the case of Burgess, among others, gave an unfortunate
degree of credence – with the relationship between Cold War treachery and 'unnatural vice'. Bowra's old joke about the 'Homintern' was
only gaining in literalistic force. The bisexual Lord Montagu and the
men who would soon be his co-defendants on another charge, his
cousin Michael Pitt-Rivers and his romantic friend the journalist
Peter Wildeblood, were quite clearly no more dangerous subversives
than John Gielgud, who was arrested in a Chelsea lavatory in October 1953. But these men were visible enough that, when they were
convicted the next year of improper conduct towards two airmen,

something appeared to be being done. Their persecution and imprisonment would come to be seen even in its own day as a petty and plodding overreaction, and ultimately an unanticipated step towards sexual liberalization.

Ten years separated the publication in 1957 of the Wolfenden Report on prostitution and homosexual offences from the implementation of its central proposal – the decriminalization of sexual relations in private between consenting men over twenty-one. For Steven Runciman, this was an exceptionally productive decade, which saw first the publication of *The Sicilian Vespers*, and then the writing of *The White Rajahs*, *The Fall of Constantinople* and *The Great Church in Captivity*. Throughout this time Steven's allusions to the climate that produced the report, to its recommendations and to its eventual adoption are vanishingly scarce; the tone of the few exceptions is notably closer to derision than to sympathy.

Writing to Stewart Perowne in November 1953, in the period between Lord Montagu's two arrests, Steven turned his mockery on the young peer, and, more to the point, on the disciples of Lord Baden-Powell:

> As you have probably seen, the press has been enjoying itself with sententious articles about Unspeakable Vices. Personally I am much less shocked by the honest dirt of the *News of the World*. But the case of Lord Montagu of Mauvais-lieu . . . is a nasty one, though gossip says that he'll get off. Bad as he was, the boy-scout was worse. As a highly respectable old lady remarked to me the other day, the first thing that should be done is to abolish the boy-scouts.

Steven is, of course, teasing, and indeed his whole correspondence with Stewart Perowne was a recurrent struggle to shock, outflank, needle and impress. The same letter also contains a clawed swipe at the expense of Israel and Jews in general: 'I've been surprised to find how many Jews are coming out now against Zionism – but they should have done it long ago. The fundamental fault of the race is a lack of moral courage.' It is noticeable that, though he may consider the press-coverage to be prurient, 'sententious' humbug, Steven seems to consider Lord Montagu both technically and morally guilty (though likely to be acquitted). This is, perhaps, reassuring, indicating Steven's aversion to what was at the time usually called 'pederasty', sexual advances towards underage boys, which is what Steven means by calling the Boy Scout allegation 'nasty'. But, more importantly, Steven's summary of the matter to the equally mischievous Perowne shows his preference for the most scandalous version of current gossip, sometimes regardless of the evidence. In 1961, on a Scottish National Trust cruise, Steven would end up befriending the notoriously scaremongering former Home Secretary Maxwell Fyfe, by then Lord Kilmuir, without any apparent qualms. In fact he was much less interested in Kilmuir's record in office than in Sylvia, Lady Kilmuir, the sister of Rex Harrison and, he thought, the mistress of Buck De La Warr (another peer, whom she went on to marry after Kilmuir's death).*

Twenty-five years later, however, writing to a much younger friend, the New York arts journalist Jeffrey Schaire, Steven was unstinting in his condemnation of the equivalent moral crusade in 1950s America:

> I remember thinking in the old days that Roy Cohn [the McCarthyite attorney] was a very handsome young man, to judge from photographs in the newspapers. But as at Senator McCarthy's orders he persecuted people whose private lives were similar to his own – and, if the gossip of the time is to be believed, the Senator's – he must have been evil, for all his present charm; and if he has AIDS, poor man, it is a divine retribution.†

---

* Leaving aside his unenlightened record on homosexuality, Kilmuir had been in most ways a distinguished and relatively liberal statesman. He had cross-examined Göring at the Nuremberg Trials with a success that surprised a press initially put off by his dry manner; he was an architect of the European Convention on Human Rights; he had stymied the reintroduction of corporal punishment and begun to moderate authorization of the capital variety; and he fought for the equal rights of Commonwealth citizens of any colour choosing to reside in Britain, race relations being a domain in which he was decidedly nearer to the present consensus than (for example) Steven.

† Joe McCarthy was persistently but never very convincingly rumoured to be homosexual; Roy Cohn was indeed secretly gay, and would die of AIDS in the summer following this letter. Steven's greater readiness to condemn American over British anti-gay witch-hunts can be attributed in part to consistent chauvinism, as when he reported to Stewart Perowne of West Berlin that 'The British are self-effacing but

Time and fashion had changed out of mind; but an important distinction is that Steven saw the American 'witch-hunters', including, with wild improbability, McCarthy himself, as hypocritical transgressors themselves. Steven's idly malicious attribution of the disease to divine discontent, even in the case of a repressed and duplicitous 'persecutor', hardly sits comfortably within the gay lexicon of 1986, let alone today. Indeed, one conclusion to be drawn from the way Steven orchestrated, concealed, revealed, flirted and adjusted throughout his long career of active sexuality is that he himself believed and continued to believe that homosexuality, ideally a private matter in the legislature of man, still constituted an inarguable offence against God. What is more, this unalterably, metaphysically criminal nature constituted, for him, a part of his sexuality's appeal.

'My life is uneventful,' Steven once told David Plante, one of a bold and inevitably disappointed few to express interest in writing his biography while he still lived. 'Uneventful and uninteresting, because I've never been in love. I've been loved, and I've hurt those who have loved me. I, myself, have never been in love.' While this insistence may come across as exaggerated and defensive, there can be little doubt that Steven himself believed it to be the whole truth. His evasion of lasting, reciprocal emotional proximity had been a conscious, willed choice. That this was so was only secondarily because he was already sixty-four when homosexuality was legalized. It was more importantly a consequence of his lifelong temperament. He was particular about good looks in others, quietly vain about his own, and specific in his demands. Those demands included an appetite for aesthetic and erotic as well as intellectual adventure, but carefully excluded the emotional domain. Emotion, or sentiment, hampered liberty, compromised clarity, and forfeited detachment and manoeuvrability, all of which were necessary for the fortified, privileged, epicurean privacy Steven had early decided that he needed.

Only in his relations with Dadie Rylands as a very young man can any neediness, any disadvantage of power, be truly discerned in

---

resented, the Americans prominent but despised. In the American zone all the nazis [Steven disdained their upper case] are scrabbling back into power, less so in ours' (SR to Stewart Perowne, 20 May 1953, Elshieshields).

Steven; and early in his Cambridge undergraduate career he seems to have determined to guard himself against ever being at another person's emotional mercy. It is significant that those mainly or entirely heterosexual young men within his early circle, as well as the women he befriended, who formed an unusual proportion of his close friends for a man of his age, class and milieu, almost all thought him a suitable confidant about their problems in love. Only his elder brother Leslie was wary of Steven's potential for malice and indiscretion; and Leslie's first wife, Rosamond Lehmann, spoke freely and intimately to Steven until he declared unambiguous war on her to her face. Christopher Chancellor and Sylvia Paget used him as their go-between until their parents approved of their match; Charles Bosanquet and Roy Harrod approached him in turn as an intermediary when they wooed his sister Kitty, as did Oliver Farrer with more success. He seemed an innately older character, a potent and impartial force who, himself free from romantic turmoil, might be able to allay it in others.

This was the somewhat steely, untouchable impression Steven liked to convey to men and women outside the initiated circle, but even in the cases of young men amenable to his flirtation he painstakingly, cautiously remained in a position of independence, and therefore, implicitly, dominance. To Cecil Beaton Steven seems to have possessed something of the same mystique that had previously made Steven himself defer to and admire Dadie Rylands. Beaton took Steven's advice on questions of visual good taste, dress sense, in social and even, where his own talent was really the surer, theatrical machinations; he cultivated Steven's company and that of his friends; all this despite a gossamer-frail suggestion that he at some point rebuffed Steven sexually – Steven refers to him in a throwaway letter of summer 1925 to Kitty as 'ridiculous amusing Cecil Beaton, who is apparently sexless and certainly soulless'. It might be thought that Steven is coyly explaining Beaton's lack of interest in most women to his young sister, but this is unlikely.* Steven's letters to Kitty in this

---

* Beaton was, in fact, very far from sexless and might easily be argued to have been a great deal less emotionally ascetic than Steven himself – he allowed himself to long for the future connoisseur Peter Watson with particularly imprudent fervour. Unlike Steven, he was also not entirely sexually averse to women; his occasional and spec-

period are unusually frank about his preferences and tendresses, sometimes through the medium of a jokey alter-ego, Kitty's childhood doll Prissy,

> I enclose a letter from Prissy who has been good on the whole, but greedy and too much inclined to make eyes at the young male peasants – they of course stare at her because she's so obviously a foreigner. I have had to reprimand her.
> [in the voice and hand of Prissy] The sheperd boys are nice here too Next time I shall come unshaproned he! He!

While detailing and sometimes boasting of his companions at lunch, tea and dinner, sometimes to Ruth but particularly to Kitty, Steven details their physical attractions and their athletic achievements ('dinner with four Blues, so alarming'), as well as his curt estimates of their social position and intellectual capacity. There is one other, much later, faint suggestion that he was resisted by an interesting object in this period – he told a younger friend in 1987 that he had reason to believe that Rex Whistler, who was then thought by Stephen Tennant's biographer Philip Hoare to have had some kind of affair with Tennant, 'wasn't that kind of boy'. In practically every other case he alludes to, then and later, Steven figures as the chaste, even slightly prudish, rejecter rather the unsatisfied pursuer. This may not always represent his conduct in love-affairs as they happened, but it does add up to a consistent view he held of himself.

During his first year at Cambridge, Steven began, but soon abandoned, a novel, tentatively entitled 'Happenings', 'about a boy and his sister. It is very irritating as I keep finding that I'm unconsciously making the boy, who isn't very nice, rather like myself.' It is no coincidence that the only person he told about this brief attempt was, presumably, the model for the female protagonist, Margie, his closest sister in age as in temperament. But Steven's frustration with this first attempt at extended fiction reveals what he rarely allowed to be seen in less intimate company, that there was much he fundamentally disliked about his own character. As he grew up at Cambridge with

---

tacularly visible girlfriends included the society courtesan Doris Castlerosse and, later on, Greta Garbo.

precocious speed, he aimed at transferring this self-distaste from the weakness of shyness to the strength of flirtatious cruelty. But this could not satisfy him either; he disliked himself for inflicting pain as much as he had despised the frailty of suffering it. Steven had a strong sense from a very young age of the passing and waste of time. This can be observed in his frustration with the endlessly self-analytical, circular conversations during Stephen Tennant's Wilsford parties, or in his jaded descriptions of Cambridge attractions that had once thrilled him, only to become routine: 'nothing happens here but a stream of pettily exciting things, that seem quite dull afterwards.'

Of the older generation whose praise meant far more to Steven than that of his undergraduate contemporaries – dons, Bloomsbury writers, hostesses and, arguably above all, E. F. Benson – the one whom he found least intimidating, and with whom, judging by the slim gossip Dadie Rylands preserved, he was likely to have carried on an intermittent physical affair, was Sebastian Sprott, sometime lover of Maynard Keynes. Steven thought Keynes himself the most awe-inspiring intelligence he had ever witnessed, but this only ratcheted up his crippling shyness. He eventually achieved friendly relations with Keynes mainly by way of intermediaries: Roy Harrod, Adrian Bishop and later Keynes's wife, Lydia Lopokova, who was even more uncertain of her reception by Bloomsbury than Steven himself. Sprott was a different matter; and in his unpublished memoirs Steven alludes to him as his closest friend among Cambridge postgraduate students: 'He was already in his later twenties, highly intelligent and accepted as an equal by the brighter dons, such as Maynard, but regarded with suspicion by the more sedate, as he studied psychology, which the academic establishment did not consider a proper object for study.' The reminiscences of David Plante imply that Steven himself disapproved of psychology, showing him in old age gently teasing his publisher at Thames & Hudson and Plante's lover, the Greek poet Nikos Stangos, about the course of analysis he had undertaken. In fact Steven's attitude was flexible; as a young man he admired Sprott's pioneering advances, and in old age, when his New Yorker friend Jeffrey Schaire admitted to him that he was undergoing psychoanalysis, he was curious but considerate.

But among both his own generation and the potential models of

Bloomsbury, when Steven conceived a distaste he could be unsparing and immovable in its expression. He was wary of, though a little dazzled by, Lytton Strachey, whose elder sister Pernel he preferred; and Lytton was renowned for his readiness to make passes, which could have played their part in Steven's caution. Steven was also disproportionately contemptuous of harmless, well-intentioned figures like Frankie Birrell (another brief attachment of Keynes's) and Raymond Mortimer. He was severe enough to Maurice Bowra, openly in print and behind his back though not generally to his face, for Bowra to maintain a grievance against him into the 1960s, declaring himself ever willing 'to pour a boiling kettle over Steven Runciman'. Steven deflected the respectful courtesies of Roger Hinks for years, insisting on interpreting him as a rival until the Second World War had passed. The deaths of so many friends and the alteration of the old world beyond recognition showed up such confected feuds as out-of-date habits of mind. Even so, Steven's remarks to Paddy Leigh Fermor, two decades after Hinks's death in 1963, in response to an essay by Leigh Fermor on their deceased acquaintance's character and qualities, were by no means confined to the generous:

> I suppose I knew him longer than any of his friends ... He was in those early days perhaps even more intolerable, and intolerant, than later on ... one always remained fond of him ... he was such good – if sometimes embarrassing – company ... what a good mind he had, though it was often wayward and shamefully prejudiced ... what a strange man he was ...

In early youth Steven writes of being 'good and nice' to Hinks, 'who doesn't deserve it', and of persistently and unavailingly turning down his (social) invitations. These glimpses combine with Steven's conflation of Hinks's 'good company' with the sense of 'embarrassment' referred to above to suggest that at various times each man had to some degree accepted as well as rejected the other, and that from Steven's perspective the old bond between them had some element of distaste and shame.

The case of Guy Burgess is an appropriately amphibious one. After Steven had signalled that his interest in Guy was amicable as well as professional, admitting him to his first parentally unsupervised house-party on Eigg, they saw each other increasingly regularly for the next three years of Burgess's sputtering postgraduate career, often daily. By 1937, after Burgess had committed himself to Communism, had then publicly denounced it and, while in the employ of the BBC, had appeared to dabble with the Tory right and even fascism, his close friendship with his old tutor had apparently waned. But the crisis of war led Steven to resort to his pupil and friend who appeared to be closest to the action, at the War Office, and they were in regular contact from January to May 1940, when Steven left for the Sofia post Burgess had procured for him. During the first long period of their friendship, at Cambridge, Steven's feelings towards Guy, which were both protective and intellectually ambitious, seem unambiguously to have sharpened his distaste for Anthony Blunt and John Cornford in a manner that shows plausible traces of sexual jealousy. Steven was certainly aware of, and amused by, the conclusions that might so easily be drawn in the later years of Burgess's notoriety – that he was believed to be linked to Burgess by sexually as well as politically suspect ties. It is in this spirit that Steven referred in the *Alphabet* to 'owing my war career to a traitor', and also that he wrote in 1986 to the intrigued, younger outsider, Schaire:

> [Blunt] certainly did not have a physical relationship with Guy Burgess. Guy disliked, physically speaking, anyone taller than himself (as he told me more than once, perhaps to deter me; if so, the precaution was quite unnecessary). Thus any suggestion that he went to bed with either Anthony Blunt or Donald Maclean, both of them exceptionally tall, is nonsense.

Steven is obviously enjoying his uniquely privileged position of knowledge here; he smoothly hints that Maclean, too, had his role to play in the homosexual parallelograms of 1930s Cambridge even while he denies the particular link to Burgess; and while he disclaims the idea of a Burgess affair in his own case as well as Blunt's and Maclean's, he evokes a world in which it was eminently possible. This rebuttal, then, functions in some ways as a confession. As evidence of Steven's physical relations, or lack of them, with Guy it is of limited value; as an example of his attitude and his teasing angle it is more revealing.

Steven's gossip to Schaire about Burgess and Maclean is also contradicted by what he told a Cambridge contemporary of Burgess's not so very long after the 1951 defection. An MI5 memo from Courtenay Young to his superior in counter-espionage, in January 1958, reports an 'informal interview' with Steven:

> The conversation inevitably got round to BURGESS, and I asked RUNCIMAN whether he had known MACLEAN. He said that BURGESS had brought MACLEAN round to see him, that is, to display MACLEAN to RUNCIMAN, as BURGESS was at that time having 'a roaring affair' with MACLEAN. RUNCIMAN dates this as being in BURGESS's fourth year at Cambridge and MACLEAN's second. According to RUNCIMAN, BURGESS and MACLEAN had met at 'Party parties' and the affair had been the direct result of their common membership of the Communist Party. RUNCIMAN said that while MACLEAN was undoubtedly good-looking, he found him slightly repellent and hardly ever saw him again. He had of course known the MACLEAN family all his life, as MACLEAN *père* and his own father were fellow Liberal politicians.
>
> He said that were he to go to Moscow he would hardly be able to resist the temptation of ringing up BURGESS and meeting him again, though he had no desire to see MACLEAN. He asked me whether it would be in order to do so. I told him that he was free, white and twenty one, and he could do what he liked, but suggested that if he was staying with the ambassador it might be tactful to move out from the ambassadorial roof before having a cosy evening with BURGESS. RUNCIMAN agreed ...

Young here contradicts his 1951 report to Robertson that Steven and Burgess were not friends and moved in different sets at Cambridge. Steven also played down, it would seem, how long or well he had known Maclean – they had met on Eigg with their respective parents, and Steven rather liked him. Most noticeably, Young has soberly briefed his superior at some length about the projected Moscow visit, which Steven certainly intended as a risqué joke and had no intention of following up; he did not visit Russia until a trip to St Petersburg in 1990, accompanied by his Russophone niece Ann Shukman, long after Burgess's early and unhappy death in 1963. The British spook in the 1950s is being teased no whit less thoroughly than the American arts journalist in the 1980s.

On Burgess and Blunt Steven's comment to Schaire is more convincing, but far from universally corroborated. Anthony Blunt's elder brother Wilfrid thought differently, but Burgess's recent biographer Andrew Lownie has cited the testimony of two lovers of both spies, Jack Hewit and Peter Pollock. According to these arguably better-informed sources, the two traitors, infamously linked in the public imagination, would have been sexually incompatible as both preferred to be the passive partner. It is intriguing that this claim is both similar in kind, and different in specifics, to Steven's. In any case Steven might have preferred to disavow any affair between Burgess and Blunt as a continuation of his old grudge. But the most important claim in this 1986 letter is that Steven himself was never even theoretically attracted to Guy Burgess.

According to his self-presentation here and elsewhere, Steven, though he *might* allow himself to toy 'physically' with a variety of interesting 'youths', never allowed his feelings genuinely to be affected. The same projection is manifest, for example, in Steven's severe, hardly even regretful accounts of the ill-fated, uncontained, sentimental alcoholic Eddie Bates. No doubt in many cases this emotional immovability was, or at least became, the truth – true enough, even, for Steven to feel guilt and regret about it in the end: 'I've been loved, and I've hurt those who have loved me.' Into his eighties, Steven seems to have retained a remarkable power to wound much younger attachments. Both Charles Turner and Jeffrey Schaire, themselves difficult men from a bibulous world full of undisciplined tempers, at times broke off their correspondence with Steven feeling slighted and hurt by him, and he had to woo them back and remonstrate with care:

I don't know what I have done wrong – some mistimed and misunderstood pleasantry, maybe . . . Dear Chuck, I have known you and have thought of you as a good friend for many years. I have always admired you as a composer – but only wish that you composed more. I am told that you are a wonderful teacher; and I know you to be intelligent and full of charm . . . I am hurt to find that you have so little faith in my affection for you.

Dear Jeff, What is fussing you? You surely realize that you are my favourite young man, or would be if you ever came to see me. Absence does not always make the heart grow fonder; on the contrary, it offers scope for alternative fondnesses.

Late in his life Steven would, very rarely, confide that he had had one more significant and deeper attachment in his youth; and he seems not to have been referring to Dadie Rylands, Douglas Davidson or Eddie Bates, as he called the brief episode 'my Naval Affair'. The abortive naval cadetship at Dartmouth of Guy Burgess can almost certainly be ruled out in this connection. Steven's only fully accredited close naval friend was his distant cousin Charles Lambe, the future First Sea Lord, who would eventually be appointed Admiral of the Fleet just before his premature death from a heart attack in 1960. Lambe, three years Steven's senior, was liked and admired by a remarkable range of friends. Lord Mountbatten would call him his 'best friend', and he seems to have brought out the humorous best, too, in King George VI; but he was also greatly loved by Freya Stark, Paddy Leigh Fermor, the composer Lennox Berkeley and the organist Boris Ord. In 1940 he married Lesbia Mylius, the divorced wife of a brother-officer, a marriage which lasted until his death, produced a son and a daughter and was by every testimony contented; but this does not entirely preclude more various habits. When his mother warned him as a very young naval officer against making a hasty marriage to a girl he had praised inordinately, Lambe stated a bracing credo: 'If you asked me, am I in love with her I should reply: "Yes – deeply." But I reply the same if you put the question to me about any of my friends ... the love of friendship is infinitely more profound [than the "love of passion"] because it embodies respect, admiration, understanding, sympathy and all the intellectual and mental ties in the world.' In this statement of belief, in his taste in paintings (he loved Edward Lear) and in his fondness for music, especially piano duets, Lambe had much in common with, and most likely much influence upon, Steven.

While Steven was a young undergraduate Lambe was in his mid-twenties, handsome, talented, kind and popular. He had seen active service as a midshipman at the end of the First World War, and continued in the service with consistent credit, but in August 1922 HMS *Raleigh*, the cruiser on which Lambe was an officer, ran aground off Newfoundland and sank, with very little loss of life. This turned out to be a happy accident at least in one way, as the navy sent Lambe to Trinity, Cambridge, for two terms. Steven was just commencing his second year and, as he later recounted in a foreword to Lambe's biography, Lambe immediately introduced himself one quiet autumn evening, claiming cousinhood. Steven greatly charmed his new kinsman by explaining that their common ancestor was, fittingly at least for the sailor, a notorious sixteenth-century Norwegian pirate, Andersen. There was a faint physical resemblance between them: Lambe's bright-red hair was an intensification of Steven's auburn. 'Charles was at once one of us, and probably the most admired,' until 'he went away, leaving all his Cambridge friends a little disconsolate.' Stewart Perowne – at this stage still wary even of Steven – felt callow and shoddy beside this omnicapable war veteran:

He seemed to create an aura of awe round him, so that he was outside, not inside, any group he happened to be talking with . . . I was afraid of Charles when I first met him: he had the glamour of having served with the Royal Navy at an age when I'd been a schoolboy . . . he had such authority, such integrity about him. He made me feel a superficial sham.

Lambe can be glimpsed years later at Steven's twenty-ninth birthday luncheon. Steven recounted the occasion in detail for Kitty, away on an Indian honeymoon:

A nice birthday . . . Mummie and Margie and Lellie and sister-in-law [by then Kay Runciman] and the Bowens and the Wansbroughs and Chula [of Siam] and Puffin [Asquith] and my naval friend Charles Lambe. Mummie gave me a bath-mat and a sponge rack for my new bathroom at Trinity, and Papa promised me a hot-rail, only it can't be managed. Vera gave me an enormous bottle of eau de cologne and the Wansbroughs some hankies and Charles Lambe expensive cigarettes . . . Chula promised me something from Paris. Lady Ottoline Morrell with whom I went to tea gave me a bit of orange-blossom from a vase in her drawing-room, but I don't think that counted.

It is interesting that Lambe is here identified not as a cousin but as a 'naval friend'. But by this point whatever could possibly have gone on was long over. Lambe was a lieutenant-commander stationed in the East Indies (he must have been on leave; perhaps the cigarettes had a decadently authentic oriental origin). His subsequent appearances in Steven's surviving correspondence are scarce, casual and simply affectionate until a faintly nippier letter to Stewart Perowne in 1955:

> As ever with Charles I am almost irritated to see that one person can combine so much energy and efficiency with so many extra talents – music, painting and so on – and so much kindness and overwhelming charm. It really isn't fair. The more I see of [Lesbia] the fonder I am of her ... supremely civilised, and does her duty as an admiral's wife superbly but so modestly and quietly that you are hardly aware of it. I used to think her a bit neurotic but there's no sign of it now.

A brother-officer of Lambe's, Sir William Davis, gives the same impression of a Renaissance exemplar in his *ODNB* biography, with a little added enigma:

> Lambe did many things well and often much better than other men, but there was something elusive about him. Endowed with much personal charm and greatly liked, he had a first-rate intellect which never tolerated insincerity – yet there was perhaps an inner sanctum in him which few penetrated but many sensed. His clear well-ordered mind saw through most problems, and also the most practical ways of solving them. His tastes were catholic and his enthusiasm infectious. Added to a love of outdoor pursuits he had a deep appreciation and understanding of many artistic things. He was a pianist quite out of the ordinary in performance, an accomplished water-colour painter, a lifelong member of the Bach Choir, and had an abiding appreciation of Shakespeare and Andrew Marvell's sonnets which he enjoyed quoting. Yet for all this, his love of the navy and sense of service took priority over all else.

It is certainly tempting, but doubtless too easy, to identify the qualities that baffled and awed Lambe's naval comrades with those that might briefly have lowered Steven's guard. Steven concluded his foreword with a sparing but superlative tribute: 'We all, I suppose, have a list of friends who are dead, whom we are grateful to Providence for having allowed us to know. My list is not the only one that has Charles at its head.'

Between the sharp crispnesses of Steven's calculated youthful resistances, the somewhat self-pitying but determined renunciation of his juvenile poetry and the weary rejoinder to David Plante lies another tantalizing memory of the regret he barely let himself express. After the war Steven had met and befriended on a Syrian dig an archaeologist named Max Mallowan and his wife, Agatha Christie. In the mid-1970s he accepted an invitation to stay with them at their house in Devon, Greenway. Patricia Ayling, a young friend of the Mallowans who helped with cooking, driving and typing, remembers Steven's impact as a guest, and a version of a rare, wounded confidence he made to his host:

> Steven was a regular visitor and an eagerly anticipated one. Although I think he was primarily Max's friend (Max always spoke to and about Steven with great admiration as well as warmth), Agatha – who was very discriminating in a rather quiet and gentle way – was also plainly fond of him ... It's possible that Steven might have been involved or consulted about some aspect of a detective story ... For his part he was generous in his response to Agatha's writing.
>
> Steven was a perfect house guest. Beautifully dressed, very charming, exquisitely polite, a performer with a good raft of anecdotes, some slightly scurrilous, about public personalities, but not outright unkind and always delivered with a rather mischievous smile as though he was also sending himself up. When not required to be entertaining (and this aspect of him appeared effortless) he was a self-entertaining and even rather withdrawn presence. He was equally nice to everyone and seemed to have time for and interest in whoever he was speaking to regardless of class or age. He gave the impression of great empathy.
>
> Although very witty and engaging, he had a melancholy air when in repose. He had rather mournful brown eyes but when something amused him his eyes changed slowly to gleeful ... I sometimes drove Max up to London for evening archaeological meetings ... On one occasion Max told me that he had taken ... a walk with Steven, and

how sad he was when Steven told him that he felt his life had been a failure because of his gayness. I remember Max saying with huge indignation how tragic and wrong it was that Steven who had such enormous achievements and such a glittering academic reputation should feel this way.

By this time years had passed since the legalization of homosexuality, but it was too late for the reforms to put any real balm on an old wound. Lord Montagu remarked in his first and last interview that he would have taken to being born in the twenty-first century like a duck to water. This is in many ways not remotely true of the more proud, self-disciplined, contained Steven. But he had indeed been born at the wrong time to rest contented with himself, even if he did live during almost the perfect period to put that discontent to good use.

Exaggeratedly effeminate men, 'exquisites' as Steven called them without admiration – Stephen Tennant above all – annoyed him; he responded aesthetically to more conventional masculine types, whether or not they were particularly likely to reciprocate. He mentions to Kitty in 1925 one Trinity rowing blue, Victor Malcolm, as being 'beautiful but dull'; in the same breath he is completely open about the nerves that a coming tête-à-tête with a new acquaintance, 'unexciting but athletic', is causing him. Steven could afford to discuss a remarkable range and procession of possibilities with his youngest sister, with whom his correspondence retained the tenor and vocabulary of Torby's school-room; he knew of Kitty's schoolgirl pashes and aversions, and would end up abetting her marriage to a younger Trinity contemporary. On both sides the siblings' language remained that of precocious childhood, while its implications could be more serious. Steven's preference for the 'athletic' at this time (it did not preclude his interest in the theatrical; he was particularly taken with Joe Ackerley's Achilles) may have had its origins in another effect of childhood. In every sphere but the intellectual, his brother was his obvious standard of quality; and until Leslie's death in 1989 Steven continued to insist (against the conclusions of some who knew both brothers) that his brother possessed superior 'glamour' and 'natural charm'. His own youthful diffidence and self-dislike perhaps left him attracted to his brother's mould rather than his own.

The austere, eventful mobility of Steven's life during, and indeed after, the war makes it harder still to guess at what distractions he may have preferred among the many combatant, neutral and diplomatic men he encountered. It is tempting to wonder about Michael Padeff, Misho to Steven, regarded even by ill-disposed acquaintances as very good-looking, mainly but not exclusively a womanizer, and extremely perceptive in his memoirs about Steven's character. Steven felt sorely responsible for Padeff's arrest not long after dining with him, and if they had been anything more than sympathetic acquaintances the guilt must have been still more oppressive. They did not meet after the war, despite Padeff's brief absorption into the Runciman family's Liberal affinity by way of his fleeting marriage to Priscilla Bibesco, Asquith's granddaughter. Steven's favourite posting during the war years was not his most conspicuous, important and superficially fitting role, as Professor of Byzantine Studies at Istanbul, but his earlier and more junior propaganda work at Jerusalem. His appreciation of life in the Holy City had, it seems, a sexual dimension: as he told David Plante, 'In the evenings, on my way home, it was rare not to pick up an Arab boy, or a Jewish boy, or even an English boy; Jerusalem was during the war rather a centre.' From his much longer Istanbul phase Steven provides one more brisk window on his rejection of a suitor; he mentioned to several different friends that he had resisted the urgent advances of a Turkish painter, Nurullah Berk. Happening on a postcard of a Berk in loud reds and yellows, he sent it in 1998 to Guy Black: 'I'm most nostalgically intrigued to see that this daub was painted by an artist who was over-fond of me (an unreciprocated passion) more than fifty years ago. *How* one's past catches up with one.'

The search for significant names is an innately futile business, and it becomes especially so during the British Council interlude. Steven's albums for 1945–7 are filled with handsome young Greek men met here and there, by chance or in the course of duty, sometimes given a first name and surname, sometimes a first name only, sometimes only an epithet or nothing at all, whose exact relation to him – whether paid tricks, fleeting objects, semi-regular arrangements or only picturesque holiday sightings – it would be interesting, but is now impossible, to discover. According to the captious gossip of Maurice

Cardiff two of Steven's subordinates in Athens, Ronald Crichton and Bill Barron, both of whom he went on seeing in later life, accompanied him on a certain amount of Greek cruising. During and after his Athens stint, Steven assisted several young men, both Greek and Turkish, with money for education in Britain (in at least two instances a musical education). These protégés often visited him in London and even Eigg, were photographed and kept in his albums with evident enthusiasm, but usually ended up as married men.

In the mid-1950s Steven befriended the composers Gian Carlo Menotti and Samuel Barber, lovers since before the war, in New York. This was an auspicious and convenient new association because Menotti shared Steven's birthday; Menotti and Barber's house in Mount Kisco, New York State, was called Capricorn, but in fact Menotti and Steven were Cancers. In 1958, when Menotti founded the Festival dei Due Mondi, for opera supplemented by dances and orchestral pieces, at Spoleto, he arranged for it to conclude at the birthday in question, 7 July. Steven could now indulge in a particularly exciting foreign adventure whenever he reached a birthday without other prevailing plans. At the second such occasion, in 1959, Steven took a strong liking to one of Barber's very few pupils, the violinist and would-be composer Charles, or Chuck, Turner, then in his early thirties. The next spring Steven invited Turner to stay with him in St John's Wood in order to accompany him to Glyndebourne, urging him with the words 'you have no social obligations – you can use the house as a hotel.' Early in 1961 both men attended a party thrown in New York by that mysterious Croesus of connoisseurship Henry McIlhenny; Steven recalled it as 'delicious', a 'pleasant little orgy'. When Turner was in England, Steven delighted in giving him ready access to his new Steinway, and, knowing that Turner planned to set *The Waves*, skilfully deflected a course of questions about Virginia and Leonard Woolf. This was a sign of things to come.

Steven, by his late fifties still a lean, able-bodied, good-looking and thorough flirt, was starting to realize that young men sought him out for his historical status as a supposed survivor of Bloomsbury. This was a process that was much accelerated by the publication of the first great post-Wolfenden Bloomsbury biography, Michael Holroyd's *Lytton Strachey*, the two volumes of whose first edition appeared in

1967–8. Steven was unusual among the book's actual and potential sources in his willingness to contribute and his friendly curiosity about the author, with whom he made contact through his old wartime connection Olivia Manning. This was partly because his own place in the story was safely marginal; he only added a few points of interest about Strachey's fleeting crush on his brother. David Garnett and Duncan Grant, much more integral protagonists, were, respectively, cautious and duplicitous towards the young biographer. But, for Steven, the main immediate effect of Wolfenden was that he was liberated to gossip with more fervour, more conspicuousness, breadth and historical proximity about *other* people.

Through the 1970s Chuck Turner hosted fairly regular New York musicological evening gatherings, made up of six of the distinguished, older intelligentsia – musical, artistic or literary – and six younger men chosen for wit, looks or both. Steven attended a few of these, and at one in 1978 he found himself alongside the composer Virgil Thomson – advising eagerly on the French components of the menu, and attracting Steven's quiet but pronounced dislike – and the painter Maurice Grosser. The younger men included several striking air stewards, an Australian musicologist, a charming but elusive Irishman named Eric, of vaguely proclaimed aristocratic extraction, and a young black writer, Darryl Pinckney. Turner himself was far gone in drink and regret relating to a slight in love and profession by Samuel Barber. Steven (a product of his age on racial matters as on others) found himself repeatedly surprised by Pinckney: a middle-class, bookish American boy, precociously established on the city's literary scene, passionately inquisitive about Bloomsbury in general and Virginia Woolf in particular; as Pinckney puts it, 'a black kid with a thing, a real jones, for Bloomsbury'. Steven took great pleasure in disillusioning him, though it proved a harder task than he had expected. No matter how often he insisted that Virginia had been a sneering, affected creature eaten up by ineffective snobbery and longing to befriend dukes, Pinckney, his faith undimmed, recited back passages of *The Waves* word for word. Years later he was still protesting, laughingly, about Steven's *lèse-majesté* towards the queen of modernist novelists: 'I'm still shocked that you can be funny about Mrs. Woolf; that someone who drew near the presence can cast a critical eye ... didn't you find her beautiful and beguiling when she was on?' But he responded with greater ease to a little ragging of Evelyn Waugh, based largely on Steven's long-ago, brief meeting with Alastair Graham ('the real Sebastian Flyte') at Sir Percy Loraine's table in Istanbul.* Their relationship thrived on paper, and, though Steven haughtily professed to other friends that Pinckney's ardent letters were 'neurotic', he was obviously flattered to command intense attention into his seventies and eighties. In 1989 Pinckney emerged as the consistent partner of the poet James Fenton, causing Steven to lament to Jeffrey Schaire with only mostly mock-ruefulness of 'Darryl's fickleness'. Pinckney remembers Steven's flirtation towards him in the flesh as having 'a courtly quality, a retreat strategy of the elderly. Not too much was risked. Pride okay. Sort of ... his flirtatiousness was also a form of good manners, of being gallant. That in no way meant he was interested.'

Steven's old friend Philip Jones, the Sarawak Public Information Officer who had instigated the commission of *The White Rajahs*, had taken holy orders in the mid-1960s. He became the chaplain of London House, a hall of residence of London University in Bloomsbury with especially reasonable rates for Commonwealth citizens. It was in this context that in 1968, after lecturing to the students at Jones's request, Steven made a new acquaintance, a New Zealander dentist, Gordon Gardiner, who would put him in touch with an intriguing younger set. Steven was free with invitations to Elshieshields to Gardiner as well as his travelling companion and fellow countryman Ross Poland: 'Can't you some day take a little time off and visit my mini-castle in Scotland? ... Do consider it – and bring your charming and intelligent young friend (or send him: but perhaps you don't let him out of your sight.)'

In fact, however, Gardiner would in general – like Nicholas Phillipson in Edinburgh – go on to play the in some ways less demanding and certainly more useful role of Steven's city host (after Steven had left the remaining lease on his London house to his Australian friend

* Steven had, however, thought Graham worth his while enough to photograph him, and pointed out this snap while showing his younger guest his albums at Elshieshields, after sufficient wine had been taken.

Mrs Dalton). Steven was enchanted by Gordon's high-rise London residence in the mid-1970s: 'I am immensely inquisitive about the Barbican and its lofty towers . . . Your eyrie is superbly placed, beautifully furnished and deliciously comfortable; and you are the kindest of hosts . . . all that luxury combined with a delectable dinner in very charming company.' He would sustain the tease by referring to 'your dizzy eyrie, so far above my station in life'. To Gordon Gardiner and several of his friends, such as the scientist Ian McDonald and the historian of Spanish courtly art Curt Noel, Steven behaved, on the whole not disingenuously, as a wise, worldly, neutral force of benevolence. Should his own offers of hospitality be accepted, he was 'known to wander', and would occasionally amuse himself by attributing nocturnal pouncing habits to his tower's ghost. But he was quick and courteous to accept any reluctance. Steven remained, justly, proud of his looks for his age (he kept dyeing his hair dark red for some decades), and would, apropos of little, talk of his 'impressive nude'; but he often admitted that 'I've always been a better friend than a lover.'

Steven's advice and mediation could be useful both when his younger friends were monopolized and harassed by possessive older lovers and when they in turn were hurt by the narcissistic cruelty of the succeeding generation (for Steven could always be relied upon to take his friends' sides):

> In my long life I have all too often seen that sort of relationship in which the young thing decides that he is being smothered by his older friend (especially if the older friend has a personality) and so behaves badly. Love alas so often ends in tears. I am glad that I have the temperament of a harlot and so am free of emotional complications. I hope you are having a happy St Valentine's Day.

Steven's bold claim of carefree 'harlotry' has a defensive ring, while the observation of a wronged older 'personality' sounds practically close enough to home to be a scarcely veiled personal identification. But it is again a little misleading, a touch insensitive to Steven's character, time and type, to be too cynical or suspicious of his clarity on the matter. He believed what he wrote about his lack of emotional fetters to be the case; he had done his best throughout a long and far from chaste life to make it so; and he had cause to regret having missed out on enviable pleasures and comforts as the price of his decision. Among his younger friends, romantic, if not necessarily physical, loyalty to a single partner was becoming the admired standard. By contrast, as Steven's Edinburgh friend Nicholas Phillipson points out, the generation and code of Steven and Dadie Rylands was by habit, circumstance and education more stratified and extreme – public courtliness and covert cruising, intertwined and sequestrated by a strict lattice of discretion. Yet friends closer to Steven's age had chosen regular ménages and benefited from a measure of public respectability and openness after legalization, notably the novelist Angus Wilson and the British Museum administrator Bentley Bridgewater. A choice to embrace the loosening spirit of the age existed, but Steven felt unable, and on balance, too, more unwilling than not, to make it.

Of Steven's part in the initiate, nocturnal world of 'adventure', even such old and close friends as Phillipson deny specific knowledge. Phillipson emphasizes his late friend's place in a specific historical and social setting:

> I think to an aristocratic, or semi-aristocratic, talented, single gay person, partners don't come into the scene even if they exist ... In that sort of Thirties, post Twenties culture, you would never dream of introducing your partner at a lunch party for the Queen Mother. It would never occur to anyone. The thing is, you can't even call it gay, this world. You really ought to call it queer ... By and large, partners are rarer. However, there may be a huge social gap, so a partner is a piece of rough trade ... You're almost in the world of Francis Bacon. I've often thought Bacon, much younger, is partly a hangover from this theme ... a sort of displaced person, that's where some of the genius comes, someone displaced from the world they ought to have lived in.
>
> ... there can be a declension from the highly respectable gay, or queer world, to a really slummy gay world. Pre-Wolfenden. That's a theme that crops up with all of those people. And if you take someone like quite a close friend of Steven's, John Gielgud ... or particularly Dadie Rylands and his friends at King's ... again, there's a displacement ... the business of sex and slumming sex is where Steven clams up completely ...

I know nothing about that, except that it's quite clear that Steven was roaring around.

. . . you need to go back to the Twenties and Thirties. The point is, this is the sort of thing that would irritate Steven . . . I do think, actually, that Steven is a type. Now Steven did not believe in types; the only times we'd actually argue about history were about this. Steven knew what I thought about history and vice versa. But the one thing he deeply distrusted was anyone who had any sort of social history mental framework . . . the trouble is I do think Steven is representative of a type, and that type is the upper-class queer.

A marginal note accidentally preserved on the back of another letter in the Elshieshields archive alludes in glancing reminiscence to an episode between Dadie, naked but for a neck-tie, and some Guardsmen in the mid-1930s; this is the earliest visual scrap to have survived Steven's 'holocausts', his practically ritual burnings of correspondence. These careful and extensive weekends of destruction may seem as shocking behaviour in a historian as they are comprehensible in a human of a certain time and place; they are also revealing in that Steven boasts of them with a glee that in itself amounts to faintly erotic nostalgia. Another phrase of Lord Montagu's is brought to mind, of how during the Maxwell Fyfe inquisition 'the sky over Chelsea was black with burning love-letters'.

In 1981, at the age of seventy-eight, Steven flew to Tulsa, Oklahoma, to visit the French-Canadian novelist David Plante, then a teacher at its University. Theirs was, as Plante well knew, a curious relationship, made distant, almost objective, by the positions of others: the Greek poet and publisher Nikos Stangos, Plante's lover, whom Steven openly preferred of the two; and Plante and Stangos's leading London patron, the poet Stephen Spender, who cordially distrusted and disliked Steven and received currency in kind. But Plante was as fascinated by Steven as he was by Stephen, analytically drawn to observing and preserving them; he awaited his celebrated guest's arrival with excitement and dread. Plante was then chastely cohabiting with Germaine Greer, who had been famous for a decade as the author of *The Female Eunuch*. The surprisingly harmonious combination that ensued Plante has preserved in his diaries, recently published. The visit won an honoured place in Steven's collection of limericks, which are usually, in contrast to the equivalent light verse of Maurice Bowra, scabrous only by pale intimation:

> They told me I ought to keep clear
> Of the formidable Dr Greer
> But now I'm discerning
> In spite of her learning
> She really is rather a dear.

Steven also made some confidences in richer flavours to Plante, over his last lunch in Tulsa:

At lunch he told me about his sex life. I found I didn't want to hear about it, but smiled as he told me. He said, 'I think I'll never make love again. I don't particularly like thinking it. I preserve the vague hope that something might happen. Some, as Bury might have said, historical contingency. And I will find myself in the arms of some young beauty. But I must say, I doubt it will happen. When I was in New York, a friend took me to a bar where he said gerontophiles gathered. Well, there were a great number of gerontos, but no philes. What upsets me most is that I will probably go to my grave without having made love with someone whose given name begins with Q. I've had all the letters of the alphabet except Q. I shall die Qless.'

I said, 'I can't think of a Z.'

'Oh,' he said, 'in the Middle East that's very easy. Once in Africa I met a rather unattractive young man whose name began with X, and thought it might be my only chance . . . Not long after in Greece, I met a delightful and very attractive young man named Xenophon. So now I've had x squared.'*

Besides being an example of the alphabetical, linguistic orderliness that went on to provide structure to *A Traveller's Alphabet*, Steven's 'partial memoirs' – and that has, to some extent, informed the organization of this biography – Plante's story, told by Steven elsewhere in

---

* On another evening Steven had told Plante that he could have resolved the Q problem at any point by succumbing to the advances of Quentin Crisp, 'but I just can't quite face that' (David Plante, conversation with author).

other variants, is mainly interesting here because it declares a regretful, natural conclusion to Steven's physical adventures. This graceful, Prospero-like renunciation is, however, unlikely to be thoroughly truthful. Later in the 1980s Steven repeatedly and with some satisfaction complains to both Charles Turner and Jeffrey Schaire of having to fend off the attentions of their friends, because he does not feel up to 'the Fate Worse than Death'. If his chastity had increased, then, it seems to have been by his own choice, not for lack of 'philes'. Besides, both his travelling and his hospitality still involved a measured and epicurean regime of such stimulation. Among his friends it was assumed that even in his last years Steven's relationships with Gerald Green in Bahrain and with Richard Brain, a witty, sharp-tongued *Times Literary Supplement* sub-editor with noble if florid features, continued to have a physical element.

More important really than the factual substance behind the alphabet story and the gerontos and philes is their real function as ripostes in a long exchange, somewhere between a game and a war. When Steven was first becoming known as a leading aesthetical Trinity undergraduate, his father had made an unwontedly boorish crack which travelled about anecdotally, along the lines of 'I put up with the rouge and the mascara and the velvet clothes, but if I ever catch him sitting down to pee, I'll cut him off with a shilling.'* Steven early learnt that it was better to make the jokes himself, and make them better. His romantic life went into his writing, and his 'life of the senses' was independent, and, even more crucially, thoroughly well defended.

---

* This remark, remembered by several sources within the Chancellor family, is contested by Walter's grandson and Steven's nephew, Garry Runciman. Lord Runciman considers its tone entirely out of character for Walter, 'a fastidious, inhibited and rather prudish person.'

# 23

# The Tower

*Texas, Austin, 1965; Dumfriesshire, Lochmaben,*
*Elshieshields Tower, Auchenbrack, Drumlanrig*
*Castle, 1966–2000; Edinburgh, 1966–2000;*
*London, Bloomsbury, Westminster, the Athenaeum*
*Club, 1966–2000*

'. . . except the Lord build the house, they labour in vain that
build it.'

Arthur Waite, *The Key to the Tarot*, 1920

Late in 1965, Steven found himself derailed from a much anticipated
first visit to Las Vegas by a summons to attend upon Lynda Bird
Johnson, the elder daughter of the President of the United States.
Lynda Bird had begun a course on English and Latin literature that
September, minoring in an obscure but increasingly fashionable
branch of history, and the boisterous US Ambassador to Australia,
Ed Clark, a Texan attorney lately in Johnson family service, had
thought Steven just the present to have couriered to her after meeting
him at dinner in Canberra:

> . . . I told him that I was going on to California and Texas . . . What!
> he exclaimed indignantly, was I going to Texas and not to Austin, to
> the University of Texas. It was his university, and it was Mrs [Lady
> Bird] Johnson's university; and why, Miss Lynda Bird Johnson was
> there at the moment. Now what was that subject in which I was inter-
> ested which began with a B? Byzantium? I ventured. Yes, that was it.
> Miss Lynda Bird was studying Byzantium.

By November Lynda Bird was still feeling a little unsettled at Austin, but that was to be nothing to the state of her unlooked-for star
lecturer. After he had missed one aeroplane on purpose and two more
due to desert storms, Steven, without time for supper, a wash or a
change of clothes, was bustled in front of the Austin audience. Owing

to a football game earlier that afternoon, he found the lecture-hall distressingly well attended, a veritable throng of 'loyal University folk'. A good-looking, attentive, well-behaved girl in the third row was chiefly recognizable as Miss Johnson by the 'two huge thugs' who flanked her; her father's predecessor had been assassinated not quite two years previously. Thus tipped off as to where to concentrate his efforts, Steven developed a reliably emotive theme, extracted from *The Fall of Constantinople* which had appeared to such acclaim the preceding summer. He noticed that by his peroration 'to my gratification' Miss Johnson 'was wiping away tears'. She had also spotted the direction of his glance directed to her bodyguards. 'These', Lynda announced to Steven after the lecture, pride overcoming trepidation, 'are the best educated detectives in the United States. They have to attend all my lectures, you see.' According to Steven, she added that the pair regarded her Byzantine history course, with its litany of plots and murders, as useful 'homework'. Steven silently compared the Byzantine security record over a millennium favourably to that of the United States Presidency. They got on to less contentious ground when Lynda was made aware of Steven's Scots origin, and he managed to elicit her family's descent from the Johnstone clan of Annandale, notorious Border reivers.\*

By the next winter, Steven himself had moved to a former Johnstone possession, the new house to which he now proudly referred as 'my mini-castle'. A topographical gazette in 1842 had described Elshieshields Tower in resonant if slightly grudging terms:

> Elshieshields, situated on an eminence overlooking the Ae, at the ter-
> mination of the wooded bank, is an old but not warlike structure, one
> part of it rising to a considerable height, and imparting to the whole,
> as seen from a distance, the appearance of a dilapidated tower . . . The

---

\* The presidential family's connection to the Johnstones was relatively distant, by way of an Ulster planter. A closer relation of the clan was Steven's uneasy friend the novelist Angus Wilson, born Angus Johnstone-Wilson. Oddly enough, Lyndon B. Johnson, Angus Wilson and Steven himself were all to be associated in the fullness of time with conspiracy theories about the shooting of John F. Kennedy: LBJ as the obvious beneficiary, and Wilson and Steven as acquaintances of Clay Shaw, a homosexual businessman and ex-CIA man from New Orleans who was prosecuted but cleared of involvement in the assassination.

parishioners, who are generally a full century behind other parts of the Lowlands in receding from the superstitions of the dark ages, have made this tower the scene of one of their most notable ghost-stories.

Steven had small patience with this chary approach. Tracing as he did the very name of Runciman – or rouncey-man, that is to say, a dealer in pack horses – to 'roughly this part of the country' (meaning Dumfriesshire), he was eager to advertise to friends his new domain's sanguinary history, and to insert himself into its story by quasi-ancestral right. He was quicker than the most eldritch-minded locals to tell of the Johnstone wife whose bairn had been burnt alive in the oldest part of the tower by reivers of the rival Maxwell affinity. She leapt into the flames and met her death trying to rescue her child; guests were regularly assured that she still returned to the tower, where Steven now constructed his latest library.

In an excited letter to Freya Stark, Steven described the tower as 'thirteenth century, rebuilt in the upper part in 1600, with a 1780 wing and an 1830 top storey added, all very compact and easy to run'. The inaccuracies in this loving, anticipatory boast are for Steven unusually moderate. In *Dumfries and Galloway*, John Gifford describes the existing tower as probably begun in the fifteenth century. Though a good deal later than Steven's first proud claim, this indicates that the tower-house's origin lies in a time of especially chronic disturbance for the Borders, never quiet for long until the Union of the Crowns. Gifford dates the old tower's most substantial reconstruction to 1567, earlier than Steven's rough approximation. This was at the very peak of the Border troubles, while the Johnstone–Maxwell feud was raging. It is tempting, even, to connect this rebuilding with the fire that consumed the Johnstone mother and child in the old ghost story. Alastair Maxwell-Irving in his *Border Towers of Scotland* (2000) notes that the tower's site is first mentioned, 'albeit fleetingly', in 1245, in a grant of 'Elsyscales' to Robert de Brus of Annandale; this actually backs up Steven's supposition of a thirteenth-century origin. Maxwell-Irving doubts the burning, rebuilding and consequent ghost, thinking 'a fairly quiet history' for the tower more likely. Steven himself is cited liberally as a source by both Gifford and Maxwell-Irving.

Gifford notes that Elshieshields shares with the slightly later Dumfriesshire towers of Repentance and Gilnockie the useful feature of a beacon-stand, to be lighted in the event of an English invasion. The Johnstone family prided itself, without obvious veracity, on confining its cattle-raiding to the English side of the border, so English reprisals were a constant hazard. The corollary was Francophilia, more evident in thought and word than deed, but having a cultural effect discernible throughout the later Scots Middle Ages, above all in architecture. In the *Alphabet* Steven would rejoice in his tower's French characteristics: 'Living as I do in a house to which a seventeenth century builder added pepper-pot turrets in the belief that they would make the house look French, I must record my loyalty to the Auld Alliance.'

Walter, Leslie and Steven had long and sedulously collected the paintings and drawings of the Runciman brothers, or as Steven happily dubbed them Uncle John and Uncle Alexander, mid-eighteenth-century Scots artists and early exponents of historical and literary subjects. These Runcimans had no recorded blood relation to Steven's family (though Steven blithely invented various specific ones uncorroborated elsewhere), but the ghoulish wit of their dim backdrops and impish figures made them congenial spiritual ancestors. In the depressed post-war art market, the work of the neo-Gothic Runcimans was unfashionable and cheap. In the same period of Attlee's high-taxation Austerity Britain, Evelyn Waugh was building up a considerable collection of Pre-Raphaelite drawings. Steven now festooned his 'ancient tower' with the creations of these improbable 'uncles'.

Steven had initially been struck not by the tower's history or appearance, but by a seductively mysterious description of its antiquity and convenience. On Easter Sunday 1966 he wrote to Ruth:

> It's not quite where I would have chosen – Dumfriesshire . . . excellent train service to Euston, so very easy to visit . . . an 18th century white-washed house attached to a 12th century pele-tower [a yet further exaggeration], on the banks of the river Annan . . . The agents haven't yet told me its name or that of its owners, but after studying the map I think it must be a house called Hoddom Castle.

Hoddom, a larger tower-house, once a stronghold of the Max-wells, some dozen miles south-east of Elshieshields, was too derelict to be saleable, never recovering from an army tenancy during the Second World War. When Steven learnt the actual name of the property, he told Ruth that 'the house is called Elshieshields Tower (it sounds as if one were drunk).' He was not at first sure what he made of the seller, a dog-breeder in marital difficulties called Mrs Harcourt Wood. But on meeting her and her collection of Labradors, which, like most furred pets, irritated both his disposition and his constitution, Steven reported (perhaps unfortunately in the circumstances) that 'we get on like a house on fire.' The handover was less than smooth. Steven professed himself:

> appalled as one always is by the sight of a dismantled house. Not that Mrs Harcourt Wood has nearly yet cleared out her belongings ... There are suitcases and books and odds and ends and bottles of wine in the cellar, to say nothing of all the Labradors. She is a very odd woman. There's nothing I don't know about her life now – about her physical ailments too in the most intimate detail. I can't help rather liking her ...

The name of Elshieshields is in truth less warlike than botanical, referring in the Lallans dialect to a grove of ash trees. Its position commanded handsome woodland and a large garden, then in a fairly wild state, as well as a descent to the Water of Ae, resonant of the folk ballad 'Annan Water'. Though he might joke to Seferis of his new home's 'suburban' qualities, in fact Steven regarded its closeness to Lockerbie and the London train – a line that would later, much to his annoyance, be moved – as one of its chief virtues, especially when he was pressing its attractions on desirable visitors. The nearest village of Lochmaben was notable as one of the putative birthplaces of Robert the Bruce, allowing Steven loftily to name the victor of Bannockburn as 'a local boy'.

Steven's choice of Elshieshields turned out to be happy and enduring, but it was precipitated by living rearrangements that caused him regret. Most important of these was the sale of Eigg. Elshieshields henceforth served as a substitute in its rural beauty, squirearchical social function, romantic historical interest, Scottish allegiance and bibliophile convenience. In all these respects, given the intensity with which Steven felt Eigg's loss Elshieshields proved surprisingly successful. Its surroundings, though lacking Eigg's captivating romance and difficulty, gave Steven a sense of homecoming, even of destiny:

> The weather has been lovely – icily cold, but cloudless every day since I came here, with sun pouring into the house, and the mountains all round (to the north and west – but on clear days I can see the Cumberland hills away to the south) gleaming with snow. There are wild geese and wild swans on my river. There's a lot of re-fencing to be done on my tiny estate and a lot of planting. I shall be kept busy for the rest of my days.

Steven was fortunate in his neighbours. At Auchenbrack, an hour's drive north-west, the laird, following the deaths of two brothers in the second war, was an amiable, gossipy, good-looking retired actor, Dan Gaskell, who shared many friends and parties with Steven. More grandly, Steven had already been for more than a decade on cheerful visiting terms with the greatest magnate in the county and, indeed, the kingdom, the Duke of Buccleuch, whose wife, Mollie, was a particular friend. His first visit to the Duke's Dumfriesshire seat, Drumlanrig, in 1955, had been overwhelming:

> the most fantastic palace . . . built in 1699, in glowing pink sandstone, with great woods all round and the moors rising behind. The stonework outside has carvings from Grinling Gibbons designs . . . In my bedroom . . . the piece de la resistance is a copy of a Claude painted, admirably, by Mme Elizabeth, sister of Louis XVI. I am writing in bed, not daring to put out the light, as I suspect the room of being haunted. My fellow guests were to have included Anthony and Clarissa Eden [Eden was then Prime Minister], but he has flu – rather a relief.

Mollie Buccleuch wrote purporting to worry that Steven had been disappointed by this 'bovine bucolic weekend'. After Steven's second visit in 1959 he wrote with unmixed, all-suffusing contentment that Drumlanrig was quite simply 'the most beautiful Great House in the world'. The Buccleuchs asked Steven for help in pursuing the provenance of their family portraits, and Mollie wrote to him with unconcealed distress on the disabling riding accident of their only son Johnny Dalkeith. Of the family's children Steven became closest to Caroline, who was married to the most cerebral of One Nation Tory grandees, Ian Gilmour. Much as Steven had enjoyed his own spell as laird of Eigg, it was at his age a pleasure to exchange demanding tenants for hospitable seigneurs.

Eigg had only ever been a partial residence, on average for about three months annually, especially in the extremes of summer and winter, and whenever Steven needed particular seclusion in order to write. Elshieshields represented a more everyday replacement – henceforth Steven lived mainly in Scotland. The Runciman brothers' renunciation of Eigg had been precipitated by the retirement of their last factor, Rutherford. Similarly when Steven's famously discreet ('indeed almost invisible') London housekeeper, an 'upmarket Frenchwoman', Madame Baudouin, returned to Normandy to care for a widower friend, he took this as the signal for a change. He let the remaining lease on his house in Elm Tree Road, St John's Wood, go to one of his closest younger female friends, Robin Dalton, an Australian beauty, sometime girlfriend of the Marquess of Milford Haven, and the widow of Steven's much admired GP Emmet Dalton. Steven accompanied this act of generosity, however, with a pertinent question: 'My dear, I will very happily give you the house, but how will you afford to live in it?', an enquiry to whose motivating force Mrs Dalton attributes some of her subsequent success as an agent and memoirist. Steven was soon reporting to Marthe Bibesco: 'I find country life much busier than life in London. It takes me far longer to finish off books now.' In fact he promptly proceeded to write three books, taking three years over each.

Steven probably did feel more at ease and socially fulfilled in his mainly rural life, where the timing and extent of excursions from, or reception of guests at, Elshieshields was entirely of his own choosing. He found it rewarding to have gained such control over his immediate, regular circumstances. His increasing sense of having adjusted more than adequately was reflected in an ever-warmer attitude to his ancestral and adopted, but not in fact native, country. As a reliable committee man he now became almost as public-spirited in Scots cultural causes as Greek ones. This was especially the case after the

beginning of his friendship with Nicholas Phillipson, a university lecturer whom Steven met in Edinburgh in the mid-1960s. As Phillipson
recalls, Steven's fondness for country retirement had, after all, its
limits:

> He was quite insatiably restless, he liked coming to Edinburgh a
> lot . . . He stayed with me on and off regularly, at least once a month,
> for about twenty years . . . He'd come through to absolutely anything,
> if there was a concert, dinner, what have you. I think he just did
> not like being alone, in the country, for more than was absolutely
> necessary . . . If you put Steven on a committee, he would turn up to
> every single bloody meeting of whatever it was. He was on the National
> Trust for Scotland for ages. He believed in it.

This sense of real, gregarious enjoyment is the reverse, and perhaps
the more accurate, side of the wry impression of public duty Steven
liked to give to friends as far-flung and worldly as Princess Bibesco: 'I
have a few days of committee meetings in Edinburgh – the Scottish
National Trust and the Scottish Museum of Antiquities (I have
become very Scottish).'

In London Steven had already by the 1960s become famous for his
birthday parties with their remarkable variety of guests, diverse in
age, rank and, unusually for those years, race. When he gave up Elm
Tree Road he told the novelist Olivia Manning, with whom he had
maintained, for all the scratchiness of her character, easy relations
since their friendship in Cairo, that 1966's birthday party, his
sixty-third, would be his last entertainment at full scale.* Perhaps he
meant it at the time, or perhaps he was teasing; in personal terms he

---

* In fact Olivia Manning still bore a specific grievance against Steven for failing to
apprise her of a party at Hatchards bookshop that February, with Violet Bonham
Carter, Edna O'Brien, Michael Frayn, A. J. P. Taylor, Robert Conquest, the biographer Lord Birkenhead and Iris Murdoch in attendance. It was most likely prudent
of Steven to collude in Manning's debarment, as she was far from reliable in the
company of Iris Murdoch, of whose success she was pathologically envious. Steven
had, though, mischievously encouraged this animus by privately agreeing with Manning that 'Miss Murdoch writes like a kitchen-maid' (SR quoted in Olivia Manning
to Francis King, 2 January 1965, Harry Ransom Center, University of Texas,
Austin).

preferred her amiable, unfaithful, Communist husband, Reggie Smith. In any case Manning believed him, lamenting to a close correspondent, the novelist Francis King (whom Steven rated below Manning as both writer and acquaintance) that 'even the oldest institutions die out at last.' This threnody, despite Steven's now mainly Caledonian life, was drastically premature. But Manning enjoyed what she took to be Steven's last garden party, describing its atmosphere to the – uninvited – Francis King:

> the party seemed smaller than usual and was marked by the appearance of the very young. One woman brought her teenage son who was dressed elegantly in the style of the '90s and had long curling hair. Very beautiful. Young FitzGerald (the Knight of Kerry) brought his fiancée who wore purple silk trousers and scarves and hangings of shocking pink – an eye-catching sight.

Manning had time to absorb and to impart various morsels of disobliging gossip, especially concerning herself, the older novelist Ivy Compton-Burnett, the fashion potentate Madge Garland and her own bitter friend, the poet Robert Liddell, a much more devoted philhellene than Steven. She got on well, too, with Bill Barron, one of Steven's British Council lieutenants in Athens who had so irked Maurice Cardiff. But her account of the party scarcely mentions her host; that tended to be the way that suited Steven. Under his aegis people met an extraordinary galère, garnered over a century's collecting. Occasionally things happened after that, but by preference never to Steven himself.

Steven continued for the moment to maintain a smaller, but 'sumptuous' – 'two *large* rooms' – London berth, a flat in Whitehall Court, 'my favourite Victorian building, overlooking the Thames', but though his summer garden parties continued here for a time, the bulk of his hostly duties and diversions shifted north of the Border. Robin Dalton, a regular visitor from the early days of Steven's tenure at Elshieshields, recalls an almost ostentatious lack of luxury about the routine and conditions at the tower. A driver existed, but guests were encouraged to subsidize the Lockerbie-to-Lochmaben bus. The bedrooms were heated not by flaming logs but by single-barred electric fires, whose overuse was quietly discouraged. The domestic auxiliaries at first constituted a husband and wife named Walker, who were easily shockable; Steven would issue in advance gentle warnings about some of his guests. The Walkers were loyal and assiduous in attending to Steven and the house's needs, and greatly preferred the new regime to the doubtful stability of Mrs Harcourt Wood, with her delinquent marriage and demanding Labradors. The couple guided Steven considerably through his first serious domestic annoyance arising from the vagaries of his predecessor. Mrs Harcourt Wood, lodged temporarily at a nearby hotel, expected Charles Walker to live up to his name in relation to her dogs, while Mrs Walker three times ambushed her sneaking back into the house to make telephone-calls. Steven was resigned and indeed amused, 'working myself up to lose my temper', while actually 'in a way almost enjoying it, it is so fantastic; and I know I have the whole locality on my side.' After a couple of months Mrs Harcourt Wood surrendered and withdrew to Ireland.

When the Lodge on Eigg was built, Steven had begged his family to avoid at all costs 'awful imitation Scots baronial'. He had been quietly critical of the castellar pretensions of Nadejda Muir, née Stancioff, at whose husband's enormous 1872 castle, Blair Drummond outside Stirling, 'an assortment of distinguished continentals liked to deck themselves in kilts in order to savour what they thought was Highland life'. Steven was now living in the real thing. Elshieshields's integrity lay partly in its accretive, organic nature; and it served in a way as a fitting image both for Steven's personality and for his career, as well as a convenient receptacle for his curious taste. Its attached eighteenth-century house was well suited to house many souvenirs of an adventurous and mobile past.* There might be found Benedict, the caged and stuffed parakeet belatedly retrieved from the family of

---

* On being asked by his final Athonite interviewer whether he would really have liked to live in the Byzantine Empire, Steven's answer was revealingly sensible, but, given his mixed feelings about the Enlightenment, unexpected. 'I don't know if I would personally fit in the time of Byzantium. I think I would rest in some monastery, living as many monks used to live, a life of an intellectual, among the wonderful libraries . . . I don't think I would like a life in Byzantine politics, but it is extremely hard to find a period in world history in which one would like to live . . . everything depends on the politics, the society, the class in which one is born. I would like to

Steven's Cambridge bedmaker; the twin candlesticks gifted by a contrite Guy Burgess after Steven had averted his dismissal from Trinity; the tall hookah that signified the respect of the Çelebi Effendi of the Mevlevi Order. The tower itself, after adjustments to accommodate the library, was kept in more chaste rapport with its rough Borders genesis. In its climbing spiral stair hung a rope, which, Steven lovingly informed his visitors regardless of their religious allegiance, would wind itself into a noose were the tower ever to be defiled by the step of Papists (the old enemies of the Johnstones, the Maxwells, had tended to the old religion). More than one guest noted that, though Steven took his new home's history as a good excuse to revel conversationally in his family Calvinism, he seldom attended the Presbyterian kirk at Lochmaben.

The first guest outside Steven's family to be invited to Elshieshields, Teoman Arica, was a young Turkish aspirant engineer whose education Steven had helped to sponsor. After Steven's death a bracelet that had belonged to Arica was discovered in one of the garden hedges by Jim Brydson, Steven's last driver and man-of-all-work. Arica makes lingering appearances in Steven's photograph albums from 1961, when he visited Eigg. He entertained Steven in Ankara not long afterwards. In 1970, four years after this visit to Elshieshields, he reappeared with a wife. But this new domestic arrangement does not seem to have impaired his friendly contact with his host until 1973. Twenty years later, he wrote to Steven apologizing for his long silence and asking for help with finding his daughter a job in Britain. This transactional anti-climax does not suggest an important bond, but Arica provides an example of the advantages that Elshieshields, as opposed to Eigg, offered Steven. The tower was entirely Steven's own, not a shared territory imbued with emotionally significant and politically charged family association. Its space for guests was strictly limited, lending itself to a policy of frequent and brisk invitations, and naturally stratified house-parties.

Over the 1960s Steven had established friendly terms with the most geographically distant avant-garde set of his wide diaspora – that of

---

live in the Britain of the 18th century if I were born an aristocrat, otherwise I wouldn't like it at all.'

Australia. His friends there included the novelist Patrick White and White's devoted, witty and good-looking Greek lover, who bore the, to Steven, intensely resonant Byzantine name of Emmanuel 'Manoly' Lascaris.* Through White and his 'housekeeper' Steven met the painter Sidney Nolan, though he really much preferred Nolan's increasingly ill-treated wife Cynthia, 'not an easy woman but a wonderful friend', who wrote several memoirs of the peripatetic marriage prior to her suicide in 1976.† It was the Nolans who gave a friend of theirs, the poet and novelist Randolph Stow, generally known as Mick, an introduction to visit Steven at Elshieshields in the summer of 1968. Mick Stow was a well-travelled, unconventional, ill-domesticated young man, a shrewd observer and an attuned listener. Though he could be uneasy in wider or grander social contexts, he was almost the ideal individual house-guest at Elshieshields, one to whom Steven could act as a benign preceptor, a cicerone straight to the past. Stow's thank-you letter after this initial visit is soaked with delight and greedy for knowledge:

> I think the house is splendid, & I enjoyed your library and picked up all sorts of odd information ... nothing as odd as I picked up from your conversation. I'm still thinking about the lady who devoured her husband, & poor Mrs Hambro & the Loch Ness Monster ‡ it would be a great loss if you don't write your memoirs, even if they have to wait as long as Lord Hervey's to be published.§ The world ought to

* White, who in 1965 confessed himself to Steven 'shockingly ignorant about your subject, in spite of having lived happily with Byzantium for twenty-five years' (Patrick White to SR, 13 September 1965, Elshieshields), liked to refer to Lascaris as 'His Imperial Highness'.

† Others found Cynthia unusually abrasive. Kenneth Clark, one of Nolan's most ardent supporters, thought her a witch.

‡ Winifred Hambro, wife of Olaf Hambro of the merchant banking dynasty, was lost in a boating accident on Loch Ness in August 1932. Her body was never recovered, and she was popularly supposed to have fallen prey to the monster.

§ John, 2nd Baron Hervey was a Georgian court wit and writer frequently attacked over his reputation for bisexuality. Alexander Pope dubbed him 'Sporus', the 'amphibious thing', in his *Epistle to Doctor Arbuthnot* (1735). Hervey's well-informed and frank memoirs were first published 105 years after his death, and even then in a somewhat bowdlerized form edited by John Wilson Croker (one of the founders of the Athenaeum).

know what happened to the Irish Crown Jewels* & about the tragedy of Princess Aspouzia [sic] and her evil eye.†

Among these diversions Stow was treated to an inspection of a case Steven kept of oddments with royal associations. One was a musical box that, Steven explained, had belonged to George III. He had acquired it from the descendants of one of the King's devoted servants during his spells of insanity. It replicated what was supposed to be the sound of the King trying to instruct caged finches to sing by way of a mouth organ. This time Stow was more than thrilled, he was struck and haunted. On returning to London he got in touch with a composer friend, Peter Maxwell Davies. An uncanny project that would lead to a great friendship – Max Davies and Steven's – was thus set in motion.

Early in 1969 Stow sent Steven the resulting libretto, *Eight Songs for a Mad King*. He explained that his composer friend was at work on a score, but that it was as yet unfinished, and that Max Davies:

> is dying to hear the musical box before he finishes the work, & has begged me [that] you would let him hear it for himself. I feel very hesitant about asking this, knowing how much you & Mr Walker have to busy yourselves, so that a visit can never be a matter of dropping in . . . but we did wonder whether, some time in late February, we might more or less drop in, before going on to Edinburgh to hear some pibroch music.

In the same letter Stow praises *The White Rajahs* effusively, slyly

---

* These jewels, strictly speaking the official regalia of the Sovereign of the Order of St Patrick, were stolen in 1907 from a safe in Dublin Castle, and never afterwards found. The world does not know their ultimate fate, and Steven's answer to the question has nowhere survived. Various rumours blame the Ulster King of Arms, Sir Arthur Vicars, over drunkenness, inattention to a rapacious mistress and/or a homosexual party infiltrated by Irish Republicans. Yet another theory insists that the whole affair was a Unionist put-up job to embarrass the Asquith government, and that the jewels are still secretly somewhere in royal possession.

† This is a reference to Aspasia Manos, the Greek commoner who was secretly married to the ill-fated King Alexander of Greece. King Alexander perished of a monkey-bite; Aspasia was retroactively recognized as a Princess of Greece and Denmark by her nephew-in-law Constantine. Steven was once again retailing a belief in popular currency about Aspasia's malign glance.

complimenting Steven on his modulated treatment of James Brooke's sexuality (a treatment several of Steven's friends, regardless of sexual tendency, had been puzzled by, in a couple of cases even obtusely seeking clarification). He explains that the *Eight Songs* are to constitute Sidney Nolan's birthday treat, but that the audience is expected to revolt 'in the form of boos, eggs, etc' at Max's modernity ('the whole thing is so outré, from staging to vocalisation'). In sum he asks Steven to accept the public dedication of this expressively advanced monodrama. He had learnt well the difficult art of flattering Steven to the right degree; the dedication was accepted at once, and Max Davies bidden to the Tower. Steven recalls that Max was even more enthralled by the royal musical box than Stow had been, twiddling with obsessive repetitions at its handle with the result that, Steven wryly noted, 'it never sounded quite the same afterwards.' Steven thought it an excellent joke to leave the mechanism to Davies in his will.

The young composer's thoughts were already turning in a northerly direction. Born in Lancashire, Davies had possessed prodigious musical energy and originality ever since being captivated by Gilbert and Sullivan at the age of four. A contemporary of Harrison Birtwistle at the Royal Manchester College of Music, he spent some years on fellowships at Princeton and Adelaide (where, in 1965, he had met Stow). By 1969 Davies was back in London but unsatisfied with the pattern of his life there. His complaints were understated but he meant what he said when he wrote to Steven, amid praise of his weekend at Elshieshields, that 'I rang the noise abatement society in London & the chairman said that the only way to avoid air noise was to go and live in the Outer Hebrides – he was very helpful, so I'll probably do just that.' Though the islands in question would turn out to be still more remote, the sentiment would not alter.

That April the Pierrot Players, the ensemble under the joint direction of Birtwistle and Davies, premiered the *Eight Songs* at the Queen Elizabeth Hall; the critical reception was as shocked, if not quite so violent, as Stow had anticipated. Davies was destined for a shock himself, one that would force his hand. In late September 1969 at that noisy London flat, 'the organ, piano, cat, some furniture, lots of books, some manuscripts (including 2 scenes of the opera, which I'll have to rework from sketches), pictures, glass as well as obvious things like floor-coverings, bedding, & clothes, went up in smoke.' As Max wrote to Steven, 'It was very much an end to something, and I hope a beginning of lots of new experience.' He felt winded but oddly refreshed by the unaccountable, impersonal nature of the fire: 'I was away at the time: it was what the firemen described as a "power surge".' At first he planned to settle abroad again, though 'still I think very kindly of Scotland.' That kindness would turn before long into a life-defining transformation. When Steven next received a letter from Max, in the January of 1971, the composer was enjoying his second trip to the Orkney Islands. In 1970 Davies had discovered the poet George Mackay Brown, and the isolated, almost deserted valley of Rackwick on north Hoy, the second largest Orkney. The next year he returned to work on the film score for Ken Russell's transgressive historical drama *The Devils*, flexibly based on Aldous Huxley's *The Devils of Loudun*. From the set Max wrote to Steven: ' . . . I love being here alone . . . it makes a quiet & even healthy rhythm to a day to have to get water from the spring, chop driftwood, make a fire, trim & re-fill the lamps, etc, before I can start on the music.'

Davies was amused to report that 'his' cottage had been kept standing not by the agency of the absentee landlord, but by the BBC, who had repaired it for use in the background to a televised play by George Mackay Brown. Max pestered Steven now to intervene on his side both with the elusive landlord and with the Scottish National Trust so that his tenancy might become permanent. Either out of annoyance or pure mischief Steven for a few months did just the reverse, telling mutual friends that Max hated Hoy and had no intention of moving there properly. Steven's devilry may have been motivated by prejudice against the rural romanticism of an acquaintance he then regarded as an indelibly urban bohemian. But the tension did not last. Max remonstrated with Steven with shrewd politesse over this 'mistaken impression', persuading him that 'nothing would please me more than to live up here all the time', and in June Steven did indeed put in a good word with the Trust, facilitating Max's permanent and productive removal to Orkney. Steven would come to regard Max, despite the undoubtedly eerie and chaotic quality of the piece that was dedicated to him, as fundamentally a 'cosy' friend, 'not such an ex-Angry Young Man'.

A less fortunate invitation to Elshieshields eventually led Steven into unsettling, if ultimately comic, difficulties. One of his favourite younger connections was Ian McDonald, Professor of Neurology at London, a New Zealander and the oldest friend of Gordon Gardiner, the young dentist Steven had met through Philip Jones. McDonald was almost universally liked, handsome, kind, slightly melancholy in love, endowed with both taste and ability in music. Not very surprisingly, Steven developed a hearty antipathy for McDonald's regular boyfriend from the early 1980s onwards, Stanley Hamilton, a dancer of doubtful success and Ulster origins (Steven tended to dismiss Ulstermen with a wince). Steven was in the habit of comparing Hamilton's facial features to those of his great-nephew's father-in-law, the writer A. N. Wilson. With indifference to conventional good taste Steven suggested that the partner in Gardiner's dental practice, a young and amiable (southern) Irishman, Gerard Cleary, might intervene: 'Can't Gerard, who must have IRA friends, persuade them that Stanley is their most dangerous enemy and must be bumped off?'

At any rate, Professor McDonald, who did not mind appeasing his illustrious older friend's whims in the interests of peace, did his best to ensure that on Steven's southern visits alternative company to Stanley was provided. One of the presentable old acquaintances from New Zealand whom McDonald correctly thought Steven would find acceptable was Wallace Waverley, a Russian-speaking blond, lately a schoolmaster in Auckland. Waverley and Steven were introduced in 1979, and soon the well-meaning McDonald was lamenting his own social forethought. Professor McDonald not only considered Waverley of 'only moderate intelligence, despite plenty of cunning', but also judged him to be, in a professional rather than idle sense, psychopathic. Gordon Gardiner adds that Waverley was 'a great flirt and adept at ingratiation'. Between 1980 and the New Year of 1983, Steven invited him to Elshieshields fourteen times, having him to stay every other month in 1981, an almost unprecedented relaxation of his preference for seeing friends at regular but extended intervals. Waverley was not only a handsome guest, but a fascinating one. He seemed educable on artistic questions, and was not without knowledge and taste of his own. His excellent spoken Russian, infinitely better than Steven's proud but never practical and now chronically rusty grip on the language, was intriguing. He more than shared Steven's interest in obscure European noble lineages, with a knack that Steven thought unexpected and charming in one from the New World.

In February 1983 after Waverley's last, New Year stay, Elshieshields was burgled. A single thief performed an operation that looked farcical in execution, but was oddly focused in its result. Steven described the local police's and his own differing conclusions in a letter to one of his friends best placed to understand the damage, the arts writer Jeffrey Schaire. But to Schaire Steven interestingly described the robbery as having taken place longer ago than was actually the case:

> Some eighteen months ago a thief broke into this house when I was away. The alarm went off at once, but before he fled in panic, leaving behind numerous finger-prints and a large black bag containing a brick for breaking the window, he knew to snatch from round the corner a small picture, or rather, two small pictures framed together, panels by Bernard van Orley. The police thought he must be a village-boy – he was so amateurish – and they thought that having landed himself with the picture he would throw it away. But I thought that a village-boy would have gone in for silver boxes, etc., of which there were many lying about and which it would be easier for him to sell. I decided that it must be some young gentleman who had been to the house (which I do open sometimes to cultured societies and groups), who knew what to go for and who, having no criminal record, did not mind about finger-prints.

Steven's evident pleasure in playing Holmes to the Dumfriesshire police force's pedestrian Lestrade is one layer of artifice in the account; still purer humbug is the protective *amour-propre* of the remark about cultured societies, undermined as it is by the wounded irony of 'young gentleman'. Jeffrey Schaire would probably have perceived what was afoot but was too deferential to call Steven's bluff. To his mutual friends with Waverley, Ian McDonald and Gordon Gardiner, Steven was soon franker about his suspicions, and after more time had passed he described the crime to Francis Russell, another friend in the art trade, as having been perpetrated by a former house-guest. He did not really want to be responsible for Waverley's prosecution, partly because, even sixteen years after the legalization of homosexuality in Britain, Steven's emotional defences baulked at the idea of such an invasive trial – a threat to his privacy far greater than the theft itself.

Steven deeply resented the loss of the van Orley panels. This Flemish Renaissance master was so dear to him that when in 1988 Darryl Pinckney, visiting Elshieshields and being regaled with the already anecdote-worthy Waverley saga, confessed to being ignorant of van Orley's work Steven put him on the Edinburgh train to bone up at the National Gallery of Scotland before resuming his stay. When the panels turned up in a Sotheby's catalogue in April 1984, having been sold by an untraceable party in Paris and then by a 'respectable dealer' in Cologne, Steven was far more assiduous in pursuing the auction house than he had been in bringing the culprit to justice. Much to his annoyance, he was advised that international law prevented his recovery of the panels short of buying them back at a reduced price of £15,000 (he had acquired them from Agnew's for £2,400 in 1958, equivalent to about £50,000 by the 1980s).

Steven was when it came to material matters a sensible and cautious man with a strong sense of his own rights, and he demurred at buying back stolen property. At the same time he could be attracted to the unreliable dash exhibited by rogues like Guy Burgess and Wallace Waverley. Waverley went on to reside through most of the 1980s in Brussels, using the command of genealogy he shared with Steven to impersonate a genuine Russian prince, Alexander Galitzine, descended from Catherine the Great. When Waverley had the impudence to ring Steven up for a chat in the mid-1990s, Steven confessed to Gordon Gardiner that he had quite enjoyed their brief conversation and awaited another in vain – 'I would have liked to hear how far his effrontery would go.'

In 1995 Steven entered into a curious correspondence relating not to crime but to punishment. 'I would guess that you do not receive too many letters from HMP Dartmoor,' began the unknown and unsolicited letter-writer, Clive Welch, a convict serving twelve years for a transgression he admitted but did not explain. Welch had been visited earlier in the year in Exeter Prison by a Benedictine monk,

Anscar Cowley, who was not uncommon among monastic readers in his enjoyment of Runciman's history.* One cell proved as good as another, and *The First Crusade* went down well with both Welch and one of his warders. Of limited education but keen amateur interest and unflagging enterprise, Welch looked up Steven's address in Dartmoor's 1987 edition of *Who's Who* and wrote without inhibition applying for more reading matter: 'The prison library seems to stock mainly thrillers and paradoxly crime books!! ... the library orderly who got me the address said "I know him ... isn't he the Rabbi who appears on Radio 4" ... this might give you an idea of the problems I have ... '

Steven was both alarmed and amused by this situation; he thought his latest penfriend an excellent subject for gossip, but also solicited advice about the likely nature of Welch's crime. His niece-in-law Ruth Runciman warned him that the length of the sentence and the reputation of Dartmoor Prison combined to indicate some kind of violence. Mark Bolland, one of Steven's smartest younger professional friends, thought a white-collar crime, possibly fraud, much more likely, and Steven agreed that this explained Welch's remarkable lack of repentance. Father Cowley, the bookish Benedictine of Exeter, was himself located; he told Steven that 'though his crime was serious [Welch] is not a hardened criminal,' considered that the long sentence owed something to a 'mistake', and made much of the prisoner's genuine thirst for education and his 'supportive wife'. While he was at it Father Cowley did his best to contribute a footnote to Steven's corpus of secular and personal interest: 'one of my own ancestors, a FitzGibbon, was in command at Jaffa in 1192 when King Richard I came down from Acre and relieved it.'

Steven's side of the exchange seems to have been playfully

---

* Despite the direct, plentiful and even gleeful vein of anti-papal political and theological thought in Runciman's work, his books received admiring notices in the *Tablet* far more often than not. John Satterthwaite, Anglican Bishop of Gibraltar (and therefore responsible for the 'diocese of Europe'), reported to Steven a 1973 visit to a Benedictine house in Catalonia: 'I lunched with the Abbot of Monserrat and his monks, and I thought you'd be pleased to know that we had your *History of the Crusades* read to us during the meal in Spanish. The monks seemed to enjoy the more gory bits!' (John Satterthwaite, Bishop of Gibraltar to SR, 10 May 1973).

conscientious. When Clive Welch discoursed in his grandest style on the consequences of his own heredity – half German, a quarter Irish and a quarter Sicilian, for which last he blamed the slothful defects of 'the Latin races' – Steven sent him first the text of his own lecture on Sicily, then the Italian translation of *The Sicilian Vespers*, wondering if he might comment on how it read. Flattered to be thus consulted, Welch offered a few judicious statements on its 'narrative flow', admitted to his rusty Italian and laid out the elaborate story of his grandparents' courtship. He had a romantically excitable conception of Steven's place in the world and the nation's body politic; when Steven innocently mentioned having recently been in London Welch beadily enquired 'if that is a euphemism for attending the House of Lords'. His last letter to Steven, dated October 1997, more than two years after the correspondence began, returns wholeheartedly to the same theme:

> I would be interested to hear what you think of Mr Blair's proposed reformation of the House of Lords, especially as it would seem to have direct implications upon your brother's hereditary seat – for what it's worth I believe that future historians may well look back upon Blair's 'Reign' as one of the most damaging for the traditions of our island . . . but then I dislike anyone who talks in soundbites!!

Clive Welch was not mistaken in imagining Steven as both concerned and informed on this constitutional question. In late 1993 Steven dined in Islington with his most frequent metropolitan host, Gordon Gardiner, a patient of Gardiner's called David Chipp, a retired journalist now working for the Press Complaints Commission, and one of Chipp's younger friends, Guy Black. Black was in his late twenties, a Peterhouse graduate with a First in history, working as a special adviser for the Conservatives, effective, amiable and personable. The next spring Steven was introduced to Mark Bolland, Black's partner and the other half of a force already being noted in political circles and the world of public relations. To Steven Guy and Mark would always be simply 'the boys'.

'Those boys are a great asset,' Steven declared to Gordon Gardiner, and indeed Guy Black and Mark Bolland constituted his last, somewhat unexpected, vantage point from which to survey the world of high political gossip that had always delighted him. He had for some years kept an affectionate eye upon the career of Gordon Brown, owing to the latter's university romance with Princess Margarita of Romania, of which he was first apprised by the once-King, and future President, Simeon of Bulgaria. But Tony Blair was a more mysterious quantity (and Steven purported to agonize over how to spell Mrs Blair's first name). Guy Black well remembers Steven's 'fascinated enquiries' on the subject of Blair, who, other than Andrew Bonar Law, 'whom nobody knew', would be the only British Prime Minister of the twentieth century to escape Steven's collection.* In the immediate aftermath of the 1997 election, Steven was more than sceptical of what he saw as nation-wide, hysterical neophilia:

> I can't say that the Election results have delighted me. I would almost have preferred a victory for Old Labour, which would have blundered on and soon lost popularity. Mr Blair does not seem to me to be lovable. (How can anyone marry a wife called Cherie and then call a daughter Kathryn – pseudo-Irish spelling!) I quite like Gordon Brown, though he is silly not to dress properly – perhaps his dinner-jacket got worn out during his liaison with Princess Margarita ... I never expected the holocaust [of Tory MPs] ... to be so thorough.

Aesthetically speaking, Steven's preferred political pin-up of the day on either side of the House was another Peterhouse Tory, Michael Portillo, about whom he composed a limerick confided to Gordon Gardiner:

> It would be such a sweet peccadillo
> To get to know Mr Portillo
> I am sure that a kiss
> From those lips would be bliss
> And his bosom might make a snug pillow.

Guy Black recalls that Steven's attitude to 'the establishment' 'was, in a word, often counter-intuitive', and that while Steven said he had often liked some politicians and admired others over the course of the century, the only one he had consistently both liked and admired was

---

* Steven had spotted Mrs Thatcher early, inviting her to a Scottish Opera production of *Nabucco* in 1972, when she was Education Secretary; he adjudged her 'hell' (SR to Nathalie Brooke, 29 March 1972, Elshieshields).

Tam Dalyell, the Labour MP of Scots High Tory lineage and unswervingly left-wing principles.

Steven dined with 'the boys' in London the night after Diana, Princess of Wales's funeral; Black, by then Director of the Press Complaints Commission, had implemented changes to respond to public outcry over the role of paparazzi in the Princess's death, as well as to help ensure the privacy of her sons. Steven's private view was that the Princess's public image, at least, had had a lucky escape. His attitude to the nation's public mourning was, as Black has it, 'punchy and sharp'. Bolland was now in the Prince of Wales's employ; on his appointment in August 1996 Steven had written with great satisfaction to Black, 'His Employer needs someone as sensible, tactful & popular as [Bolland] is.' By 1999, Black was involved in Lords reform working for the Royal Commission Tony Blair had granted the recently ennobled Conservative former minister John Wakeham. Steven was eager for news of royalty from Bolland and of nobility from Black. He did not trouble to hide his conviction that hereditary peers, though illogical, were Good Things: 'Surely it is useful to have one body in the state whose members are chosen by God and not by man.' When the Wakeham Report recommended a hybrid, partly elected Second Chamber Steven denounced this result to Black as 'unhelpful and rather silly'.

Though Steven was thrilled by his 'most distinguished younger friends' and their access to channels of the most up-to-date privilege, the real importance he located in the highly professional, immaculately urban and relatively informal Black–Bolland set-up was symbolic and generational. 'The boys' lived in Bloomsbury, and while Steven teased them about having become 'the heirs to those Bloomsbury figures, Virginia, Vanessa, Lytton, Duncan, Maynard, etc., whom I used to know when I was young, long ago', in a sense he meant it. Guy Black and Mark Bolland entered into an early civil partnership in February 2006, and in 2010 Black was himself ennobled, becoming the first openly gay Conservative peer. This was indeed a very different Bloomsbury; the fact that Steven survived to converse with and entertain it is a remarkable instance of historical connection.

After less than a year at Elshieshields, in October 1967, Steven had written to his niece Ann, Margie's daughter, who had by now been married for a decade to Harry Shukman, like her a scholar of Russian, to tell her of an important expectation:

> I feel that I should tell you (in case I fall out of an aeroplane one of these days) that I have just signed a new Will. According to it, you get Elshieshields with the request (not binding) that if you don't want it, you offer it to each of my other nieces in turn. If they don't want it you are free to dispose of it and contents (apart from specific legacies) as you please ... You are anyhow my residuary legatee. I trust (and I hope you do too) that the circumstances won't arise for some time to come. But I thought you ought to be warned.

Ann herself found this proposal unreal and impractical at the time, and did not seriously pay it much mind until decades later. But Steven was increasingly aware that, though he kept lecturing and writing, he was potentially nearing the end of his professional life and of life itself. He did not pay quite as much heed as he pretended to the fortune-teller who had in 1925 promised him many illnesses but a long life. His response to the consciousness of mortality was, at least, financially careful; by 1975 he had surrendered two comfortable service flats in London, in Whitehall Court and St James Court, in favour of lodging at his club, the Athenaeum, where he had offered Donald Nicol his 'after-service' supervision. Steven had been a member since 1928, proposed by Lord Grey of Fallodon and seconded by the then Archbishop of Canterbury, Randall Davidson. He was, as he told Leslie, surprised to find how well it now suited him on a more permanent basis: 'like a nice old fashioned hotel, a little shabby but perfectly comfortable – and by present standards rather cheap'. The Club, like almost all its competitors at the time, excluded women from full membership, but it was equipped with a Ladies' Annexe where female visitors might be entertained. At some point, Steven scented a chance for an ambush and put into practice a plan that developed into an annual ritual.

Steven's relationship to the British royal family was not dreamlessly tranquil or unthinkingly reverent; had it been, it would scarcely have kept him so consistently interested. In the early years of the new Elizabethan reign, he could be sceptical and derisive about the Queen Mother, and indeed about both her daughters. After the Coronation (which he heard about second-hand from his brother and sister-in-law, who attended as a peer and peeress: 'I, not being at all official, haven't been to any official parties'), Steven wrote a more than faintly satirical account to Stewart Perowne:

> The ceremonies ... all went off without a hitch, once a drunken American-born Countess was removed from the Abbey. Princess Marie Louise was, of course, reeling, with a bottle of brandy in her coach, but she didn't quite fall out ... *
>
> Lord Halifax's page, who is a limb of Satan, hid his coronet, in order to see all the more important Lordships on their knees searching for it, but he revealed it in time.† Prince Charles behaved beautifully, though he was terribly shocked to see his father walk backwards, and protested to his grandmothers.‡ My brother, who had an excellent view, said that when a sudden ray of sun struck the duchesses and their tiaras, everyone was literally blinded ... the litter left behind by the duchesses and marchionesses was awful. The humble baronesses were far tidier.
>
> Apart from the Queen herself, with whom it is clear that the whole British public is desperately in love, the success of it all was the Queen of Tonga, who would not allow the roof of her carriage to be closed despite the pouring rain. The little Sultan of Kelantan, who was sitting opposite, was furious with her ... a pathetic figure, scowling and green with cold, his nice silks all ruined; while she was having the time of her life ... §

Two months later, in August 1953, Steven reported to Perowne (who was off the scene designing model Palestinian villages in Israel) that he had 'detected a slight whispering campaign against the Queen

---

* A granddaughter of Queen Victoria, Princess Marie Louise had endured a brief, farcical marriage to the homosexual Duke of Anhalt. After the House of Saxe-Coburg-Gotha became that of Windsor, she and her sister Princess Helena Victoria decided to remain princesses but do without surnames altogether.
† Master Benedick Peake. As Chancellor of the Order of the Garter, Lord Halifax had to process in just behind the chaplains with the other knightly officers.
‡ Prince Charles was then four years old.
§ This highly visible couple was (apocryphally) rumoured to have inspired Noël Coward's quip to Princess Marina, 'Oh, that's her lunch, my dear.'

on the grounds that she is a martinet', bullying a colonel of Guards and snubbing the socially ambitious, 'but I approve of all that.' At the same time he criticized the Queen Mother for her extravagance. Much as he affected indifference to it, Steven's knighting was a great turning point in his courtly career. In the furore of August 1957, when John Grigg, the reluctant 2nd Baron Altrincham, lambasted the Queen's public image as that of a 'priggish schoolgirl', Steven's sympathies were entirely with Grigg, a friend through the London Library, and with Grigg's almost solitary defender on the right, Ian Gilmour, then editor of the *Spectator*. But after he had accepted his honour – albeit with a waspish grace – Steven felt that he ought, broadly, to rally round. After 1958 he moderated his jibes at royal figures with the enduring exception of Princess Margaret, whom, though he was occasionally flattered by her attention and liked to show off about the demands she made upon him, he thought 'common-looking', abrasive, dictatorial and wearying.

For all this increased cosiness, Steven himself must have been taken aback by the extent of the true friendship he developed by the 1970s with the Queen Mother – once mocked as 'Grinning Lizzie'. The crucial pivot between them was Nathalie Brooke, née von Benckendorff, granddaughter of the last Tsarist ambassador to the Court of St James's, a thoroughly connected and discreet court intimate. With such an auxiliary Steven almost inadvertently crossed the line with the Queen Mother, as he had done previously with the Greek dynasty and Princess Marina, between a stylized, anecdotal connection and a human bond. With the Queen – though he had a certain limited success in making her laugh at formal occasions – Steven was more nervous and distant; but he took to squiring the Queen Mother about grand parties, such as one given by the French Ambassador in 1976, when she appeared to him to be conversationally neglected. By the mid-1980s things had proceeded so pleasantly that he thought he had better ask her to his Club.* There was no question that the Ladies' Annexe would do in this instance; the Athenaeum's traditional

---

* David Plante recalls Steven telling him that he made this decision after a direct question from Her Majesty: 'What do you men *do* in your Clubs?' (David Plante, conversation with author).

mainstay of the higher Anglican clergy were ambushed in their heart-
land. Frowns turned to bows and the occasional instinctive curtsey.

This surprise was to be diluted by custom, as the first lunch was
such a success that Steven decided to repeat it every summer. The
Queen Mother would be attended by Mrs Brooke and occasionally
too by Sir Ralph Anstruther, her Equerry and Treasurer, who amiably retailed back that his Employer would 'talk of nothing else for
weeks afterwards'. But Steven preferred in fact to discourage Anstruther's attendance, theoretically out of consideration for the Equerry's
hectic round of duties and never-ending difficulties as Treasurer in
restricting regal expenditure, but really because Anstruther played a
role in another side of Steven's life, and Steven regarded him as seedy,
bibulous, increasingly absent-minded and an unwanted source of
competition for royal favour. Anstruther set the wrong tone, for
these lunches were not to be stuffy court occasions, as was indicated
in the first instance by Queen Elizabeth's only 'feminine support'
there being a mutual close friend, Mrs Brooke, rather than a
semi-professional lady-in-waiting. Steven sought to introduce the
Queen Mother to new company that she would find genuinely refreshing, and indeed vice versa.

Oddly, this formal, courtly coup of attracting the monarch's mother
to lunch every year became a context in which Steven was at his least
circumscribed and where he could invite particularly heterogeneous
combinations. The catalogues of guests – about half a dozen annually
besides Steven, Her Majesty and Mrs Brooke – mingled the claims of
talent, flirtation and even family loyalty. There was often a representative from the Runcimans at large, whether Garry and Ruth
Runciman, who were as prominent figures as Steven himself, or Margie's grandson, Geoffrey Pooley, who, it occurred to Steven, as a keen
equestrian had much to discuss with Queen Elizabeth on the subject
of the turf. The choice of guests was not nearly as simple or exclusive
as the rather easy joke, circulated by Steven among many others, that
'the Queen Mother likes queens,' might indicate.

On the one occasion Steven had to give up on the lunch for reasons
of health, in 1999, his Principal Guest sent him a somewhat loaded
present in hospital, Michael Ignatieff's life of Isaiah Berlin, a rival
admirer of hers whom Steven had never entirely ceased to dislike. Yet

Steven, who had at first groused in a puzzled way, wondering whether the Queen Mother was tactless or merely lazy, found the choice when it came to it a wholly perceptive and pleasurable one:

> ... I think the Ignatieff life of Isaiah is a remarkably good book. It makes sense of his political thought and it makes him out to be a very exceptional person. One begins to understand why he had this remarkable effect on us all. I wish that I had known him better. I had one moment of triumph over him, when I was able to tell him that I had bought a slim volume of Anna Akhmatova's poetry in 1923, before he had heard of her, and was able to quote to him in Russian a short poem of hers ... being no Wagner fan, I was delighted to read in the book Stravinsky's remark to Isaiah: 'If you listen to Parsifal you hear many disagreeable sounds.'

The Queen Mother made no claim to highbrow literary or artistic sensibility, certainly not to historical learning, but a number of Steven's various and distinguished lunch-guests gained richly, as Steven had intended they should, from more than the mere fact of her company. Richard Jarman, the Director of Scottish Opera, had a false start when he found that Queen Elizabeth 'had no great love' for his professional medium, but thought her enthusiastic on the history of ballet and positively gossipy about Freddie Ashton. The charming young Director of the National Gallery, Neil MacGregor, by contrast felt that they had conversed lengthily and intimately without his being able to recall a syllable of what had transpired – 'I suppose that must be the effect of the Royal Aura!' Most moved, and moving, was Steven's old academic ally the Professor, Prince and knight Dimitri Obolensky. Coming, as did Nathalie Brooke, from a lost White Russian world, he discovered in the Queen Mother a sudden ingress to a distant and irrecoverable past:

> I still feel the after-glow of the lunch ... I thought I would 'play the Duchess card', and am glad I did. The QM knew all about the departure of the Russian Empress-Mother from the Crimea on board HMS Marlborough in the spring of 1919 (we followed on a humbler craft), remembered Serge Obolensky ('such a handsome man') and his marriage to Alice Astor, and spoke warmly of the Grand Duchess Xenia,

whom she helped to befriend, a childhood friend of my maternal grandmother.

In the last year of his life Steven would lament to Nathalie Brooke, 'Oh, how everyone is dying. The only friend I now have who is older than me is the Queen Mother.'

The Queen Mother had entered a particular category, far separate from and above the game of polished reverence, with much reason. Although anointed with majestic chrism as Queen, as Elizabeth Bowes-Lyon she was also a Scottish girl born into what might be called the upper-middle-class nobility. Pondering the career in royal service of his starry young acquaintance Mark Bolland, Steven was soberly precise about the circumstances and qualities that set the Queen Mother aside:

> one knows not to put any trust in Royals; the Bible warns us so. Indeed, it is the sign of a born Royal that he or she cannot believe that any of their employees – or friends – can have any engagement that might conflict with the Royal convenience. Even Queen Mary, who was not fully Royal, (who were those Tecks, with their vulgar Hungarian blood?) held that view. Our dear Queen Mother fortunately, while born into a family that maintained a sense of *noblesse oblige* but did realize that lesser folk had obligations of their own, is a bit more realistic.

Runciman was a great romantic historian; but in his personal affairs Steven had come to be more admiring of that epithet 'realistic' than of any height of romance.

# 24

# The Grand Orator

The Eastern Schism *(lectures delivered 1954–5, published 1955)*; The Great Church in Captivity *(lectures delivered 1960–61, 1966, written 1966–8, published 1968)*; Mistra *(written 1977–9, published 1980)*

> Something very special on the other side:
> some discus-thrower, young, good-looking.
> Above all I urge you to see to it
> (Sithaspis, for God's sake don't let them forget)
> that after 'King' and 'Savior,'
> they engrave 'Philhellene' in elegant characters.
>
> Constantine Cavafy, 'Philhellene', 1912

Steven Runciman's obituarists were free with the laudatory honorific 'philhellene', so longingly and unconvincingly sought by Cavafy's vestigially Hellenistic, fundamentally Barbarian ruler. Steven proved himself by distancing himself from it, with a wry satire that concealed quiet satisfaction. Even in adolescence he had teased his parents and his old governess Torby by disparaging the glories of the Parthenon. He never entirely retracted his mischievous but genuinely inquisitive view that Europe might have ended up a more historically interesting, culturally various continent had the Persians won the Battle of Marathon. In letters to friends such as Freya Stark, well versed in the legacy of Hellenistic Asia Minor, he was prone to express a languidly ironical refrain about his duties 'as a good philhellene'; in private he called the Anglo-Hellenic League, the pro-Greek cultural charity of which he was Chairman from 1951 to 1967, by the more concise sobriquet 'Anglo-Hell'. *The Fall of Constantinople* includes a swipe at the nineteenth-century Romantic philhellenism that animated the Greek War of Independence: 'The Philhellenes spoke of

Themistocles and Pericles but never of Constantine.' George Seferis understood and agreed. In a fan-letter about Steven's next great work on Greek Orthodoxy, *The Great Church in Captivity*, the poet added an urgent aside: 'I don't mean, for God's sake, to praise your philhellenism – I am not attracted by philhellenes!'

On his final visit to the Mount Athos in 2000, Steven made a bleak prediction to the monastic magazine *Pemptousia*. 'Sometimes I feel very disappointed by the other Churches of the west, but I am happy in the thought that in the next 100 years the Orthodox Church will be the only historical church that will exist.' For all this – despite an enterprising late play for his soul by a breakaway order of ultra-Orthodox nuns from Colorado – Steven returned to, or remained in, the Church of Scotland at his death. One Greek admirer, Angelos Delivorias of the Benaki Museum, Athens, declared that Steven would be remembered as 'a pure-bred Scot but one with an unlikely idiosyncrasy, a sympathy with the Mediterranean world; in others words as one of us and a faithful friend'. This epitaph was mostly misleading (or misled), but it nicely displays Steven's ability to claim parallel yet cohesive allegiances. In fact his Scottishness was as mixed, and quite as deliberately assumed and as detachable, as his philhellenism.

The fascination that each country held for him had aesthetic elements in common. Steven wrote from his beloved retreat on Eigg: 'my western isle is looking like one of the isles of Greece, with a burning sun, parched yellow grass and empty river-beds'. Steven was by doctrine as well as origin far from being a 'pure-bred' anything. He was proud of his family's canny record as 'Geordies of Scots descent who came south to do well out of the English'. While this Scots strain set him apart from Northumbrians of a similarly upwardly mobile class, like Hugh Trevor-Roper, who adhered with romantic virulence to the English side of the old Border debates, it did not make him unmodulatedly Scottish, or, as he often said, Scotch. If Scottishness was in part a guise, so too was Orthodoxy – a creed Steven could admire precisely because it transcended 'ethnicist' concerns. It was splendidly suitable that he died Grand Orator to the Patriarch of Constantinople, a Gold Medallist and Honorary Citizen and Soldier of Athens, and a Knight Commander of the (Greek) Order of the

Phoenix, with a (modest) street named after him in Mistra. But it was not necessarily fitting for the reasons the admirers who formed what Steven himself gently mocked as his 'cult' in Greece always assumed.

When he claimed in the *Alphabet* that 'Greece is to me a second country,' Steven was not being altogether histrionic. But he kept this full-throated loyalty to the country that had passed through so many destabilizing troubles over his lifetime separate from his historical writing and his attraction, part expedient, part temperamental, to Orthodoxy. It was, relatively unusually in his life, a tie of duty rather than pleasure, begun in a time of war, just as the war services of most of his friends were quietening down. Steven's war, barring the near miss of the bomb planted on the Sofia–Istanbul royal express train and the irreparable wound of his elder sister's death, had by the standards of his generation been comfortable, productive and filled with interest. By contrast his work for the British Council in Athens from autumn 1945 to spring 1947 brought him into actual contact with twentieth-century total war. Greece was in a divided, uncertain and frightening state. The enemy was now Communist rather than Nazi – indeed, to a greater extent than Steven knew or acknowledged, former Nazi collaborators were enlisted by the equally tottering British Empire and the Greek monarchy. That the war was local and civil rather than global did not diminish its bitterness.

The work Steven was now engaged upon, propping up shaky governments, opening schools, funding lectures, marshalling and reprimanding subordinates, might often enough feel dull, but possessed tangible importance and visible results. He could not come through such a period without feeling that Greece had a particularly strong claim on his attention (for all that he might twitch with annoyance or satire at such a claim). In Turkey Steven's loyalty was to the country's cultural, historical and geographical past in the form of Byzantium; but his academic struggles left him disillusioned with the Turkish elite. In Athens, it was his own country, government and, in the form of the British Council, employers who incurred his annoyance. The Greeks, in their many different, contradictory incarnations – their Danish imported monarchy, their Great Church with its historic ties to what had become the second city of modern Turkey, their literature with its conflicting traditions and nostalgias towards remote antiquity and Byzantium, and their people, attractive, maddening, touchy and affectionate – offered a tempting alternative to everything Steven found lowering in post-war, socialist, Austerity Britain.

Although Runciman was regarded before the war as a promising Byzantinist, and would by the end of his life enjoy a more than somewhat exaggerated reputation as one of the first rehabilitators of Byzantine history in English, his first real achievements, following Bury, had been in the even more obscure field of Balkan history. *Romanus Lecapenus* had impressed and even baffled the dons of Trinity in its comprehension, unprecedented in a scholar of Steven's youth, of Slavonic sources. *The First Bulgarian Empire*, while arguably in large part derivative of Zlatarski, was at least in English pioneering. *The Medieval Manichee* drew its original power and force of argument far more from Balkan thorniness than from Byzantine order. In contrast, *Byzantine Civilization*, Runciman's first formal work on the Byzantine Empire unweighted towards Balkan concerns, was a slight, fallible and rushed work that failed to play to its author's strengths. It was natural at the outset of war that Steven be regarded by Guy Burgess and the War Office as, in the first instance, a solid Sofia man. It was the Athenian experience – more than the Istanbul chair itself – that fixed Steven, in the sight of others and in his own estimation, as a writer interested not just in Byzantinism, especially at its furthest Slavic fringes, but in Greekness, too.

The first subject in which this new cause manifested itself was that of the Orthodox Church. In the academic year of 1954–5 Steven delivered the Waynflete Lectures at Oxford on the subject of the Great Schism between the Eastern and Western Churches; they emerged the next year as his first book after the *Crusades* trilogy, *The Eastern Schism*. To Freya Stark Steven lamented, a little disingenuously, that the hardened opinions continuing to predominate on both sides would inevitably cause his intention to miss its mark: 'The new book won't be a success. The Romans will view it with kindly sorrow . . . the Orthodox will think it insufficiently partisan.'* But to

---

* As Steven put it with lengthier protestation in a 1962 article, 'Nothing is more dangerous than to try to be eirenical in matters of religion. Blessed indeed are the

other friends Steven spoke freely of his 'anti-papal' book, and the burden of conciliation in his preface gives a clear indication of his position: 'I hope that none of my words will cause offence . . . If my personal sympathies incline towards Byzantium, it is because I have tried to understand the Byzantine point of view.'

Later, in the first chapter of *The Great Church in Captivity* (1968), Runciman would concede with pre-emptive, insincere humility that 'It may well be that no one who has not been nurtured in the atmosphere of the Orthodox Church is in a position to understand it fully.' It was in *The Eastern Schism* that he first set out to prove precisely the reverse and, judging by the reception of his published lectures, he was substantially successful. Constantine Trypanis, still Bywater Professor of Medieval and Modern Greek at Oxford and not so long past Steven's bitterly resented rival, led the handsome acknowledgements which in fact were forthcoming from both sides – but especially the Greek one – in the Schism:

> As the story of the schism has, on the whole, been treated by arid theologians or bigoted lay historians, this book is most refreshing and welcome. Mr. Runciman displays a deep understanding of both sides, an admirable grasp of the profound cultural as well as psychological differences between East and West, and the inevitable historical forces that led to the schism . . . I know no other account of this vexed problem which is as clear, as fair-minded or as readable as Mr. Runciman's present book.

The course of lectures and their texts were fair-minded in that the dogmatists of the Orthodox side – especially the Patriarch Michael

---

peacemakers; for they obtain no reward here below. If you adopt an air of entire impartiality in telling of a religious dispute, both sides will call you cynical if not anti-religious. If you reveal sympathies with one side but attempt to be just, that side will call you insufficiently loyal and the other hopelessly prejudiced' (SR, 'The Schism between the Eastern and Western Churches', *Anglican Theological Review*, October 1962). Early in his career Steven tended to take the first course and was indeed labelled a cynic in his stuffier notices; but in his post-war writings on Orthodoxy his alignment with the Greeks over the Roman Catholics was certainly evident enough to evade the charge of 'insufficient loyalty', if not always that of unprofessional partiality.

Cerularius, 'who saw himself as an Emperor' – received quite as scathing a report as the predictable array of politically interested and dictatorial Roman prelates. But in his summing-up Steven quite clearly attributed to the Greek Orthodox those characteristics that he admired, and to the Roman Catholics those that repelled him: 'the agelong difference in temperament between Rome and Greece, the former legalistic and authoritarian, the latter philosophical and individualistic'. Only two years earlier, Steven had laid out his candid view of the contemporary Roman Catholic Church for the benefit of Stewart Perowne: ' . . . I can't stomach Rome. It's too unscrupulous, too ready to falsify history, too political (and Franco-Italian;) and the Uniate churches don't have too good a time – have you ever got the Maronites to talk really frankly to you? It's illuminating.'

Steven's increasingly comfortable post-war position, philhellene as well as Orthodox, had much to do with two Greek friendships, one more exalted, the other deeper. These were respectively with Patriarch Athenagoras of Constantinople, and the poet and diplomat George Seferis. Athenagoras, born Matthew Spyrou, was translated from the Archdiocese of North America to Constantinople in January 1949. He arrived in his new Oecumenical See on the aeroplane of his friend and fellow Freemason President Truman. His appointment was not a popular choice in the city either with less far-flung Orthodox clergy or with the Turkish government, who argued that the new Patriarch was in breach of an old but unrepealed Ottoman law. This ordained that the Oecumenical Patriarch, as leader of the Greek *milet* or community in Turkey, must swear allegiance to – what had once been the Sublime Porte – the Presidency, and therefore must take Turkish citizenship. Spyrou had in fact been born within the bounds of the old Ottoman Empire, at Iannina, but for the Empire's successors this was not good enough. So, after Truman's intercession, the Turkish Interior Minister was flown out to Washington, accompanied the new Patriarch on the presidential plane and granted Athenagoras updated Turkish citizenship during the flight. The aircraft in question was at the time called not *Air Force One* but *Sacred Cow*.

Steven met Athenagoras in Istanbul in the autumn after this legendary descent; he found himself comparing the new Patriarch to Cardinal Roncalli (who would be elected to the Papacy nine years later). Both men, he reflected, came from backgrounds of rural obscurity; but Athenagoras, unlike Roncalli, did not look the part of the holy peasant. Rather, he resembled a Byzantine God the Father, tall and commanding, with a long white beard. As the presidential aviation incident had indicated, the Patriarch had a sense of humour and a flair for showmanship. On one occasion when Steven paid him a visit in the early 1950s during Orthodox Easter, Athenagoras placed his favoured Byzantinologue on a lesser throne beside his great Patriarchal seat, and they received the homage of the faithful together – including that of a family of grand Kolonaki Athenians, who knew Steven well and could not restrain their mirth. When the Patriarch then took Steven's hand and gripped it throughout several petitions, Steven glimpsed the raised eyebrow of a Greek minister. In due course Athenagoras would give substance to this symbolically intimate enthronement.

In 1965, the year in which *The Fall of Constantinople* appeared, Steven's two favourite Christian hierarchs, Roncalli, now Pope John, and Athenagoras, issued the Catholic–Orthodox Joint Declaration. This was a grand expression of the forgiving ecumenism Steven had actively been preaching since the publication of the *Crusades* trilogy. In 1969, in response to *The Great Church in Captivity*, Athenagoras named Steven his Grand Orator. 'In the good old Ottoman days,' Steven pointed out with care, 'that would have made me the senior lay member of the Holy Synod of the Patriarchate, and would have allowed me to bear the hereditary title of Prince. But in these secular days it was an empty, though deeply appreciated, honour.' In fact the title would prove far from empty in Steven's subsequent engagements with the politics of Orthodoxy.

The influence of George Seferis on Steven's sympathies, and on his writing, was more subtle, but far more important. Seferis's friendship was the vial which transmuted Steven's day-to-day, conformist frustration with Greek corruption, intrigue and inefficiency, during his British Council days, into increasingly considered scepticism about British rectitude. Steven liked to attribute to the poet a similar sense of romantic Byzantine nostalgia to his own (one easier, in fact, to locate in Cavafy, whose poetry was really more to Steven's taste). But after Seferis's death Steven criticized the Nobel laureate's posthumous reputation as 'a Man of Sorrows':

It is true that any great poet must be sensitive to the tragedies and cruelties of life. It is true that [Seferis's] last years were made miserable by the drab and nasty dictatorship [the Colonels' regime from 1967 to 1974] that had taken over his beloved country. My memories of George are . . . of laughter, of appreciation of the natural beauties of the world and the man-made monuments of the past, and of all the whims and traditions of history.

When Seferis was serving as Greek Ambassador in Lebanon in 1953, Steven imagined him deriving the *ci-devant* satisfactions that he himself felt for such glorious baubles as his later Grand Oratorship:

[The Beirut Embassy] was a post which I think he enjoyed. It involved no serious political worries at that date; and Beirut was still a pleasant city in which to live. Moreover, the Greek Ambassador, in those countries where there was a large native Orthodox population, enjoyed a special position. In the eyes of the Orthodox believers the King of Greece was heir to the Emperor of Byzantium, God's viceroy on earth; and the Greek Ambassador was thus entitled to royal honours. George fully appreciated that historic role.

Steven, at any rate, fully appreciated the idea of Seferis fully appreciating it. But their friendship proved to be a true meeting and moderation of attitudes. Seferis was indeed a royalist in politics, and he yearned for a broad concept of Greekness evincing a wound of exile unsurprising in a son of Smyrna, lost to the Turks in 1922. Thoroughly Anglophile in his tastes, he came to find British Imperial manoeuvring and the proxies it supported equally unpalatable. It was through his affinity with Seferis that Steven evolved from a wilfully partial British observer, who even in August 1949 hymned the unsavoury anti-Communist re-education camp on the island of Makronisos as a place where 'the old spirit is being reborn, vital, eager, and full of faith and hope', to a gloomy observer of British blunders on Cyprus and a determined critic of the Colonels' regime.

Seferis kept Steven minutely informed of developments on Cyprus, under British rule since 1878 and after the Second World War in ferment over the desire of the Greek majority to unite with mainland

Greece. Steven was thus one of the first British observers to be informed of the oath declared by the Cypriot terrorist organization EOKA, who pledged in April 1955 'to free Cyprus from the British yoke'. Seferis had broken with many English friends over the matter – notably, though not permanently, Lawrence Durrell, who was Director of Public Relations for the British Governor there from 1952 to 1956. With Steven, as with Paddy Leigh Fermor, Seferis seems to have felt assured of a more understanding ear. As Steven's subsequent correspondence with Stewart Perowne shows, Seferis was about half right in this assumption; but Steven approached nearer to his Greek friend's position over the course of 1955:

> I'm interested to hear that you think of retiring eventually to Cyprus. It's a lovely and liveable place and the people charming in spite of the way that we've mishandled it and them. The Athens government is not making things easier, and I spend my time trying to explain to Greek friends that provocative broadcasts to Cyprus are exactly the wrong method of building up philhellene sentiments among the British . . . [6 April]

> The Archbishop's hobnobbing with Amin Husseini should certainly be shown up at its true worth. I hope Larry Durrell will make use of it . . . * [20 May]

> One can hardly bear to think about Cyprus. We are being so stupid, the Greeks so frivolous and irresponsible and the Turks so truculent. Our only chance was surely to say: make self-government work, and

---

* Lawrence Durrell, as has been seen, was in British government service on the island, and still in 1955 directly responsible for pro-British propaganda operations there. The Archbishop was Makarios III of Cyprus, the figurehead of the Cypriot independence movement, who would become in 1960 the first President of the Cypriot Republic. Amin al-Husseini was the notoriously anti-British, anti-Semitic and, when expedient, Nazi-amenable Palestinian nationalist and former Grand Mufti of Jerusalem. As religious ethnarchs opposed to British policy in the twilight of empire, the two had a certain amount in common, but by 1955 the sometime Mufti was unavoidably tarnished by his support for Nazi Germany, and Makarios, whose star was rising, had little to gain from open association with him. Steven's accusation that the pair were active collaborators is a plausible if gossipy piece of British invective, without overmuch factual basis.

then in so many years you can have a plebiscite or whatever you like. Now it is too late. I am told the Foreign Office was ready for some such move. It was the army that made them utter that stupid word 'Never' . . . The Greeks are bound to win in the end, like the Irish, the Indians, the Egyptians and all . . . [14 October]

[Eden's] waffling platitudes raise hopes and promise nothing. On the other hand he is uncompromising about Cyprus – it seems because he has a personal hatred of Greece. He was appallingly rude to the King when he was there last, with the result that the King has stopped trying to moderate the Queen's anti-British feelings . . . [11 December]

As these observations to Perowne, an Englishman similar to Steven in background, experience and political complexion, suggest, Steven did not (despite what he hinted to Seferis) really desire the union of Cyprus to Greece. But the diplomat-poet convinced him that Britain's policy was ramshackle. That same spring, pestered by an old acquaintance, Peter Quennell, to provide something for *History Today*, Steven offered a brief condensation of his account of Richard I in *The Kingdom of Acre*. The article took a more definite line than the trilogy had on two aspects of the King's character – his homosexuality, and the bilious short-termism with which he had captured Cyprus, a fit of bad temper and sea-sickness on account of which 'the Cypriots were never to be ruled by fellow-Greeks again.' Five years later, this melancholy reflection had ceased to apply.

Not long after *The Fall of Constantinople*'s successful publication, Steven's relations with his 'second country' of Greece underwent a drastic change for the worse. The high standing he enjoyed with the King and Queen, Paul and Frederika, survived the Cyprus crisis unscathed, and in 1961, a year after Cyprus became independent, Steven was created by King Paul, who as Crown Prince had crushed his foot fourteen years earlier, a Knight Commander of the Order of the Phoenix. But Paul died, after several botched operations, in 1964. His son Constantine II was thought to be too much under the influence of his politically active mother Queen Frederika, who in republican circles was pilloried as a former Nazi sympathizer; Steven himself had on Paul's accession called Frederika too clever to make for a safe Queen Consort. This cleverness was an air rather than an asset; Frederika was famous for gathering intellectual dinner-parties at which she could demonstrate her impressionistic grasp of the guests' wide-ranging oeuvres. Where Frederika was uncompromising in her meddling, her son seemed indecisive and inexperienced in his. A series of weak Prime Ministers the young King appointed in 1965 earned the nickname of the Apostasia, as they were felt to have apostatized from the leadership of George Papandreou Sr, the centrist, republican-leaning, liberal 'old man of democracy' loathed by Constantine. But in 1967 the King was defeated on quite another political flank, in the form of the coup of the Colonels' junta.

Steven's distaste for the Colonels was almost surprisingly instinctive. They were not, after all, so different from many military figures, such as Colonel Tsigantes, whom he had befriended in his British Council days, and to whom he had looked as a bulwark against Greek Communism. In his tribute to Seferis, Steven states that after the coup 'I had no wish to go to Greece, and [Seferis] wrote to tell me to stay away.' That implies that his attitude was reinforced, rather than formed, by Seferis's information. By now he had come to regret his public support for the re-Hellenization project on Makronisos, and claimed unreliably to Anthony Bryer that he had disapproved of it all along. His employment of an anachronism in *The Fall of Constantinople* might very well be interpreted as a deliberate barb: 'Greeks who refused to understand the decree of union must be sent to Rome for re-education.' From his sources of royal gossip Steven was well aware that, though Constantine II had, disastrously, lent the new regime the stamp of his legitimacy, he was in truth scrabbling to foment a counter-coup. He went so far as to miss the Inaugural Lecture given by his last and most faithful pupil, Donald Nicol, as Koraes Professor at London, so as to avoid encountering the Colonels' Ambassador (and Steven had, after all, been relatively relaxed about meeting even Nazi diplomats, both before the war and, in neutral Turkey, during it).

The most likely cause of Steven's unwavering antipathy towards the Colonels – which arguably preceded even that of Seferis – lies with Steven's friends and sources in the international hierarchy of the Greek Orthodox Church, and, closer to home, the Church of

England. Steven was a friend and admirer of Michael Ramsey, Archbishop of Canterbury from 1961. After the death of the Patriarch Athenagoras in 1972, Steven confided to the Archbishop a 'disquieting rumour' whose origin, he implies, was Athenagoras himself, about the Colonels' intentions towards the Patriarchate: 'the Greek Colonels were hoping to do a deal with the Turks which would include the removal of the Patriarchate to Greek territory. I hope and believe that the idea has been abandoned. It would ruin the *Oecumenical* role of the Patriarchate.' When it came to the Orthodox hierarchy, if called upon to choose between Greekness and ecumenicity Steven would always defend the latter. In several cases, such as the ecclesiastical set-up of the Orthodox faithful in Palestine, this even led him to adopt a broadly anti-Greek position. As he had written to Stewart Perowne in 1952:

> The Armenians are I think the best community in Jerusalem (I confess I am not so fond of them elsewhere, and I remember Cyril [Israelian, their Patriarch in the 1940s, a friend of Steven and of Perowne] himself shaking his head over the Armenians of Constantinople.) The Greeks at Jerusalem always disappointed me – The Orthodox church isn't meant to be Universal but particular, and Orthodoxy in Palestine should have gone Arabic-speaking. Greek was all right so long as Byzantium still existed as the great Orthodox power, and so long too, I think, as the Greek Church was so to speak the official church of the Ottoman Empire, but it is now out of date in Palestine.

The Colonels' version of Greekness, on the other hand, was aggressive and expansive – especially on the matter of Cyprus – but Steven found its nationalism narrow, ignorant and ahistorical. The junta dubbed itself, for all its reactionary anti-Communism, the Ethnosotirios Epanastasis, 'revolution to save the nation'. Such a slogan held no appeal for Steven.

During the chaos of the junta's seven years' rule and for some time afterwards, especially after Athenagoras had made him Grand Orator, Steven was regularly importuned by deposed Greek Orthodox hierarchs who believed he might be able to put in a good word for them. He exchanged wry jokes about these intercessions with another Anglican friend, John Satterthwaite, Bishop of Gibraltar, whose

23. (*above*) SR at the British Ministry in Sofia, where he was employed as Press Attaché, 1940. The Minister, George Rendel, would later describe his own operation to Anthony Eden, the Foreign Secretary, as generally assumed to be 'the centre of a widespread system of espionage'. Next to SR on the left of the picture is Magdalene 'Lena' Bone; opposite, between Rendel's daughter Ann and a Ministry secretary, Norman Davis. Both fulfilled covert duties with SOE.

24. (*left*) SR in the house by Herod's Gate, Jerusalem, a traditional Arab construction rented from a Palestinian nationalist and equipped with an Armenian landlady, 1941, inspecting a new icon for his collection.

25. (*below*) The cyclamen garden SR planted at Herod's Gate, described by his successor there, John Connell, as 'delicate, trembling, indestructible, spring after spring, fragile in appearance, extremely tough in reality'.

26. (*top*) SR with a Byzantine Art class at the University of Istanbul, 1941. Seated to his right in the white hat is his assistant Münire Çelebi, a sophisticated city cousin of the Kings of Egypt.

27. (*bottom left*) Münire's husband, Bakir Çelebi, hereditary head of the Mevlevi Order, better known as the Whirling Dervishes, in 1942.

28. (*bottom right*) Stewart Perowne, Iraq, 1944, demonstrating the classical heritage of British imperial rule *sine fine*.

29. (*left*) Lawrence Durrell and his second wife Ruth Cohen, supping on Rhodes, 1946.

30. (*below*) Ronald Crichton (*left*) and Bill Barron (*right*), 1946: the young British Council pair whom Steven's assistant, Maurice Cardiff, privately considered to constitute the core of a 'very nasty set'.

31. (*left*) Freya Stark at Asolo, 1947. In her memoirs Stark wrote that 'there is a distinction about Asolo which dates back through centuries, ever since the last Queen of Cyprus received it from Venice in exchange for her island, and kept a gay and learned country court.'

32. (*right*) SR, 1949, at the Runciman laird's Lodge at Eigg. Designed in the mid-1920s by the family architect Robert Mauchlen with the addition of certain suggestions from Steven, the Lodge was intended to give a summery, Italianate impression. Though well emphasized in this picture with its Mediterranean columns, the continental touches did not always translate.

33. (*below*) SR watching a Jesuit school production of *Macbeth* in the Philippines, 1956. His host, George Clutton, Britain's man in Manila, does not appear to be enjoying himself.

34. (*above*) SR celebrating Christmas with Robin Dalton, an Australian-born society beauty, wife of his much admired GP Emmet Dalton and an increasingly close friend, in the mid-1950s.

35. (*left*) SR on Eigg as co-laird conversing with his recently appointed factor, Rutherford (*centre*), in the mid-1950s.

36. (*left*) The poet and diplomat Georgios Seferiades, or George Seferis, and his wife Maro, visiting Eigg in 1960.

37. (*above*) SR, newly knighted in 1959, enjoying a VIP tour around Sydney Zoo, where a koala bear pays its respects. Steven claimed to have narrowly evaded ravishment not long afterwards by an excitable buck-kangaroo.

38. (*below*) SR at the St Demetrius' Day Parade, Thessalonica, mid-1960s.

39. (*left*) SR bought Elshieshields Tower, by Lochmaben in Dumfriesshire, in 1966, to replace both Eigg as his Scottish retreat and his house in St John's Wood as his primary residence.

40. (*above*) SR and a young lady-friend, visiting the ruins of Caerlaverock, 1970s.

41. (*left*) SR and the composer Peter Maxwell Davies, Elshieshields, 1980s – as Steven described him, 'cosy … not such an ex-Angry Young Man'.

42. SR at the unveiling of the street named in his honour at Mistra, 1976.

43. Cartoon of SR by Hugh Trevor-Roper (by this point, 1993, Baron Dacre of Glanton), with a dedicatory Greek epigram in honour of Steven's ninetieth birthday.

diocese included Anglicans in Greece. One particularly persistent ex-Metropolitan, Panteleimon, once of Thessalonica, attracted the mockery of Satterthwaite, like Steven a bachelor aficionado of crowned heads with an intermittently acidic turn of phrase: 'I have called on the Metropolitan consistently since his "exile" . . . He obviously feels that since the latest coup the Judgement of the Lord is now nigh at hand and that there may even be a chance of his being returned to Thessalonika (of this, however, I myself am not very certain . . . ).' Steven also received with weary politeness the many manifestos from sympathizers, often Greek American, of competing claimants to vacant Greek sees. His letterbox abounded with eager analyses of the chances at ecclesiastical Synod or dictatorial whim of many a Hieronimos or Meliton, complete with righteous classical allusions to wronged characters like Aristides the Just of ancient Athens.

True to his assurances to Seferis, Steven did not set foot in Greece for the seven years the Colonels lasted. He hurried back in the autumn of 1974, after their fall and the monarchy's final, democratically confirmed exile, by which time Seferis had died (in 1971), transformed into a martyr to liberty, his very funeral a rallying point. But Greece and Orthodoxy continued to preoccupy Runciman's written work, most monumentally in *The Great Church in Captivity*. Steven's personal knowledge of and friendship with Athenagoras, and Athenagoras's own relative freedom from the junta as a globally prominent figure with Turkish citizenship and a residence at Istanbul, afforded Steven a worthy object for his continuing love of the Greek language, rite, history and culture, even in a time of neo-totalitarian eclipse for Greece itself. It was consoling to concentrate for a time on the reassuring continuities of the Orthodox Church's history, rather than the secular tragedy of Empire he had already brought to its polished conclusion.

*The Great Church in Captivity: A Study of the Patriarchate of Constantinople from the Eve of the Turkish Conquest to the Greek War of Independence*, to give it its full and cumbersome title was based, too, on an encumbering and limiting form. Steven had given one lecture series on the Church of Constantinople from 1261 (the date of the city's recapture from the Franks by Michael Palaeologus) to 1821, at St Andrews, in the winter of 1960–61, and another back at his own Trinity in 1966 on the negotiations between the Constantinopolitan Church and the various Protestant Churches. These locations fittingly illustrated two sides of him: his original intellectual world of Cambridge was offered an intriguingly recondite and detailed forgotten corner of ecclesiastical might-have-beens, while the Scots University was treated to Runciman the world authority, master of the grand sweep. But, while evidently related, the two series conjoined into a structurally awkward book. The idea of the 'eve of the Turkish conquest' is stretched up to and beyond its absolute maximum, with Runciman covering 160 pages before he reaches 1453 and its consequences. By contrast to this loving if hardly ground-breaking comprehensiveness, the book's last chapters on the early nineteenth century, with the exception of *The White Rajahs*, Runciman's one foray into the fringes of modern history, are rushed and flawed.* But the whole work has strengths, arguments and attractions that transcend its difficult shape.

The longer second, more pertinent part of the book that treats the Greek Church after the Turkish Conquest has a unifying moral. To Lord Acton's axiom that absolute power corrupts absolutely – which Runciman accepts, considering it illustrated by the Ottoman Sultanate – he now presents an analogue: 'the corruption of absolute impotence', applied to the Greek Patriarchate, hierarchy, priesthood and even, eventually, monasteries. Runciman is careful to leave the still-powerful Russian Church at the edge of his picture; yet he has not called his book 'The *Greek* Church in Captivity' – even though that is mostly what its contents deliver. The 'Great Church' is a high-vaunting Greek phrase, unfamiliar to English readers. For a writer justly considered light on metaphor, Runciman has adopted this usage for wide, flexible conceptual reasons. The Great Church applies to the whole of Orthodoxy, the claim rooted in Empire of a single universal Christianity, and so raises his besetting questions: 'Could the Church sincerely accept Turkish rule in perpetuity? . . .

---

* But the most serious fault of the first half is less its broad familiarity than its occasional and apologetic gambits after perverse shock value, including perhaps Runciman's silliest statement in print – 'Byzantium was fundamentally a democracy' (SR, *The Great Church in Captivity* (Cambridge University Press, 1968), p. 73).

Could Hellenism be combined with Oecumenicity? . . . Would there not inevitably be a narrowing of [the Patriarch's] vision?' But at the same time the Great Church is in fact an actual building, Hagia Sofia, lost to Islam at the Conquest: 'more than a church; the symbol of the old Christian Empire'. And, as such, its story continues to remain the story of the Greek people by other means. This involves both felicities and blemishes. To the reader of *The Fall of Constantinople*, the second part of *The Great Church in Captivity* at first feels partly recapitulative and redundant, but comes to offer the deeper relish of an organic, sustained theme.

One of Runciman's most affectionate critics, Anthony Bryer, would after Steven's death describe *The Great Church in Captivity* – which he had been kinder about at the time – as 'like a history of the Anglican Church seen through the eyes of Patriarch Dositheos of Jerusalem'. Steven himself was uneasily conscious that perhaps his most abstrusely exotic-sounding book yet was written from what, for him, was an unusually occidental and even Britannic perspective; but he argued in his preface that this arose from the nature of his material (more assiduous archival researchers, Bryer among them, have outstripped him in this respect): 'A detailed account of everything that is known about the later Greek church would fill many volumes and at the same time be curiously uneven in its detail . . . Were it not for the reports and the accounts of foreign diplomats, churchmen and travellers, there are whole periods about which we should be very ignorant.'

There is a positive aspect to the wilful-seeming oddity of Runciman's point of view in *The Great Church in Captivity*, for those readers willing to enjoy it. The book represents Runciman himself finally coming to terms, in youthful old age, with a period and a cast of mind that had left him cold and impatient as an undergraduate – the domestic and intellectual history of Britain in the seventeenth and eighteenth centuries. There is palpable pleasure in his deployment of English prose and observation, and his insistence on drawing heavily upon that second, 1966 course of lectures at Trinity, his beloved old college – on the relationship between Orthodoxy and Protestantism – is not the barrenly high-political rabbit-hole that some ill-disposed professionals considered it to be, but a lasting, and personal, parable.

The English diplomat who gets the most prominent position in *The*

*Great Church in Captivity* is Sir Paul Ricaut, in his youth an assistant to Charles II's Ambassador to the Sublime Porte, and himself of mixed Flemish and Spanish origin. Later in his career Ricaut played a reasonable and conciliatory part in the government of Ireland, was the confidant of the age's most sensible and witty politician, the Marquess of Halifax, helped William III to perpetrate economic sabotage against the Scots, and was credited with the invention of the duvet. He did not marry owing to a long, heartfelt and faithful arrangement with his sister-in-law. Ricaut's greatest literary success, *The Present State of the Ottoman Empire*, became a much translated best-seller despite being originally published in 1666 during the Great Fire of London. Runciman quotes from an obscurer work of 1678, *The Present State of the Greek and Armenian Churches*:

> Tragical the subversion of the Sanctuaries of Religion, the Royal Priesthood expelled from their Churches, and these converted into Mosques; the Mysteries of the altar concealed in secret and dark places ... rather like Vaults and Sepulchres than Churches, having their roofs almost levelled with the Superficies of the Earth, lest the most ordinary Exsurgency of Structure should be accused for Triumph of Religion, and stand in competition with the lofty Spires of the Mahometan Mosque ...
>
> ... It is no wonder to human reason that considers the Oppression and the Contempt that good Christians are exposed to, and the Ignorance in their Churches occasioned through Poverty in the Clergy, that many should be found who retreat from the Faith; but it is, rather, a Miracle, and a true Verification of those Words of Christ, That the Gates of Hell shall not be able to prevail ... that there is conserved ... in despite of all Tyranny and Arts contrived against it, an open and public Profession of the Christian Faith.

There were further incidental reasons why Ricaut might be expected to have drawn Steven's interest. He travelled widely all his life, spoke nine languages and was the youngest son of a highly successful shipowner mixed up, to the whole family's detriment, in royalist politics. Runciman accords him straightforward approval, calling him 'deeply moved by the position of the Greeks', 'well informed', 'tactful', 'shrewd', and allowing that 'his censure was mitigated by real sympathy ... alone among Western writers of the seventeenth and eighteenth centuries' (Robert Burton and Lady Mary Wortley Montagu, by contrast, are lightly reproved for their anti-Greek prejudice). But the highest honour Runciman accords this earlier polyglot shipping scion is to remember him within the conclusion of the whole book, invoking his Scriptural allusion to balance a less charitable but equally pithy fellow countryman:

> The grand achievement of the Patriarchate was that in spite of humiliation and poverty and disdain the Church endured and endures as a great spiritual force. The Candlestick had been darkened and obscured, as the Englishman Peter Heylyn, who disliked the Greeks, noted in the early seventeenth century, but God had not taken it away. The light still burns, and burns brighter. The Gates of Hell have not prevailed.

Some of the eccentricities of Orthodox–Protestant ententes were evidently too delicious for Runciman to omit. There is the compressed epic of the Greek scoundrel James Basilicus Marchetti, 'the Heraclid', a prodigious genealogical forger who managed for a fraught two years to become the first Lutheran sovereign in Eastern Europe; there is the introduction of coffee to Britain by an otherwise idle young Greek at Balliol, Oxford, and the fiasco of the attempted formation of a Greek College on what would eventually be the site of Worcester – both stories that bring out in Steven the happily acerbic Cambridge loyalist. There is the case of the Jacobite Non-Juring Anglicans scheming for union with Constantinople. But the episode that becomes the most involving human drama in the book is that of Cyril I Lucaris, the 'Calvinist Patriarch' of Constantinople. Several reviewers felt that Steven had allowed his own Church of Scotland upbringing to affect his view of this radical and ill-fated hierarch, sensing a touch of individual regret in his version, a hankering after some less 'obscurantist' path the Greek Church might have taken; but this charge is only borne out in part by the substance of his study of Lucaris.

Within The Great Church in Captivity's incrementally, even covertly chronological construction, Runciman's telling of the life, career and death of Cyril Lucaris immediately appeals because it is a fresh sliver of his historical art at its narrative best. Yet readability does not equate to approval in Runciman's work, even if it can sometimes denote affinity. There is an ironic distance to the formal similarity of his account of Lucaris to a hagiography. It is based, once again, on robustly English and Protestant if not frankly secular sources from the later seventeenth century: the research of a one-time chaplain to the English Embassy at Constantinople, Thomas Smith, who would end up a Non-Juring Fellow of Magdalen, and the more direct testimony of an English Arabist scholar, Edward Pococke. Cyril I's religious persuasion is most memorably summed up by a 'somewhat Calvinistic' Archbishop of Canterbury, George Abbott: 'As for the Patriarke himself, I do not doubt but that in opinion of religion he is, as we terme him, a pure Calvinist, and so the Jesuites in these parts do brande him.' Nonetheless, from such thoroughgoing English material Runciman constructs a traditional Byzantine tale of martyrdom. He offers up the signs of Lucaris's singularity and precocity in childhood, which he attributes to the influence of a free-spirited headmaster, 'a man of independent mind . . . in trouble with the Orthodox authorities for suspected Latinizing tendencies . . . and later in difficulties with the Inquisition for being anti-Latin'.

This is basically Runciman's analysis of Lucaris: a man of impressive but ultimately impossible individuality. As usual Runciman incorporates every traceable visual note. The young Lucaris is glimpsed as a foppish student at Padua, running up debts, skipping lectures and buying an imprudently decorative sword to wear; but this is balanced by a local tradition that, in proper Galilean spirit, he worked hard for a time as a fisherman. Once embarked on his ecclesiastical career, Cyril is indeed portrayed by Runciman as highly intelligent, competent, politically tactful and physically brave, and the historian also defends him against accusations of corruption within what elsewhere in *The Great Church in Captivity* seems a milieu of almost unavoidable embezzlement. But when it comes to the beliefs Runciman is criticized for holding too warmly in common with Lucaris, he is more dextrously neutral.

In fact Lucaris in his most Protestant, and therefore arguably least traditionally Greek, role is not quite to Steven's taste. There is something priggish in the young Patriarch (Cyril was elected to the see of Alexandria, initially, at the age of twenty-nine) who describes the Orthodox practices at Jerusalem as 'almost pagan' (this is mainly a reference to the Miracle of the Holy Fire at the Holy Sepulchre on Easter, which Steven adored and attended as often as possible, and in which he professed fiercely sober belief). Runciman begins to show the Patriarch's doctrinal eclecticism weakening his human judgement – he emphasizes Lucaris's brief association with the plurally renegade prelate Marcantonio de Dominis, 'a very disreputable character who after doing well out of the Anglican Church, thanks to his flattery of James I, in the end reverted to Catholicism'. Then Runciman does not entirely exculpate Lucaris from the charge of poisoning his predecessor as Patriarch of Constantinople, merely adding in worldly temper that 'If this were so, the Holy Synod certainly did not object. Cyril was promptly and unanimously elected Patriarch.' But once he reaches Lucaris's actual beliefs his urbane, Machiavellian admiration wanes. 'The Orthodox Church has never cared for compendia of doctrine,' Runciman warns, very much in his capacity as an honorary Greek rather than a cradle Scots Calvinist. Later on he concludes sadly that Lucaris was 'an intellectual by temperament, with a logical mind and no sympathy with the apophatic attitude traditionally followed by Orthodox theologians'. In Runciman's discourse 'anti-intellectual' and 'intellectual' are both perilous epithets, and 'brilliance' can end up being quite as unsatisfactory as 'philistinism'. In the last analysis he has little more faith in the Calvinist Patriarch Lucaris than he did in the equally non-conformist 'national socialist' philosopher Plethon:

> Cyril Lucaris failed ... His was the only attempt to bring the Orthodox Church into line with the livelier Churches of the West ... the hard, logical intellectualism of Calvinism attracted the realistic and cerebral side of the Greek character. Had Cyril achieved his objects the intellectual level of the Orthodox Church might have been immeasurably raised and much of its later obscurantism checked. But the Greek character has its other side, its taste for the Mysteries ... [The Orthodox Church's] power of survival through worldly disasters lay largely in its acceptance of the transcendental mystery of the divine. This Cyril never understood.

It takes a serious misreading to interpret this verdict as partisan regret in the cause of Protestantism, rather than enigmatic resignation in the tradition of Orthodoxy.

All the same, one reason why it is easy and natural to accuse Runciman of a partial and blinkered Protestantism (as Jonathan Riley-Smith has done in the context of the Crusades) is that he does often lay into the Church of Rome with the hungry vigour of a keen blood sportsman and the melodrama of a Jacobean dramatist. During his Lucaris chapter the Jesuits, their pawns, the French and Imperial ambassadors, and their distant figurehead, the Pope, all perform and express deeds and phrases of villainy that trespass into pantomime. This is a serious consequence of Bryer's fair complaint that *The Great Church in Captivity* represents a weirdly, and uncharacteristically, skewed view, bigoted towards Anglican or at least British expectations. But, especially in combination with Runciman's deepening affection for seventeenth-century English prose, the effect is superbly readable.

The Jesuits make their entrance oozing urbane perfidy, 'well-trained, cultivated and courteous men'. Runciman had expressed his views of the Jesuits operating in the period in a lecture three years previously. Speaking before the ecumenically minded Archbishop Ramsey, Runciman described the Order as 'lying in wait' for young Greek scholars who would then be 'lured away by mysterious strangers and kidnapped to Rome for indoctrination'; the Greek Church, he asserted, had been by turns 'wooed and harassed' by such agents. Runciman also claimed in this lecture that the Western embassies co-operated along confessional lines, Protestant England and Holland thus consistently and necessarily against Catholic France and Austria – a fallible generalization which he moderates in *The Great Church in Captivity*, noting that the embassies' religious intrigues were 'not in unison'. Here Jesuits appear as masters of a soi-disant, untraceable public relations network, spreading exaggerated or at least emphatic reports among Greeks as to Cyril Lucaris's frank Protestantism, while contriving to plant a rumour at London that some visiting Greek Orthodox Metropolitans were themselves Roman Catholic spies in disguise. The Catholic Ambassadors of France and Austria make a less impressive but equally dastardly showing. The Comte de Cési libels Cyril Lucaris to the Grand Vizier as a traitor and blasphemer against Islam, commenting to his Jesuit friends that 'this will add sauce to the dishes'. The Habsburg envoy, Rudolf

Schmid-Scharzenhorn, casuistically supports a prelate he privately considers 'good and virtuous . . . good towards the wicked and severe towards the good'. The far-off Pope seems petulant, impotent, ill informed and shrill, dubbing Lucaris 'the son of darkness and athlete of hell'. Runciman had sadly noted that the Orthodox–Anglican proposed reunions could never have succeeded because their only, shallow foundation was 'a mutual fear and hatred of Rome'. For all the sincerity of his ecumenical instinct, and despite his several close Roman Catholic and even Jesuit friends, Steven's narrative of the Greek Church is often fuelled by that same age-old animus.

By 1976, two years after the Colonels and the King had alike fallen, Greece, in the new form of the Third Hellenic Republic, had returned to Steven's favour. Nevertheless he was pleasantly surprised to hear of a proposal that a street in the picturesque town of Mistra, perched above the site of ancient and modern Sparta, be named after him. This was not, like his office of Grand Orator, a piece of Patriarchal largesse, but a good deed coming home to roost from his British Council days. The Greek Deputy for Sparta had benefited as a boy from a scholarship instituted by Steven, enabling a British university education, and wanted to show his gratitude. Among his superiors was the Minister for Culture in the new democratic government, the erstwhile Bywater Professor at Oxford, Constantine Trypanis – once Steven's academic rival but for decades an obliging, even slightly oleaginous friend. The naming of the street was not, therefore, so very strange; but the site was more unexpected.

Even in its days of greatest pomp Mistra had never felt populous; in *The Fall of Constantinople* Runciman writes of the then provincial capital of about twenty thousand citizens, 'Mistra ... though it boasted of a palace and a castle, and several churches, monasteries and schools, was little more than a village.' In a way Mistra served as a symbol for the kind of Greekness Steven felt had too long been neglected in favour of classical Greek myth-making. English travellers throughout the Ottoman hegemony had mistaken the hill-top town and its high medieval ruins for the remains of classical Sparta. After the Greek War of Independence even this small Turkish hill-town was abandoned, eclipsed by the revivified modern city of Sparta.

Steven's own practical knowledge of Mistra was limited, though he was increasingly drawn to its history; he had visited its ruins twice, in 1928 and 1947. The first time he had been entertained by the convent of nuns at the Pantanassa, in the shadow of the Byzantine Despots' Palace; they served him coffee within their convent, a liberty at which he purported to Kitty to be shocked, and asked solicitously after the health of Queen Victoria. Steven called the scenery 'like Switzerland, only nice'. The second time he inspected the city's remains in his capacity as the British Council's Representative in Athens. On both occasions he felt a powerful and contradictory emotional response. Overcome by the romance of overlooked Mistra, he still saw that conservation work of a kind both unusually sensitive and costly was urgently needed if its loveliness was to be preserved. By the 1970s the state of the ruins had improved, but their history was still relatively unknown. Steven himself was the deserted hill-town's most prominent votary in the Anglosphere, but even he had mainly concentrated on the high politics of its Despots and the intellectual radicalism of its philosophers, rather than aiming to recover a sense of the place itself. It was thus with restoration and reorientation, art and narrative alike in mind that Steven guided his political Greek friends towards fêting him, if fêted he was to be, at Mistra.

The International Congress of Byzantine Studies fell to Athens in 1976, so it was convenient for the Mistra ceremony to be arranged not long before. Three cars left the Greek capital for the one-time citadel of the Morea. Steven rode in Trypanis's ministerial Daimler, feeling rather overshadowed by this poet turned professor turned politician's physical bulk; behind them Madame Trypanis was escorted by the representative of Oxford University, Steven's old friend and ally Dimitri Obolensky, Prince and Professor, while the Director of Antiquities from Sparta took the envoy from Cambridge. This last was Stavros Papastavrou, brother of the virtuoso cellist Eleftherios, whose education Steven had in part funded, a Byzantinist lecturer attached to Peterhouse. This Papastavrou brother was as gifted academically as his brother was musically, but had disappointed the expectations of his friends, publishing nothing and declining into alcoholic and marital catastrophe. All the same Steven was extremely fond of him, and of his estranged wife Flora, something of a white witch in a way Steven found worthy of respect. Stavros was integral to the Mistra ceremony as he had substantially redrafted Steven's grateful oration in demotic modern Greek. Steven enjoyed watching the Greek police shunt buses full of tourists to the roadside as their calvacade passed.

On arrival in the little town's centre, Palaeologos Square, named for the last great Byzantine dynasty who had ruled as Despots in Mistra as well as Emperors at Constantinople, Steven saw assembled what he took to be the whole population. Hardly had he stepped down from the Daimler when 'a buxom blonde lady came up and presented me with a bouquet of pink roses, in the name of the women of Sparta – an undeserved tribute, as I had never done anything for them.'* Mindful of how his favourite deceased British royal consort, Queen Mary (May of Teck), would have behaved in the circumstances, Steven coolly passed this garland over to Madame Trypanis. In general he experienced an unusual sense of mistaken identity, as if he had suddenly and unwittingly been transformed into the lesser royal role he would have carried off with such dignity. He wondered idly whether any of the modern inhabitants of Mistra had really heard of him. His eponymous street was small, ran westerly, and looked, he thought, a trifle insalubrious. It was bedecked with Greek and British flags, which when withdrawn revealed plaques, bearing the new street-name in Greek and English. Steven heard out baffling addresses in refined *katharevousa*, delivered Stavros's piece in return – to the surprise and delight of his hosts – then when he could sidled off to share a sticky cake and a half-bottle of lemonade with the General responsible for the Sparti District and the Bishop of Lacedaemonia. He now felt slightly feverish, but this worked to his advantage – 'as slight intoxication or great rage releases inhibitions, so does a fever. I found myself chatting and making jokes in Greek . . . ' The Mayor, a local schoolmaster, bestowed on him a parchment by which he was made Mistra's

---

* As he would soon show in his book on Mistra, Steven was well aware of the legendary licence of Spartan womanhood, who 'enjoyed a freedom remarkable in ancient Greece' (SR, *Mistra* (Thames & Hudson, 1980), p. 10).

first ever honorary citizen. 'I did not know how to show my grateful appreciation, except by writing a book.'

*Mistra: Byzantine Capital of the Peloponnese* duly made its appearance in 1980. For its publication Steven defected from Cambridge University Press, about whose dealings he had ever groused, to Thames & Hudson, under the guidance of its art history editor, the charming, sensitive and good-looking Greek poet Nikos Stangos. Stangos, though by birth Athenian, was, like Seferis, attached by family heritage to the wider Greek world which had been dissevered after the Greco-Turkish War of the early 1920s. Steven's latest work, which he identified in its preface as 'not a guidebook, nor just an essay in appreciation', but an attempt at a 'full history', continued to convey his scepticism about straightforward, nationalistic philhellenism. In one particular way Mistra was the ideal subject for this parable, because of its close association with Sparta. This allows Runciman to make hay at the expense of Sparta's ancient rival Athens, that city most beloved of Western European romantics, now a modern capital that stood in for Greek chauvinism in general: 'To later philhellenes, dazzled by the superb achievements of Athenian genius, Sparta has always seemed deplorable . . . They forget that Athenian democracy was made possible by a vast slave population, and that Athenian women were little better off than those slaves.' Athens, the Greek city Steven perforce knew best of all, having lived there during his British Council spell, was always to be the part of Greece about which he was most irreverent, even after it had awarded him its Gold Medal, Citizenship and the rank of an honorary soldier ('my first ever military role') in 1991. Mock-irritation elegantly enswathing his self-satisfaction, Steven complained to Donald Nicol that 'I must now speak with affection of that noisy polluted city.' The overlooked beauties of Sparta in legend, as of Mistra in history, were far more to his taste. In introducing his history of Mistra with a discussion of Sparta, both its ancestor and successor city, Runciman counters its familiar, militaristic image with a softer and more bewitching tradition:

> Here Helen, the loveliest of the queens of history, lived and reigned till she eloped to Troy . . . Here she lies along with Menelaus, the husband whom she wronged and to whom she returned . . . Before Christian

saints replaced her, her tomb was a shrine at which one prayed to be granted beautiful children . . . *

. . . In Sparta the fierce contests which had initiated boys into manhood were [after the Roman conquest] enacted before tourists in a theatre. The severity had vanished from Spartan life; the valley of the Eurotas was noted for its indolent, easy-going luxury. The ghost of Helen had triumphed over the ghost of Lycurgus.†

Runciman was always attuned to the local, the specific, the personal and the familial, to coincidences of place, kinship and alliance that were no coincidences at all. But his minutiae always served to adorn a larger view, even as he declared that view unjustifiable without them: 'Your theory may provide you with – so to say – a huge mosaic picture, but a mosaic is composed of individual tesserae, or cubes, some more important for the design than others.' In the case of Mistra, he was concerned to show both that an apparent 'backwater', distant from 'the mainstream of history', had its own crucial part to play, and that its history in turn had often been determined by events apparently far distant in both time and place. In this way, with signal fair-mindedness, Runciman shows in this, his last published, full historical work, some unintended but nonetheless beneficial consequences of the Fourth Crusade – the very expedition whose climax he had condemned as the greatest ever crime against humanity. Runciman still did not deviate from that position – except on occasion to describe the 1204 sack of Constantinople as a 'tragedy' as much as a crime – but his sense of justice, as well as his liking for unexpected contingency, urged him to point out that, on the bright side, that immoral disaster 'was to lead to the two most brilliant centuries in the history of Lacedaemon'. All the slaughter and the looting had,

* Steven was always well versed in pagan shrines; in the *Alphabet* he refers to 'the Zoodochos Pigi, the Fountain of Life . . . known to the ancients as Canathus, in which the goddess Hera used to bathe every year to recover her virginity. I have never been able to persuade any of my lady friends to see if the magic still works' (SR, *Alphabet*, p. 101).
† The traditional founder of the harsh Spartan warrior code; Runciman with deliberate and delighted mischief dismisses Lycurgus as a 'dim mythical figure', while endowing the Homeric Helen with lavishly grave historicity (SR, *Mistra*, p. 10).

apparently, brought forth the silverest of linings. Without the brief, partial and ill-conceived Frankish seizure of the Byzantine Empire, the vital principality of the Morea or Peloponnese, with its brand-new fortress of Mistra on a conical promontory named Myzithra, 'probably because it was thought to resemble a local cheese', would never have emerged.

The fate of that fortress and its eventual transformation into the 'Byzantine Capital' of Runciman's subtitle (nine years after his death the book was reissued with the even grander designation of 'Lost Capital of Byzantium') was in turn, he emphasized, decided by two geographically far-off dramas: 'a battle in northern Macedonia' and 'a massacre in a distant island'. The first was the Battle of Pelagonia in 1259, where an alliance led by William de Villehardouin, the Frankish Prince of Achaea and the original founder of Mistra, was defeated by the resurgent Byzantines. Prince William was forced to cede Mistra, Monemvasia and the Mani to the Emperor Michael VIII Palaeologus. After it had passed under Byzantine rule, the castle at Mistra expanded into a thriving provincial capital, eclipsing and effectively replacing Sparta, which was abandoned by Greek citizens seeking 'a governor of their own race and religion' and was also populated by those of mixed Greek and Frank blood, the so-called *gasmoules*, attracted by the Byzantines' 'lack of racial prejudice' and their willingness 'to welcome as equals anyone who would accept the Orthodox faith'. This state of affairs was confirmed by the island massacre – no other than the Sicilian Vespers of 1272, which Runciman had introduced twenty-three years earlier to the Anglophone general reading public. The Vespers, by destroying the power of Charles of Anjou, ended the prospect of a Frankish resurgence in the Peloponnese. Inevitably some of Runciman's ground here is familiar, but he shows an interesting suppleness about absorbing some of the arguments of his critics. Rather than aiming to replace the exiled Latin Emperors, in *Mistra* he has Charles of Anjou planning 'to put his son-in-law upon the Imperial throne, which he would then control' – a graceful formula for acceding to some of the evidence Runciman had ignored, without really compromising his original version of Charles as a chilly megalomaniac. In general, Runciman's dictum that 'A history of Mistra must range across many lands' is of a piece with the whole tendency and direction of his lifelong historical corpus. During the fiasco of the Sudetenland affair of 1938, in which Steven's father had played his doleful part, Neville Chamberlain had called Czechoslovakia 'a far-away country' with 'people of whom we know nothing'. The achievement of Runciman's life, and century, stood as a rebuke to this cramped parochial purblindness. It was his pleasure to demonstrate that scattered-looking lands and countries could be shown, by a sharp-eyed inspection expressed in plain clarity of language, to be intimately bound up.

Runciman's favourite themes of cultural complexity, religious tolerance, political integration and imaginative accommodation, strongly discernible already (if sometimes by their absence) in *A History of the Crusades* and *The Fall of Constantinople*, are laid out in *Mistra* in a final, far-reaching display. The book covers a long, uneasy but surprisingly fruitful period of Greek and Frankish co-residence in the Peloponnese. The early, successful Frankish Princes of Achaea of the house of Villehardouin are notable for the regard they won from their Greek subjects, despite the difference in religion. The Villehardouins, Runciman points out, imposed Latin Bishops but left the Greek parish priests in peace. He also dwells on these Princes' genuine appreciation of and identification with their new domain, practically implying that their motives were at least as aesthetic as avaricious: 'The vale of Sparta was at its loveliest in the early spring weather, and Geoffrey was enchanted by it.' Of all the 'futile' line of Latin Emperors of Constantinople, Runciman can approve only of Henry of Flanders, 'ablest and most attractive' of his family, 'popular with his Greek as well as his Frankish subjects'.

When the Peloponnese peninsula passes back into Greek rule, Runciman's standards of civilized statesmanship are unchanged. The first Despot of the Peloponnese, or Morea, Manuel Cantacuzenus, is praised in identical terms to Geoffrey de Villeharduoin and Henry of Flanders; he had married a wife who was Latin by birth, from the Crusader kingdom of Cyprus, and showed friendliness to both Frankish lords and Latin clergy, even conducting a regular correspondence with the Pope. Under his rule in Mistra, Runciman notes, names begin to recur among the Greek nobility that suggest a Frankish origin being reabsorbed into an Orthodox world – Phrangopoulos,

Raoul, Phrantzes (for Francis) or, in the most glorious instance of all, Syryannis Gilopoulos (which Runciman gleefully renders in almost Falstaffian idiom as Sir John, son of Giles). The greatest intellectual court at Mistra, where 'philosophy and letters flourished for the last time at Byzantium', was presided over by the 'strange and neurotic' Despot Theodore II Palaeologos and his Italian wife, Cleope Malatesta, a niece of Pope Martin V. Cleope, as Runciman has it, 'identified completely with her adopted country', probably converted despite her uncle's remonstrances to the Orthodox Church, and 'provided a harmonious influence' on her husband and his quarrelsome brothers. Her premature death was 'mourned by all the Greek scholars of the time and deeply sorrowed her husband, who had come to value and love her'. Bigots on both sides – including, unsurprisingly, the Knights Hospitaller in the Catholic camp, and Cleope's 'violent and neurotic' daughter Helena, who became Queen of Cyprus, among the Orthodox – are correspondingly reprimanded.

Over his long and celebrated historical career, Runciman had attained the respect of many notable readers, including both professional historians and more general lay writers, who objected to what they saw as the colonialist drift of much Western narrative history – among them Edward Said, Eric Hobsbawm, Christopher Hitchens and Richard J. Evans. It comes then as a surprise to read one of his most boldly old-fashioned generalizations in *Mistra*: 'As usually happens in a colonizing society, the authorities at the top were benevolent and considerate towards their native subjects. It was the invaders of lesser rank that were contemptuous and arrogant.' There is undeniably much straightforward snobbery in this pronouncement, as well as nostalgia for numerous experiences facilitated by imperial peregrinations throughout Steven's life. He had benefited from extremely unusual colonial perspectives in China in his youth, and in Sarawak as a distinguished knight in early old age; Steven had loved the heterogeneous Palestine of the British Mandate and Syria of the French, though he never cared much for British India. But sometimes Runciman's location of enduring cultural and racial division at the level of the lesser clergy, the local populations, the merchant classes and the lesser soldiery has the welcome result of making him concentrate, to a degree, on these groups as well as upon the nobility and prelates.

Runciman is as surefooted and broadminded in his conclusions on intermarriage at large as he is in pursuing any temptingly thorny dynastic lineage. In discussing the mixed Greek–Frank class of *gasmoules*, he productively interweaves confessional allegiance, material prosperity and social position: 'The children of knights and sergeants tended to identify themselves with their father's kin, speaking French and adhering to the Latin Church. The children of poorer soldiers were more apt to speak Greek and follow their mothers' religion.' Admittedly – and with a certain careless honesty – Runciman does not really trouble to conceal his own prejudices. In comparing the lesser clergy of the Catholic and Orthodox rites, he allows to the Greeks a certain disinherited dignity, losing 'cultural standards, but never . . . the allegiance of the people', while the Latin priests are, so to speak, frankly caricatured, 'stalking arrogantly through the streets, stirring up resentment'. He even implies that his increasingly admired Villehardouins had little time for the Latin clerical hierarchy themselves.

Essentially Runciman is an advocate of benevolent good order from any source; he is impatient with the rebellious petty Greek nobility, 'resentful and short-sighted as ever', and his harshest judgements fall on the most lawless elements in his story, Catalan mercenaries and Maniot bandits.* The question of whence peace, authority, culture and continuity came was far more real to him than any partisan purity. More tactfully than the brilliant but alcoholically polemical scholar Romilly Jenkins had done, Runciman carefully and inarguably asserted that the modern Greek people owed much not just to Frankish but to Slav, Albanian and, of course, Turkish extraction.

The choice of Thames & Hudson for *Mistra* had signified a different sort of book from Runciman's previous output, for all his insistence that he was still writing a full history and not a guidebook. His latest work was emerging under an imprint best known for its artistic expertise and generous illustrations. For the book's alluring photography of Mistra's prospects, remains, architecture and art, Steven enlisted the help of a friend at the Benaki Museum in Athens, Dr

---

* Steven never has a good word to say about the peninsula of the Mani or its inhabitants; this consistently stern view is probably at least in part a running joke aimed at Paddy Leigh Fermor, as devoted an encomiast of the Mani as Steven of Mistra.

Fani-Maria Tsigakou; but he was aware that his text, too, required a more than usually visual accompaniment. Flashes of this purpose emerge in the straight narrative that constitutes the first two-thirds of *Mistra*, though these perhaps are of best service to a reader who already knows a little of the Peloponnese. Any visitor to Monemvasia will be awed at Runciman's playful information that its besieged citizens contrived on one occasion to eat all the coastal fortress-city's mice and cats. As always, Runciman is free with the use and quotation of sources that, while quite often uncorroborated, are a gift in terms of plausibility, vitality and background exactitude. *The Chronicle of the Morea* is a contemporary reportage constructed like a chivalric romance, equipped with giants, lovely damsels, maddened suicides and every kind of amatory and political enmity. A more fragmentary, less grand, but equally pictorial point of view is lent to the narrative by the journal of the Venetian notary Nicola di Martoni, threading his way home through a war-torn Morea in 1395, glumly noting 'the appalling state of the countryside', 'infested by Turkish soldiers who lived as brigands'. But, in keeping both with his new publisher and with the ludic side of his nature, maddening to professional scholars, that he had never troubled entirely to restrain, Runciman is in *Mistra* wholly cavalier about his footnotes and citations; these are scarcely hinted at by an appendix as genially meandering as it is brief.

Runciman had always been at his best when in the midst of the story; but in this last history book he outstripped his traditional pattern, aiming to excel in analysis after concluding his chronicle of personalities, schemes and events. His summary of the glittering intellectual life at Mistra, culminating in the outstanding quasi-totalitarian and sometimes bizarre work of Plethon, is a condensation of a decade-old but excellent little book, *The Last Byzantine Renaissance*; but his physical description of the old city's remaining monuments is an altogether fresh accomplishment.* Steven had

---

* *The Last Byzantine Renaissance* had its origins in the Wiles lectures Steven gave at Belfast in 1968. He was unnecessarily apologetic about its quality to his pupil Donald Nicol: 'Not a very good book – but if ever you should give them you should remember that you aren't paid for them until your typescript has gone to the publishers. The natural result is that you want to get it there as soon as possible and not to waste time in putting it into a better form' (SR to Donald Nicol, 26 July 1970, KCL).

always regarded himself as a qualified authority on Byzantine art at need – and he had harsh words for more regular and in-depth commentators on Byzantine art and architecture, including Thomas Whittemore, Robert Byron and David Talbot-Rice. But his writing, though its plainness and fearlessness in the face of intricacy could serve visual description very well, as in *The Fall of Constantinople*, still tended to favour event and personality at the expense of the physical world. In the *Crusades* trilogy, the whole third volume begins to feel like an unwieldy revenge tragedy with universal, dispiriting lessons, that could be set at almost any period, with the art, architecture and culture of the Crusader States confined to an inadequate appendix. As in *The Kingdom of Acre*, in *Mistra* Runciman's engagement with the visible and tangible comes late, but in this, final, case its quality makes up for its tardiness.

The situation Runciman treats is complicated by the many stages through which Mistra evolved: a bare cheese-shaped hill above Sparta; a strategic Frankish outpost; a Byzantine town and then capital; a forgotten Turkish village misinterpreted by passing antiquarians; and finally the beautiful ruin a mile north of the small modern town that contained the Odos Sir Steven Runciman off Palaeologos Square – the whole eclipsed again by reborn Sparta, designed by King Otto's Bavarian neo-classical experts. Runciman must negotiate through the layers of the visible and the imaginable, the surviving, the reputed and the forgotten:

> It is not easy now to envisage Mistra as it must have been under the Despots . . . one leaves the bustle of modern life in the pleasant little town . . . In the old walled city . . . only a few churches stand out intact as buildings, and the great shell of the Palace of the Despots dominates the middle scene . . .
>
> . . . As one wanders through the ruined streets and alleyways one begins to see what must have been the great houses of the nobility, the poorer houses, the shops, and the barracks . . .

Runciman praises the 'tactful restoration' carried out by the Greek

---

Nicol, among others, recalled that Steven delighted in lingering on his ecumenical argument as a deliberate reproach to the sectarian tenor of his Belfast hosts.

government, but he also enacts it himself in verbal form, as he reconstructs the lived, everyday, practical experience involved at various levels, geographical as much as social, of Byzantine Mistra's existence. Because the context is more general than technical a vein of comic charm persists in his description; the lower city below the castle and the Despots' Palace is said to be 'shaped like a sort of apron'; and there is both pleasure and profit in his no-nonsense summaries of the cramped hill-town's logistical shortcomings. In sharp contrast to the waning garden-city of Constantinople (and Runciman has already announced that 'The beauty of Greece lies mainly in contrast'), Mistra, 'not entirely a suitable site for a town', as it began to thrive for political reasons forced its new citizens to struggle with natural problems: 'the terrain obliged the houses to jostle against each other.' In the upper city water could be provided only by cisterns of rain (fortunately plentiful), and 'wheeled transport was impossible.' The Despot and his family by way of the Nauplia back gate beside their palace 'could have ridden out into the countryside', while noblewomen could always rely on litters, but otherwise even the quite prosperous citizens in the 'steep, winding lanes of the lower city' 'must have gone about their business on foot'.

In his interpretation of the origin and calibre of Mistra's architecture and its restored frescoes, Runciman sustains his depiction of the town as a vigorous meeting place between Greek and Frankish styles. But he does not quite keep up his even-handed defence of this combination, revealing at the last his irrepressible Byzantine preferences. The ecclesiastical buildings are called the town's 'chief glory', 'remaining true to the Byzantine tradition', while the Despots' Palace is rebuked as 'closer in conception to the smaller old palaces in Italy', a comparison surely less insulting than he intended. Following the development of the frescoes in Mistra's monasteries, Runciman produces some of his very best writing – and some of his most deterministic and inflexible conclusions. Three styles in three different churches, the Hodeghetria, the Peribleptos and the Pantanassa, are under discussion, and Runciman tackles them in the order of their construction to indicate a teleological direction:

Here [at the Hodeghetria] ... the workmanship is excellent. The drawing is good. There is a touch of humanity, of human drama and human pathos, about the figures, though their dignity is unimpaired. There is a strong sense of movement. The colours are rich but not too lavish, with something of the disregard for realism that originated with the painters of Trebizond ...

It is tempting to see the paintings of the Peribleptos as the work of a native school, as they have an individuality of their own ... The drawing is still excellent, though the artists now like to soften outlines by subtler gradations in colour. There is still an austere dignity in many of the figures, but here and there a touch of wistfulness comes in. There is a slight loss of vigour. People seem not so much to move as float ...

The Church of the Pantanassa, built in 1428, shows in its decoration how taste had changed in the intervening half-century. The artists were still highly accomplished, with a use of colour that is almost riotous in its variety ... but somehow the religious intensity of earlier Byzantine work is gone. It is almost as though we were looking at the illustrations of a book of fairy stories ... There is a great charm about it all; but it is the art of a civilization that has outlived its political basis ... of wistful nostalgia for which there was no future ... the last important monument of the medieval free world.

The casually derogatory use of the word 'charm' here recalls Anthony Blanche in *Brideshead Revisited*, who is also warning of the end of an overbred, bloodless artistic school: 'Charm is the great English blight. It does not exist outside these damp islands. It spots and kills anything it touches. It kills love; it kills art.' Steven, who had always been deceptively willing, despite his own exoticizing impulse, to find remembrances of Northumberland, the Scottish Border and the Isles however far from home he had strayed, found this same mortal charm in melancholy, impoverished, damp Byzantium, and even in rainy Mistra with its 'final taste of glory'. With the 'illustrations in a book of fairy stories' of the Peribleptos, all unknowing of the twenty years he himself had left, he bade farewell both to Byzantine art and to the Empire's long story.

# 25

# The Magician

*Mount Athos, 1937, 1992, 2000*

> ... it shews the descent of grace, virtue and light, drawn from
> things above and derived to things below. The suggestion
> throughout is therefore the possession and communication of
> the Powers and Gifts of the Spirit.
>
> Arthur Waite, *The Key to the Tarot*, 1920

According to legend, the Holy Mountain of the Orthodox began with
a giant who defied the gods. The gigantic Athos either flung his mountainous namesake into the Aegean, or was himself buried beneath it by
the wrath of Poseidon. Both Herodotus and Strabo note the existence
of some towns on the slopes of the mountain's inaccessible peninsula,
but no one paid their rise or waning much mind. When, so the Athonite
story has it, the Blessed Virgin herself, along with St John the Evangelist for good measure, was blown off course on to the mountain's shores,
and delighted in its beauty, she was the only woman upon it; and, in
response to her prayer, her Son ordained that no more creatures of the
female sex should follow her, keeping it for her garden only. It may
have taken some centuries for these commandments, and Christianity
itself, to come fully into effect on the Mountain – a temple to Zeus is
recorded there in the fifth century AD – but by 883 the usurping
Emperor Basil the Macedonian could formalize what was probably an
existing situation: reserving the mountain for its multiplying monasteries, debarring laymen, breeders of cattle and, doubtless, their cows.

By the Crusader sack of Constantinople in 1204, the monasteries of
the Mountain had become numerous, rich and argumentative. In the
centuries to come, whether the mainland was ruled by Greek, Frank or

Turk, the rights of the twenty great monastic houses were recognized. They commanded the respect of the Greek populace and wielded a certain amount of power. Runciman mentions them in *The Great Church in Captivity* as supporting the scholarly usurper John VI Cantacuzenus, and after 1453 as exerting critical influence in the elections of the Patriarchs of Constantinople. By the eighteenth and nineteenth centuries the monks represented a particularly picturesque challenge to the British traveller loose upon the Levant, but were regarded by Westerners as barbarously uneducated – how the wheel had come around – and inhospitable. In 1856 Edward Lear expostulated against them: 'muttering, miserable, mutton-hating, man-avoiding, Misogynic, morose and merriment-marring, monotoning, many-mule-making, mocking, mournful, minced fish and marmalade-masticating Monx!' Then he added, with one of his moving and slightly alarming turns into sympathy, 'Poor old pigs.'

By the 1920s, Byzantium was quietly becoming a facet of avant-garde fashionable and intellectual taste in the former Roman province furthest from her influence. This could not be attributed to the enthusiasms of the young Steven Runciman, rather to the Oxford amateur Byzantinist Robert Byron, a personal and literary rival of Steven. Robert Byron had been an Etonian two years Steven's junior, odd-looking with goggling, watery eyes in a moonish face, lacking in obvious academic ability but unconventionally talented, with a vicious tongue and a penchant for dressing up, disconcertingly convincingly, as Queen Victoria. At Oxford he had run with the Hypocrites crowd, notorious in its day and later to be overemphasized as part of the Brideshead generation. So outspoken was his homosexuality that some considered it confected for effect. Byron (who claimed to be a distant connection of the poet) was exactly the sort of person Steven had in mind when he put himself, but really Oxford, down, writing to his closest Oxonian friend, Roy Harrod: 'Oxford might not appreciate me enough . . . the prospect of going there at all makes me quite incredibly frightened. If you have me, you must be very kind to me and show me the less terrifying people. Remember, I prefer people to be beautiful and dislike the young & precocious.'*

---

* It is scarcely necessary to add that Steven was twenty-one when he wrote this letter and had just learnt of his (as he maintained, scraped) First in history.

Byron certainly was precocious; even Harold Acton felt a little subdued next to his volubility, publicity seeking and prolific journalistic output. In 1925, at the age of twenty, Byron first travelled to Greece. The next spring he was commissioned by the highly cultivated editor of *Vogue*, Dorothy 'Dody' Todd, to write two articles on the monasteries of Athos. Miss Todd had been editor since 1922, increasingly assisted by a brilliant Australian-born protégée, Madge Garland.* The four years of her tenure saw Aldous Huxley, Clive Bell and Virginia Woolf recruited to the cadre of *Vogue* contributors, but also a drop in sales that proved unacceptable to Condé Nast. The Athos commission was typical of Todd's approach, original, visionary, desperately uncommercial; Byron's biographer James Knox remarks that Miss Todd 'could hardly have picked a less suitable subject for her readers'. But by the time the maligned editor was fired in the summer of 1926, Byron's adventure was well under way. While Steven was befriending both Dody Todd and Madge Garland in London among the Sitwells, Byron had, that April, arrived on Athos.

Byron was the lodestar of a whole party of Oxford rakehells to make pilgrimages to the Holy Mountain over the next year, including Bryan Guinness, Mark Ogilvie-Grant, David Talbot-Rice, Alastair Graham and Alfred Duggan. Duggan, though at this point in his life given over to drink, nursed a scholar's disposition that would much later find its most successful expression in his historical fiction. Talbot-Rice became an authority on Byzantine art (not one of whom Steven would ever approve). Byron was something else altogether, and his book on Athos, entitled with defiant opacity *The Station*, was hard to categorize. It was, he insisted, 'intended only for people totally ignorant of the subject', but it would in practice baffle the general public while appealing, in a fraught, qualified sort of way, to

* Madge Garland, née McHarg, later Lady Ashton, would remain an oracle on fashion and a friend of Steven's until she died in 1990. In 1994, Steven sent her book *The Changing Face of Beauty* as a birthday present to Guy Black: 'It is not that I think you to be in serious need of this little book. But when one passes into a decade when prettiness, precocity and pertness no longer suffice, one can perhaps still find helpful hints in unexpected places. Madge may be a wee bit out of date (nearly 100 years) but to her near contemporaries (like myself) she produces gems of lasting value' (SR to Guy Black, 5 August 1994).

specialists. Steven, for his part, was catty about Byron's work when writing to Marthe Bibesco in 1959, seventeen years after his rival's death: 'very enthusiastic and valuable as the first piece of at all effective *vulgarisation* of Byzantine studies to appear in English'. But in the immediate aftermath of *The Station*'s publication in 1928 he admitted to Byron's close friend Christopher Sykes that he was impressed by the book. His exact feelings about Byron's achievement – as opposed to his personality, which he definitely disliked – are thus difficult to calibrate, but they almost certainly included envy. Over the succeeding decade reaching Athos, and claiming it back from the Oxford dilettanti for sober Cambridge, remained to Steven a frustratingly elusive goal.

After a couple of false starts, Steven arrived on the Holy Mountain late in the June of 1937, overcoming both adverse elements and the truculence of a Greek sea-captain:

> It is wonderful how rage rids one of inhibitions. I found myself shouting in Greek with a fluency that I never knew that I possessed about his incompetence and general nastiness; and I turned angrily on an amiable Greek colonel, berating him for belonging to a country that allowed its ships to be captained by such idiots. He merely smiled sadly and congratulated me on my eloquence.

Finding the port of Athos, Daphne, to be 'cold and raining . . . we might have been in the Hebrides', Steven settled to await a reliable muleteer. During this stop he fell in with a Mr Melfos, an elderly Greek MP out of work since the dictator Metaxas had abolished the Parliament. 'He was occupying himself, he told me not once but many times, in writing the history of Macedonia from the fourth millennium BC until modern times.' Of more interest to Steven was his companion Jordani Papazoglou, a young photographer of Christian Turkic descent, who 'decided that I was less boring than his patron and transferred his attentions to me'.

The first monastery upon which Steven and this attractive new Sancho Panza happened was Xeropotamou; it took in travellers with an ill grace, until Steven mentioned the subject of his first book, for the house had been founded by the Emperor Romanus Lecapenus. From then on Steven and Jordani had the run of uncatalogued relics, bean soup, mulberries and 'hungry bed bugs'. At Karyes, the village that serves as the Mountain's capital, Steven lunched with the deputy Governor and the local bank-manager; women might be excluded from Athos, but Mammon had his place there. The brief rage-driven fluency of Steven's Greek quite deserted him for the purposes of polite conversation. Next to come was Vatopedi, tenth century in origin but extremely up to date. It even had electricity, which had become widespread for domestic use in Britain only the decade before; and 'in consequence all the other monasteries considered it to be heretical.' Vatopedi was built above a discreet cove, perfect for a dip, and Steven and Jordani took decorous pictures of each other on this hidden strand.

Mr Melfos, parliamentarian and historian, was following at a slower pace but slipped off his mule and sprained a leg, forcing Jordani to turn back. Just before they separated, Steven made the disconcerting discovery of a cat feeding kittens, in clear defiance of the Virgin Mary's ban. A monk explained (with the help of Jordani's translation from Greek to French) that 'about a hundred years ago' Athos had been faced with a vexing dilemma. 'Mice and snakes would not obey the rules and were breeding too plentifully,' and, while the monks did employ tomcats, the cat-merchants of Thessalonica had started to cash in and hike up their prices. After the Holy Synod devoted an evening of prayer to the Blessed Virgin for a solution, in the morning it was found that all the tomcats had given birth to kittens. Some were, and would continue to be, female, but as gifts of the Mother of God they could hardly be rejected. 'Which was the sex of the cats I subsequently saw', Steven notes soberly, 'I had no means of telling.' After Jordani Steven found at first less pleasant company on the road; one brawny monk pinched him 'hard, for emphasis', whenever his Greek faltered; and a doctor at the monastery of Iviron laid on medicinally lavish retsina and sent Steven reeling to 'the worst bed-bugs on the Mountain'. He had a better time at Karakallou, 'the most charming of all the small monasteries ... beautifully kept, with a pretty garden', and Lavra, where he stumbled on an Englishman equipped with a rubber bath, who 'only spoke English and liked to talk unceasingly. So he ... kindly allowed me to share in his amenities.'

After returning to the mainland, following a gloomy track from a hut-like quay to the small town of Ierissos, Steven called for help in hesitant Greek to a rustic silhouette, and was answered 'in broad Lancashire English'. He had run into a goat-herd who had fled the Pontic genocide during the Greco-Turkish War of 1919–22, passed an unhappy period as a mill-hand in Britain and fetched up in Macedonia.

The most elemental drama was yet to come. The bus from Ierissos contained mainly monks keen to visit Thessalonica, but also an Ierissan girl, unescorted and far gone in pregnancy. The road was rocky and shaded by pines, which swayed about eerily to either side as a thunderstorm began. The driver mutinied and came to blows with the conductor; the girl went into labour; the conductor reasserted control. By happy chance one of the monks with a taste for city life was the drunken doctor from Iviron. The conductor deposited the girl, the doctor, Steven, 'as I seemed to be the cleanest of those present', and a boy who happened to have a spirit-lamp, at the roadside, while he drove off for a midwife. Steven boiled some water to sterilise the instruments, and avoided the makeshift operating table, but nonetheless 'saw sights that no innocent bachelor should have been permitted to see'.

Steven never visited Athos during his post-war years working in Athens for the British Council; his letters from Athens give a full account of his movements, and show that he contemplated a trip to the Holy Mountain in the June of 1946, but was unable to find the time. Of a fleeting stop in the 1950s he says little in his correspondence, only hankering plaintively after 'creature comforts'; during his 2000 interview with the Athonite magazine, he added that the 'state of decay' in the monasteries by the 1950s had saddened him. Athos does not receive extended attention in his work until 1968 in *The Great Church in Captivity*, the book that had the momentous consequence of Steven's elevation to Grand Orator of the Patriarchate of Constantinople, the first such appointment outside the Orthodox faithful.

This new eminence aside, Steven's later and more intense involvement with Athos, like his earlier foray, may have derived some of its force from competitiveness. One of his longest and least appreciated acquaintances was with the painter Derek Hill, who had in 1970 painted a portrait of him which resembled, Steven thought, 'a crucified martyr'. Steven always and in a way sincerely described Hill as one of his oldest friends. He approved of his elder brother, John, a Cambridge contemporary who became a decorator, but never quite took to the younger Hill. Derek died a month after Steven's ninety-seventh and final birthday, in July 2000, at which point Steven was able to articulate most of his real feelings without much restraint:

> Derek's death has come as rather a shock to me. In spite of his appall-ing self-indulgence and lack of consideration for others, there was something lovable about him, and he was really fond of his friends, no matter how appallingly he treated them. He was not a good portrait painter: though one or two of his male portraits are not bad. But I think his early Italian landscapes are charming, and so are his sketches of Mt Athos. I am less keen on his Irish pictures . . . his elder brother John was as cadaverous as Derek was gross . . . I suppose there will be a grandiose memorial service to which we shall all have to go . . .

Despite a certain residual friendship, Steven thought Hill a syba-rite, a crass and pompous social operator, to a fairly serious degree an artistic fraud (the Irish paintings he denigrates are the works on which Hill's reputation most securely rests) and, always important to Steven, physically repellent. But one advantage Hill had over Steven was a close and regular knowledge of the Holy Mountain. By the 1980s this was a particularly bright feather in Hill's plumage, as the most fervent votaries of Athos included the Duke of Edinburgh and the Prince of Wales.

So it must have been gratifying when, in 1989, Hill approached Steven with a request for his help in a matter that affected the Holy Mountain. Also concerned were the academic publisher Graham Speake and Bishop Kallistos of Diakleia, né Timothy Ware. Kallistos is an Oxford theologian who embraced Orthodoxy at the age of twenty-four, later became tonsured as a priest and monk, and as aux-iliary bishop to the Archbishop of Thyateira and Great Britain is the second personage in the Greek Orthodox Church in Britain, while remaining a don at Pembroke. Kallistos had cited Runciman with respect in *The Orthodox Church* (1963). Dr Speake, Kallistos and

Hill were anxious about the independence of the Athonite State under the Patriarchate, and especially about reports that monks of non-Greek nationality, often from Communist countries, were receiving prejudicial treatment from both the Patriarchal authorities and the Greek civil government. They correctly calculated that they would find in Steven a sympathetic ear, one situated to make an impact – for Steven was still the Patriarchate's Grand Orator.

Since a chrysobull, or decree, of the Emperor Constantine IX Monomachus in 1046, both the prohibition on women and the temporal independence of the Holy Mountain as a monastic republic had possessed official legal status. The Emperor protected but did not rule the peninsula. After Byzantium's destruction a Turkish governor replaced the Imperial representative, but stayed just as detached from the local administration; this luckless posting naturally involved the governor's separation from his harem. The Hellenic Kingdom and then Republic succeeded to the Turkish position. But Athos was never truly part of the Ottoman Empire, Greece or indeed the European Union. The monks acknowledged the Patriarch of Constantinople – after 1453 the secular as well as spiritual leader of the Greek community in the Ottoman Empire – as their ecclesiastical, but not their governmental, superior. Now, in the 1990s, the Patriarch was accused of overstepping his boundaries. The house on the Mountain reserved especially for Russians, the Rossikon or St Panteleimon, was reduced to a dozen monks because of the Patriarch's connivance with the Greek state in restricting Russian immigrants, and even pilgrims.

Derek Hill struck the first blow, drawing attention to the problem in *The Times*; Graham Speake then suggested to him the formation of a Society of Friends of Mount Athos. Hill agreed, but insisted on the inclusion of Bishop Kallistos; and Kallistos pointed out that Steven would be a suitably dignified and useful President. The Society was formed in November 1990, and at first saw more merriment than controversy. Between them Steven and Hill (who preferred to forgo official rank in the Society – 'I'm just an artist, I can't *do* anything') accrued a formidable and amusing muster of old friends as Patrons, including Patrick Leigh Fermor, Dimitri Obolensky, James Lees-Milne and Donald Nicol. Meetings were held three times a year at Oxford – Dimitri Conomos, a younger friend of Obolensky's who joined a couple of years into the Society's existence, pointed out that 'Oxford' and 'Bosphorus' mean exactly the same thing – and annually in London.

In accordance with his new presidential position, Steven now prepared, in September 1992, to revisit the Holy Mountain. He had concocted certain plans to ensure that things would be more comfortable than they had been in the 1950s (he was, after all, very nearly ninety): the British Embassy at Athens had agreed to send a young attaché to act as his 'equerry'; Steven would stay for five days and no more, and had arranged to recuperate at 'a splendid villa on a hill top with magnificent views down the Macedonian coast', looked after by the son of its owners, his Greek friends Costa and Lydia Carras, 'a handsome, very intelligent and blond youth of 19'. At the same time and rather in the same spirit, Steven accepted the David Livingstone Medal from the Royal Scottish Geographical Society: 'ridiculous, I think, as I have nothing in common with great missionary explorers. But I am always ready to accept what is offered to me.' To the Friends of Mount Athos he was no mere worthy figurehead or tame dignitary; unity over a good cause did not stop his barbs at Derek Hill's expense, while his private name for Graham Speake was 'Dr. Unspeakable'.

In 1991 the Patriarch Demetrios had died, to be replaced by Bartholomew, the 270th and (at the time of writing) present Patriarch, previously Metropolitan of Chalcedon and Philadelphia, but not known to Steven. Two years later they met for the occasion of the new Patriarch's visit to the Diocese of Great Britain. Steven felt that he was bearing the brunt of the visit along with Prince Philip; but he intimated to Nathalie Brooke that of their duties Steven, who had to introduce a lecture by the Patriarch at the British Museum, had a less onerous task ahead of him than the Duke of Edinburgh, who had to have lunch with him. Prince Philip and Prince Charles were both, by this point, members of the Society. Prince Charles was so taken with the Athonite life that the largest cell in the Vatopedi came to be nick-named after him (according to Dimitri Conomos, 'a palatial suite', but according to Steven 'not at all princely'). Steven liked to inform his Athonite friends that Prince Charles deliberately made excuses to escape his royal duties and stay with them for as long as he could contrive. He even joked to Gordon Gardiner that he himself, as President of the Friends of Mount Athos, 'seemed to be one of Prince Charles's spiritual gurus', and to Nathalie Brooke that 'I almost think that we shall hear some day that the Prince of Wales has turned Orthodox and is retiring to a monastery on Mt Athos or perhaps Mt Sinai.'

But in February 1994 the wound which had called the Society into being was reopened. The Patriarch dispatched an 'exarchate' of three bishops to Karyes; these, with Patriarchal authority, deposed one abbot and the representatives of three of the twenty great monasteries at the Mountain's Holy Council, or Parliament. According to Steven, 'the deposed fathers were among the most outspoken on matters of minority rights.' This move, according to Dr Speake, 'threw the Holy Mountain into crisis and schism'. Thirteen of the twenty monasteries defied the exarchate, six obeyed, while one, the northernmost Esphigmenou, notorious since the 1970s for its rebelliousness, declined to vote at all.* Fourteen votes were necessary for any decision and, as Dr Speake relates, 'relations with Constantinople were at an all-time low.' Under these circumstances the 'thirteen' opposed to the depositions appealed to the Friends of Mount Athos. A fresh letter to *The Times* was fired off, signed (although not drafted) by Steven as President. The moment had been well chosen: British, Greek, American and other foreign papers re-echoed the outcry, and the Patriarch Bartholomew, so visibly rebuked by his own Grand Orator, for the time being retreated over the depositions. In the immediate aftermath of this outcome Dr Speake optimistically averred that the relationship between the Patriarchate and the monks 'may even have been improved by the upset'.

Battle was rejoined all the same in March 1995, when the Great Lavra, the oldest monastery on Athos, appeared to be on the point of joining the rebel houses on the question of definite temporal independence, so bringing them to the required majority of fourteen. The

---

* The Esphigmenou, however, represented in many ways the reverse of Steven and the Friends' position; it was fiercely protective of its independence but also wildly anti-ecumenical, having always disapproved of Steven's favourite Patriarch, the reforming Athenagoras.

Patriarch sent five bishops to undermine the Abbot of Lavra's position, at a trial conducted in camera, over the heads of the Holy Council. This time Steven took to the barricades himself, in his last article for *The Times*; his first had been his travel-pieces from the Far East in 1939. In this piece, published in mid-April, he lays emphasis upon the pan-Orthodox, rather than simply Greek, character of the Mountain, fostered by Byzantine Emperors and Russian Tsars and sanctioned in Holy Scripture:

> Irrespective of national origin, monks have lived out their austere lives of holy service in a territory that offered hospitality and opportunity to all spiritual growth . . . the Holy Mountain was destined from the outset to play an influential role in the shaping of Orthodox monastic tradition throughout Eastern Europe. Its continued ability to do so, even in times of persecution, invasion and subjugation, can be attributed to its aloofness from political and ethnic disputes; its privileged status of self-government with respect to administrative and domestic affairs, and its commitment to the Christian ideal that recognises neither Jew nor Greek but rather a holy nation and a royal priesthood.

Steven accused the Greek press and Foreign Ministry – with which he was ordinarily on excellent terms – of mealy-mouthed and menacing euphemisms, calling the monks 'unpatriotic' when they meant 'un-Greek'. When the Foreign Ministry and the Patriarchate – which, Steven noted, drew its funding not from Ankara but from Athens – guaranteed the Holy Mountain's continuing administrative independence and attached privileges, 'so long as these are interpreted correctly', he attacked them over such equivocations. He declared that the Holy Council was outraged, and charged the Patriarchate with allowing itself to be degraded in turn while it demeaned the monasteries, manipulated by a Greek government 'that cannot itself afford to be accused of ethnic cleansing or constitutional violation'. He does not hesitate to employ the word 'racism' when criticizing a plan to vet non-Greek novices before allowing them into the Athonite houses. Steven's own non-Greek extraction, combined implicitly with his high standing in Greece, is used to his side's advantage. He can write of the Holy Council's 'embarrassment' at having to turn in its hour of need to friends in the West. He insists without entire accuracy, bearing in mind the purist and exclusionist Esphigmenou, that the tradition and power of Athos lies in its unity and ecumenism: 'the very heart and strength of Athonite monasticism is its ecumenical profile. As a federation of monastic houses, its belief in supra-national parity is not a separatist movement but simply a traditional reality. The fathers' common Orthodox faith transcends and conquers ethnic differences.'

Steven's external British perspective also comes in useful for commenting on the EU and delivering a side-swipe to another adopted country of his, by now fallen from favour, Turkey:

> Mount Athos should not be the bugbear but the boast of modern Greece. As a member state of the multinational EU, Greece alone can point to this unique republic under God as a paradigm of harmonious collaboration among different peoples striving for a common cause. The Ecumenical Patriarchate in Turkey, itself a persecuted entity, should rejoice in this most valuable adornment in its spiritual jurisdiction.

Steven ends stylishly, with another scriptural, faintly self-referential allusion: 'for monks to practise their vocation they must be left alone. Then they can toil and pray not only for themselves but "for the life of the world".' As a whole the letter is a rare return to the pragmatic efficiency of his post-war British Council days. Steven's taste inclined towards more languorous and ironical rhetoric, but if necessary, even into his tenth decade, he did not disdain straightforward fisticuffs.

This intervention was not, and probably could never have been, conclusive. Steven had embroiled himself at the very end of his life in the kind of institutional war he had ducked at Cambridge and loathed at the British Council, and such wars tend to last as long as the institutions themselves; in the case of Athos, the struggle had already been prosecuted for nearly a millennium. In 1996, Steven could be found plotting with a younger Greek historian, Aristeides Papadakis. Papadakis shared 'your misgivings about the Patriarchate, although initially I was optimistic. And it is not just the Holy Mountain. More recently, the handling of the Estonia problem, I'm convinced, does not bode well.'* The Abbots of Athos now believed that they could turn to the

---

* This was the problem of whether the Estonian Orthodox Church, which had been dissolved entirely between 1978 and 1996, should now answer to Moscow – its

President of their Friends as a regular champion, and Steven received correspondence from them with mingled exasperation and curiosity. He was especially taken with one abbot who addressed him as 'Your Honesty' – 'endearing, I think – I suppose he thinks that is what "The Hon." stands for.'

In his very last years, no longer writing much except the odd teasing and brief review on a royal subject and his own understandably underpowered memoirs, 'Footnotes to a Long Life', relying upon first a walking stick and then a wheelchair for his mobility, it was hardly surprising that Steven mellowed. Most of those who had dealings with him, including Patriarch Bartholomew, the Greek authorities and even the Young Turks among professional historians, were also inclined to be irenic, feeling that by now, however profound their differences, Steven's achievements should be celebrated and his honours enjoyed. In 1997 Michael Llewellyn-Smith, a British Ambassador to Athens who befriended Steven after meeting him with Costa and Lydia Carras, was instrumental in conferring on him another accolade, putting his name forward for an International Onassis Award for Culture. It amounted to some $300,000, and when Steven duly won it no one could deny the handsomeness of his action in putting the whole sum at the disposal of the Athonite Holy Council. With his enthusiastic approval, it was decided that the prize should be spent on the restoration of the Protaton Tower in Karyes, to fit it up as both an archive for the Holy Synod and a treasury of icons – a fitting metonymy, in its usefulness to learning, physical beauty, venerability and holiness, for everything he valued. In the meantime he cheerfully groused about the award ceremony in Athens to Nathalie Brooke:

> My Greek visit went off quite well . . . the Foundation provided a huge Mercedes car for my sole use . . . so much grander than the Embassy car that the Ambassadress liked to travel in it to functions with me, leaving the Ambassador to follow humbly behind us.* The functions

---

historic superior – or Constantinople, which had overseen the Church from 1923 until its suppression.

* In mischievously upstaging the British Ambassador to Greece while squiring his Ambassadress, Steven was gaily reprising his excursions with Lady ('Peter') Norton in 1940s Athens.

were overlong but I managed to last them out – vast receptions where
I searched and searched for a chair, and when I found one all the more
boring Greeks at once settled like flies on me . . .

So it was that Steven found himself invited upon his very last excursion, to A for Athos, or Abroad. The Patriarch Bartholomew, for all his Grand Orator's naughtiness, had agreed to dedicate the now restored, but anciently constructed, Protaton Tower himself, in a ceremony in the mid-July of the millennial year, not long after Steven's ninety-seventh birthday. As Steven wrote with ill-concealed excitement to Gordon Gardiner in May: 'They have promised to provide me with all the comforts that the Holy Mountain can provide (which are not very great), even making use of a helicopter, provided by the Greek government . . . I am not sure that I approve – one ought not to descend from heaven to the Holy Mountain – the journey should surely be in the other direction.' In fact the chopper was laid on at the expense of the grateful Athonite State, as Steven was slightly less pleased to learn. On a bright Friday evening he descended to the monastery of the Vatopedi, where he was to lodge, accompanied in the little whirling craft by Graham Speake (who had benefited from Steven's general amnesty in recent years: Steven told Nathalie Brooke that 'I am now devoted to Dr. Unspeakable'); Dimitri Conomos with his young son, whom Steven looked upon with fondness and was in the habit of presenting with Elshieshields eggs in Smartie tubes; and Simon Jennings, the Society's Treasurer. Musing on this journey, Anthony Bryer, the younger Byzantinist who had known Steven ever since his own wartime childhood in Palestine, reflected that

> . . . Sir Steven flew from the Scottish border tower which housed his
> own library to a curiously similar one on the Holy Mountain of Athos,
> a living community of Byzantium, to inaugurate its monastic archive . . .
> Carried enthroned amid abbots and archimandrites, Steven Runci-
> man was in his element. It was an astonishingly appropriate final act.
> The romance, the style and the scholarship, had been consistently
> authentic.

But Steven did not know at the time that he was engaged in such a fitting and symbolic inverted apotheosis. He had joked to many friends about the spiritual consequences of his death during or after this planned descent, but such witticisms were, by now, reasonably, one of his staple devices. When it came to the flight he was thrilled, able to take in the beauty of the peninsula's woods as he had never done from the ferry. He was relieved by Vatopedi's relative comfort, with its lifts and 'up-to-date loos'. The Abbot was 'a dear old man', he thought, 'and many of the monks Cypriots and eager to talk in English. I spent the afternoon lying down in my cell but emerging for a long religious service and a short, not very alluring meal – then a pleasant evening on a balcony with the Abbot, with a wonderful view and a splendid sunset . . . ' The morning he had passed hurtling up and down the lifts of Vatopedi. Everything seemed in ferment; the library had just been reorganized and a museum was under construction, with empty and crowded glass cases scattered about as if by the Latin looters of 1204. Steven still thought the Athonite larder rather lowering: 'I find lentils unattractive.' But 'the great heat wave that had descended on South-East Europe had tactfully receded.' The coming Sabbath was the real test of his mettle:

Sunday was almost more than I could manage. At 8 am a helicopter appeared to take us over the forested hills to the village which is the capital of the Mountain, for the consecration and opening of the tower . . . a reception at 9 am, to which the Greek Government had sent its Ministers of Finance and Education to greet me (but also to greet the Patriarch of Constantinople . . . ) Then there was a long religious service blessing the building, followed by a speech praising me and my reply . . . And then I had to be shown the whole building – the museum containing the remarkable collection of icons and manuscripts owned by the Holy Synod, in a pleasant room with a large fresco in praise of me . . . The tower had no lift, and I was carried in my wheelchair by my British colleagues, aided by stalwart young monks, upstairs and downstairs (the latter rather alarming). Then at last we moved to have lunch, provided by the civil governor of the Mountain – a bit more edible than the monastic meals – over which we could not sit for long, as we had to take the helicopter back to Salonica . . .

I don't imagine that I shall ever go abroad again – but I am glad that I managed this last rather splendid journey.

Graham Speake reported that 'the assembled monks, government ministers and pilgrims were astonished when Sir Steven addressed them formally in good ecclesiastical Greek.' Dimitri Conomos thought Steven's brief speech in response 'high-level, if a little rusty', detecting in it 'Erasmian pronunciation'.* It had in truth been composed by the Greek poet Nikos Stangos, Steven's last publisher. This fact, in its way, was just as characteristic of Steven as the consecrated descent from tower to tower that had so struck Anthony Bryer.

---

* The pronunciation of ancient Greek taught by Erasmus is still followed in slightly variant forms by students and scholars of the language in Western Europe; it differs significantly from that of Byzantine and modern Greek.

# 26

# Judgement

Paradise Regained *(supposedly written 1935,
actually c. 1990s, privately printed 1992)*; A
Traveller's Alphabet *(written 1989–90, published
1991)*; Elshieshields, 1980–2000; Romania, 1969,
1971; Bulgaria, 1975–2003; Wolfsgarten, 1937–97;
Sanlúcar de Barrameda, 1951; London, 1997;
Bahrain, 1985–2000; Iraq 1956; Cairo 1951;
Istanbul, 1986; Warwickshire, Radway, 2000

... all the figures are as one in the wonder, adoration and
ecstacy expressed by their attitudes.

Arthur Waite, *The Key to the Tarot*, 1920

*Mistra* in 1980 was Runciman's last full-length historical work, and
not, at that, over-full or long. Steven was confessedly a writer before
he was a historian or traveller. His last two decades were to be punctuated by *jeux d'esprit*, both literary and historical. He continued to
lecture all over the world until the end of 1988, when, with decided
relief, he gave his last lecture on Patmos as a tribute to the monastery
of St John the Divine, then celebrating the 900th year since its foundation by the Emperor Alexius I Comnenus. In October 1992 Steven
offered Dadie Rylands a more playful present for his ninetieth birthday, *Paradise Regained*, a novella he claimed to have written in
1935 and lately rediscovered. Like *Mistra*, *Paradise Regained* aspired
to material as well as literary refinement; it was privately printed by
Rampant Lions Press, a letterpress firm headed by Will Carter,
younger brother of the bibliophile John Wayneflete Carter, a lately
deceased schoolfriend of both Steven and Dadie. The novella's action
concerned an assortment of allusively named archaeologists, explorers and scientists who stumble upon the Earthly Paradise in Kurdistan,
and pay the price accordingly. One of the most memorably silly of the

rechristened authorities who play a part in the story is Dame Helga Shark; Freya Stark was not endamed until 1972, but more importantly, for his proleptic, appropriating eye cannot be entirely discounted, Steven did not actually know her until the early years of the Second World War.* He distributed copies of this work among favoured friends, including some of very recent standing, unlike Dadie, such as the royal dressmaker Hardy Amies and the precocious gallery director Neil MacGregor. Despite his youth MacGregor was quietly wise to the joke, suggesting with sly courtliness, 'You should discover more things you wrote in 1935.'

At the beginning of the previous year, Steven had completed a seemingly more substantial undertaking; but A Traveller's Alphabet resisted classification. It was not a history book, a full autobiography, a travel book or a conventional memoir; it was playfully subtitled Partial Memoirs, punning with a vengeance. He imagined that it would in time be followed by a more formal production. In the meantime with careful self-deprecation he described to his friends what would turn out to be his last published book, telling Donald Nicol in the summer of 1989, 'I am amusing myself by writing an anecdotal account of some of my travels . . . It will all be trivial and full of digressions – self-indulgence, really. No more learned articles ever . . . ' This slippery biography-as-parlour-game was actually an announcement of some finality. The Alphabet marked the formal end of Steven's active academic life, and his willingness henceforth to let himself be beheld, interviewed, summarized, mischaracterized and chased, almost always in vain, as both a witness to his long era and a sort of historical actor in his own right. From now on he theoretically colluded in becoming what he had in 1989 gloomily remarked to Dadie the pair of them seemed: 'relicts of a past age . . . left-overs from more gracious days'.

There was, Steven felt, a kind of record to be set straight. He could be sensitive to written impressions about him that he considered inaccurate, or unsympathetic. This was especially the case when the writers were admiring would-be acolytes, well intentioned bordering on reverent. Steven took sternly against a 1986 New Yorker profile of

---

* Stark herself was still alive when Steven released Paradise Regained, but was not sent it; she had been suffering from dementia since the late 1980s.

him by David Plante, by now a friend of over a decade's standing as well as the companion of Steven's editor Nikos Stangos. Plante had acquired a reputation for mischief with his disconcertingly frank triple portrait of Sonia Orwell, Jean Rhys and Germaine Greer in *Difficult Women* (1983). His profile of Steven was not even a slightly related exercise. Plante quoted Steven accurately and abundantly, in a deliberate, mutually agreed attempt at conversational realism. But Steven recoiled from the result, which he damned to several friends as 'unlovable'; many took his part, stigmatizing the French-Canadian outsider Plante as a bitchy offender against Steven's steely code. Steven had been worried by Plante's piece – not in the long run at all damaging – because he recognized in it faithfully observed characteristics that, rather to his inward credit, Steven could display in the moment but regret in retrospect – 'I sounded governessy, irascible, long-winded and rather humourless.' It was the last that cut the deepest. Steven now determined to rectify this with an essay in his historically specific, and by now endangered, but still seductive mode of wit, diaphanously veiled as travel-memoir.

Steven's works of recreational fiction, from his schooldays onwards, had always been ordered by a firm, formal conceit. 'The She-Devil', with its deliberately irrelevant and alluring title for the delectation of his fellow Collegers at Eton and his sisters at home, had followed a faithless wife who was all too conveniently assumed dead at sea; 'Victoria Robinson: Saint and Martyr' was the fantasy novella of 'an English spinster who battled werewolves in Slavonic lands'; 'The Wish-Bone' – like 'Victoria Robinson' an adventure featuring a heroine caught somewhere between Torby's intellect and Vera Donnet's glamour – was a governess's ascent to the throne of a cannibal kingdom; *Paradise Regained* was a skit on Milton and a boatload of renowned acquaintances. All were light, clever and deliberately juvenile, preserving an air of precocity in aspic; their appeal and limits derived from strict rules. They lacked entirely the amplitude and addictive potential of Runciman's historical writing.*

---

* One younger correspondent in May 1996, an intimidated but evidently charmed would-be historical novelist and clergyman named Jonathan Price, alludes to the lost manuscript of a full historical novel by Steven, on the life and career of Humphrey

But *A Traveller's Alphabet* is the last, most practised and most successful of these games. Despite observing many and strict self-denying
ordinances, it is able, sometimes because of as much as in spite
of them, to sparkle and startle. Its underlying rules are simple but
contain a tease especially comprehensible to Steven's inner circle.
Twenty-seven chapters each describe a place beginning with a letter
of the alphabet – with a supplementary ampersand to sweep up odds
and sods. Various forms of circumvention occur. There is wilful
antiquation and exoticism – Cochin-China for Vietnam, Ur of the
Chaldees standing in for Iraq and Xanadu for China, Yucatan for
Mexico, and Zion for Jerusalem. Geography and orthography allow
for one doublet and two sets of triplets, Cambodia and Cochin-China,
Hamburg, Hildesheim and Hesse, and Morea, Monemvasia and
Mistra. Sometimes Steven's titular locations are precise, tending to
the obscure, where the chapter's matter is more general; Kodiak
Island does the work of Alaska. Naughtiest of all is the reference for
those in the know to Steven's elaborate anecdote, repeated in suitable
company, of collecting lovers whose name began with every letter of
the alphabet. In his *Partial Memoirs*, unlike in life, Steven did not
struggle with X nor omit Q (Queensland).

Rather, as Steven's history serves both to challenge and provoke
experts, and to compel and hold general readers, the *Alphabet* alerted
those who knew Steven only by repute or not at all to the existence
of a habit of mind and sense of humour they might have already
thought extinct. It also stirred memories in old and grateful friends.
The critic Janet Adam Smith was reminded by 'Roumania' of the first
rumour she had heard of Steven, while she was at Cambridge; one
of Steven's Stevenson cousins had soberly reported to her that this
brilliant young don in the family had been taken as a lover by Queen
Marie. Enrico d'Assia, a painter, set designer and great-great-grandson

---

IV of Toron, a baron of the Kingdom of Jerusalem rumoured to be bisexual. Steven
may well have been teasing when he told Price he had ever completed such a thing;
and, unlike many other works of fiction he claimed out of embarrassment to have
lost (like 'Victoria Robinson'), it has not resurfaced since his death. It would otherwise have been interesting to see whether it more closely resembled his short fiction
or his history, with the the ambitious reach of the Tolstoy–Zoé Oldenbourg school
of historical fiction he most admired.

of Queen Victoria, born Prince Heinrich of Hesse-Kassel, expressed his thorough enjoyment of so many 'stories about our family'; and Enrico was no mean judge, as the chief source for Steven's theory that the Old Queen's illegitimate daughter Jean Brown had enjoyed a quiet life in Italy. John Grigg, the ex-Lord Altrincham who had eventually managed to renounce his title and was now an acclaimed political historian, the biographer of Lloyd George and President of the London Library, was more enthusiastic than attentive:

> What I particularly admire is the combination of romantic and ironic vision which you share with some of my favourite authors (e.g. Byron and Stendhal). It makes all your experiences, whether in palaces and government houses or roughing it on the road, supremely enjoyable to read about . . . you convey an enormous amount of information in the lightest possible way.

As a description of Steven's *Partial Memoirs* this is more flattering than ept; it sounds more like an encomium to the travel narratives of Patrick Leigh Fermor. Steven scarcely ever claimed to 'rough it on the road', and in the *Alphabet* he did not really intend to convey information – rather to advertise, then withhold it.

Steven's contemporaries whose own adventurous lives had overlapped with some of the action in his *Alphabet* responded to what it evoked for them, more or less independently of its author's own mysterious career and personality. The sometime songwriter and journalist David Yates Mason, one of Dadie's pupils and favourites at King's, described the 'pleasantness of meeting old friends', in particular Eddie Bates; he recalled an all-night carousal with Bates, Noel Annan and Arthur Marshall, though Steven's own references to Bates in the *Alphabet* had been curt to the point of repression. James Earl Jewell, one of Steven's last guests on Eigg, a set-designer from Los Angeles, sent Steven a doubtless unsolicited summary of his own erotic adventures in pre-war China. The diplomat Sir William Hayter, whose sister Alethea, a writer, Steven had always liked, had his own maddening recollections of flirting with Queen Marie. Sometimes familiarity with Steven occluded rather than elucidated the book; Martin Palmer, an academic in Alaska and himself a prominent supporting character in 'Kodiak Island', was baffled by the sheer plenitude and casualness of the ghost stories distributed over the rest of the *Alphabet*. Several friends guilelessly wondered at Steven's miraculously continuing existence, given the extreme frequency, severity and oddity of his illnesses on various far-flung emprises.

One of the best-suited and most limber readers of these *Partial Memoirs* was Leslie Perowne, Stewart Perowne's surviving younger brother. The fan-letter he wrote to Steven, whom he had befriended in 1938 more than a decade after his brother had become one of Steven's Cambridge intimates, represents the spirit of the *Alphabet*, its corset momentarily, tantalizingly removed:

> so much of the book reminded me of the Steven I first knew, more than fifty years ago, of 'all the difference in the world', 'that's what you think', and of course, your shattering put-down, when we were allotting cars, 'I'm not going in a car with that Miss Horror' . . .
>
> . . . that naughty Charles Lambe (nobody ever told me you and he were related) introduced me to Mt Athos with a fascinating book called, I think, the Seven Thousand Beards of Mt Athos. It starts with a description of a trek, on donkeys, up to a monastery and the little boy leading the creatures went into the monastery and was never seen again. I have here, among Stewart's letters, a *laisser-passer* to enter Mt A, but I have never had the opportunity to go. I do know a young man, English, who spent five years there and is now a monk of an odd community of the Greek Church, based in Brookwood Cemetery, who signs himself now, Niphon, Monk & Sinner. Well, he certainly was a very naughty boy, but is now tonsured and bearded and Good.

Perowne reckoned that:

> . . . Only Harry Luke* had been to so many places as you, in my knowledge, but you have the advantage in having known so many

---

* Sir Harry Luke was a British colonial governor of Hungarian-Polish birth, with an exceptionally eventful and mobile career. Sir Ronald Storrs said that Luke had passed 'the most unwasted life of any man I have known' (see *ODNB*), a verdict that Steven's much younger lady-friend Robin Dalton would later pass on him in not dissimilar words – 'I would hate to cope with boredom . . . at least you cannot say that *any* of your time has been wasted *merely* on frivolities . . . maybe you feel less old in the time sense than I do' (Robin Dalton to SR, 29 October 2000, Elshieshields). Steven never received this rallying-cry, as he died away from home two days after it was written.

queens, or perhaps I should say Queens; it looks better. I have been reading your book in bed, and . . . talking of all those Splendid Queens . . . I really had a belly-laugh at the bits about the face-lift: that was the Old Steven.*

. . . Many years ago I took Stewart on a Greyhound tour of the USA, coast to coast, and on the way stopped in the middle of the night at a place called State Line, between Utah and Nevada. One side was Dry and the other swam in drink and gambling machines. Only you would have had two jackpots at a first attempt. I am no gambler and have never had any luck.†

Steven's reply was comparatively mild but he tipped the wink back: 'I am so glad that you enjoyed my rather frivolous Alphabet. I wish that Stewart could have seen it – it shows, I think, how much I owed to him in the enjoyment of my life.'

One paradox was that the publication of so very contained a kind of memoir itself necessitated for Steven a programme of unprecedented performance and public relations. To Nikos Stangos he complained with less than convincing plaintiveness that the Thames & Hudson publicity department was 'bullying' him; he found the prospect of an interview with Ned Sherrin vulgar, and thought the Foyle's Library Luncheon 'a crowning horror'. To Elizabeth Wansbrough he lamented the onset of an unsought 'celebrity', while to Dadie he was resigned, but even more mutinous: 'I suppose publicity is considered necessary nowadays; I don't think I like the modern world.' But small sign of such resentment and fatigue emerged in the interviews on television and in print that emerged. Steven had learnt from what he considered the unsatisfactory David Plante experience. Now he charmed and bamboozled journalistic visitors with a less literary and comprehensive

---

* 'Queen Elisabeth of the Belgians, Bavarian by birth but heroically loyal to her adopted country when it was overrun by the Germans . . . was also a first-class violinist, and had the further distinction of being the first queen to have her face lifted, in those early days when a lift left one with starry eyes and a permanent smile; tragically so in her case, as a few days later her husband, King Albert, was killed in a climbing accident, and the smile had to be let down for the funeral' (from 'Roumania', *Alphabet*, p. 129).

† See 'Nevada', *Alphabet*.

grip, appearing to show to them what they thought they wanted, while politely enjoying himself at their expense.*

Steven affected bemusement to Dadie at his latest book's wider success: 'My new book seems to be doing well, with wonderfully kind reviews.' There was one notable exception – Steven's old Trinity neighbour in Nevile's Court, Enoch Powell, with whom he had kept up polite but cool relations, wrote a 'very stern' notice, thinking the *Alphabet* 'deplorably silly. I was fascinated by his reaction.' Powell's distinctly envious splutter, carried by the *Daily Telegraph*, about the pleasant but aimless career, as he saw it, of a soft-living, undisciplined and sybaritic Byzantinist was exactly the kind of attack Steven enjoyed provoking. Nettled Puritans showed his own coolness to advantage. Powell's grievances ranged from his bitterness against the easy advantages of Steven's connected family circumstances, to incomprehension of his ironic visual style and vigilant sense of humour, to frustration at his taunting omission of an index. His review constituted an old-fashioned and virulent instance of the objections Runciman had always attracted from scholars in his own field, of sloppiness, partiality, mendacity and preciosity. Runciman's reputation (and, especially, his sales) continued to weather such assaults, even though their greater ferocity after his death rendered redundant the courtesy Steven's age, position and embodiment of a now nearly mythical era had so long commanded.

Runciman's most sophisticated critics could adopt, and on occasion best, his preferred rhetorical weapon, the light rapier-touch *en passant*. Frank Kermode, in the *Guardian*, applied an exact and exacting scalpel to which Steven himself could not honestly have objected:

> The style of the book is the produce of an easy confidence that anything the author says about himself is intrinsically likely to be interesting, and that dissent from this position would be without significance.
>
> . . . These great things are not to be had by jostling in the street; if one called them gifts of grace Sir Steven would probably not demur.

Fiona MacCarthy at the *Observer* was perceptive enough to take

---

* Steven's interview with James Shirley at the *Observer*, 10 February 1991, is a good example of this effortless, indeed really extroverted hiding in plain sight.

Runciman more seriously. She acknowledged, with an analytical rather than adversarial purpose, the significance of his upbringing and milieu:

> The privilege-span is as important as the time-span ... Almost from the age of infancy, Runciman was in the role of roving VIP ...
>
> ... this is not a snob of the old school we have to deal with; it is something infinitely more ingenious and subtle. Runciman is interested in the usefulness of friends in influential places in easing the way towards the things he really cares about. Solitude; comfort; the sheer oddness of experience that only great reserves of discrimination bring you ...
>
> Runciman's bashfulness is, in its way, convincing. But what makes these memoirs so surprising and enchanting is their revelation of another Runciman: Runciman the reckless, even the ruthless ... When he hits the jack-pot he scoops up his winnings and he runs.
>
> The affectation of incompetence is striking in a historian so astute and so wide-ranging ... His pose of affability is similarly suspect ... Not for nothing are these memoirs labelled partial: they are partly sweet nostalgia ... partly wilful and exhilarating insolence.
>
> This is a book of nuances, in which the half-said or barely hinted is often more important than the actually stated: the terse reference to his mother's death, which he felt deeply; the sardonic little portrait of his brother, flirting and ennervé in wartime Tehran. Reading between the lines with Runciman is one of the pleasures he proffers us, with Calvinist backhandedness.

MacCarthy provides the best, most distilled account of Runciman's character, motivation and style since Peter Green's review of *The Sicilian Vespers*.

Green considered Steven to be a great historian and a stylist in the mode of Lytton Strachey, even one who surpassed his master in the range of his conception. He thought the decisive flaw in *The Sicilian Vespers* to be its author's cold-bloodedness, a shortage of empathy and compassion when confronted with tragedy:

> Sir Steven is apt to see every Western move in terms of ecclesiastical cynicism or political self-advantage ... but – and this is the crux of the

matter – the Machiavellian crust was only skin deep. *The Sicilian Vespers* is a superb exercise in historical scholarship and creative skill; but it misses that extra dimension of understanding which would make it truly great. *Sunt lacrimae rerum* . . . but Sir Steven remains dry-eyed amid the ruins of a world.

This was not an argument that applied to Runciman's threnodies for Byzantium, and even for the Latin settlers of Outremer. Wanton and short-sighted as he considered the Crusaders, he had reserved for them some admiration, mingled with condemnation, at the conclusion of his trilogy. In the *Alphabet*, he dealt directly less with his own life than with the passing of the world he had known.

This process of decorous mourning, dry-eyed perhaps but not the less deeply felt, is most immediately obvious in the 'Bulgaria' and 'Roumania' chapters, concerning that far-off Balkan world where Runciman had first made his name in his twenties and thirties. Despite his usually unbending rule against revisiting places where he had long ago been happy, despite his description to Marthe Bibesco of the Communist ascendancy over Eastern Europe as 'the cataclysm', Steven did return to both Bulgaria and Ro(u)mania after the onset of the Iron Curtain (he had small time for resonant Churchillian coinages).

Steven was first invited to the Socialist Republic of Romania in 1969, four years after Ceauşescu's ascension to power and two years after his assumption of the Presidency. Though shocked by the reducing of the streets of Bucharest to 'drabness, shabbiness, and inappropriate heavy industry', Steven felt at first surprisingly optimistic about the republic's future. The new regime, not unlike Tito's Yugoslavia, appeared to place more importance on establishing a course independent from Russia than on exchanging catcalls with the West. The national Orthodox Church had proceeded, Steven thought, along an adroit middle way between the party and the Faith, and he was particularly interested in one unexpected result of this compromise, that in the three government-backed seminaries 'many of the ordinands were black young men from Africa.' He easily befriended a government chauffeur whom a young Bucharest scholar had warned him was a party agent, and let the Abbot of the monastery at Putna drink him into bewilderment with much replenished slivova, 'the seductive plum brandy of the Balkans'; the Abbot confided that professors of archaeology were a much greater nuisance than state officials. Queen Marie seemed to be widely remembered with gratifying fondness, having 'passed into local legend', and when Steven called at Princess Bibesco's beloved palace of the Mogoşoea, he was asked 'innumerable questions, not all of which I could answer' about how it had been run in his friend's time (Marthe herself was still alive, having retired, like Prince Chula of Siam, to Cornwall with her daughter, Valentine, Princess Ghika). Even life in the Romanian academy, so far as Steven discerned, could be led undisturbed, 'so long as professors steered clear of politics'. It looked too to be a good sign that the entirely non-Communist, indeed on occasion rather fascistic, Professor and one-time Prime Minister Nicolae Iorga – the man who had encouraged Steven to pursue *Byzance après Byzance*, the idea and period which had resulted in *The Great Church in Captivity*, published just before this visit – was acknowledged as Romania's greatest historian. But two years later, at another Bucharest conference, Steven realized that these encouraging signs had been utterly misleading. 'Our Roumanian colleagues were still very cordial, but less at their ease.' He describes encountering a bugging device by his hotel lavatory seat, 'as though it was there that I conducted secret conversations'. He met the Dictator and thought him and his whole suite 'scruffy'. 'The night is ended at last,' Steven would venture, writing in early 1990 after the Christmas that had seen the execution of Nicolae and Elena Ceauşescu, 'but the dawn is stormy and uncertain.'

It had taken Steven longer to return to Bulgaria, though he still had friends there. An invitation to lecture issued by the Bulgarian Academy in 1975 was suddenly 'superseded' by the proffered hospitality of Liudmilla Zhivkova, the daughter, 'First Lady' and rumoured heir-designate of the Bulgarian President Todor Zhivkov. Steven had gathered from the British Ambassador to Sofia, Edwin Bolland, that Madame Zhivkova was partial to incognito shopping expeditions at Harrods. She and her husband ran Friday soirées, much endearing themselves to the intellectual scene in Sofia. Zhivkova's interests were searching and persistent, and it was particularly to Steven's advantage that they included history – especially that of the Bulgar people – and, more broadly, occult power. To Nathalie Brooke Steven described with astonished pleasure his first return to Bulgaria. For all that the country's 'simple charm' had yielded, in the capital at least, to a 'clumsy Soviet style',

> My Bulgarian visit was extraordinary. The Government did me proud – everything paid for – even when I wanted to buy a picture postcard . . . the Bulgarian First Lady, the President's beloved daughter, in her capacity as cultural dictatress, gave a dinner for me (she had never entertained a visiting scholar before) and came to a dinner given by the Ambassador for me (she has never accepted to dine in a Western Embassy before). I came back staggering under the weight of books given to me and bottles and bottles of Bulgarian wine and slivova – but my luggage had been provided with such an enormous label stating VIP that the Heathrow customs officials gasped and passed me on.

For the next three years, Steven was in favour at Sofia as he had never been even in the glory-days of King Boris's Anglophile period. He reports in the *Alphabet* that Zhivkova, almost entirely on the grounds of 'personal liking', treated him 'as an honorary Minister of Culture'. He felt able to make useful contributions, advocating the funding of fresco-restorers, urging on archaeological digs and protecting the ruins of Sardica beneath Sofia when an underground railway was planned there. But in July 1981, in the aftermath of the 1,300th anniversary of the Bulgars' arrival in the Balkans whose celebrations she had herself planned, Zhivkova died at the age of thirty-eight, officially of a brain tumour. Steven makes it fairly clear he lent credence to the idea of her murder by the Kremlin, writing of a 'mysterious illness' and pointing out that Zhivkova's cultural nationalism was unacceptable to Moscow, as it alluded to Bulgaria's more ancient Orthodox tradition.

Steven's own attachment to Bulgaria was not yet over, especially as the fall of Communism also involved the homecoming of the Stancioff family. Johnny Stancioff, the son of Steven's old friends Ivan and Marion, was appointed Ambassador from the new democratic republic to Britain in 1991; one of his earliest childhood memories was of meeting Steven in Sofia before the war. He lost little time in ensuring

Steven was well rewarded for his long relationship with what Steven called in the *Alphabet* 'that beautiful and interesting country':

> I had the honour as Ambassador of convincing the Bulgarian government that Steven, who had written the best history of Bulgaria in the English language, should receive something for his endeavours, and contacted the presidential office which hands out gongs. After a while I got a letter back saying they had prepared the highest one [the Order of the Madara Horseman, First Class], which I hadn't dared suggest! I called Steven and asked, would you like to have an official presentation at the Embassy? He said, let's make it a family thing. So we had a dinner, I put the thing around his neck, and he smiled and said, Johnny, they thought they'd get away with not giving it to me, but I got through them!

In July 2001, less than a year after Steven died, another Bulgarian come home from exile, a keen correspondent of Steven, was elected President Sakskoburggotski. This was the former King Simeon of Bulgaria, son of Boris III. In 2003, during the reign of the resulting 'Tsar's Cabinet', a Stancioff kinsman serving as a Bulgarian deputy had a street-name in Sofia altered to commemorate Steven, seconding the existing tribute in Mistra. Bulgaria had not turned out to constitute 'the ruins of a world' after all, and it was felt that some of the credit for its well-preserved heritage and national consciousness was due to its first English-language historian, as much by way of his salutary influence upon Zhivkova as because of his early work.

The *Alphabet* is less about Steven's life than about his sometimes baffled survival, amid the gradual alteration or entire demise of societies and individuals he has known. In the German triple-H chapter, Steven surveys the social echelon whose gossip brought him most pleasure, and which had suffered the most dramatic reversals over his century – the international family of royalty. Among his most remote but useful relatives he counted Margaret Geddes, 'a distant cousin but a cousin twice, if not three times, over, as Scottish families in former days retained a clan spirit and only knew and intermarried with their relatives'. At any rate this relative, the daughter of a formidable ambassador, Sir Auckland Geddes, had herself broken the family tendency by marriage a long way out, to Prince Louis of Hesse, younger son of the Grand Duke of Hesse. Owing to a disastrous aeroplane crash at Ostend in 1937, caused by the attempt of the pilot to land so that a heavily pregnant Hessian princess could go safely into labour, almost the whole family of Hesse was killed on the way to the Hesse–Geddes wedding. Louis became the legitimist Grand Duke, but never used the title, which had in any case been abolished by the German state.

Steven's kinswoman thus involuntarily became Peg of Hesse, the unlikely chatelaine of 'the old grand-ducal hunting-box', Wolfsgarten.* Steven describes the young couple's subsequent predicament:

> [Peg] had to go to live with him in Germany, under a regime that they detested, and which detested them, and soon to face a war in which their loyalties were cruelly divided. But courage and integrity saw them through it all ... [Louis] was, I think, the most civilized man that I have ever known, with a wide and sensitive knowledge of all the arts. He wrote beautifully, but far too little, in both German and English. His humour was delicious ... Music was always the main delight of the Prince and Princess. Benjamin Britten was a close friend ...

Partly because Peg of Hesse was still alive when he wrote the *Alphabet*, but mainly in deference to the code of a family that was not only Scots nor merely royal, Steven did not treat the question of Louis ('Lu') of Hesse's sexuality. Like Henry McIlhenny's Glenveagh, Wolfsgarten was a dignified and cultivated bower where conduct could be relaxed without needing to be discussed. Steven first met Benjamin Britten and Peter Pears there; and judging by the evidence of his photograph albums he seems now and again to have taken recently befriended young men on his regular stays with the Hesses. As for the ominous background of the war, Lu of Hesse was indeed impeccably unbesmirched by Nazism, but Steven's emphasis on this proud and pleasurable friendship also functions as a cry for European reconciliation: 'After having lived through two world wars in which the Germans were our savage enemies, I felt for a time a little uneasy in Germany. But it is better to discard bitter memories.' Steven's special

* Philip Mansel, Peg of Hesse's obituarist, described Wolfsgarten as 'a "hunting lodge" the size of a small Oxford college' (*Independent*, 30 January 1997).

fondness for the Hesses, 'my royal relatives', was regarded as faintly risible by various old friends such as Henry Maxwell and Robin Dalton, but it always proved impossible to make him rise to any tease on the subject.

A certain inevitability gathers in Steven's section 'Ampersand', largely dealing with Spain, when he mentions at an initially quiet tempo 'the couple who were to become my closest Spanish friends'. These were grander royal catches yet, the Orleanses, the Infante Alfonso and his British-born Infanta Beatrice, Marie of Roumania's little sister. Alfonso had not evaded embroilment in totalitarian rule so adeptly as Lu of Hesse; Steven says he 'became disillusioned with Franco's aims and methods and went into retirement, but remained in Spain'. Miriam James, Elizabeth Wansbrough's daughter, the sister of Steven's godson Henry, and herself a god-daughter of the Infanta, remembers meeting Steven in the summer of 1951 at the Orleans house in Sanlúcar de Barrameda:

> We were an odd assembly: the Infantes; an elderly duchess and her daughter; Princess Dolly of Hohenlohe-Langenburg, on a prolonged visit to her aunt and lamenting the downfall of Hitler; a former governess who had lost her job as teacher to a sherry-producing family when the youngest daughter 'came out', and who was welcomed by the Infantes while she planned her future; a pianist called Lucas Moreno; a series of visiting members of the family of two generations. Steven's arrival was very welcome and excitedly anticipated. One of the entertainments on offer was a bull-fight in Cadiz, where we sat side by side, and at a gruesome moment (not much padding for horses then) he said to me 'I think we'd better look at my camera for a bit': a revelation to me that other – grown-up – people might share my squeamish attitude.

Steven himself in the *Alphabet* lists, among other notable visitors to Sanlúcar over the years, 'Professor Messerschmitt, the aeroplane designer, a dear, gentle old man, quite unsuitable to be the creator of such deadly machines'. Mrs James's 'odd assembly' arrives at the heart of the matter – it was the oddness of the Spanish Orleans household, as much as or more than its regality, that attracted Steven's notice. He noticed people and situations that would soon be beyond recall, and, finding to his surprise that he had outlasted them, he committed them to his archive of observations and jokes. This growing consciousness of being left to witness and record an old world for the delectation of an often uncomprehending new one began to rise into an undemonstrative strain of melancholy for Steven. 'There is no one left with whom I can compare memories of these journeys. I like to travel alone; but one pays a price for it in the end.'

Steven had worked hard throughout his active academic life on writing in the first place and lecturing in the second, and he also busily reviewed his Byzantinist peers, usually through the patchy anonymity of the *Times Literary Supplement.* By the late 1980s he had given most of this up, and was in turn granted an apparently reverend amnesty that he recognized as a doubtful accolade; as was said of Steven's friend the philanthropist Belinda Norman-Butler, 'in her later years she was honoured as much for being as for doing.' In 1986 King's College London named an annual lecture on Hellenic subject matter after him, though the Runciman Lecture was funded not by Steven but by Nicholas and Mattie Egon, respectively Hungarian and Greek benefactors who had long known and admired him. Steven's reaction to this unasked-for elder statesmanhood was salted with the anarchic and the unaccountable. If he was perforce to be regarded as an exalted repository of precious historical evidence, he intended to derive what entertainment he could from it. He still placed occasional pieces, more than ever at the *Spectator,* and especially on royal topics; but even when theoretically fulfilling the function of a review, these were now personal reminiscences, even elliptical short stories and self-portraits. He slipped into place as the last remaining link, however insubstantial looking, in a great and golden chain. Invested with this authority Steven could comment on the unhappy marriage of Queen Ena of Spain (the generous employer of the long dead friend of his youth, Baba Brougham); opine that the House of Bourbon-Parma had a superior Jacobite claim on Britain to that of Bavaria; chide outlasted rival sages, such as Noël Coward, 'never a good listener'; and occasionally present his favourite carbuncles – the illegitimacy of the King of Norway, or King Zog of Albania's pre-war assassination in a brothel, and substitution (this plot surely borrowed from *The Prisoner of Zenda*) by a double – as verifiable truths denied only by obstinate dullards.

Behind this cloth-of-gold sheen of anecdotage, Steven superficially appeared – not least to a younger generation of medieval historians struggling in vain to dislodge the overbearing influence of, in particular, his *Crusades* trilogy – to be separated from the actual present, into which he had, after all, accidentally strayed. But to dismiss him thus was to succumb to the trap he had laid for all but his most intimate friends (of any age). The cannier Runcimanosceptics perceived what was afoot, and did their best not to be taken unawares by the act. Christopher Tyerman, who five years after Runciman's death published *God's War*, a magisterial analysis of the Crusades which would supersede the Runciman trilogy in the academy and even the bookshop, realized that there was nothing to be gained from direct antagonism against Runciman and what he purported to represent: he sums it up as 'civilised scepticism, wisdom, moderation, learning, and all that'. He considers Runciman to have been 'very successful in rebranding himself as some superior and separate being. The whole Olympian tone that he adopts . . . It's very hard – without becoming a caricature of what he criticises – to actually take Runciman apart, as the only way you can do it is to dig into your fort [that is, to adopt the dry specialism deprecated by Runciman].' In Tyerman's view, the division between the position Runciman adopted in his work and his life – between what this book has described respectively as 'Runciman' and 'Steven' – is vanishingly small; the whole being is coherent, self-aware and to be expected:

> Runciman always gave the impression, whenever I encountered him, of being rather ludic. He was playing games. He actually was well aware of the acts that he was putting up. He liked to tease people. He liked to fulfil people's expectations of who he was. The first time I heard him give a paper, sometime in the mid Seventies, at Christ Church, Obolensky was there, all the grandees were there. Runciman after dinner sat there, with his hooded eyes, and all that, and said 'When I was at school' . . . and he started to pick out a silk handkerchief from his sleeve, it was a sort of generational thing. And then he said – everyone was riveted on this very slow act – he timed it brilliantly,

he said, 'I was told in 1453, the Turks captured Constantinople, and fleeing scholars from Constantinople came to the West, and in their luggage, they carried something called . . . the Renaissance.'

And the handkerchief flicked out. Everyone thought 'what on earth is going on', and tittered rather nervously. Then he went on to give a rather technical paper about how this was completely wrong, how there were all these Greek scholars, Basilian monks, in Calabria, teaching people Greek in the 14th century . . . but that was his way. He would tease people. He would give the impression that he was – and of course in some sense he was – this ever so refined, snobbish, aristocratic figure – though of course he wasn't aristocratic at all – and he caricatured himself. He loved teasing his audiences. That was very characteristic. As long as he had the attention, that was really what he wanted.

Though Tyerman, who says that he 'observed Steven, rather than knew him', had noticed much that was insightful, he had, too, been more than a little misled. Steven, who detested speaking in public but lectured into his eighties, who felt most comfortable in private study and threw a ninetieth-birthday party for four hundred guests, was a puzzle not quite so easily unravelled, although Tyerman's courteous and cunning introduction to *God's War* was a riposte of stylish disingenuousness worthy of the master – 'It would be folly and hubris to pretend to compete, to match, as it were, my clunking computer keyboard with [Runciman's] pen, at once a rapier and a paintbrush; to pit one volume, however substantial, with the breadth, scope and elegance of his three.'

Had Steven in fact frozen his ideals, taste and ambition at some given historical point, and altogether surrendered to nostalgia for it, he would have relinquished both the enjoyment and the duty involved in his unsleeping consciousness of period and evolution. His interest in his surroundings never ebbed and his faculty of observation remained exceptionally keen; he was still better informed than many and his instincts were less fallible than most. His sense of fashions past and contemporary, aesthetic and intellectual, remained sure. His personal preferences tended incrementally to the conservative, but their development was shaped by curiosity, not ignorance. In 1989 he complained to Nikos Stangos that a production of *Boris Godunov* 'might have been daring in the 1960s but was now old-fashioned, silly and vulgar', and throughout the 1990s he grumbled that in opera 'kinky productions are now felt to be necessary ... kinky enough to be slightly irritating.'* In 1997 he attended the private view at the London National Portrait Gallery of Maggi Hambling's *Sculpture for Oscar Wilde* and, though he judged the statue itself 'ugly and absurd', he was thrilled still to have a prospect on 'the smart intellectual world'; both socially and artistically he found the accompanying exhibition 'strange but interesting', evocative of a particular haunting sensation: ' ... I keep thinking of the old Scots ballad which begins "Gin I were young, as I once ha'e been" ... '

Steven's attitude to the utterly changed world he now experienced might be said to have had two predominant modes, the temporal and the spiritual. In his temporal mode he was easily but at times idly witty, strongly receptive to comfort, if not necessarily luxury, appreciative of worldly standing; he indulged in an oddly consistent amalgam of naive optimism and pragmatic cynicism. This temper is best exemplified in the regular, convenient and not very attractive relationship he built up with the insular Gulf Kingdom of Bahrain. He had never fallen straightforwardly into blind advocacy of British policy in the Middle East; he had always dissented from the Lawrence of Arabia myth, and in 1953 he exclaimed to Stewart Perowne, 'What a blot on the royal horizon the Saoudis are. Everything I hear about that family shocks me. Can they survive once the old man is gone?' Yet Steven was to become a useful and respectable spokesman for the scarcely more enlightened Bahraini monarchy, writing irate letters on that kingdom's behalf to *The Times* in the late 1990s, and

---

* Steven gave one particularly scathing account of a production at Glyndebourne in the summer of 1996 to Gordon Gardiner: 'I did not enjoy *Theodora* ... The story is of Christian martyrdom under the Romans in Alexandria. Here the Roman governor wore a lounge suit and sat at a desk in front of a long row of metal chairs on which sat people dressed as though to attend a minor football match in bright ugly colours. The Xian throng was a little better dressed. Soldiers in red track suits occasionally ran pointlessly across the stage. The martyrdom scene was really nasty – the victims were not led away to be executed off stage but were tied down on frames on the stage and given lethal injections' (SR to Gordon Gardiner, 19 May 1996).

devoting to the Emir of Bahrain one of his few unacceptably sucrose paragraphs in the *Alphabet*:

> The Ruler, Shaikh Isa bin Salman al-Khalifa ... is physically a small man. Seen standing next to our Queen he makes her appear like a giantess. But such is the dignity that he radiates that he dominates any gathering he attends. Bahrain is not a democracy in the Western pattern.* The Ruler still rules. But, in the age-long Islamic tradition, every one of his subjects, however humble, can have direct access to him ...

Steven allowed himself to be thus compromised partly for the sake of a very old friendship and, at least at some point, a casual sexual attachment with General Gerald Green, the Emir's right hand, himself noted in his *Telegraph* obituary for his belief in the efficacy of removing hands as a punishment for theft. Steven also sincerely believed that the only alternative to the Emir was an extreme Shia theocracy along the lines of revolutionary Iran, which he imagined would be much less congenial – and harder to visit. But it must also be admitted that Steven, old, tired and more than slightly complacent, could be grotesquely susceptible to flattery. He was, at least, aware of and wry about so being, and to the very end his letters to friends about Bahrain are exercises in quiet comedy: 'Everyone there was immensely kind. Indeed, His Highness the Ruler presented me with an expensive (and rather vulgar) Rolex watch, just to thank me for visiting his country ... '

Steven was undeceived, too, about the circumstances of his old Athens friend General Green's employment. He knew he was bestowing a favour

---

* Steven – doubtless partly as a result of his over-parliamentary family background and childhood – was never enamoured of democracy. To his last interviewer on Mount Athos, he posed the question of what it even was: 'I never understood what exactly "democracy" is supposed to mean. In most places in the world today, democracy means to be governed by mass media, newspapers and television. It seeks to have what we call "the popular vote", but from the moment that people cannot judge themselves – and there are many people in the modern world that don't think – then they transport the authority in the hands of those who control the media, which, with the power they possess, should have chosen to select the hard road and educate people. But many of them, fortunately not all, are irresponsible. Democracy can exist only if we have a highly educated public' (SR, *Pemptousia* interview, 2000).

as much as receiving a jolly; and that the Bahraini scene, pleasant and diverting as it could be to him, had its purgatorial aspects:

> If you work for an Arab family you become one of the family and can never leave – it would be desertion: and they have no conception of retirement with a pension. So he has to remain in what you might call gilded imprisonment there, in great comfort but without enough really to do; so he loves having old friends to stay. The British there are either tycoons (because it is the one off-shore banking centre that permits alcohol to be drunk) or members of a second-rate Embassy and a third-rate British Council. So as an old friend it is my duty – and no hardship – to visit him.

Gerald Green liked to boast to another friend, his professional counterpart Sir Ralph Anstruther, that he, unlike Sir Ralph, would benefit when the time came from more tender services than those of the NHS. But Steven could see the loneliness of his predicament beneath such boasts. Green had originally taken service in Bahrain following the failure of his marriage as a consequence of his sexuality, in pre-Wolfenden days, and Steven, as was his way, masked but did not omit this from his account in the *Alphabet*, alluding to 'domestic difficulties'. Of his and Green's own attachment he wrote to Jeffrey Schaire that 'at one point it was more amiable than I could manage, but we have settled down long since to an easy friendship.' Steven understood his old friend's boredom and isolation, and palliating it while soaking up thorough sunbathing and the occasional adventure suited him perfectly. It was in Bahrain that he wrote much of the *Alphabet* and nearly all of his extant, unpublished 'Footnotes to a Long Life'.

Such was the temporal mode; it did not overwhelm the spiritual one. This side of Steven was neither naive nor cynical, not easy or comfortable; it was the heartfelt ardour for which the coolly Olympian tempo throughout most of the *Crusades* trilogy, observed and criticized by Tyerman, ultimately served as handmaiden. Occasionally it manifested itself in Steven's pride in his family extraction and Scottishness (though his father, who unlike Steven adored Sir Walter Scott without reservation, had been more prone to this form of romance). Of such a kind had been Steven's mingled passion and responsibility towards Eigg, and it had settled later into his satisfaction with his accidental Dumfriesshire eyrie. At other times he was truly animated by his affection for Greece, and throughout his life his affinity with the unbroken tradition and unitive ideal of Orthodoxy sustained his most serious purpose. But nearly all of his particular sympathies and causes led him back to larger allegiances and principles. He was loyal to local peculiarity; to interlocking hybridity; and to sensitivity towards the past.

This loyalty could provoke exasperation from true believers in other quarters. Alfred Duggan, who devoured Runciman's histories and leant upon them for the construction of his own historical fictions, had in 1958 attacked *The Sicilian Vespers* on grounds of the author's, as Duggan thought, inflexible atavism: 'he regards religion as entirely a matter of ancestral piety, almost as though he had been raised in Belfast. To him it is unthinkable that a Greek should wish to heal the breach with Rome, or that a Moslem King of Tunis should desire baptism. But if no one had ever abandoned the religion of his forefathers we should still be worshipping Thor.' Steven, serial tease at the expense of Ulstermen that he was, cannot have been much pleased by that Belfast jibe. The accusation comes oddly and a trifle defensively from Duggan, who had himself renounced and then returned to childhood Catholicism. No reader of Runciman's later work, such as *The Great Church in Captivity*, could have denied its writer's genuine ecumenism. But that there was a certain – not uncomplimentary – truth in Duggan's intended criticism would be revealed at Steven's death, when Steven surprised many and disappointed some Orthodox observers by leaving instructions for his burial according to the rite of the Church of Scotland.

Steven's involved history with the Athonite monks of the Holy Mountain, whom he supported against their and (as Grand Orator) his own Patriarch, was an evident instance of his threefold loyalty to oddity, unity and history. Another, sadder consequence of this position was the intense distress he felt at the Blair government's war in Kosovo. His early books had displayed much enthusiasm for the valiant Serbian people and their distinctive ecclesiastical, political and cultural independence. His previous wrangle with the Patriarchate of Constantinople in 1995 had concerned, among many other grievances, the high-handed treatment which both the Patriarch's administration and the Greek civil authorities had meted out to Serbian pilgrims. To Nathalie Brooke, perhaps his closest remaining friend to be herself of Orthodox persuasion, Steven wrote in April 1999 that 'I hate the Balkan bombing. I learn from reliable sources that the American bombs have damaged the loveliest of Serbian medieval churches, Gracenica.' His attitude to Islam, quite as much as to Orthodoxy, was informed by this manoeuvrably romantic, and aesthetic, pluralism.

Steven was always most enchanted by congruence, the deeper logic that overcomes apparently irreconcilable division. His spirits and his pen responded to the pious Byzantine iconoclasts who created mosaics for the Caliph at Damascus, which 'obedient to Moslem rules contain no human figures, but show houses and trees and gardens through which rivulets are flowing'; to Turks of Cretan origin who dreamed in Greek; to Russian Orthodox missionaries in Alaska, modifying animist customs with tact and gradualism while reaching out with 'candles, icons and simple dignity'; to the Muslim dynasty of doorkeepers to the Church of the Holy Sepulchre. In 1956 Steven had much enjoyed visiting the villages of the Marsh Arabs by punt, and felt an innate sympathy when he came across a secluded settlement of the syncretist Yazidis: 'This strictly Dualist sect ... regard the Devil, whom they treat with respect but in fact do not worship, to be as powerful as God. There are few of them left now ... they seemed to be gentle self-effacing folk, taught by centuries of cruel persecution not to draw attention to themselves.'

Steven lived through an era when the most destructive creeds were, at least in theory, rationalist and anti-religious. He did not take religious fundamentalism as seriously as secular totalitarianism in his own time; but his writing had been ground-breaking and unambiguous in linking the two habits of thought. Muslim and Christian fundamentalism were automatically bracketed in his mind, and Christian fundamentalism in his own day was, he thought, usually a subject apt for comedy, as when he visited Oral Roberts University with David Plante:

We went through the Journey of Faith in the Prayer Tower. Oral Roberts was a fundamentalist minister who earned so much money he built a university. A Christian fundamentalist university. Walking through the campus Steven said, 'It is all fantasy. Not even the Roman Church at the height of its power was capable of so much fantasy. This is where I want to lecture.'

Lecturing in Cairo in 1951, just after the publication of *The First Crusade*, Steven insisted, despite hand-wringing from the British Ambassador, on speaking about medieval Christian–Muslim relations. As he explained in the 'Egypt' section of the *Alphabet*, he reasoned that 'unless one is faced with fundamentalists – and Christian fundamentalists are almost as savage as Moslems – it is easy to discuss religion with Moslems, so long as one is obviously sincere.' Steven now began with a gentle but decisive emphasis on the enduring effect of historical religious differences:

> Many people think that medieval history is a pleasantly remote subject, and its study so far removed from modern problems as to be hardly worth serious attention – rather just a harmless and romantic pastime. I personally hope that it is harmless – I would not like to be devoting my life to a harmful profession! – and I personally see nothing wrong in savouring its romance. But there is more even to medieval history than that. I have concentrated my studies in particular on the relations of Islam and Christendom in those by-gone centuries, and I have found that they have left legacies behind them, direct and indirect, which still exercise a real if unconscious effect on human minds.

He went on to speculate about how he himself might really have reacted to the Crusading cause in its time:

> I like to think that even had I lived in the Middle Ages I would not have responded to the call to the Crusade . . . I would have seen the movement as heroic, maybe, and inspired by faith – but faith based on ignorance, arrogance and intolerance. However one must be honest, especially in history. I know that had I lived in Western Europe at that time I should probably have been as ignorant about Islam as anyone else . . .

This is an honesty that oddly recalls Steven's British Council colleague, Rex Warner, uncertainly contrasting the Marxism of his youth with the student radicalism at the University of Connecticut, where he was teaching in 1968: 'I like to think that we of the old left were at least more rational, but perhaps we weren't.'

In the autumn of 1994, Steven learnt that a symposium at Istanbul he had planned, unusually by this late point in his career, to attend had been suddenly cancelled. Local elections in the summer had delivered the city into the control of the Islamist Welfare Party, 'to whom anything to do with Byzantine Constantinople is anathema. They informed the worthy Turkish lady who was organising the symposium that they would organise demonstrations against it and would not guarantee the safety of any of the delegates. I find it shocking and ominous . . . ' At this time Steven made a throwaway prediction to David Sox, an Anglican priest and writer who had been a playful confederate of his Catholic-baiting over the years: ' . . . I find Muslim Fundamentalism very frightening but I fear it is on the increase. I doubt if it will take over any more whole countries, but it will do a mass of harm.'

Steven had last visited Istanbul in 1986, for the film about his career by Lydia Carras, *Bridge to the East*. 'The weather was lovely, with a hazy sunshine giving a cloak of mystery to the whole city.' He paid his respects to the Patriarch Demetrios (he had not yet fallen out with the Patriarchate of which he was Grand Orator). He visited St Mary of the Mongols, the last undesecrated Christian church from before the conquest; it had been rebuilt by an emperor's bastard daughter who married a 'marginally Buddhist' Mongol Khan, and then preserved by the carefully timed petitions of two Greek architects to the Conquering Sultan and his heir. Steven dropped into his 'favourite Ottoman mosque, that of Sokullu Pasha, the loveliest, I think, of all the buildings of the great architect Sinan'. To his even greater contentment, he was housed that week in a proper wooden *yali* on the shore of the Bosphorus, just like that in which his long-dead friends the Ostrorog brothers had once lived. After the cancellation of the 1994 symposium, he never saw the city again.

In Steven's last two years at Elshieshields, his niece, the tower's long-designated heiress, Ann Shukman, moved in to ensure that he was properly attended; by now he was wheelchair bound and had to be helped up to his library on increasingly rare occasions, even if he only wanted to look up a poem of Cavafy. Guests from outside the

family no longer stayed the night, but in September 2000 Paddy Leigh
Fermor and Pamela, the Dowager Lady Egremont came up for lunch.
They found Steven, as Paddy subsequently wrote in the *Spectator*,

> not very mobile physically, but mentally he was as active as he had
> ever been, and there was much laughter. My grubby apparition of
> 66 years earlier was joyfully recalled – it always was – and the three of
> us talked for hours. Upright in his armchair, he was still, as it were,
> encfouded in Athonite glory. He told us that he was determined, if he
> was spared for another three years, to celebrate his 100th birthday by
> a large and cheerful party in Madame Tussaud's. He gave us a cheerful
> wave as we left, and, assisted by his mood as we drove south, we
> played with the idea of Steven's warlock privilege of summoning
> shades from the past to ask them to his centenary festival, and we
> wondered, could this sorcery be switched to the returning of such
> supernatural visits? Where would these imaginary journeys carry
> him? Whom would he choose?
>
> As we motored through the Cumbrian dusk, we imagined him help-
> ing to plot the circumference of the dome of St Sophia, before a late
> supper with the Empress Theodora, or – he had a soft spot for crowned
> heads – advising Princess Anna about the accuracy of the *Alexiad*. In
> other scenes, he was shaking his head over the wilder tenets of the
> Bogomils and persuading a team of iconoclasts to drop their ham-
> mers; or calming rebellious prelates at the Council of Ephesus. In yet
> other scenes, he was reasoning with Bohemond at Antioch; or coun-
> selling Richard Coeur de Lion about his policy at Acre; or playing
> chess with Saladin, in his tent; then, a bit later, rallying Bessarion for
> accepting the *filioque* clause at the same time as a cardinal's hat; con-
> soling the eastern Comnenes for the loss of Trebizond; or, under
> Mount Taygetus, exchanging syllogisms with Gemistos Plethon as
> they strolled along the future Runciman Street. Later on still, we
> imagined him hobnobbing with Phanariot hospodars in the snows
> beyond the Danube . . . It was hard to stop.

But stop it had to do, and Steven, along with some of his closest
remaining friends, well knew it. Richard Brain, who had visited every
Easter for many years, thought already that spring that Steven no
longer had much desire to go on. The end was a merciful, indeed a

graceful one. Steven was in the south, visiting the young married couple among his collateral descendants who were his acknowledged favourites: Ann's son Henry Shukman, then a travel-writer, and his wife Clare, née Dunne, a niece-in-law of George Jellicoe, Steven's favourite undergraduate pupil. The Jellicoes came over for dinner one evening. Another guest, who had noticed the sometimes melancholy cast of Steven's eyes, asked him when they chanced to be alone if he was afraid of death. After a short pause Steven replied that he was not really, but merely wished he knew when it might come; it was so tiresome waiting. Two days later he developed pneumonia. When he was no longer in much of a position to make his desires felt his relatives called a nurse, doing so with some measure of dread, as they knew him for a man of settled prejudices, 'allergic to nurses – bossy or flirtatious or both'. So many times Steven had recovered, to complain and to itemize. When a beautiful young Thai male nurse answered the emergency call, it was a benign sort of portent that things would be different this time.

Dying as he did on 1 November 2000, wisely pessimistic as he had been both about the millennial celebrations and about the century likely to follow them, it is unquestionable that Steven was spared many torments. He missed 11 September and the inception of the War on Terror; the mismanaged invasion and vandalistic aftermath of the Iraq war, in the land that he had hymned to the end as the ancient seat of 'Ur of the Chaldees'; the ahistorical expectations of the Arab Spring and the end of the mosaic he had loved across the Levant, that seaboard which, as Duncan Fallowell has written, Steven once 'made his own'; the bloody implosion of Syria, in recent memory a delicately balanced model of what counted for Steven infinitely above democracy – variety and multivalence. Steven was spared these sufferings; but Runciman also escaped in death, as he had not always in life, hearing his work, especially his volumes on the Crusades, being misquoted and manipulated by those with small understanding or real interest in his views, and even less in the reality and validity of the past itself.

# Notes

## CHAPTER 1: THE HIGH PRIESTESS

2 'a vast edifice': Steven Runciman, 'Footnotes to a Long Life', unfinished memoirs up to 1938, Elshieshields Archive, p. 19

2 'the most important': ibid., p. 20

2 'her first duty': ibid.

3 'a lady with red hair': ibid., p. 28

3 'I've lived a great': David Plante profile of Steven Runciman, *New Yorker*, 3 November 1986, p. 59

4 'more or less bi-lingual': SR, 'Footnotes', p. 28

5 'she could not bring': ibid., p. 31

6 'Leslie is an observant': Hilda Runciman to Walter Runciman, 6 April 1913, Elshieshields

6 'essentially English': SR, 'Footnotes', p. 29

7 'She would talk': ibid.

7 'Don't ever write': SR to Stewart Perowne, 7 July 1958, Elshieshields

8 'perfunctory': SR, 'Footnotes', p. 29

8 'temper that could': ibid., p. 28

8 'having a sow': ibid., p. 30

9 'large ... dressed in scarves': ibid., p. 29

## CHAPTER 2: THE EMPRESS

10 'We all have': SR, 'Footnotes', p. 4

10 '11 November 1911 AD': SR to HR, 11 November 1911, Elshieshields

11 'We have been': ibid.

11 'a charmless bearded': SR, 'Footnotes', p. 31

11 'Margie and I': ibid.

11 'carelessness': HR to WR, 6 April 1913, Elshieshields

11  'humiliating to be': ibid.

11  'Why have you': SR to HR, 11 November 1911, Elshieshields

11  'H'aint I wrote': ibid.

12  'Leslie was a beautiful': SR, 'Footnotes', p. 24

12  'because divorce sounded': ibid., p. 25

12  'Soon afterwards both': ibid.

12  'owing to our liking': ibid.

13  'ritual books': ibid., p. 26

13  'they do not seem': SR, *A Traveller's Alphabet* (Thames & Hudson, 1991), p. 40

14  'Steven is full': HR to WR, 1 April 1913, Elshieshields

14  'seeking pleasant tours': HR to WR, 8 April 1913, Elshieshields

14  'We saw dungeons': HR to WR, 7 April 1913, Elshieshields

15  'Arles has its fascination': HR to WR, 8 April 1913, Elshieshields

15  'How sadly undignified': HR to WR, 12 April 1913, Elshieshields

16  'Keep my letters': HR to Leslie Runciman, 14 April 1914, Elshieshields

16  'At Corfu we went': ibid.

17  'pretentious and a bit': SR, 'Footnotes', p. 33

17  'stern and orderly': ibid.

17  'I was not': ibid., p. 34

17  'Besides this I': SR to WR, 14 December 1913, Elshieshields

17  'He had enormous': SR, 'Footnotes', p. 34

19  'suited her thin': ibid., p. 36

20  'terrible consequences': ibid., p. 35

20  'Puffin scored a Duck': SR to WR, 14 December 1913, Elshieshields

20  'Dovey, sweety, lovebird': SR to Anthony Asquith, 19 March 1916, Elshieshields


## CHAPTER 3: THE EMPEROR

22  'The experience did not': SR, 'Footnotes', p. 21

22  'a long sea voyage': Steven Runciman quoted in David Plante, *Becoming a Londoner* (Bloomsbury, 2013), p. 232

22  'What I really hated': SR, 'Footnotes', p. 23

23  'My father's relations': ibid., p. 12

23  'On leaving Cambridge': ibid., p. 13

24  'He was a remarkable': ibid., p. 10

24  'the curse that kills': ibid.

25  'a typical Scottish': ibid.

25  'Will you whack': SR to WR, 15 November 1911, Elshieshields

25 'What fun the rows': SR to WR, 18 November 1911, Elshieshields

25 'charming and erudite': SR, 'Footnotes', p. 4

25 'a little goose': Roy Jenkins, *Churchill* (Macmillan, 2001), p. 151

26 'were in the pay': David Lloyd George to Frances Stevenson, *My Darling Pussy: The Letters of Lloyd George and Frances Stevenson 1913–41*, ed. A. J. P. Taylor (Weidenfeld & Nicolson, 1975), p. 68

26 'How can you find': Margot Asquith, 2 January 1916, quoted in Lady Cynthia Asquith, *Diaries* (Hutchinson, 1968), p. 123

26 'By this time': SR, 'Footnotes', p. 35

27 'I may have disliked': ibid., p. 38

28 'My games are much': SR to WR, 18 November 1916, Elshieshields

28 'one of the few': SR, 'Footnotes', p. 38

29 'I greatly resented': ibid.

31 'red-haired and freckled': Steven Runciman quoted in Clive Fisher, *Cyril Connolly* (Macmillan, 1995), p. 45

31 'a quiet unexciting': SR, 'Footnotes', p. 47

31 'a good comic': ibid., p. 70

32 'Blair, though he always': Steven Runciman quoted in Bernard Crick, *George Orwell: A Life* (Secker & Warburg, 1980), p. 59.

33 'pity for the human': Steven Runciman quoted in Jeffrey Meyers, *Orwell: Wintry Conscience of a Generation* (W. W. Norton, 2000), p. 287.

33 'the world will be': Steven Runciman interviewed by Piers Brendon 1993, in Churchill College Archive, Cambridge

34 'an able accountant': Arthur Balfour on Reginald McKenna, quoted in *Geoffrey Madan's Notebooks*, ed. J. A. Gere and John Sparrow (Oxford University Press, 1981), p. 27

34 'not disgraceful, but': H. H. Asquith quoted in Roy Jenkins, *Asquith* (Collins, 1964), p. 239

34 'as if it were': ibid., pp. 340–41

## CHAPTER 4: TEMPERANCE

35 'Alington . . . had a capacity': Christopher Hollis, 'John Bull's Schooldays', *Spectator*, 13 June 1958

35 'quite the ugliest': Steven Runciman quoted in Fisher, *Connolly*, p. 41

35 'the thrill, not untinged': Cyril Connolly, *Enemies of Promise* (Routledge, 1938), p. 248

35 'I could not give': ibid.

37 'our own senior election': ibid., p. 238

37 'Don't bother ducking': see e.g. http://www.longfordatwar.ie/soldiers/ 379

37 'a silly boy': Brendon interview, Churchill College

37 'difficult to forgive': ibid.

38 'worldliness, insincerity, meanness': Cyril Connolly to Noel Blakiston, quoted in *A Romantic Friendship: The Letters of Cyril Connolly to Noel Blakiston*, ed. Noel Blakiston (Constable, 1975), p. 35

38 'aloof and unsympathetic': letter from George Rylands to Gordon Bowker, quoted in Bowker, *George Orwell* (Little, Brown, 2003), p. 51

38 'With a sad mixture': SR, 'Footnotes', p. 40

38 'a very simple fugue': ibid.

38 'The She-Devil': unsigned Steven Runciman short story in *The Election Times*, no. 4, 3 June 1918, p.102, digitally accessible from University College London Archive

39 'How is your story': SR to Margaret Runciman, 10 November 1918, Elshieshields

39 'eccentric temporary masters': SR, 'Footnotes', p. 40

39 'French was so meanly thought': Hollis, 'John Bull's Schooldays'

39 'elegance of his English': SR, 'Footnotes', p. 40

39 'he taught us': Steven Runciman quoted in Crick, *Orwell*, p. 59

40 'learning far more': SR, 'Footnotes', p. 39

40 'She was far': ibid.

40 'the ape-like virtues': Connolly, *Enemies of Promise*, p. 249

41 'didn't really like': Steven Runciman quoted in Bowker, *Orwell*, p. 54

41 'He was a Jesuitical': Cyril Connolly quoted in Jeremy Lewis, *Cyril Connolly* (Jonathan Cape, 1997), p. 54

41 'A. R.D. – After rooms': unsigned notice in *College Days* magazine, 1 April 1920, quoted in Crick, *Orwell*, p. 59

41 'a baited hook': ibid.

42 'a thrilling dream': SR to HR, 26 October 1919, Elshieshields

42 'a good but not': Steven Runciman quoted in Meyers, *Orwell*, p. 42

42 'taken the trouble': SR, 'Footnotes', p. 47

42 'some of my most': Fisher, *Connolly*, p. 41

43 'a lot of manual': Anthony Powell quoted in Lewis, *Connolly*, p. 118

43 'the Old Testament': Connolly, *Enemies of Promise*, p. 249

43 'there was a strange': Hollis, 'John Bull's Schooldays'

43 'I decided to quit': SR, 'Footnotes', p. 41

43 'Doubtless I shall': G. W. Headlam quoted in Hollis, 'John Bull's Schooldays'

44 'None of us took': ibid.

44 'I wish this boy': ibid.

44 'This week, instead': SR to HR, 19 October 1919, Elshieshields

45 'would have been': SR to HR, 26 October 1919, Elshieshields

45 'a large lady': SR, 'Footnotes', p. 42

47 'We all thought': James Butler to WR, 16 December 1920, Elshieshields

47 'Steven's very remarkable': John Crace to WR, 17 December 1920, Elshieshields

48 'I have always found': SR, 'Footnotes', p. 42

48 'The Evil Eye': paper preserved in Eton College Library

## CHAPTER 5: THE LOVERS

49 'I am really very': SR to Ann Margaret Runciman, 4 May 1922, Elshieshields

49 'It has come': SR to George Rylands, 5 August 1921, King's College Cambridge Archive (hereafter King's)

50 'I've found a tea': ibid.

50 'beautiful manners': Roland Penrose quoted in Antony Penrose, *Roland Penrose: The Friendly Surrealist* (Prestel, 2001), p. 22

51 'doing a Dadie': see Michael De-La-Hoy, *Eddy: The Life of Eddy Sackville-West* (Arcadia, 1999), p. 129

51 'Dadie has an ingratiating': *The Diary of Virginia Woolf*, vol. 2: *1920–1924*, ed. Anne Olivier Bell (Hogarth Press, 1978), p. 268

51 'Dadie in his silver-grey': ibid.

51 'condescension towards us ... pink-shirted to match': Frances Partridge, *Independent* obituary of George Rylands, 20 January 1999

51 'My one grief': SR to George Rylands, 5 August 1921, King's

52 'I haven't properly': SR to George Rylands, 22 September 1921, King's

52 'married to the college': SR, 'Footnotes', p. 49

52 'were a by-product': Gordon A. Fletcher, *Dennis Robertson: Essays on his Life and Work* (Palgrave Macmillan, 2007), p. 15

52 'realised later that': SR, 'Footnotes', p. 51

53 'We have been undergoing': SR to George Rylands, 22 September 1921, King's

54 'my only whim': SR, 'Footnotes', p. 45

54 'Chinese porcelain': SR to George Rylands, 22 September 1921, King's

54 'I dread the future': ibid.

54 'Spy Harrison': Vladimir Nabokov quoted in Andrew Field, *VN: The Life and Art of Vladimir Nabokov* (University of Queensland Press, 1986), p. 64

55 'pure Cambridge': *The Letters of Virginia Woolf*, vol. 5: *The Sickle Side of the Moon 1932–1935*, ed. Nigel Nicolson and Joanne Trautmann (Hogarth Press, 1975), p. 357

55 'the tone of life': Rebecca West, *New Statesman*, 23 October 1920, p. 82, quoted in Nicola Beauman, 'Jones, Emily Beatrix Coursolles', *Oxford Dictionary of National Biography*

56 'It is impossible': Raymond Mortimer, 'London Letter', *The Dial*, February 1928

57 'moments of loneliness': Emily Lucas to George Rylands, undated letter from the 1920s, King's

57 'I love Steven': ibid.

57 'It was a perfectly': SR, 'Footnotes', p. 48

57 'unwilling to join': Emily Lucas to George Rylands, 1926, King's

58 'Douglas had a charming': SR, 'Footnotes', p. 48

58 'we had many': ibid.

58 'roughly speaking, a dulcimer': ibid., p. 46

58 'a rather dull': Penelope Fitzgerald, *The Knox Brothers* (Macmillan, 1977), p. 93

58 'admired his talents': SR, 'Footnotes', p. 54

59 'I have been working': SR to WR, 5 June 1922, Elshieshields

59 'a hospitable little man': SR, 'Footnotes', p. 50

59 'a most valuable member': Ernest Harrison to WR, 28 April 1922, Elshieshields

59 'for economics he has': ibid.

59 'Steven is thought': ibid.

60 'shamelessly, almost stridently': SR, 'Footnotes', p. 55

60 'wilfully eager to shock': ibid.

60 'affected clever conceited': SR to Ruth Runciman, 18 November 1923, Elshieshields

60 'Cecil had none': Stewart Perowne quoted in Hugo Vickers, *Cecil Beaton* (Weidenfeld & Nicolson, 1985), p. 32

60 'I don't want people': ibid.

60 'absurd-looking . . . He really is rather': ibid., p. 30

61 'Nowadays I am': Edward Bates to Noel Annan, undated, King's

62 'exotic taste': Steven Runciman quoted in Vickers, *Beaton*, p. 42

62 'a dear, ridiculous': SR to Kitty Runciman, 25 January 1925, Elshieshields

62 'stuffed out with cushions': SR, 'Footnotes', p. 55

62 'a hilarious production': ibid.

63 'he would try': SR to MR, 22 October 1922, Elshieshields

63 'very well. His green': SR to MR, 5 November 1922, Elshieshields

63 'pursing up his mouth': Vickers, *Beaton*, p. 41

63 'glittering like a diamond': A. C. Benson on Gaillard Lapsley, quoted in David Newsome, *On the Edge of Paradise: A. C. Benson, the Diarist* (John Murray, 1980), p. 175

64 'withering lecture': SR, 'Footnotes', p. 55

64 'that terrific snob': SR to RR, 23 October 1923, Elshieshields

64 'my great friend': SR to WR, 5 May 1930, Elshieshields

64 'grammar-school boys': SR, 'Footnotes', p. 50

64 'the soulful poetess': SR to RR, 23 October 1923, Elshieshields

65 'the putting off': Ermengard Maitland, foreword to Fredegond Shove, *Poems* (Cambridge University Press, 1956), p. viii

65 'In particular she': SR, 'Footnotes', p. 86

66 'horrid Mr Hinks': SR to RR, 11 November 1923, Elshieshields

66 'I lunched with': SR to RR, 16 June 1924, Elshieshields

66 'my little enemy': SR to KR, 27 October 1926, Elshieshields

66 'I don't like him': SR to RR, 18 November 1923, Elshieshields

66 'apt to be boring': SR to KR, 25 January 1925, Elshieshields

66 'a fine historian': SR, 'Footnotes', p. 55

67 'apposite and severe': ibid., p. 56

67 'the small but amusing': ibid., p. 52

67 'I thought then': Steven Runciman quoted in Michael Holroyd, *Lytton Strachey* (William Heinemann, 1968), vol. 2, p. 652n

68 'a ridiculous old': SR to RR, 2 December 1923, Elshieshields

69 'one or two': SR, 'Footnotes', p. 57

69 'from whom our material': ibid., p. 60

69 'the most glamorous': ibid., p. 73

69 'Rosamond Lehmann has': SR to MR, 12 November 1922, Elshieshields

70 'This continual effort': LR to Rosamond Lehmann, 27 May 1923, King's

70 'Is Rosamond catching': Steven Runciman quoted in LR to Rosamond Lehmann, 30 May 1923, King's

71 'in the course': LR to Rosamond Lehmann, 3 July 1923, King's

71 'I've been out': SR to RR, 16 June 1924, Elshieshields

71 'The plains are': SR, 'The Loveless', 'Juvenilia' notebook, Elshieshields

## CHAPTER 6: THE HIEROPHANT

74 'was a frail shy': SR, *Alphabet*, p. 16

75 'distinctive, but somewhat': Norman Baynes (ed.), *A Bibliography of the Works of J. B. Bury* (Cambridge University Press, 1929), p. 53

75 'a talk with Bury': ibid., p. 51

75 'the release of history': ibid.

75 'History is not': ibid., p. 109

75 'so long as history': J. B. Bury, Inaugural Lecture, 'The Science of History', 26 January 1903, Cambridge

75 'History belongs': Steven Runciman quoted by David Plante, conversation with author, 28 January 2012

75 'wished to put Clio': Harold Temperley, introduction to J. B. Bury, *Selected Essays* (Cambridge University Press, 1930), p. xxiv

75 'an awful snob': SR, Royal Society of Literature lecture, 'Medieval History and the Romantic Imagination', 13 December 1962

76 'He told me': SR, *Alphabet*, p. 16

76 'it was ridiculous': ibid.

76 'from that interview': Norman Baynes in Bury *Bibliography*, p. 50

76 'enjoyed having company': SR, 'Footnotes', p. 58

77 'shock when I said': ibid.

77 'The idea of writing': Bury, 'The Science of History'

77 'genetic history . . . the present condition': ibid.

77 'Thought was rendered': ibid.

78 'Elisha': Robert Byron, *New Statesman*, 1 April 1933

78 'Justice was administered': SR, *The Emperor Romanus Lecapenus and his Reign* (Cambridge University Press, 1929), p. 114

78 'I am quite unfit': Francis Birrell, *Nation and Athenaeum*, 21 August 1929

78 'Mr. Runciman has a feline': ibid.

78 'Mr. Runciman . . . is readable': *Times Literary Supplement*, 29 August 1929

78 'Gibbon's dark shadow': SR, *Romanus Lecapenus*, p. 10

79 'a dreadful book . . . the same effect': SR, 'Medieval History and the Romantic Imagination'

79 'Neither Anglican nor Roman': Steven Runciman interviewed by Jonathan Riley-Smith, December 1995

79 'what Walter Scott': Jonathan Riley-Smith, *The Crusades, Christianity and Islam* (Columbia University Press, 2008), p. 304

80 'I interview and teach': SR to Lady Bonham Carter, 27 January 1929, Hampshire Archives, Winchester

80 'One of my bright': SR to HR, 3 February 1929, Elshieshields

80 'I fear I'm not': SR to Lady Bonham Carter, 1 March 1929, Hants

81 'my dull Byz book': ibid.

81 'horizontal rather than': SR, *Romanus Lecapenus*, pp. 5, 10

81 *'une pétulance un peu'*: Henri Grégoire, *Byzantion*, 1929

81 'the pedant must': E. H. Minns, *Cambridge Review*, 11 October 1929

81 'a certain modish': *Journal of Hellenic Studies*, 1930

81 'miasma of dullness': *New Statesman*, 3 August 1929

82 'unattractive, conceited but': SR to RR, 15 November 1927, Elshieshields

82 'to look at,': SR to KR, 20 November 1927, Elshieshields

82 'it is not strict': SR to Donald Nicol, 28 December 1957, King's

82 'In the battles': SR, *Romanus Lecapenus*, p. 10

82 'The commander-in-chief': ibid., p. 54

83 'interesting, and never': J. B. Bury quoted by SR to RR, 8 June 1924, Elshieshields

83 'Romanus, instead of begging': SR, *Romanus Lecapenus*, p. 93

84 'some rather vehement': F. H. Marshall, *History*, 1930

84 'garbled': SR, *Romanus Lecapenus*, p. 139

84 'fantastic nonsense': ibid., p. 165

85 'Liudprand . . . twice visited': ibid., p. 4

85 'was on a much lower': ibid., p. 166

86 'Prejudice has descended': ibid., p. 121

86 'to a nation': ibid., p. 117

86 'a civilized potentate': ibid., p. 116

86 'Eunuchs were an ideal': ibid., p. 19

87 'it seems unreasonable': ibid. p. 77

87 'Greek heretics': ibid., 129

87 'In the West': ibid., p. 29

88 'a lack of snobbishness': ibid., p. 20

88 'the task of making': *Near East and India*, 12 September 1929

88 'I've just finished': Lytton Strachey to Roger Senhouse, *The Letters of Lytton Strachey*, ed. Paul Levy (Viking, 2005), p. 608

## CHAPTER 7: THE SUN

90 'Oh, life is a glorious': Dorothy Parker, 'Comment', quoted in SR, *Alphabet*, p. 129

90 'I want to go': SR to Lady Bonham Carter, 10 May 1929, Hants

91 'a work which I doubt': SR, 'Footnotes', p. 62

91 'philosophy . . . was never': ibid.

91 'Clare has the face': ibid., p. 63

91 'giving the impression': ibid.

92 'the stupids and the sillies': Connolly, *Enemies of Promise*, p. 249

92 'another beautiful young': James Owen, 'A Meeting with Sir Steven Runciman', *Spectator*, 15 August 1998

92 'what would happen': Steven Runciman quoted in Philip Hoare, *Serious Pleasures* (Hamish Hamilton, 1990), p. 22

92 'dear Mr. Beaton': SR to RR, 19 January 1927, Elshieshields

93 'a very fetching': Steven Runciman quoted in Hoare, *Serious Pleasures*, p. 50

93 'I don't think': ibid.

93 'that most valuable': SR, 'Footnotes', p. 61

93 'In London a group': ibid.

94 'and on the whole': ibid.

94 'It was the golden ... writers such as': ibid.

94 'All this fuss': Evelyn Waugh, *Vile Bodies* (Chapman & Hall, 1930), p. 87

94 'As an outcome': SR, 'Footnotes', p. 64

95 'the youngest and': ibid., p. 63

95 'love of fantasy': ibid., p. 64

96 'looking like a large': SR to Tony Reavell, 16 June 1984, Elshieshields

96 'father thinks she's': Hoare, *Serious Pleasures*, p. 67n

96 'That afternoon we': SR to KR, 28 June 1925, Elshieshields

97 'no chicken and': SR to RR, 19 January 1927, Elshieshields

97 'never expecting that': Cecil Beaton, *The Wandering Years* (Weidenfeld & Nicolson, 1961), p. 154

97 'all the young men': Jane Schenkar, *Truly Wilde: The Unsettling Story of Dolly Wilde, Oscar's Unusual Niece* (Virago, 2000), p. 136

97 'raven hair shingled': Beaton, *Wandering Years*, p. 153

97 'painted and powdered': Schenkar, *Truly Wilde*, p. 136

97 'historical anecdotes ... regaled us with': Beaton, *Wandering Years*, p. 154

98 'All the weekend': SR to RR, 19 January 1927, Elshieshields

98 'Baba was remarkably': ibid.

98 'society young ladies': ibid.

98 'with her page's': Beaton, *Wandering Years*, p. 154

99 'My Skeleton: a kind': ibid.

99 'soft-voiced and ingenuous ... Everyone was very': SR to RR, 19 January 1927, Elshieshields

99 'paedophobia': Selina Hastings, *Rosamond Lehmann* (Chatto & Windus, 2002), p. 67

100 'the inevitable Wogan': SR to RR, 6 February 1927, Elshieshields

100 'irritated to find': SR, 'Footnotes', p. 75

101 'Mr and Mrs R.': Holroyd, *Lytton Strachey*, p. 912

102 'mushroom growth': Dora Carrington to Lytton Strachey, 16 January 1928, *Carrington: Letters*, ed. David Garnett (Jonathan Cape, 1970), p. 385

102 'Robot Runciman': Maynard Keynes to Lydia Lopokova, 17 May 1925, *Lydia & Maynard: The Letters of Lydia Lopokova and John Maynard Keynes*, ed. Polly Hill and Richard Keynes (André Deutsch, 1989), p. 324

102 'such a public': SR to KR, 25 June 1925, Elshieshields

103 'I was never': SR, undated lecture text, Elshieshields

103 'Rosamond's novel is': SR to RR, 12 June 1927, Elshieshields

103 'unco' spinsterish': Hastings, *Rosamond Lehmann*, p. 99

104 'for about twenty': SR to RR, 6 February 1927, Elshieshields

104 'Rumour maintained': SR, 'Footnotes', p. 76

104 'Our darling sister-in-law': SR to RR, 19 June 1927, Elshieshields

105 'there was – is – so': Rosamond Lehmann to SR, 12 June 1987, Elshieshields

107 'EFB always seemed': SR to Tony Reavell, 17 January 1984, Elshieshields

107 'gracefully puritanical . . . eager – a loveable': Newsome, *On the Edge of Paradise*, p. 360

107 'thought haughty': ibid., p. 361

107 'bird-like morals': ibid., p. 365

108 'E. F. never lived': Madan, *Notebooks*, p. 46

108 'idea of a good': ibid., p. 47

108 'was, I think': Steven Runciman quoted in Cynthia and Tony Reavell, *E. F. Benson* (Martello Bookshop, 1984) p. 67

109 'I remember now': SR to Cynthia Reavell, undated, 1994, Elshieshields

109 'delight in the ridiculous': SR to Tony Reavell, 1 July 1983, Elshieshields

109 'EFB certainly "believed"': SR to Cynthia Reavell, undated, 1990, Elshieshields

111 'after the silly': SR to George Rylands, 17 August 1927, King's

111 'one could not follow': *Edith Olivier: From her Journals 1924–48*, ed. Penelope Middelboe (Weidenfeld & Nicolson, 1989), p. xii

112 'I was not allowed': SR, 'Footnotes', p. 66

112 'She enjoyed nothing': Edith Olivier, *Without Knowing Mr. Walkley* (Reader's Union, 1939), p. 254

113 'convulsive laughter': Olivier, *Journals*, p. 56

113 'spoke of nothing': ibid.

113 'untrue to her': ibid.

113 'of jibing at her': ibid.

113 'completely mad': SR to RR, 9 July 1927, Elshieshields

113 'my only friends': Elinor Wylie quoted in Stanley Olson, *Elinor Wylie: A Life Apart* (Dial Press, 1979), p. 325

113 'best poetry of': ibid.

113 'Zakaznija No. 10': ibid., p. 308

114 'How I loved ... who would leave ... and be good': Elinor Wylie to SR, 30 May 1928, Smith College

114 'One has to be': Elinor Wylie to SR, 7 March 1928, Smith College

114 'Personally I think': Elinor Wylie to SR, 8 February 1928, Smith College

114 'possessed the blood': Olson, *Elinor Wylie*, p. 296

114 'A guest noticed': SR, 'Footnotes', p. 66

115 'In the evening': SR to RR, 29 November 1927, Elshieshields

115 'preferable to the smarter': SR, 'Footnotes', p. 80

115 'restful and happy': ibid.

115 'enchanting house': SR, *Alphabet*, p. 41

115 'a nice looking': R. W. B. Lewis, *Edith Wharton* (Constable, 1975), p. 483

116 'brilliance and erudition': ibid.

116 'an exquisite *pavillon*': SR, *Alphabet*, p. 41

116 'extremely charming': SR to KR, 20 November 1926, Elshieshields

116 'a wealthy stage-struck ... the flirtatious lightness': Stanley Dunn quoted in Victoria Price, *Vincent Price* (St Martin's Press, 2000), p. 68

116 'the strain of living': SR, *Alphabet*, p. 41

116 'I feel eternal': SR, 'Footnotes', p. 80

117 'To one who saw': SR, 'Repentance', 'Juvenilia' notebook, Elshieshields

117 'I have a passion': Hermione Lee, *Edith Wharton* (Chatto & Windus, 2007), p. 701

117 'novels are about': ibid., p. 732

118 'she descended from': SR review of Mary Blume, *Côte d'Azur*, *Spectator*, 17 July 1992

118 'Cubist château': Christian Arthaud and Eric Paul, *La Côte d'Azur des écrivains* (Edisud, 1999), p. 22

118 'Picasso collage': ibid.

119 'Oh, il aime': Alexis von Rosenberg, *Baron de Redé, Alexis: The Memoirs of the Baron de Rédé*, ed. Hugo Vickers (Dovecote Press, 2005), p. 62

119 'redoubtable viscountess ... undistinguished Cubist extravaganza ... I told her': James Lord, *Picasso & Dora* (Weidenfeld & Nicolson, 1993), p. 258

119 'She was not': *Redé, Alexis*, p. 62

121 'I fancy she': HR to SR, quoted in Lee, *Edith Wharton*, p. 700
121 'evil-tempered Pekinese': Lee, *Edith Wharton*, p. 701
121 'from the bedroom': SR to HR, 18 September 1934, Elshieshields


## CHAPTER 8: THE MOON

122 'one of the few': SR, 'Footnotes', p. 59
122 'I had no wish': ibid., p. 60
122 'faith in the sea's': SR, *Alphabet*, p. 189
122 'I realised that': ibid.
123 'had no intention': Meyers, *Orwell*, p. 45
123 'lonely and apprehensive . . . and felt sure . . . reading unsociably': SR, *Alphabet*, p. 189
123 'They are my little': SR to HR, 12 October 1925, Elshieshields
124 'slightly Levantine . . . curiously untraceable accent': SR to HR, 27 October 1925, Elshieshields
124 'jolly manly man': ibid.
124 'the famous emporium': SR, *Alphabet*, p. 35
125 'in patterns on': ibid.
125 'I had my fortune': SR to HR, 27 October 1925, Elshieshields
125 'I was always': ibid.
125 'which has improved': SR to KR, 2 November 1925, Elshieshields
125 'the inevitable fancy-dress': SR, *Alphabet*, p. 190
125 'I was not': ibid.
126 'It is a remarkable': SR to HR, 17 November 1925, Elshieshields
127 'mass of brilliant': SR to WR, 5 November 1925, Elshieshields
127 'the vastest and': SR to HR, 11 November 1925, Elshieshields
127 'a tall voracious': SR to KR, 10 November 1925, Elshieshields
127 'the kind agent': ibid.
127 'There was a glamorous': SR, *Alphabet*, p. 190
128 'a twin city': SR to HR, 17 November 1925, Elshieshields
128 'I heard that': SR to KR, 17 November 1925, Elshieshields
128 'ornamented with tree-clumps': SR to HR, 29 November 1925, Elshieshields
128 'no more Yellow': SR to HR, 11 November 1925, Elshieshields
129 'The journey that': SR, *Alphabet*, p. 192
129 'they bore no': ibid., p. 193
129 'One met most': ibid.
129 'The monde of Tientsin': SR to KR, 1 December 1925, Elshieshields

130 'a shy hesitating-hurried-voiced': SR to LR, 2 December 1925, Elshieshields

130 'quite learned in Chinese': SR to HR, 29 November 1925, Elshieshields

130 'Living in a consular': ibid.

131 'We live in the midst': SR to AMR, 1 December 1925, Elshieshields

131 'There were bright': SR to KR, 1 December 1925, Elshieshields

131 'hideous to look at ... rumours come rushing ... Statesmen and generals': SR to HR, 4 December 1925, Elshieshields

132 'his understudy ... I cannot, alas': SR, *Alphabet*, p. 193

132 'the Emperor had': ibid.

132 'a large villa ... a frail, etiolated ... sadly revealed ... adequate English': ibid.

133 'He called himself': ibid., p. 194

133 'I left China': SR to KR, 5 February 1926, Elshieshields

134 'I feel republican!': SR to LR, undated, 1926, Elshieshields

134 'Links with the past ... comfortable to contemplate': SR, 'Footnotes', p. 1

135 'a tempting idea': SR, *Alphabet*, p. 193

135 'importing antiques from': ibid., p. 75

135 'a wonderful opportunity': ibid.

135 'I am to be taken': SR to HR, 11 December 1925, Elshieshields

136 'wars consist of': SR to HR, 4 December 1925, Elshieshields

136 'They are fighting': SR to HR, 11 December 1925, Elshieshields

136 'I am in a beleaguered': SR to KR, 22 December 1925, Elshieshields

136 'the shopkeepers in': SR to HR, 21 December 1925, Elshieshields

137 'I went down': SR to KR, 16 December 1925, Elshieshields

137 'shuffling along in ... solemnly and courteously': SR, *Alphabet*, p. 194

137 'I am undergoing': SR to WR, 24 December 1925, Elshieshields

138 'the most interesting': SR to AMR, 1 December 1925, Elshieshields

138 'I'm glad the war': SR to KR, 1 January 1926, Elshieshields

138 'The sensationally minded': SR to HR, 31 December 1925, Elshieshields

138 'At last, at last!': SR to KR, 4 January 1926, Elshieshields

139 'the wickedest and smartest': SR to HR, 6 January 1926, Elshieshields

139 'among the most enjoyable': SR, *Alphabet*, p. 195

139 'badly, even unpleasantly': ibid.

139 'The great walls': ibid.

140 'a pathetic figure': SR to WR, 13 January 1926, Elshieshields

140 'liberal ideas': John MacMurray, *How the Peace Was Lost* (Hoover Press, 1992), p. 75

140 'a passée beauty': SR to WR, 13 January 1926, Elshieshields

140 'You need not think': SR, *Alphabet*, p. 195

140 'eager, well-informed': ibid., p. 196

140 'The vast park': SR to HR, 6 January 1926, Elshieshields

140 'inside the Imperial City': SR to WR, 13 January 1926, Elshieshields

141 'Social life is': SR to KR, 11 January 1926, Elshieshields

141 'a dear old man': SR, *Alphabet*, p. 196

141 'One object which': SR to HR, 18 January 1926, Elshieshields

141 'who seemed to have': SR, *Alphabet*, p. 196

141 'The latter was': ibid.

142 'a strange place': SR to WR, 13 January 1926, Elshieshields

142 'He travels fastest': Earl Albert Selle, biographer of W. H. Donald, 1948 interview, New York (http://donaldofchina.com/Don_Who_/ Press2/press2.html)

143 'so indispensable that': SR, *Alphabet*, p. 195

143 'the Lloyd George': SR to KR, 27 January 1926, Elshieshields

143 'an elegant and lively ... As his first wife ... the finer points': SR, *Alphabet*, p. 196

143 'The Wall was ... Suddenly the foothills': ibid.

144 'the Ladder to': SR to KR, 27 January 1926, Elshieshields

144 'from which one could': SR, *Alphabet*, p. 197

144 'I might have liked': ibid., p. 74

144 'one had seen it ... erroneous belief ... they were determined': ibid.

144 'my bear-leader': ibid., p. 75

144 'just like a Cook's': SR to HR, 10 February 1926, Elshieshields

144 'an ex-Geisha girl': ibid.

144 'In the evening': ibid.

145 'a wonderful place': SR to HR, 15 February 1926, Elshieshields

145 'I am enjoying Japan ... the leading *antiquaire*': ibid.

146 'old-fashioned English ... determined to see': SR, *Alphabet*, p. 77

146 'Being a foreigner': SR, undated account, 'The Ningyo Joruri of Osaka', Elshieshields

146 'the slow progress': SR, *Alphabet*, p. 77

147 'one of the greatest': ibid., p. 74

147 'It seemed to be': ibid., p. 77

## CHAPTER 9: THE WORLD

148 'She has painted lips': SR to RR, 15 May 1924, Elshieshields

148 'I had fallen': SR, *Alphabet*, p. 129

148 'was not as classically': SR, review of Christine Sutherland, *Enchantress: Marthe Bibesco and her World*, *Spectator*, 11 April 1997

149  'She acted her role': SR, *Alphabet*, p. 130

149  'I was shown': SR, *Enchantress* review, *Spectator*

150  'but he was homosexual': ibid.

150  'She had huge green': ibid.

150  'I know that': SR to Princess Marthe Bibesco, 28 April 1934, Harry Ransom Center, University of Texas, Austin

150  'the most romantic': SR to Princess Bibesco, 7 May 1934, Austin

150  'I hope that you': SR to Princess Bibesco, 25 August 1934, Austin

151  'the Bulgar Lady': SR to Lady Bonham Carter, 7 January 1929, Hants

151  'lovely pair of Balkan': SR to HR, 17 September 1934, Elshieshields

152  'totally unfit . . . delicate': Queen Victoria to the Marquess of Salisbury, 10 July 1887, quoted in Theo Aronson, *Crowns in Conflict* (John Murray, 1986), p. 83

152  'I liked Ivan': SR to WR, undated, 1930, Elshieshields

152  'I thought that he': SR to RR, 18 April 1930, Elshieshields

153  'I don't think': SR to RR, 20 April 1930, Elshieshields

153  'an apoplectic looking': SR to HR, 15 April 1930, Elshieshields

153  'Tell me, is it . . . There was a pause': SR, *Alphabet*, p. 18

153  'which I thought': ibid.

153  'a Bulgarian savant': SR to HR, 15 April 1930, Elshieshields

154  'when the royal children': Johnny Stancioff, conversation with author, 21 January 2014

154  'I saw all the royal': SR to HR, 8 August 1933, Elshieshields

155  'tall, upright, gentlemanly': Johnny Stancioff, conversation with author

155  'still a handsome': SR, *Alphabet*, p. 19

155  'acres of grapes': SR to HR, 10 September 1934, Elshieshields

155  'I have only one': ibid.

156  'a banquet that lasted': ibid.

156  'My week in Sofia': SR to HR, 17 September 1934, Elshieshields

157  'His Eminence spent': SR to HR, 18 September 1934, Elshieshields

157  'He was a man': SR, *Alphabet*, p. 57

158  'eccentric English dream': Hilary Spurling, *Matisse the Master* (Hamish Hamilton, 2005), p. 350

158  'This museum is closed': Patrick Balfour, Baron Kinross, *Hagia Sophia* (W. W. Norton, 1972), p. 128

158  'very wholly mad': Isaiah Berlin to Joseph Alsop, 11 February 1944, in Isaiah Berlin, *Flourishing: Letters 1928–1946*, ed. Henry Hardy (Chatto & Windus, 2004), p. 481

158  'the most memorable . . . a young man': SR, *Alphabet*, p. 19

159 'anyone gifted with': SR to Patrick Leigh Fermor, 11 February 2000, National Library of Scotland, Edinburgh (hereafter NLS)

159 'the dead spit . . . erudite and shrewish': Patrick Leigh Fermor, 'Remembering Steven Runciman', *Spectator*, 13 January 2001

159 'both of them impeccable': ibid.

159 'kind, under his provisos . . . pleasantly feline': Patrick Leigh Fermor, *The Broken Road*, ed. Artemis Cooper and Colin Thubron (John Murray, 2013), p. 9

159 'with one of those beautiful': Leigh Fermor, 'Remembering Steven Runciman', *Spectator*

159 'a pretty, fair-haired': Leigh Fermor, *The Broken Road*, p. 14

160 'a market town': SR, *Alphabet*, p. 17

160 'Bucharest was at that . . . It was not a': ibid., p. 130

161 'It was exciting': Leigh Fermor, *The Broken Road*, p. 188

161 'ornately splendid, but': SR, *Alphabet*, p. 131

161 'A young peacock': ibid.

162 'a vision of Mogoşoea': SR to Princess Bibesco, 20 October 1934, Austin

162 'Queen Marie always': SR, *Alphabet*, p. 213

162 'a palace built': SR to HR, 18 September 1934, Elshieshields

162 'I feel that I must': SR to Walter, Baron Runciman, 17 September 1934, Elshieshields

163 'We waited in': SR to HR, 18 September 1934, Elshieshields

163 'The palace was': SR, *Alphabet*, p. 132

163 'in favour of frankness . . . poor nineteenth century': ibid.

163 'the best of all': ibid., p. 133

164 'a handsome, voluptuous': SR, review of Prince Paul of Hohenzollern, *King Carol II*, *Spectator*, 23 September 1988

165 'energy as king . . . seems mostly to have': ibid.

165 'a very bad . . . his one memorable': SR to HR, 24 September 1934, Elshieshields

165 'it was [Iorga] who': SR, *Alphabet*, p. 133

165 'At the first mention': Sacheverell Sitwell, *A Roumanian Journey* (B. T. Batsford, 1938), p. 1

166 'Roumania has never': ibid., p. 3

166 'all I asked': Hector Bolitho, *A Biographer's Notebook* (Macmillan, 1950), p. 3

166 'The abiding good': ibid., p. 5

166 'She had the rare': ibid., p. 8

166 'such a tragedy': ibid., p. 16

167 'I tried to describe': ibid.

167 'unkind, unreliable': SR, *Carol II* review, *Spectator*

167  'It is, it seems': SR, *Alphabet*, p. 134

167  'white walls and red . . . I can frankly . . . On the contrary': Sitwell, *A Roumanian Journey*, p. 14

168  'a flustered nun . . . with nothing to do': SR, *Alphabet*, p. 134

168  'Tuscan Roumania . . . the same blue': Sitwell, *A Roumanian Journey*, p. 17

168  'a Russian prince': SR, *Alphabet*, p. 135

169  'This is going': SR to Princess Bibesco, 20 October 1934, Austin

170  'lying in the clutches': SR, *Alphabet*, p. 139


## CHAPTER 10: SAILING TO BULGARIA

171  'The first shadows': SR, *A History of the First Bulgarian Empire* (Cambridge University Press, 1930), p. 259

171  'The only Occultist': SR, *The Medieval Manichee* (Cambridge University Press, 1947), p. 187

171  'I am busy': SR to WR Sr, 25 April 1936, Elshieshields

172  'To the ordinary': SR, *The Medieval Manichee*, p. vii

172  'In future the average': ibid., p. 17

172  'Bulgaria's most curious . . . The Cathars': SR, 'Byzantium and the Slavs', in Norman Baynes and Henry St Leger Moss (eds), *Byzantium* (Clarendon Press, 1947), p. 352

173  'I was glad': SR, *Alphabet*, p. 56

173  'There were no more': ibid.

174  'the fruit of much': William Miller, *English Historical Review*, Vol. 36, No. 184, October 1931

174  'it was absurd': SR, *Alphabet*, p. 17

176  'to belittle your': SR, *First Bulgarian Empire*, p. v

176  'In Western Europe': ibid.

176  'It is not for': ibid., p. vi

176  'lacunae are excellent': ibid.

177  'Once upon a time': ibid., p. 1

177  'Some say they were': ibid., p. 4

177  'Avitokhol, of the house': ibid., p. 11

178  'The Bulgars were': ibid., p. 66

178  'they made their attempts': ibid., p. 5

178  'There was a king': ibid., p. 7

178  'the primary significance': George Seferis, unpublished review of Steven Runciman, *The Kingdom of Acre* (1954), Gennadius Library, Athens For all subsequent quotations and translations from the Runciman/Seferis

correspondence in the Gennadius Library I am indebted to Katerina Krikos-Davis's article, 'Sir Steven Runciman and "The Nicest Greek" he knew: the chronicle of his friendship with George Seferis', published in *"His Words Were Nourishment and His Counsel Food" – a Festschrift for David W. Holton*, ed. Efrosini Camatsos, Tassos A. Kaplanis, Jocelyn Pye (Cambridge Scholars Publishing, 2014).

179 'Not long ago': SR, *First Bulgarian Empire*, p. 4

179 'were only the land-owning': ibid., p. 34

180 'Theophanes's conclusion': ibid., p. 62

180 'Barbarian that he was': ibid., p. 70

180 'The episode that': ibid., p. 63

181 'The Empress-Regent Irene': ibid., p. 47

181 'her white horses': ibid., p. 50

181 'Women's Liberation': SR, 'The Empress Irene', *Conspectus of History*, Vol. 1, No. 1 (1974), p. 1

182 'realized now that he': SR, *First Bulgarian Empire*, p. 171

182 'Benjamin's life was': ibid., p. 189

183 'Dualism has always . . . Pope Bogomil . . . genius': ibid., p. 191

183 'this intricate Armenian': ibid., p. 192

183 'equally but passively': ibid., p. 256

183 'A faith that teaches': ibid., p. 194

184 'their abstention from women': ibid.

184 'dualism was associated': SR, *The Medieval Manichee*, p. 175

184 'certain of the Gnostics': ibid., p. 176

184 'Casual promiscuity': ibid., p. 177

184 'Was there some Secret': ibid.

184 'the somewhat inarticulate': ibid., p. 179

185 'if Runciman's learning': Lynn White, *Journal of Bible and Religion*, Vol. 16, No. 2, April 1948, p. 118

185 'Photius was prodigiously': SR, *First Bulgarian Empire*, p. 100

185 'Historians ever since': ibid., p. 107

186 'who ever afterwards': SR, 'Footnotes', p. 94

186 'whatever the defects': *Oxford Magazine*, 19 October 1933

186 'Mr. Runciman lacks': Robert Byron, *New Statesman*, 1 April 1933

187 'That man Yeats': SR, 'Byzantine Art and Western Medieval Taste', lecture at Athens, 1966

188 'So it was that one': SR, *The Medieval Manichee*, p. 171

188 'They thought, he added': ibid., p. 33

188 'Heresies, like civilisation': ibid., p. 94

188 'the recent circumstances': ibid., p. vii

189 'Tolerance is a social': ibid., p. 1

189 'orthodox doctrine is': ibid., p. 2

189 'created medieval Latin': SR to Stewart Perowne, 6 January 1967, Elshieshields

190 'Beware of Steven Runciman': Anthony Bryer, 'The Spider, the Owl and the Historian', *History Today*, 5 May 2001

190 'it is the State': SR, *The Medieval Manichee*, p. 3

190 'Kill them all': see e.g. Zoé Oldenbourg, *Massacre at Montségur*, trans. Peter Green (Weidenfeld & Nicolson, 1961), p. 109

190 'I am interested': *Pemptousia* interview with Steven Runciman, 14 July 2000

191 'sin was a very': SR, *The Medieval Manichee*, p. 5

191 'careful and mildly': *Church Times*, 20 June 1947

191 'light, bemused style': Allen Cabaniss, *Journal of Religion*, Vol. 37, No. 2, April 1957, p. 128

191 'Sects arose that': SR, *The Medieval Manichee*, p. 10

192 'spiritual aristocracy . . . the initiate became': ibid.

192 'Gnostic extravagancies': ibid., p. 23

192 'taste for fairy-stories': ibid., p. 21

192 'as an Armenist . . . I disagree with': ibid., p. viii

193 'My first impression': F. C. Conybeare, *The Key of Truth* (Clarendon Press, 1898), p. v

193 'investigated the creed': Edward Gibbon, *The Decline and Fall of the Roman Empire*, vol. 10 (Cadell & Davies, 1807), p. 169

193 'their liberty was enlarged': ibid., p. 171

193 'It is not unpleasing': ibid., p. 180

193 'the seeds of reformation': ibid., p. 167

193 'Even them who kept': John Milton, 'On the Late Massacre in Piedmont' (1655)

194 'The Armenian Church': SR, *The Medieval Manichee*, p. 31

194 'must be either the followers': ibid., p. 47

194 'The history of the Paulicians': ibid., p. 46

194 'a free-booting state': ibid., p. 39

194 'in happy anarchy': ibid., p. 36

194 'Chrysocheir came': ibid., p. 41

195 'justifiably annoyed': ibid., p. 44

195 'remained merely military': ibid., p. 50

195 'had sufficient truck': ibid., p. 88

195 'found it a more . . . Their struggle was': ibid.

195 'There happened to be': ibid., p. 106

195 'the political impulse': ibid., p. 171

195 'a national dress': ibid., p. 115

195 'Weak and evanescent': ibid., p. 112

196 'land of high lakes ... Comforts might be': SR, *First Bulgarian Empire*, p. 245

196 'made no complaint': ibid., p. 231

196 'Their passivity was': SR, *The Medieval Manichee*, p. 68

197 'Modern occultists have': ibid., p. 177

197 'There has been so': ibid., p. 186

197 'Before me floats': W. B. Yeats, 'Byzantium', included in *The Winding Stair* (1933)


## CHAPTER II: DEATH

198 'Best cut out': John Cornford, *Collected Writings*, ed. Jonathan Galassi (Carcanet, 1986), p. 29

198 'When first I returned ... undergraduates remain': SR, 'Footnotes', p. 88

199 'with delight': SR to HR, 6 January 1926, Elshieshields

199 'first-class pianist ... a wonderful purveyor': SR, 'Footnotes', p. 83

200 'middle-aged bachelors ... where one will best ... is not suitable': SR to KR, 27 May 1932, Elshieshields

200 'I quite often': SR, 'Footnotes', p. 92

200 'the undergraduate whom': SR to KR, 27 May 1932, Elshieshields

201 'And yet Time': Lord Justice Crewe, 1626; see e.g. Samuel Bent, *Familiar Short Sayings of Great Men (Ticknor, 1887), p. 166

201 'the most moving': Michael Burn, *Turned towards the Sun* (Michael Russell, 2003), p. 63

202 'He was gross': Goronwy Rees, *A Chapter of Accidents* (Chatto & Windus, 1972), p. 113

202 'master–pupil relationship': ibid., p. 131

202 'a bit grubby': Steven Runciman quoted in Plante profile, *New Yorker*

202 'showing no wish': SR, 'Footnotes', p. 92

203 'The truth is that': Rees, *Chapter of Accidents*, p. 121

204 'altogether rather bitter': SR to WR, 16 October 1929, Elshieshields

204 'If I'm going in': SR to WR, 5 May 1930, Elshieshields

205 'the most distinguished': SR, 'Footnotes', p. 80

205 'I am being filled': SR to HR, 9 March 1930, Elshieshields

206 'I received a letter': SR to WR, 1 May 1932, Elshieshields

206 'I no longer': SR, 'Footnotes', p. 87

207 'proceeded to embellish': ibid.

207 'a celebrated study': Enoch Powell, review of SR, *A Traveller's Alphabet, Daily Telegraph*, 28 February 1991

207 'the son and heir . . . all the right': SR, 'Footnotes', p. 91

208 'his knowledge and genuine': ibid., p. 93

208 'had been proposed': ibid.

208 'pleased with himself . . . supercilious': Steven Runciman quoted in Miranda Carter, *Anthony Blunt: His Lives* (Macmillan, 2001), p. 99

208 'His manner towards me': SR, 'Footnotes', p. 93

208 'I never fully realized': information from Nicholas Phillipson, conversation with author, 16 September 2012

210 'almost sylphlike': Alan Strachan, *Secret Dreams: A Biography of Michael Redgrave* (Weidenfeld & Nicolson, 2004), p. 76

211 'was terse in speech': Alan G. Jamieson, 'Bates, Sir Percy Elly', *ODNB*

212 'naïf youths': Edward Bates to Noel Annan, undated, King's

212 'the cleverest boy': SR, 'Footnotes', p. 92

212 'very unattractive': Steven Runciman quoted in Carter, *Anthony Blunt*, p. 121

212 'intelligent . . . grim . . . having looked forward . . . a disappointing experience': SR, 'Footnotes', p. 93

212 'The essays that [Cornford]': ibid.

213 'absolutely glamorised': Steven Runciman quoted in Carter, *Anthony Blunt*, p. 121

213 'relentless': Steven Runciman quoted in Barrie Penrose and Simon Freeman, *Conspiracy of Silence* (Grafton Books, 1986), p. 108

214 'In his early days': Steven Runciman quoted in Plante profile, *New Yorker*

215 'I don't like Madrid': SR to HR, 21 March 1936, Elshieshields

216 'They are all vehement': ibid.

216 'The house-party consists': SR to HR, 28 March 1936, Elshieshields

217 'two or three other': SR, *Alphabet*, p. 212

218 'I think Spain': SR to WR Sr, 25 April 1936, Elshieshields

218 'Everywhere I met': ibid.

218 'Heart of the heartless': Cornford, *Collected Writings*, p. 40

219 'guru': SR, 'Footnotes', p. 93

219 'He was the stuff': Anthony Blunt quoted in Carter, *Anthony Blunt*, p. 121

219 'Strange . . . extremely clever . . . forceful': Steven Runciman quoted in ibid.

219 'Love of the arts': Rees, *Chapter of Accidents*, p. 100

220 'particularly recommended': SR to HR, 23 July 1937, Elshieshields

220 'above the bleak': SR, *Alphabet*, p. 57

220 'a silly man': SR to HR, 23 July 1937, Elshieshields

221 'There, amid the sugar-cake': SR, *Alphabet*, p. 58

221 'how enjoyable life': ibid.

222 'comfortably endowed': SR, 'Footnotes', p. 12.

## CHAPTER 12: THE DEVIL

224 'I shouldn't really ': SR to George Rylands, 17 August 1927, King's

224 'I suppose that I': SR, 'Footnotes', p. 79

225 'distinguished and ridiculous': SR to KR, 31 May 1925, Elshieshields

225 'Well the plunge': Edward Bates to George Rylands, 24 September 1937, King's

225 'I know when': Edward Bates to George Rylands, 26 October 1937, King's

226 'Don't take Cambridge': Edward Bates to Anne Barnes, undated, King's

226 'Life seems to': Edward Bates to George Rylands, undated, 1938, King's

226 'not love in any . . . I think I nearly': Edward Bates to George Rylands, 18 May 1938, King's

226 'I am not supposed': Edward Bates to George Rylands, 27 June 1938, King's

226 'I believe even': Edward Bates to George Rylands, 1 July 1938, King's

227 'Dinner with Roger H: Edward Bates to George Rylands, 25 July 1938, King's

227 'long, involved, and unabridged . . . And now, I must': Edward Bates to George Rylands, 11 September 1938, King's

228 'A young man': SR, *Alphabet*, p. 153

228 'no beauty, looking': SR, 'Footnotes', p. 90

229 'interesting rather than': SR, *Alphabet*, p. 152

229 'a good Regent': ibid.

229 'I fear after you': Prince Birabongse of Siam to SR, 5 January 1938, Elshieshields

229 'before I settled': SR, *Alphabet*, p. 153

230 'all is for the best': Edward Bates to George Rylands, 14 September 1938, King's

230 'the old and lovely . . . every other person': SR, *Alphabet*, p. 153

230 'though not really': Edward Bates to George Rylands, 1 December 1938, King's

231 'We went to the Watson': ibid.

231 'Eddie was very good': SR to George Rylands, 2 March 1939, King's

232 'it got underneath': Edward Bates to George Rylands, 1 December 1938, King's

232 'It was beautiful': SR, *Alphabet*, p. 153

232 'a rather ugly': SR, ibid., p. 154

233 'nearly all the market': ibid., p. 155

233 'royal white elephants': ibid.

233 'charming and elegant': ibid., p. 156

233 'really we have not': Edward Bates to George Rylands, 3 January 1939, King's

234 'Chula is terrific in Siam': SR to George Rylands, 2 March 1939, King's

234 '[Chula's] English wife': ibid.

234 'I am rather sorry': SR to RR, 16 January 1939, Elshieshields

234 'When I had talks': SR to WR, 4 January 1939, Elshieshields

235 'the old owl': Prince Birabongse of Siam to SR, 8 January 1939, Elshieshields

235 'clean, unhurrying train': SR, *Alphabet*, p. 26

235 'Malay peacocks are': ibid.

235 'I can only record': ibid.

236 'Where the superb': ibid., p. 27

236 'Love is a terrible': SR, 'Angkor: Jungle Poems', 'Juvenilia' notebook, Elshieshields

237 'On dirait un autre . . . a soft blue': Edward Bates to George Rylands, 3 January 1939, King's

237 'not a suitable': SR, *Alphabet*, p. 28

237 'two unknown Britishers . . . memorable deliciousness . . . The view up': ibid., p. 29

238 'he was only 13 . . . the most *énervant*': Edward Bates to George Rylands, 3 January 1939, King's

238 'Well, dear, somehow': ibid.

238 'young lady . . . laden': SR, *Alphabet*, p. 153

239 'In receiving the high': Field Marshal Plaek Phibunsongkhram to SR, 17 January 1940, Elshieshields

## CHAPTER 13: THE CHARIOT

240 'When [Papa] saw Ramsay': SR to RR, 5 November 1931, Elshieshields

241 'legalistic brain': SR to Stewart Perowne, 18 November 1953, Elshieshields

241 'a wedding cake': see https://www.martinrandall.com/gardens-and-villas-of-the-italian-lakes

241 'The Villa Taranto': SR, *Alphabet*, p. 108

242 'a handsome old': ibid.

243 '[Hoesch was] one of': Günther Henle, quoted in James and Patience Barnes, *Nazis in Pre-War London 1930–1939* (Sussex Academic Press, 2010), p. 88

243 'style and furnishings': ibid., p. 93

243 'that ubiquitous fellow ... arch-Hitler spy': quoted in Anne Edwards, *Matriarch: The Life of Queen Mary* (Rowman & Littlefield, 2014), p. 378

244 'hostile to, or at least': Barnes and Barnes, *Nazis in Pre-War London*, p. 85

244 'a complete homosexual': Jeremy Lewis, *Shades of Greene* (Jonathan Cape, 2010), p. 63

246 'The conductor woke': SR to HR, 14 March 1938, Elshieshields

247 'not very ambassadorial ... a risqué French': ibid.

247 'Small, dark, overflowing': Sir Maurice Peterson, *Both Sides of the Curtain* (Constable, 1950), p. 64

248 '[Lawrence] gave me': SR, *Alphabet*, p. 32

248 'as president of the British': SR to HR, 20 March 1938, Elshieshields

249 'it was a happy': SR, *Alphabet*, p. 31

249 'frightful': SR to HR, 27 March 1938, Elshieshields

250 'a splendid host': SR, *Alphabet*, p. 31

250 'suddenly there was': ibid.

250 'lacking in sparkle': SR, 'Footnotes', p. 83

251 'I've visited innumerable': SR to MR, 7 April 1938, Elshieshields

251 'I'm terribly glad': ibid.

251 'I have been interested': SR to HR, 15 April 1938, Elshieshields

253 'lacked practical experience': Paul Vyšný, *The Runciman Mission to Czechoslovakia, 1938* (Palgrave Macmillan, 2003), p. 74

253 'a strong impression': Clifford Norton quoted in ibid., p. 8

253 'a fictitious country': Sir Joseph Addison quoted in ibid., p. 10

253 'Friends? They eat': Addison quoted in Shiela Grant Duff, *The Parting of the Ways* (Peter Owen, 1982), p. 127

254 'record that would impress': Sir Horace Wilson quoted in Vyšný, *The Runciman Mission*, p. 76

254 'I quite understand': Walter Runciman, Cabinet meeting, 27 July 1938, The National Archives, Kew (hereafter TNA), CAB 23/94, Cab 35 (38)

254 'what a cockpit': Walter Runciman quoted in Vyšný, *The Runciman Mission*, p. 143

255 'delightful chief': Frank Ashton-Gwatkin quoted in ibid., p. 144

255 'Good Lord Runciman': ibid., p. 350

256 'would have to accompany': ibid., p. 76

256 'Doesn't sound like': HR journal, quoted in Karina Urbach, *Go-Betweens for Hitler* (Oxford University Press, 2015), p. 289

256 'It could, of course, be': Vyšný, *The Runciman Mission*, p. 331

258 'a fruitless diplomatic': SR, *Alphabet*, p. 103

258 'I was horrified': Oliver Harvey, 18 September 1938, *Diplomatic Diaries* (Collins, 1970), p. 186

259 'this is making way': ibid., p. 216

259 'vacillating and weak': King George VI quoted in Vyšný, *The Runciman Mission*, p. 334

259 'We don't listen': Rose Macaulay to Jean Smith, 15 September 1938, *Dearest Jean: Rose Macaulay's Letters to a Cousin*, ed. Martin Ferguson Smith (Manchester University Press, 2011)

259 'able, honest . . . high office': Hobhouse, 13 August 1912, *Inside Asquith's Cabinet*, p. 122

260 'For all its beauty': SR, *Alphabet*, p. 211

260 'Rather to my relief': ibid., p. 20

260 'advanced . . . somewhat . . . left-wing': references to BBC from Basil Nicholls, 15 November 1935; G. M. Trevelyan, 5 December 1935; J. Burnaby, 10 August 1936; all digitally accessible in BBC Archives

262 'I'll get rid': King Farouk quoted in Artemis Cooper, *Cairo in the War 1939–1945* (Hamish Hamilton, 1989), p. 60

262 'the boy': Michael Haag, *Alexandria: City of Memory* (Yale University Press, 2004), p. 159

263 'It certainly looks': SR to Freya Stark, 28 October 1940, Austin

263 'A lot of my work': SR to RR, 5 January 1941, Elshieshields

263 'I'll always be glad': ibid.

263 'Nobody could really': *Time*, 10 March 1941

263 'did a great deal': Sir George Rendel, *The Sword and the Olive* (John Murray, 1957), p. 169

264 'I wonder if': SR to RR, 5 January 1941, Elshieshields

264 'I have been racking': Courtenay Young to J. C. Robertson, 27 June 1951, TNA KV 2/4104

266 'preferred making history': *Time*, 12 February 1945

266 'a stupid man': Rendel, *The Sword and the Olive*, p. 179

266 'King Jekyll and King Hyde': ibid., p. 153

267 'almost everyone in Bulgaria . . . very few . . . any inherited': ibid., p. 140

267 'I felt embarrassed': SR, *Alphabet*, p. 21

267 'I do rather feel': SR to RR, 5 January 1941, Elshieshields

267 'undistinguished appearance': James McNeish, *Dance of the Peacocks: New Zealanders in Exile in the Time of Hitler and Mao Tse-tung* (Virago, 2003), p. 53

269 'Dining with Steven': Michael Padeff, *Escape from the Balkans* (Cassell, 1943), p. 13

269 'in dealing with people': ibid.

270 'I do not know': Rendel quoted in Padeff, *Escape from the Balkans*, p. 12

271 'It's getting rather hot': Cedric Salter quoted in Padeff, *Escape from the Balkans*, p. 13

271 'Like the perfect host': ibid.

271 'the most charming man': Prince Antoine Bibesco quoted in Simon Blow, obituary of Priscilla Bibesco, *Independent*, 27 November 2004

271 'Misho's arrest': SR, engagement diary for 1941, Elshieshields

272 'magnificent specimens, obviously': SR, *Alphabet*, p. 21

273 'a ghastly shambles': ibid., p. 22

273 'Her legs are gone': *Time*, 24 March 1941

274 'had time to see': SR, *Alphabet*, p. 22

274 'fantastic': Rendel, statement to press, 24 March 1941, transcription at Elshieshields

274 'that H. M. Legation': Rendel, report to Anthony Eden, 26 March 1941, Elshieshields


## CHAPTER 14: THE WHEEL OF FORTUNE

275 'Cairo had become': Olivia Manning, *Friends and Heroes* (William Heinemann, 1965), p. 12

275 'We did not suppose': Olivia Manning, *Modern Reading* (Phoenix House, 1943), p. 74

276 'Members of the Embassy': SR, *Alphabet*, p. 35

276 'None of the men': Manning, *Modern Reading*, p. 78

276 'These people would': ibid., p. 76

276 'stuffed ... against a shed': Anthony Powell, *The Military Philosophers* (William Heinemann, 1968), p. 190

277 'the Cairene scene': Henry Channon, 3 January 1941, *Chips: The Diaries of Sir Henry Channon*, ed. Robert Rhodes James (Weidenfeld & Nicolson, 1967), p. 280

277 'There was a sense': Manning, *Friends and Heroes*, p. 57

277 'It had an unreal': SR, *Alphabet*, p. 36

278 'Royalty is most': SR to WR, 3 April 1931, Elshieshields

279 'military camps ... an informal': SR, *Alphabet*, p. 203

279 'a wonderful place': SR to WR, 3 April 1931, Elshieshields

279 'dignified, and of Imperial': SR, *Alphabet*, p. 203

279 'the most sensational': ibid., p. 206

279 'Several years later': ibid.

279 'I am glad to have known ... a fair-haired, fair-skinned girl': ibid., p. 209

280 'It was a great asset ... What I most enjoyed': ibid., p. 208

280 'the more unyielding': John Connell, *The House by Herod's Gate* (Sampson Low, 1947), p. 135

280 'masterful': ibid., p. 137

280 'a certain sumptuous': ibid., p. 138

281 'Queen Mary I came': Michael Grant, *My First Eighty Years* (Aidan Ellis, 1994), p. 47

281 'And so, by remaining': ibid.

281 'İnönü ... had been driving': SR, *Alphabet*, p. 59

281 'the post has very': Michael Grant to SR, 17 October 1941, Elshieshields

282 'I may of course': SR to RR, 22 February 1942, Elshieshields

282 'there were, in amongst': Connell, *House by Herod's Gate*, p. 140

283 'the lecherous advances': SR, *Alphabet*, p. 60

283 'which had recovered': ibid., p. 62

283 'as a matter': ibid., p. 60

284 'a good scholar': ibid.

284 'high, old-fashioned': ibid., p. 61

285 'The leading young': ibid., p. 69

285 'vague and unreal': ibid., p. 68

285 'When a former': ibid., p. 66

286 'the richest expedition': SR to HR, 2 October 1943, Elshieshields

286 'a large wooden': SR, *Alphabet*, p. 61

286 'I can't honestly': SR to HR, 3 September 1943, Elshieshields

287 'The story was told': SR, *Alphabet*, p. 69

288 'One of the reasons': Grant, *My First Eighty Years*, p. 65

288 'Why, I believe you': Nicholas Elliott quoted in Ben Macintyre, *A Spy among Friends: Kim Philby and the Great Betrayal* (Bloomsbury, 2014), p. 79

288 'In fact I think': SR, *Alphabet*, p. 67

289 'The idea was that': David Abulafia, *Mediterranean Studies*, Vol. 9 (2000), p. 6

290 'non-Aryan and echt ... I was audible': SR to HR, 16 November 1943, Elshieshields

290 'Like all committees': SR to HR, 9 January 1944, Elshieshields

290 'It is even one': ibid.

290 '[The party] was made': ibid.

290 'I gave an enormous': SR to HR, 24 March 1944, Elshieshields

291 'Lectures were supposed': SR to HR, 16 November 1943, Elshieshields

291 '[Michael Grant] tells me ': SR to HR, 9 January 1944, Elshieshields

292 'However, a fortune-teller': SR to HR, 22 April 1944, Elshieshields

293 'Son Altesse le Çelebi': *laisser-passer* covering the Free French Mandate in Syria and the Lebanon, issued by Count Stanislas Ostrorog, 28 April 1944, Elshieshields

294 'I love you better': Giles Whittell, *Spitfire Women of World War II* (Harper Press, 2007), p. 223

294 'I had for weeks ': SR to HR, 10 May 1944, Elshieshields

295 'Alexandria is an extraordinary': SR to HR, 16 July 1944, Elshieshields

295 'the tenseness had': SR, *Alphabet*, p. 36

295 'It's all a poor': SR to HR, 16 July 1944, Elshieshields

296 'set an example': SR, *Alphabet*, p. 209

296 'I am staying . . . in a lovely': SR to HR, 9 August 1944, Elshieshields

297 'though nearly seventy . . . very vivacious': ibid.

## CHAPTER 15: THE STAR

298 'Nor law, nor duty': Yeats, 'An Irish Airman Foresees his Death', included in *The Wild Swans at Coole* (1919)

299 'the Cold Front': Whittell, *Spitfire Women*, p. 66

300 'blow-flies in their': Reader Bullard, *Letters from Tehran*, ed. Edward Christian Hodgkin (I. B. Tauris, 1991), p. 216

300 'a pathetic figure': Leslie Runciman quoted in Abbas Milani, *The Shah* (Macmillan, 2011), p. 140

300 'that vile stinking': Robert Byron quoted in James Buchan, *Days of God: The Revolution in Iran and its Consequences* (John Murray, 2012), p. 80

301 'One evening soon': SR, *Alphabet*, p. 167

301 'Tehran itself': SR to HR, 21 September 1944, Elshieshields

303 'Ah, the machine': Leslie Runciman quoted in Bullard, 24 September 1944, *Letters from Tehran*, p. 256

303 'One could have wished ': SR to HR, 21 September 1944, Elshieshields

303 'To the people ': 'Caractacus', a.k.a. Norman Daniel, *Revolution in Iraq* (Victor Gollancz, 1959), p. 23

304 'the Italian combinazione': Stewart Perowne memorandum to Ernest Bevin, quoted in William Roger Louis, *The British Empire in the Middle East: 1945–51* (Clarendon Press, 1984), p. 320

304 'I was asked': SR to HR, 18 October 1944, Elshieshields

305 'Agriculture was particularly': SR to HR, 5 March 1945, Elshieshields

305 'No city is': SR, *Alphabet*, p. 70

306 'as many Byzantines': ibid.

306 'young Turk who': SR to HR, 5 March 1945, Elshieshields

306 'I realized then': SR, *Alphabet*, p. 71

307 'molto intelligente': ibid., p. 66

307 'To look at': ibid., p. 67

308 'took the easy way . . . bundled . . . dining out': Michael Asher, *Thesiger* (Viking, 1994), p. 248

309 'to teach Arabic ': Bertram Thomas quoted in Leslie McLoughlin, *In a Sea of Knowledge: British Arabists in the 20th Century* (Ithaca Press, 2002), p. 120

309 'the Caliph Hakim': SR, *The First Crusade* (Cambridge University Press, 1951), p. 35

311 'They tell me': Steven Runciman quoted in Noel Annan, letter to George Rylands, 12 January 1945, King's

312 'this may give . . . Dear Steven always': ibid.

313 'long-haired, effeminate': *Evening Standard*, 22 March 1948

313 'mummified': Manning, *Friends and Heroes*, p. 49

313 'pretty pair': ibid., p. 35

313 'the old soul': ibid., p. 20

313 'I feel very strongly': C. F. W. Dundas to Lord Lloyd, 31 October 1940, quoted in Frances Donaldson, *The British Council: The First Fifty Years* (Jonathan Cape, 1984), p. 95

314 'We must be ': R. Seymour to Kenneth Johnstone, 2 December 1944, quoted in Sir Michael Llewellyn-Smith, 'Steven Runciman at the British Council', lecture at Athens, February 2012

## CHAPTER 16: JUSTICE

316 'We have forced': SR to HR, 28 November 1945, Elshieshields

317 'a charming erudite': Maurice Cardiff, *Friends Abroad* (Radcliffe Press, 1991), p. 1

317 'I had imagined I': ibid., p. 2

317 'much less conventional': Geoffrey Wheatcroft, obituary of Maurice Cardiff, *Guardian*, 20 June 2006

318 'I was pleased ': SR to HR, 7 October 1945, Elshieshields

318 'friendly and charming': Cardiff, *Friends Abroad*, p. 17

318 'The whole organisation': SR to HR, 16 October 1945, Elshieshields

319 'I was prompted': Cardiff, *Friends Abroad*, p. 17

319 'Naples is shabby': SR to HR, 7 October 1945, Elshieshields

320 'he looked like': Bevis Hillier, 'Lancaster, Sir Osbert', *ODNB*

320 'almost ostentatiously recognisable': Osbert Lancaster quoted in Richard Boston, *Osbert* (Collins, 1989), p. 136

321 'the most popular': SR to HR, 31 October 1945, Elshieshields

322 'the Regent Archbishop's': SR to HR, 18 April 1946, Elshieshields

322 'very meagre and ugly ... Anyhow it is ... I am giving': SR to HR, 24 October 1945, Elshieshields

322 'a large gentle': SR to Stewart Perowne, 12 October 1952, Elshieshields

322 'No doubt ... I must': Cardiff, *Friends Abroad*, p. 17

323 'very nasty set': Maurice Cardiff conversation with Ann Shukman, June 2002

323 'did become something': Wheatcroft, Cardiff obituary

324 'we are to have eighty': Rex Warner quoted in Stephen Tabachnick, *Fiercer than Tigers: The Life and Works of Rex Warner* (Michigan State University Press, 2002), p. 229

324 'Quick to spot': Cardiff, *Friends Abroad*, p. 11

324 'A for Personality': Llewellyn-Smith, 'Steven Runciman at the British Council'

324 'though very charming': Tabachnick, *Fiercer than Tigers*, p. 215

325 'one kept seeing': SR to HR, 31 October 1945, Elshieshields

325 'all the great ... not very good': SR to HR, 31 October 1945, Elshieshields

325 'The political situation': SR to HR, 28 November 1945, Elshieshields

326 'I don't think': Cardiff conversation with Ann Shukman

326 'I had also to say ... Almost all of them': SR to HR, 14 December 1945, Elshieshields

326 'scarcely commendable ... the sight': ibid.

327 'like travelling in ... I gave them': SR to HR, 17 December 1945, Elshieshields

327 'E.A.M., the Communist': SR to HR, 8 January 1946, Elshieshields

327 'He was very cordial': ibid.

327 'a liking for Greece': SR to HR, 12 April 1946, Elshieshields

327 'mostly in circles': SR to HR, 14 January 1946, Elshieshields

328 '[The Embassy] are determined': ibid.

328 'a dockers' strike': SR to HR, 3 February 1946, Elshieshields

329 'I had two Orthodox ... a praiseworthy institution ... a portentous gentleman': SR to HR, 10 February 1946, Elshieshields

329 'the private army': Hugh Seton-Watson quoted in Stephen Dorril, *MI6: Inside the Covert World of Her Majesty's Secret Intelligence Service* (Simon & Schuster, 2002), p. 309

330 'Ann darling': SR to Ann Shukman, 9 August 1944, Elshieshields

330 'state of non-being ... undoubtedly would find ... loved spying out': Ann Shukman to author, 30 April 2014

330 'she was not very': SR to HR, 13 March 1946, Elshieshields

330 'what difference the new': SR to HR, 17 March 1946, Elshieshields

330 'the Russian Ambassador ... It was a dreary': SR to HR, 24 March 1946, Elshieshields

331 'The impression that ': SR to HR, 31 March 1946, Elshieshields

331 'A heavy-built blear-eyed': SR to HR, 24 March 1946, Elshieshields

331 'It was her intention': Cardiff, *Friends Abroad*, p. 6

331 'Lady N. goes about': SR to HR, 31 March 1946, Elshieshields

332 'the whole campaign': ibid.

333 'would abdicate in favour': SR to HR, 12 April 1946, Elshieshields

333 'just the type': SR to HR, 18 April 1946, Elshieshields

333 'Justinian and Theodora': Cardiff conversation with Ann Shukman

333 'altogether (unlike the British': SR to HR, 18 April 1946, Elshieshields

333 'My literary party': ibid.

334 'though I very much': SR to LR, 21 April 1946, Elshieshields

335 'we rowed out ': SR to HR, 4 May 1946, Elshieshields

335 ' ... I spent yesterday ... I hope by then ': SR to HR, 12 May 1946, Elshieshields

335 'She is almost': SR to HR, 18 May 1946, Elshieshields

336 'mere Battenberg ... As Queen Victoria's': SR, *Alphabet*, p. 46

336 'which governs them ': SR to HR, 31 May 1946, Elshieshields

336 'all the priests ... I feel that ... that colourful old': ibid.

337 'suddenly launched into': Ian S. MacNiven, *Lawrence Durrell* (Faber & Faber, 1998), p. 332

337 'in the ruins': Artemis Cooper, *Patrick Leigh Fermor: An Adventure* (Hachette, 2012), p. 211

337 'As if by heaven': John Craxton to Richard Morphet, 16 June 1986, Tate Archives, London

338 'Oh Quee! I can't': John Craxton to E. Q. Nicholson, undated, 1946, Tate

338 'I have absolutely ... a nice Anichist': ibid.

338 'I must say': SR to HR, 7 June 1946, Elshieshields

338 ' ... I don't know ... They are quick': SR to Nigel Logan, 29 September 1946, Elshieshields

339 'very pleasant simple': SR to HR, 24 June 1946, Elshieshields

339 'for Greece, a large ... looking rather shabby': ibid.

339 'we had to go': SR to HR, 29 July 1946, Elshieshields

340 'the good bandit': Nigel Clive obituary of Steven Runciman, *Guardian*, 3 November 2000

340 'an unalluring figure ... I doubt': SR to HR, 4 August 1946, Elshieshields

340 'Marooned in his': Cardiff, *Friends Abroad*, p. 22

340 'that terrible fellow': ibid.

341 'The Crown Prince': SR to HR, 2 November 1946, Elshieshields

341 'He has grown up ': SR to HR, 15 November 1946, Elshieshields

341 'worldly-wise, amusing, scholarly': John Lehmann, *The Ample Proposition* (Eyre & Spottiswoode, 1966), p. 59

341 'Gigantic, brilliantly coloured': ibid., p. 60

342 'a dear old man ... no trouble at all ... a grim humourless': SR to HR, 28 November 1946, Elshieshields

342 'we have fought': SR to HR, 4 August 1946, Elshieshields

342 'amiable, pompous, boring': SR to HR, 28 November 1946, Elshieshields

342 'Dr Morgan ... is': SR to HR, 6 December 1946, Elshieshields

343 'Mr Lee-Fermore is': Maurice Bowra, report to British Council, quoted in Llewellyn-Smith, 'Steven Runciman at the British Council'

343 'little irregularities': Cooper, *Patrick Leigh Fermor*, p. 206

343 'older than the rocks': ibid., p. 213

344 'is coming all out': SR to LR, 15 December 1956, Elshieshields

344 'charming, gay and disreputable': SR to HR, 26 December 1946, Elshieshields

344 'a good-looking young ... I think there': ibid.

345 'icons, tanagras, Mycenean': Nigel Clive, *A Greek Experience* (Michael Russell, 1985), p. 180

345 'The Princess again': SR to HR, 15 January 1947, Elshieshields

346 'descended upon us': SR to HR, 31 January 1947, Elshieshields

346 'If he's a good': SR to HR, 7 June 1946, Elshieshields

346 'He is not difficult': SR to HR, 31 January 1947, Elshieshields

346 'we opened an Exhibition ... very royal': ibid.

347 'laughed more heartily': SR to HR, 6 February 1947, Elshieshields

347 'Our great event ... He was not': SR to HR, 4 April 1947, Elshieshields

347 'snivelled quite sadly ... excellently managed ... I was surprised': ibid.

348 'was very well ... The King's lady': ibid.

348 'We are still': SR to HR, 9 April 1947, Elshieshields

## CHAPTER 17: THE HERMIT

349 'private means': Ronald Montagu Burrows, Principal of King's College London, quoted in Richard Clogg, *Politics and the Academy: Arnold Toynbee and the Koraes Chair* (Routledge, 2013), p. 25

350 'If they want': SR to HR, 19 January 1947, Elshieshields

350 'I don't like': ibid.

350 'I can't say': SR to HR, 21 February 1947, Elshieshields

351 'would be very': Maurice Bowra recalled by Cardiff, conversation with Ann Shukman

351 'some worthless British . . . a worthless Cambridge . . . knew how to': Isaiah Berlin to Noel Annan, 31 August 1973, in Berlin, *Building: Letters 1960–1975*, ed. Henry Hardy and Mark Pottle (Chatto & Windus, 2013), p. 548

351 'dallying . . . I'm terribly shocked': SR to Freya Stark, 18 February 1947, Austin

352 'I love this country': SR to Princess Bibesco, 8 January 1946, Austin

352 'I believe it': SR to HR, 27 February 1947, Elshieshields

352 'a letter pleading . . . The escapades . . . as he visited': ibid.

353 'the most beautiful': SR to Princess Bibesco, 8 January 1946, Austin

353 'heart-broken to leave': SR to Freya Stark, 24 April 1947, Austin

353 'I gave a lecture': SR to HR, 6 March 1947, Elshieshields

353 'the poor man': ibid.

354 'a very civilized': SR to Freya Stark, 18 October 1953, Austin

354 'Truman's declaration on Greece': SR to HR, 28 March 1947, Elshieshields

355 'He took up': SR to HR, 7 May 1947, Elshieshields

355 'She is extremely': SR to HR, 31 May 1947, Elshieshields

355 'Though mad and rather': SR to HR, 23 April 1947, Elshieshields

356 'you are the only . . . I do like diplomats': SR to HR, 10 June 1947, Elshieshields

356 'which I was incorrectly . . . The officer of gendarmerie': ibid.

357 'That Madonna is': SR to Freya Stark, 24 April 1947, Austin

357 'too hot for . . . the excellent and not': SR to HR, 21 June 1947, Elshieshields

357 'a pale, gentle . . . We are chaperoned': ibid.

358 'The place has': Freya Stark, *Traveller's Prelude* (John Murray, 1950), p. 31

359 'we made one': SR to HR, 29 June 1947, Elshieshields

359 'stream of people . . . a quiet little': Freya Stark to Sir Sydney Cockerell, *Letters*, vol. 6: *The Broken Road 1947–52*, ed. Lucy Moorehead (Michael Russell, 1981), p. 16

359 'a very amiable': SR to HR, 29 June 1947, Elshieshields

360 'pathetic . . . with his minor': ibid.

360 'My visit to Asolo': SR to Freya Stark, 4 July 1947, Austin

360 'I can't help': SR to Freya Stark, 28 September 1947, Austin

361 'Of the two': SR to Freya Stark, 4 July 1947, Austin

361 'I am doing': SR to Freya Stark, 28 September 1947, Austin

361 'would start the whole': Philip Ziegler, *Diana Cooper* (Faber & Faber, 2011), p. 309

362 'a quiet literary': SR to LR, 21 July 1946, Elshieshields

363 'I am much enjoying': SR to Stewart Perowne, 15 February 1954, Elshieshields

364 'Can you write . . . That is almost': J. C. Masterman, *On the Chariot Wheel* (Oxford University Press, 1975), p. 206

364 'Very limited intelligence . . . by and large': Hugh Trevor-Roper, quoted in Mark Hollingsworth and Nick Fielding, *Defending the Realm: MI5 and the Shayler Affair* (André Deutsch, 1999), p. 18

364 'a serpentine character': Adam Sisman, *Hugh Trevor-Roper* (Weidenfeld & Nicolson, 2010), p. 93

365 'unambitious archivists': Hugh Trevor-Roper to J. C. Masterman, 13 December 1956, Christ Church, Oxford

365 'our present Regius': ibid.

365 'a plebeian character': Hugh Trevor-Roper to Bernard Berenson, 22 March 1957, Trevor-Roper, *Letters from Oxford*, ed. Richard Davenport-Hines (Weidenfeld & Nicolson, 2006), p. 220

365 'as clever as . . . no gentleman': V. H. Galbraith quoted in Sisman, *Hugh Trevor-Roper*, p. 194

365 'I fear I should': SR to Roy Harrod, 2 December 1924, British Library, London

366 'Mr. Runciman's learning': Hugh Trevor-Roper, *Guardian*, 23 February 1951

366 'A great movement': Hugh Trevor-Roper, *New Statesman*, 3 March 1951

366 'Medieval Manchester Mice': Hugh Trevor-Roper to Bernard Berenson, 22 March 1957, Trevor-Roper, *Letters from Oxford*, p. 220

366 'For mere interest': Hugh Trevor-Roper to J. C. Masterman, 13 December 1956, Christ Church

367 'there is one English': Hugh Trevor-Roper to Bernard Berenson, 18 February 1951, Trevor-Roper, *Letters from Oxford*, p. 61

368 'Having once escaped': SR to Hugh Trevor-Roper, 21 July 1956, Elshieshields

369 ' . . . [Runciman] can write': Hugh Trevor-Roper to J. C. Masterman, 13 December 1956, Christ Church

369 'My suspicion is': Sisman, *Hugh Trevor-Roper*, p. 280

370 'I'm interested in': SR to LR, 12 February 1957, Elshieshields

371 'Runciman is my man': Hugh Trevor-Roper to J. C. Masterman, 13 December 1956, Christ Church

371 'I love this city . . . the sheerest fantasy': SR to LR, 12 February 1957, Elshieshields

371 'I learn from yesterday's': SR to Hugh Trevor-Roper, 21 February 1957, Elshieshields

371 'If [A. J. P.] Taylor is': Hugh Trevor-Roper to Wallace Notestein, *One Hundred Letters from Hugh Trevor-Roper*, ed. Richard Davenport-Hines and Adam Sisman (Oxford University Press, 2014), p. 64

371 'Macmillan and Masterman': V. H. Galbraith quoted in Kathleen Burk, *Troublemaker: The Life and History of A. J. P. Taylor* (Yale University Press, 2002), p. 211

372 'the only people': Donald Nicol recalled by Ruth Macrides, conversation with author, December 2014

373 'Something prevented me': ibid.

373 'Thank you for': SR to Donald Nicol, 20 June 1952, King's College Archives, London (hereafter KCL)

374 'fairly business-like': SR to Donald Nicol, 23 June 1955, KCL

374 "Dölger . . . is very': SR to Donald Nicol, 20 June 1952, KCL

374 'to be ordered': SR to Donald Nicol, 5 August 1958, KCL

374 'a man of intense': SR, *Alphabet*, p. 107

374 'Yesterday I saw': SR to Donald Nicol, 25 February 1953, KCL

374 'Grégoire moves in': SR to Donald Nicol, 6 October 1953, KCL

374 ' . . . you must surely ': SR to Donald Nicol, 23 June 1955, KCL

375 'a fussy and incurably': SR to Donald Nicol, 25 November 1955, KCL

375 'Lemerle's effusion . . . is': SR to Donald Nicol, 16 April 1959, KCL

375 'It's very impressive': SR to Donald Nicol, 13 March 1957, KCL

376 'remarkable man': SR, *The Greek Church in Captivity* (Cambridge University Press, 1968), p. 392

376 'monster': Steven Runciman quoted in Plante profile, *New Yorker*

376 'I was offered': SR to Donald Nicol, 20 April 1962, KCL

## CHAPTER 18: THE TRILOGY

379 'the wars of the Crusaders': see e.g. John Wolfe, *Religion in History* (Manchester University Press, 2004), p. 61

379 'Isaac and the elephant': SR, 'Charlemagne and Palestine', *English Historical Review*, Vol. 50, No. 200, October 1935, p. 608

380 'hoping to write ... come and see ... [Wavell] kindly had': SR, *Alphabet*, p. 31

381 'Their enterprise itself': W. B. Stevenson, *Crusaders in the East* (Cambridge University Press, 1907), p. 1

381 'he had fought': SR, *The First Crusade*, p. 4

381 'died of a broken': ibid., p. 5

381 'His style is': ibid., p. 331

381 'modern historians are': ibid., p. 327

382 '*Beau Geste*': Robert Irwin, review of Christopher Tyerman, *God's War*, *Times Literary Supplement*, 8 September 2006, p. 4

383 'In truth Alexius ... Roussel disappears': SR, *The First Crusade*, p. 67

384 '[Peter the Hermit] was': ibid., p. 113

384 'The brothers formed': ibid, p. 146

384 'About the middle': SR, *The Kingdom of Jerusalem* (Cambridge University Press, 1952), p. 369

385 'Though an utter': ibid., p. 480

385 'William ... is one': ibid., p. 477

386 'accurate and reliable': ibid., p. 475

386 'It seems to me': R. C. Smail, Third Programme broadcast, 6 April 1951

387 'blend of scholarly ... provides, indirectly': Bruce Bain, *Tribune*, 29 October 1954

387 'All over the Empire': SR, *The First Crusade*, p. 16

387 'Unlike Christianity, which': ibid., p. 15

387 'I came not': Matthew 10: 34 (Authorized Version)

388 'a disastrous and evil': Steven Runciman quoted in Robert Thicknesse, 'No Holding Back', *Tablet*, 7 December 2013

388 'didn't really approve': SR to Leslie Perowne, 24 November 1939, Elshieshields

388 'The Christian citizen': SR, *The First Crusade*, p. 83

388 'The Byzantine soldier': ibid.

389 'He was a bad': SR, *The Kingdom of Acre* (Cambridge University Press, 1954), p. 75

389 'The code of chivalry': SR, *The First Crusade*, p. 84

389 'one of the most ... a shameful thing': ibid.

389 'Godfrey of Bouillon ... appears': ibid., p. 145

390 'blackmail': ibid., p. 136

390 'a certain Volkmar ... a multitude of simple': ibid., p. 64

390 'It was not a very ... Small as was': ibid., p. 65

390 'the Germans, with': SR, *The Kingdom of Acre*, p. 16

391 'communities of will': Kenneth Clark, 'Protest and Communication', part 6 of *Civilisation*

392 'it was only': SR, *The First Crusade*, p. 78

392 'His policy was': ibid., p. 80

392 'it is probable that Bohemond's': ibid., p. 87

393 'His person was': ibid., p. 81

393 'not so-suppressed ... mischievous ... That remark': Christopher Tyerman, conversation with author, May 2012

393 'If Anna admired': Georgina Buckler, *Anna Comnena: A Study* (Oxford University Press, 1929), p. 57

394 'I have followed': SR, *The Kingdom of Jerusalem*, p. 47

394 'Even in the private': ibid., p. 20

394 'It is probable that Alexius': ibid., p. 137

394 'It may be that': ibid., p. 213

395 'Had the Mongols': SR, *The Kingdom of Acre*, p. 313

395 'There they killed': SR, *The Kingdom of Jerusalem*, p. 20

395 'The fate of the Margravine': ibid., p. 29

395 'Rudel seems certainly': SR, *The Kingdom of Acre*, p. 410

396 'It was not the little': ibid., p. 144

396 'cites Munro's article': Peter Raedts, 'The Children's Crusade of 1213', *Journal of Medieval History*, Vol. 3, issue 4, 1977

396 'Comedy militates against': Alfred J. Andrea and Andrew Holt, *Seven Myths of the Crusades* (Hackett, 2015), p. xxvi

397 'scrupulous in their study': SR, preface to Reavell and Reavell, *E. F. Benson*, p. 7

397 'There, at the end': SR, *The Kingdom of Jerusalem*, p. 178

397 'In choosing a husband': ibid., p. 332

397 'Andronicus, though already': ibid., p. 377

398 'Mohammed in his turn': ibid., p. 41

398 'He was succeeded': ibid., p. 127

398 'Since the loss': ibid., p. 365

399 'A more delicate': SR, *The Kingdom of Acre*, p. 40

399 'a conspiracy of silence': John Harvey, *The Plantagenets* (Batsford, 1948), p. 33

399 'given over to venery': SR, *The First Crusade*, p. 72

399 'Baldwin was fond': SR, *The Kingdom of Jerusalem*, p. 102

400 'The Countess set out ... All the country': ibid., p. 103

400 'a renegade Moslem': ibid., p. 92

401 'There was never': SR, *The Kingdom of Acre*, p. 130

401 're-opening of the African': Resolutions of the Republican Convention, Chicago, 1860

401 'There is no greater': SR, *Alphabet*, p. 91

402 'He was profoundly': SR, *The Kingdom of Acre*, p. 128

402 'Did you ever': Uri Avnery, 'On Crusaders and Zionists', *Tikkun*, 11 October 2014

403 'The triumphs of the Crusade': SR, *The Kingdom of Acre*, p. 480

403 'we cannot withhold ... At any moment': SR, 'The Families of Outremer', Creighton Lecture, King's College London, 1959

## CHAPTER 19: STRENGTH

406 'Upon the earth': SR to Charles Turner, 7 March 1961, New York Public Library, New York

406 'LIBERAL ELDER STATESMAN ... one of those who lent': *The Times* obituary of Viscount Runciman of Doxford, 15 November 1949

407 'at best a thankless ... killed flying in': ibid.

407 'My father's death': SR to Freya Stark, 30 November 1949, Austin

408 'Mamma's life being': SR to LR, 21 July 1946, Elshieshields

408 'the embarrassment of the baronetcy': LR to SR, 25 November 1949, Elshieshields

408 'I never much cared': SR to Freya Stark, 30 September 1950, Austin

411 'my mother and brother': SR to Freya Stark, 7 December 1948, Austin

411 'the sweetheart of Eigg': Miriam James to author, 15 September 2014

412 'There was an evil': Steven Runciman recalled by John Chancellor, conversation with author, May 2012

412 'we didn't get on': John Chancellor, conversation with author

412 'immoral earnings': ibid.; see also SR to Leslie Perowne, 24 November 1939, Elshieshields

412 'On a February day': SR, *The First Crusade*, p. 1

413 'sitting in solitude': SR to Stewart Perowne, 3 August 1951, Elshieshields

413 'a more stimulating': SR to LR, 21 April 1946, Elshieshields

414 'Hail to thee': Camille Dressler, *Eigg: The Story of an Island* (Polygon, 1998), p. 50

414 'Pity me, oh': SR to KR, 2 April 1930, Elshieshields

415 'a lady who': SR to Charles Turner, 7 March 1961, NYPL

416 'Papa, Uncle Jack': SR to KR, 5 October 1926, Elshieshields

416 'lovely days of slaughter': SR to LR, 15 December 1946, Elshieshields

416 'the British Liberace': Clive Lythgoe obituary, *Daily Telegraph*, 18 September 2006

416 'a handy man': Noel Banks, *Six Inner Hebrides* (David & Charles, 1977), p. 105

417 'You may talk': SR, 'A Drop of Scotch', *Listener*, 15 January 1959

418 'velvet caps, parakeets': Simon Elliot, conversation with author, May 2012

418 'Before I knew it': ibid.

419 'to have conversation ... he was a kind': Elliot, conversation with author

419 'towering, incandescent ... This young professor': ibid.

419 '[Steven's] mood did': ibid.

419 'How well are you ... the deeply obscure': ibid.

420 'he certainly could ... He was a snob': ibid.

420 'He had a tongue ... He didn't talk ... one of the great': ibid.

421 'arduous passage ... trying not to slip ... a boat designed': SR, 'Some Personal Memories', *Labrys*, 1983

421 'hardly had they arrived': ibid.

421 'The strange thing': George Seferis, *Meres 1956–1960*, ed. Theano Michaelidou (Ikaros, 1990), p. 206

421 'Celts are the Romans': George Seferis recalled by Steven Runciman in *Pemptousia* interview, 2000

421 'the west coast': SR, 'Some Personal Memories'

421 'The isles of Scotland!': Edwin Morgan, *Sonnets from Scotland* (Mariscat, 1984)

422 'tawdry Ulysses': ibid.

422 'After interviewing a number': SR to Stewart Perowne, 14 October 1955, Elshieshields

422 'ran Rutherford ... insolent son of Eli': SR to LR, 7 May 1958, Elshieshields

423 'The situation over the dog-slain': SR to LR, 24 May 1959, Elshieshields

424 'There were no real ... a mixed-up kid': Steven Runciman quoted in Duncan Fallowell, *How to Disappear* (Aurum, 2013), p. 132

424 'dangerous, rotten, barmy': Keith Schellenberg, quoted in the *Guardian*, 20 April 1999

425 'I hope you will': SR to LR, 22 August 1960, Elshieshields

425 'recovering remarkably well': SR to Freya Stark, 3 September 1954, Austin

425 'ghastly family tragedy ... Oliver shot himself': SR to Stewart Perowne, 28 January 1954, Elshieshields

425 'after eighty-seven years ... There should have': SR to Princess Bibesco, 12 November 1956, Austin

427 'You will want': SR to LR, 20 July 1961, Elshieshields

428 'one cannot honestly': ibid.

428 'Mrs John Angus': ibid.

428 'Garry seems to want': SR to LR, 23 March 1963, Elshieshields

429 'sentimental': SR to LR, 23 November 1961, Elshieshields

429 'I am a little': ibid.

429 'Though nominally fond': SR to Elizabeth Wansbrough, 26 May 1966, Bodleian Library, Oxford

429 'I shall have to break': ibid.

429 'a Border tower': ibid.

430 'after Eigg, [the tower]': SR to George Rylands, 10 January 1967, King's

430 'my next-door neighbour': Robert MacNeil of Barra to SR, 20 November 1958, Elshieshields

430 'that admirable Campbell': SR to LR, 22 February 1959, Elshieshields

430 'Arts and Crafty': SR to KR, 8 October 1926, Elshieshields

430 'a temporary man': SR to LR, 11 January 1962, Elshieshields

431 'Peter Wormell of the Nature': ibid.

431 ' . . . George Orwell in Jura': Dressler, *Eigg*, p. 144

432 'It is very melancholy': SR to RR, 16 September 1966, Elshieshields

433 'I don't really feel': SR to Guy Black, undated, before May 1996

433 'I wish the new': SR to Guy Black, 9 August 1997

## CHAPTER 20: A WIDE CANVAS

435 'The canvas is wide': SR, *The Sicilian Vespers* (Cambridge University Press, 1958), p. x

435 'That was an unfortunate': SR, *The Sicilian Vespers*, p. ix

435 'largely because I': SR to Freya Stark, 20 September 1954, Austin

436 'the whole history of the Mediterranean world': ibid.

436 'within three pages': SR to William Dalrymple, 'The Last Crusader', *Country Life*, March 1991

436 'I know the eastern': SR to Freya Stark, 20 September 1954, Austin

437 'a chapter for the nightmarish': SR to Freya Stark, 3 November 1954, Austin

437 'It's such a good': SR to Stewart Perowne, 6 April 1955, Elshieshields

437 'Some of the Hohenstaufen . . . the recently published': SR, *The Sicilian Vespers*, p. x

437 'entire ... wanton': see e.g. Robert M. Edsel, *Saving Italy* (W. W. Norton, 2013), p. 78

438 'an immense void': Riccardo Filangieri, *American Archivist*, Vol. 7, No. 4, October 1944, p. 255

438 'to give some account': SR to Freya Stark, 29 April 1956, Austin

438 'Italy without Sicily': Johann von Goethe, *Italian Journey* (1787), quoted in SR, 'Sicily: An Introduction', lecture text, February 1957

438 'In the whole history of the Mediterranean world': ibid.

439 'It is not surprising': ibid.

439 'more leisurely and massive': C. V. Wedgwood, *London Magazine*, August 1958

439 'This book demonstrates': Peter Green, *Times Literary Supplement*, 11 April 1958

440 'Few islands have been': SR, *The Sicilian Vespers*, p. 1

440 'Man has been less': ibid.

440 'very little is known': SR, 'Sicily' lecture text

440 'Who the Siculi': SR, *The Sicilian Vespers*, p. 1

440 'petty wars ... endemic pastime': ibid.

440 'now and then a Tyrant': ibid., p. 2

441 'when he was taking': ibid., p. 4

441 'William II [Norman King': ibid., p. 7

441 'something like a *Who's Who*': Aubrey Gwynn, *Irish Historical Studies*, Vol. 11, No. 44, September 1959, p. 368

441 'the race of vipers': Pope Innocent IV, quoted in SR, *The Sicilian Vespers*, p. 16

442 'rather stuck ... unable to decide': SR to Freya Stark, 11 February 1953, Austin

442 'His conversation, when': SR, *The Kingdom of Acre*, p. 175

442 'Runciman is now': Kenneth Rexroth, *Nation*, 17 May 1958

443 'readable': David Abulafia, *Frederick II* (Oxford University Press, 1988), p. 455

443 'thorough-going conservative ... man of his time': ibid., p. 438

443 'Though [Frederick] was by blood': SR, *The Kingdom of Acre*, p. 176

443 '[Runciman] is quietly and effectively': Wedgwood, *London Magazine* review

443 'not a Sicilian, nor a Roman': Abulafia, *Frederick II*, p. 439

444 're-do the history ... one does not impudently': Abulafia, *Mediterranean Studies* review, 2000

444 'a brilliant and glamorous': SR, *The Sicilian Vespers*, p. 35

445 'Dante describes [Manfred]': ibid., p. 297

445 'Belles qualités, affabilité': Emile Léonard, *Les Angevins de Naples* (Presses Universitaires de France, 1954), p. 40

445 '[Manfred] had already': SR, *The Sicilian Vespers*, p. 35

446 'embarrassing papal opposition': ibid., p. 298

446 'With little family': ibid., p. 71

447 'guilt at loving': ibid., p. 77

447 'His personal ambition': ibid., p. 255

447 'unkind ... too occupied with rescuing ... his contemporaries': Jean Dunbabin, *Charles I of Anjou* (Longman, 1998), p. 235

447 'The new king': SR, *The Sicilian Vespers*, p. 97

447 'neither visible nor audible': Pope Clement IV, quoted in ibid., p. 98

448 'nothing so much': Green, *TLS* review

448 'Gossip attributed his': SR, *The Sicilian Vespers*, p. 70

448 'When last they had': ibid., p. 71

448 'Charles's ambition was': ibid., p. 136

448 'still the best': ibid., p. 200

449 'Its fall was an insult': ibid., p. 284

449 'Charles was put': ibid., p. 141

450 'The Greek element': ibid., p. 212

450 'of all the peoples': ibid.

450 'It is remarkable': ibid., p. 292

450 'Bloodshed is an evil': ibid., p. 287

450 'Should I dare': the Emperor Michael VIII Palaeologus quoted in ibid., p. 219

451 'The barons of Outremer': ibid., p. 101

451 'On 15th September 1267': ibid., p. 103

451 'muttering hopefully that': ibid., p. 108

452 'Crowds met him': ibid.

452 'It is often impossible': SR, *Alphabet*, p. 71

452 'behind the fold': SR, *The Sicilian Vespers*, p. 111

452 'After a disastrous': ibid., p. 113

452 'Conradin's boyish charm': ibid., p. 115

453 'It was the only': ibid.

453 'What you [that is': Heinrich Heine, 'Religion and Philosophy in Germany', first pub. 1835, included in *The Romantic School and Other* Essays, ed. Jost Hermand, trans. Robert C. Holub (Continuum, 1998), p. 226

453 'The rebellion in Sicily': SR, *The Sicilian Vespers*, p. 227

453 'The real duel': ibid., p. 240

454 'It is not till': T. S. R. Boase, *English Historical Review*, April 1959

454 'Easter fell early': SR, *The Sicilian Vespers*, p. 213

455 'Among them was': ibid., p. 215

455 'Sicilian girls who': ibid.

455 'the lesson of the Vespers': Green, *TLS* review

456 'the grandest conception': SR, *The Sicilian Vespers*, p. x

456 'no mean ideal': ibid., p. 22

456 'gradual suicide': ibid., p. x

456 'Runciman intersperses his account': Palmer A. Throop, *American Historical Review*, Vol. 65, No. 1, October 1959, p. 104

456 'The Lady Machalda': SR, *The Sicilian Vespers*, p. 231

457 'The emir [of Jerba]': ibid., p. 253

457 'It would have helped': Hélène Wieruszowski, *Speculum – A Journal of Mediaeval Studies*, Vol. 34, No. 2, April 1959, p. 323

457 'my first outstanding pupil': A. L. Rowse quoted in G. R. Batho, 'Wedgwood, Dame (Cecily) Veronica', *ODNB*

458 'rather priggish and self-righteous': SR to C. V. Wedgwood, 22 May 1950, Elshieshields

458 'although the understanding': C. V. Wedgwood, *Times Literary Supplement*, 6 January 1956

459 'Steven Runciman's wise': ibid.

459 '*The Decline and Fall*': Alfred Duggan, *Tablet*, 24 December 1960

459 'The historical novelist': ibid.

460 'Most historians, I suspect . . . the braid, braid road': SR, 'Medieval History and the Romantic Imagination'

460 'O see ye not': Thomas the Rhymer (trad.), *The Romance and Prophecies of Thomas of* Ercildoune, ed. Sir James Murray (Early English Text Society, 1875), p. lv

460 'the chief lesson . . . For myself, I am': SR, 'Medieval History and the Romantic Imagination'

461 'the novels of Mme Oldenbourg': ibid.

461 'that most romantic': ibid.

461 'History is an art . . . the language of the Gothic': ibid.

462 'The great scientist . . . We should be careful': ibid.

462 'alien to the sparkling . . . never more terrible': ibid.

462 'I feel a certain . . . a form of history . . . more than just': ibid.

463 'To my surprise': SR to Freya Stark, 20 July 1965, Austin

464 'What gave me': SR to George Seferis, 30 December 1954, Gennadeion

464 'it is the first': George Seferis to SR, 3 September 1963, Gennadeion

464 'What a splendid': George Seferis to SR, 17 December 1966, Gennadeion

464 'In many districts': SR, *The Fall of Constantinople 1453* (Cambridge University Press, 1965), p. 10

464 ' . . . Nearby the Hippodrome': ibid.

465 ' . . . You might still': ibid., p. 11

465 'The splendid civilization': ibid., p. xii

465 'fallen with his fallen': ibid., p. xiii

465 'with the Empire as': ibid., p. 191

465 'In this story': ibid., p. xiii

465 'a distinguished guest . . . for all his high . . . lawful heir of Augustus . . . Emperor of the Greeks': ibid., p. 1

465 'I reflected how grievous': ibid.

466 'In the days when ': ibid., p. xi

466 'The stream of history': ibid.

467 'vitally important . . . two peoples': ibid., p. xii

467 'The history of Byzantine ': SR, 'Byzantine and Hellene in the Fourteenth Century', lecture at Thessalonica, 1951

467 'Hellenic blood . . . the last decades': ibid.

467 'The history of the last . . . The advocates of Hellenism': ibid.

468 'To the humanists': SR, *The Fall of Constantinople*, p. 21

468 'that epic story': SR, 'Byzantine and Hellene in the Fourteenth Century'

468 'Hellas meant something': ibid.

469 'it offers a very': Steven Runciman quoted in *Pemptousia* interview

469 'the primary significance': George Seferis, unpublished review of SR, *The Kingdom of Acre*, Gennadius Library, Athens

469 'The Greek world': SR, 'Byzantine and Hellene in the Fourteenth Century'

469 'the old, lay': ibid.

469 'in its last decades': SR, *The Fall of Constantinople*, p. 15

470 'In the orchards': ibid., p. 86

470 'Fading Hope': ibid., p. 112

470 'Next day . . . the whole city': ibid., p. 121

470 'the exquisite music': C. P. Cavafy, 'The God Abandons Antony', *Selected Poems*, trans. Edmund Keeley and Philip Sherrard (Princeton University Press, 2015), p. 16

470 'The month of May': SR, *The Fall of Constantinople*, p. 122

471 'half in ruins': ibid., p. 152

471 'A frontier divides': SR, 'Life on the Frontier between Islam and Eastern Christendom in the Middle Ages', lecture at University of Peshawar, March 1965

471 'But . . . none of them': ibid.

471 'an able *ghazi*': SR, *The Fall of Constantinople*, p. 30

471 'sought to impress': ibid.

472 'later legend, not': ibid., p. 55

472 'peculiarly disappointing': ibid., p. 197

472 'Moslems of the old': ibid., p. 56

472 'a man of peace . . . longed to retire': ibid., p. 44

472 'old and trusted': ibid., p. 56

472 'had always been': ibid., p. 125

472 'a pensioner of the Greeks': ibid., p. 170

472 'even the most highly': ibid., p. 169

472 'upstart renegades': ibid., p. 125

473 'aggressive converts . . . without vested interests': ibid., p. 170

473 'Notaras sent [Halil]': ibid., p. 230

473 'hoping that his perfect': ibid., p. 150

473 'the Bashi-bazouks': ibid., p. 134

474 'little would have changed . . . If Sultan Mehmet': ibid., p. 188

474 'of the two great': ibid.

474 'Mehmet Pasha [a convert': ibid., p. 184

474 'the end of an old': ibid.

475 'remains the best': ibid., p. xiii

475 'a seriously flawed': John W. Barker, *Speculum – A Journal of Mediaeval Studies*, Vol. 41, No. 3, July 1966, p. 571

475 'the greatest of living': Gervase Mathew, *Oxford Magazine*, August 1965

475 'shows, perhaps more': David Knowles, *Spectator*, 2 July 1965

475 'as we read': ibid.

476 'For almost half': ibid.

476 'on equal terms': Gore Vidal, *Point to Point Navigation* (Little, Brown, 2006), p. 16

476 'To read an historian': Gore Vidal, *Reporter*, 7 October 1965

477 'in nature there can': ibid.

477 'national socialist dictatorship': SR, *Mistra* (Thames & Hudson, 1980), p. 100

477 'his most perceptive': Anthony Bryer, memoir, 'James Cochran Stevenson Runciman', for Cambridge University Press, accessed Cambridge University Press website

478 'historians, not content': Vidal, *Reporter* review

## CHAPTER 21: THE FOOL

479 'An historian dealing': SR, *The White Rajahs* (Cambridge University Press, 1960), p. ix

480 'a genius for friendship': Malcolm MacDonald quoted in Clyde Sanger, *Malcolm MacDonald: Bringing an End to Empire* (McGill-Queen's Press, 1995), p. 325

480 'With Greece and now': SR to Donald Nicol, 13 March 1957, KCL

481 'that ineffectual Man': SR to Hugh Trevor-Roper, 12 December 1956, Elshieshields

481 'jungle-covered mountains': SR to Princess Bibesco, 20 April 1957, Austin

481 'I never wanted': SR, *Alphabet*, p. 140

481 'From what I already': ibid.

481 'whether a hack': ibid.

482 'He was a wonderfully': SR to Gordon Gardiner, 27 February 1984, quoted with permission of Gordon Gardiner

482 'seriously suggested in 1960': Nigel Barley, *White Rajah: A Biography of Sir James Brooke* (Hachette, 2013), p. 13

482 'some of the ladies': Nigel Barley to author, 28 April 2015

483 'He was not an easy': SR, *Alphabet*, p. 146

483 'as part of a long': Judith M. Heimann, *The Most Offending Soul Alive: Tom Harrisson and his Remarkable Life* (University of Hawaii Press, 1998), p. 312

483 'Tom's real objection': ibid.

483 'felt greatly flattered . . . remembered that there': SR, *Alphabet*, p. 84

484 'received us in black': ibid.

484 'prostitution . . . My name . . . I rather liked': ibid.

484 'lousy': ibid.

485 'I did not think . . . I was not prepared': ibid., p. 85

486 'At Cukor's house': Patrick McGilligan, *George Cukor: A Double Life* (St Martin's Griffin, 1997), p. 124

487 'the kindest of hosts . . . presented a problem . . . a not very noteworthy': SR, *Alphabet*, p. 85

487 'the whole film world': SR to LR, 12 February 1957, Elshieshields

487 'Film circles themselves': SR to Princess Bibesco, 20 April 1957, Austin

487 'the archest funfair . . . the biggest ever': SR to LR, 12 February 1957, Elshieshields

488 'hilariously horrifying . . . I was soon made': SR, *Alphabet*, p. 86

488 'Just as in England . . . If, like George': ibid.

490 'The MacArthy [sic] probe': SR to Stewart Perowne, 14 November 1952, Elshieshields

490 'none of them wildly': SR to RR, 12 February 1957, Elshieshields

490 'Grand historical spectacles': SR to Princess Bibesco, 20 April 1957, Austin

491 'I wouldn't mind': SR to LR, 12 February 1957, Elshieshields

491 'It is from the East': SR, *Alphabet*, p. 181

491 'especially interested in the theatre': ibid., p. 113

492 'austere and astigmatic': Mark J. Gasiorowski and Malcolm Byrne (eds), *Mohammed Mossadeq and the 1953 Coup in Iran* (Syracuse University Press, 2004), p. 162

493 'a very quiet middle-aged . . . who is tragically': SR to RR, 26 February 1957, Elshieshields

493 'Rather frail and lonely . . . who seemed glad': SR, *Alphabet*, p. 113

494 'unending': ibid.

494 'each worse than the last': SR to Princess Bibesco, 20 April 1957, Austin

494 'I was worked': SR to LR, 16 March 1957, Elshieshields

495 'whether the Great Man': Donald Nicol to Anthony Bryer, 4 May 2001, Elshieshields

495 'Britain's cultural ambassador . . . after giving nine': SR to RR, 10 March 1957, Elshieshields

495 'I have never seen': SR, *Alphabet*, p. 114

496 'nothing between aeroplanes': SR to RR, 6 April 1957, Elshieshields

496 'said to be difficult . . . perfectly affable': SR to RR, 10 March 1957, Elshieshields

496 'tiny, whispering man': SR to LR, 16 March 1957, Elshieshields

496 'The Sultan was not': SR, *Alphabet*, p. 141

497 'an absurd little state . . . outwardly meek . . . a very corrupt . . . his insults covered': SR to RR, 1 February 1959, Elshieshields

497 'The Sultan's increasing wealth': SR, *Alphabet*, p. 142

497 'an unpretentious town': ibid., p. 145

497 'One's vision of the tropics': ibid., p. 142

497 'a most eclectic building': SR to LR, 16 March 1957, Elshieshields

497 'his tact and geniality': SR, *Alphabet*, p. 145

498 'The set-up is interesting': SR to LR, 16 March 1957, Elshieshields

498 'the wives of British Governors . . . basking in the warm glow': SR, *Alphabet*, p. 145

498 'much less melancholy': ibid., p. 146

498 'eerie but not actually': ibid., p. 145

499 'in the hope that I': ibid., p. 147

499 'rather like a registered ... decanted into a speed-boat': SR to RR, 6 April 1957, Elshieshields

499 'I walked four miles': ibid.

499 'terribly like Ireland': SR to LR, 14 March 1958, Elshieshields

500 'I had hardly ... It had a sort': SR, *Alphabet*, p. 147

500 'scrappy, curious collection': ibid., p. 145

500 'I'm enjoying my': SR to LR, 16 March 1957, Elshieshields

500 'I think I'm going': SR to RR, 6 April 1957, Elshieshields

501 'how delicious it is': SR to Freya Stark, 3 April 1955, Austin

501 'Jean indefatigably took': SR to Princess Bibesco, 3 April 1955, Austin

501 'I am full': SR, *Alphabet*, p. 211

502 'a certain understanding': ibid.

502 'an Islamic Colloquium': SR to Freya Stark, 29 November 1957, Austin

502 'One ought, when invited': ibid.

502 'As you know better': SR to Stewart Perowne, 1 May 1957, Elshieshields

502 'like most women-lecturers': SR to Stewart Perowne, 10 March 1954, Elshieshields

502 'to have a Jew': SR to RR, 3 January 1958, Elshieshields

502 'the doyen of Orientalists': ibid.

502 'The Colloquium itself': ibid.

503 'conversation with the Pakistanis': SR to RR, 7 January 1958, Elshieshields

503 'crazy Islamic Congress': SR to Leslie Perowne, 22 January 1958, Elshieshields

503 'dull and elementary': SR to RR, 7 January 1958, Elshieshields

503 'when I read': SR to RR, 3 January 1958, Elshieshields

503 'You could have knocked': SR to Leslie Perowne, 22 January 1958, Elshieshields

503 'I oughtn't to assume': SR to Donald Nicol, 22 January 1958, Elshieshields

503 'that blousy woman': SR to Lady Ottoline Morrell, postcard, 6 December 1936, Austin

504 'Now I know': John Chancellor, conversation with author

504 'a country about which': SR to Freya Stark, 29 November 1957, Austin

504 'gave me lunch': SR, *Alphabet*, p. 119

504 'I don't like being': SR to RR, 15 March 1958, Elshieshields

504 'somewhat delinquent': SR, *Alphabet*, p. 119

505 'I suppose that no one': ibid., p. 120

505 'hideous, except in': SR to RR, 15 March 1958, Elshieshields

505 'I spent a heavenly': ibid.

505 'We went first': SR, *Alphabet*, p. 120

505 'very odd, clever': SR to LR, 23 March 1958, Elshieshields

506 'She reminded me': SR, *Alphabet*, p. 148

506 'the only capital': ibid.

507 'rather to the puzzlement': ibid., p. 143

507 'The Japanese concentrated': SR, *The White Rajahs*, p. 256

508 'Two dried heads': SR, *Alphabet*, p. 149

508 'It showed me': Sir Anthony Abell to SR, 1 November 1960, Elshieshields

509 'the most monstrous': SR to LR, 23 March 1958, Elshieshields

510 'It is likely': SR, *The White Rajahs*, p. 45

510 'The great advantage': ibid., p. 46

510 '[James] had long discussions': ibid., p. 50

510 'He was at his best': ibid., p. 89

511 'there is little doubt': Barley, *White Rajah*, p. 208

511 'The British Liberal': SR, *The White Rajahs*, p. 96

## CHAPTER 22: THE HANGED MAN

512 'witch-hunt': Lord Montagu of Beaulieu, interview in *Evening Standard*, 14 July 2007

513 'As you have probably seen': SR to Stewart Perowne, 22 November 1953, Elshieshields

513 'I've been surprised': ibid.

514 'I remember thinking': SR to Jeffrey Schaire, 1 January 1986, Firestone Library, Princeton

515 'My life is uneventful': Steven Runciman quoted in David Plante, *Worlds Apart* (Bloomsbury, 2015), p. 258

516 'ridiculous amusing Cecil': SR to KR, 6 May 1925, Elshieshields

517 'I enclose a letter': SR to KR, 10 April 1930, Elshieshields

517 'dinner with four Blues': SR to KR, 3 November 1932, Elshieshields

517 'wasn't that kind': SR to Gordon Gardiner, 15 October 1987

517 'about a boy': SR to MR, 22 January 1922, Elshieshields

518 'nothing happens here': ibid.

518 'He was already': SR, 'Footnotes', p. 53

519 'to pour a boiling': Maurice Bowra to Patrick Leigh Fermor, undated, 1950s, NLS

519 'I suppose I knew': SR to Patrick Leigh Fermor, 12 February 1982, NLS

520 'owing my war': SR, *Alphabet*, p. 20

520 '[Blunt] certainly did': SR to Jeffrey Schaire, 1 January 1936, Princeton

521 'The conversation inevitably': Courtenay Young to J. C. Robertson, 29 January 1958, TNA KV 2/4123

522 'I don't know': SR to Charles Turner, 12 October 1984, NYPL

522 'Dear Jeff, What': SR to Jeffrey Schaire, 5 January 1985, Princeton

523 'my Naval Affair': information from Darryl Pinckney, December 2015

523 'best friend': Earl Mountbatten of Burma quoted in Oliver Warner, *Admiral of the Fleet: The Life of Charles Lambe* (Sidgwick & Jackson, 1969), p. ix

523 'If you asked': ibid., p. 23

524 'Charles was at once ... he went away': SR, foreword to Warner, *Admiral of the Fleet*, p. xii

524 'He seemed to create': Stewart Perowne quoted in ibid., p. 31

524 'A nice birthday': SR to KR, 19 July 1932, Elshieshields

525 'As ever with Charles': SR to Stewart Perowne, 18 February 1955, Elshieshields

525 'Lambe did many': William Davis, 'Lambe, Sir Charles Edward', *ODNB*

525 'We all, I suppose': SR, foreword to Warner, *Admiral of the Fleet*, p. xiii

526 'Steven was a regular': Patricia Ayling to author, 20 January 2015

527 'beautiful but dull ... unexciting but athletic': SR to KR, 10 May 1925, Elshieshields

528 'In the evenings': Steven Runciman recalled by David Plante, conversation with author

528 'I'm most nostalgically': SR to Guy Black, 17 January 1998

529 'you have no social': SR to Charles Turner, 24 June 1960, NYPL

529 'delicious ... pleasant little orgy': SR to Charles Turner, 21 February 1961, NYPL

530 'a black kid': Darryl Pinckney to author, 16 May 2012

530 'I'm still shocked': Darryl Pinckney to SR, 3 November 1987, Elshieshields

531 'neurotic': SR to Jeffrey Schaire, 20 June 1987, Princeton

531 'Darryl's fickleness': SR to Charles Turner, 29 January 1989, NYPL

531 'a courtly quality': Darryl Pinckney to author, December 2015

531 'Can't you some': SR to Gordon Gardiner, 31 July 1973

532 'I am immensely': SR to Gordon Gardiner, 27 October 1976

532 'your dizzy eyrie': SR to Gordon Gardiner, 4 February 1978

532 'known to wander . . . impressive nude . . . I've always been': Gordon Gardiner, conversation with author, 9 February 2015

532 'In my long': SR to Gordon Gardiner, 14 February 1978

533 'I think to': Nicholas Phillipson, conversation with author

534 'the sky over': Lord Montagu, *Standard* interview

535 'They told me ': Plante, *Becoming a Londoner*, p. 444

535 'At lunch he': David Plante, conversation with author

536 'the Fate Worse': SR to Jeffrey Schaire, 15 October 1983, Princeton

536 'I put up': Walter Runciman according to John Chancellor, conversation with author

## CHAPTER 23: THE TOWER

537 ' . . . I told him': SR, *Alphabet*, p. 103

538 'loyal University folk': ibid.

538 'two huge thugs': ibid., p. 104

538 'to my gratification . . . was wiping away . . . These are the best . . . homework': ibid.

538 'Elshieshields, situated on': *Topographical, Statistical and Historical Gazetteer of Scotland* (A. Fullarton, 1853), p. 289

539 'roughly this part': SR to RR, 11 April 1966, Elshieshields

539 'thirteenth century, rebuilt': SR to Freya Stark, 26 October 1966, Austin

539 'albeit fleetingly . . . a fairly quiet': Alastair Maxwell-Irving, *The Border Towers of Scotland: The West March* (Alastair Maxwell-Irving, 2000), p. 136

540 'Living as I do': SR, *Alphabet*, p. 42

540 'ancient tower': SR to Gordon Gardiner, 8 June 1987

540 'It's not quite': SR to RR, 11 April 1966, Elshieshields

541 'the house is': SR to RR, undated, 1966, Elshieshields

541 'we get on ': SR to RR, 21 April 1966, Elshieshields

541 'appalled as one': SR to RR, 11 October 1966, Elshieshields

541 'suburban': SR to George Seferis, 11 January 1967, Gennadeion

541 'a local boy': SR to Patrick Leigh Fermor, 29 November 1983, NLS

542 'The weather has': SR to RR, 6 January 1967, Elshieshields

542 'the most fantastic': SR to Stewart Perowne, 16 September 1955, Elshieshields

542 'bovine bucolic weekend': Duchess of Buccleuch to SR, 4 October 1955, Elshieshields

542 'the most beautiful': SR to Leslie Perowne, 22 September 1959, Elshieshields

543 'indeed almost . . . upmarket Frenchwoman': Robin Dalton, conversation with author, June 2013

543 'My dear, I will': ibid.

543 'I find country': SR to Princess Bibesco, 6 September 1972, Austin

544 'He was quite insatiably': Nicholas Phillipson, conversation with author

544 'I have a few': SR to Princess Bibesco, 6 September 1972, Austin

545 'even the oldest': Olivia Manning to Francis King, undated, 1966, Austin

545 'the party seemed': Olivia Manning to Francis King, undated, later in 1966, Austin

545 'sumptuous . . . two *large* . . . my favourite Victorian': SR to Freya Stark, 26 October 1966, Austin

546 'working myself up . . . in a way almost': SR to RR, 6 January 1967, Elshieshields

546 'awful imitation Scots': Fallowell, *How to Disappear*, p. 132

546 'an assortment of': SR, *Alphabet*, p. 17

548 'I think the house': Randolph Stow to SR, 18 August 1968, Elshieshields

549 'is dying to hear': Randolph Stow to SR, 25 January 1969, Elshieshields

550 'in the form of boos . . . the whole thing': ibid.

550 'it never sounded': SR to Gordon Gardiner, undated

550 'I rang the noise': Peter Maxwell Davies to SR, 22 March 1969, Elshieshields

550 'the organ, piano . . . It was very much': Peter Maxwell Davies to SR, 25 September 1969, Elshieshields

551 'I was away . . . still, I think': ibid.

551 ' . . . I love being here': Peter Maxwell Davies to SR, 17 January 1971, Elshieshields

551 'mistaken impression . . . nothing would please': Peter Maxwell Davies to SR, 2 June 1971, Elshieshields

552 'cosy . . . not such an ex-Angry': SR to Gordon Gardiner, undated

552 'Can't Gerard, who': SR to Gordon Gardiner, 26 November 1986

552 'only moderate intelligence': Gordon Gardiner to author, 18 February 2015

552 'a great flirt': ibid.

553 'Some eighteen months': SR to Jeffrey Schaire, 10 April 1984, Princeton

554 'I would have liked': SR to Gordon Gardiner, 15 March 1996

554 'I would guess': Clive Welch to SR, undated correspondence over 1995, Elshieshields

555 'The prison library': ibid.

555 'though his crime ... mistake ... supportive wife': Father Anscar Cowley to SR, 10 August 1995, Elshieshields

555 'one of my own': ibid.

556 'the Latin races': Clive Welch to SR, Elshieshields

556 'narrative flow': ibid.

556 'if that is a euphemism': ibid.

556 'I would be interested': Clive Welch to SR, 26 October 1997, Elshieshields

556 'Those boys are': SR to Gordon Gardiner, 14 April 1994

557 'fascinated enquiries': Lord Black and Mark Bolland, conversation with author, 19 March 2015

557 'whom nobody knew': see The Times obituary of Sir Steven Runciman, 2 November 2000

557 'I can't say that': SR to Mark Bolland, 14 May 1997, quoted with permission of Mark Bolland

557 'It would be such': SR to Gordon Gardiner, 19 September 1999

557 'was, in a word': Lord Black, conversation with author

558 'punchy and sharp': ibid.

558 'His Employer needs': SR to Guy Black, 17 August 1996

558 'Surely it is useful': SR to Guy Black, 4 February 1999

558 'unhelpful and rather': SR to Guy Black, 8 March 2000

558 'most distinguished younger': SR to Guy Black, 26 August 1997

558 'the heirs to those': SR to Guy Black, 14 June 1995

559 'I feel that I should': SR to Ann Shukman, 15 October 1967, Elshieshields

559 'like a nice old fashioned': SR to LR, 2 July 1975, Elshieshields

560 'I, not being at all': SR to Stewart Perowne, 9 June 1953, Elshieshields

560 'The ceremonies ... all went': ibid.

560 'detected a slight': SR to Stewart Perowne, 14 August 1953, Elshieshields

561 'priggish schoolgirl': John Grigg, National and English Review, August 1957

561 'common-looking': SR to Gordon Gardiner, 21 October 1991

562 'talk of nothing else': Sir Ralph Anstruther to SR, 7 May 1994, Elshieshields

563 ' ... I think the Ignatieff': SR to Nathalie Brooke, 10 March 1999, Elshieshields

563 'had no great love': Richard Jarman to SR, 26 June 1996, Elshieshields

563 'I suppose that must': Neil MacGregor, 5 June 1995, Elshieshields

563 'I still feel': Sir Dimitri Obolensky to SR, 6 June 1995, Elshieshields

564 'Oh, how everyone': SR to Nathalie Brooke, 8 March 2000, Elshieshields

564 'one knows not': SR to Guy Black, 29 August 1998

## CHAPTER 24: THE GRAND ORATOR

565 'Something very special': Cavafy, *Selected Poems*, p. 20

565 'as a good philhellene': SR to Freya Stark, 13 February 1953, Austin

565 'Anglo-Hell': SR to LR, 24 May 1959, Elshieshields

565 'The Philhellenes spoke': SR, *The Fall of Constantinople*, p. 190

566 'I don't mean': George Seferis to SR, 2 September 1969, Gennadeion

566 'Sometimes I feel': Steven Runciman quoted in *Pemptousia* interview

566 'a pure-bred Scot': Angelos Delivorrias, 'Farewell to a Friend', in *New Griffon* (Gennadius Library, 2002), accessed online at http://www.myriobiblos.gr/texts/english/delivorias_friend.html

566 'my western isle': SR to Freya Stark, 20 August 1955, Austin

566 'Geordies of Scots': see *The Times* obituary of Sir Steven Runciman

567 'cult': SR to Gordon Gardiner, 26 November 1987

567 'Greece is to me': SR, *Alphabet*, p. 90

568 'The new book': SR to Freya Stark, 20 August 1955, Austin

569 'anti-papal': SR to Princess Bibesco, 30 December 1955, Austin

569 'I hope that': SR, *The Eastern Schism* (Cambridge University Press, 1955), p. vi

569 'It may well': SR, *The Great Church in Captivity* (Cambridge University Press, 1968), p. 4

569 'As the story': Constantine Trypanis, *Spectator*, 7 October 1955

570 'who saw himself': SR, *The Eastern Schism*, p. 54

570 'the agelong difference': ibid., p. 169

570 ' ... I can't stomach': SR to Stewart Perowne, 5 December 1952, Elshieshields

571 'In the good old': SR, *Alphabet*, p. 72

572 'It is true': SR, 'Some Personal Memories'

572 '[The Beirut Embassy] was': Steven Runciman quoted in Roderick Beaton, *George Seferis: Waiting for the Angel* (Yale University Press, 2003), p. 300

572 'The old spirit': SR, 'The Makronesos Experiment', *Guardian*, 17 August 1949

573 'to free Cyprus': EOKA pledge, April 1955, quoted in Lawrence Durrell, *Bitter Lemons* (Faber & Faber, 1957), p. 183

573 'I'm interested to hear': SR to Stewart Perowne, 6 April 1955, Elshieshields

573 'The Archbishop's hobnobbing': SR to Stewart Perowne, 20 May 1955, Elshieshields

573 'One can hardly': SR to Stewart Perowne, 14 October 1955, Elshieshields

574 '[Eden's] waffling platitudes': SR to Stewart Perowne, 11 December 1955, Elshieshields

574 'the Cypriots were': SR, 'Richard Coeur-De-Lion', *History Today*, April 1955

575 'I had no wish': SR, 'Some Personal Memories'

575 'Greeks who refused': SR, *The Fall of Constantinople*, p. 63

576 'disquieting rumour ... the Greek Colonels were': SR to Michael Ramsey, Archbishop of Canterbury, 17 July 1972, Elshieshields

576 'The Armenians are': SR to Stewart Perowne, 5 December 1952, Elshieshields

577 'I have called': John Satterthwaite, Bishop of Gibraltar, to SR, 2 January 1973, Elshieshields

578 'Could the Church': SR, *The Great Church in Captivity*, p. 182

579 'more than a church': ibid., p. 187

579 'like a history': Anthony Bryer, Runciman memoir for Cambridge University Press

579 'A detailed account': SR, *The Great Church in Captivity*, p. viii

580 'Tragical the subversion': Sir Paul Ricaut quoted in ibid., p. 204

580 'deeply moved ... well informed ... tactful ... shrewd ... his censure was': ibid., p. 205

581 'The grand achievement': ibid., p. 412

581 'obscurantist': *Christchurch Press*, 14 June 1969

582 'somewhat Calvinistic ... "As for the Patriarke': SR, *The Great Church in Captivity*, p. 269

582 'a man of independent': ibid., p. 260

582 'almost pagan': ibid., p. 267

583 'a very disreputable': p. 268

583 'If this were so': ibid., p. 269

583 'The Orthodox Church': ibid., p. 276

583 'an intellectual by': ibid., p. 282

583 'Cyril Lucaris failed': ibid., p. 288

584 'well-trained, cultivated': ibid., p. 230

584 'lying in wait ... lured away ... wooed and harassed': SR, 'The Church of England and the Orthodox in the 17th and 18th Centuries',

in E. G. W. Bill (ed.), *Anglican Initiatives in Christian Unity* (Lambeth Palace Library, 1967), p. 4

584 'not in unison': SR, *The Great Church in Captivity*, p. 203
584 'this will add': ibid., p. 273
585 'good and virtuous': ibid., p. 283
585 'the son of darkness': ibid., p. 271
585 'a mutual fear': SR, 'The Church of England and the Orthodox in the 17th and 18th Centuries', p. 17
585 'Mistra . . . though it boasted': SR, *The Fall of Constantinople*, p. 12
586 'like Switzerland, only': SR to KR, 2 April 1930, Elshieshields
587 'a buxom blonde': SR, *Alphabet*, p. 98
587 'as slight intoxication . . . I did not know': ibid., p. 99
588 'not a guidebook . . . full history': SR, *Mistra*, p. 7
588 'To later philhellenes': ibid., p. 10
588 'my first ever military': SR to Donald Nicol, 29 September 1991, KCL
588 'I must now speak': SR to Donald Nicol, undated, 1991, KCL
588 'Here Helen, the loveliest': SR, *Mistra*, p. 10
589 'Your theory may ': SR, lecture draft, 1976, Elshieshields
589 'backwater . . . the mainstream of history': SR, *Mistra*, p. 11
589 'tragedy . . . was to': ibid., p. 14
590 'probably because it': ibid., p. 30
590 'a battle in northern': ibid., p. 7
590 'a massacre in a distant': ibid., p. 43
590 'a governor of their own': ibid., p. 36
590 'lack of racial . . . to welcome as equals': ibid., p. 37
590 'to put his son-in-law': ibid., p. 42
590 'A history of Mistra': ibid., p. 7
591 'The vale of Sparta': ibid., p. 21
591 'futile': ibid., p. 39
591 'ablest and most attractive . . . popular with his Greek': ibid., p. 22
592 'philosophy and letters': ibid., p. 72
592 'strange and neurotic . . . identified completely with': ibid., p. 65
592 'provided a harmonious . . . mourned by all': ibid., p. 70
592 'violent and neurotic': ibid., p. 66
592 'As usually happens': ibid., p. 26
593 'The children of knights': ibid.
593 'cultural standards': ibid., p. 27
593 'stalking arrogantly through': ibid.
593 'resentful and short-sighted': ibid., p. 63
594 'the appalling state . . . infested by Turkish': ibid., p. 58

595 'It is not easy': ibid., p. 95
595 'tactful restoration': ibid.
596 'shaped like a sort': ibid., p. 96
596 'The beauty of Greece': ibid., p. 9
596 'not entirely a suitable': ibid., p. 36
596 'the terrain obliged': ibid., p. 103
596 'wheeled transport . . . could have ridden . . . steep, winding . . . must have gone': ibid., p. 104
596 'chief glory . . . remaining true . . . closer in conception': ibid., p. 105
596 'Here [at the Hodeghetria]': ibid., pp. 107–8
597 'Charm is the great': Evelyn Waugh, *Brideshead Revisited* (Chapman & Hall, 1945), p. 260
597 'final taste of glory': SR, *Mistra*, p. 82

## CHAPTER 25: THE MAGICIAN

599 'muttering, miserable, mutton-hating': Vivien Noakes, *Edward Lear* (Houghton Mifflin, 1969), p. 146
599 'Oxford might not': SR to Roy Harrod, 1 November 1924, British Library
600 'could hardly have': James Knox, *Robert Byron* (John Murray, 2003), p. 98
600 'intended only for': ibid., p. 149
601 'very enthusiastic and valuable': SR to Princess Bibesco, 17 August 1959, Austin
601 'It is wonderful': SR, *Alphabet*, p. 11
601 'cold and raining': ibid.
601 'He was occupying': ibid.
601 'decided that I was': ibid.
602 'hungry bed bugs': ibid., p. 12
602 'in consequence all': ibid.
602 'about a hundred': ibid., p.13
602 'Mice and snakes': SR, *The Great Church in Captivity*, p. 45
602 'Which was the sex': SR, *Alphabet*, p. 13
602 'hard, for emphasis . . . the worst bed-bugs': ibid.
602 'the most charming': ibid.
602 'only spoke English': ibid., p. 14
603 'in broad Lancashire': ibid.
603 'as I seemed to be': ibid., p. 15
603 'saw sights that no': ibid.
603 'creature comforts': SR to Gordon Gardiner, undated
603 'state of decay': SR quoted in *Pemptousia* interview

604 'a crucified martyr': Bruce Arnold, *Derek Hill* (Quartet, 2010)

604 'Derek's death has': SR to Nathalie Brooke, 1 August 2000, Elshieshields

605 'I'm just an artist': Derek Hill recalled by Graham Speake, *Pemptousia* interview, 30 July 2013

606 'equerry': SR to Gordon Gardiner, undated, 1992

606 'a splendid villa': ibid.

606 'a handsome, very intelligent': ibid.

606 'ridiculous, I think': ibid.

606 'a palatial suite': Dimitri Conomos, conversation with author, 1 June 2015

606 'not at all princely': SR to Gordon Gardiner, 18 July 2000

607 'seemed to be one': SR to Gordon Gardiner, 4 August 1996

607 'I almost think': SR to Nathalie Brooke, undated, 1997, Elshieshields

607 'the deposed fathers': SR, 'Trouble on holy mountain', *The Times*, 17 April 1995

607 'threw the Holy Mountain': Graham Speake, *Friends of Mount Athos Newsletter*, August 1994

607 'relations with Constantinople': ibid.

607 'may even have been': ibid.

608 'Irrespective of national': SR, 'Trouble on holy mountain'

608 'unpatriotic . . . un-Greek': ibid.

608 'so long as these': ibid.

608 'that cannot itself . . . racism . . . embarrassment': ibid.

609 'the very heart': ibid.

609 'Mount Athos should': ibid.

609 'for monks to practise': ibid.

609 'your misgivings about': Aristeides Papadakis to SR, 4 May 1996, Elshieshields

610 'Your Honesty . . . endearing, I think': SR to Nathalie Brooke, 13 March 1996, Elshieshields

610 'My Greek visit': SR to Nathalie Brooke, 1 October 1997, Elshieshields

611 'They have promised': SR to Gordon Gardiner, 4 May 2000

611 'I am now devoted': SR to Nathalie Brooke, 1 August 2000, Elshieshields

611 ' . . . Sir Steven flew': Bryer, 'The Spider, the Owl and the Historian', p. ?

612 'up-to-date loos . . . a dear old man': SR to Gordon Gardiner, 23 July 2000

612 'and many of the monks': ibid.

612 'I find lentils': SR to Nathalie Brooke, 1 August 2000, Elshieshields

612 'the great heat': ibid.

612 'Sunday was almost': SR to Gordon Gardiner, 23 July 2000

612 'the assembled monks': Graham Speake, letter to *The Times*, 6 November 2000

613 'high-level . . . Erasmian': Dimitri Conomos, conversation with author

## CHAPTER 26: JUDGEMENT

615 'You should discover': Neil MacGregor to SR, 9 January 1993, Elshieshields

615 'I am amusing': SR to Donald Nicol, 16 July 1989, KCL

615 'relicts of a past': SR to George Rylands, undated, 1991, King's

616 'unlovable . . . I sounded governessy': SR to Gordon Gardiner, 26 November 1986

616 'an English spinster': SR, 'Footnotes', p. 84

617 'stories about our family': Enrico D'Assia to SR, undated 1991, Elshieshields

617 'What I particularly': John Grigg to SR, 10 March 1991, Elshieshields

617 'pleasantness of meeting': David Yates Mason to SR, 1 May 1991, Elshieshields

619 'so much of the book': Leslie Perowne to SR, 3 May 1991, Elshieshields

620 'I am so glad': SR to Leslie Perowne, 29 May 1991, Elshieshields

620 'bullying . . . a crowning horror': SR to Nikos Stangos, 6 March 1991, Princeton

620 'celebrity': SR to Elizabeth Wansbrough, 15 June 1991, Bodleian

620 'I suppose publicity': SR to George Rylands, undated, 1991, King's

621 'My new book . . . very stern . . . deplorably silly': SR to George Rylands, 4 March 1991, King's

621 'The style of the book': Frank Kermode, *Guardian*, 14 February 1991

622 'The privilege-span': Fiona MacCarthy, *Observer*, 17 February 1991

622 'Sir Steven is apt': Green, *TLS* review

623 'the cataclysm': SR to Princess Bibesco, 12 November 1956, Austin

623 'drabbness, shabbiness and inappropriate': SR, *Alphabet*, p. 136

623 'many of the ordinands': ibid.

624 'the seductive plum': ibid., p. 137

624 'passed into local . . . innumerable questions': ibid., p. 138

624 'so long as professors': ibid., p. 136

624 'Our Roumanian colleagues': ibid., p. 138

624 'as though it was there . . . scruffy': ibid.

624 'The night is ended': ibid., p. 139

624 'superseded': ibid., p. 22

625 'simple charm . . . clumsy Soviet style': ibid., p. 23

625 'My Bulgarian visit': SR to Nathalie Brooke, 27 March 1975, Elshieshields

625 'personal liking . . . as an honorary Minister': SR, *Alphabet*, p. 23

625 'mysterious illness': ibid., p. 24

626 'that beautiful and interesting': ibid., p. 25

626 'I had the honour': Johnny Stancioff, conversation with author

626 'a distant cousin': SR, *Alphabet*, p. 54

627 'the old grand-ducal': ibid.

627 '[Peg] had to go': ibid.

627 'After having lived': ibid., p. 55

628 'my royal relatives': Steven Runciman paraphrased in Henry Maxwell to Robin Dalton, 29 May 1986, Elshieshields

628 'the couple who': SR, *Alphabet*, p. 212

628 'became disillusioned with': ibid., p. 213

628 'We were an odd': Miriam James to author, 15 September 2014

628 'Professor Messerschmitt': SR, *Alphabet*, p. 213

629 'There is no one': ibid., p. 117

629 'in her later years': *The Times* obituary, 3 January 2009

629 'never a good listener': SR, *Spectator*, 10 August 1984

630 'civilised scepticism, wisdom': Christopher Tyerman, conversation with author

630 'very successful in rebranding': ibid.

630 'Runciman always gave': ibid.

631 'observed Steven, rather': ibid.

631 'It would be folly': Tyerman, *God's War*, p. xv

632 'might have been daring': SR to Nikos Stangos, 31 August 1989, Princeton

632 'kinky productions are': SR to Gordon Gardiner, 12 October 1994

632 'ugly and absurd . . . the smart intellectual': SR to Gordon Gardiner, 10 April 1997

632 'strange but interesting . . . I keep thinking': SR to Gordon Gardiner, 30 May 1997

632 'What a blot': SR to Stewart Perowne, 20 May 1953, Elshieshields

633 'The Ruler, Shaikh': SR, *Alphabet*, p. 47

633 'Everyone there was ': SR to Gordon Gardiner, 6 March 1989

634 'If you work for': SR to Guy Black, 8 March 2000

634 'domestic difficulties': SR, *Alphabet*, p. 46

634 'at one point': SR to Jeffrey Schaire, 14 January 1985, Princeton

635 'he regards religion': Alfred Duggan, *Daily Telegraph*, 7 March 1958

636 'I hate the Balkan': SR to Nathalie Brooke, 10 April 1999, Elshieshields

636 'obedient to Moslem': SR, *Alphabet*, p. 30

636 'candles, icons and simple': ibid., p. 80

636 'This strictly Dualist': ibid., p. 172

636 'We went through': Plante, *Worlds Apart*, p. 253

637 'unless one is faced': SR, *Alphabet*, p. 37

637 'Many people think': SR, 'Europe and Islam: The Historical Legacy', lecture at Cairo, March 1951

637 'I like to think that even had I lived': ibid.

638 'I like to think that we of the old left': Rex Warner to SR, 14 December 1968, Elshieshields

638 'to whom anything': SR to Gordon Gardiner, undated, September 1994

638 '. . . I find Muslim': SR to David Sox, undated 1994, Elshieshields

638 'The weather was lovely': SR, *Alphabet*, p. 73

638 'marginally Buddhist': SR, 'The Ladies of the Mongols', lecture at Athens, February 1960

638 'favourite Ottoman mosque': SR, *Alphabet*, p. 73

639 'not very mobile': Leigh Fermor, 'Remembering Steven Runciman'

640 'allergic to nurses': SR to Guy Black, 8 April 2000

640 'made his own': Fallowell, *How to Disappear*, p. 185

# Select Bibliography

## MANUSCRIPT

Annan, Noel, letters to Dadie Rylands, 1942–5, King's College Archives, Cambridge

Bates, Edward, letters to Noel Annan, undated, 1930s, King's

——, letters to Anne Barnes, undated, 1930s, King's

——, letters to Dadie Rylands, 1937–8, King's

Bowra, Maurice, letters to Patrick Leigh Fermor, 1950s, National Library of Scotland, Edinburgh

Brendon, Piers, interview with Steven Runciman, 1993, Churchill College Archives, Cambridge

Brougham, Eleanor, letters to Lord Berners, 1945, St John's College Archives, Cambridge

Craxton, John, letters to E. Q. Nicholson, 1946–8, Tate Archives, London

——, letter to Richard Morphet, 1986, Tate

Dacre Papers, Christ Church, Oxford

Jones, Emily Beatrix Coursolles, letters to Dadie Rylands, 1920s–55, King's

Llewellyn-Smith, Michael, lecture at British School at Athens, February 2012, 'Steven Runciman at the British Council'

Manning, Olivia, letters to Francis King, 1965–71, Harry Ransom Center, University of Texas, Austin

Runciman, Hilda, correspondence, 1911–56, Elshieshields Archive, Lochmaben

Runciman, Leslie, letters to Rosamond Lehmann, 1923, King's

Runciman, Steven, 'Footnotes to a Long Life', unfinished memoirs up to 1938, Elshieshields

——, correspondence with family and friends, 1911–2000, Elshieshields

——, lecture texts, Elshieshields

——, 'Juvenilia' verses, Elshieshields

——, 'The She-Devil', unsigned short story, digitally accessible, University College London Special Collections

——, letters to Marthe Bibesco and Valentine Ghika, 1934–73, Austin

——, letters to Guy Black and Mark Bolland, 1994–2000

——, letters to Charlotte Bonham-Carter, 1929–39, Hampshire Archives, Winchester

——, letters to Nathale Brooke, 1972–2000, Elshieshields

——, letters to Gordon Gardiner, 1973–2000

——, letters to Roy Harrod, 1922–59, British Library, London

——, letters to Patrick and Joan Leigh Fermor, 1980–2000, National Library of Scotland

——, postcards to Lady Ottoline Morrell, 1936, Austin

——, letters to Donald Nicol, 1951–97, King's College Archives, London

——, letters to Dadie Rylands, 1921–93, King's

——, letters to Jeffrey Schaire, 1983–91, Firestone Library, Princeton

——, letters to Nikos Stangos, 1975–2000, Firestone Library, Princeton

——, letters to Freya Stark, 1940–68, Austin

——, letters to Charles Turner, 1960–92, New York Public Library, New York

——, letters to Elizabeth Wansbrough, 1932–87, Bodleian Library, Oxford

Seferis, George, correspondence with SR, 1952–71, Gennadius Library, Athens

Wylie, Elinor, correspondence with SR, 1925–8, Smith College, Northampton, Massachusetts

Young, Courtenay, memos to J. C. R. Robertson, 1950s, Security Service Files, The National Archives, Kew, KV 2/4104, 4123

## PUBLISHED

Abulafia, David, *Frederick II* (Oxford University Press, 1988)

Allfrey, Anthony, *Man of Arms: The Life and Legend of Sir Basil Zaharoff* (Weidenfeld & Nicolson, 1989)

Andrea, Alfred J. and Holt, Andrew, *Seven Myths of the Crusades* (Hackett, 2015)

Arnold, Bruce, *Derek Hill* (Quartet, 2010)

Aronson, Theo, *Crowns in Conflict* (John Murray, 1986)

Arthaud, Christian and Paul, Eric, *La Côte d'Azur des écrivains* (Edisud, 1999)

Asher, Michael, *Thesiger* (Viking, 1994)

Asquith, Lady Cynthia, *Diaries* (Hutchinson, 1968)

Banks, Noel, *Six Inner Hebrides* (David & Charles, 1977)

Barley, Nigel, *White Rajah: A Biography of Sir James Brooke* (Hachette, 2013)

Barnes, James and Patience, *Nazis in Pre-War London 1930–1939* (Sussex Academic Press, 2010)

Baynes, Norman (ed.), *A Bibliography of the Works of J. B. Bury* (Cambridge University Press, 1929)

—— and Henry St Leger Moss (eds), *Byzantium* (Clarendon Press, 1947)

Beaton, Cecil, *The Wandering Years* (Weidenfeld & Nicolson, 1961)

Beaton, Roderick, *George Seferis: Waiting for the Angel* (Yale University Press, 2003)

Benaïm, Laurence, *Marie-Laure de Noailles* (Grasset, 2001)

Bent, Samuel, *Familiar Short Sayings of Great Men (Ticknor, 1887)*

Berlin, Isaiah, *Flourishing: Letters 1928–1946*, ed. Henry Hardy (Chatto & Windus, 2004)

——, *Building: Letters 1960–1975*, ed. Henry Hardy and Mark Pottle (Chatto & Windus, 2013)

Bill, E. G. W. (ed.), *Anglican Initiatives in Christian Unity* (Lambeth Palace Library, 1967)

Bolitho, Hector, *A Biographer's Notebook* (Macmillan, 1950)

Boston, Richard, *Osbert* (Collins, 1989)

Bowker, Gordon, *George Orwell* (Little, Brown, 2003)

Buchan, James, *Days of God: The Revolution in Iran and its Consequences* (John Murray, 2012)

Buckler, Georgina, *Anna Comnena: A Study* (Oxford University Press, 1929)

Bullard, Reader, *Letters from Tehran*, ed. Edward Christian Hodgkin (I. B. Tauris, 1991)

Burk, Kathleen, *Troublemaker: The Life and History of A. J. P. Taylor* (Yale University Press, 2002)

Burn, Michael, *Turned towards the Sun* (Michael Russell, 2003)

Bury, John Bagnell, *Selected Essays* (Cambridge University Press, 1930)

Camatsos, Efrosini, *"His Words Were Nourishment and His Counsel Food" – a Festschrift for David W. Holton*, ed. Efrosini Camatsos, Tassos A. Kaplanis, Jocelyn Pye (Cambridge Scholars Publishing, 2014)

Campbell, John, *Lloyd George* (Jonathan Cape, 1977)

Cardiff, Maurice, *Friends Abroad* (Radcliffe Press, 1991)

Carrington, Dora, *Carrington: Letters*, ed. David Garnett (Jonathan Cape, 1970)

Carter, Miranda, *Anthony Blunt: His Lives* (Macmillan, 2001)

Cavafy, C. P., *Selected Poems*, trans. Edmund Keeley and Philip Sherrard (Princeton University Press, 2015)

Channon, Henry, *Chips: The Diaries of Sir Henry Channon*, ed. Robert Rhodes James (Weidenfeld & Nicolson, 1967)

Churchill, Clementine and Winston, *Speaking for Themselves: The Personal Letters of Winston & Clementine Churchill*, ed. Mary Soames (Doubleday, 1998)

Clive, Nigel, *A Greek Experience* (Michael Russell, 1985)

Clogg, Richard, *Politics and the Academy: Arnold Toynbee and the Koraes Chair* (Routledge, 2013)

Connell, John, *The House by Herod's Gate* (Sampson Low, 1947)

Connolly, Cyril, *Enemies of Promise* (Routledge, 1938)

——, *A Romantic Friendship: The Letters of Cyril Connolly to Noel Blakiston*, ed. Noel Blakiston (Constable, 1975)

Conybeare, Frederick Cornwallis, *The Key of Truth* (Clarendon Press, 1898)

Cooper, Artemis, *Cairo in the War 1939–1945* (Hamish Hamilton, 1989)

——, *Patrick Leigh Fermor: An Adventure* (Hachette, 2012)

Cornford, John, *Collected Writings*, ed. Jonathan Galassi (Carcanet, 1986)

Crick, Bernard, *George Orwell: A Life* (Secker & Warburg, 1980)

Daniel, Norman (pseud. as 'Caractacus'), *Revolution in Iraq* (Victor Gollancz, 1959)

Davenport-Hines, Richard, *Universal Man: The Lives of John Maynard Keynes* (HarperCollins, 2015)

De-La-Hoy, Michael, *Eddy: The Life of Eddy Sackville-West* (Arcadia, 1999)

Donaldson, Frances, *The British Council: The First Fifty Years* (Jonathan Cape, 1984)

Dorril, Stephen, *MI6: Inside the Covert World of Her Majesty's Secret Intelligence Service* (Simon & Schuster, 2002)

Dressler, Camille, *Eigg: The Story of an Island* (Polygon, 1998)

Dunbabin, Jean, *Charles I of Anjou* (Longman, 1998)

Durrell, Lawrence, *Bitter Lemons* (Faber & Faber, 1957)

Edsel, Robert M., *Saving Italy* (W. W. Norton, 2013)

Edwards, Anne, *Matriarch: The Life of Queen Mary* (Rowman & Littlefield, 2014)

Empson, William, *Milton's God* (Chatto & Windus, 1961)

Fallowell, Duncan, *How to Disappear* (Aurum, 2013)

Field, Andrew, *VN: The Life and Art of Vladimir Nabokov* (University of Queensland Press, 1986)

Fisher, Clive, *Cyril Connolly* (Macmillan, 1995)

Fitzgerald, Penelope, *The Knox Brothers* (Macmillan, 1977)

Fletcher, Gordon A., *Dennis Robertson: Essays on his Life and Work* (Palgrave Macmillan, 2007)

Gasiorowski, Mark J. and Byrne, Malcolm (eds), *Mohammed Mossadeq and the 1953 Coup in Iran* (Syracuse University Press, 2004)

Gibbon, Edward, *The Decline and Fall of the Roman Empire* (Cadell & Davies, 1807)

Gifford, John, *Dumfries and Galloway* (Penguin/Buildings of Scotland Trust, 1996)

Glassheim, Eagle, *Noble Nationalists* (Harvard University Press, 2005)

Grant, Michael, *My First Eighty Years* (Aidan Ellis, 1994)

Grant Duff, Shiela, *The Parting of the Ways* (Peter Owen, 1982)

Haag, Michael, *Alexandria: City of Memory* (Yale University Press, 2004)

Harvey, John, *The Plantagenets* (B. T. Batsford, 1948)

Harvey, Oliver, *Diplomatic Diaries*, ed. John Harvey (Collins, 1970)

Hastings, Selina, *Rosamond Lehmann* (Chatto & Windus, 2002)

Heimann, Judith M., *The Most Offending Soul Alive: Tom Harrisson and his Remarkable Life* (University of Hawaii Press, 1998)

Heine, Heinrich, 'Religion and Philosophy in Germany', first pub. 1835, included in *The Romantic School and Other Essays*, ed. Jost Hermand, trans. Robert C. Holub (Continuum, 1998)

Hoare, Philip, *Serious Pleasures* (Hamish Hamilton, 1990)

Hobhouse, Charles, *Inside Asquith's Cabinet*, ed. Edward David (John Murray, 1977)

Hollingsworth, Mark and Fielding, Nick, *Defending the Realm: MI5 and the Shayler Affair* (André Deutsch, 1999)

Hollis, Christopher, *A Study of George Orwell* (Hollis & Carter, 1956)

Holroyd, Michael, *Lytton Strachey* (William Heinemann, 1968)

Jenkins, Roy, *Asquith* (Collins, 1964)

——, *Churchill* (Macmillan, 2001)

Keynes, John Maynard and Lopokova, Lydia, *Lydia & Maynard: The Letters of Lydia Lopokova and John Maynard Keynes*, ed. Polly Hill and Richard Keynes (André Deutsch, 1989)

Kinross, Patrick Balfour, Baron, *Hagia Sophia* (W. W. Norton, 1972)

Knox, James, *Robert Byron* (John Murray, 2003)

Lee, Hermione, *Edith Wharton* (Chatto & Windus, 2007)

Lees-Milne, James, *Diaries 1984–1897*, ed. Michael Bloch (Hachette, 2011)

Lehmann, John, *The Ample Proposition* (Eyre & Spottiswoode, 1966)

Leigh Fermor, Patrick, *The Broken Road*, ed. Artemis Cooper and Colin Thubron (John Murray, 2013)

Léonard, Emile, *Les Angevins de Naples* (Presses Universitaires de France, 1954)

Lewis, Jeremy, *Cyril Connolly* (Jonathan Cape, 1997)

——, *Shades of Greene* (Jonathan Cape, 2010)

Lewis, R. W. B., *Edith Wharton* (Constable, 1975)

Lloyd George, David, *My Darling Pussy: The Letters of Lloyd George and Frances Stevenson 1913–41*, ed. A. J. P. Taylor (Weidenfeld & Nicolson, 1975)

Lord, James, *Picasso & Dora* (Weidenfeld & Nicolson, 1993)

Louis, William Roger, *The British Empire in the Middle East: 1945–51* (Clarendon Press, 1984)

Lownie, Andrew, *Stalin's Englishman: The Lives of Guy Burgess* (Hodder & Stoughton, 2015)

Luke, Michael, *David Tennant and the Gargoyle Years* (Weidenfeld & Nicolson, 1991)

Macaulay, Rose, *Dearest Jean: Rose Macaulay's Letters to a Cousin*, ed. Martin Ferguson Smith (Manchester University Press, 2011)

McGilligan, Patrick, *George Cukor: A Double Life* (St Martin's Griffin, 1997)

Macintyre, Ben, *A Spy among Friends: Kim Philby and the Great Betrayal* (Bloomsbury, 2014)

McLoughlin, Leslie, *In a Sea of Knowledge: British Arabists in the 20th Century* (Ithaca Press, 2002)

MacMurray, John, *How the Peace Was Lost* (Hoover Press, 1992)

McNeish, James, *Dance of the Peacocks: New Zealanders in Exile in the Time of Hitler and Mao Tse-tung* (Virago, 2003)

MacNiven, Ian S., *Lawrence Durrell* (Faber & Faber, 1998)

Madan, Geoffrey, *Geoffrey Madan's Notebooks*, ed. J. A. Gere and John Sparrow (Oxford University Press, 1981)

Manning, Olivia, *Modern Reading* (Phoenix House, 1943)

——, *Friends and Heroes* (William Heinemann, 1965)

Masterman, J. C., *On the Chariot Wheel* (Oxford University Press, 1975)

Maxwell-Irving, Alastair, *The Border Towers of Scotland: The West March* (Alastair Maxwell-Irving, 2000)

Meyers, Jeffrey, *Orwell: Wintry Conscience of a Generation* (W. W. Norton, 2000)

Milani, Abbas, *The Shah* (Macmillan, 2011)

Milton, John, *Major Works*, ed. Stephen Orgel (Oxford University Press, 2003)

Morgan, Edwin, *Sonnets from Scotland* (Mariscat, 1984)

Mulvagh, Jane, *Madresfield* (Doubleday, 2008)

Nabokov, Vladimir, *Speak, Memory* (Victor Gollancz, 1951)

Newsome, David, *On the Edge of Paradise: A. C. Benson, the Diarist* (John Murray, 1980)

Noakes, Vivien, *Edward Lear* (Houghton Mifflin, 1969)

Oldenbourg, Zoé, *Massacre at Montségur*, trans. Peter Green (Weidenfeld & Nicolson, 1961)

Olivier, Edith, *Without Knowing Mr. Walkley* (Reader's Union, 1939)

——, *Edith Olivier: From her Journals 1924–48*, ed. Penelope Middelboe (Weidenfeld & Nicolson, 1989)

Olson, Stanley, *Elinor Wylie: A Life Apart* (Dial Press, 1979)

Padeff, Michael, *Escape from the Balkans* (Cassell, 1943)

Parker, Peter, *Ackerley* (Constable, 1989)

Penrose, Antony, *Roland Penrose: The Friendly Surrealist* (Prestel, 2001)

Penrose, Barrie and Freeman, Simon, *Conspiracy of Silence* (Grafton Books, 1986)

Peterson, Maurice, *Both Sides of the Curtain* (Constable, 1950)

Plante, David, *Difficult Women* (Victor Gollancz, 1983)

——, *Becoming a Londoner* (Bloomsbury, 2013)

——, *Worlds Apart* (Bloomsbury, 2015)

Powell, Anthony, *The Military Philosophers* (William Heinemann, 1968)

Price, Victoria, *Vincent Price* (St Martin's Press, 2000)

Reavell, Cynthia and Tony, *E. F. Benson* (Martello Bookshop, 1984)

Redé, Alexis von Rosenberg, *Baron de, Alexis: The Memoirs of the Baron de Rédé*, ed. Hugo Vickers (Dovecote Press, 2005)

Rees, Goronwy, *A Chapter of Accidents* (Chatto & Windus, 1972)

Rendel, George, *The Sword and the Olive* (John Murray, 1957)

Riley-Smith, Jonathan, *The Crusades, Christianity and Islam* (Columbia University Press, 2008)

Runciman, Steven, *The Emperor Romanus Lecapenus and his Reign* (Cambridge University Press, 1929)

——, *A History of the First Bulgarian Empire* (Cambridge University Press, 1930)

——, *Byzantine Civilization* (Cambridge University Press, 1933)

——, *The Medieval Manichee* (Cambridge University Press, 1947)

——, *The First Crusade* (Cambridge University Press, 1951)

——, *The Kingdom of Jerusalem* (Cambridge University Press, 1952)

——, *The Kingdom of Acre* (Cambridge University Press, 1954)

——, *The Eastern Schism* (Cambridge University Press, 1955)

——, *The Sicilian Vespers* (Cambridge University Press, 1958)

——, *The White Rajahs* (Cambridge University Press, 1960)

——, *The Fall of Constantinople 1453* (Cambridge University Press, 1965)

——, *The Great Church in Captivity* (Cambridge University Press, 1968)

——, *Mistra* (Thames & Hudson, 1980)

——, *A Traveller's Alphabet* (Thames & Hudson, 1991)

——, *Paradise Regained* (Rampant Lions Press, 1993)

Runciman, Walter, Baron, *Windjammers and Sea Tramps* (Walter Scott, New York, 1905)

Sanger, Clyde, *Malcolm MacDonald: Bringing an End to Empire* (McGill-Queen's Press, 1995)

Sebba, Anne, *That Woman* (Weidenfeld & Nicolson, 2011)

Schenkar, Joan, *Truly Wilde: The Unsettling Story of Dolly Wilde, Oscar's Unusual Niece* (Virago, 2000)

Seferis, George, *Meres 1956–1960*, ed. Theano Michaelidou (Ikaros, 1990)

Shove, Fredegond, *Poems* (Cambridge University Press, 1956)

Sisman, Adam, *Hugh Trevor-Roper* (Weidenfeld & Nicolson, 2010)

Sitwell, Sacheverell, *A Roumanian Journey* (B. T. Batsford, 1938)

Spurling, Hilary, *Matisse the Master* (Hamish Hamilton, 2005)

Stark, Freya, *Traveller's Prelude* (John Murray, 1950)

——, *Letters*, vol. 6: *The Broken Road 1947–52*, ed. Lucy Moorehead (Michael Russell, 1981)

Stevenson, W. B., *Crusaders in the East* (Cambridge University Press, 1907)

Strachan, Alan, *Secret Dreams: A Biography of Michael Redgrave* (Weidenfeld & Nicolson, 2004)

Strachey, Lytton, *The Letters of Lytton Strachey*, ed. Paul Levy (Viking, 2005)

Tabachnick, Stephen, *Fiercer than Tigers: The Life and Works of Rex Warner* (Michigan State University Press, 2002)

Thomas the Rhymer (trad.), *The Romance and Prophecies of Thomas of Ercildoune*, ed. Sir James Murray (Early English Text Society, 1875)

*Topographical, Statistical and Historical Gazetteer of Scotland* (A. Fullarton, 1853)

Trevor-Roper, Hugh, *Letters from Oxford*, ed. Richard Davenport-Hines (Weidenfeld & Nicolson, 2006)

——, *One Hundred Letters from Hugh Trevor-Roper*, ed. Richard Davenport-Hines and Adam Sisman (Oxford University Press, 2014)

Tyerman, Christopher, *God's War* (Penguin, 2006)

Urbach, Karina, *Go-Betweens for Hitler* (Oxford University Press, 2015)

Vickers, Hugo, *Cecil Beaton* (Weidenfeld & Nicolson, 1985)

Vidal, Gore, *Point to Point Navigation* (Little, Brown, 2006)

Vyšný, Paul, *The Runciman Mission to Czechoslovakia, 1938* (Palgrave Macmillan, 2003)

Waite, Arthur, *The Key to the Tarot* (W. Rider, 1920)

Warner, Oliver, *Admiral of the Fleet: The Life of Charles Lambe* (Sidgwick & Jackson, 1969)

Wasserstein, Bernard, *Herbert Samuel* (Clarendon Press, 1992)

Waugh, Evelyn, *Vile Bodies* (Chapman & Hall, 1930)

——, *Brideshead Revisited* (Chapman & Hall, 1945)

Wharton, Edith, *The Letters of Edith Wharton*, ed. Nancy and R. W. B. Lewis (Simon & Schuster, 1988)

Whittell, Giles, *Spitfire Women of World War II* (Harper Press, 2007)

Wolfe, John, *Religion in History* (Manchester University Press, 2004)

Woolf, Virginia, *The Letters of Virginia Woolf*, ed. Nigel Nicolson and Joanne Trautmann (Hogarth Press, 1975)

——, *The Diary of Virginia Woolf*, ed. Anne Olivier Bell (Hogarth Press, 1978)

Yeats, William Butler, *Major Works*, ed. Edward Larrissy (Oxford University Press, 2008)

Ziegler, Philip, *Diana Cooper* (Faber & Faber, 2011)


## ONLINE

Borromean Islands: https://www.martinrandall.com/gardens-and-villas-of-the-italian-lakes

Anthony Bryer memoir, 'James Cochran Stevenson Runciman (1903–2000)': http://assets.cambridge.org/052183/4457/excerpt/0521834457_excerpt.htm

Donald of China: http://donaldofchina.com/Don_Who_/Press2/press2.html

5th Earl of Longford: http://www.longfordatwar.ie/soldiers/379

Eva Palmer Sikelianos: http://jacketmagazine.com/27/w-sike.html

*Oxford Dictionary of National Biography*, online edition: 'Bates, Sir Percy Elly', Alan G. Jamieson

——, 'Baynes, Norman Hepburn', J. M. Hussey

——, 'Bury, John Bagnell', Michael Whitby

——, 'Fachiri [née D'Arányi], Adila Adrienne Adalbertina Maria', Ivor Newton, rev. Robert Brown

——, 'Fisher, Herbert Albert Laurens', Alan Ryan

——, 'Jones, Emily Beatrix Coursolles', Nicola Beauman

——, 'Lambe, Sir Charles Edward', William Davis

——, 'Lancaster, Sir Osbert', Bevis Hillier

——, 'Luke, Sir Harry Charles', Robert Holland

——, 'Wedgwood, Dame (Cecily) Veronica', G. R. Batho

*Dictionary of Art Historians*, online edition: Georges Duthuit

——, Matthew Prichard

# Acknowledgements

Late in the autumn of 2011 I was stopping with friends in Dumfriesshire. Not long out of university and lacking any committed professional plans, I talked to my hostess about reading. I discovered that her brother had been the god-son of my favourite historian, and that this historian's niece lived not far off in her uncle's Border tower. In this way one of the people responsible for the origin of this book, Susanna Johnston, was able to direct me to the other, the Reverend Dr Ann Shukman, Sir Steven Runciman's niece and literary executor. Without Ann Shukman's hospitality, friendship, information and initiative, I could not have contemplated this book in its present form. Its dedication recognizes four and a half years during which she has lent me both purpose and delight.

Over those succeeding years I was to benefit from the help, conversation and suggestions of David Abulafia, Michael Angold, Lady Avon, Patricia Ayling, Michael Barber, Nigel Barley, Roderick Beaton, Gordon Bowker, the late Richard Brain, Christopher Brooke, Jim Brydson, Duncan Bull, Gabriella Bullock, Averil Cameron, Jeremy Catto, the late John Chancellor, Gerard Cleary, Isabelle Cole, Dimitri Conomos, Dame Robin Dalton, Nicholas and Mattie Egon, the late Lady Egremont, Simon Elliott, Duncan Fallowell, James and Maggie Fergusson, Karsten Fledelius, Gordon Fletcher, Peter Green, Michael Haag, James Holloway, James Howard-Johnston, Miriam James, Michael Jamieson, James Knox, the late Andro Linklater, John McEwen, Leslie McLoughlin, Peter Mackridge, Charles Mackworth-Young, Paul Magdalino, Philip Mansel, Bob Moore, James Morwood, Rudolf Muhs, Curt Noel, John Julius Norwich, Mark Gregory Pegg,

Nicholas Phillipson, Darryl Pinckney, David Plante, Keith Robbins, Charlotte Roueche, Lord Runciman, Francis Russell, Ivan (Johnny) Stancioff, Lord Strathcona, Colin Thubron, Nigel Tully, Christopher Tyerman, Fr Henry Wansbrough, Hywel Williams, Vincent Yorke and Sir George Young.

I owe substantial debts for allowing me access to, or pointing me towards, indispensable primary material to Lord Black, Mark Bolland, Nathalie Brooke, Tristram Clark, Gordon Gardiner, Charles King-Farlow, Katerina Krikos-Davis, Sir Michael Llewellyn-Smith, Andrew Lownie, Ruth Macrides and Robert Preece. Euan Adamson, Louise Bands, Raphael Cormack and Carmel Richmond carried out crucial, painstaking research in the Elshieshields archives, transferring the copious but opaque evidence of engagement diaries, photograph albums and address books into more digestible incarnations. Flora Scrymgeour gave a subtle eye to winnowing and selecting the ensuing pictures. Adam Sisman, one of my models in the enterprise I envisaged for this book from the start, and one of the first writers I consulted about it, gave me invaluable pointers as to tightened prose. Paul Lay's interest in Steven Runciman was welcome, cheering and thought-provoking. Peter Parker has offered unfailing help and reassurance both in word and deed, and by example. Frances Wilson has brightened many a story, standing up or sitting down. Emily Bearn's rapid consumption of *The Sicilian Vespers* was a promising portent. Flora Fraser has been a friend and a guide, across and about the Atlantic and the city. Richard Davenport-Hines has been free-handed with kindness, research and advice. His writing constitutes an ever-lucid beacon ahead; I can only apologize to him for not obeying his sensible precepts on biographical pithiness.

I wish to acknowledge the generous and conscientious assistance of King's and St John's College Libraries, Cambridge, the Bodleian and Christ Church Libraries, Oxford, Eton College Archives, the Harry Ransom Center, University of Texas, Austin, Smith College, Massachusetts, the Philadelphia Museum of Art, the New York Public Library, the Firestone Library, Princeton, the Beinecke Library, Yale, the Tate Archive, the National Library of Scotland, the British Library, the Royal

Society of Literature and the Jerwood Foundation and, what Steven Runciman called 'that most valuable institution', the London Library.

I am grateful for assistance of a miscellaneous nature better recalled than detailed from Andrew Bernhardt, Katie Bowden, Clare Bullock, David Jones, Nakul Krishna, Henry Mason, Hussein Omar, Anna Sander, Karl Sternberg, Giles Tully and Philip Womack.

I am grateful to David Abulafia, Frances Osborne, Lord Runciman, Johnny and Alexandra Stancioff and Norman Stone for drawing my attention to necessary corrections.

Friends who read and reacted to parts of the manuscript with an interest and attention to detail that was both encouraging and materially helpful include Charlotte Goldney, Anna Kullmann, Maria Paz Mendez Hodes, Oliver Rowse and Yasmine Seale. Friends in whose company and under whose roofs I wrote or pursued large parts of this book include Jacob Goodwin, Hugo Gye, Allegra FitzHerbert, Constance Watson, Michael Webb, Larkin Ozro Griffin, Daniel Craigmille, James Rosenheim, Mark and Georgie Rowse, Mary Beard and Robin Cormack, and Gilles and Sophie-Caroline de Margerie. A decade or so ago I began my serious acquaintance with Steven Runciman in the library of the last two named.

Rupert Christiansen became a stablemate as well as a dear friend when he put me in touch with Caroline Dawnay, who is now my agent. Caroline and her exceedingly efficient left-hand woman Sophie Scard tempered my intentions into reality over a disciplined year, culminating in my book's acceptance by Simon Winder at Penguin. No editor could be more sympathetic, both to a beginner and his subject. The verbal sensitivity of Peter James, the book's copy-editor, has been indispensable for its good order and refinement. Richard Duguid superintended the proofing process and expedited it to a remarkable degree.

I have profited from the company and counsel of a varied kin-group, including Quentin and Annabel Portsmouth, my aunt Avi Dinshaw, and my siblings, step-half-sister, and step-siblings, Oliver, Clem, Rose, Yvo and Xavier.

In history, in reading and in writing, the most faithful and enlivening of pleasures and practices, I will not forget the lessons, in particular, of Paul Dean, Ralph Oliphant-Callum, David Evans, Gareth Mann, Seamus Perry and Colin Burrow. But my first teachers and my most unstinting are my parents, Fram Dinshaw and Candia McWilliam, with the frequent and galvanizing addition of Claudia FitzHerbert. I will record some concluding gratitude to Sammy Jay, who only ever distracts me at exactly the right moment.

# *Permissions*

All quotations from the papers, lectures, published writings and unpublished correspondence of Steven Runciman and his family are reproduced by permission of the Executor of Sir Steven Runciman's Estate, as are photographs from Sir Steven's albums. A photograph from the effects of Denys King-Farlow is reproduced by permission of his Estate. Photographs taken by Cecil Beaton are reproduced by permission of the Executor of Sir Cecil Beaton's Estate. Quotations from an unpublished letter by Noel Annan are reproduced by permission of the Executors of Lord Annan's Estate. Quotations from unpublished material by Olivia Manning are by permission of the Executors of Olivia Manning's Estate. Quotations from unpublished letters by Randolph Stow are by permission of the Executors of Randolph Stow's Estate. Every effort has been made to reach other copyright holders, and the author would be grateful to receive communications from any who have been involuntarily overlooked, for correction in subsequent editions.

# Index